D0204932

The Tales of

HENRY JAMES

The opening page of the manuscript of 'Four Meetings', reproduced by permission of the Huntington Library, San Marino, California

The Tales of
HENRY JAMES

VOLUME THREE
1875-1879

EDITED BY
MAQBOOL AZIZ

CLARENDON PRESS · OXFORD
1984

Oxford University Press, Walton Street, Oxford OX2 6DP
London New York Toronto
Delhi Bombay Calcutta Madras Karachi
Kuala Lumpur Singapore Hong Kong Tokyo
Nairobi Dar es Salaam Cape Town
Melbourne Auckland
and associated companies in
Beirut Berlin Ibadan Mexico City Nicosia

Oxford is a trade mark of Oxford University Press

Published in the United States
by Oxford University Press, New York

British Library Cataloguing in Publication Data

James, Henry, 1843-1916
The tales of Henry James.
Vol. 3: 1875-1879
I. Title II. Aziz, Maqbool
813' .4 PS2116

ISBN 0-19-812573-9

Library of Congress Cataloging in Publication Data
(Revised for volume 3)

James, Henry, 1843-1916.
The tales of Henry James.

Includes bibliographical references.
Contents: v. 1. 1864-1869.--v. 2. 1870-1874.--
v. 3. 1875-1879.
I. Aziz, Maqbool, ed. II. Title.
PS2110.F73 813' .4 74-155805
ISBN 0-19-812573-9

Typeset by DMB (Typesetting), Oxford
and printed in Great Britain
at the Alden Press, Oxford

ACKNOWLEDGEMENTS

IT GIVES ME PLEASURE TO HAVE THIS OPPORTUNITY OF RECORDING my debt of gratitude to many friends, colleagues, libraries and other institutions of learning. Once again, I am particularly grateful to the Princeton University Library for permission to quote from manuscript letters in the Scribner Archive; to the Huntington Library for providing information about the manuscript of 'Four Meetings' and for permission to reproduce a page from that manuscript; to the Harvard University Press, Cambridge, Massachusetts, for permission to quote from *Henry James Letters*, so excellently edited by Dr. Leon Edel.

I am deeply grateful to the Social Sciences and Humanities Research Council of Canada for awarding me a Leave Fellowship which has enabled me to complete work on the present volume and advance work on those to come. I am grateful also to the Arts Research Board of McMaster University for a Summer Research Award given me in the summer of 1979. To the staff of the Mills Memorial Library at McMaster and the Secretaries of the Department of English there, I owe thanks for their unfailing courtesy and help.

I record with pleasure a very helpful discussion on 'Daisy Miller' I had with my friend and colleague, Dr. Gabriele Erasmi, of the Department of Italian at McMaster University. My very special thanks must once again go to my family for their continued patience and perseverance.

CONTENTS

Frontispiece ii

REFERENCES AND ABBREVIATIONS ix

THE COMPLETE TALES: A CHRONOLOGICAL LIST xi

INTRODUCTION 1
- Benvolio 23
- Crawford's Consistency 60
- The Ghostly Rental 86
- Four Meetings 114
- Théodolinde 138
- Daisy Miller: A Study 154
- Longstaff's Marriage 203
- An International Episode 228
- The Pension Beaurepas 290
- The Diary of a Man of Fifty 334

TEXTUAL VARIANTS 361
- Introduction 363
- Benvolio 365
- Four Meetings 373
- Théodolinde 396
- Daisy Miller: A Study 398
- Longstaff's Marriage 434
- An International Episode 438
- The Pension Beaurepas 482

APPENDIX I:
- Some Contemporary Notices of the Tales 509

APPENDIX II:
- James's Preface to 'Four Meetings', 'Daisy Miller', 'An International Episode' and 'The Pension Beaurepas' 514

APPENDIX III:
- 'Americans Abroad'—An Uncollected Essay by Henry James 518

APPENDIX IV:
- 'Daisy Miller': A Comedy in Three Acts—by Henry James 523

REFERENCES AND ABBREVIATIONS

A Passionate Pilgrim	Henry James, *A Passionate Pilgrim and Other Tales* (Boston: James R. Osgood and Company, 1875).
Daisy Miller	Henry James, *Daisy Miller, An International Episode, Four Meetings*, 2 volumes (London: Macmillan and Company, 1878).
The Madonna of the Future	Henry James, *The Madonna of the Future and Other Tales*, 2 volumes (London: Macmillan and Company, 1879).
Washington Square, Etc.	Henry James, *Washington Square, The Pension Beaurepas, A Bundle of Letters*, 2 volumes (London: Macmillan and Company, 1881).
The Author of Beltraffio, Etc.	Henry James, *The Author of Beltraffio, Georgina's Reasons, The Path of Duty, Four Meetings* (Boston: James R. Osgood and Company, 1885).
Stories Revived	Henry James, *Stories Revived* 3 volumes (London: Macmillan and Company, 1885).
Henry James Letters	*Henry James Letters*, ed. Leon Edel, vol. i, 1843-1875; vol. ii, 1875-1883 (Cambridge, Massachusetts: Harvard University Press, 1974, 1975).
Letters	*The Letters of Henry James*, 2 volumes, ed. Percy Lubbock (New York: Charles Scribner's Sons, 1920).
The Art of the Novel	*The Art of the Novel*, Critical Prefaces by Henry James, with an Introduction by R. P. Blackmur (New York: Charles Scribner's Sons, 1934). Quotations are from the paperback edition of 1962.
Bibliography	Leon Edel and Dan H. Laurence, *A Bibliography of Henry James* (London: Rupert Hart-Davis, 1957; revised, 1961). References are to the edition of 1961.

The James Family	F. O. Matthiessen, *The James Family* (New York: Alfred A. Knopf, 1961).

COLLECTED EDITIONS OF JAMES'S TALES AND NOVELS

Collective Edition	Collective Edition of 1883, 14 volumes (London: Macmillan and Company, 1883). 13 tales were included in their revised state.
New York Edition	*The Novels and Tales of Henry James*, 'New York Edition', 24 volumes (New York: Charles Scribner's Sons, 1907-9). 55 tales were included in this 'definitive' edition, for which James heavily revised the tales for the last time.
	The Novels and Stories of Henry James, 35 volumes, ed. Percy Lubbock (London: Macmillan and Company, 1921-3). 91 tales were included in a variety of textual states.
	The Complete Tales of Henry James, 12 volumes, ed. Leon Edel (London: Rupert Hart-Davis, 1962-4). The text follows the first book editions.

THE COMPLETE TALES: A CHRONOLOGICAL LIST

THE 112 TALES OF HENRY JAMES ARE LISTED BELOW IN ORDER OF their first publication. The original form of the titles is mentioned. The place and date of publication for each tale is given against the title. A brief parenthetical note identifies the works James did not serialize in magazines but first published in a collection or a book edition. The starred tales were included in the New York edition.

1.	'A Tragedy of Error'	*The Continental Monthly* (1864)
2.	'The Story of a Year'	*The Atlantic Monthly* (1865)
3.	'A Landscape Painter'	(1866)
4.	'A Day of Days'	*The Galaxy* (1866)
5.	'My Friend Bingham'	*The Atlantic Monthly* 1867)
6.	'Poor Richard'	(1867)
7.	'The Story of a Masterpiece'	*The Galaxy* (1868)
8.	'The Romance of Certain Old Clothes'	*The Atlantic Monthly* (1868)
9.	'A Most Extraordinary Case'	(1868)
10.	'A Problem'	*The Galaxy* (1868)
11.	'De Grey: A Romance'	*The Atlantic Monthly* (1868)
12.	'Osborne's Revenge'	*The Galaxy* (1868)
13.	'A Light Man'	(1869)
14.	'Gabrielle De Bergerac'	*The Atlantic Monthly* (1869)
15.	'Travelling Companions'	(1870)
*16.	'A Passionate Pilgrim'	(1871)
17.	'At Isella'	*The Galaxy* (1871)
18.	'Master Eustace'	(1871)
19.	'Guest's Confession'	*The Atlantic Monthly* (1872)
*20.	'The Madonna of the Future'	(1873)
21.	'The Sweetheart of M. Briseux'	*The Galaxy* (1873)
22.	'The Last of the Valerii'	*The Atlantic Monthly* (1874)

*23.	'Mme. De Mauves'	*The Galaxy* (1874)
24.	'Adina'	*Scribner's Monthly* (1874)
25.	'Professor Fargo'	*The Galaxy* (1874)
26.	'Eugene Pickering'	*The Atlantic Monthly* (1874)
27.	'Benvolio'	*The Galaxy* (1875)
28.	'Crawford's Consistency'	*Scribner's Monthly* (1876)
29.	'The Ghostly Rental'	(1876)
*30.	'Four Meetings'	(1877)
31.	'Théodolinde'	*Lippincott's Magazine* (1878)
*32.	'Daisy Miller: A Study'	*The Cornhill Magazine* (1878)
33.	'Longstaff's Marriage'	*Scribner's Monthly* (1878)
*34.	'An International Episode'	*The Cornhill Magazine* (1878-9)
*35.	'The Pension Beaurepas'	*The Atlantic Monthly* (1879)
36.	'The Diary of a Man of Fifty'	*Harper's New Monthly Magazine & Macmillan's Magazine* (1879)
*37.	'A Bundle of Letters'	*The Parisian* (1879)
*38.	'The Point of View'	*The Century Magazine* (1882)
*39.	'The Siege of London'	*The Cornhill Magazine* (1883)
40.	'The Impressions of a Cousin'	*The Century Magazine* (1883)
*41.	'Lady Barberina'	(1884)
*42.	'The Author of Beltraffio'	*The English Illustrated Magazine* (1884)
*43.	'Pandora'	*The New York Sun* (1884)
44.	'Georgina's Reasons'	(1884)
45.	'A New England Winter'	*The Century Magazine* (1884)
46.	'The Path of Duty'	*The English Illustrated Magazine* (1884)
47.	'Cousin Maria'	*Harper's Weekly* (1887)
*48.	'Louisa Pallant'	*Harper's New Monthly Magazine* (1888)
*49.	'The Aspern Papers'	*The Atlantic Monthly* (1888)
*50.	'The Liar'	*The Century Magazine* (1888)
51.	'Two Countries'	*Harper's New Monthly Magazine* (1888)

*52.	'A London Life'	*Scribner's Magazine* (1888)
*53.	'The Lesson of the Master'	*The Universal Review* (1888)
*54.	'The Patagonia'	*The English Illustrated Magazine* (1888)
55.	'The Solution'	*The New Review* (1889-90)
*56.	'The Pupil'	*Longman's Magazine* (1891)
*57.	'Brooksmith'	*Harper's Weekly & Black and White* (1891)
*58.	'The Marriages'	*The Atlantic Monthly* (1891)
*59.	'The Chaperon'	(1891)
*60.	'Sir Edmund Orme'	*Black and White* (1891)
61.	'Nona Vincent'	*The English Illustrated Magazine* (1892)
*62.	'The Private Life'	*The Atlantic Monthly* (1892)
*63.	'The Real Thing'	*Black and White* (1892)
64.	'Lord Beauprey'	*Macmillan's Magazine* (1892)
65.	'The Visit'	*Black and White* (1892)
66.	'Jersey Villas'	*Cosmopolitan Magazine* (1892)
67.	'Collaboration'	*The English Illustrated Magazine* (1892)
*68.	'Greville Fane'	*The Illustrated London News* (1892)
69.	'The Wheel of Time'	*Cosmopolitan Magazine* (1892-3)
*70.	'Owen Wingrave'	*The Graphic* (1892)
*71.	'The Middle Years'	*Scribner's Magazine* (1893)
*72.	'The Death of the Lion'	*The Yellow Book* (1894)
*73.	'The Coxon Fund'	(1894)
*74.	'The Altar of the Dead'	*Terminations* (first appeared in this collection of tales by James) (1895)
*75.	'The Next Time'	*The Yellow Book* (1895)
*76.	'The Figure in the Carpet'	*Cosmopolis* (1896)
77.	'Glasses'	*The Atlantic Monthly* (1896)
*78.	'The Way It Came'	*The Chap Book & Chapman's Magazine of Fiction* (1896)
79.	'John Delavoy'	*Cosmopolis* (1898)
*80.	'The Turn of the Screw'	*Collier's Weekly* (1898)

*81.	'In the Cage'	*In the Cage* (first appeared in a book edition) (1898)
82.	'Covering End'	*The Two Magics* (first appeared in this collection of two tales by James) (1898)
83.	'The Given Case'	*Collier's Weekly* (1898-9)
84.	'The Great Condition'	*The Anglo-Saxon Review* (1899)
*85.	'Europe'	*Scribner's Magazine* (1899)
*86.	'Paste'	*Frank Leslie's Popular Monthly* (1899)
*87.	'The Real Thing'	*Collier's Weekly* (1899)
*88.	'The Great Good Place'	*Scribner's Magazine* (1900)
89.	'Maud-Evelyn'	*The Atlantic Monthly* (1900)
*90.	'Miss Gunton of Poughkeepsie'	*The Cornhill Magazine and The Truth* (1900)
91.	'The Special Type'	*Collier's Weekly* (1900)
*92.	'The Tree of Knowledge'	*The Soft Side* (first appeared in this collection of tales by James) (1900)
*93.	'The Abasement of the Northmores'	*The Soft Side* (1900)
94.	'The Third Person'	(1900)
95.	'The Tone of Time'	*Scribner's Magazine* (1900)
*96.	'Broken Wings'	*The Century Magazine* (1900)
*97.	'The Faces'	*Harper's Bazaar* (1900)
*98.	'Mrs. Medwin'	*Punch* (1901)
*99.	'The Beldonald Holbein'	*Harper's New Monthly Magazine* (1901)
*100.	'The Story in it'	*Anglo-American Magazine* (1902)
*101.	'Flickerbridge'	*Scribner's Magazine* (1902)
*102.	'The Beast in the Jungle'	*The Better Sort* (first appeared in this collection of tales by James) (1903)
*103.	'The Birthplace'	*The Better Sort* (1903)
104.	'The Papers'	(1903)
*105.	'Fordham Castle'	*Harper's Magazine* (1904)

*106.	'Julia Bride'		(1908)
*107.	'The Jolly Corner'	*The English Review*	(1908)
108.	'The Velvet Glove'		(1909)
109.	'Mora Montravers'		(1909)
110.	'Crapy Cornelia'	*Harper's Magazine*	(1909)
111.	'The Bench of Desolation'	*Putnam's Magazine*	(1909)
112.	'A Round of Visits'	*The English Review*	(1910)

INTRODUCTION

1.

DURING HIS LONG AND RICHLY VARIED CAREER HENRY JAMES published 112 works of short fiction varying in length between seven thousand and fifty thousand words. All were called 'tales' by James. It was with one of these that he launched himself as a writer in 1864; and it was with a collection of these that, a decade later, he made his first book, *A Passionate Pilgrim*. More than five decades after his first published tale, the work which closed his career as a writer of fiction was also a collection of reprinted short stories, *The Uniform Tales of Henry James*.[1] The first volume of this work appeared in 1915, less than a year before his death. There are only eight years in the forty-six years of his story-telling when he did not publish any tale. More than two dozen of the many volumes of fiction published by James are collections or selections of tales. The 'shorter form', then, 'the beautiful and blest *nouvelle*', the 'small circular frame',[2] was no diversion from novel writing: 'to write a series of good little tales' was, young James once told C. E. Norton, 'ample work for a lifetime'.[3]

All but nine of the 112 tales were originally published in thirty-four different periodicals on both sides of the Atlantic. Most were given book status by James himself, some receiving the honour more than once, in the collections he issued from time to time. Only fifty-five stories, however, found their way into the 'definitive' New York Edition. Many—but not all—of the pieces 'rejected' were resurrected by Percy Lubbock in his edition of *The Novels and Stories of Henry James*. The tales included therein number ninety-five. The stories first appeared in their entirety in *The Complete Tales of Henry James*, edited by Leon Edel.

It was James's lifelong practice to revise his magazine writings for book publication and, not infrequently, the book texts for subsequent

[1] (London: Martin Secker, 1915-20). The New York Edition text of thirteen, and one newly revised tale, are reproduced in this collection in fourteen separate volumes.

[2] These and several other terms are used by James to describe his fictions which do not qualify as novels. But within 'the shorter form' there are other, finer, distinctions; these are explored and stated in the Prefaces to the volumes of tales in the New York Edition. The Prefaces are also available in a separate volume, *The Art of the Novel*.

[3] Letter of 16 January 1871, to C. E. Norton. *Henry James Letters*, i, p. 253. In a letter to R. L. Stevenson, dated 31 July 1888, James reiterated his faith in the shorter form. He told Stevenson that after *The Tragic Muse*, which he was then writing for the *Atlantic*, 'with God's help, I propose, for a longish period to do nothing but short lengths. I want to leave a multitude of pictures of my time, projecting my small circular frame upon as many different spots as possible and going in for number as well as quality, so that the number may constitute a total having a certain value as observation and testimony.' *Letters*, i, p. 138.

reprints. As a result, most of the tales, as well as many novels and other prose writings, now exist in multiple versions.[4] This textual multiplicity is an aspect which no serious student of James can afford to ignore.[5] In the existing state of the texts, when the multiple versions are scattered in old periodicals and early collections of the stories, it is not easy to assemble different versions of a work together for comparison and examination. This new edition of the tales is designed to meet this difficulty. Its principal aim is to provide the reader with a chronologically consistent text of the tales, together with a complete record of substantive textual variants for the stories revised.

The copy-text for the present edition is the original, serial text of the tales. For those James did not serialize the edition will reprint *their* original form in the book editions. The decision to reprint the original versions has been influenced by a variety of factors which I shall now try to explain. But I should first like to attempt a brief survey of the present state of the texts, and of the problems that are likely to confront an editor looking for a suitable basic text for a complete chronological edition.

The texts of James's tales are available in the following forms:

A. Manuscripts and typescripts—only seven tales appear to have survived in this form.[6]

B. The serial versions—all but nine tales are available in this state.

C. Manuscript revisions—one complete manuscript revision of a tale and a half-finished revision appear to have survived.[7]

D. The first authorized book versions—eighty-seven tales are available in this state. Most are revised forms of the serial versions.

E. Revised reprints (excluding the New York Edition) of the first book versions—over two dozen tales are available in this state.

F. The New York Edition—fifty-five tales were included in this definitive edition.

If we disregard categories A and C, which are of no relevance to the present purpose, we are left with four categories to choose from. All carry James's authority. As three of the four (D, E, and F) do not

[4] It is difficult to decide when a new edition of a text becomes a separate version. For the purpose of this essay, however, any new edition of a tale showing substantive variants introduced by James constitutes a new version.

[5] See 'Henry James Reprints' [by Simon Nowell-Smith], *The Times Literary Supplement*, 5 February 1949, p. 96; and my paper '"Four Meetings": A Caveat for James Critics' in *Essays in Criticism*, xviii (July 1968), pp. 258-74.

[6] See the *Bibliography*, pp. 390-3.

[7] The only complete manuscript revision of a tale to have survived is that of 'A Light Man'. The incomplete manuscript revision which has been preserved is that of 'At Isella'. This item is not mentioned in the *Bibliography*, but I found six heavily revised magazine pages of the tale in the Houghton Library. One of the pages is reproduced in the first volume of this edition as an illustration.

represent all the tales, they may be considered only *as possible bases* for a copy-text.

Viewed from the author's point of view, the question as to which of the four has the greater authority poses no serious difficulty. In the New York Edition James has given us a 'definitive' edition of his fiction: if his wishes are to be respected, then the text of the tales in that edition is the one which the editor is obliged to reprint. In other words, if the New York Edition texts are being used as the basis, a new edition of the tales would reprint fifty-five works in that text and the remaining fifty-seven in *their* final form. On the face of it this seems a perfectly sensible approach. But there is an inherent contradiction in it. If the principle behind such a policy is to respect the author's own final plan, then common sense would demand that it be accepted in full—in all its detail. The New York Edition is what it is because of three closely interrelated factors: its particular thematic design, the exclusions and rejections which are an integral part of that design, and extensive revisions especially carried out to give the whole an overall unity of style and structure.[8] The editor cannot claim superior authority for the definitive text without also accepting the principles of exclusion and revision which give the definitive text that authority. In practical terms, he cannot, without violating James's intention, give the rejected tales the status the author himself wished to deny them.

It could be argued that James excluded many of his stories not because he thought they were of inferior quality, but because he did not have space for them, or they did not seem to belong in the grand design he had in mind. For some tales not included this might well have been the case. However, we do know that the number of volumes for the edition was decided upon by James himself, and he was quite perturbed when his original choice of twenty-three came to be twenty-four.[9] It is difficult to believe James was not aware of the implications of the limit he so insistently wanted to impose upon the final edition. The limit was, indeed, partly dictated by the fact that he simply could not reread some of his early works.[10] Therefore, it cannot be denied that critical judgement—'the whole growth of one's "taste"',[11] as James put it—played a large role in his decision to limit the number to stories to be included to fifty-five.

[8] See Leon Edel, 'The Architecture of Henry James's "New York Edition"', the *New England Quarterly*, xxiv (June 1951), pp. 169-78; as well as the note on the New York Edition in the second volume of this edition.

[9] Ibid., pp. 177-8.

[10] Ibid., p. 172.

[11] *The Art of the Novel*, p. 340.

The selections made, James proceeded to consolidate the exclusive design of his plan by giving the selected works a uniform style. The stories and novels, especially of the early and middle periods, were so drastically revised for the edition that, in matters of detail, their 'definitive' form bears little relation to their original, in which many had first seen the light several decades before the New York Edition. The final revision is thus a case of 'renewals of vision', the 'exploring tread' taking the author, not back over 'the original tracks', but forcing him to 'break the surface in other places'.[12]

In short, the form in which the fifty-five tales have been revised and arranged in the definitive edition places them in a class by itself from which, if the wishes of the designer of the edition are to be respected, they may not be disengaged. In any case, the problem of textual and chronological inconsistency is not resolved if we decide to reprint one tale in the high manner of the final phase, one in the 'middle style', and one in its early revised state—which is precisely the form the new edition would take with the definitive texts as its textual basis.

This latter difficulty stays with us when we turn to an alternative possibility: an edition based on the final versions of the revised tales—categories E and D—but excluding the New York Edition. As the number of tales to have undergone two separate revisions prior to the definitive edition is rather small, such an edition would once again end up with a text in three different states. Some stories will appear in their unrevised state, some in their first (and only) revised form, and some in their second revised form. The stylistic difference, however, will be as great now as it might be with the New York Edition joining in. The one advantage of this approach is that it strikes a good compromise: while allowing the definitive edition its special status, it offers the tales in a text which would have been their final had James not embarked upon a definitive edition of his fictional writings. The major drawback of this approach, as we have said, is that it too cannot cope with the chronological problem. Also, like the definitive texts, the second revised versions, as well as the first, of some tales are far removed from their originals.

For a revised copy-text, the first book versions—category D—seem to offer a more satisfactory alternative. The arguments in favour of this text are the obvious ones. Other than the serial form, this is the text in which *most* tales are available in a theoretically uniform state. And in this state the revised works have had the benefit of a revision. An edition based on the first book versions would, therefore, be a much simpler, and, in a sense, more logical affair. A great many of the tales would appear in it in their first (and only) revised form, and

[12] Ibid., p. 336.

some in their unrevised form—only two different texts. But this apparently simple policy is not without its problems, which begin to crop up when we examine the character of the first revision in particular cases. To take one example, James revised and reprinted 'The Romance of Certain Old Clothes' (1868) in his first collection of tales, *A Passionate Pilgrim* (1875). Some years later he revised the 1875 text and reprinted the story in *Stories Revived* (1885).[13] Now, if our reason for reprinting the text of 1875 is that in that form the tale has had the benefit of revision then we must be using the term in a very restricted sense, to mean 'mild alteration'. For the text of 1875 is far more a case of small alterations in several places than of revision proper; it is the text of 1885 which gives us a revised text in any significant sense of the term. If, however, we argue that 'mild alteration' is precisely the sense in which we are applying the term, then what are we to do with tales such as 'A Light Man', or 'Poor Richard', the first revised form of which, appearing more than a decade after first publication, is radically different from their original? So it is only in theory that this textual policy promises to offer the whole corpus in two different textual states. In actual fact, because of the varying scale of the first revisions, the final design of an edition based on the first book versions would not be any different than the possibilities considered above.

We may now turn to the last of the four possibilities—category B—the first published versions. This is the only form in which *all* of James's writings are available in an historically, chronologically, and textually uniform state—in which, that is, the texts of the tales are simply there in their right original order. From a strictly historical point of view, this is the only entirely satisfactory alternative for a complete edition of the tales. Yet, obviously, if we apply the authorial point of view here, as we did while considering the New York Edition texts, it is not. For we cannot now decide to go against James's wishes and select the original form of a work which has been revised by him.

The moral to be drawn from the foregoing is that, if we are looking for a copy-text which does not present any chronological difficulties, has been revised and re-revised to the author's complete satisfaction, does no violence to any other of his plans and intentions, conveys a sense of development, etc., is, in short, satisfactory on all counts, then we are not likely to find one in the maze of James's texts. James revised some of his tales only once, some twice, some three times, and some never at all. The gaps of time, moreover, between different classes of revision, and between the original and revised form, or forms, of individual works range from a month or so to thirty-five

[13] See the first volume of this edition.

years. The result of this process of 'fingering' is a state of textual multiplicity in James to which order can now be given only by an outside hand.[14]

There are, in the final analysis, three courses open to the editor of James—or, for that matter, of any constantly revising author—who wants to make a single-text edition of the tales. All involve the editor's own judgement, choice, and decision. He can either approach the question from the author's point of view and, disregarding the demands of history and chronology, prepare an edition based on the final texts; or he can take a purely critical view and, disregarding not only the historical principle but also James's final revisions, base his edition on the versions he considers (from his particular point of view) the best; or he can take the historical approach and, completely ignoring the revisions, make an edition based on the original texts. There is one other solution—and it seems the ideal possibility. The editor can combine the three approaches in a 'variant edition' of the works: an edition based on any one version but providing, within the single framework, all the other available textual evidence.

It is this last course which I have chosen for this edition. The decision to use the serial versions of the tales as the basic text for the edition is based on the theory that the *first published* form, in manuscript or print, of a multiple-version work is the only one which may be said to have the 'right' authority. The manuscript, when it exists, which is not the case with the tales, cannot claim this authority simply because, essentially, it is the author's message to the printer, and remains a private document until it is translated into print and thus allowed to become public. If, however, the author allows the manuscript to circulate in public in that form then the manuscript would obviously have definite priority.

The revised versions cannot make such a claim for different reasons. The creative activity which originates with the inception of a new idea culminates when, having been realized in the finished artefact, the idea is given to the public. Any authorial alterations or revisions which may appear in a future version of the artefact, following the original event, cannot be considered as anything but the author's second thoughts, his comment and gloss upon the published work. No revision of a published work is ever an integral part of the

14 The image comes from James himself. Dencombe, the writer in the tale 'The Middle Years' (1893), 'was a passionate corrector, a fingerer of style; the last thing he ever arrived at was a form final for himself. His ideal would have been to publish secretly, and then, on the published text, treat himself to the terrified revise, sacrificing always a first edition and beginning for posterity and even for the collectors, poor dears, with a second.'

chain of events which make up the original creative sequence. All published revisions are, therefore, afterthoughts and represent a conciousness other than the one which created the original work. The last remark is of special significance in a consideration of multiple-version works by James, who carried out his major revisions years after their first publication.

In making these observations, it is of course not my intention to suggest that the revised versions of the tales are in any way inferior in quality, or are less authoritative and representative. The distinction I am proposing is that, while most instances of revision in James make for better literary effects, in his case—as well as in that of any other 'revisionist'—a revised version can be said to possess representative authority only in so far as it represents a new phase of his developing consciousness—'the growth', as James put it, 'of the immense array of terms, perceptional and expressional'.[15] The alterations in the third text of 'The Madonna of the Future', for instance, which came in 1879, small though they are, cannot claim to represent the writer who first issued the tale in 1873. The authority likewise of the text of 1879 is fixed in time. In other words, when an editor is confronted with a multiple-version work, he cannot afford to think of textual authority in any absolute terms—even the so-called final version is a tentative final with a compulsive revisionist. The only textual authority that he can single out and establish is the 'right' authority of the first published version.

In view of all these considerations, and because an historical principle seems to me to be inherent in the idea of a variant edition, I have decided to reprint the serial texts of the tales. It is, for this edition, a happy coincidence that in their original form—the form in which they were known to contemporary readers[16]—most of the tales have never been reprinted before.

The serial text is here reprinted without any major editorial interference. All misprints found in the text have been silently corrected. Similarly, missing punctuation marks—for the most part involving commas, hyphens for compound words, quotation marks, etc.,—have been supplied where the text appeared to need them. Words and phrases appearing in different spelling, at different places, have been normalized according to current English usage. Full stops after the titles have been deleted. Spaced contractions—*had n't*, *could n't*,

[15] *The Art of the Novel*, p. 339.

[16] In the first decade of his career, James did not publish any volume and was known to his contemporaries as a writer of magazine stories even after his work began to be reprinted in book editions, simply because the magazines had a much larger circulation than any of his collections or book editions.

etc.,—which, incidentally, disappear in most early book versions but come back in the New York Edition, have been normalized. Where applicable, the notes about the division of texts into parts, which may have had James's tacit approval but may not have been a feature of the manuscripts, have been preserved. In order to preserve some flavour of James's early treatment of foreign expressions and foreign place-names, no attempt is made to normalize these—or impose consistency where James is inconsistent—according to current usage; however, obvious printing errors in this category have been corrected. English spellings have been substituted for American, and single quotation marks for double. All illustrations accompanying the serial texts will be reproduced.

Since it is difficult to determine the dates of composition for many of the tales, I have decided to follow throughout the chronology of publication. The ten tales in the present volume are arranged in the order in which they were first published in magazines. Each tale carries a brief headnote which provides its complete publishing history during James's lifetime. Textual variants for the revised tales in this volume will be found in the textual section. The present volume covers the years in which James came of age—became an author of novels and *volumes* of tales, and acquired, on both sides of the Atlantic, a large public recognition ('the flourishing condition of my fame', as he called it) with such early novellas as 'Daisy Miller' and 'An International Episode'. It closes with the year in which his first 'big' book, *The Portrait of a Lady*, came into being.

2.

In James's long creative life the five years with which the present volume concerns itself stand out as a display of remarkable intellectual as well as physical energy. During the five years, he managed to put out no fewer than twelve volumes of prose fiction, literary criticism, and travel writing. He wrote four new novels, completely revised another, published two novellas, eight shorter tales, and contributed some two hundred pieces of miscellaneous prose to periodicals on both sides of the Atlantic. Needless to add, always a faithful correspondent, he continued to write copious letters to his family and friends abroad.

In the same five years, moreover, he crossed the Atlantic twice, changed his residence three times, and dined out, as the legend says, more than two hundred times. Faced with a flurry of activity of such vast and various proportions, the task of dating only ten, out of over two hundred, pieces of writing acquires special difficulties. These are compounded by the fact that, with his confidence and reputation on the increase, James now felt little need to make announcements about his latest published tale, or the one in progress.

The ten tales divide themselves into two distinct groups. 'Benvolio', 'Crawford's Consistency', and 'The Ghostly Rental', the first three in order of publication, have little in common with the semi-international stories James had lately been sending home for publication. The tales suggest a break taken by their author from his early explorations in the international theme. In the remaining seven, however, with a renewed sense of its literary significance, he appears to be returning to the international theme and setting. The division nicely corresponds to James's year away from Europe, and his subsequent decision to return to it 'for a term of years'. It is tempting to suggest, therefore, that 'Benvolio', 'Crawford's Consistency', and 'The Ghostly Rental' might all three have originated during his stay in New York—even though the latter two were sent to their magazine publisher from Paris. But we must first take an account of James's transatlantic crossings of those years: we may pick up the thread from the second volume of this edition.

After two years in Europe (1872-4), with mixed feelings and mixed motives, James returned to America in the summer of 1874. He wanted to give America another chance; for some time he had been hankering for the domestic hearth, for its 'tomatoes, ice cream, melons, cranberries, and other indigenous victuals'.[17] As if the fictional character were supposed to anticipate its creator's own future course, the first-person narrator of the last tale James wrote before he sailed westward, 'Professor Fargo', finds himself strolling in the streets of New York.

The home-coming had been meticulously planned well before it actually occured; and James seemed to have a sense it would do little for the writer in him. As early as 17 May 1874 he had written to his mother:

> Tell Willy [William James] I thank him greatly for setting before me so vividly the question of my going home or staying. I feel equally with him the importance of the decision. I have been meaning, as you know, for some time past to return in the autumn, and I see as yet no sufficient reason for changing my plan. I shall go with the full prevision that I shall not find life at home *simpatico*, but rather painfully, and as regards literary work, obstructively the reverse, and not even with the expectation that time will make it easier . . . If at the

[17] See the Introductions to the first two volumes of this edition.

end of a period at home, I don't feel an overwhelming desire to come back, it will be so much gained; but I should prepare myself for great deceptions if I don't take the possibility of such desire into account.[18]

And within weeks he was ready to announce to Sarah Butler Wister:

I sail for America on the 25th of August . . . I am extremely impatient to have it over, to start and to arrive . . . I have no plans of liking or disliking, of being happy or the reverse; I shall take what comes, make the best of it and dream inveterately, I foresee, of going back for a term of years, as the lawyers say, to Italy. I shall spend two or three months at Cambridge, but I expect to dispose of the winter in New York . . .[19]

James followed the plan he had outlined to Mrs. Wister with no small precision: he started, arrived, and, after spending 'two or three months at Cambridge', set himself up in New York as a writer and reviewer for the *Nation*. From New York, on 23 January 1875, he reported to Mrs. Wister:

I have been out tonight among some people who were telling ghost stories, and heard for the first time a young woman maintain that she had seen a ghost with her own eyes. It was a very pretty story—only too pretty to be true. But I see ghosts all the while here; I live among them: the ghosts of old world and the old things I left *là-bas*.[20]

For the writer in James the home-coming performed a crucial function; it crystallized his subject for him; made him locate it in the very ghost of Europe of which he had spoken to Mrs. Wister: as that ghost haunted and teased (it still does) the American sensibility. Thus *came into prominence*, and a new satirical, cultural, and moral focus, the international theme in the novels and stories of the years 1874-9. The theme had already been tested in earlier stories such as 'A Passionate Pilgrim' and 'Madame de Mauves'.

Since 'Professor Fargo', written in the spring of 1874, until the time James arrived in New York, apart from routine reviewing for magazines, his literary labours were confined to work on his first major novel, *Roderick Hudson*, and the launching of his first two books, a collection of tales and another of travel sketches. The only other work of fiction he completed during those many months was his first and last allegorical tale, 'Benvolio', which appeared in the *Galaxy* of August 1875. The tale was written in the early months of 1875, and the manuscript sent off to the editors in New York.

Before 'Benvolio' saw the light of day, however, its author's American experiment was already coming to an end. By July 1875

18 *Henry James Letters*, i, p. 449.'
19 Letter of 29 July 1874. Ibid., p. 461.
20 Ibid., p. 471.

James was back in Cambridge, with plans to return to 'the old world and the old things'. He had managed to obtain a commission from the *New York Tribune* to act as its correspondent in Paris. And before the winter set in, he had arrived in Paris. He stayed in Paris until the winter of 1876, when he moved to London and settled down in the British metropolis, more or less permanently, as an American expatriate, a writer, a bachelor.

It was from Paris, not long after his arrival there, that James sent to the *Scribner's Monthly Magazine* a package containing two manuscripts for publication. On 11 April 1876 he told Henry James Senior:

> I have lately sent two short tales to Scribner, which you will see when they are printed, and I trust judge according to their pretensions, which are small. One by the way (much the better) is on the history of your friend Webster in Albany, according to the account of it you gave me three years ago. I had had it in mind ever since, and had thoughts of using it for a longer story; but then I decided it was too lugubrious to be spun out. As it is, however, you will probably think I have been brutally curt.[21]

The 'history' of 'Webster' of the letter was the tale of 'Crawford's Consistency', which appeared in the *Scribner's* of August 1876. The manuscript accompanying this was the story of 'The Ghostly Rental', which came out in the same magazine a month later. The history of Matthew Henry Webster, 'a cultivated and accomplished young man in Albany', was first related to James by his father as early as 1873.[22]

[21] Ibid., ii, p. 39.

[22] *The James Family*, p. 126. Henry James Senior's account of the life of Webster reads thus: 'Matthew Henry Webster was a very cultivated and accomplished young man in Albany, at the time I [HJS] was growing up. He belonged to a respectable family, . . . was himself bred to the law, but had such a love of literature and, especially, of the natural sciences, that he never devoted himself very strictly to his profession. He was . . . *a polished gentleman, of perfect address, brave as Caesar, utterly unegotistic*, and one's wonder was how he ever grew up in Albany or reconciled himself to living in the place. One day he invested some money in a scheme much favoured by the President of the Bank in which he deposited, and his adventure proved a fortune.

There lived also a family in Albany of the name of Kane and this family reckoned upon a great social sensation in bringing out their youngest daughter, (Lydia Sybil Kane) who had never been seen by mortal eye outside of her own family, except that of a physician, who reported that she was fabulously beautiful. She *was* the most beautiful girl I think I ever saw, at a little distance. Well, she made her sensation, and brought Mr. Webster incontinently to her feet. Her family wanted wealth above all things for her; but here was wealth and something more, very much more, and they smiled upon his suit. Everything went merrily for a while. Webster was profoundly intoxicated with his prize. Never was man so enamoured, and never was beauty better fitted to receive adoration. She was an exquisite Grecian outline as to face, with a countenance like the tender dawn, and form and manners ravishingly graceful. But Webster was not content with his adventure—embarked again and lost all he owned almost. Mr. Oliver Kane (or Mrs., for she was the ruler of the family and as hard as

The subject had even then made an impression upon James, who had asked his mother, on 24 March 1873, to

> thank [father] meanwhile greatly for his story of *Mr. Webster*. It is admirable material, and excellently presented. I have transcribed it in my note book with religious care, and think that some day something will come of it. It would require much thinking out. But it is a first class theme.[23]

It is clear from James's two letters of 1873 and 1876 that he had been brooding over the 'theme' for quite some time. The finished tale of Crawford—as also its sister piece, 'The Ghostly Rental', which latter may have been prompted by the ghost stories James had heard in New York—does, indeed, appear to be of an earlier vintage; and the two works together products of a mental climate other than the one

---

the nether world in heart) gave the cue to her daughter, and my friend was dismissed. He couldn't believe his senses. He raved and cursed his fate. But it was inexorable. What was to be done? With a bitterness of heart inconceivable he plucked his revenge by marrying instantly a stout and blooming jade who in respect to Miss Kane was a peony to a violet, and who was absolutely nothing but flesh and blood. Her he bore upon his arm at fashionable hours through the streets; her he took to church, preserving his exquisite ease and courtesy to everyone, as if absolutely nothing had occurred; and her he pretended to take to bosom in private, with what a shudder one can imagine. Everybody stood aghast. He went daily about his affairs, as serene and unconscious as the moon in the heavens. Soon his poverty showed itself in certain economy of his wardrobe which had always been very recherché. Soon again he broke his leg, and went about on crutches, but neither poverty nor accident had the *least* power to ruffle his perfect repose. He was always superior to his circumstances, met you exactly as he had always done, impressed you invariably as the best bred man you ever saw, and left you wondering what a heart and what a brain lay behind such a fortune.

One morning we all read in the paper at breakfast that Mr. Webster had appealed the day before to the protection of the police against his wife, who had beaten him, and whom as a woman he could not degrade by striking in return: and the police responded promptly to his appeal. He went about his affairs as usual that day and every day, never saying a word to any one of his trouble, nor even indirectly asking sympathy, but compelling you to feel that here if anywhere was a novel height of manhood, a self-respect so eminent as to look down with scorn upon every refuge open to ordinary human infirmity. This lasted for five or six years. He never drank, had no vice, in fact of any kind, and lived a life of such decorum, so far as his own action was concerned, a life of such interest in science and literature as to be the most delightful and unconscious of companions even when his coat was shabby beyond compare, and you dare not look at him for fear of betraying your own vulgar misintelligence.

Finally, Sybil died smitten with small pox, and all her beauty gone to hideousness. He lingered awhile, his beautiful manners undismayed still, his eye as undaunted as at the beginning, and then he suddenly died. I never knew his equal in manhood, sheer, thorough, manly force, competent to itself in every emergency, and seeking none of the ordinary subterfuges which men seek in order to hide their own imbecility. I think it is a good basis for a novel.' *The James Family*, pp. 123-5.

[23] *Henry James Letters*, i, p. 357.

invoked either by James's fresh experience of Paris, or by his current, major literary preoccupation: work on his latest novel, *The American.*

While there is no clear evidence to support such a proposition, it is quite likely the two works were sketched out during James's stay in New York, and completed in Paris. It is hard to believe the writing of two tales with small pretensions would acquire such a priority with him so soon after his arrival in Paris. The stories are closer to the mood of 'Benvolio' and 'Professor Fargo', rather than to that of the international tales which preceded them, or the seven of the same kind which followed—led by 'Four Meetings'.

With greater justification, and authority of evidence, similar observations *need* to be made about the five tales which follow 'The Ghostly Rental' in the chronology of publication: 'Four Meetings' (November 1877), 'Théodolinde' (May 1878), 'Daisy Miller: A Study' (June-July 1878), 'Longstaff's Marriage' (August 1878), 'An International Episode' (December-January 1878-9). Once again, James's eagerness to sell as many of his wares as quickly as possible has, in the present case very definitely, confused the chronology of his tales.

The chronology of publication indicates a gap of almost a year between 'Four Meetings' and 'Longstaff's Marriage' and, because of the latter's particular placing in the chronology, a brief break occurring between the otherwise similar concerns of 'Daisy Miller' and 'An International Episode'. While no definite date of composition can be assigned to either 'Four Meetings', 'Théodolinde', or 'Longstaff's Marriage', we have evidence to prove that 'Longstaff's Marriage' existed as a completed manuscript, in fact, long *before* the inception both of 'Daisy Miller' and 'Théodolinde'; and that, therefore, there was, in fact, no discontinuity between 'Daisy Miller' and 'An International Episode'. As James himself claimed, the latter work was written straight after the former and was, in every sense, a pendant to 'Daisy Miller'.

The evidence comes from a 'strictly business' letter James wrote to his mother on 17 February 1878. In it he speaks of a draft (for $300.00) which the family had received in August 1877, and goes on to add: 'The draft was from Scribner for two stories I had sent him: one the tale of *Four Meetings* which you read: the second another tale which has not yet appeared.'[24] The tale 'not yet appeared' is not named in the letter. But there is no doubt the reference is to 'Longstaff's Marriage', which is the only other tale of the period by James to appear in the *Scribner's*, following the publication there of 'Four Meetings'. It is clear the two works were sent to their magazine publisher under the same cover, probably sometime in the spring of 1877—the draft was

[24] Ibid., ii, p. 155.

made in the summer; while 'Four Meetings' managed to get into print in the issue of that November, 'Longstaff's Marriage' had to wait yet another year to get its turn, in the number for August 1878. The editor's decision to give priority to 'Four Meetings' must have been dictated by that work's decidedly more striking and superior character.

By November 1877, when 'Four Meetings' appeared in the pages of the *Scribner's*, as we have seen, James had yet another manuscript of a tale awaiting publication with that periodical. The *Atlantic* had then only recently finished serializing *The American* (May 1877). The *Galaxy* was in the process of being taken over by the *Atlantic*. But James had yet another tale ready seeking a publisher! As he came to describe the condition later, in the 'strictly business' letter to his mother quoted above, he was facing a temporary 'stoppage of chance to publish' his shorter tales. In the circumstances, it was only natural that his latest effort should end up with a new magazine: 'Théodolinde' appeared in the *Lippincott's Magazine* for May 1878. Circumstantial evidence points to the summer of 1877—not long after the package that went to the *Scribner's*—as the most likely date of composition for this tale. There is, indeed, an obvious French connection between the three stories 'Four Meetings', 'Longstaff's Marriage', and 'Theodolinde'. Unlike 'Crawford's Consistency' and 'The Ghostly Rental', these three works are very clearly by-products of the Parisian year. James appears to have written the tales when he had moved from Paris to London—had already become, as he told his brother, 'an established Londoner'.[25]

3.

Contrary to the impression given by some of his commentators, James's conquest of London was less than swift. If anything, it was slow and fraught with doubts and difficulties. In the initial stages at any rate, the ritual of 'making acquaintances' had been somewhat dreary:

> All the Englishmen I meet are of the 'useful information' prosaic sort, and I don't think in an equal lot of people I ever received such an impression of want of imagination. Sometimes I feel as if this process of 'making acquaintances' in a strange country were very dreary work: it is so empirical and experimental, and you have to try one by one so many uninteresting people to hit upon even the *possibly* interesting ones. I hope it won't be often repeated, and that I shall be able to settle down in England long enough to keep, and profit by, any sense of domestication that I may acquire.[26]

25 Letter to William James, 12 January 1877. Ibid., p. 89.

26 Letter to William James, 28 February 1877. Ibid., p. 100.

His conquest of literary London was even slower. Though already a professional writer of considerable standing, and soon to become 'an established Londoner', in 1877 James did not feel confident enough to try his luck with British magazines. Eventually, however, when he did make his début in 1878, the occasion had something of an accident about it—an accident with a couple of 'firsts' attached to it. The work in question, 'Daisy Miller', was his first tale to be rejected by an American magazine; ironically, it was also the first of his works to win him what he was to call 'the flourishing condition of [his] fame'. It is interesting to note that James won real popular acclaim in a foreign land, fifteen years after he started as a writer, with a work a minor literary periodical of his own country had promptly turned down.

In the autumn of 1877, having dispatched his French tales to America, and completed a good part of *The Europeans*—his 'brightest possible sun-spot' (for 1878),[27] the child of his 'buxom muse'—James decided to take a vacation in Italy. He spent several weeks in Rome, 'lodging in the bosom of a Roman family; that of the Cavaliere Avvocato Spinetti—a rather ragged and besmirched establishment.'[28] Weeks later, he returned to London with material for a novella, which he proceeded to write in the early months of 1878. The work was called 'Daisy Miller: A Study'.

In the Preface to the New York Edition of this work,[29] James speaks of a friend who, 'in Rome during the autumn of 1877', had told him the story of a 'simple and uninformed lady of the previous winter, whose young daughter, a child of nature and of freedom', had acted in a manner so unconventional that it pointed to James 'a familiar moral'. He felt it could be dramatized. The ladies in question 'weren't named' to him.

Some eight or nine months before 'the previous winter', on 4 April 1876, the death had occured in Rome of Julia Newberry, the daughter of a wealthy, highly placed Chicago family. Julia had died quite suddenly, at the age of twenty-two, and was buried in the Protestant Cemetery in Rome. For several years, with her mother and a sister, moving from hotel to hotel, she had been travelling all over Europe. Vevey was familiar to her; so was Rome. And she had a 'snip'—an admirer—who had followed her to Nice and Naples. She was sprightly, full of opinions, naïve, talkative, and a real charmer. Sixty years after her death, in 1933, when her diary was discovered and published, the reviewer for *The Times Literary Supplement* for 26 October

[27] Letter to William Dean Howells, 30 March 1877. Ibid., p. 105.

[28] Letter to Alice James, 2 November 1877. Ibid., p. 141.

[29] See Appendix II below.

1933 described the young diarist as a person having a 'great spirit, a dashing style, and very definite opinions.'[30] Others spoke of a sense of tragedy inherent in Julia Newberry's life and diary.

In the years 1872-4, together with her mother and sister, she was doing the European round. So was Henry James: their paths might have—could have—crossed. He turned up in Rome only a year and a half after her death.

It is difficult to believe that from the small American community in Rome he had heard nothing about the recent death in Rome of so familiar a figure of the Roman-American scene. James's informant of the autumn of 1877 simply could not have left the characters of his 'anecdote'—as James's own account in the Preface has come to be called—'unnamed'. The close correspondence between the real-life Julia Newberry and Daisy Miller of James's fiction is difficult to ignore. It could be argued that the chain of events that led to the 'vogue' of 'Daisy Miller' was, at least in part, owing to this fact!

James's original choice for the most fortunate and prosperous of his works was a second-rate American magazine, the *Lippincott's Magazine*. He sent the manuscript off to its editor sometime in March 1878, two months before another tale by him, 'Thédolinde', was to appear in its pages. Presumably, James did not sell the story to the *Atlantic* because, in spite of W. D. Howells there, that magazine was now somewhat reluctant to pay the higher price James had begun to ask for his tales. The *Scribner*, meanwhile, already had 'Longstaff's Marriage' awaiting publication. At the time, James did not feel his story was fit, or good enough, for publication in a British magazine. The *Lippincott's* seemed the most obvious and lucrative choice.

John Foster Kirk, the editor of the *Lippincott's*, turned down the manuscript *without any comment*. In later years it was believed, by James as well as Howells, that the work had been rejected because it was seen to be presenting an unfavourable image of American girlhood. It is quite likely Kirk had rejected the tale for a different reason: James's account of the last days of Daisy Miller corresponded too closely to the real-life story of Julia Newberry!

Not expecting the response he actually received, James offered the rejected manuscript to his closest literary acquaintance in London, Sir Leslie Stephen, who accepted it for the *Cornhill* in April 1878—

30 *The Times Literary Supplement*, p. 725. With an Introduction by Margaret Ayer Barnes and Janet Ayer Fairbank, the *Diary* of Julia Newberry was first published by the firm of Norton (by Selwyn and Blount, in Britain). The extraordinary correspondence between the real-life portrait of Julia and James's fiction was first pointed out by Edgar J. Goodspeed in a short note, 'A Footnote to "Daisy Miller"', the *Atlantic Monthly*, 153 (February 1934), pp. 252-3.

and not without some 'effusion'. James conveyed the news from the *Cornhill* to his father in a letter of 19 April 1878: 'Leslie Stephen has just accepted, with effusion, a short story of mine for the *Cornhill*. It is in two parts and comes out probably in June and July. I will of course immediately send it you . . .'[31]

In two instalments 'Daisy Miller' was published in the *Cornhill* for June and July 1878, and, as James reported to William, shortly after the second instalment was out, it instantly 'made a great hit'. James became famous almost overnight. The 'vogue' of 'Daisy Miller' which followed, the ire, the interest, and the admiration that it aroused on both sides of the Atlantic, was, at least in some measure, due to the fact that the particular countenance of the American Daisy had surfaced in a prestigious British periodical. To James, however, the publication gave 'a capital start' in England.

Several different factors appear to have gone into the making of James's next tale, yet another novella, again in two parts, and published again in the *Cornhill*, in its issues of December 1878-January 1879. From the very start of Daisy Miller's career, James had felt that his delicate point, his subtle satire, would be misunderstood by at least a portion of his American, as well as British, reading public. This feeling was confirmed by the response of John Foster Kirk. And when the tale actually appeared, it seemed to have stepped into a controversy over the conduct of American, in particular American women, travellers abroad. The tale seemed to be giving an unfortunate incentive to the already misguided discussion. James was giving vent to these feelings when he wrote to Mrs. William Dean Howells on 14 August 1878:

> I must thank you very tenderly for your generous little despatch on the subject of 'Daisy Miller'. I am charmed to think that she struck a sympathetic chord in your imagination, and that having been, in fact, so harshly treated by fate and public opinion, she has had it made up to her in posthumous honours. She appears to have made something of a hit; for people appear to have found time to talk of her a little even in this busy and not particularly nimble-witted England.[32]

It was certainly not James's intention to show up American womanhood: though that is precisely how a large segment of his 'nimble-witted' readers had understood the story. The need for a corrective was, therefore, urgent: this James provided with 'An International Episode'.[33]

[31] *Henry James Letters*, ii, p. 166.

[32] Ibid., p. 182.

[33] See also Howell Daniels, 'Henry James and "An International Episode"' in *British Association for American Studies Bulletin*, i (1960), pp. 3-35; James's own, little-known, 'Americans Abroad' is reprinted in this volume.

In his letters of the period, James repeatedly speaks of his new novella as a '*pendant*', a 'counterpart' to 'Daisy Miller'. Evidently, he started writing the story very soon after 'Daisy Miller' had been placed with the *Cornhill*; it is even likely that he had discussed the idea of his projected counterpart with Sir Leslie Stephen. The work was completed in the month in which the second instalment of 'Daisy Miller' came out in print.

The publication of 'An International Episode', in which the satire is more direct, the irony more pungent, caused an even bigger misunderstanding and furore—this time, largely, among his British readers, who failed to see any point in the satire being directed *at them*, with the advantage going to a herione, Bessie Alden, who was, after all, a sister of Daisy Miller. Thus, within days of the publication of 'An International Episode', James had heard enough grumbling to have felt the need to report to Grace Norton in a letter of 4 January 1879:

> You may be interested to know that I hear my little 'International Episode' has given offence to various people of my acquaintance here. Don't you wonder at it? So long as one serves up Americans for their entertainment it is all right—but hands off the sacred natives! They are really, I think, thinner-skinned than we![34]

With an added note of caution, he had similar feelings to express to his mother in a letter written two weeks later:

> You will have read the second part by this time [of 'An International Episode'], and I hope that you won't, like many of my friends here (as I partly know and partly suspect) take it ill of me as against my 'British entertainers'. It seems to me myself that I have been very delicate; but I shall keep off dangerous ground in future. It is an entirely new sensation for them (the people here) to be (at all delicately) *ironised* or satirised, from the American point of view, and they don't at all relish it. Their conception of the normal in such a relation is that the satire should be all on their side against the Americans; and I suspect that if one were to push this a little further one would find that they are extremely sensitive. But I like them too much and feel too kindly to them to go into the satire-business or even the light-ironical in any case in which it would wound them—even if in such a case I should see my way to it very clearly.[35]

The popular success, as well as notoriety, of 'Daisy Miller' and 'An International Episode', augmented as it was by their controversial aspect, led directly and immediately to the publication, for the first

[34] *Henry James Letters*, ii, pp. 209-10.

[35] Letter to Mrs. Henry James Senior, 18 January 1879. Ibid., pp. 212-13. See also James's defence of his tale in his letter to Mrs. F. H. Hill, who reviewed the first book edition of the tale for the *Daily News*. *Henry James Letters*, ii, pp. 219-23.

time in England, of a collection of tales by James, *Daisy Miller, An International Episode, Four Meetings*, which came out within weeks of the second instalment of 'An International Episode'. All three works had been lightly revised for their book publication. To 'An International Episode' James gave a unique revision: while he otherwise touched up the text only in a dozen places, he inserted a completely new scene into the book edition of the novella. This first collection was followed later in 1879 by the publication of yet another collection, *The Madonna of the Future*, through which James introduced his British readers to some of his earlier international tales. The year 1878 was coming to be his finest hour:[36] he was now an 'established Londoner' with an international literary reputation.

If 'An International Episode' was a '*pendant*' to 'Daisy Miller', James's next tale, 'The Pension Beaurepas', was a natural outcome, and extension, of the climate generated by the two novellas, and the controversy surrounding American travellers abroad. What could be more conducive to international episodes than the setting of a French *pension*! James wrote the tale in the satiric mode of 'An International Episode' not long after the latter work was completed—perhaps in September-October 1878. The manuscript of it was dispatched to the *Atlantic* in the middle of November. With a sense of the interest already in the air, the *Atlantic* did not waste time to offer its readers what *it* had from the author of 'Daisy Miller' and 'An International Episode'. 'The Pension Beaurepas', later described by James himself as 'a mere pretext . . . *en tête*',[37] came out within a few months, in the *Atlantic* for April 1879—an unusually quick disposal of a manuscript for that magazine. The first published text, however, was rather badly bruised.

The theme of contrast, the controversial cultural aspect of the international subject, with which James had been preoccupied for a better part of 1877 and 1878—'Four Meetings', *The Europeans*, 'Daisy Miller', 'An International Episode', and 'The Pension Beaurepas'—had served James well: it had made him famous. Yet, as he told Howells, it had also left him just a little disappointed:

> My fame indeed seems to do very well everywhere—the proportions it has acquired here are a constant surprise to me; it is only my fortune that leaves to be desired . . . The aforesaid fame, expanding through two hemispheres, is represented by a pecuniary equivalent almost grotesquely small. Your [Howells's] account of the vogue of *Daisy Miller* and the *International Episode*, for instance, embittered my spirit when I reflected that it had awakened no

36 The reputation of 1878 as the most productive year of James's life is not well founded: many of the fictions published that year were written, in fact, in 1877.

37 *Henry James Letters*, ii, p. 243. Letter to W. D. Howells, 17 June 1879.

echo (to speak of) in my pocket. I have made $200 by the whole American career of D.M. and nothing at all by the Episode . . .[38]

For the final tale collected in this volume, 'The Diary of a Man of Fifty', which followed 'The Pension Beaurepas', we have little need to make conjectures. Since about the early seventies James had been jotting down ideas to be developed into novels and stories. The earliest of such Notebooks to survive carries an entry for 'The Diary of a Man of Fifty', according to which a note for the tale was made on 12 December 1878. The tale was completed on 14 January 1879.[39] It was the first tale by James to be published simultaneously in Britain (*Macmillan's Magazine*, July 1879) and America (*Harper's New Monthly Magazine*, July 1879). He was, in short, fast becoming a name worth watching. There was more than a touch of foresight in the advice Edward L. Burlingame gave to the head of his firm, Charles Scribner, in a letter written on 19 August 1879:

Doesn't it seem to you—as it certainly does to me—that it is worth while to make him [James] a decidedly good offer . . . He is (thus far) almost entirely

[38] Ibid.

[39] See *The Notebooks of Henry James* edited by F. O. Matthiessen and Kenneth B. Murdock (New York: Oxford University Press, 1961), pp. 8-9. James's working Note for the tale reads thus: 'It has often occurred to me [James] that the following would be an interesting situation.—A man of certain age (say 48) who has lived and thought, sees a certain situation of his own youth reproduced before his eyes and hesitates between his curiosity to see at what issue it arrives in this particular case and the prompting to interfere, in the light of his own experience, for the benefit of the actors. Mortimer, for instance, goes abroad and in some foreign town he finds the daughter of a lady—the Contessa G—whom, when he was five and twenty, on a visit to the same place, he had known and fallen in love with. That episode of his youth comes back to him with peculiar vividness—the daughter is a strange, interesting reproduction of the mother. The mother had been a dangerous woman and had entangled him in a flirtation; an unscrupulous charmer—an imperious circe—on the brink of whose abysmal coquetry he trembled for an hour; or rather for many days. After a great struggle he took himself off, escaped from his danger by flight and breathed more freely. Then he had greatly regretted his discretion—he wished that he might have known what it was to love such a woman. Afterwards, however, he hears things that make him think he has had a great escape. The Contessa G. has an intrigue with another man, with whom, in consequence, her husband fights a duel. The Conte G. is killed and the Countess marries her lover. She is now dead—all this, for Mortimer, is a memory. But her daughter, as I say, strongly resembles her and stirs up in Mortimer's mind the depths of the past. She is a beautiful dangerous coquette. Hovering near her Mortimer finds a young Englishman who is evidently much in love with her, and who seems to Mortimer a sort of reproduction of himself at twenty-five—the image of his own early innocence—his own timid and awkward passion. The young man interests him and he watches the progress of his relations with the lady. They seem to him to correspond at all points with his own relations with the mother—so that at last he determines to warn him and open his eyes. (The above sketch worked out and finished January 17th.—*The Diary of a Man of Fifty*).'

> unattached in the matter of publishing; and his future is certainly valuable enough to make an effort to connect him here—But of course all this 'goes without saying' after all.[40]

Only six days before this letter was written, James had sent Howells a letter outlining his plans for his first 'big' book—to be called *The Portrait of a Lady*;[41] and, it is worth adding, a quarter of a century later, the same Burlingame arranged the publication of the New York Edition of James's fiction.[42]

[40] MS. letter, the Scribner Archive, Princeton University Library.

[41] '. . . my title would (probably) be "The Portrait of a Lady". But on this meanwhile please observe complete silence.' Letter of 23 August 1879. *Henry James Letters*, ii, p. 253.

[42] For an account of the making of the New York Edition, as well as the earlier revised editions of the tales, see the Introduction to the second volume of this edition. In connection with the New York Edition of 'Four Meetings', 'Daisy Miller', 'An International Episode', and 'The Pension Beaurepas', however, it is worth adding that these works came to occupy their present positions in that edition after a good deal of rearranging and reconsideration. At one point 'Daisy Miller' was to appear as the last tale in volume xvii, and not the title story of volume xviii, as came to be the case with it in the final edition. Similarly, originally 'Four Meetings' was to go with 'The Altar of the Dead', rather than with 'The Author of Beltraffio', under which title it is grouped in the published arrangement. James was unhappy that

> a *strict* following of chronological order has been impossible. One of my greatest reasons for desiring an edition was, from the first, that I might in a measure *classify* and (more or less illuminatingly) juxtapose; and this I have tried for—the more easily that it hasn't happened to involve, luckily, any great chronological violence and then, to repeat, I have had, as I said the other day, to fit in lengths, to arrange Quantity for each Volume in a comparative and accommodating way. Also the illustration-question has led me a little of a dance, modifying at best an *ideally* systematic sequence. [MS. letter to Scribner, 10 March 1908, the Scribner Archive.]

The final decision to give a place of honour to 'Daisy Miller—as the title story of the volume in which it appears in the New York Edition—was taken by the publisher. James had had an alternative in mind, 'Julia Bride', although he, too, had wished the novella should receive some distinction. The publisher's argument, however, was decisive:

> In spite of the attractiveness of 'Julia Bride', which is such in our eyes as to make it seem almost questionable to yield precedence over her even to 'Daisy Miller' herself, we feel that the latter has the advantage of so many years of fame as to entitle her at least to lead the volume which includes her. Furthermore, she will then not be torn from the congenial companionship of 'Pandora', etc. [MS. letter to James, from W. C. Brownell of Scribner, 12 January 1909, the Scribner Archive.]

Benvolio

[First appeared in the *Galaxy*, vol. xx (August 1875), pp. 209-35. The tale was revised and reprinted in volume ii of *The Madonna of the Future* (1879).]

I.

ONCE UPON A TIME (AS IF HE HAD LIVED IN A FAIRY TALE) THERE was a very interesting young man. This is not a fairy tale, and yet our young man was, in some respects, as pretty a fellow as any fairy prince. I call him interesting because his type of character is one I have always found it agreeable to observe. If you fail to consider him so, I shall be willing to confess that the fault is mine and not his; I shall have told my story with too little skill.

His name was Benvolio; that is, it was not; but we shall call him so for the sake both of convenience and of picturesqueness. He was more than twenty-five years old, but he was not yet thirty-five; he had a little property; he followed no regular profession. His personal appearance was in the highest degree prepossessing. Having said this, it were perhaps well that I should let you—you especially, madam—suppose that he exactly corresponded to your idea of a well-favoured young man; but I am bound to explain definitely wherein it was that he resembled a fairy prince, and I need furthermore to make a record of certain little peculiarities and anomalies in which it is probable that your brilliant conception would be deficient. Benvolio was slim and fair, with clustering locks, remarkably fine eyes, and such a frank, expressive smile that, on the journey through life, it was almost as serviceable to its owner as the magic key, or the enchanted ring, or the wishing-cap, or any other bauble of necromantic properties. Unfortunately this charming smile was not always at his command, and its place was sometimes occupied by a very dusky and ill-conditioned frown, which rendered the young man no service whatever—not even that of frightening people; for though it expressed extreme irritation and impatience, it was characterized by the brevity of contempt, and the only revenge upon disagreeable things and offensive people that it seemed to express a desire for on Benvolio's part was that of forgetting and ignoring them with the utmost possible celerity. It never made any one tremble, though now and then it perhaps made sensitive people murmur an imprecation or two. You might have supposed from Benvolio's manner, when he was in good humour (which was the greater part of the time), from his brilliant, intelligent glance, from his easy, irresponsible step, and in especial from the sweet, clear, lingering, caressing tone of his voice—the voice as it were of a man whose fortune has been made for him, and who assumes, a trifle egotistically, that the rest of the world is equally at leisure to share with him the sweets of life, to pluck the wayside flowers and chase the butterflies afield—you might have supposed, I say, from all this luxurious assurance of demeanour, that our hero really had the wishing-cap sitting invisible on his handsome brow, or was obliged only to close his knuckles together a moment to exert an effective pressure upon the magic ring. The young man, I have said, was compounded of many anomalies; I may say more exactly that he was a tissue of absolute contradictions. He did possess the magic ring, in a certain fashion; he possessed, in other words, the poetic imagination. Everything that fancy could do for him was done in perfection. It gave him immense satisfactions; it transfigured the world; it made very common objects sometimes seem radiantly beautiful, and it converted beautiful ones into infinite sources of intoxication. Benvolio had what is called the poetic temperament. It is rather out of fashion to describe a man in these terms; but I believe, in spite of much evidence to the contrary, that there are poets still; and if we may call a spade a spade, why should we not call such a person as Benvolio a poet?

These contradictions that I speak of ran through his whole nature, and they were perfectly apparent in his habits, in his manners, in his conversation, and even in his person. It was as if the souls of two very different men had been thrown together in the same mould and they had agreed, for convenience' sake, to use the very vulgar phrase of the day, to run the machine in alternation. The machine with Benvolio was always the imagination; but in his different moods it kept a very different tune. To an acute observer his face itself would have betrayed these variations; and it is certain that his dress, his talk, his way of spending his time, one day and another, abundantly indicated them. Sometimes he looked very young—rosy, radiant, blooming, younger than his years. Then suddenly, as the light struck his head in a particular manner, you would see that his golden locks contained a surprising number of silver threads; and with your attention quickened by this discovery, you would proceed to detect something grave and discreet in his smile—something vague and ghostly, like the dim adumbration of the darker half of the lunar disk. You might have met Benvolio, in certain moods, dressed like a man of the highest fashion—wearing his hat on his ear, a rose in his buttonhole, a wonderful intaglio or an antique Syracusan coin, by way of a pin, in his cravat. Then, on the morrow, you would have espied him braving the sunshine in a rusty scholar's coat, with his hat pulled over his brow—a costume wholly at odds with flowers and gems. It was all a matter of fancy; but his fancy was a weather-cock and faced east or west, as the wind blew. His conversation matched his coat and trowsers; he talked one day the talk of the town; he chattered, he gossiped, he asked questions and told stories; you would have said that he was a charming fellow for a dinner party or the pauses of a cotillon. The next he either talked philosophy or politics, or said nothing at all; he was absent and indifferent; he was thinking his own thoughts; he had a book in his pocket, and evidently he was composing one in his head. At home he lived in two chambers. One was an immense room hung with pictures, lined with books, draped with rugs and tapestries, decorated with a multitude of ingenious devices (for of all these things he was very fond); the other, his sleeping-room, was almost as bare as a monastic cell. It had a meagre little strip of carpet on the floor, and a dozen well-thumbed volumes of classic poets and sages on the mantel-shelf. On the wall hung three or four coarsely engraved portraits of the most exemplary of these worthies; these were the only ornaments. But the room had the charm of a great window, in a deep embrasure, looking out upon a tangled, silent, moss-grown garden, and in the embrasure stood the little ink-blotted table at which Benvolio did most of his poetic scribbling. The windows of his sumptuous sitting-room commanded a wide public square, where people were always passing and lounging, where military music used to play on vernal nights, and half the life of the great town went forward. At the risk of your thinking our hero a sad idler, I will say that he spent an inordinate amount of time in gazing out of these windows (on either side), with his elbows on the sill. The garden did not belong to the house which he inhabited, but to a neighbouring one, and the proprietor, a graceless old miser, was very chary of permits to visit his domain. But Benvolio's fancy used to wander through the alleys without stirring the long arms of the untended plants, and to bend over the heavy-headed flowers without leaving a footprint on their beds. It was here that his happiest thoughts came to him—that inspiration (as we may say, speaking of a man of the poetic temperament) descended upon him in silence, and for certain divine, appreciable moments stood poised along the course of his scratching quill. It was not, however, that he had not spent some very charming hours in the larger, richer apartment. He used to receive his friends there—sometimes in great numbers, sometimes at boisterous, many-voiced suppers, which lasted far into the night. When these entertainments were over he never made a direct transition to his little scholar's cell, with its garden view. He went out and wandered for an hour through the dark, sleeping streets of the town, ridding himself of the fumes of wine, and feeling not at all tipsy, but intensely, portentously sober. More than once, when he came back and prepared to go to bed, he had seen the first faint glow of dawn trembling upward over the tree tops of his garden. His friends, coming to see him, often found the greater room empty, and, advancing, pounded at the door of his chamber. But he frequently kept quiet, not desiring in the least to see them, knowing exactly what they were going to say, and not thinking it worth hearing. Then, hearing them stride away, and the outer door close behind them, he would come forth and take a turn in his slippers, over his Persian carpets, and glance out of the window and see his defeated visitant stand scratching his chin in the sunny square, and then laugh lightly to himself—as is said to be the habit of the scribbling tribe in moments of production.

Although he had a family he enjoyed extreme liberty. His family was so large, his brothers and sisters so numerous, that he could absent himself constantly and be little missed. Sometimes he used this privilege freely; he tired of people whom he had seen very often, and he had seen, of course, an immense deal of his family. At others he was extremely domestic; he suddenly found solitude depressing, and it seemed to him that if one sought society as a refuge, one needed to be on familiar terms with it, and that with no one was familiarity so natural as among people who had grown up at a common fireside. Nevertheless it frequently occurred to him—for sooner or later everything occurred to him—that he was too independent and irresponsible; that he would be happier if his hands were sometimes tied, so long as the knot were not too tight. His curiosity about all things was great, and he satisfied it largely whenever the occasion offered itself; but as the years went by this pursuit of impartial science appeared to produce a singular result. He became conscious of an intellectual condition similar to that of a palate which has lost its relish. To a man with a disordered appetite all things taste alike, and so it seemed to Benvolio that his imagination was losing its sense of a better and a worse. It had still its glowing moments, its feasts and its holidays; but, on the whole, the spectacle of human life was growing flat and stale. This is simply a wordy way of expressing that pregnantly synthetic fact—Benvolio was *blasé.* He knew it, he knew it betimes, and he regretted it acutely. He believed that such a consummation was not absolutely necessary—especially at his time of life; for he said to himself that there *must* be a way of using one's faculties which will keep their edges sharp. There was a certain possible economy in one's dealings with life which would make the two ends meet at the last. What was it? The wise man's duty was to find it out.

One of its rudiments, he believed, was that one grows tired of one's self sooner than of anything else in the world. Idleness, every one admitted, was the greatest of follies; but idleness was subtle and exacted tribute under a hundred plausible disguises. One was often idle when one seemed to be ardently occupied; one was always idle (it might be concluded) when one's occupations had not a high aim. One was idle therefore when one was working simply for one's self. Curiosity for curiosity's sake, art for art's sake, these were essentially broken-winded steeds. *Ennui* was at the end of everything that did not entangle us somehow with human life. To get entangled, therefore, pondered Benvolio, should be the wise man's aim. Poor Benvolio had to ponder all this, because, as I say, he was a poet and not a man of action. A fine fellow of the latter stamp would have solved the problem without knowing it, and bequeathed to his fellow men not cold formulas but vivid examples. But Benvolio had often said to himself that he was born to imagine great things—not to do them; and he had said this by no means sadly, for, on the whole, he was very well content with his portion. Imagine them he determined he would, and on a most magnificent scale. He would entangle himself at least in a mesh of work—work of the most profound and elaborate sort. He would handle great ideas, he would enunciate great truths, he would write immortal verses. In all this there was a large amount of talent and a liberal share of ambition. I will not say that Benvolio was a man of genius; it may seem to make the distinction too cheap; but he was at any rate a man with an intellectual passion; and if, being near him, you had been able to listen intently enough, he would, like the great people of his craft, have seemed to emit something of that vague, magical murmur—the voice of the infinite—which lurks in the involutions of a sea-shell. He himself, by the way, had once made use of this little simile, and had written a poem in which it was melodiously set forth that the poetic minds scattered about the world correspond to the little shells one picks up on the beach, all resonant with the echo of ocean. The whole thing was of course rounded off with the sands of time, the waves of history, and other harmonious conceits.

II.

But (as you are naturally expecting to hear) Benvolio knew perfectly well that there is one way of getting entangled which is far more effectual than any other—the way that a charming woman points out. Benvolio was of course in love. Who was his mistress, you ask (I flatter myself with some impatience), and was she pretty, was she kind, was he successful? Hereby hangs my tale, which I must relate categorically.

Benvolio's mistress was a lady whom (as I cannot tell you her real name) it will be quite in keeping to speak of as the Countess. The Countess was a young widow, who had some time since divested herself of her mourning weeds—which indeed she had never worn but very lightly. She was rich, extremely pretty, and free to do as pleased her. She was passionately fond of pleasure and admiration, and they gushed forth at her feet in unceasing streams. Her beauty was not of the conventional type, but it was dazzlingly brilliant; few faces were more expressive, more fascinating. Hers was never the same for two days together; it reflected her momentary circumstances with extraordinary vividness, and in knowing her you had the advantage of knowing a dozen different women. She was clever and accomplished, and had the credit of being perfectly amiable; indeed, it was difficult to imagine a person combining a greater number of the precious gifts of nature and fortune. She represented felicity, gaiety, success; she was made to charm, to play a part, to exert a sway. She lived in a great house, behind high verdure-muffled walls, where other Countesses, in other years, had been the charm and the envy of their time. It was an antiquated quarter, into which the tide of commerce had lately begun to roll heavily; but the turbid waves of trade broke in vain against the Countess's enclosure, and if in her garden and her drawing-room you heard the deep uproar of the city, it was only as a vague undertone to sweeter things—to music, and witty talk, and tender dialogue. There was something very striking in this unyielding, elegant privacy, in the midst of public toil and traffic.

Benvolio was a great deal at this lady's house; he rarely desired better entertainment. I spoke just now of privacy; but privacy was not what he found there, nor what he wished to find. He went there when he wished to learn with the least trouble what was going on in the world, for the talk of the people the Countess generally had about her was an epitome of the gossip, the rumours, the interests, the hopes and fears of polite society. She was a thoroughly liberal hostess; all she asked was to be entertained; if you would contribute to the common fund of amusement, of discussion, you were a welcome guest. Sooner or later, among your fellow-guests, you encountered every one of consequence. There were frivolous people and wise people; people whose fortune was in their pockets, and people whose fortune was in their brains; people deeply concerned in public affairs, and people concerned only with the fit of their garments or with the number of the people who looked round when their names were announced. Benvolio, who liked a large and various social spectacle, appreciated all this; but he was best pleased, as a general thing, when he found the Countess alone. This was often his fortune, for the simple reason that when the Countess expected him, she invariably had herself refused to every one else. This is almost an answer to your inquiry whether Benvolio was successful in his suit. As yet, strictly speaking, there was no suit. Benvolio had never made love to the Countess. This sounds very strange, but it is nevertheless true. He was in love with her; he thought her the most charming creature conceivable; he spent hours with her alone by her own orders; he had had opportunity—he had been up to his neck in opportunity—and yet he had never said to her, as would have seemed so natural, 'Dear Countess, I beseech you to be my wife.' If you are surprised, I may also confide to you that the Countess was; and surprise under the circumstances very easily became displeasure. It is by no means certain that Benvolio had made the little speech we have just imagined, the Countess would have fallen into his arms, confessed to a mutual flame, and rung in *finis* to our tale, with the wedding bells. But she nevertheless expected him in civility to pay her this supreme compliment. Her answer would be—what it might be; but his silence was a permanent offence. Every man, roughly speaking, had asked the Countess to marry him, and every man had been told that she was much obliged, but had no idea of marrying. Now here, with the one man who failed to ask her, she had a great idea of it, and his forbearance gave her more to think about than all the importunities of all her other suitors. The truth was she liked Benvolio extremely, and his independence rendered him excellent service. The Countess had a very lively fancy, and she had fingered, nimbly enough, the volume of the young man's merits. She was by nature a trifle cold; she rarely lost her head; she measured each step as she took it; she had had little fancies and incipient passions; but on the whole she had thought much more about love than felt it. She had often tried to form an image mentally of the sort of man it would be well for her to love—for so it was she expressed it. She had succeeded but indifferently, and her imagination had gone a-begging until the day she met Benvolio. Then it seemed to her that her quest was ended—her prize gained. This nervous, ardent, deep-eyed youth struck her as the harmonious counterpart of her own facile personality. This conviction rested with the Countess on a fine sense of propriety which it would be vain to attempt to analyse; he was different from herself and from the other men who surrounded her, and to be complete it seemed to her that she ought to have something of that sort in her train. In the old days she would have had it in the person of a troubador or a knight-errant; now, a woman who was in her own right a considerable social figure might conveniently annex it in the form of a husband. I don't know how good a judge the Countess was of such matters, but she believed that the world would hear of Benvolio. She had beauty, ancestry, money, luxury, but she had not genius; and if genius was to be had, why not secure it, and complete the list? This is doubtless a rather coarse statement of the Countess's argument; but you have it thrown in gratis, as it were; for all I am bound to tell you is that this charming young woman took a fancy to this clever young man, and that she used to cry sometimes for a quarter of a minute when she imagined he didn't care for her. Her tears were wasted, because he did care for her—more even than she would have imagined if she had taken a favourable view of the case. But Benvolio, I cannot too much repeat, was an exceedingly complex character, and there was many a hiatus in the logic of his conduct. The Countess charmed him, excited him, interested him; he did her abundant justice—more than justice; but at the end of all he felt that she failed to satisfy him. If a man could have half a dozen wives—and Benvolio had once maintained, poetically, that he ought to have—the Countess would do very well for one of them—possibly even for the best of them. But she would not serve for all seasons and all moods; she needed a complement, an alternative—what the French call a *repoussoir*. One day he was going to see her, knowing that he was expected. There was to be a number of other people—in fact, a very brilliant assembly; but Benvolio knew that a certain touch of the hand, a certain glance of the eye, a certain caress of the voice, would be reserved for him alone. Happy Benvolio, you will say, to be going about the world with such charming secrets as this locked up in his young heart! Happy Benvolio indeed; but mark how he trifled with his happiness. He went to the Countess's gate, but he went no further; he stopped, stood there a moment, frowning intensely, and biting the finger of his glove; then suddenly he turned and strode away in the opposite direction. He walked and walked and left the town behind him. He went his way till he reached the country, and here he bent his steps towards a little wood which he knew very well, and whither indeed, on a spring afternoon, when she had taken a fancy to play at shepherd and shepherdess, he had once come with the Countess. He flung himself on the grass, on the edge of the wood—not in the same place where he had lain at the Countess's feet, pulling sonnets out of his pocket and reading them one by one; a little stream flowed beside him; opposite, the sun was declining; the distant city lay before him, lifting its towers and chimneys against the reddening western sky. The twilight fell and deepened and the stars came out. Benvolio lay there thinking that he preferred them to the

Countess's wax candles. He went back to town in a farmer's wagon, talking with the honest rustic who drove it.

Very much in this way, when he had been on the point of knocking at the gate of the Countess's heart and asking ardently to be admitted, he had paused, stood frowning, and then turned short and rambled away into solitude. She never knew how near, two or three times, he had come. Two or three times she had accused him of being rude, and this was nothing but the backward swing of the pendulum. One day it seemed to her that he was altogether too vexatious, and she reproached herself with her good nature. She had made herself too cheap; such conduct was beneath her dignity; she would take another tone. She closed her door to him, and bade her people say, whenever he came, that she was engaged. At first Benvolio only wondered. Oddly enough, he was not what is commonly called sensitive; he never supposed you meant to offend him; not being at all impertinent himself, he was not on the watch for impertinence in others. Only, when he fairly caught you in the act he was immensely disgusted. Therefore, as I say, he simply wondered what had suddenly made the Countess so busy; then he remembered certain other charming persons whom he knew, and went to see how the world wagged with them. But they rendered the Countess eminent service: she gained by comparison, and Benvolio began to miss her. All that other charming women were, who led the life of the world (as it is called), the Countess was in a superior, in a perfect degree; she was the ripest fruit of a high civilization; her companions and rivals, beside her, had but a pallid bloom, an acrid savour. Benvolio had a relish in all things for the best, and he found himself breathing sighs under the Countess's darkened windows. He wrote to her asking why in the world she treated him so cruelly, and then she knew that her charm was working. She was careful not to answer his letter, and to have him refused at her gate as inexorably as ever. It is an ill wind that blows nobody good, and Benvolio, one night after his dismissal, wandered about the moonlit streets till nearly morning, composing the finest verses he had ever produced. The subscribers to the magazine to which he sent them were at least the gainers. But unlike many poets, Benvolio did not on this occasion bury his passion in his poem; or if he did, its ghost was stalking abroad the very next night. He went again to the Countess's gate, and again it was closed in his face. So, after a very moderate amount of hesitation, he bravely (and with a dexterity which surprised him) scaled her garden wall and dropped down in the moonshine, upon her lawn. I don't know whether she was expecting him, but if she had been, the matter could not have been better arranged. She was sitting in a little niche of shrubbery, with no protector but a microscopic lap-dog. She pretended to be scandalized at his audacity, but his audacity carried the hour. 'This time certainly,' thought the Countess, 'he will make his declaration. He didn't jump that wall, at the risk of his neck, simply to ask me for a cup of tea.' Not a bit of it; Benvolio was devoted, but he was not more explicit than before. He declared that this was the happiest hour of his life; that there was a charming air of romance in his position; that, honestly, he thanked the Countess for having made him desperate; that he would never come to see her again but by the garden wall; that something, to-night—what was it?—was vastly becoming to her; that he devoutly hoped she would receive no one else; that his admiration for her was unbounded; that the starts, finally, had a curious pink light! He looked at her, through the flower-scented dusk, with admiring eyes; but he looked at the stars as well; he threw back his head and folded his arms, and let the conversation flag while he examined the constellations. He observed also the long shafts of light proceeding from the windows of the house, as they fell upon the lawn and played among the shrubbery. The Countess had always thought him a strange man, but to-night she thought him stranger than ever. She became satirical, and the point of her satire was that he was after all but a dull fellow; that his admiration was a poor compliment; that he would do well to turn his attention to astronomy! In answer to this he came perhaps (to the Countess's sense) as near as he had ever come to making a declaration.

'Dear lady,' he said, 'you don't begin to know how much I admire you!'

She left her place at this, and walked about the lawn, looking at him askance while he talked, trailing her embroidered robe over the grass, and fingering the folded petals of her flowers. He made a sort of sentimental profession of faith; he assured her that she represented his ideal of a certain sort of woman. This last phrase made her pause a moment and stare at him, wide-eyed. 'Oh, I mean the finest sort,' he cried—'the sort that exerts the widest sway. You represent the world and everything that the world can give, and you represent them at their best—in their most generous, most graceful, most inspiring form. If a man were a revolutionist, you would reconcile him to society. You are a divine embodiment of all the amenities, the refinements, the complexities of life! You are the flower of urbanity, of culture, of tradition! You are the product of so many influences that it widens one's horizon to know you; of you too it is true that to admire you is a liberal education! Your charm is irresistible; I never approach you without feeling it.'

Compliments agreed with the Countess, as we may say; they not only made her happier, but they made her better. It became a matter of conscience with her to deserve them. These were magnificent ones, and she was by no means indifferent to them. Her cheek faintly flushed, her eyes vaguely glowed, and though her beauty, in the literal sense, was questionable, all that Benvolio said of her had never seemed more true. He said more in the same strain, and she listened without interrupting him. But at last she suddenly became impatient; it seemed to her that this was after all a tolerably inexpensive sort of tribute. But she did not betray her impatience with any petulance; she simply shook her finger a moment, to enjoin silence, and then she said, in a voice of extreme gentleness—'You have too much imagination!' He answered that to do her perfect justice, he had too little. To this she replied that it was not of her any longer he was talking; he had left her far behind. He was spinning fancies about some highly subtilized figment of his brain. The best answer to this, it seemed to Benvolio, was to seize her hand and kiss it. I don't know what the Countess thought of this form of argument; I incline to think it both pleased and vexed her; it was at once too much and too little. She snatched her hand away and went rapidly into the house. Although Benvolio immediately followed her, he was unable to overtake her; she had retired into impenetrable seclusion. A short time afterward she left town and went for the summer to an estate which she possessed in a distant part of the country.

III.

Benvolio was extremely fond of the country, but he remained in town after all his friends had departed. Many of them made him say he would come and see them. He promised, or half promised, but when he reflected that in almost every case he would find a house full of fellow-guests, to whose pursuits he would have to conform, and that if he rambled away with a valued duodecimo in his pocket to spend the morning alone in the woods, he would be denounced as a marplot and a selfish brute, he felt no great desire to pack his bag. He had, as we know, his moods of expansion and of contraction; he had been tolerably expansive for many months past, and now the tide of contraction had set in. And then I suspect the foolish fellow had no money to travel withal. He had lately put all his available funds into the purchase of a picture—an estimable work of the Venetian school, suddenly thrown into the market. It was offered for a moderate sum, and Benvolio, who was one of the first to see it, secured it and hung it triumphantly in his room. It had all the classic Venetian glow, and he used to lie on his divan by the hour, gazing at it. It had, indeed, a peculiar property, of which I have known no other example. Most pictures that are remarkable for their colour (especially if they have been painted a couple of centuries) need a flood of sunshine on the canvas to bring it out. But this one seemed to have a hidden radiance of its own, which showed brightest when the room was half darkened. When Benvolio wished especially to enjoy his treasure he dropped his Venetian blinds, and the picture glowed forth into the cool dusk with enchanting effect. It represented, in a fantastic way, the story of Perseus and Andromeda—the beautiful naked maiden chained to a rock, on which, with picturesque incongruity, a wild fig-tree was growing; the green Adriatic tumbling at her feet, and a splendid brown-limbed youth in a curious helmet hovering near her on a winged horse. The journey his fancy made as he lay and looked at his picture Benvolio preferred to any journey he might make by the public conveyances.

But he resorted for entertainment, as he had often done before, to the windows overlooking the old garden behind his house. As the summer deepened, of course, the charm of the garden increased. It grew more tangled and bosky and mossy, and sent forth sweeter and heavier odours into the neighbouring air. It was a perfect solitude: Benvolio had never seen a visitor there. One day, therefore, at this time, it puzzled him most agreeably to perceive a young girl sitting under one of the trees. She sat there a long time, and though she was at a distance, he managed, by looking long enough, to make out that she was pretty. She was dressed in black, and when she left her place her step had a kind of nun-like gentleness and demureness. Although she was alone, she seemed shy and half-startled. She wandered away and disappeared from sight, save that here and there he saw her white parasol gleaming in the gaps of the foliage. Then she came back to her seat under the great tree, and remained there for some time, arranging in her lap certain flowers that she had gathered. Then she rose again and vanished, and Benvolio waited in vain for her return. She had evidently gone into the house. The next day he saw her again, and the next, and the next. On these occasions she had a book in her hand, and she sat in her former place a long time, and read it with an air of great attention. Now and then she raised her head and glanced towards the house as if to keep something in sight which divided her care; and once or twice she laid down her book and tripped away to her hidden duties with a lighter step than she had shown the first day. Benvolio had a fancy that she had an invalid parent, or a relation of some kind, who was unable to walk, and had been moved into a window overlooking the garden. She always took up her book again when she came back, and bent her pretty head over it with charming earnestness. Benvolio had already discovered that her head was pretty. He fancied it resembled a certain exquisite little head on a Greek silver coin which lay, with several others, in an agate cup on his table. You see he had also already taken to fancying, and I offer this as the excuse for his staring at his modest neighbour by the hour in this inordinately idle fashion. But he was not really idle, because he was—I can't say falling in love with her: he knew her too little for that, and besides, he was in love with the Countess—but because he was at any rate cudgelling his brains about her. Who was she? what was she? why had he never seen her before? The house in which she apparently lived was on another street from Benvolio's own, but he went out of his way on purpose to look at it. It was an ancient, grey, sad-faced structure, with grated windows on the ground floor; it looked like a convent or a prison. Over a wall, beside it, there tumbled into the street some stray tendrils of a wild vine from Benvolio's garden. Suddenly Benvolio began to fancy that the book the young girl in the garden was reading was none other than a volume of his own, put forth some six months before. His volume had a white cover and so had this; white covers are rather rare, and there was nothing impossible either in this young lady's reading his book or in her finding it interesting. Very many other women had done the same. Benvolio's neighbour had a pencil in her pocket, which she every now and then drew forth, to make with it a little mark on her page. This quiet gesture gave the young man an exquisite pleasure

I am ashamed to say how much time he spent, for a week, at his window. Every day the young girl came into the garden. At last there befell a rainy day—a long, warm summer's rain—and she stayed within doors. He missed her quite acutely, and wondered, half smiling, half frowning, at her absence making such a difference with him. He actually depended upon her. He didn't know her name; he knew neither the colour of her eyes nor the shade of her hair, nor the sound of her voice; it was very likely that if he were to meet her face to face elsewhere, he would not recognize her. But she interested him; he liked her; he found her little indefinite, black-dressed figure sympathetic. He used to find the Countess sympathetic, and certainly the Countess was as unlike this quiet garden nymph as she could very well be and be yet a charming woman. Benvolio's sympathies, as we know, were broad. After the rain the young girl came out again, and now she had another book, having apparently finished Benvolio's. He was gratified to observe that she bestowed upon this one a much more wandering attention. Sometimes she let it drop listlessly at her side, and seemed to lose herself in maidenly revery. Was she thinking how much more beautiful Benvolio's verses were than others of the day? Was she perhaps repeating them to herself? It charmed Benvolio to suppose she might be; for he was not spoiled in this respect. The Countess knew none of his poetry by heart; she was nothing of a reader. She had his book on her table, but he once noticed that half the leaves were uncut.

After a couple of days of sunshine the rain came back again, to our hero's infinite annoyance, and this time it lasted several days. The garden lay dripping and desolate; its charm had quite departed. These days passed gloomily for Benvolio; he decided that rainy weather, in summer, in town, was intolerable. He began to think of the Countess again. He was sure that over her broad lands the summer sun was shining. He saw them, in envious fancy, studded with joyous Watteau groups, feasting and making music under the shade of ancestral beeches. What a charming life! he thought—what brilliant, enchanted memorable days! He had said the very reverse of all this, as you remember, three weeks before. I don't know that he had ever formulated the idea that men of imagination are not bound to be consistent, but he certainly conformed to its spirit. We are not, however, by any means at the end of his inconsistencies. He immediately wrote a letter to the Countess asking her if he might pay her a visit.

Shortly after he had sent his letter the weather mended, and he went out to take a walk. The sun was near setting; the streets were all ruddy and golden with its light, and the scattered rain-clouds, broken into a thousand little particles, were flecking the sky like a shower of opals and amethysts. Benvolio stopped, as he sauntered along, to gossip a while with his friend the bookseller. The bookseller was a foreigner and a man of taste; his shop was on the corner of the great square. When Benvolio went in he was serving a lady, and the lady was dressed in black. Benvolio just now found it natural to notice a lady who was dressed in black, and the fact that this lady's face was averted made observation at once more easy and more fruitless. But at last her errand was finished; she had been ordering several books, and the bookseller was writing down their names. Then she turned round, and Benvolio saw her face. He stood staring at her most inconsiderately, for he felt an immediate certainty that she was the bookish damsel of the garden. She gave a glance round the shop, at the books on the walls, at the prints and busts, the apparatus of learning, in various forms, that it contained, and then, with the gentle, half-furtive step which Benvolio now knew so well, she took her departure. Benvolio seized the startled bookseller by the two hands and besieged him with questions. The bookseller, however, was able to answer but few of them. The young girl had been in his shop but once before, and had simply left an address, without any name. It was the address of which Benvolio had assured himself. The books she had ordered were all learned works—disquisitions on philosophy, on history, on the natural sciences. She seemed an expert in such matters. For some of the volumes that she had just bespoken the bookseller was to send to foreign countries; the others were to be despatched that evening to the address which the young girl had left. As Benvolio stood there the bibliophilist gathered these latter together, and while he was so engaged he uttered a little cry of distress: one of the volumes of a set was missing. The book was a rare one, and it would be hard to repair the loss. Benvolio on the instant had an inspiration; he demanded leave of his friend to act as messenger: he would carry the books, as if he came from the shop, and he would explain the absence of the lost volume, and the bookseller's views about replacing it, far better than one of the hirelings. He asked leave, I say, but he did not wait till it was given: he snatched up the pile of books and strode triumphantly away!

IV.

As there was no name on the parcel, Benvolio, on reaching the old grey house, over the wall of whose court an adventurous creeper stretched its long arm into the street, found himself wondering in what terms he should ask to have speech of the person for whom the books were intended. At any hazard he was determined not to retreat until he had caught a glimpse of the interior and its inhabitants; for this was the same man, you must remember, who had scaled the moonlit wall of the Countess's garden. An old serving woman in a quaint cap answered his summons, and stood blinking out at the fading daylight from a little wrinkled white face, as if she had never been compelled to take so direct a look at it before. He informed her that he had come from the bookseller's, and that he had been charged with a personal message for the venerable gentleman who had bespoken the parcel. Might he crave licence to speak with him? This obsequious phrase was an improvisation of the moment: of course it was hit or miss. But Benvolio had an indefinable conviction that it was rightly aimed; the only thing that surprised him was the quiet complaisance of the old woman.

'If it's on a bookish errand you come, sir,' she said with a little wheezy sigh, 'I suppose I only do my duty in admitting you!'

She led him into the house, through various dusky chambers, and at last ushered him into an apartment of which the side opposite to the door was occupied by a broad, low casement. Through its small old panes there came a green dim light—the light of the low western sun shining through the wet trees of the famous garden. Everything else was ancient and brown; the walls were covered with tiers upon tiers of books. Near the window, in the still twilight, sat two persons, one of whom rose as Benvolio came in. This was the young girl of the garden—the young girl of an hour since at the bookseller's. The other was an old man who turned his head, but otherwise sat quite still.

Both his movements and his stillness immediately announced to Benvolio's fine sense that he was blind. In his quality of poet Benvolio was inventive; a brain that is constantly cudgelled for rhymes is tolerably alert. In a few moments, therefore, he had given a vigorous push to the wheel of fortune. Various things had happened. He had made a soft, respectful speech, he hardly knew about what; and the old man had told him he had a delectable voice—a voice that seemed to belong rather to a person of education than to a tradesman's porter. Benvolio confessed to having picked up an education, and the old man had thereupon bidden the young girl offer him a seat. Benvolio chose his seat where he could see her, as she sat at the low-browed casement. The bookseller on the square thought it likely Benvolio would come back that evening and give him an account of his errand, and before he closed his shop he looked up and down the street, to see whether the young man was approaching. Benvolio came, but the shop was closed. He didn't notice it: he walked three times round the great Place without noticing it. He was thinking of something else. He had sat all the evening with the blind old scholar and his daughter, and he was thinking intently, ardently of them. When I say of them, of course I mean of the daughter.

A few days afterward he got a note from the Countess saying it would give her pleasure to receive his visit. He immediately wrote to her that, with a thousand regrets, he found himself urgently occupied in town and must beg leave to defer his departure for a day or two. The regrets were perfectly sincere, but the plea was none the less valid. Benvolio had become deeply interested in his tranquil neighbours, and, for the moment, a certain way the young girl had of looking at him—fixing her eyes, first, with a little vague, half-absent smile, on an imaginary point above his head, and then slowly dropping them till they met his own—was quite sufficient to make him happy. He had called once more on her father, and once more, and yet once more, and he had a vivid prevision that he would often call again. He had been in the garden and found its mild mouldiness even more delightful on a nearer view. He had pulled off his very ill-fitting mask, and let his neighbours know that his trade was not to carry parcels, but to scribble verses. The old man had never heard of his verses; he read nothing that had been published later than the sixth century; and nowadays he could read only with his daughter's eyes. Benvolio had seen the little white volume on the table, and assured himself it was his own; and he noted the fact that in spite of its well-thumbed air, the young girl had never given her father a hint of its contents. I said just now that several things had happened in the first half hour of Benvolio's first visit. One of them was that this modest maiden fell most positively in love with him. What happened when she learned that he was the author of the little white volume I hardly know how to express; her innocent passion, I suppose, passed from the positive to the superlative degree. Benvolio possessed an old quarto volume, bound in Russia leather, about which there clung an agreeable pungent odour. In this old quarto he kept a sort of diary—if that can be called a diary in which a whole year had sometimes been allowed to pass without an entry. On the other hand, there were some interminable records of a single day. Turning it over you would have chanced, not infrequently, upon the name of the Countess; and at this time you would have observed on every page some mention of 'the Professor' and of a certain person named Scholastica. Scholastica, we immediately guess, was the Professor's daughter. Very likely this was not her own name, but it was the name by which Benvolio preferred to know her, and we needn't be more exact than he. By this time of course he knew a great deal about her, and about her venerable sire. The Professor, before the loss of his eyesight and his health, had been one of the stateliest pillars of the University. He was now an old man; he had married late in life. When his infirmities came upon him he gave up his chair and his classes and buried himself in his library. He made his daughter his reader and his secretary, and his prodigious memory assisted her clear young voice and her steady-moving pen. He was held in great honour in the scholastic world; learned men came from afar to consult the blind sage, and to appeal to his wisdom as to the ultimate law. The University settled a pension upon him, and he dwelt in a dusky corner, among the academic shades. The pension was small, but the old scholar and the young girl lived with conventual simplicity. It so happened, however, that he had a brother, or rather a half brother, who was not a bookish man, save as regarded his ledger and daybook. This personage had made money in trade, and had retired, wifeless and childless, into the old grey house attached to Benvolio's garden. He had the reputation of a skinflint, a curmudgeon, a bloodless old miser who spent his days in shuffling about his mouldy old house, making his pockets jingle, and his nights in lifting his money-bags out of trapdoors, and counting over his hoard. He was nothing but a chilling shadow, an evil name, a pretext for a curse: no one had ever seen him, much less crossed his threshold. But it seemed that he had a soft spot in his heart. He wrote one day to his brother, whom he had not seen for years, that the rumour had come to him that he was blind, infirm, and poor; that he himself had a large house with a garden behind it, and that if the Professor was not too proud, he was welcome to come and lodge there.

The Professor had come in this way a few weeks before, and though it would seem that to a sightless old ascetic all lodgings might be the same, he took a great satisfaction in this one. His daughter found it a paradise, compared with their two narrow chambers under the old gable of the University, where, amid the constant coming and going of students, a young girl was compelled to lead a cloistered life.

Benvolio had assigned as his motive for intrusion, when he had been obliged to confess to his real character, an irresistible desire to ask the old man's opinion on certain knotty points of philosophy. This was a pardonable fiction, for the event, at any rate, justified it. Benvolio, when he was fairly launched in a philosophical discussion, forgot that there was anything in the world but metaphysics; he revelled in transcendent abstractions, and became unconscious of all concrete things—even of that most brilliant of concrete things, the Countess. He longed to embark on a voyage of discovery on the great sea of pure reason. He knew that from such voyages the deep-browed adventurer rarely returns; but if he finds an El Dorado of thought, why should he regret the dusky world of fact? Benvolio had much high discourse with the Professor, who was a devout Neo-Platonist, and whose venerable wit had spun to subtler tenuity the ethereal speculations of the Alexandrian school. Benvolio at this season vowed that study and science were the only game in life worth the candle, and wondered how he could ever for an instant have thought otherwise. He turned off a little poem in the style of Milton's 'Penseroso', which, if it had not quite the merit of that famous effusion, was at least the young man's own happiest performance. When Benvolio liked a thing he liked it as a whole—it appealed to all his senses. He relished its accidents, its accessories, its material envelope. In the satisfaction he took in his visits to the Professor it would have been hard to say where the charm of philosophy began or ended. If it began with a glimpse of the old man's mild, sightless blue eyes, sitting fixed beneath his shaggy white brows like patches of pale winter sky under a high-piled cloud, it hardly ended before it reached the little black bow on Scholastica's slipper; and certainly it had taken a comprehensive sweep in the interval. There was nothing in his friends that the appreciative fellow did not feel an immense kindness for. Their seclusion, their stillness, their super-simple notions of the world and the world's ways, the faint, musty perfume of the University which hovered about them, their brown old apartment, impenetrable to the rumours of the town—all these things were part of the charm. Then the essence of it perhaps was that in this silent, simple life the intellectual key, if you touched it, was so finely resonant. In the way of thought there was nothing into which his friends were not initiated—nothing they could not understand. The mellow light of their low-browed room, streaked with the moted rays that slanted past the dusky bookshelves, was the atmosphere of culture. All this made them, humble folk as they were, not so simple as they at first appeared. They, too, in their own fashion, knew the world; they were not people to be patronized; to visit them was not a condescension but a privilege.

In the Professor this was not surprising. He had passed fifty years in arduous study, and it was proper to his character and his office that he should be erudite, impressive, and venerable. But sweet Scholastica seemed to Benvolio at first almost grotesquely wise. She was an anomaly, a prodigy, a charming monstrosity. Charming, at any rate, she was, and as pretty, I must lose no more time in saying, as had seemed likely to Benvolio at his window. And yet, even on a nearer view, her prettiness shone forth slowly and half-dimly. It was as if it had been covered with a series of film-like veils, which had to be successively drawn aside. And then it was such a homely, shrinking, subtle prettiness, that Benvolio, in the private record I have mentioned, never thought of calling it by the arrogant name of beauty. He called it by no name at all; he contented himself with enjoying it—with looking into the young girl's mild grey eyes and saying things, on purpose, that caused her candid smile to deepen until (like the broadening ripple of a lake) it reached a certain dimple in her left cheek. This was its maximum; no smile could do more, and Benvolio desired nothing better. Yet I cannot say he was in love with the young girl; he only liked her. But he liked her, no doubt, as a man likes a thing but once in his life. As he knew her better the oddity of her learning quite faded away; it seemed delightfully natural, and he only wondered why there were not more women of the same pattern. Scholastica had imbibed the wine of science instead of her mother's milk. Her mother had died in her infancy, leaving her cradled in an old folio, three-quarters opened, like a wide V. Her father had been her nurse, her playmate, her teacher, her life-long companion, her only friend. He taught her the Greek alphabet before she knew her own, and fed her with crumbs from his own scholastic revels. She had taken submissively what was given her, and, without knowing it, she grew up a learned maiden.

Benvolio perceived that she was not in the least a woman of genius. The passion for knowledge, of its own motion, would never have carried her far. But she had a clear, tranquil, natural mind, which gave back an exact, definite image of everything that was presented to it; the sort of intelligence, Benvolio said, which had been, as a minimum, every one's portion in the golden age, and would be again the golden mean in the millennium. And then she was so teachable, so diligent, so indefatigable. Slender and meagre as she was, and rather pale too, with being much within doors, she was never tired, she never had a headache, she never closed her book or laid down a pen with a sigh. For helping a man, Benvolio thought it was an exquisite organism. What a work he might do on summer mornings and winter nights with that brightly demure little creature at his side, transcribing, recollecting, sympathizing! He wondered how much she cared for these things herself; whether a woman could care for them without being dry and harsh. It was in a great measure for information on this point that he used to question her eyes with the frequency that I have mentioned. But they never gave him a perfectly direct answer, and this was why he came and came again. They seemed to him to say, 'If you could lead a student's life for my sake, I could be a life-long household scribe for yours.' Was it divine philosophy that made Scholastica charming, or was it she that made philosophy divine? I cannot relate everything that came to pass between these young people, and I must leave a great deal to your imagination. The summer waned, and when the autumnal shadow began to gnaw the bright edge of the days, the quiet couple in the old grey house had expanded to a talkative trio. For Benvolio the days had passed very fast; the trio had talked of so many things. He had spent many an hour in the garden with the young girl, strolling in the weedy paths, or resting on a moss-grown bench. She was a delightful listener, because while she was perfectly deferential, she was also perfectly attentive. Benvolio had had women fix very beautiful eyes upon him, and watch with an air of ecstasy the movement of his lips, and yet had found them three minutes afterward quite incapable of saying what he was talking about. Scholastica followed him and, without effort or exultation, understood him.

V.

You will say that my description of Benvolio has done him injustice, and that, far from being the sentimental weathercock I have depicted, he is proving himself a model of constancy. But mark the sequel. It was at this moment, precisely, that, one morning, having gone to bed the night before singing pæans to divine philosophy, he woke up with a headache, and in the worst of humours with it. He remembered Scholastica telling him that she never had headaches, and the memory quite annoyed him. He was in the mood for declaring her a neat little mechanical toy, wound up to turn pages and write a pretty hand, but with neither a head nor a heart that was capable of human ailments. He fell asleep again, and in one of those brief but vivid dreams that sometimes occur in the morning hours, he had a brilliant vision of the Countess. *She* was human beyond a doubt, and duly familiar with headaches and heartaches. He felt an irresistible desire to see her and to tell her that he adored her. This satisfaction was not unattainable, and before the day was over he was well on his way towards enjoying it. He found the Countess holding her usual court, and making a merry world of it. He had meant to stay with her a week; he stayed two months—the most entertaining months of his life. I cannot pretend of course to enumerate the diversions of this fortunate circle, nor to say just how Benvolio spent every hour of his time. But if the summer had passed quickly with him, the autumn moved with a tread as light. He thought once in a while of Scholastica and her father—once in a while, I say, when present occupations suffered his thoughts to wander. This was not often, for the Countess had always, as the phrase is, a dozen irons on the fire. You see the negative, with Benvolio, always implied as distinct a positive, and his excuse for being inconstant on one side was that he was at that time very constant on another. He developed at this period a talent as yet untried and unsuspected: he proved himself capable of writing brilliant dramatic poetry. The long autumn evenings, in a great country house, offered the ideal setting for the much-abused pastime known as private theatricals. The Countess had a theatre, and abundant material for a troupe of amateur players; all that was lacking was a play exactly adapted to her resources. She proposed to Benvolio to write one; the idea took his fancy; he shut himself up in the library, and in a week produced a masterpiece. He had found the subject one day when he was pulling over the Countess's books in an old MS. chronicle written by the chaplain of one of her late husband's ancestors. It was the germ of an admirable drama, and Benvolio enjoyed vastly the work of bringing it to maturity. All his genius, all his imagination went into it. This was their proper mission, he cried to himself—the study of warm human passions, the painting of rich dramatic pictures, not the bald excogitation of cold metaphysical formulas. His play was acted with brilliant success, the Countess herself representing the heroine. Benvolio had never seen her act, and had no idea she possessed the talent; but she was inimitable, she was a natural artist. What gives charm to life, Benvolio hereupon said to himself, is the element of the unexpected, the unforeseen; and this one finds only in women of the Countess's type. And I should do wrong to imply that he here made an invidious comparison, because he did not even think of Scholastica. His play was repeated several times, and people were invited to see it from all the country round. There was a great bivouac of servants in the castle court; in the cold November nights a bonfire was lighted to keep the servants warm. It was a great triumph for Benvolio, and he frankly enjoyed it. He knew he enjoyed it, and how great a triumph it was, and he felt every disposition to drain the cup to the last drop. He relished his own elation, and found himself excellent company. He began immediately another drama—a comedy this time—and he was greatly interested to observe that when his work was fairly on the stocks he found himself regarding all the people about him as types and available figures. Everything paid tribute to his work; everything presented itself as possible material. Life, really, on these terms was becoming very interesting, and for several nights the laurels of Molière kept Benvolio awake.

Delightful as this was, however, it could not last for ever. At the beginning of the winter the Countess returned to town, and Benvolio came back with her, his unfinished comedy in his pocket. During much of the journey he was silent and abstracted, and the Countess supposed he was thinking of how he should make the most of that capital situation in his third act. The Countess's perspicuity was just sufficient to carry her so far—to lead her, in other words, into plausible wrong conjectures. Benvolio was really wondering what in the name of mystery had suddenly become of his inspiration, and why his comedy had turned as stale on his hands as the cracking of the post-boy's whip. He looked out at the scrubby fields, the rusty woods, the sullen sky, and asked himself whether *that* was the world to which it had been but yesterday his high ambition to hold up the mirror. The Countess's *dame de compagnie* sat opposite to him in the carriage. Yesterday he thought her, with her pale, discreet face, and her eager movements that pretended to be indifferent, a finished specimen of an entertaining genus. To-day he could only say that if there was a whole genus, it was a thousand pities, for the poor lady struck him as miserably false and servile. The real seemed hideous; he felt homesick for his dear familiar rooms between the garden and the square, and he longed to get into them and bolt his door and bury himself in his old arm-chair and cultivate idealism for evermore. The first thing he actually did on getting into them was to go to the window and look out into the garden. It had greatly changed in his absence, and the old maimed statues, which all summer had been comfortably muffled in verdure, were now, by an odd contradiction of propriety, standing white and naked in the cold. I don't exactly know how soon it was that Benvolio went back to see his neighbours. It was after no great interval, and yet it was not immediately. He had a bad conscience, and he was wondering what he should say to them. It seemed to him now (though he had not thought of it sooner) that they might accuse him of neglecting them. He had cultivated their friendship, he had professed the highest esteem for them, and then he had turned his back on them without farewell, and without a word of explanation. He had not written to them; in truth, during his sojourn with the Countess, it would not have been hard for him to pursuade himself that they were people he had only dreamed about, or read about, at most, in some old volume of memoirs. People of their value, he could now imagine them saying, were not to be taken up and dropped in that summary fashion; and if friendship was not to be friendship as they themselves understood it, it was better that he should forget them at once, for all time. It is perhaps too much to affirm that he could imagine them saying all this; they were too mild and civil, too unused to acting in self-defence. But they might easily receive him in a way that would irresistibly imply it, for a man of any delicacy. He felt profaned, dishonoured, almost contaminated; so that perhaps when he did at last return to his friends, it was because that was the simplest way to be purified. How did they receive him? I told you a good way back that Scholastica was in love with him, and you may arrange the scene in your fancy in any manner that best accords with this circumstance. Her forgiveness, of course, when once that chord was touched, was proportionate to her resentment. But Benvolio took refuge both from his own compunctions and from the young girl's reproaches, in whatever form these were conveyed, in making a full confession of what he was pleased to call his frivolity. As he walked through the naked garden with Scholastica, kicking the wrinkled leaves, he told her the whole story of his sojourn with the Countess. The young girl listened with bright intentness, as she would have listened to some thrilling chapter of romance; but she neither sighed, nor looked wistful, nor seemed to envy the Countess, or to repine at her own dull fashion of life. It was all too remote for comparison; it was not, for Scholastica, among the things that might have been. Benvolio talked to her about the Countess, without reserve. If she liked it, he found on his side that it eased his mind; and as he said nothing that the Countess would not have been flattered by, there was no harm done. Although, however, Benvolio uttered nothing but praise of this distinguished lady, he was very frank in saying that she and her way of life always left him at the end in a worse humour than when they found him. They were very well in their way, he said, but their way was not his way, or could not be in the long run; for him, he was convinced, the only happiness was in seclusion, meditation, concentration. Scholastica answered that it gave her extreme pleasure to hear this, for it was her father's belief that Benvolio had a great aptitude for philosophical research, and that it was a sacred duty with him to devote his days and his nights to it.

'And what is your own belief?' Benvolio asked, remembering that the young girl knew several of his poems by heart.

Her answer was very simple: 'I believe you're a poet'.

'And a poet oughtn't to run the risk of turning pedant?'

'No,' she answered; 'a poet ought to run all risks—even that one which for a poet, perhaps, is the most cruel. But he ought to evade them all!'

Benvolio took great satisfaction in hearing that the Professor deemed that he had in him the making of a philosopher, and it gave an impetus to the zeal with which he returned to work.

VI.

Of course even the most zealous student cannot work always, and often, after a very philosophical day, Benvolio spent with the Countess a very sentimental morning. It is my duty as a veracious historian not to conceal the fact that he discoursed to the Countess about Scholastica. He gave such a puzzling description of her that the Countess declared that she must be a delightfully quaint creature, and that it would be vastly amusing to know her. She hardly supposed Benvolio was in love with this little book-worm in petticoats, but to make sure—if that might be called making sure—she deliberately asked him. He said No; he hardly saw how he could be, since he was in love with the Countess herself! For a while this answer satisfied her, but as the winter went by she began to wonder whether there was not such a thing as a man being in love with two women at once. During many months that followed Benvolio led a kind of double life. Sometimes it charmed him and gave him an inspiring sense of personal power. He haunted the domicile of his gentle neighbours, and drank deep of philosophy, history, and all the garnered wisdom of the ages; and he made appearances as frequent in the Countess's drawing-room, where he played his part with magnificent zest and ardour. It was a life of alternation, and variation, and contrast, and it really demanded a vigorous and elastic temperament. Sometimes his own seemed to him quite inadequate to the occasion—he felt fevered, bewildered, exhausted. But when it came to the point, it was impossible to give up either his worldly habits or his studious aspirations. Benvolio raged inwardly at the cruel limitations of the human mind, and declared it was a great outrage that a man should not be personally able to do everything he could imagine doing. I hardly know how she contrived it, but the Countess was at this time a more engaging woman than she had ever been. Her beauty acquired an ampler and richer cast, and she had a manner of looking at you, as she slowly turned away, which had lighted a hopeless flame in many a youthful breast. Benvolio one day felt in the mood for finishing his comedy, and the Countess and her friends acted it. Its success was no less brilliant than that of its predecessor, and the manager of the theatre immediately demanded the privilege of producing it. You will hardly believe me, however, when I tell you that on the night that his comedy was introduced to the public its eccentric author sat discussing the absolute and the relative with the Professor and his daughter. Benvolio had all winter been observing that Scholastica never looked so pretty as when she sat, of a winter's night, plying a quiet needle in the mellow circle of a certain antique brass lamp. On the night in question he happened to fall a-thinking of this picture, and he tramped out across the snow for the express purpose of looking at it. It was sweeter even than his memory promised, and it drew every thought of his theatrical honours from his head. Scholastica gave him some tea, and her tea, for mysterious reasons, was delicious; better, strange to say, than that of the Countess, who, however, it must be added, recovered her ground in coffee. The Professor's miserly brother owned a ship which made voyages to China, and brought him goodly chests of the incomparable plant. He sold the cargo for great sums, but he kept a chest for himself. It was always the best one, and he had at this time carefully measured a part of his annual quantum into a piece of flossy tissue paper, made it into a little parcel, and presented it to Scholastica. This is the secret history of Benvolio's fragrant cups. While he was drinking them on the night I speak of—I am ashamed to say how many he drank—his name, at the theatre, was being tossed across the footlights to a brillant, clamorous multitude, who hailed him as the redeemer of the national stage.But I am not sure that he even told his friends that his play was being acted. Indeed, this was hardly possible, for I meant to say just now that he had forgotten it.

It is very certain, however, that he enjoyed the criticisms the next day in the newspapers. Radiant and jubilant, he went to see the

Countess. He found her looking terribly dark. She had been at the theatre, prepared to revel in his triumph—to place on his head with her own hand, as it were, the laurel awarded by the public; and his absence had seemed to her a sort of personal slight. Yet his triumph had nevertheless given her an exceeding pleasure, for it had been the seal of her secret hopes of him. Decidedly he was to be a great man, and this was not the moment for letting him go! At the same time there was something impressive in this extraordinary lapse in his eagerness—in his finding it so easy to forget his honours. It was only an intellectual Crœsus, the Countess said to herself, who could afford to keep so loose an account. But she insisted on knowing where he had been, and he told her he had been discussing philosophy and tea with the Professor.

'And was not the daughter there?' the Countess demanded.

'Most sensibly!' he cried. And then added in a moment—'I don't know whether I ever told you, but she's almost as pretty as you.'

The Countess resented the compliment to Scholastica much more than she enjoyed the compliment to herself. She felt an extreme curiosity to see this inky-fingered little nobody, who was spoken of thus freely in the same breath with herself; and as she seldom failed, sooner or later, to compass her desires, she succeeded at last in catching a glimpse of her innocent rival. To do so she was obliged to set a great deal of machinery in motion. She made Benvolio give a lunch, in his rooms, to some ladies who professed a desire to see his works of art, and of whom she constituted herself the chaperon. She took care that he threw open the room that looked into the garden, and here, at the window, she spent much of her time. There was but a chance that Scholastica would come forth into the garden, but it was a chance worth staking something upon. The Countess gave to it time and temper, and she was finally rewarded. Scholastica came out. The poor girl strolled about for half an hour, in profound unconsciousness that the Countess's fine eyes were devouring her. The impression she made was singular. The Countess found her both pretty and ugly: she did not admire her herself, but she understood that Benvolio might. For herself personally she detested her, and when Scholastica went in and she turned away from the window, her first movement was to pass before a mirror, which showed her something that, impartially considered, seemed to her a thousand times more beautiful. The Countess made no comments, and took good care Benvolio did not suspect the trick she had played him. There was something more she promised herself to do, and she impatiently awaited her opportunity.

In the middle of the winter she announced to him that she was going to spend ten days in the country: she had received the most attractive accounts of the state of things on her estate. There had been great snowfalls, and the sleighing was magnificent; the lakes and streams were solidly frozen, there was an unclouded moon, and the resident gentry were skating, half the night, by torch-light. The Countess was passionately fond both of sleighing and skating, and she found this picture irresistible. And then she was charitable, and observed that it would be a kindness to the poor resident gentry, whose usual pleasures were of a frugal sort, to throw open her house and give a ball or two, with the village fiddlers. Perhaps even they might organize a bear-hunt—an entertainment at which, if properly conducted, a lady might be present as spectator. The Countess told Benvolio all this one day as he sat with her in her boudoir, in the fire-light, during the hour that precedes dinner. She had said more than once that he must decamp—that she must go and dress for dinner; but neither of them had moved. She did not invite him to go with her to the country; she only watched him as he sat gazing with a frown at the fire-light—the crackling light of the great logs which had been cut in the Countess's bear-haunted forests. At last she rose impatiently, and fairly turned him out. After he had gone she stood for a moment looking at the fire with the tip of her foot on the fender. She had not to wait long; he came back within the minute—came back and begged her leave to go with her to the country—to skate with her in the crystal moonlight and dance with her to the sound of the village fiddles. It hardly matters in what terms his petition was granted: the notable point is that he made it. He was her only companion, and when they were established in the castle the hospitality extended to the resident gentry was less abundant than had been promised. Benvolio, however, did not complain of the absence of it, because, for the week or so, he was passionately in love with his hostess. They took long sleigh-rides and drank deep of the poetry of winter. The blue shadows on the snow, the cold amber lights in the west, the leafless twigs against the snow-charged sky, all gave them extraordinary pleasure. The nights were even better, when the great silver stars, before the moonrise, glittered on the polished ice, and the young Countess and her lover, firmly joining hands, launched themselves into motion and into the darkness and went skimming for miles with their winged steps. On their return, before the great chimney-place in the old library, they lingered a while and drank little cups of wine heated with spices. It was perhaps here, cup in hand—this point is uncertain—that Benvolio broke through the last bond of his reserve, and told the Countess that he loved her, in a manner that quite satisfied her. To be his in all solemnity, his only and his for ever—this he explicitly, passionately, imperiously demanded of her. After this she gave her ball to her country neighbours, and Benvolio danced, to a boisterous, swinging measure, with a dozen ruddy beauties dressed in the fashions of the year before last. The Countess danced with the lusty male counterparts of these damsels, but she found plenty of chances to watch Benvolio. Towards the end of the evening she saw him looking grave and bored, with very much such a frown in his forehead as when he had sat staring at the fire that last day in her boudoir. She said to herself for the hundredth time that he was the oddest of mortals.

On their return to the city she had frequent occasion to say it again. He looked at moments as if he had repented of his bargain—as if it did not at all suit him that his being the Countess's only lover should involve her being his only mistress. She deemed now that she had acquired the right to make him give an account of his time, and he did not conceal the fact that the first thing he had done after his return was to go to see his eccentric neighbours. She treated him hereupon to a passionate outburst of jealousy; called Scholastica a dozen harsh names—a dingy little Quakeress, a little underhand, hypocritical Puritan; demanded he should promise never to speak to her again, and summoned him to make a choice once for all. Would he belong to her, or that odious little blue-stocking? It must be one thing or the other; he must take her or leave her; it was impossible she should have a lover who could be so little depended upon. The Countess did not say this made her unhappy, but she repeated a dozen times that it made her ridiculous. Benvolio turned very pale; she had never seen him so before; a great struggle was evidently taking place within him. A terrible scene was the consequence. He broke out into reproaches and imprecations; he accused the Countess of being his bad angel, of making him neglect his best faculties, mutilate his genius, squander his life; and yet he confessed that he was committed to her; that she fascinated him beyond resistance, and that, at any sacrifice, he must still be her slave. This confession gave the Countess uncommon satisfaction, and made up in a measure for the unflattering remarks that accompanied it. She on her side confessed—what she had always been too proud to acknowledge hitherto—that she cared vastly for him, and that she had waited for long months for him to say something of this kind. They parted on terms which it is hard to define— full of mutual resentment and devotion, at once adoring and hating each other. All this was deep and stirring emotion, and Benvolio, as an artist, always in one way or another found his profit in emotion, even when it lacerated or suffocated him. There was, moreover, a sort of elation in having burnt his ship behind him, and vowed to seek his fortune, his intellectual fortune, in the tumult of the life and action.

He did not work; his power of work, for the time at least, was paralysed. Sometimes this frightened him; it seemed as if his genius were dead, his career cut short; at other moments his faith soared supreme; he heard, in broken murmurs, the voice of the muse, and said to himself that he was only resting, waiting, storing up knowledge. Before long he felt tolerably tranquil again; ideas began to come to him, and the world to seem entertaining. He demanded of the Countess that, without further delay, their union should be solemnized. But the Countess, at that interview I have just related, had in spite of her high spirit received a great fright. Benvolio, stalking up and down with clenched hands and angry eyes, had seemed to her a terrible man to marry; and though she was conscious of a strong will of her own, as well as of robust nerves, she had shuddered at the thought that such scenes might recur. She had hitherto seen little but the mild and caressing, or at most the joyous and fantastic side of her friend's disposition; but it now appeared that there was another side to be taken into account, and that if Benvolio had talked of sacrifices, these were not all to be made by him. They say the world likes its master—that a horse of high spirit likes being well ridden. This may be true in the long run; but the Countess, who was essentially a woman of the world, was not yet prepared to surrender her own luxurious liberty in tribute. She admired Benvolio the more now that she was afraid of him, but at the same time she liked him a trifle less. She answered that marriage was a very serious matter; that they had lately had a taste of each other's tempers; that they had better wait a while longer; that she had made up her mind to travel for a year, and that she strongly recommended him to come with her, for travelling was notoriously an excellent test of friendship.

VII.

She went to Italy, and Benvolio went with her; but before he went he paid a visit to his other mistress. He flattered himself that he had burned his ships behind him, but the fire was still visibly smouldering. It is true, nevertheless, that he passed a very strange half-hour with Scholastica and her father. The young girl had greatly changed; she barely greeted him; she looked at him coldly. He had no idea her face could wear that look; it vexed him to find it there. He had not been to see her in many weeks, and he now came to tell her that he was going away for a year: it is true these were not conciliatory facts. But she had taught him to think that she possessed in perfection the art of trustful resignation, of unprotesting, cheerful patience—virtues that sat so gracefully on her bended brow that the thought of their being at any rate supremely becoming took the edge from his remorse at making them necessary. But now Scholastica looked older, as well as sadder, and decidedly not so pretty. Her figure was meagre, her movements angular, her complexion, even, not so pure as he had fancied. After the first minute he avoided her eye; it made him uncomfortable. Her voice she scarcely allowed him to hear. The Professor, as usual, was serene and frigid, impartial and transcendental. There was a chill in the air, a shadow between them. Benvolio went so far as to wonder that he had ever found a charm in the young girl, and his present disillusionment gave him even more anger than pain. He took leave abruptly and coldly, and puzzled his brain for a long time afterwards over the mystery of Scholastica's reserve.

The Countess had said that travelling was a test of friendship; in this case friendship (or whatever the passion was to be called) bade fair for some time to resist the test. Benvolio passed six months of the liveliest felicity. The world has nothing better to offer to a man of sensibility than a first visit to Italy during those years of life when perception is at its keenest, when discretion has arrived, and yet youth has not departed. He made with the Countess a long, slow progress through the lovely land, from the Alps to the Sicilian Sea; and it seemed to him that his imagination, his intellect, his genius, expanded with every breath and ripened with every glance. The Countess was in an almost equal ecstasy, and their sympathy was perfect in all points save the lady's somewhat indiscriminate predilection for assemblies and receptions. She had a thousand letters of introduction to deliver, and they entailed a vast deal of social exertion. Often, on balmy nights when he would have preferred to meditate among the ruins of the Forum, or to listen to the moonlit ripple of the Adriatic, Benvolio found himself dragged away to kiss the hand of a decayed princess, or to take a pinch from the snuff-box of an epicurean cardinal. But the cardinals, the princesses, the ruins, the warm southern tides which seemed the voice of history itself—these and a thousand other things resolved themselves into a vast pictorial spectacle—the very stuff that inspiration is made of. Everything he had written before coming to Italy now appeared to him worthless; this was the needful stamp, the consecration of talent. One day, however, this pure felicity was clouded; by a trifle you will say, possibly, but you must remember that in men of Benvolio's disposition primary impulses are almost always produced by trifles light as air. The Countess, speaking of the tone of voice of some one they had met, happened to say that it reminded her of the voice of that queer little woman at home—the daughter of the blind professor. Was this pure inadvertence, or was it malicious design? Benvolio never knew, though he immediately demanded of her, in surprise, when and where she had heard Scholastica's voice. His whole attention was aroused; the Countess perceived it, and for a moment she hesitated. Then she bravely proclaimed that she had seen the young girl in the musty old book-room where she spent her dreary life. At these words, uttered in a profoundly mocking tone, Benvolio had an extraordinary sensation. He was walking with the Countess in the garden of a palace, and they had just approached the low balustrade of a terrace which commanded a magnificent view. On one side were violet Apennines, dotted here and there with a gleaming castle or convent; on the other stood the great palace through whose galleries the two had just been strolling, with its walls incrusted with medallions and its cornice charged with statues. But Benvolio's heart began to beat; the tears sprang to his eyes; the perfect landscape around him faded away and turned to nothing, and there rose before him, distinctly, vividly present, the old brown room that looked into the dull northern garden, tenanted by the quiet figures he had once told himself that he loved. He had a choking sensation and a sudden, overwhelming desire to return to his own country.

The Countess would say nothing more than that the fancy had taken her one day to go and see Scholastica. 'I suppose I may go where I please!' she cried in the tone of the great lady who is accustomed to believe that her glance confers honour wherever it falls. 'I'm sure I did her no harm. She's a good little creature, and it's not her fault if she's so unfortunately plain.' Benvolio looked at her intently, but he saw that he would learn nothing from her that she did not choose to tell. As he stood there he was amazed to find how natural or at least how easy it was to disbelieve her. She had been with the young girl: that accounted for anything; it accounted abundantly for Scholastica's painful constraint. What had the Countess said and done? what infernal trick had she played upon the poor girl's simplicity? He helplessly wondered, but he felt that she could be trusted to hit her mark. She had done him the honour to be jealous, and to alienate Scholastica she had invented some infernally plausible charge against himself. He felt sick and angry, and for a week he treated his companion with the coldest civility. The charm was broken, the cup of pleasure was drained. This remained no secret to the Countess, who was profoundly vexed at her own indiscretion. At last she abruptly told Benvolio that the test had failed; they must separate; he would please her by taking his leave. He asked no second permission, but bade her farewell in the midst of her little retinue, and went journeying out of Italy with no other company than his thick-swarming memories and projects.

The first thing he did on reaching home was to repair to the Professor's abode. The old man's chair, for the first time, was empty, and Scholastica was not in the room. He went out into the garden, where, after wandering hither and thither, he found the young girl seated on a secluded bench. She was dressed, as usual, in black; but her head was drooping, her empty hands were folded, and her face was sadder even than when he had last seen her. If she had been changed then, she was doubly changed now. Benvolio looked round, and as the Professor was nowhere visible, he immediately guessed the cause of her affliction. The good old man had gone to join his immortal brothers, the classic sages, and Scholastica was utterly alone. She seemed frightened at seeing him, but he took her hand, and she let him sit down beside her. 'Whatever you were once told that made you think ill of me is detestably false,' he said. 'I have a boundless friendship for you, and now more than ever I should like to show it.' She slowly gathered courage to meet his eyes; she found them reassuring, and at last, though she never told him in what way her mind had been poisoned, she suffered him to believe that her old confidence had come back. She told him how her father had died and how, in spite of the high philosophical maxims he had bequeathed to her for her consolation, she felt very lonely and helpless. Her uncle had offered her a maintenance, meagre but sufficient; she had the old serving-woman to keep her company, and she meant to live where she was and occupy herself with collecting her father's papers and giving them to the world according to a plan for which he had left particular directions. She seemed irresistibly appealing and touching and yet full of secret dignity and self-support. Benvolio fell in love with her on the spot, and only abstained from telling her so because he remembered just in time that he had an engagement with the Countess which had not yet been formally rescinded. He paid her a long visit, and they went in together and rummaged over her father's books and papers. The old scholar's literary memoranda proved to be extremely valuable. It would be a great work and a most interesting enterprise to give them to the world. When Scholastica heard Benvolio's high estimate of them her cheek began to glow and her spirit to revive. The present then was secure, she seemed to say to herself, and she would have occupation for many a month. He offered to give her every assistance in his power, and in consequence he came daily to see her. Scholastica lived so much out of the world that she was not obliged to trouble herself about gossip. Whatever jests were aimed at the young man for his visible devotion to a mysterious charmer, he was very sure that her ear was never wounded by base insinuations. The old serving-woman sat in a corner, nodding over her distaff, and the two friends held long confabulations over yellow manuscripts in which the commentary, it must be confessed, did not always adhere very closely to the text. Six months elapsed, and Benvolio found an ineffable charm in this mild mixture of sentiment and study. He had never in his life been so long of the same mind; it really seemed as if, as the phrase is, the fold was taken for ever, as if he had done with the world and were ready to live henceforth in the closet. He hardly thought of the Countess, and they had no correspondence. She was in Italy, in Greece, in the East, in the Holy Land, in places and situations that taxed the imagination.

One day, in the darkness of the vestibule, after he had left Scholastica, he was arrested by a little old man of sordid aspect, of whom he could make out hardly more than a pair of sharply-glowing little eyes and an immense bald head, polished like an ivory ball. He was a quite terrible little figure in his way, and Benvolio at first was frightened. 'Mr. Poet,' said the old man, 'let me say a single word. I give my niece a maintenance. She may do what she likes. But she forfeits every stiver of her allowance and her expectations if she is fool enough to marry a fellow who scribbles rhymes. I'm told they are sometimes an hour finding two that will match! Good evening, Mr. Poet!' Benvolio heard a sound like the faint jingle of loose coin in a trowsers pocket, and the old man abruptly retreated into his domiciliary gloom. Benvolio had never seen him before, and he had no wish ever to see him again. He had not proposed to himself to marry Scholastica, and even if he had, I am pretty sure he would now have taken the modest view of the matter, and decided that his hand and heart were an insufficient compensation for the forfeiture of a miser's fortune. The young girl never spoke of her uncle: he lived quite alone apparently, haunting his upper chambers like a restless ghost, and sending her, by the old serving-woman, her slender monthly allowance, wrapped up in a piece of old newspaper. It was shortly after this that the Countess at last came back. Benvolio had been taking one of his long customary walks, and passing through the park on his way home, he had sat down on a bench to rest. In a few moments a carriage came rolling by; in it sat the Countess—beautiful, sombre, solitary. He rose with a ceremonious salute, and she went her way. But in five minutes she passed back again, and this time her carriage stopped. She gave him a single glance, and he got in. For a week afterwards Scholastica vainly awaited him. What had happened? It had happened that though she had proved herself both false and cruel, the Countess again asserted her charm, and our precious hero again succumbed to it. But he resumed his visits to Scholastica after an interval of neglect not long enough to be unpardonable; the only difference was that now they were not so frequent.

My story draws to a close, for I am afraid you have already lost patience with our young man's eternal comings and goings. Another year ran its course, and the Professor's manuscripts were arranged in great piles and almost ready for the printer. Benvolio had had a constant hand in the work, and had found it exceedingly interesting; it involved inquiries and researches of the most stimulating and profitable kind. Scholastica was very happy. Her friend was often absent for many days, during which she knew he was leading the great world's life; but she had learned that if she patiently waited, the pendulum would swing back and he would reappear and bury himself in their books and papers and talk. And it was not all work and no play between them either; they talked of everything that came into their heads, and Benvolio by no means forbade himself to descant on those things touching which this sacred vow of personal ignorance had been taken for his companion. He took her wholly into his poetic confidence, and read her everything he had written since his return from Italy. The more he worked the more he desired to work; and so, at this time, occupied as he was with editing the Professor's manuscripts, he had never been so productive on his own account. He wrote another drama, on an Italian subject, which was performed with magnificent success; and this he had discussed with Scholastica scene by scene and speech by speech. He proposed to her to come and see it acted from a covered box, where her seclusion would be complete. She seemed for an instant to feel the force of the temptation; then she shook her head with a frank smile, and said it was better not. The play was dedicated to the Countess, who had suggested the subject to him in Italy, where it had been imparted to her, as a family anecdote, by one of her old princesses. This easy, fruitful double life might have lasted for ever but for two most regrettable events. *Might* have lasted I say; you observe I do not affirm it positively. Scholastica became preoccupied and depressed; she was suffering a secret annoyance. She concealed it as far as she might from her friend, and with some success; for although he suspected something and questioned her, she persuaded him that it was his own fancy. In reality it was no fancy at all, but the very uncomfortable fact that her shabby uncle, the miser, was making himself excessively disagreeable to her. He had told Benvolio that she might do as pleased her, but he had recently revoked this amiable concession. He informed her one day by means of an illegible note, scrawled with a blunt pencil, on the back of an old letter, that her beggarly friend the poet came to see her altogether too often; that he was determined she never should marry a crackbrained rhymester; and that before the sacrifice became too painful she would be so good as to dismiss Mr. Benvolio. This was accompanied by an intimation, more explicit than gracious, that he opened his money bags only for those who deferred to his incomparable wisdom. Scholastica was poor, and simple, and lonely; but she was proud, for all that, with a silent pride of her own, and her uncle's charity, proffered on these terms, became intolerably bitter to her soul. She sent him word that she thanked him for his past liberality, but she would no longer be a charge upon him. She said to herself that she could work; she had a superior education; many women, she knew, supported themselves. She even found something inspiring in the idea of going out into the world of which she knew so little, to seek her fortune. Her great desire, however, was to keep her situation a secret from Benvolio, and to prevent his knowing the sacrifice she was making for him. This it is especially that proves she was proud. It so befell that circumstances made secrecy possible. I don't know whether the Countess had always an idea of marrying Benvolio, but her unquenchable vanity still suffered from the spectacle of his divided allegiance, and it suggested to her a truly malignant revenge. A brilliant political mission, for a particular purpose, was about to be despatched to a neighbouring government, and half a dozen young men of eminence were to be attached to it. The Countess had influence at court, and without saying anything to Benvolio, she immediately urged his claim to a post, on the ground of his distinguished services to literature. She pulled her wires so cleverly that in a very short time she had the pleasure of presenting him his appointment, on a great sheet of parchment, from which the royal seal dangled by a blue ribbon. It involved an exile of but a few weeks, and to this, with her eye on the sequel of her project, she was able to resign herself. Benvolio's imagination took fire at the thought of spending a month at a foreign court, in the very hotbed of consummate diplomacy; this was a phase of experience with which he was as yet unacquainted. He departed, and no sooner had he gone that the Countess, at a venture, waited upon Scholastica. She knew she was poor, and she believed that in spite of her homely virtues she would not, if the opportunity was placed in a certain light, prove implacably indisposed to better her fortunes. She knew nothing of the young girl's contingent expectations from her uncle, and her interference, at this juncture, was simply a remarkable coincidence. She laid before her a proposal from a certain great lady, whose husband, an eminent general, had just been dubbed governor of an island on the other side of the globe. This lady desired a preceptress for her children; she had heard of Scholastica's merit, and she ventured to hope that she might persuade her to accompany her to the Antipodes and reside in her family. The offer was brilliant; to Scholastica it seemed mysteriously and providentially opportune. Nevertheless she hesitated, and demanded time for reflection; without telling herself why, she wished to wait till Benvolio returned. He wrote her two or three letters, full of the echoes of his actual life, and without a word about the things that were nearer her own experience. The month elapsed, but he was still absent. Scholastica, who was in correspondence with the governor's wife, delayed her decision from week to week. She had sold her father's manuscripts to a publisher, at a very poor bargain, and gone, meanwhile, to live in a convent. At last the governor's lady demanded her ultimatum. The poor girl scanned the horizon, and saw no rescuing friend; Benvolio was still at the court of Illyria! What she saw was the Countess's fine eyes eagerly watching her over the top of her fan. They seemed to contain a horrible menace, and to hold somehow her happiness at their mercy. Her heart sank; she gathered up her few possessions and set sail, with her illustrious protectors, for the Antipodes. Shortly after her departure Benvolio returned. He felt a terrible pang of rage and grief when he learned that she had gone; he went to the Countess, prepared to accuse her of the basest treachery. But she checked his reproaches by arts that she had never gone so far as to use before, and promised him that if he would trust her, he should never miss that pale-eyed little governess. It can hardly be supposed that he believed her, but he appears to have been guilty of letting himself be persuaded without belief. For some time after this he almost lived with the Countess. He had, with infinite pains, purchased from his neighbour, the miser, the right of occupancy of the late Professor's apartment. The repulsive old man, in spite of his aversion to rhymesters, had not resisted the financial argument, and seemed greatly amazed that a poet should have a dollar to spend. Scholastica had left all things in their old places, but Benvolio, for the present, never went into the room. He turned the key in the door, and kept it in his waistcoat pocket, where, while he was with the Countess his fingers fumbled with it. Several months rolled by and the Countess's promise was not verified. He missed Scholastica intensely, and missed her more as time elapsed. He began at last to go to the old room with the garden, and to try to do some work there. He succeeded in a fashion, but it seemed dreary—doubly dreary when he reflected what might have been. Suddenly he ceased to visit the Countess; a long time passed without her seeing him. She met him at another house, and had some remarkable words with him. She covered him with reproaches that were doubtless deserved, but he made her an answer that caused her to open her eyes and flush, and admit afterwards that, for a clever woman, she had been a great fool. 'Don't you see,' he said—'can't you imagine that I cared for you only by contrast? You took the trouble to kill the contrast, and with it you killed everything else. For a constancy I prefer *this!*' And he tapped his poetic brow. He never saw the Countess again. I rather regret now that I said at the beginning of my story that it was not to be a fairy tale; otherwise I should be at liberty to say, with harmonious geniality, that if Benvolio missed Scholastica he missed the Countess also, and led an extremely fretful and unproductive life, until one day he sailed for the Antipodes and brought Scholastica home. After this he began to produce again; only, many people said, his poetry had become dismally dull. But excuse me; I am writing as if this *were* a fairy tale!

Crawford's Consistency

[First appeared in the *Scribner's Monthly*, vol. xii (August 1876), pp. 569-84. Not reprinted during James's lifetime.]

WE WERE GREAT FRIENDS, AND IT WAS NATURAL THAT HE SHOULD have let me know with all the promptness of his ardour that his happiness was complete. Ardour is here, perhaps, a misleading word, for Crawford's passion burned with a still and hidden flame; if he had written sonnets to his mistress's eyebrow, he had never declaimed them in public. But he was deeply in love; he had been full of tremulous hopes and fears, and his happiness, for several weeks, had hung by a hair—the extremely fine line that appeared to divide the yea and nay of the young lady's parents. The scale descended at last with their heavily-weighted consent in it, and Crawford gave himself up to tranquil bliss. He came to see me at my office—my name, on the little tin placard beneath my window, was garnished with an M. D., as vivid as new gilding could make it—long before that period of the morning at which my irrepressible buoyancy had succumbed to the teachings of experience (as it usually did about twelve o'clock), and resigned itself to believe that that particular day was not to be distinguished by the advent of the female form that haunted my dreams—the confiding old lady, namely, with a large account at the bank, and a mild, but expensive chronic malady. On that day I quite forgot the paucity of my patients and the vanity of my hopes in my enjoyment of Crawford's contagious felicity. If we had been less united in friendship, I might have envied him; but as it was, with my extreme admiration and affection for him, I felt for half an hour as if I were going to marry the lovely Elizabeth myself. I reflected after he had left me that I was very glad I was not, for lovely as Miss Ingram was, she had always inspired me with a vague mistrust. There was no harm in her, certainly; but there was nothing else either. I don't know to what I compared her—to a blushing rose that had no odour, to a blooming peach that had no taste. All that nature had asked of her was to be the prettiest girl of her time, and this request she obeyed to the letter. But when, of a morning, she had opened wide her beautiful, candid eyes, and half parted her clear, pink lips, and gathered up her splendid golden tresses, her day, as far as her own opportunity was concerned, was at an end; she had put her house in order, and she could fold her arms. She did so invariably, and it was in this attitude that Crawford saw her and fell in love with her. I could heartily congratulate him, for the fact that a blooming statue would make no wife for me, did not in the least discredit his own choice. I was human and erratic; I had an uneven temper and a prosaic soul. I wished to get as much as I gave— to be the planet, in short, and not the satellite. But Crawford had really virtue enough for two—enough of vital fire, of intelligence and devotion. He could afford to marry an inanimate beauty, for he had the wisdom which would supply her shortcomings, and the generosity which would forgive them.

Crawford was a tall man, and not particularly well made. He had, however, what is called a gentlemanly figure, and he had a very fine head—the head of a man of books, a student, a philosopher, such as he really was. He had a dark colouring, thin, fine black hair, a very clear, lucid, dark grey eye, and features of a sort of softly-vigorous outline. It was as if his face had been cast first in a rather rugged and irregular mould, and the image had then been lightly retouched, here and there, by some gentler, more femine hand. His expression was singular; it was a look which I can best describe as a sort of intelligent innocence—the look of an absent-minded seraph. He knew, if you insisted upon it, about the corruptions of this base world; but, left to himself, he never thought of them. What he did think of, I can hardly tell you: of a great many things, often, in which I was not needed. Of this, long and well as I had known him, I was perfectly conscious. I had never got behind him, as it were; I had never walked all round him. He was reserved, as I am inclined to think that all first rate men are; not capriciously or consciously reserved, but reserved in spite of, and in the midst of, an extreme frankness. For most people he was a clear-visaged, scrupulously polite young man, who, in giving up business so suddenly, had done a thing which required a good deal of charitable explanation, and who was not expected to express any sentiments more personal than a literary opinion re-inforced by the name of some authority, as to whose titles and attributes much vagueness of knowledge was excusable. For me, his literary opinions were the lightest of his sentiments; his good manners, too, I am sure, cost him nothing. Bad manners are the result of irritability, and as Crawford was not irritable he found civility very easy. But if his urbanity was not victory over a morose disposition, it was at least the expression of a very agreeable character. He talked a great deal, though not volubly, stammering a little, and casting about him for his words. When you suggested one, he always accepted it thankfully,—though he sometimes brought in a little later the expression he had been looking for and which had since occurred to him. He had a great deal of gaiety, and made jokes and enjoyed them—laughing constantly, with a laugh that was not so much audible as visible. He was extremely deferential to old people, and among the fairer sex, his completest conquests, perhaps, were the ladies of sixty-five and seventy. He had also a great kindness for shabby people, if they were only shabby enough, and I remember seeing him, one summer afternoon, carrying a baby across a crowded part of Broadway, accompanied by its mother,—a bewildered pauper, lately arrived from Europe. Crawford's father had left him a very good property; his income, in New York, in those days, passed for a very easy one. Mr. Crawford was a cotton-broker, and on his son's leaving college, he took him into his business. But shortly after his father's death he sold out his interest in the firm—very quietly, and without asking any one's advice, because, as he told me, he hated buying and selling. There were other things, of course, in the world that he hated too, but this is the only thing of which I remember to have heard him say it. He had a large house, quite to himself (he had lost his mother early, and his brothers were dispersed); he filled it with books and scientific instruments, and passed most of his time in reading and in making awkward experiments. He had the tastes of a scholar, and he consumed a vast number of octavos; but in the way of the natural sciences, his curiosity was greater than his dexterity. I used to laugh at his experiments and, as a thrifty neophyte in medicine, to deprecate his lavish expenditure of precious drugs. Unburdened, independent, master of an all-sufficient fortune, and of the best education that the country could afford, good-looking, gallant, amiable, urbane—Crawford at seven and twenty might fairly be believed to have drawn the highest prizes in life. And, indeed, except that it was a pity he had not stuck to business, no man heard a word of disparagement either of his merit or of his felicity. On the other hand, too, he was not envied—envied at any rate with any degree of bitterness. We are told that though the world worships success, it hates successful people. Certainly it never hated Crawford. Perhaps he was not regarded in the light of a success, but rather of an ornament, of an agreeable gift to society. The world likes to be pleased and there was something pleasing in Crawford's general physiognomy and position. They rested the eyes; they were a gratifying change. Perhaps we were even a little proud of having among us so harmonious an embodiment of the amenities of life.

In spite of his bookish tastes and habits, Crawford was not a recluse. I remember his once saying to me that there were some sacrifices that only man of genius was justified in making to science, and he knew very well that he was not a man of genius. He was not, thank heaven; if he had been, he would have been a much more difficult companion. It was never apparent, indeed, that he was destined to make any great use of his acquisitions. Every one supposed, of course, that he would 'write something;' but he never put pen to paper. He liked to bury his nose in books for the hour's pleasure; he had no dangerous *arrière pensée*, and he was simply a very perfect specimen of a class which has fortunately always been numerous—the class of men who contribute to the advancement of learning by zealously opening their ears and religiously closing their lips. He was fond of society, and went out, as the phrase is, a great deal,—the mammas in especial, making him extremely welcome. What the daughters, in general, thought of him, I hardly know; I suspect that the younger ones often preferred worse men. Crawford's merits were rather thrown away upon little girls. To a considerable number of wise virgins, however, he must have been an object of high admiration, and if a good observer had been asked to pick out in the whole town, the most propitious victim to matrimony, he would certainly have designated my friend. There was nothing to be said against him—there was not a shadow in the picture. He himself, indeed, pretended to be in no hurry to marry, and I heard him more than once declare, that he did not know what he should do with a wife, or what a wife would do with him. Of course we often talked of this matter, and I—upon whom the burden of bachelorhood sat heavy—used to say, that in his place, with money to keep a wife, I would change my condition on the morrow. Crawford gave a great many opposing reasons; of course the real one was that he was very happy as he was, and that the most circumspect marriage is always a risk.

'A man should only marry in self-defence,' he said, 'as Luther became Protestant. He should wait till he is driven to the wall.'

Some time passed and our Luther stood firm. I began to despair of ever seeing a pretty Mrs. Crawford offer me a white hand from my friend's fireside, and I had to console myself with the reflection, that some of the finest persons of whom history makes mention, had been celibates, and that a desire to lead a single life is not necessarily a proof of a morose disposition.

'Oh, I give you up,' I said at last. 'I hoped that if you did not marry for your own sake, you would at least marry for mine. It would make your house so much pleasanter for me. But you have no heart! To avenge myself, I shall myself take a wife on the first opportunity. She shall be as pretty as a picture, and you shall never enter my doors.'

'No man should be accounted single till he is dead,' said Crawford. 'I have been reading Stendhal lately, and learning the philosophy of the *coup de foudre*. It is not impossible that there is a *coup de foudre* waiting for me. All I can say is that it will be lightning from a clear sky.'

The lightning fell, in fact, a short time afterwards. Crawford saw Miss Ingram, admired her, observed her, and loved her. The impression she produced upon him was indeed a sort of summing up of the impression she produced upon society at large. The circumstances of her education and those under which she made her first appearance in the world, were such as to place her beauty in extraordinary relief. She had been brought up more in the manner of an Italian princess of the middle ages—sequestered from conflicting claims of ward-ship—than as the daughter of a plain American citizen. Up to her eighteenth year, it may be said, mortal eye had scarcely beheld her; she lived behind high walls and triple locks, through which an occasional rumour of her beauty made its way into the world. Mrs. Ingram was a second or third cousin of my mother, but the two ladies, between whom there reigned a scanty sympathy, had never made much of the kinship; I had inherited no claim to intimacy with the family, and Elizabeth was a perfect stranger to me. Her parents had, for economy, gone to live in the country—at Orange—and it was there, in a high-hedged old garden, that her childhood and youth were spent. The first definite mention of her loveliness came to me from old Dr. Beadle, who had been called to attend her in a slight illness. (The Ingrams were poor, but their daughter was their golden goose, and to secure the most expensive medical skill was but an act of common prudence.) Dr. Beadle had a high appreciation of a pretty patient; he, of course, kept it within bounds on the field of action, but he enjoyed expressing it afterwards, with the freedom of a profound anatomist, to a younger colleague. Elizabeth Ingram, according to this report, was perfect in every particular, and she was being kept in cotton in preparation for her *début* in New York. He talked about her for a quarter of an hour, and concluded with an eloquent pinch of snuff; whereupon I remembered that she was, after a fashion, my cousin, and that pretty cousins are a source of felicity, in this hard world, which no man can afford to neglect. I took a holiday, jumped into the train, and arrived at Orange. There, in a pretty cottage, in a shaded parlour, I found a small spare woman with a high forehead and a pointed chin, whom I immediately felt to be that Sabrina Ingram, in her occasional allusions to whom my poor mother had expended the very small supply of acerbity with which nature had entrusted her.

'I am told my cousin is extremely beautiful,' I said. 'I should like so much to see her.'

The interview was not prolonged. Mrs. Ingram was frigidly polite; she answered that she was highly honoured by my curiosity, but that her daughter had gone to spend the day with a friend ten miles away.

On my departure, as I turned to latch the garden gate behind me, I saw dimly through an upper window, the gleam of a golden head, and the orbits of two gazing eyes. I kissed my hand to the apparition, and agreed with Dr. Beadle that my cousin was a beauty. But if her image had been dim, that of her mother had been distinct.

They came up to New York the next winter, took a house, gave a great party, and presented the young girl to an astonished world. I succeeded in making little of our cousinship, for Mrs. Ingram did not approve of me, and she gave Elizabeth instructions in consequence. Elizabeth obeyed them, gave me the tips of her fingers, and answered me in monosyllables. Indifference was never more neatly expressed, and I wondered whether this was mere passive compliance, or whether the girl had put a grain of her own intelligence into it. She appeared to have no more intelligence than a snowy-fleeced lamb, but I fancied that she was, by instinct, a shrewd little politician. Nevertheless, I forgave her, for my last feeling about her was one of compassion. She might be as soft as swan's-down, I said; it could not be a pleasant thing to be her mother's daughter, all the same. Mrs. Ingram had black bands of hair, without a white thread, which descended only to the tops of her ears and were there spread out very wide, and polished like metallic plates. She had small, conscious eyes, and the tall white forehead I have mentioned, which resembled a high gable beneath a steep roof. Her chin looked like her forehead reversed, and her lips were perpetually graced with a thin, false smile. I had seen how little it cost them to tell a categorical fib. Poor Mr. Ingram was a helpless colossus; an immense man with a small plump face, a huge back to his neck, and a pair of sloping shoulders. In talking to you, he generally looked across at his wife, and it was easy to see that he was mortally afraid of her.

For this lady's hesitation to bestow her daughter's hand upon Crawford, there was a sufficiently good reason. He had money, but he had not money enough. It was a very comfortable match, but it was not a splendid one, and Mrs. Ingram, in putting the young girl forward, had primed herself with the highest expectations. The marriage was so good that it was a vast pity it was not a little better. If Crawford's income had only been twice as large again, Mrs. Ingram would have pushed Elizabeth into his arms, relaxed in some degree the consuming eagerness with which she viewed the social field, and settled down, possibly, to contentment and veracity. That was a bad year in the matrimonial market, for higher offers were not freely made. Elizabeth was greatly admired, but the ideal suitor did not present himself. I suspect that Mrs. Ingram's charms as a mother-in-law had been accurately guaged. Crawford pushed his suit, with low-toned devotion, and he was at last accepted with a good grace. There had been, I think, a certain amount of general indignation at his being kept waiting, and Mrs. Ingram was accused here and there, of not knowing a first-rate man when she saw one. 'I never said she was honest,' a trenchant critic was heard to observe, ''but at least I supposed she was clever.' Crawford was not afraid of her; he told me so distinctly. 'I defy her to quarrel with me,' he said, 'and I don't despair of making her like me.'

'Like you!' I answered. 'That's easily done. The difficulty will be in your liking her.'

'Oh, I do better—I admire her,' he said. 'She knows so perfectly what she wants. It's a rare quality. I shall have a very fine woman for my mother-in-law.'

Elizabeth's own preference bore down the scale in Crawford's favour a little, I think; how much I hardly know. She liked him, and thought her mother took little account of her likes (and the young girl was too well-behaved to expect it). Mrs. Ingram reflected probably that her pink and white complexion would last longer if she were married to a man she fancied. At any rate, as I have said, the engagement was at last announced, and Crawford came in person to tell me of it. I had never seen a happier-looking man; and his image, as I beheld it that morning, has lived in my memory all these years, as an embodiment of youthful confidence and deep security. He had said that the art of knowing what one wants was rare, but he apparently possessed it. He had got what he wanted, and the sense of possession was exquisite to him. I see again my shabby little consulting-room, with an oil-cloth on the floor, and a paper, representing seven hundred and forty times (I once counted them) a young woman with a pitcher on her head, on the walls; and in the midst of it I see Crawford standing upright, with his thumbs in the arm-holes of his waistcoat, his head thrown back, and his eyes as radiant as two planets.

'You are too odiously happy,' I said. 'I should like to give you a dose of something to tone you down.'

'If you could give me a sleeping potion,' he answered, 'I should be greatly obliged to you. Being engaged is all very well, but I want to be married. I should like to sleep through my engagement—to wake up and find myself a husband.'

'Is your wedding-day fixed?' I asked.

'The twenty-eighth of April—three months hence. I declined to leave the house last night before it was settled. I offered three weeks, but Elizabeth laughed me to scorn. She says it will take a month to make her wedding-dress. Mrs. Ingram has a list of reasons as long as your arm, and every one of them is excellent; that is the abomination of it. She has a genius for the practical. I mean to profit by it; I shall make her turn my mill-wheel for me. But meanwhile it's an eternity!'

'Don't complain of good things lasting long,' said I. 'Such eternities are always too short. I have always heard that the three months before marriage are the happiest time of life. I advise you to make the most of these.'

'Oh, I am happy, I don't deny it,' cried Crawford. 'But I propose to be happier yet.' And he marched away with the step of a sun-god beginning his daily circuit.

He was happier yet, in the sense that with each succeeding week he became more convinced of the charms of Elizabeth Ingram, and more profoundly attuned to the harmonies of prospective matrimony. I, of course, saw little of him, for he was always in attendance upon his betrothed, at the dwelling of whose parents I was a rare visitor. Whenever I did see him, he seemed to have sunk another six inches further into the mystic depths. He formally swallowed his words when I recalled to him his former brave speeches about the single life.

'All I can say is,' he answered, 'that I was an immeasurable donkey. Every argument that I formerly used in favour of not marrying, now seems to me to have an exactly opposite application. Every reason that used to seem to me so good for not taking a wife, now seems to me the best reason in the world for taking one. I not to marry, of all men on earth! Why, I am made on purpose for it, and if the thing did not exist, I should have invented it. In fact, I think I *have* invented some little improvements in the institution—of an extremely conservative kind—and when I put them into practice, you shall tell me what you think of them.'

This lasted several weeks. The day after Crawford told me of his engagement, I had gone to pay my respects to the two ladies, but they were not at home, and I wrote my compliments on a card. I did not repeat my visit until the engagement had become an old story—some three weeks before the date appointed for the marriage—I had then not seen Crawford in several days. I called in the evening, and was ushered into a small parlour reserved by Mrs. Ingram for familiar visitors. Here I found Crawford's mother-in-law that was to be, seated, with an air of great dignity, on a low chair, with her hands folded rigidly in her lap, and her chin making an acuter angle than ever. Before the fire stood Peter Ingram, with his hands under his coat-tails; as soon as I came in, he fixed his eyes upon his wife. 'She has either just been telling, or she is just about to tell, some particularly big fib,' I said to myself. Then I expressed my regret at not having found my cousin at home upon my former visit, and hoped it was not too late to offer my felicitations upon Elizabeth's marriage.

For some moments, Mr. Ingram and his wife were silent; after which, Mrs. Ingram said with a little cough, 'It *is* too late.'

'Really?' said I. 'What has happened?'

'Had we better tell him, my dear?' asked Mr. Ingram.

'I didn't mean to receive any one,' said Mrs. Ingram. 'It was a mistake your coming in.'

'I don't offer to go,' I answered, 'because I suspect that you have some sorrow. I couldn't think of leaving you at such a moment.'

Mr. Ingram looked at me with huge amazement. I don't think he detected my irony, but he had a vague impression that I was measuring my wits with his wife. His ponderous attention acted upon me as an incentive, and I continued,

'Crawford has been behaving badly, I suspect?—Oh, the shabby fellow!'

'Oh, not exactly behaving,' said Mr. Ingram; 'not exactly badly. We can't say that, my dear, eh?'

'It is proper the world should know it,' said Mrs. Ingram, addressing herself to me; 'and as I suspect you are a great gossip, the best way to diffuse the information will be to entrust it to you.'

'Pray tell me,' I said bravely, 'and you may depend upon it the world shall have an account of it.' By this time I knew what was coming. 'Perhaps you hardly need tell me,' I went on. 'I have guessed your news; it is indeed most shocking. Crawford has broken his engagement!'

Mrs. Ingram started up, surprised into self-betrayal. 'Oh, really?' she cried, with a momentary flash of elation. But in an instant she perceived that I had spoken fantastically, and her elation flickered down into keen annoyance. But she faced the situation with characteristic firmness. 'We have broken the engagement,' she said. 'Elizabeth has broken it with our consent.'

'You have turned Crawford away?' I cried.

'We have requested him to consider everything at an end.'

'Poor Crawford!' I exclaimed with ardour.

At this moment the door was thrown open, and Crawford in person stood on the threshold. He paused an instant, like a falcon hovering; then he darted forward at Mr. Ingram.

'In heaven's name,' he cried, 'what is the meaning of your letter?'

Mr. Ingram looked frightened and backed majestically away. 'Really, sir,' he said; 'I must beg you to desist from your threats.'

Crawford turned to Mrs. Ingram; he was intensely pale and profoundly agitated. 'Please tell me,' he said, stepping towards her with clasped hands. 'I don't understand—I can't take it this way. It's a thunderbolt!'

'We were in hopes you would have the kindness not to make a scene,' said Mrs. Ingram. 'It is very painful for us, too, but we cannot discuss the matter. I was afraid you would come.'

'Afraid I would come!' cried Crawford. 'Could you have believed I would not come? Where is Elizabeth?'

'You cannot see her!'

'I cannot see her?'

'It is impossible. It is her wish,' said Mrs. Ingram.

Crawford stood staring, his eyes distended with grief, and rage, and helpless wonder. I have never seen a man so thoroughly agitated, but I have also never seen a man exert such an effort at self-control. He sat down; and then, after a moment—'What have I done?' he asked.

Mr. Ingram walked away to the window, and stood closely examining the texture of the drawn curtains. 'You have done nothing, my dear Mr. Crawford,' said Mrs. Ingram. 'We accuse you of nothing. We are very reasonable; I'm sure you can't deny that, whatever you may say. Mr. Ingram explained everything in the letter. We have simply thought better of it. We have decided that we can't part with our child for the present. She is all we have, and she is so very young. We ought never to have consented. But you urged us so, and we were so good-natured. We must keep her with us'.

'Is that all you have to say?' asked Crawford.

'It seems to me it is quite enough,' said Mrs. Ingram.

Crawford leaned his head on his hands. 'I must have done something without knowing it,' he said at last. 'In heaven's name tell me what it is, and I will do penance and make reparation to the uttermost limit.'

Mr. Ingram turned round, rolling his expressionless eyes in quest of virtuous inspiration. 'We can't say that you have done anything; that would be going too far. But if you had, we would have forgiven you.'

'Where is Elizabeth?' Crawford again demanded.

'In her own apartment,' said Mrs. Ingram majestically.

'Will you please to send for her?'

'Really, sir, we must decline to expose our child to this painful scene.'

'Your tenderness should have begun farther back. Do you expect me to go away without seeing her?'

'We request that you will.'

Crawford turned to me. 'Was such a request ever made before?' he asked, in a trembling voice.

'For your own sake,' said Mrs. Ingram, 'go away without seeing her.'

'For my own sake? What do you mean?'

Mrs. Ingram, very pale, and with her thin lips looking like the blades of a pair of scissors, turned to her husband. 'Mr. Ingram,' she said, 'rescue me from this violence. Speak out—do your duty.'

Mr. Ingram advanced with the air and visage of the stage manager of a theatre, when he steps forward to announce that the favourite of the public will not be able to play. 'Since you drive us so hard, sir, we must tell the painful truth. My poor child would rather have had nothing said about it. The truth is that she has mistaken the character of her affection for you. She has a high esteem for you, but she does not love you.'

Crawford stood silent, looking with formidable eyes from the father to the mother. 'I must insist upon seeing Elizabeth,' he said at last.

Mrs. Ingram gave a toss of her head. 'Remember it was your own demand!' she cried and rustled stiffly out of the room.

We remained silent; Mr. Ingram sat slowly rubbing his knees, and Crawford, pacing up and down, eyed him askance with an intensely troubled frown, as one might eye a person just ascertained to be liable to some repulsive form of dementia. At the end of five minutes, Mrs. Ingram returned, clutching the arm of her daughter, whom she pushed into the room. Then followed the most extraordinary scene of which I have ever been witness.

Crawford strode towards the young girl, and seized her by both hands; she let him take them, and stood looking at him. 'Is this horrible news true?' he cried. 'What infernal machination is at the bottom of it?'

Elizabeth Ingram appeared neither more nor less composed than on most occasions; the pink and white of her cheeks was as pure as usual, her golden tresses were as artistically braided, and her eyes showed no traces of weeping. Her face was never expressive, and at this moment it indicated neither mortification nor defiance. She met her lover's eyes with the exquiste blue of her own pupils, and she looked as beautiful as an angel. 'I am very sorry that we must separate,' she said. 'But I have mistaken the nature of my affection for you. I have the highest esteem for you, but I do not love you.'

I listened to this, and the clear, just faintly trembling, child-like tone in which it was uttered, with absorbing wonder. Was the girl the most consummate of actresses, or had she, literally, no more sensibility than an expensive wax doll? I never discovered, and she has remained to this day, one of the unsolved mysteries of my experience. I incline to believe that she was, morally, absolutely nothing but the hollow reed through which her mother spoke, and that she was really no more cruel now than she been kind before. But there was something monstrous in her quiet, flute-like utterance of Crawford's damnation.

'Do you say this from your own heart, or have you been instructed to say it? You use the same words your father has just used.'

'What can the poor child do better in her trouble than use her father's words?' cried Mrs. Ingram.

'Elizabeth,' cried Crawford, 'you don't love me?'

'No, Mr. Crawford.'

'Why did you ever say so?'

'I never said so.'

He stared at her in amazement, and then, after a little—'It is very true,' he exclaimed. 'You never said so. It was only I who said so.'

'Good-bye!' said Elizabeth; and turning away, she glided out of the room.

'I hope you are satisfied, sir,' said Mrs. Ingram. 'The poor child is before all things sincere.'

In calling this scene the most extraordinary that I ever beheld, I had particularly in mind the remarkable attitude of Crawford at this juncture. He effected a change of base, as it were, under the eyes of the enemy—he descended to the depths and rose to the surface again. Horrified, bewildered, outraged, fatally wounded at heart, he took the full measure of his loss, gauged its irreparableness, and, by an amazing effort of the will, while one could count fifty, superficially accepted the situation.

'I have understood nothing!' he said. 'Good-night.'

He went away, and of course I went with him. Outside the house, in the darkness, he paused and looked around at me.

'What were you doing there?' he asked.

'I had come—rather late in the day—to pay a visit of congratulation. I rather missed it.'

'Do you understand—can you imagine?' He had taken his hat off, and he was pressing his hand to his head.

'They have backed out, simply!' I said. 'The marriage had never satisfied their ambition—you were not rich enough. Perhaps they have heard of something better.'

He stood gazing, lost in thought. 'They,' I had said; but he, of course, was thinking only of *her*; thinking with inexpressible bitterness. He made no allusion to her, and I never afterwards heard him make one. I felt a great compassion for him, but knew not how to help him, nor hardly, even, what to say. It would have done me good to launch some objurgation against the precious little puppet, within doors, but this delicacy forbade. I felt that Crawford's silence covered a fathomless sense of injury; but the injury was terribly real, and I could think of no healing words. He was injured in his love and his pride, his hopes and his honour, his sense of justice and of decency.

'To treat *me* so!' he said at last, in a low tone. 'Me! me!—are they blind—are they imbecile? Haven't they seen what I have been to them—what I was going to be?'

'Yes, they are blind brutes!' I cried. 'Forget them—don't think of them again. They are not worth it.'

He turned away and, in the dark empty street, he leaned his arm on the iron railing that guarded a flight of steps, and dropped his head upon it. I left him standing so a few moments—I could just hear his sobs. Then I passed my arm into his own and walked home with him. Before I left him, he had recovered his outward composure.

After this, so far as one could see, he kept it uninterruptedly. I saw him the next day, and for several days afterwards. He looked like a man who had had a heavy blow, and who had yet not been absolutely stunned. He neither raved nor lamented, nor descanted upon his wrong. He seemed to be trying to shuffle it away, to resume his old occupations, and to appeal to the good offices of the arch-healer, Time. He looked very ill—pale, preoccupied, heavy-eyed, but this was an inevitable tribute to his deep disappointment. He gave me no particular opportunity to make consoling speeches, and not being eloquent, I was more inclined to take one by force. Moral and sentimental platitudes always seemed to me particularly flat upon my own lips, and, addressed to Crawford, they would have been fatally so. Nevertheless, I once told him with some warmth, that he was giving signal proof of being a philosopher. He knew that people always end by getting over things, and he was showing himself able to traverse with a stride a great moral waste. He made no rejoinder at the moment, but an hour later, as we were separating, he told me, with some formalism, that he could not take credit for virtues he had not.

'I am not a philosopher,' he said; 'on the contrary. And I am not getting over it.'

His misfortune excited great compassion among all his friends, and I imagine that this sentiment was expressed, in some cases, with well-meaning but injudicious frankness. The Ingrams were universally denounced, and whenever they appeared in public, at this time, were greeted with significant frigidity. Nothing could have better proved the friendly feeling, the really quite tender regard and admiration that were felt for Crawford, than the manner in which every one took up his cause. He knew it, and I heard him exclaim more than once with intense bitterness that he was that abject thing, an 'object of sympathy.' Some people flattered themselves that they had made the town, socially speaking, too hot to hold Miss Elizabeth and her parents. The Ingrams anticipated by several weeks their projected departure for Newport—they had given out that they were to spend the summer there—and, quitting New York, quite left, like the gentleman in 'The School for Scandal,' their reputations behind them.

I continued to observe Crawford with interest, and, although I did full justice to his wisdom and self-control, when the summer arrived I was ill at ease about him. He led exactly the life he had led before his engagement, and mingled with society neither more nor less. If he disliked to feel that pitying heads were being shaken over him, or voices lowered in tribute to his misadventure, he made at least no visible effort to ignore these manifestations, and he paid to the full the penalty of being 'interesting.' But, on the other hand, he showed no disposition to drown his sorrow in violent pleasure, to deafen himself to its echoes. He never alluded to his disappointment, he discharged all the duties of politeness, and questioned people about their own tribulations or satisfactions as deferentially as if he had had no weight upon his heart. Nevertheless, I knew that his wound was rankling—that he had received a dent, and that he would keep it. From this point onward, however, I do not pretend to understand his conduct. I only was witness of it, and I relate what I saw. I do not pretend to speak of his motives.

I had the prospect of leaving town for a couple of months—a friend and fellow-physician in the country having offered me his practice while he took a vacation. Before I went, I made a point of urging Crawford to seek a change of scene—to go abroad, to travel and distract himself.

'To distract myself from what?' he asked, with his usual clear smile.

'From the memory of the vile trick those people played you.'

'Do I look, do I behave as if I remembered it?' he demanded with sudden gravity.

'You behave very well, but I suspect that it is at the cost of a greater effort than it is wholesome for a man—quite unassisted—to make.'

'I shall stay where I am,' said Crawford, 'and I shall behave as I have behaved—to the end. I find the effort, so far as there is an effort, extremely wholesome.'

'Well, then,' said I, 'I shall take great satisfaction in hearing that you have fallen in love again. I should be delighted to know that you were well married.'

He was silent a while, and then—'It is not impossible,' he said. But, before I left him, he laid his hand on my arm, and, after looking at me with great gravity for some time, declared that it would please him extremly that I should never again allude to his late engagement.

The night before I left town, I went to spend half an hour with him. It was the end of June, the weather was hot, and I proposed that instead of sitting indoors, we should take a stroll. In those days, there stood, in the centre of the city, a concert-garden, of a somewhat primitive structure, into which a few of the more adventurous representatives of the best society were occasionally seen—under stress of hot whether—to penetrate. It had trees and arbours, and little fountains and small tables, at which ice-creams and juleps were, after hope deferred, dispensed. Its musical attractions fell much below the modern standard, and consisted of three old fiddlers playing stale waltzes, or an itinerant ballad-singer, vocalizing in a language perceived to be foreign, but not further identified, and accompanied by a young women who performed upon the triangle, and collected tribute at the tables. Most of the frequenters of this establishment were people who wore their gentility lightly, or had none at all to wear; but in compensation (in the latter case), they were generally provided with a substantial sweetheart. We sat down among the rest, and had each a drink with a straw in it, while we listened to a cracked Italian tenor in a velvet jacket and ear-rings. At the end of half an hour, Crawford proposed we should withdraw, whereupon I busied myself with paying for our juleps. There was some delay in making change, during which, my attention wandered; it was some ten minutes before the waiter returned. When at last he restored me my dues, I said to Crawford that I was ready to depart. He was looking another way and did not hear me; I repeated my observation, and then he started a little, looked round, and said that he would like to remain longer. In a moment I perceived the apparent cause of his changing mind. I checked myself just in time from making a joke about it, and yet—as I did so—I said to myself that it was surely not a thing one could take seriously.

Two persons had within a few moments come to occupy a table near our own. One was a weak-eyed young man with a hat poised into artful crookedness upon a great deal of stiffly brushed and much-anointed straw-coloured hair, and a harmless scowl of defiance at the world in general from under certain bare visible eyebrows. The defiance was probably prompted by the consciousness of the attractions of the person who accompanied him. This was a woman, still young, and to a certain extent pretty, dressed in a manner which showed that she regarded a visit to a concert-garden as a thing to be taken seriously. Her beauty was of the robust order, her colouring high, her glance unshrinking, and her hands large and red. These last were encased in black lace mittens. She had a small dark eye, of a peculiarly piercing quality, set in her head as flatly as a button-hole in a piece of cotton cloth, and a lower lip which protruded beyond the upper one. She carried her head like a person who pretended to have something in it, and she from time to time surveyed the ample expanse of her corsage with a complacent sense of there being something in that too. She was a large woman, and, when standing upright, must have been much taller than her companion. She had a certain conscious dignity of demeanour, turned out her little finger as she ate her pink ice-cream, and said very little to the young man, who was evidently only her opportunity, and not her ideal. She looked about her, while she consumed her refreshment, with a hard, flat, idle stare, which was not that of an adventuress, but that of a person pretentiously and vulgarly respectable. Crawford, I saw, was observing her narrowly, but his observation was earnestly exercised, and she was not—at first, at least,—aware of it. I wondered, nevertheless, why he was observing her. It was not his habit to stare at strange women, and the charms of this florid damsel were not such as to appeal to his fastidious taste.

'I see you are struck by our lovely neighbour,' I said. 'Have you ever seen her before?'

'Yes!' he presently answered. 'In imagination!'

'One's imagination,' I answered, 'would seem to be the last place in which to look for such a figure as that. She belongs to the most sordid reality.'

'She is very fine in her way,' said Crawford. 'My image of her was vague; she is far more perfect. It is always interesting to see a supreme representation of any type, whether or no the type be one that we admire. That is the merit of our neighbour. She resumes a certain civilization; she is the last word—the flower.'

'The last word of coarseness, and the flower of commonness,' I interrupted. 'Yes, she certainly has the merit of being unsurpassable, in her own line.'

'She is a very powerful specimen,' he went on. 'She is complete.'

'What do you take her to be?'

Crawford did not answer for some time, and I suppose he was not heeding me. But at last he spoke. 'She is the daughter of a woman who keeps a third-rate boarding-house in Lexington Avenue. She sits at the foot of the table and pours out bad coffee. She is considered a beauty, in the boarding-house. She makes out the bills—"for three weeks' board," with *week* spelled *weak*. She has been engaged several times. That young man is one of the boarders, inclined to gallantry. He has invited her to come down here and have ice-cream, and she has consented, thought she despises him. Her name is Matilda Jane. The height of her ambition is to be "fashionable." '

'Where the duece did you learn all this?' I asked. 'I shouldn't wonder if it were true.'

'You may depend upon it that it is very near the truth. The boarding-house may be in the Eighth avenue, and the lady's name may be Araminta; but the general outline that I have given is correct.'

We sat awhile longer; Araminta—or Matilda Jane—finished her ice-cream, leaned back in her chair, and fanned herself with a newspaper, which her companion had drawn from his pocket, and she had folded for the purpose. She had by this time, I suppose, perceived Crawford's singular interest in her person, and she appeared inclined to allow him every facility for the gratification of it. She turned herself about, placed her head in attitudes, stroked her glossy tresses, crooked her large little finger more than ever, and gazed with sturdy coquetry at her incongruous admirer. I, who did not admire her, at last, for a second time, proposed an adjournment; but, to my surprise, Crawford simply put out his hand in farewell, and said that he himself would remain. I looked at him hard; it seemed to me that there was a spark of excitement in his eye which I had not seen for many weeks. I made some little joke which might have been taxed with coarseness; but he received it with perfect gravity, and dismissed me with an impatient gesture. I had not walked more than half a block away when I remembered some last word—it has now passed out of my mind—that I wished to say to my friend. It had, I suppose, some importance, for I walked back to repair my omission. I re-entered the garden and returned to the place where we had been sitting. It was vacant; Crawford had moved his chair, and was engaged in conversation with the young woman I have described. His back was turned to me and he was bending over, so that I could not see his face, and that I remained unseen by him. The lady herself was looking at him strangely; surprise, perplexity, pleasure, doubt as to whether 'fashionable' manners required her to seem elated or offended at Crawford's overture, were mingled on her large, rosy face. Her companion appeared to have decided that his own dignity demanded of him grimly to ignore the intrusion; he had given his hat another cock, shouldered his stick like a musket, and fixed his eyes on the fiddlers. I stopped, embraced the group at a glance, and then quietly turned away and departed.

As a physician—as a physiologist—I had every excuse for taking what are called materialistic views of human conduct; but this little episode led me to make some reflections which, if they were not exactly melancholy, were at least tinged with the irony of the moralist. Men are all alike, I said, and the best is, at bottom, very little more delicate than the worst. If there was a man I should have called delicate, it had been Crawford; but he too was capable of seeking a vulgar compensation for an exquisite pain—he also was too weak to be faithful to a memory. Nevertheless I confess I was both amused and re-assured; a limit seemed set to the inward working of his resentment—he was going to take his trouble more easily and naturally. For the next few weeks I heard nothing from him; good friends as we were, we were poor correspondents, and as Crawford, moreover, had said about himself—What in the world had he to write about? I came back to town early in September, and on the evening after my return, called upon my friend. The servant who opened the door, and who showed me a new face, told me that Mr. Crawford had gone out an hour before. As I turned away from the house it suddenly occured to me—I am quite unable to say why—that I might find him at the concert-garden to which we had gone together on the eve of my departure. The night was mild and beautiful, and—though I had not supposed that he had been in the interval a regular *habitué* of those tawdry bowers—a certain association of ideas directed my steps. I reached the garden and passed beneath the arch of paper lanterns which formed its glittering portal. The tables were all occupied, and I scanned the company in vain for Crawford's familiar face. Suddenly I perceived a countenance which, if less familiar, was, at least, vividly impressed upon my memory. The lady whom Crawford had ingeniously characterized as the daughter of the proprietress of a third-rate boarding-house was in possession of one of the tables where she was enthroned in assured pre-eminence. With a garland of flowers upon her bonnet, an azure scarf about her shoulders, and her hands flashing with splendid rings, she seemed a substantial proof that the Eighth avenue may, after all, be the road to fortune. As I stood observing her, her eyes met mine, and I saw that they were illumined with a sort of gross, good humoured felicity. I instinctively connected Crawford with her transfiguration, and concluded that he was effectually reconciled to worldly joys. In a moment I saw that she recognized me; after a very brief hesitation she gave me a familiar nod. Upon this hint I approached her.

'You have seen me before,' she said. 'You have not forgotten me.'

'It's impossible to forget you,' I answered, gallantly.

'It's a fact that no one ever does forget me?—I suppose I oughtn't to speak to you without being introduced. But wait a moment; there is a gentleman here who will introduce me. He has gone to get some cigars.' And she pointed to a gaily bedizened stall on the other side of the garden, before which, in the act of quitting it, his purchase made, I saw Crawford.

Presently he came up to us—he had evidently recognized me from afar. This had given him a few moments. But what, in such a case, were a few moments? He smiled frankly and heartily, and gave my hand an affectionate grasp. I saw, however, that in spite of his smile he was a little pale. He glanced towards the woman at the table, and then, in a clear, serene voice: 'You have made acquaintance?' he said.

'Oh, I know him,' said the lady; 'but I guess he don't know me! Introduce us.'

He mentioned my name, ceremoniously, as if he had been presenting me to a duchess. The woman leaned forward and took my hand in her heavily begemmed fingers. 'How d'ye do, Doctor?' she said.

Then Crawford paused a moment, looking at me. My eyes rested on his, which, for an instant, were strange and fixed; they seemed to defy me to see anything in them that he wished me not to see. 'Allow me to present you,' he said at last, in a tone I shall never forget—'allow me to present you to my wife.'

I stood staring at him; the woman still grasped my hand. She gave it a violent shake and broke into a loud laugh. 'He don't believe it! There's my wedding-ring!' And she thrust out the ample knuckles of her left hand.

A hundred thoughts passed in a flash through my mind, and a dozen exclamations—tragical, ironical, farcical—rose to my lips. But I happily suppressed them all; I simply remained portentously silent, and seated myself mechanically in the chair which Crawford pushed towards me. His face was inscrutable, but in its urbane blankness I found a reflection of the glaring hideousness of his situation. He had committed a monstrous folly. As I sat there, for the next half-hour—it seemed an eternity—I was able to take its full measure. But I was able also to resolve to accept it, to respect it, and to side with poor Crawford, so far as I might, against the consequences of his deed. I remember of that half-hour little beyond a general, rapidly deepening sense of horror. The woman was in a talkative mood; I was the first of her husband's friends upon whom she had as yet been able to lay hands. She gave me much information—as to when they had been married (it was three weeks before), what she had had on, what her husband (she called him 'Mr. Crawford') had given her, what she meant to do during the coming winter. 'We are going to give a great ball,' she said, 'the biggest ever seen in New York. It will open the winter, and I shall be introduced to all his friends. They will want to see me, dreadfully, and there will be sure to be a crowd. I don't know whether they will come twice, but they will come once, I'll engage.'

She complained of her husband refusing to take her on a wedding-tour—was ever a woman married like that before? 'I'm not sure it's a good marriage, without a wedding-tour,' she said. 'I always thought that to be really man and wife, you had to go to Niagara, or Saratoga, or some such place. But he insists on sticking here in New York; he says he has his reasons. He gave me that to keep me here.' And she made one of her rings twinkle.

Crawford listened to this, smiling, unflinching, unwinking. Before we separated—to say something—I asked Mrs. Crawford if she liked music? The fiddlers were scraping away. She turned her empty glass upside down, and with a thump on the table—'I like that!' she cried. It was most horrible. We rose, and Crawford tenderly offered her his arm; I looked at him with a kind of awe.

I went to see him repeatedly, during the ensuing weeks, and did my best to behave as if nothing was altered. In himself, in fact, nothing was altered, and the really masterly manner in which he tacitly assumed that the change in his situation had been in a high degree for the better, might have furnished inspiration to my more bungling efforts. Never had incurably wounded pride forged itself a more consummately impenetrable mask; never had bravado achieved so triumphant an imitation of sincerity. In his wife's absence, Crawford never alluded to her; but, in her presence, he was an embodiment of deference and attentive civility. His habits underwent little change, and he was punctiliously faithful to his former pursuits. He studied—or at least he passed hours in his library. What he did—what he was—in solitude, heaven only knows; nothing, I am happy to say, ever revealed it to me. I never asked him a question about his wife; to feign a respectful interest in her would have been too monstrous a comedy. She herself, however, more than satisfied my curiosity, and treated me to a bold sketch of her life and adventures. Crawford had hit the nail on the head; she was veritably, at the time he made her acquaintance, residing at a boarding-house, not in the capacity of a boarder. She even told me the terms in which he had made his proposal. There had been no love-making, no nonsense, no flummery. 'I have seven thousand dollars a year,' he had said—all of a sudden;—'will you please to become my wife? You shall have four thousand for your own use.' I have no desire to paint the poor woman who imparted to me these facts in blacker colours than she deserves; she was to be pitied certainly, for she had been lifted into a position in which her defects acquired a glaring intensity. She had made no overtures to Crawford; he had come and dragged her out of her friendly obscurity, and placed her unloveliness aloft upon the pedestal of his contrasted good-manners. She had simply taken what was offered her. But for all one's logic, nevertheless, she was a terrible creature. I tried to like her, I tried to find out her points. The best one seemed to be that her jewels and new dresses—her clothes were in atrocious taste—kept her, for the time, in loud good-humour. Might they never be wanting? I shuddered to think of what Crawford would find himself face to face with in case of their failing;—coarseness, vulgarity, ignorance, vanity, and, beneath all, something as hard and arid as dusty bricks. When I had left them, their union always seemed to me a monstrous fable, an evil dream; each time I saw them the miracle was freshly repeated.

People were still in a great measure in the country, and though it had begun to be rumoured about that Crawford had taken a very strange wife, there was for some weeks no adequate appreciation of her strangeness. This came, however, with the advance of the autumn and those beautiful October days when all the world was in the streets. Crawford came forth with his terrible bride upon his arm, took every day a long walk, and ran the gauntlet of society's surprise. On Sundays, he marched into church with his incongruous consort, led her up the long aisle to the accompaniment of the opening organ-peals, and handed her solemnly into her pew. Mrs. Crawford's idiosyncrasies were not of the latent and lurking order, and, in the view of her fellow-worshipers of her own sex, surveying her from a distance, were sufficiently summarized in the composition of her bonnets. Many persons probably remember with a good deal of vividness the great festival to which, early in the winter, Crawford convoked all his friends. Not a person invited was absent, for it was a case in which friendliness and curiosity went most comfortably, hand in hand. Every one wished well to Crawford and was anxious to show it, but when they said they wouldn't for the world seem to turn their backs upon the poor fellow, what people really meant was that they would not for the world miss seeing how Mrs. Crawford would behave. The party was very splendid and made an era in New York, in the art of entertainment. Mrs. Crawford behaved very well, and I think people were a good deal disappointed and scandalized at the decency of her demeanour. But she looked deplorably, it was universally agreed, and her native vulgarity came out in the strange bedizenment of her too exuberant person. By the time supper was served, moreover, every one had gleaned an anecdote about her bad grammar, and the low level of her conversation. On all sides, people were putting their heads together, in threes and fours, and tittering over each other's stories. There is nothing like the bad manners of good society, and I, myself, acutely sensitive on Crawford's behalf, found it impossible, by the end of the evening, to endure the growing exhilaration of the assembly. The company had rendered its verdict; namely, that there were vulgar people one could, at a pinch accept, and the vulgar people one couldn't, and that Mrs. Crawford belonged to the latter class. I was savage with every one who spoke to me. 'Yes, she is as bad as you please,' I said; 'but you are worse!' But I might have spared my resentment, for Crawford, himself, in the midst of all this, was simply sublime. He was the genius of hospitality in person; no one had ever seen him so careless, so free, so charming. When I went to bid him good-night, as I took him by the hand—'You will carry it through!' I said. He looked at me, smiling vaguely, and not showing in the least that he understood me. Then I felt how deeply he was attached to the part he had undertaken to play; he had sacrificed our old good-fellowship to it. Even to me, his oldest friend, he would not raise a corner of the mask.

Mrs. Ingram and Elizabeth were, of course, not at the ball; but they had come back from Newport, bringing an ardent suitor in their train. The event had amply justified Mrs. Ingram's circumspection; she had captured a young Southern planter, whose estates were fabled to cover three-eights of the State of Alabama. Elizabeth was more beautiful than ever, and the marriage was being hurried forward. Several times, in public, to my knowledge, Elizabeth and her mother, found themselves face to face with Crawford and his wife. What Crawford must have felt when he looked from the exquisite creature he had lost to the full-blown dowdy he had gained, is a matter it is well but to glance at and pass—the more so, as my story approaches its close. One morning, in my consulting-room, I had been giving some advice to a little old gentleman who was as sound as a winter-pippin, but, who used to come and see me once a month to tell me that he felt a hair on his tongue, or, that he had dreamed of a blue-dog, and to ask to be put upon a 'diet' in consequence. The basis of a diet, in his view, was a daily pint of port wine. He had retired from business, he belonged to a club, and he used to go about peddling gossip. His wares, like those of most peddlers, were cheap, and usually, for my prescription, I could purchase the whole contents of his tray. On this occasion, as he was leaving me, he remarked that he supposed I had heard the news about our friend Crawford. I said that I had heard nothing. What was the news?

'He has lost every penny of his fortune,' said my patient. 'He is completely cleaned out.' And, then, in answer to my exclamation of dismay, he proceeded to inform me that the New Amsterdam Bank had suspended payment, and would certainly never resume it. All the world knew that Crawford's funds were at the disposal of the bank, and that two or three months before, when things were looking squally, he had come most generously to the rescue. The squall had come, it had proved a hurricane, the bank had capsized, and

Crawford's money had gone to the bottom. 'It's not a surprise to me,' said Mr. Niblett, 'I suspected something a year ago. It's true, I am very sharp.'

'Do you think any one else suspected anything?' I asked.

'I dare say not; people are so easily humbugged. And, then, what could have looked better, above board, than the New Amsterdam?'

'Nevertheless, here and there,' I said, 'an exceptionally sharp person may have been on the watch.'

'Unquestionably—though I am told that they are going on to-day, down town, as if no bank had ever broken before.'

'Do you know Mrs. Ingram?' I asked.

'Thoroughly! She is exceptionally sharp, if that is what you mean.'

'Do you think it is possible that she foresaw this affair six months ago?'

'Very possible; she always has her nose in Wall Street, and she knows more about stocks than the whole board of brokers.'

'Well,' said I, after a pause, 'sharp as she is, I hope she will get nipped, yet!'

'Ah,' said my old friend, 'you allude to Crawford's affairs? But you shouldn't be a better royalist than the king. He has forgiven her—he has consoled himself. But what will console him now? Is it true his wife was a washerwoman? Perhaps she will not be sorry to know a trade.'

I hoped with all my heart that Mr. Niblett's story was an exaggeration, and I repaired that evening to Crawford's house, to learn the real extent of his misfortune. He had seen me coming in, and he met me in the hall and drew me immediately into the library. He looked like a man who had been thrown by a vicious horse, but had picked himself up and resolved to go the rest of the way on foot.

'How bad is it?' I asked.

'I have about a thousand a year left. I shall get some work, and with careful economy we can live.'

At this moment I heard a loud voice screaming from the top of the stairs. 'Will *she* help you?' I asked.

He hesitated a moment, and then—'No!' he said simply. Immediately, as a commentary upon his answer, the door was thrown open and Mrs. Crawford swept in. I saw in an instant that her good-humour was in permanent eclipse; flushed, disheveled, inflamed, she was a perfect presentation of a vulgar fury. She advanced upon me with a truly formidable weight of wrath.

'Was it you that put him up to it?' she cried. 'Was it you that put it into his head to marry me? I'm sure I never thought of him—he isn't the twentieth part of a man! I took him for his money—four thousand a year, clear; I never pretended it was for anything else. To-day, he comes and tells me that it was all a mistake—that we must get on as well as we can on twelve hundred. And he calls himself a gentleman—and so do you, I suppose! There are gentlemen in the State's prison for less. I have been cheated, insulted and ruined; but I'm not a woman you can play that sort of game upon. The money's mine, what is left of it, and he may go and get his fine friends to support him. There ain't a thing in the world he can do—except lie and cheat!'

Crawford, during this horrible explosion, stood with his eyes fixed upon the floor; and I felt that the peculiarly odious part of the scene was that his wife was literally in the right. She had been bitterly disappointed—she had been practically deceived. Crawford turned to me and put out his hand. 'Good-bye,' he said 'I must forego the pleasure of receiving you any more in my own house.'

'I can't come again?' I exclaimed.

'I will take it as a favour that you should not.'

I withdrew with an insupportable sense of helplessness. In the house he was then occupying, he, of course, very soon ceased to live; but for some time I was in ignorance of whither he had betaken himself. He had forbidden me to come and see him, and he was too much occupied in accommodating himself to his change of fortune to find time for making visits. At last I disinterred him in one of the upper streets, near the East River, in a small house of which he occupied but a single floor. I disobeyed him and went in, and as his wife was apparently absent, he allowed me to remain. He had kept his books, or most of them, and arranged a sort of library. He looked ten years older, but he neither made nor suffered me to make an allusion to himself. He had obtained a place as clerk at a wholesale chemist's, and he received a salary of five hundred dollars. After this, I not infrequently saw him; we used often, on a Sunday, to take a long walk together. On our return we parted at his door; he never asked me to come in. He talked of his reading, of his scientific fancies, of public affairs, of our friends—of everything except his own troubles. He suffered, of course, most of his purely formal social relations to die out; but if he appeared not to cling to his friends, neither did he seem to avoid them. I remember a clever old lady saying to me at this time, in allusion to her having met him somewhere—'I used always to think Mr. Crawford the most agreeable man in the world, but I think now he has even improved!' One day—we had walked out into the country, and were sitting on a felled log by the roadside, to rest (for in those days New Yorkers could walk out into the country),—I said to him that I had a piece of news to tell him. It was not pleasing, but it was interesting.

'I told you six weeks ago,' I said, 'that Elizabeth Ingram had been seized with small-pox. She has recovered, and two or three people have seen her. Every ray of her beauty is gone. They say she is hideous.'

'I don't believe it!' he said, simply.

'The young man who was to marry her does,' I answered. 'He has backed out—he has given her up—he has posted back to Alabama.'

Crawford looked at me a moment, and then—'The idiot!' he exclaimed.

For myself, I felt the full bitterness of poor Elizabeth's lot; Mrs. Ingram had been 'nipped,' as I had ventured to express it, in a grimmer fashion than I hoped. Several months afterwards, I saw the young girl, shrouded in a thick veil, beneath which I could just distinguish her absolutely blasted face. On either side of her walked her father and mother, each of them showing a visage almost as blighted as her own.

I saw Crawford for a time, as I have said, with a certain frequency; but there began to occur long intervals, during which he plunged into inscrutable gloom. I supposed in a general way, that his wife's temper gave him plenty of occupation at home; but a painful incident—which I need not repeat—at last informed me how much. Mrs. Crawford, it appeared, drank deep; she had resorted to liquor to console herself for her disappointments. During her periods of revelry, her husband was obliged to be in constant attendance upon her, to keep her from exposing herself. She had done so to me, hideously, and it was so that I learned the reason of her husband's fitful absences. After this, I expressed to Crawford my amazement that he should continue to live with her.

'It's very simple,' he answered. 'I have done her a great wrong, and I have forfeited the right to complain of any she may do to me.'

'In heaven's name,' I said, 'make another fortune and pension her off.'

He shook his head. 'I shall never make a fortune. My working-power is not of a high value.'

One day, not having seen him for several weeks, I went to his house. The door was opened by his wife, in curl-papers and a soiled dressing-gown. After what I can hardly call an exchange of greetings,—for she wasted no politeness upon me,—I asked for news of my friend.

'He's at the New York Hospital,' she said.

'What in the world has happened to him?'

'He has broken his leg, and he went there to be taken care of—as if he hadn't a comfortable home of his own! But he's a deep one; that's a hit at me!'

I immediately announced my intention of going to see him, but as I was turning away she stopped me, laying her hand on my arm. She looked at me hard, almost menacingly. 'If he tells you,' she said, 'that it was me that made him break his leg—that I came behind him, and pushed him down the steps of the back-yard, upon the flags, you needn't believe him. I could have done it; I'm strong enough'—and with a vigorous arm she gave a thump upon the door-post. 'It would have served him right, too. But it's a lie!'

'He will not tell me,' I said. 'But you have done so!'

Crawford was in bed, in one of the great, dreary wards of the hospital, looking as a man looks who has been laid up for three weeks with a compound fracture of the knee. I had seen no small amount of physical misery, but I had never seen anything so poignant as the sight of my once brilliant friend in such a place, from such a cause. I told him I would not ask him how his misfortune occurred: I knew! We talked awhile, and at last I said, 'Of course you will not go back to her!'

He turned away his head, and at this moment, the nurse came and said that I had made the poor gentleman talk enough.

Of course he did go back to her—at the end of a very long convalescence. His leg was permanently injured; he was obliged to move about very slowly, and what he had called the value of his working-power was not thereby increased. This meant permanent poverty, and all the rest of it. It lasted ten years longer—until 185-, when Mrs. Crawford died of *delirium tremens*. I cannot say that this event restored his equanimity, for the excellent reason that to the eyes of the world—and my own most searching ones—he had never lost it.

The Ghostly Rental

[First appeared in the *Scribner's Monthly*, vol. xii (September 1876), pp. 664-79. Not reprinted during James's lifetime.]

I WAS IN MY TWENTY-SECOND YEAR, AND I HAD JUST LEFT COLLEGE. I was at liberty to choose my career, and I chose it with much promptness. I afterwards renounced it, in truth, with equal ardour, but I have never regretted those two youthful years of perplexed and excited, but also of agreeable and fruitful experiment. I had a taste for theology, and during my college term I had been an admiring reader of Dr. Channing. This was theology of a grateful and succulent savour; it seemed to offer one the rose of faith delightfully stripped of its thorns. And then (for I rather think this had something to do with it), I had taken a fancy to the Old Divinity School. I have always had an eye to the back scene in the human drama, and it seemed to me that I might play my part with a fair chance of applause (from myself at least), in that detached and tranquil home of mild casuistry, with its respectable avenue on one side, and its prospect of green fields and contact with acres of woodland on the other. Cambridge, for the lovers of woods and fields, has changed for the worse since those days, and the precinct in question has forfeited much of its mingled pastoral and sholastic quietude. It was then a College-hall in the woods—a charming mixture. What it is now has nothing to do with my story; and I have no doubt that there are still doctrine-haunted young seniors who, as they stroll near it in the summer dusk, promise themselves, later, to taste of its fine leisurely quality. For myself, I was not disappointed. I established myself in a great square, low-browed room, with deep window-benches; I hung prints from Overbeck and Ary Scheffer on the walls; I arranged my books, with great refinement of classification, in the alcoves beside the high chimney-shelf, and I began to read Plotinus and St. Augustine. Among my companions were two or three men of ability and of good fellowship, with whom I occasionally brewed a fireside bowl; and with adventurous reading, deep discourse, potations conscientiously shallow, and long country walks, my initiation into the clerical mystery progressed agreeably enough.

With one of my comrades I formed an especial friendship, and we passed a great deal of time together. Unfortunately he had a chronic weakness of one of his knees, which compelled him to lead a very sedentary life, and as I was a methodical pedestrian, this made some difference in our habits. I used often to stretch away for my daily ramble, with no companion but the stick in my hand or the book in my pocket. But in the use of my legs and the sense of unstinted open air, I have always found company enough. I should, perhaps, add that in the enjoyment of a very sharp pair of eyes, I found something of a social pleasure. My eyes and I were on excellent terms; they were indefatigable observers of all wayside incidents, and so long as they were amused I was contented. It is, indeed, owing to their inquisitive habits that I came into possession of this remarkable story. Much of the country about the old College town is pretty now, but it was prettier thirty years ago. That multitudinous eruption of domiciliary pasteboard which now graces the landscape, in the direction of the low, blue Waltham Hills, had not yet taken place; there were no genteel cottages to put the shabby meadows and scrubby orchards to shame—a juxtaposition by which, in later years, neither element of the contrast has gained. Certain crooked cross-roads, then, as I remember them, were more deeply and naturally rural, and the solitary dwellings on the long grassy slopes beside them, under the tall, customary elm that curved its foliage in mid-air like the outward dropping ears of a girdled wheatsheaf, sat with their shingled hoods well pulled down on their ears, and no prescience whatever of the fashion of French roofs—weather-wrinkled old peasant women, as you might call them, quietly wearing the native coif, and never dreaming of mounting bonnets, and indecently exposing their venerable brows. That winter was what is called an 'open' one; there was much cold, but little snow; the roads were firm and free, and I was rarely compelled by the weather to forego my exercise. One grey December afternoon I had sought it in the direction of the adjacent town of Medford, and I was retracing my steps at an even pace, and watching the pale, cold tints—the transparent amber and faded rose-colour—which curtained, in wintry fashion, the western sky, and reminded me of a sceptical smile on the lips of a beautiful woman. I came, as dusk was falling, to a narrow road which I had never traversed and which I imagined offered me a short cut homeward. I was about three miles away; I was late, and would have been thankful to make them two. I diverged, walked some ten minutes, and then perceived that the road had a very unfrequented air. The wheel-ruts looked old; the stillness seemed peculiarly sensible. And yet down the road stood a house, so that it must in some degree have been a thoroughfare. On one side was a high, natural embankment, on the top of which was perched an apple-orchard, whose tangled boughs made a stretch of coarse black lace-work, hung across the coldly rosy west. In a short time I came to the house, and I immediately found myself interested in it. I stopped in front of it gazing hard, I hardly knew why, but with a vague mixture of curiosity and timidity. It was a house like most of the houses thereabouts, except that it was decidedly a handsome specimen of its class. It stood on a grassy slope, it had its tall, impartially drooping elm beside it, and its old black well-cover at its shoulder. But it was of very large proportions, and it had a striking look of solidity and stoutness of timber. It had lived to a good old age, too, for the wood-work on its door-way and under its eaves, carefully and abundantly carved, referred it to the middle, at the latest, of the last century. All this had once been painted white, but the broad back of time, leaning against the door-posts for a hundred years, had laid bare the grain of the wood. Behind the house stretched an orchard of apple-trees, more gnarled and fantastic than usual, and wearing, in the deepening dusk, a blighted and exhausted aspect. All the windows of the house had rusty shutters, without slats, and these were closely drawn. There was no sign of life about it; it looked blank, bare and vacant, and yet, as I lingered near it, it seemed to have a familiar meaning—an audible eloquence. I have always thought of the impression made upon me at first sight, by that grey colonial dwelling, as a proof that induction may sometimes be near akin to divination; for after all, there was nothing on the face of the matter to warrant the very serious induction that I made. I fell back and crossed the road. The last red light of the sunset disengaged itself, as it was about to vanish, and rested faintly for a moment on the time-silvered front of the old house. It touched, with perfect regularity, the series of small panes in the fan-shaped window above the door, and twinkled there fantastically. Then it died away, and left the place more intensely sombre. At this moment, I said to myself with the accent of profound conviction—'The house is simply haunted!'

Somehow, immediately, I believed it, and so long as I was not shut up inside, the idea gave me pleasure. It was implied in the aspect of the house, and it explained it. Half an hour before, if I had been asked, I would have said, as befitted a young man who was explicitly cultivating cheerful views of the supernatural, that there were no such things as haunted houses. But the dwelling before me gave a vivid meaning to the empty words; it had been spiritually blighted.

The longer I looked at it, the intenser seemed the secret that it held. I walked all round it, I tried to peep here and there, through a crevice in the shutters, and I took a puerile satisfaction in laying my hand on the door-knob and gently turning it. If the door had yielded, would I have gone in?—would I have penetrated the dusky stillness? My audacity, fortunately, was not put to the test. The portal was admirably solid, and I was unable even to shake it. At last I turned away, casting many looks behind me. I pursued my way, and, after a longer walk than I had bargained for, reached the high-road. At a certain distance below the point at which the long lane I have mentioned entered it, stood a comfortable, tidy dwelling, which might have offered itself as the model of the house which is in no sense haunted—which has no sinister secrets, and knows nothing but blooming prosperity. Its clean white paint stared placidly through the dusk, and its vine-covered porch had been dressed in straw for the winter. An old, one-horse chaise, freighted with two departing visitors was leaving the door, and through the undraped windows, I saw the lamp-lit sitting-room, and the table spread with the early 'tea,' which had been improvised for the comfort of the guests. The mistress of the house had come to the gate with her friends; she lingered there after the chaise had wheeled creakingly away, half to watch them down the road, and half to give me as I passed in the twilight, a questioning look. She was a comely, quick young woman, with a sharp, dark eye, and I ventured to stop and speak to her.

'That house down that side-road,' I said, 'about a mile from here—the only one—can you tell me whom it belongs to?'

She stared at me a moment, and, I thought, coloured a little. 'Our folks never go down that road,' she said, briefly.

'But it's a short way to Medford,' I answered.

She gave a little toss of her head. 'Perhaps it would turn out a long way. At any rate, we don't use it.'

This was interesting. A thrifty Yankee household must have good reasons for this scorn of time-saving processes. 'But you know the house, at least?' I said.

'Well, I have seen it.'

'And to whom does it belong?'

She gave a little laugh and looked away as if she were aware that, to a stranger, her words might seem to savour of agricultural superstition. 'I guess it belongs to them that are in it.'

'But is there any one in it? It is completely closed.'

'That makes no difference. They never come out, and no one ever goes in.' And she turned away.

But I laid my hand on her arm, respectfully. 'You mean,' I said, 'that the house is haunted?'

She drew herself away, coloured, raised her finger to her lips, and hurried into the house, where, in a moment, the curtains were dropped over the windows.

For several days, I thought repeatedly of this little adventure, but I took some satisfaction in keeping it to myself. If the house was not haunted, it was useless to expose my imaginative whims, and if it was, it was agreeable to drain the cup of horror without assistance. I determined, of course, to pass that way again; and a week later—it was the last day of the year—I retraced my steps. I approached the house from the opposite direction, and found myself before it at about the same hour as before. The light was failing, the sky low and grey; the wind wailed along the hard, bare ground, and made slow eddies of the frost-blackened leaves. The melancholy mansion stood there, seeming to gather the winter twilight around it, and mask itself in it, inscrutably. I hardly knew on what errand I had come, but I had a vague feeling that if this time the door-knob were to turn and the door to open, I should take my heart in my hands, and let them close behind me. Who were the mysterious tenants to whom the good woman at the corner had alluded? What had been seen or heard—what was related? The door was as stubborn as before, and my impertinent fumblings with the latch caused no upper window to be thrown open, nor any strange, pale face to be thrust out. I ventured even to raise the rusty knocker and give it half-a-dozen raps, but they made a flat, dead sound, and aroused no echo. Familiarity breeds contempt; I don't know what I should have done next, if, in the distance, up the road (the same one I had followed), I had not seen a solitary figure advancing. I was unwilling to be observed hanging about this ill-famed dwelling, and I sought refuge among the dense shadows of a grove of pines near by, where I might peep forth, and yet remain invisible. Presently, the new-comer drew near, and I perceived that he was making straight for the house. He was a little, old man, the most striking feature of whose appearance was a voluminous cloak, of a sort of military cut. He carried a walking-stick, and advanced in a slow, painful, somewhat hobbling fashion, but with an air of extreme resolution. He turned off from the road, and followed the vague wheel-track, and within a few yards of the house he paused. He looked up at it, fixedly and searchingly, as if he were counting the windows, or noting certain familiar marks. Then he took off his hat, and bent over slowly and solemnly, as if he were performing an obeisance. As he stood uncovered, I had a good look at him. He was, as I have said, a diminutive old man, but it would have been hard to decide whether he belonged to this world or to the other. His head reminded me, vaguely, of the portraits of Andrew Jackson. He had a crop of grizzled hair, as stiff as a brush, a lean, pale, smooth-shaven face, and an eye of intense brilliancy, surmounted with thick brows, which had remained perfectly black. His face, as well as his cloak, seemed to belong to an old soldier; he looked like a retired military man of a modest rank; but he struck me as exceeding the classic privilege of even such a personage to be eccentric and grotesque. When he had finished his salute, he advanced to the door, fumbled in the folds of his cloak, which hung down much further in front than behind, and produced a key. This he slowly and carefully inserted into the lock, and then, apparently, he turned it. But the door did not immediately open; first he bent his head, turned his ear, and stood listening, and then he looked up and down the road. Satisfied or reassured, he applied his aged shoulder to one of the deep-set panels, and pressed a moment. The door yielded—opening into perfect darkness. He stopped again on the threshold, and again removed his hat and made his bow. Then he went in, and carefully closed the door behind him.

Who in the world was he, and what was his errand? He might have been a figure out of one of Hoffman's tales. Was he vision or a reality—an inmate of the house, or a familiar, friendly visitor? What had been the meaning, in either case, of his mystic genuflexions, and how did he propose to proceed, in that inner darkness? I emerged from my retirement and observed narrowly, several of the windows. In each of them, at an interval, a ray of light became visible in the chink between the two leaves of the shutters. Evidently, he was lighting up; was he going to give a party—a ghostly revel? My curiosity grew intense, but I was quite at a loss how to satisfy it. For a moment I thought of rapping peremptorily at the door; but I dismissed this idea as unmannerly, and calculated to break the spell, if spell there was. I walked round the house and tried, without violence, to open one of the lower windows. It resisted, but I had better fortune, in a moment, with another. There was a risk, certainly, in the trick I was playing—a risk of being seen from within, or (worse) seeing, myself, something that I should repent of seeing. But curiosity, as I say, had become an inspiration, and the risk was highly agreeable. Through the parting of the shutters I looked into a lighted room—a room lighted by two candles in old brass flambeaux, placed upon the mantel-shelf. It was apparently a sort of back parlour, and it had retained all its furniture. This was of a homely, old-fashioned pattern, and consisted of hair-cloth chairs and sofas, spare mahogany tables, and framed samplers hung upon the walls. But although the room was furnished, it had a strangely uninhabited look; the tables and chairs were in rigid positions, and no small, familiar objects were visible. I could not see everything, and I could only guess at the existence, on my right, of a large folding-door. It was apparently open, and the light of the neighbouring room passed through it. I waited for some time, but the room remained empty. At last I became conscious that a large shadow was projected upon the wall opposite the folding-door—the shadow, evidently, of a figure in the adjoining room. It was tall and grotesque, and seemed to represent a person sitting perfectly motionless, in profile. I thought I recognized the perpendicular bristles and far-arching nose of my little old man. There was a strange fixedness in his posture; he appeared to be seated, and looking intently at something. I watched the shadow a long time, but it never stirred. At last, however, just as my patience began to ebb, it moved slowly, rose to the ceiling, and became indistinct. I don't know what I should have seen next, but by an irresistible impulse, I closed the shutter. Was it delicacy?—was it pusillanimity? I can hardly say. I lingered, nevertheless, near the house, hoping that my friend would re-appear. I was not disappointed; for he at last emerged, looking just as when he had gone in, and taking his leave in the same ceremonious fashion. (The lights, I had already observed, had disappeared from the crevice of each of the windows.) He faced about before the door, took off his hat, and made an obsequious bow. As he turned away I had a hundred minds to speak to him, but I let him depart in peace. This, I may say, was pure delicacy;—you will answer, perhaps, that it came too late. It seemed to me that he had a right to resent my observation; though my own right to exercise it (if ghosts were in the question) struck me as equally positive. I continued to watch him as he hobbled softly down the bank, and along the lonely road. Then I musingly retreated in the opposite direction. I was tempted to follow him, at a distance, to see what became of him; but this, too, seemed indelicate; and I confess, moreover, that I felt the inclination to coquet a little, as it were, with my discovery—to pull apart the petals of the flower one by one.

I continued to smell the flower, from time to time, for its oddity of perfume had fascinated me. I passed by the house on the cross-road again, but never encountered the old man in the cloak, or any other wayfarer. It seemed to keep observers at a distance, and I was careful not to gossip about it: one inquirer, I said to myself, may edge his way into the secret, but there is no room for two. At the same time, of course, I would have been thankful for any chance side-light that might fall across the matter—though I could not well see whence it was to come. I hoped to meet the old man in the cloak elsewhere, but as the days passed by without his reappearing, I ceased to expect it. And yet I reflected that he probably lived in that neighbourhood, inasmuch as he had made his pilgrimage to the vacant house on foot. If he had come from a distance, he would have been sure to arrive in some old deep-hooded gig with yellow wheels—a vehicle as venerably grotesque as himself. One day I took a stroll in Mount Auburn cemetery—an institution at that period in its infancy, and full of a sylvan charm which it has now completely forfeited. It contained more maple and birch than willow and cypress, and the sleepers had ample elbow room. It was not a city of the dead, but at the most a village, and a meditative pedestrian might stroll there without too importunate reminder of the grotesque side of our claims to posthumous consideration. I had come out to enjoy the first foretaste of Spring—one of those mild days of late winter, when the torpid earth seems to draw the first long breath that marks the rupture of the spell of sleep. The sun was veiled in haze, and yet warm, and the frost was oozing from its deepest lurking-places. I had been treading for half an hour the winding ways of the cemetery, when suddenly I perceived a familiar figure seated on a bench against a southward-facing evergreen hedge. I call the figure familiar, because I had seen it often in memory and in fancy; in fact, I had beheld it but once. Its back was turned to me, but it wore a voluminous cloak, which there was no mistaking. Here, at last, was my fellow-visitor at the haunted house, and here was my chance, if I wished to approach him! I made a circuit, and came towards him from in front. He saw me, at the end of the alley, and sat motionless, with his hands on the head of his stick, watching me from under his black eyebrows as I drew near. At a distance these black eyebrows looked formidable; they were the only thing I saw in his face. But on a closer view I was re-assured, simply because I immediately felt that no man could really be as fantastically fierce as this poor old gentleman looked. His face was a kind of caricature of martial truculence. I stopped in front of him, and respectfully asked leave to sit and rest upon his bench. He granted it with a silent gesture, of much dignity, and I placed myself beside him. In this position I was able, covertly, to observe him. He was quite as much an oddity in the morning sunshine, as he had been in the dubious twilight. The lines in his face were as rigid as if they had been hacked out of a block by a clumsy wood-carver. His eyes were flamboyant, his nose terrific, his mouth implacable. And yet, after awhile, when he slowly turned and looked at me, fixedly, I perceived that in spite of this portentous mask, he was a very mild old man. I was sure he even would have been glad to smile, but, evidently, his facial muscles were too stiff—they had taken a different fold, once for all. I wondered whether he was demented, but I dismissed the idea; the fixed glitter in his eye was not that of insanity. What his face really expressed was deep and simple sadness; his heart perhaps was broken, but his brain was intact. His dress was shabby but neat, and his old blue cloak had known half a century's brushing.

I hastened to make some observation upon the exceptional softness of the day, and he answered me in a gentle, mellow voice, which it was almost startling to hear proceed from such bellicose lips.

'This is a very comfortable place,' he presently added.

'I am fond of walking in graveyards,' I rejoined deliberately; flattering myself that I had struck a vein that might lead to something.

I was encouraged; he turned and fixed me with his duskily glowing eyes. Then very gravely,—'Walking, yes. Take all your exercise now. Some day you will have to settle down in a graveyard in a fixed position.'

'Very true,' said I. 'But you know there are some people who are said to take exercise even after that day.'

He had been looking at me still; at this he looked away.

'You don't understand?' I said, gently.

He continued to gaze straight before him.

'Some people, you know, walk about after death,' I went on.

At last he turned, and looked at me more portentously than ever. 'You don't believe that,' he said simply.

'How do you know I don't'.

'Because you are young and foolish.' This was said without acerbity—even kindly;but in the tone of an old man whose consciousness of his own heavy experience made everything else seem light.

'I am certainly young,' I answered; 'but I don't think that, on the whole, I am foolish. But say I don't believe in ghosts—most people would be on my side.'

'Most people are fools!' said the old man.

I let the question rest, and talked of other things. My companion seemed on his guard, he eyed me defiantly, and made brief answers to my remarks; but I nevertheless gathered an impression that our meeting was an agreeable thing to him, and even a social incident of some importance. He was evidently a lonely creature, and his opportunities for gossip were rare. He had had troubles, and they had detached him from the world, and driven him back upon himself; but the social chord in his antiquated soul was not entirely broken, and I was sure he was gratified to find that it could still feebly resound. At last, he began to ask questions himself; he inquired whether I was a student.

'I am a student of divinity,' I answered.

'Of divinity?'

'Of theology. I am studying for the ministry.'

At this he eyed me with peculiar intensity—after which his gaze wandered away again. 'There are certain things you ought to know, then,' he said at last.

'I have a great desire for knowledge,' I answered. 'What things do you mean?'

He looked at me again awhile, but without heeding my question.

'I like your appearance,' he said. 'You seem to me a sober lad.'

'Oh, I am perfectly sober!' I exclaimed—yet departing for a moment from my soberness.

'I think you are fair-minded,' he went on.

'I don't any longer strike you as foolish then?' I asked.

'I stick to what I said about people who deny the power of departed spirits to return. They *are* fools!' And he rapped fiercely with his staff on the earth.

I hesitated a moment, and then, abruptly, 'You have seen a ghost!' I said.

He appeared not at all startled.

'You are right, sir!' he answered with great dignity. 'With me it's not a matter of cold theory—I have not had to pry into old books to learn what to believe. *I know!* With these eyes I have beheld the departed spirit standing before me as near as you are!' And his eyes, as he spoke, certainly looked as if they had rested upon strange things.

I was irresistibly impressed—I was touched with credulity.

'And was it very terrible?' I asked.

'I am an old soldier—I am not afraid!'

'When was it?—where was it?' I asked.

He looked at me mistrustfully, and I saw that I was going too fast.

'Excuse me from going into particulars,' he said. 'I am not at liberty to speak more fully. I have told you so much, because I cannot bear to hear this subject spoken of lightly. Remember in future, that you have seen a very honest old man who told you—on his honour—that he had seen a ghost!' And he got up, as if he thought he had said enough. Reserve, shyness, pride, the fear of being laughed at, the memory, possibly, of former strokes of sarcasm—all this, on one side, had its weight with him; but I suspected that on the other, his tongue was loosened by the garrulity of old age, the sense of solitude, and the need of sympathy—and perhaps, also, by the friendliness which he had been so good as to express towards myself. Evidently it would be unwise to press him, but I hoped to see him again.

'To give greater weight to my words,' he added, 'let me mention my name—Captain Diamond, sir. I have seen service.'

'I hope I may have the pleasure of meeting you again,' I said.

'The same to you, sir!' And brandishing his stick portentously—though with the friendliest intentions—he marched stiffly away.

I asked two or three persons—selected with discretion—whether they knew anything about Captain Diamond, but they were quite unable to enlighten me. At last, suddenly, I smote my forehead, and, dubbing myself a dolt, remembered that I was neglecting a source of information to which I had never applied in vain. The excellent person at whose table I habitually dined, and who dispensed hospitality to students at so much a week, had a sister as good as herself, and of conversational powers more varied. This sister, who was known as Miss Deborah, was an old maid in all the force of the term. She was deformed, and she never went out of the house; she sat all day at the window, between a bird-cage and a flower-pot, stitching small linen articles—mysterious bands and frills. She wielded, I was assured, an exquisite needle, and her work was highly prized. In spite of her deformity and her confinement, she had a little, fresh, round face, and an imperturbable serenity of spirit. She had also a very quick little wit of her own, she was extremely observant, and she had a high relish for a friendly chat. Nothing pleased her so much as to have you —especially, I think, if you were a young divinity student—move your chair near her sunny window, and settle yourself for twenty minutes' 'talk'. 'Well, sir,' she used always to say, 'what is the latest monstrosity in Biblical criticism?'—for she used to pretend to be horrified at the rationalistic tendency of the age. But she was an inexorable little philosopher, and I am convinced that she was a keener rationalist than any of us, and that, if she had chosen, she could have propounded questions that would have made the boldest of us wince. Her window commanded the whole town—or rather, the whole country. Knowledge came to her as she sat singing, with her little, cracked voice, in her low rocking-chair. She was the first to learn everything, and the last to forget it. She had the town gossip at her fingers' ends, and she knew everything about people she had never seen. When I asked her how she had acquired her learning, she said simply—'Oh, I observe!' 'Observe closely enough,' she once said, 'and it doesn't matter where you are. You may be in a pitch-dark closet. All you want is something to start with; one thing leads to another, and all things are mixed up. Shut me up in a dark closet and I will observe after a while, that some places in it are darker than others. After that (give me time), and I will tell you what the President of the United States is going to have for dinner.' Once I paid her a compliment. 'Your observation,' I said, 'is as fine as your needle, and your statements are as true as your stitches.'

Of course Miss Deborah had heard of Captain Diamond. He had been much talked about many years before, but he had survived the scandal that attached to his name.

'What was the scandal?' I asked.

'He killed his daughter.'

'Killed her?' I cried; 'how so?'

'Oh, not with a pistol, or a dagger, or a dose of arsenic! With his tongue. Talk of women's tongues! He cursed her—with some horrible oath—and she died!'

'What had she done.'

'She had received a visit from a young man who loved her, and whom he had forbidden the house.'

'The house,' I said—'ah yes! The house is out in the country, two or three miles from here, on a lonely cross-road.'

Miss Deborah looked sharply at me, as she bit her thread.

'Ah, you know about the house?' she said.

'A little,' I answered; 'I have seen it. But I want you to tell me more.'

But here Miss Deborah betrayed an incommunicativeness which was most unusual.

'You wouldn't call me superstitious, would you?' she asked.

'You?—you are the quintessence of pure reason.'

'Well, every thread has its rotten place and every needle its grain of rust. I would rather not talk about that house.'

'You have no idea how you excite my curiosity!' I said.

'I can feel for you. But it would make me very nervous.'

'What harm can come to you?' I asked.

'Some harm came to a friend of mine.' And Miss Deborah gave a very positive nod.

'What had your friend done?'

'She had told me Captain Diamond's secret, which he had told her with a mighty mystery. She had been an old flame of his, and he took her into his confidence. He bade her tell no one, and assured her that if she did, something dreadful would happen to her.'

'And what happened to her?'

'She died.'

'Oh, we are all mortal!' I said. 'Had she given him a promise?'

'She had not taken it seriously, she had not believed him. She repeated the story to me, and three days afterwards, she was taken with inflammation of the lungs. A month afterwards, here where I sit now, I was stitching her grave-clothes. Since then, I have never mentioned what she told me.'

'Was it very strange?'

'It was strange, but it was ridiculous too. It is a thing to make you shudder and to make you laugh, both. But you can't worry it out of me. I am sure that if I were to tell you, I should immediately break a needle in my finger, and die the next week of lock-jaw.'

I retired, and urged Miss Deborah no further; but every two or three days, after dinner, I came and sat down by her rocking-chair.

I made no further allusion to Captain Diamond; I sat silent, clipping tape with her scissors. At last, one day, she told me I was looking poorly. I was pale.

'I am dying of curiosity,' I said. 'I have lost my appetite. I have eaten no dinner.'

'Remember Bluebeard's wife!' said Miss Deborah.

'One may as well perish by the sword as by famine!' I answered.

Still she said nothing, and at last I rose with a melodramatic sigh and departed. As I reached the door she called me and pointed to the chair I had vacated. 'I never was hard-hearted,' she said. 'Sit down, and if we are to perish, may we at least perish together.' And then, in very few words, she communicated what she knew of Captain Diamond's secret. 'He was a very high-tempered old man, and though he was very fond of his daughter, his will was law. He had picked out a husband for her, and given her due notice. Her mother was dead, and they lived alone together. The house had been Mrs. Diamond's own marriage portion; the Captain, I believe, hadn't a penny. After his marriage they had come to live there, and he had begun to work the farm. The poor girl's lover was a young man with whiskers from Boston. The Captain came in one evening and found them together; he collared the young man, and hurled a terrible curse at the poor girl. The young man cried that she was his wife, and he asked her if it was true. She said, No! Thereupon Captain Diamond, his fury growing fiercer, repeated his imprecation, ordered her out of the house, and disowned her forever. She swooned away, but her father went raging off and left her. Several hours later, he came back and found the house empty. On the table was a note from the young man telling him that he had killed his daughter, repeating the assurance that she was his own wife, and declaring that he himself claimed the sole right to commit her remains to earth. He had carried the body away in a gig! Captain Diamond wrote him a dreadful note in answer, saying that he didn't believe his daughter was dead, but that, whether or no, she was dead to him. A week later, in the middle of the night, he saw her ghost. Then, I suppose, he was convinced. The ghost reappeared several times, and finally began regularly to haunt the house. It made the old man very uncomfortable, for little by little his passion had passed away, and he was given up to grief. He determined at last to leave the place, and tried to sell it or rent it; but meanwhile the story had gone abroad, the ghost had been seen by other persons, the house had a bad name, and it was impossible to dispose of it. With the farm, it was the old man's only property, and his only means of subsistence; if he could neither live in it nor rent it, he was beggared. But the ghost had no mercy, as he had had none.

He struggled for six months, and at last he broke down. He put on his old blue cloak and took up his staff, and prepared to wander away and beg his bread. Then the ghost relented, and proposed a compromise. "Leave the house to me!" it said; "I have marked it for my own. Go off and live elsewhere. But to enable you to live, I will be your tenant, since you can find no other. I will hire the house of you and pay you a certain rent." And the ghost named a sum. The old man consented, and he goes every quarter to collect his rent!'

I laughed at this recital, but I confess I shuddered too, for my own observation had exactly confirmed it. Had I not been witness of one of the Captain's quarterly visits, had I not all but seen him sit watching his spectral tenant count out the rent-money, and when he trudged away in the dark, had he not a little bag of strangely gotten coin hidden in the folds of his old blue cloak? I imparted none of these reflections to Miss Deborah, for I was determined that my observations should have a sequel, and I promised myself the pleasure of treating her to my story in its full maturity. 'Captain Diamond,' I asked, 'has no other known means of subsistence?'

'None whatever. He toils not, neither does he spin—his ghost supports him. A haunted house is valuable property!'

'And in what coin does the ghost pay?'

'In good American gold and silver. It has only this peculiarity—that the pieces are all dated before the young girl's death. It's a strange mixture of matter and spirit!'

'And does the ghost do things handsomely; is the rent large?'

'The old man, I believe, lives decently, and has his pipe and his glass. He took a little house down by the river; the door is sidewise to the street, and there is a little garden before it. There he spends his days, and has an old coloured woman to do for him. Some years ago, he used to wander about a good deal, he was a familiar figure in the town, and most people knew his legend. But of late he has drawn back into his shell; he sits over his fire, and curiosity has forgotten him. I suppose he is falling into his dotage. But I am sure, I trust,' said Miss Deborah in conclusion, 'that he won't outlive his faculties or his powers of locomotion, for, if I remember rightly, it was part of the bargain that he should come in person to collect his rent.'

We neither of us seemed likely to suffer any especial penalty for Miss Deborah's indiscretion; I found her, day after day, singing over her work, neither more nor less active than usual. For myself, I boldly pursued my observations. I went again, more than once, to the great graveyard, but I was disappointed in my hope of finding Captain Diamond there. I had a prospect, however, which afforded me compensation. I shrewdly inferred that the old man's quarterly pilgrimages were made upon the last day of the old quarter. My first sight of him had been on the 31st of December, and it was probable that he would return to his haunted home on the last day of March. This was near at hand; at last it arrived. I betook myself late in the afternoon to the old house on the cross-road, supposing that the hour of twilight was the appointed season. I was not wrong. I had been hovering about for a short time, feeling very much like a restless ghost myself, when he appeared in the same manner as before, and wearing the same costume. I again concealed myself, and saw him enter the house with the ceremonial which he had used on the former occasion. A light appeared successively in the crevice of each pair of shutters, and I opened the window which had yielded to my importunity before. Again I saw the great shadow on the wall, motionless and solemn. But I saw nothing else. The old man reappeared at last, made his fantastic salaam before the house, and crept away into the dusk.

One day, more than a month after this, I met him again at Mount Auburn. The air was full of the voice of Spring; the birds had come back and were twittering over their Winter's travels, and a mild west wind was making a thin murmur in the raw verdure. He was seated on a bench in the sun, still muffled in his enormous mantle, and he recognized me as soon as I approached him. He nodded at me as if he were an old Bashaw giving the signal for my decapitation, but it was apparent that he was pleased to see me.

'I have looked for you here more than once,' I said. 'You don't come often.'

'What did you want of me?' he asked.

'I wanted to enjoy your conversation. I did so greatly when I met you here before.'

'You found me amusing?'

'Interesting!' I said.

'You didn't think me cracked?'

'Cracked?—My dear sir—!' I protested.

'I'm the sanest man in the country. I know that is what insane people always say; but generally they can't prove it. I can!'

'I believe it,' I said. 'But I am curious to know how such a thing can be proved.'

He was silent awhile.

'I will tell you. I once committed, unintentionally, a great crime. Now I pay the penalty. I give up my life to it. I don't shirk it; I face it squarely, knowing perfectly what it is. I haven't tried to bluff it off; I haven't begged off from it; I haven't run away from it. The penalty is terrible, but I have accepted it. I have been a philosopher!'

'If I were a Catholic, I might have turned monk, and spent the rest of my life in fasting and praying. That is no penalty; that is an evasion. I might have blown my brains out—I might have gone mad. I wouldn't do either. I would simply face the music, take the consequences. As I say, they are awful! I take them on certain days, four times a year. So it has been these twenty years; so it will be as long as I last. It's my business; it's my avocation. That's the way I feel about it. I call that reasonable!'

'Admirably so!' I said. 'But you fill me with curiosity and with compassion.'

'Especially with curiousity,' he said, cunningly.

'Why,' I answered, 'if I know exactly what you suffer I can pity you more.'

'I'm much obliged. I don't want your pity; it won't help me. I'll tell you something, but it's not for myself; it's for your own sake.' He paused a long time and looked all round him, as if for chance eavesdroppers. I anxiously awaited his revelation, but he disappointed me. 'Are you still studying theology?' he asked.

'Oh, yes,' I answered, perhaps with a shade of irritation. 'It's a thing one can't learn in six months.'

'I should think not, so long as you have nothing but your books. Do you know the proverb, "A grain of experience is worth a pound of precept?" I'm a great theologian.'

'Ah, you have had experience,' I murmured sympathetically.

'You have read about the immortality of the soul; you have seen Jonathan Edwards and Dr. Hopkins chopping logic over it, and deciding, by chapter and verse, that it is true. But I have seen it with these eyes; I have touched it with these hands!' And the old man held up his rugged old fists and shook them portentously. 'That's better!' he went on; 'but I have bought it dearly. You had better take it from the books—evidently you always will. You are a very good young man; you will never have a crime on your conscience.'

I answered with some juvenile fatuity, that I certainly hoped I had my share of human passions, good young man and prospective Doctor of Divinity as I was.

'Ah, but you have a nice, quiet little temper,' he said. 'So have I—now! But once I was very brutal—very brutal. You ought to know that such things are. I killed my own child.'

'Your own child?'

'I struck her down to the earth and left her to die. They could not hang me, for it was not with my hand I struck her. It was with foul and damnable words. That makes a difference; it's a grand law we live under! Well, sir, I can answer for it that *her* soul is immortal. We have an appointment to meet four times a year, and then I catch it!'

'She has never forgiven you?'

'She has forgiven me as the angels forgive! That's what I can't stand—the soft, quiet way she looks at me. I'd rather she twisted a knife about in my heart—O Lord, Lord, Lord!' and Captain Diamond bowed his head over his stick, and leaned his forehead on his crossed hands.

I was impressed and moved, and his attitude seemed for the moment a check to further questions. Before I ventured to ask him anything more, he slowly rose and pulled his old cloak around him. He was unused to talking about his troubles, and his memories overwhelmed him. 'I must go my way,' he said; 'I must be creeping along.'

'I shall perhaps meet you here again,' I said.

'Oh, I'm a stiff-jointed old fellow,' he answered, 'and this is rather far for me to come. I have to reserve myself. I have sat sometimes a month at a time smoking my pipe in my chair. But I should like to see you again.' And he stopped and looked at me, terribly and kindly. 'Some day, perhaps, I shall be glad to be able to lay my hand on a young, unperverted soul. If a man can make a friend, it is always something gained. What is your name?'

I had in my pocket a small volume of Pascal's *Thoughts*, on the fly-leaf of which were written my name and address. I took it out and offered it to my old friend. 'Pray keep this little book,' I said. 'It is one I am very fond of, and it will tell you something about me.'

He took it and turned it over slowly, then looking up at me with a scowl of gratitude, 'I'm not much of a reader,' he said; 'but I won't refuse the first present I shall have received since—my troubles; and the last. Thank you, sir!' And with the little book in his hand he took his departure.

I was left to imagine him for some weeks after that sitting solitary in his arm-chair with his pipe. I had not another glimpse of him. But I was awaiting my chance, and on the last day of June, another quarter having elapsed, I deemed that it had come. The evening dusk in June falls late, and I was impatient for its coming. At last, towards the end of a lovely summer's day, I revisted Captain Diamond's property. Everything now was green around it save the blighted orchard in its rear, but its own immitigable greyness and sadness were as striking as when I had first beheld it beneath a December sky. As I drew near it, I saw that I was late for my purpose, for my purpose had simply been to step forward on Captain Diamond's arrival, and bravely ask him to let me go in with him. He had preceded me, and there were lights already in the windows. I was unwilling, of course, to disturb him during his ghostly interview, and I waited till he came forth. The lights disappeared in the course of time; then the door opened and Captain Diamond stole out. That evening he made no bow to the haunted house, for the first object he beheld was his fair-minded young friend planted, modestly but firmly, near the door-step. He stopped short, looking at me, and this time his terrible scowl was in keeping with the situation.

'I knew you were here,' I said. 'I came on purpose.'

He seemed dismayed, and looked round at the house uneasily.

'I beg your pardon if I have ventured too far,' I added, 'but you know you have encouraged me.'

'How did you know I was here?'

'I reasoned it out. You told me half your story, and I guessed the other half. I am a great observer, and I had noticed this house in passing. It seemed to me to have a mystery. When you kindly confided to me that you saw spirits, I was sure that it could only be here that you saw them.'

'You are mighty clever,' cried the old man. 'And what brought you here this evening?'

I was obliged to evade this question.

'Oh, I often come; I like to look at the house—it fascinates me.'

He turned and looked up at it himself. 'It's nothing to look at outside.' He was evidently quite unaware of its peculiar outward appearance, and this odd fact, communicated to me thus in the twilight, and under the very brow of the sinister dwelling, seemed to make his vision of the strange things within more real.

'I have been hoping,' I said, 'for a chance to see the inside. I thought I might find you here, and that you would let me go in with you. I should like to see what you see.'

He seemed confounded by my boldness, but not altogether displeased. He laid his hand on my arm. 'Do you know what I see?' he asked.

'How can I know, except as you said the other day, by experience? I want to have the experience. Pray, open the door and take me in.'

Captain Diamond's brilliant eyes expanded beneath their dusky brows, and after holding his breath a moment, he indulged in the first and last apology for a laugh by which I was to see his solemn visage contorted. It was profoundly grotesque, but it was perfectly noiseless. 'Take you in?' he softly growled. 'I wouldn't go in again before my time's up for a thousand times that sum.' And he thrust out his hand from the folds of his cloak and exhibited a small agglomeration of coin, knotted into the corner of an old silk pocket-handkerchief. 'I stick to my bargain no less, but no more!'

'But you told me the first time I had the pleasure of talking with you that it was not so terrible.'

'I don't say it's terrible—now. But it's damned disagreeable!'

This adjective was uttered with a force that made me hesitate and reflect. While I did so, I thought I heard a slight movement of one of the window-shutters above us. I looked up, but everything seemed motionless. Captain Diamond, too, had been thinking; suddenly he turned towards the house. 'If you will go in alone,' he said, 'you are welcome.'

'Will you wait for me here?'

'Yes, you will not stop long.'

'But the house is pitch dark. When you go you have lights.'

He thrust his hand into the depths of his cloak and produced some matches. 'Take these,' he said. 'You will find two candlesticks with candles on the table in the hall. Light them, take one in each hand and go ahead.'

'Where shall I go?'

'Anywhere—everywhere. You can trust the ghost to find you.'

I will not pretend to deny that by this time my heart was beating. And yet I imagine I motioned the old man with a sufficiently dignified gesture to open the door. I had made up my mind that there was in fact a ghost. I had conceded the premise. Only I had assured myself that once the mind was prepared, and the thing was not a surprise, it was possible to keep cool. Captain Diamond turned the lock, flung open the door, and bowed low to me as I passed in. I stood in the darkness, and heard the door close behind me. For some moments, I stirred neither finger nor toe; I stared bravely into the impenetrable dusk. But I saw nothing and heard nothing, and at last I struck a match. On the table were two brass candlesticks rusty from disuse. I lighted the candles and began my tour of exploration.

A wide staircase rose in front of me, guarded by an antique balustrade of that rigidly delicate carving which is found so often in old New England houses. I postponed ascending it, and turned into the room on my right. This was an old-fashioned parlour meagrely furnished, and musty with the absence of human life. I raised my two lights aloft and saw nothing but its empty chairs and its blank walls. Behind it was the room into which I had peeped from without, and which, in fact, communicated with it, as I had supposed, by folding doors. Here, too, I found myself confronted by no menacing spectre. I crossed the hall again, and visited the rooms on the other side; a dining-room in front, where I might have written my name with my finger in the deep dust of the great square table; a kitchen behind with its pots and pans eternally cold. All this was hard and grim, but it was not formidable. I came back into the hall, and walked to the foot of the staircase, holding up my candles; to ascend required a fresh effort, and I was scanning the gloom above. Suddenly, with an inexpressible sensation, I became aware that this gloom was animated; it seemed to move and gather itself together. Slowly—I say slowly, for to my tense expectancy the instants appeared ages—it took the shape of a large, definite figure, and this figure advanced and stood at the top of the stairs. I frankly confess that by this time I was conscious of a feeling to which I am in duty bound to apply the vulgar name of fear. I may poetize it and call it Dread, with a capital letter; it was at any rate the feeling that makes a man yield ground. I measured it as it grew, and it seemed perfectly irresistible; for it did not appear to come from within but from without, and to be embodied in the dark image at the head of the staircase. After a fashion I reasoned—I remember reasoning. I said to myself, 'I had always thought ghosts were white and transparent; this is a thing of thick shadows, densely opaque.' I reminded myself that the occasion was momentous, and that if fear were to overcome me I should gather all possible impressions while my wits remained. I stepped back, foot behind foot, with my eyes still on the figure and placed my candles on the table. I was perfectly conscious that the proper thing was to ascend the stairs resolutely, face to face with the image, but the soles of my shoes seemed suddenly to have been transformed into leaden weights. I had got what I wanted; I was seeing the ghost. I tried to look at the figure distinctly so that I could remember it, and fairly claim, afterwards, not to have lost my self-possession. I even asked myself how long it was expected I should stand looking, and how soon I could honourably retire. All this, of course, passed through my mind with extreme rapidity, and it was checked by a further movement on the part of the figure. Two white hands appeared in the dark perpendicular mass, and were slowly raised to what seemed to be the level of the head. Here they were pressed together, over the region of the face, and then they were removed, and the face was disclosed. It was dim, white, strange, in every way ghostly. It looked down at me for an instant, after which one of the hands was raised again, slowly, and waved to and fro before it. There was something very singular in this gesture; it seemed to denote resentment and dismissal, and yet it had a sort of trivial, familiar motion. Familiarity on the part of the haunting Presence had not entered into my calculations, and did not strike me pleasantly. I agreed with Captain Diamond that it was 'damned disagreeable.' I was pervaded by an intense desire to make an orderly, and, if possible, a graceful retreat. I wished to do it gallantly, and it seemed to me that it would be gallant to blow out my candles. I turned and did so, punctiliously, and then I made my way to the door, groped a moment and opened it. The outer light, almost extinct as it was, entered for a moment, played over the dusty depths of the house and showed me the solid shadow.

Standing on the grass bent over his stick, under the early glimmering stars, I found Captain Diamond. He looked up at me fixedly for a moment, but asked no questions, and then he went and locked the door. This duty performed, he discharged the other—made his obeisance like the priest before the altar—and then without heeding me further, took his departure.

A few days later, I suspended my studies and went off for the summer's vacation. I was absent for several weeks, during which I had plenty of leisure to analyse my impressions of the supernatural. I took some satisfaction in the reflection that I had not been ignobly terrified; I had not bolted nor swooned—I had proceeded with dignity. Nevertheless, I was certainly more comfortable when I had put thirty miles between me and the scene of my exploit, and I continued for many days to prefer the daylight to the dark. My nerves had been powerfully excited; of this I was particularly conscious when, under the influence of the drowsy air of the sea-side, my excitement began slowly to ebb. As it disappeared, I attempted to take a sternly rational view of my experience. Certainly I had seen *something*—that was not fancy; but what had I seen? I regretted extremely now that I had not been bolder, that I had not gone nearer and inspected the apparition more minutely. But it was very well to talk; I had done as much as any man in the circumstances would have dared; it was indeed a physical impossibility that I should have advanced. Was not this paralysis of my powers in itself a supernatural influence? Not necessarily, perhaps, for a sham ghost that one accepted might do as much execution as a real ghost. But why had I so easily accepted the sable phantom that waved its hand? Why had it so impressed itself? Unquestionably, true or false, it was a very clever phantom. I greatly preferred that it should have been true—in the first place because I did not care to have shivered and shaken for nothing, and in the second place because to have seen a well-authenticated goblin is, as things go, a feather in a quiet man's cap. I tried, therefore, to let my vision rest and to stop turning it over. But an impulse stronger than my will recurred at intervals and set a mocking question on my lips. Granted that the apparition was Captain Diamond's daughter; if it was she it certainly was her spirit. But was it not her spirit and something more?

The middle of September saw me again established among the

theologic shades, but I made no haste to revisit the haunted house.

The last of the month approached—the term of another quarter with poor Captain Diamond—and found me indisposed to disturb his pilgrimage on this occasion; though I confess that I thought with a good deal of compassion of the feeble old man trudging away, lonely, in the autumn dusk, on his extraordinary errand. On the thirtieth of September, at noonday, I was drowsing over a heavy octavo, when I heard a feeble rap at my door. I replied with an invitation to enter, but as this produced no effect I repaired to the door and opened it. Before me stood an elderly negress with her head bound in a scarlet turban, and a white handkerchief folded across her bosom. She looked at me intently and in silence; she had that air of supreme gravity and decency which aged persons of her race so often wear. I stood interrogative, and at last, drawing her hand from her ample pocket, she held up a little book. It was the copy of Pascal's *Thoughts* that I had given to Captain Diamond.

'Please, sir,' she said, very mildly, 'do you know this book?'

'Perfectly,' said I, 'my name is on the fly-leaf.'

'It is your name—no other?'

'I will write my name if you like, and you can compare them,' I answered.

She was silent a moment and then, with dignity—'It would be useless, sir,' she said, 'I can't read. If you will give me your word that is enough. I come,' she went on, 'from the gentleman to whom you gave the book. He told me to carry it as a token—a token—that is what he called it. He is right down sick, and he wants to see you.'

'Captain Diamond—sick?' I cried. 'Is his illness serious?'

'He is very bad—he is all gone.'

I expressed my regret and sympathy, and offered to go to him immediately, if his sable messenger would show me the way. She assented deferentially, and in a few moments I was following her along the sunny streets, feeling very much like a personage in the Arabian Nights, led to a postern gate by an Ethiopian slave. My own conductress directed her steps towards the river and stopped at a decent little yellow house in one of the streets that descend to it. She quickly opened the door and led me in, and I very soon found myself in the presence of my old friend. He was in bed, in a darkened room, and evidently in a very feeble state. He lay back on his pillow staring before him, with his bristling hair more erect than ever, and his intensely dark and bright old eyes touched with the glitter of fever. His apartment was humble and scrupulously neat and I could see that my dusky guide was a faithful servant. Captain Diamond, lying there rigid and pale on his white sheets, resembled some ruggedly carven figure on the lid of a Gothic tomb. He looked at me silently, and my companion withdrew and left us alone.

'Yes, it's you,' he said, at last, 'it's you, that good young man. There is no mistake, is there?'

'I hope not; I believe I'm a good young man. But I am very sorry you are ill. What can I do for you?'

'I am very bad, very bad; my poor old bones ache so!' and, groaning portentously, he tried to turn towards me.

I questioned him about the nature of his malady and the length of time he had been in bed, but he barely heeded me; he seemed impatient to speak of something else. He grasped my sleeve, pulled me towards him and whispered quickly:

'You know my time's up!'

'Oh, I trust not,' I said, mistaking his meaning. 'I shall certainly see you on your legs again.'

'God knows!' he cried. 'But I don't mean I'm dying; not yet a bit. What I mean is, I'm due at the house. This is rent-day.'

'Oh, exactly! But you can't go.'

'I can't go. It's awful. I shall lose my money. If I am dying, I want it all the same. I want to pay the doctor. I want to be buried like a respectable man.'

'It is this evening?' I asked.

'This evening at sunset, sharp.'

He lay staring at me, and, as I looked at him in return, I suddenly understood his motive for sending for me. Morally, as it came into my thought, I winced. But, I suppose I looked unperturbed, for he continued in the same tone. 'I can't lose my money. Some one else must go. I asked Belinda; but she won't hear of it.'

'You believe the money will be paid to another person?'

'We can try, at least. I have never failed before and I don't know. But, if you say I'm as sick as a dog, that my old bones ache, that I'm dying, perhaps she'll trust you. She don't want me to starve!'

'You would like me to go in your place, then?'

'You have been there once; you know what it is. Are you afraid?'

I hesitated.

'Give me three minutes to reflect,' I said, 'and I will tell you.' My glance wandered over the room and rested on the various objects that spoke of the threadbare, decent poverty of its occupant. There seemed to be a mute appeal to my pity and my resolution in their cracked and faded sparseness, Meanwhile Captain Diamond continued, feebly:

'I think she'd trust you, as I have trusted you; she'll like your face;

she'll see there is no harm in you. It's a hundred and thirty-three dollars, exactly. Be sure you put them into a safe place.'

'Yes,' I said at last, 'I will go, and, so far as it depends upon me, you shall have the money by nine o'clock tonight.'

He seemed greatly relieved; he took my hand and faintly pressed it, and soon afterwards I withdrew. I tried for the rest of the day not to think of my evening's work, but, of course, I thought of nothing else. I will not deny that I was nervous; I was, in fact, greatly excited, and I spent my time in alternately hoping that the mystery should prove less deep than it appeared, and yet fearing that it might prove too shallow. The hours passed very slowly, but, as the afternoon began to wane, I started on my mission. On the way, I stopped at Captian Diamond's modest dwelling, to ask how he was doing, and to receive such last instructions as he might desire to lay upon me. The old negress, gravely and inscrutably placid, admitted me, and, in answer to my inquiries, said that the Captain was very low; he had sunk since the morning.

'You must be right smart,' she said, 'if you want to get back before he drops off.'

A glance assured me that she knew of my projected expedition, though, in her own opaque black pupil, there was not a gleam of self-betrayal.

'But why should Captain Diamond drop off?' I asked. 'He certainly seems very weak; but I cannot make out that he has any definite disease.'

'His disease is old age,' she said, sententiously.

'But he is not so old as that; sixty-seven or sixty-eight, at most.'

She was silent a moment.

'He's worn out; he's used up; he can't stand it any longer.'

'Can I see him a moment?' I asked; upon which she led me again to his room.

He was lying in the same way as when I had left him, except that his eyes were closed. But he seemed very 'low,' as she had said, and he had very little pulse. Nevertheless, I further learned the doctor had been there in the afternoon and professed himself satisfied. 'He don't know what's been going on,' said Belinda, curtly.

The old man stirred a little, opened his eyes, and after some time recognized me.

'I'm going, you know,' I said. 'I'm going for your money. Have you anything more to say?' He raised himself slowly, and with a painful effort, against his pillows; but he seemed hardly to understand me. 'The house, you know,' I said. 'Your daughter.'

He rubbed his forehead, slowly, awhile, and at last, his comprehension awoke. 'Ah, yes,' he murmured, 'I trust you. A hundred and thirty-three dollars. In old pieces—all in old pieces.' Then he added more vigorously, and with a brightening eye: 'Be very respectful—be very polite. If not—if not—' and his voice failed again.

'Oh, I certainly shall be,' I said, with a rather forced smile. 'But, if not?'

'If not, I shall know it!' he said, very gravely. And with this, his eyes closed and he sunk down again.

I took my departure and pursued my journey with a sufficiently resolute step. When I reached the house, I made a propitiatory bow in front of it, in emulation of Captain Diamond. I had timed my walk so as to be able to enter without delay; night had already fallen. I turned the key, opened the door and shut it behind me. Then I struck a light, and found the two candlesticks I had used before, standing on the tables in the entry. I applied a match to both of them, took them up and went into the parlour. It was empty, and though I waited awhile, it remained empty. I passed then into the other rooms on the same floor, and no dark image rose before me to check my steps. At last, I came out into the hall again, and stood weighing the question of going upstairs. The staircase had been the scene of my discomfiture before, and I approached it with profound mistrust. At the foot, I paused, looking up, with my hand on the balustrade. I was acutely expectant, and my expectation was justified. Slowly, in the darkness above, the black figure that I had seen before took shape. It was not an illustion; it was a figure, and the same. I gave it time to define itself, and watched it stand and look down at me with its hidden face. Then, deliberately, I lifted up my voice and spoke.

'I have come in place of Captain Diamond, at his request,' I said. 'He is very ill; he is unable to leave his bed. He earnestly begs that you will pay the money to me; I will immediately carry it to him.' The figure stood motionless, giving no sign. 'Captain Diamond would have come if he were able to move.' I added, in a moment, appealingly; 'but, he is utterly unable.'

At this the figure slowly unveiled its face and showed me a dim, white mask; then it began slowly to descend the stairs. Instinctively I fell back before it, retreating to the door of the front sitting-room. With my eyes still fixed on it, I moved backward across the threshold; then I stopped in the middle of the room and set down my lights. The figure advanced; it seemed to be that of a tall woman, dressed in vaporous black crape. As it drew near, I saw that it had a perfectly human face, though it looked extremely pale and sad. We stood gazing at each other; my agitation had completely vanished; I was only deeply interested.

'Is my father dangerously ill?' said the apparition.

At the sound of its voice—gentle, tremulous, and perfectly human—I started forward; I felt a rebound of excitement. I drew a long breath, I gave a sort of cry, for what I saw before me was not a disembodies spirit, but a beautiful woman, an audacious actress. Instinctively, irresistibly, by the force of reaction against my credulity, I stretched out my hand and seized the long veil that muffled her head. I gave it a violent jerk, dragged it nearly off, and stood staring at a large fair person, of about five-and-thirty. I comprehended her at a glance; her long black dress, her pale, sorrow-worn face, painted to look paler, her very fine eyes,—the colour of her father's,—and her sense of outrage at my movement.

'My father, I suppose,' she cried, 'did not send you here to insult me!' and she turned away rapidly, took up one of the candles and moved towards the door. Here she paused, looked at me again, hesitated, and then drew a purse from her pocket and flung it down on the floor. 'There is your money!' she said majestically.

I stood there, wavering between amazement and shame, and saw her pass out into the hall. Then I picked up the purse. The next moment, I heard a loud shriek and a crash of something dropping, and she came staggering back into the room without her light.

'My father—my father!' she cried; and with parted lips and dilated eyes, she rushed towards me.

'Your father—where?' I demanded.

'In the hall, at the foot of the stairs.'

I stepped forward to go out, but she seized my arm.

'He is in white,' she cried, 'in his shirt. It's not he!'

'Why, your father is in his house, in his bed, extremely ill,' I answered.

She looked at me fixedly, with searching eyes.

'Dying?'

'I hope not,' I stuttered.

She gave a long moan and covered her face with her hands.

'Oh, heavens, I have seen his ghost!' she cried.

She still held my arm; she seemed too terrified to release it. 'His ghost!' I echoed, wondering.

'It's the punishment of my long folly!' she went on.

'Ah,' said I, 'it's the punishment of my indiscretion—of my violence!'

'Take me away, take me away!' she cried, still clinging to my arm. 'Not there'—as I was turning towards the hall and the front door—'not there, for pity's sake! By this door—the back entrance.' And snatching the other candles from the table, she led me through the neighbouring room into the back part of the house. Here was a door opening from a sort of scullery into the orchard. I turned the rusty lock and we passed out and stood in the cool air, beneath the stars. Here my companion gathered her black drapery about her, and stood for a moment, hesitating. I had been infinitely flurried, but my curiosity touching her was uppermost. Agitated, pale, picturesque, she looked, in the early evening light, very beautiful.

'You have been playing all these years a most extraordinary game,' I said.

She looked at me sombrely, and seemed disinclined to reply. 'I came in perfect good faith,' I went on. 'The last time—three months ago—you remember?—you greatly frightened me.'

'Of course it was an extraordinary game,' she answered at last. 'But it was the only way.'

'Had he not forgiven you?'

'So long as he thought me dead, yes. There have been things in my life he could not forgive.'

I hesitated and then—'And where is your husband?' I asked.

'I have no husband—I have never had a husband.'

She made a gesture which checked further questions, and moved rapidly away. I walked with her round the house to the road, and she kept murmuring—'It was he—it was he!' When we reached the road she stopped, and asked me which way I was going. I pointed to the road by which I had come, and she said—'I take the other. You are going to my father's?' she added.

'Directly,' I said.

'Will you let me know tomorrow what you have found?'

'With pleasure. But how shall I communicate with you?'

She seemed at a loss, and looked about her. 'Write a few words,' she said, 'and put them under that stone.' And she pointed to one of the lava slabs that bordered the old well. I gave her my promise to comply, and she turned away. 'I know my road,' she said. 'Everything is arranged. It's an old story.'

She left me with a rapid step, and as she receded into the darkness, resumed, with the dark flowing lines of her drapery, the phantasmal appearance with which she had at first appeared to me. I watched her till she became invisible, and then I took my own leave of the place. I returned to town at a swinging pace, and marched straight to the little yellow house near the river. I took the liberty of entering without a knock, and, encountering no interruption, made my way to Captain Diamond's room. Outside the door, on a low bench, with folded arms, sat the sable Belinda.

'How is he?' I asked.

'He's gone to glory.'

'Dead?' I cried.

She rose with a sort of tragic chuckle.

'He's as big a ghost as any of them now!'

I passed into the room and found the old man lying there irredeemably rigid and still. I wrote that evening a few lines which I proposed on the morrow to place beneath the stone, near the well; but my promise was not destined to be executed. I slept that night very ill—it was natural—and in my restlessness left my bed to walk about the room. As I did so I caught sight, in passing my window, of a red glow in the north-western sky. A house was on fire in the country, and evidently burning fast. It lay in the same direction as the scene of my evening's adventures, and as I stood watching the crimson horizon I was startled by a sharp memory. I had blown out the candle which lighted me, with my companion, to the door through which we escaped, but I had not accounted for the other light, which she had carried into the hall and dropped—heaven knew where—in her consternation. The next day I walked out with my folded letter and turned into the familiar cross-road. The haunted house was a mass of charred beams and smouldering ashes; the well-cover had been pulled off, in quest of water, by the few neighbours who had had the audacity to contest what they must have regarded as a demon-kindled blaze, the loose stones were completely displaced, and the earth had been trampled into puddles.

Four Meetings

[First appeared in the *Scribner's Monthly*, vol. xv (November 1877), pp. 44-56. The tale was revised and reprinted in volume ii of *Daisy Miller: A Study* (1879). This text was later reproduced in volume xiii of James's first 'Collective Edition' (1883); and, in America, in a collection of tales entitled *The Author of Beltraffio, Etc.* (Boston, James R. Osgood and Company, 1885). Using the 1879 text, James finally revised the tale for the New York Edition where it appears in volume xvi (*The Author of Beltraffio, Etc.*, 1909).]

I SAW HER BUT FOUR TIMES, BUT I REMEMBER THEM VIVIDLY; SHE made an impression upon me. I thought her very pretty and very interesting—a charming specimen of a type. I am very sorry to hear of her death, and yet, when I think of it, why should I be sorry? The last time I saw her she was certainly not —. But I will describe all our meetings in order.

I.

The first one took place in the country, at a little tea-party, one snowy night. It must have been some seventeen years ago. My friend Latouche, going to spend Christmas with his mother, had persuaded me to go with him, and the good lady had given in our honour the entertainment of which I speak. To me it was really entertaining. I had never been in the depths of New England at that season. It had been snowing all day and the drifts were knee-high. I wondered how the ladies had made their way to the house, but I perceived that at Grimwinter a *conversazione* offering the attraction of two gentlemen from New York was felt to be worth an effort.

Mrs. Latouche in the course of the evening asked me if I 'didn't want to' show the photographs to some of the young ladies. The photographs were in a couple of great portfolios, and had been brought home by her son, who, like myself, was lately returned from Europe. I looked round and was struck with the fact that most of the young ladies were provided with an object of interest more absorbing than the most vivid sun-picture. But there was a person standing alone near the mantel-shelf, and looking round the room with a small, gentle smile, which seemed at odds, somehow, with her isolation. I looked at her a moment, and then said, 'I should like to show them to that young lady.'

'Oh yes,' said Mrs. Latouche, 'she is just the person. She doesn't care for flirting; I will speak to her.'

I rejoined that if she did not care for flirting, she was, perhaps, not just the person; but Mrs. Latouche had already gone to propose the photographs to her.

'She's delighted,' she said, coming back. 'She is just the person, so quiet and so bright.' And then she told me the young lady was, by name. Miss Caroline Spencer, and with this she introduced me.

Miss Caroline Spencer was not exactly a beauty, but she was a charming little figure. She must have been close upon thirty, but she was made almost like a little girl, and she had the complexion of a child. She had a very pretty head, and her hair was arranged as nearly as possible like the hair of a Greek bust, though it was presumable that she had never seen a Greek bust save in plaster. She was 'artistic,' I suspected, so far as Grimwinter allowed such tendencies. She had a soft, surprised eye, and thin lips, with very pretty teeth. Round her neck she wore what ladies call, I believe, a 'ruche,' fastened with a very small pin in pink coral, and in her hand she carried a fan made of plaited straw and adorned with pink ribbon. She wore a scanty black silk dress. She spoke with a kind of soft precision, showing her white teeth between her narrow but tender-looking lips, and she seemed extremely pleased, even a little fluttered at the prospect of my demonstrations. These went forward very smoothly, after I had moved the portfolios out of their corner, and placed a couple of chairs near a lamp. The photographs were usually things I knew,—large views of Switzerland, Italy and Spain, landscapes, copies of famous buildings, pictures and statues. I said what I could about them, and my companion, looking at them as I held them up, sat perfectly still, with her straw fan raised to her under lip. Occasionally, as I laid one of the pictures down, she said very softly, 'Have you seen that place?' I usually answered that I had seen it several times (I had been a great traveller), and then I felt that she looked at me askance for a moment with her pretty eyes. I had asked her at the outset whether she had been to Europe; to this she answered, 'No, no, no,' in a little quick, confidential whisper. But after that, though she never took her eyes off the pictures, she said so little that I was afraid she was bored. Accordingly, after we had finished one portfolio, I offered, if she desired it, to desist. I felt that she was not bored, but her reticence puzzled me and I wished to make her speak. I turned round to look at her, and saw that there was a faint flush in each of her cheeks. She was waving her little fan to and fro. Instead of looking at me she fixed her eyes upon the other portfolio, which was leaning against the table.

'Wont you show me that?' she asked, with a little tremor in her voice. I could almost have believed she was agitated.

'With pleasure,' I answered, 'if you are not tired.'

'No, I am not tired,' she affirmed. 'I like it—I love it.'

And as I took up the other portfolio she laid her hand upon it rubbing it softly.

'And have you been here too?' she asked.

On my opening the portfolio it appeared that I had been there. One of the first photographs was a large view of the Castle of Chillon, on the Lake of Geneva.

'Here,' I said, 'I have been many a time. Is it not beautiful?' And I pointed to the perfect reflection of the rugged rocks and pointed towers in the clear, still water. She did not say, 'Oh, enchanting!' and push it away to see the next picture. She looked awhile, and then she asked if it was not where Bonnivard, about whom Byron wrote, was confined. I assented, and tried to quote some of Byron's verses, but in this attempt I floundered, helpless.

She fanned herself a moment and then repeated the lines correctly, in a soft, flat, and yet agreeable voice. By the time she had finished, she was blushing. I complimented her and told her she was perfectly equipped for visiting Switzerland and Italy. She looked at me askance again to see whether I was serious, and I added, that if she wished to recognize Byron's descriptions she must go abroad speedily; Europe was getting sadly dis-Byronized.

'How soon must I go?' she asked.

'Oh, I will give you ten years.'

'I think I can do it within ten years,' she answered very soberly.

'Well,' I said, 'you will enjoy it immensely; you will find it very charming.' And just then I came upon a photograph of some nook in a foreign city which I had been very fond of, and which recalled tender memories. I discoursed (as I suppose) with a certain eloquence; my companion sat listening, breathless.

'Have you been *very* long in foreign lands?' she asked, some time after I had ceased.

'Many years,' I said.

'And have you travelled everywhere?'

'I have travelled a great deal. I am very fond of it; and, happily, I have been able.'

Again she gave me her sidelong gaze.

'And do you know the foreign languages?'

'After a fashion.'

'Is it hard to speak them?'

'I don't believe you would find it hard,' I gallantly responded.

'Oh, I shouldn't want to speak—I should only want to listen,' she said, Then, after a pause, she added: 'They say the French theatre is so beautiful.'

'It is the best in the world.'

'Did you go very often?'

'When I was first in Paris I went every night.'

'Every night!' And she opened her clear eyes very wide. 'That to me is—' and she hesitated a moment—'is very wonderful.' A few minutes later she asked: 'Which country do you prefer?'

'There is one country I prefer to all others. I think you would do the same.'

She looked at me a moment, and then she said softly—'Italy?'

'Italy,' I answered softly, too, and for a moment we looked at each other. She looked as pretty as if, instead of showing her photographs, I had been making love to her. To increase the analogy, she glanced away, blushing. There was a silence, which she broke at last by saying:

'That is the place which—in particular—I have thought of going to.'

'Oh! that's the place—that's the place!' I said.

She looked at two or three photographs in silence.

'They say it is not so dear.'

'As some other countries? Yes, that is not the least of its charms.'

'But it is all pretty dear, is it not?'

'Europe, you mean?'

'Going there and travelling. That has been the trouble. I have very little money. I teach.' said Miss Spencer.

'Of course one must have money,' I said, 'but one can manage with a moderate amount.'

'I think I should manage. I have laid something by, and I am always adding a little to it. It's all for that.' She paused a moment, and then went on with a kind of suppressed eagerness, as if telling me the story were a rare, but a possibly impure satisfaction. 'But it has not been only the money; it has been everything. Everything has been against it. I have waited and waited. It has been a mere castle in the air. I am almost afraid to talk about it. Two or three times it has been a little nearer, and then I have talked about it and it has melted away. I have talked about it too much,' she said, hypocritically; for I saw that such talking was now a small, tremulous ecstasy. 'There is a lady who is a great friend of mine; she doesn't want to go; I always talk to her about it. I tire her dreadfully. She told me once she didn't know what would become of me. I should go crazy if I did not go to Europe, and I should certainly go crazy if I did.'

'Well,' I said, 'you have not gone yet, and nevertheless you are not crazy.'

She looked at me a moment, and said:

'I am not so sure. I don't think of anything else. I am always thinking of it. It prevents me from thinking of things that are nearer home—things that I ought to attend to. That is a kind of craziness.'

'The cure for it is to go,' I said.

'I have a faith that I shall go. I have a cousin there.'

We turned over some more photographs, and I asked her if she had always lived at Grimwinter.

'Oh, no, sir,' said Miss Spencer. 'I have spent twenty-three months in Boston.'

I answered, jocosely, that in that case foreign lands would probably prove a disappointment to her; but I quite failed to alarm her.

'I know more about them than you might think,' she said, with her shy, neat little smile. 'I mean by reading; I have read a great deal. I have not only read Byron; I have read histories and guide-books. I know I shall like it!'

'I understand your case,' I rejoined. 'You have the native American passion—the passion for the picturesque. With us, I think, it is primordial—antecedent to experience. Experience comes and only shows us something we have dreamt of.'

'I think that is very true.' said Caroline Spencer. 'I have dreamt of everything; I shall know it all.'

'I am afraid you have wasted a great deal of time.'

'Oh yes, that has been my great wickedness.'

The people about us had begun to scatter; they were taking their leave. She got up and put out her hand to me, timidly, but with a peculiar brightness in her eyes.

'I am going back there.' I said, as I shook hands with her. 'I shall look out for you.'

'I will tell you,' she answered, 'if I am disappointed.'

And she went away, looking delicately agitated and moving her little straw fan.

II.

A few months after this I returned to Europe, and some three years elapsed. I had been living in Paris, and, towards the end of October, I went from that city to Havre, to meet my sister and her husband, who had written me that they were about to arrive there. On reaching Havre I found that the steamer was already in; I was nearly two hours late. I repaired directly to the hotel, where my relatives were already established. My sister had gone to bed, exhausted and disgusted by her voyage; she was a wretchedly poor sailor, and her sufferings on this occasion had been extreme. She wished, for the moment, for undisturbed rest, and was unable to see me for more than five minutes. It was agreed that we should remain at Havre until the next day. My brother-in-law, who was anxious about his wife, was unwilling to leave her room; but she insisted upon his going out with me to take a walk and recover his land-legs. The early autumn day was warm and charming, and our stroll through the bright-coloured, busy streets of the old French sea-port was sufficiently entertaining. We walked along the sunny, noisy quays and then turned into a wide, pleasant street which lay half in sun and half in shade—a French provincial street, that looked like an old water-colour drawing: tall, grey, steep-roofed, red-gabled, many-storied houses; green shutters on windows and old scroll-work above them; flower-pots in balconies and white caps in doorways. We walked in the shade; all this stretched away on the sunny side of the street and made a picture. We looked at it as we passed along, then, suddenly, my brother-in-law stopped, pressing my arm and staring. I followed his gaze and saw that we had paused just before coming to a café, where, under an awning, several tables and chairs were disposed upon the pavement. The windows were open behind; half a dozen plants in tubs were ranged beside the door; the pavement was besprinkled with clean bran. It was a nice little, quiet, old-fashioned café; inside, in the comparative dusk, I saw a stout, handsome woman, with pink ribbons in her cap, perched up with a mirror behind her back smiling at someone who was out of sight. All this, however, I perceived afterwards; what I first observed was a lady sitting alone outside at one of the little marble-topped tables. My brother-in-law had stopped to look at her. There was something on that table, but she was leaning back quietly, with her hands folded, looking down the street, away from us. I saw her only in something less than profile; nevertheless, I instantly felt that I had seen her before.

'The little lady of the steamer!' exclaimed my brother-in-law.

'Was she on your steamer?' I asked.

'From morning till night. She was never sick. She used to sit perpetually at the side of the vessel with her hands crossed that way, looking at the eastward horizon.'

'Are you going to speak to her?'

'I don't know her. I never made acquaintance with her. I was too seedy. But I used to watch her and—I don't know why—to be interested in her. She's a dear little Yankee woman. I have an idea she is a schoolmistress taking a holiday,—for which her scholars have made up a purse.'

She turned her face a little more into profile, looking at the steep, grey house-fronts opposite to her. Then I said:

'I shall speak to her myself.'

'I wouldn't; she is very shy,' said my brother-in-law.

'My dear fellow, I know her. I onced showed her photographs a whole winter's evening, at a tea-party.'

And I went up to her. She turned and looked at me, and I saw she was in fact Miss Caroline Spencer. But she was not so quick to recognize me; she looked startled. I pushed a chair to the table and sat down.

'Well,' I said, 'I hope you are not disappointed!'

She stared, blushing a little; then she gave a small jump which betrayed recognition.

'It was you who showed me the photographs—at Grimwinter!'

'Yes, it was I. This happens very charmingly, for I feel as if it were for me to give you a formal reception here—an official welcome. I talked to you so much about Europe.'

'You didn't say too much. I'm so happy!' she softly exclaimed.

Very happy she looked. There was no sign of her being older; she was as gravely, decently, demurely pretty as before. If she had seemed before a thin-stemmed, mild-hued flower of Puritanism, it may be imagined whether in her present situation this delicate bloom was less apparent. Beside her an old gentleman was drinking absinthe; behind her the *dame de comptoir* in the pink ribbons was calling '*Alcibiade! Alcibiade!*' to the long-aproned waiter. I explained to Miss Spencer that my companion had lately been her ship-mate, and my brother-in-law came up and was introduced to her. But she looked at him as if she had never seen him before, and I remembered that he had told me that her eyes were always fixed upon the eastward horizon. She had evidently not noticed him, and, still timidly smiling, she made no attempt whatever to pretend that she had. I stayed with her at the café door, and he went back to the hotel and to his wife. I said to Miss Spencer that this meeting of ours in the first hour of her landing was really very strange; but that I was delighted to be there and receive her first impressions.

'Oh, I can't tell you,' she said: 'I feel as if I were in a dream. I have been sitting here for an hour, and I don't want to move. Everything is so picturesque. I don't know whether the coffee has intoxicated me; it's so delicious.'

'Really,' said I, 'if you are so pleased with this poor old prosaic shabby Havre, you will have no admiration left for better things.

Don't spend your admiration all the first day; remember it's your intellectual letter of credit. Remember all the beautiful places and things that are waiting for you; remember that lovely Italy!'

'I'm not afraid of running short,' she said gaily, still looking at the opposite houses. 'I could sit here all day, saying to myself that here I am at last. It's so dark, and old, and different.'

'By the way,' I inquired, 'how come you to be sitting here? Have you not gone to one of the inns?' For I was half amused, half alarmed at the good conscience with which this delicately pretty woman had stationed herself in conspicuous isolation at a café door.'

'My cousin brought me here,' she answered. 'You know I told you I had a cousin in Europe. He met me at the steamer this morning.'

'It was hardly worth his while to meet you if he was to desert you so soon.'

'Oh, he has only left me for half an hour.' said Miss Spencer. 'He has gone to get my money.'

'Where is your money?'

She gave a little laugh.

'It makes me feel very fine to tell you! It is in some circular notes.'

'And where are your circular notes?'

'My cousin has them.'

This statement was very serenely uttered, but—I can hardly say why—it gave me a certain chill. At the moment, I should have been utterly unable to say why. I knew nothing of Miss Spencer's cousin, and the presumption was in his favour, since he *was* her cousin. But I felt suddenly uncomfortable at the thought that half an hour after her landing her scanty funds should have passed into his hands.

'Is he to travel with you?' I asked.

'Only as far as Paris. He is an art student there. I wrote to him that I was coming, but I never expected him to come off to the ship. I supposed he would only just meet me at the train in Paris. It is very kind of him. But he *is* very kind—and very bright.'

I instantly became conscious of an extreme curiosity to see this bright cousin who was an art student.

'He is gone to the banker's?' I asked.

'Yes, to the banker's. He took me to an hotel—such a queer, quaint delicious little place, with a court in the middle, and a gallery all round, and a lovely landlady, in such a beautifully fluted cap, and such a perfectly fitting dress! After a while we came out to walk to the banker's, for I haven't got any French money. But I was very dizzy from the motion of the vessel, and I thought I had better sit down. He found this place for me here, and he went off to the banker's himself. I am to wait here till he comes back.'

It may seem very fantastic, but it passed through my mind that he would never come back. I settled myself in my chair beside Miss Spencer and determined to await the event. She was extremely observant; there was something touching in it. She noticed everything that the movement of the street brought before us—the peculiarities of costumes, the shapes of vehicles, the big Norman horses, the fat priests, the shaven poodles. We talked of these things. There was something charming in her freshness of perception and the way her book-nourished fancy recognized and welcomed everything.

'And when your cousin comes back what are you going to do?' I asked.

She hesitated a moment.

'We don't quite know.'

'When do you go to Paris? If you go by the four o'clock train I may have the pleasure of making the journey with you.'

'I don't think we shall do that. My cousin thinks I had better stay here a few days.'

'Oh!' said I, and for five minutes said nothing more. I was wondering what her cousin was, in vulgar parlance, 'up to.' I looked up and down the street, but saw nothing that looked like a bright American art student. At last I took the liberty of observing that Havre was hardly a place to choose as one of the æsthetic stations of a European tour. It was a place of convenience, nothing more; a place of transit, through which transit should be rapid. I recommended her to go to Paris by the afternoon train, and meanwhile to amuse herself by driving to the ancient fortress at the mouth of the harbour—that picturesque, circular structure which bore the name of Francis the First, and looked like a small castle of St. Angelo. (It has lately been demolished.)

She listened with much interest; then for a moment she looked grave.

'My cousin told me that when he returned he should have something particular to say to me, and that we could do nothing or decide nothing until I should have heard it. But I will make him tell me quickly, and then we will go to the ancient fortress. There is no hurry to get to Paris; there is plenty of time.'

She smiled with her softly severe little lips as she spoke those last words. But I, looking at her with a purpose, saw just a tiny gleam of apprehension in her eye.

'Don't tell me now,' I said, 'that this wretched man is going to give you some bad news!'

'I suspect it is a little bad, but I don't believe it is very bad. At any rate, I must listen to it.'

I looked at her again an instant. 'You didn't come to Europe to listen,' I said, 'You came to see!' But now I was sure her cousin would come back; since he had something disagreeable to say to her, he certainly would come back. We sat a while longer, and I asked her about her plans of travel. She had them on her fingers' ends, and she told over the names with a kind of solemn distinctness: From Paris to Dijon and to Avignon, from Avignon to Marseilles and the Cornice road; thence to Genoa, to Spezia, to Pisa, to Florence, to Rome. It apparently had never occurred to her that there could be the least incommodity in her travelling alone; and since she was unprovided with a companion, I, of course, religiously abstained from kindling her suspicions.

At last her cousin came back. I saw him turn towards us out of a side street, and from the moment my eyes rested upon him I felt that this was the bright American art student. He wore a slouch hat and a rusty black velvet jacket, such as I had often encountered in the Rue Bonaparte. His shirt-collar revealed a large portion of a throat which, at a distance, was not strikingly statuesque. He was tall and lean; he had red hair and freckles. So much I had time to observe while he approached the café, staring at me with natural surprise from under his umbrageous coiffure. When he came up to us I immediately introduced myself to him as an old acquaintance of Miss Spencer. He looked at me hard with a pair of little red eyes, then he made me a solemn bow in the French fashion, with his sombrero.

'You were not on the ship?' he said.

'No, I was not on the ship. I have been in Europe these three years.'

He bowed once more, solemly, and motioned me to be seated again. I sat down, but it was only for the purpose of observing him an instant. I saw it was time I should return to my sister. Miss Spencer's cousin was a queer fellow. Nature had not shaped him for a Raphaelesque or Byronic attire, and his velvet doublet and naked throat were not in harmony with his facial attributes. His hair was cropped close to his head; his ears were large and ill adjusted to the same. He had a lackadaisical carriage and a sentimental droop, which was peculiarly at variance with his small, strange-coloured eyes. Perhaps I was prejudiced, but I thought his eyes treacherous. He said nothing for some time; he leaned his hands on his cane and looked up and down the street. Then at last, slowly lifting his cane and pointing with it, 'That's a very nice bit,' he remarked, softly. He had his head on one side, and his little eyes were half closed. I followed the direction of his stick; the object it indicated was a red cloth hung out of an old window. 'Nice bit of colour.' he continued, and without moving his head he transferred his half-closed gaze to me. 'Composes well,' he pursued. 'Make a nice thing.' He spoke in a strange, weak drawl.

'I see you have a great deal of eye,' I replied. 'Your cousin tells me you are studying art?' He looked at me in the same way without answering, and I went on with deliberate urbanity: 'I suppose you are at the studio of one of those great men.'

Still he looked at me, and then he said softly—'Gérôme.'

'Do you like it?' I asked.

'Do you understand French?' he said.

'Some kinds,' I answered.

He kept his little eyes on me; then he said—'*Je l'adore!*'

'Oh, I understand that kind!' I rejoined. Miss Spencer laid her hand upon her cousin's arm with a little pleased and fluttered movement; it was delightful to be among people who were so easily familiar with foreign tongues. I got up to take leave, and asked Miss Spencer where, in Paris, I might have the honour of waiting upon her. To what hotel should she go?

She turned to her cousin inquiringly, and he honoured me again with his little languid leer. 'Do you know the *Hotel des Princes*?'

'I know where it is.'

'I shall take her there.'

'I congratulate you,' I said to Caroline Spencer. 'I believe it is the best inn in the world; and in case I should still have a moment to call upon you here, where are you lodged?'

'Oh, it's such a pretty name,' said Miss Spencer, gleefully. '*À la Belle Cuisinière*,—the Beautiful Cook.'

As I left them her cousin gave me a great flourish with his picturesque hat. My sister, as it proved, was not sufficiently restored to leave Havre by the afternoon train; so that, as the autumn dusk began to fall, I found myself at liberty to call at the sign of the 'Beautiful Cook.' I must confess that I had spent much of the interval in wondering what the disagreeable thing was that my charming friend's disagreeable cousin had been telling her. The *Belle Cuisinière* was a modest inn in a shady by-street, where it gave me satisfaction to think Miss Spencer must have encountered local colour in abundance. There was a crooked little court where much of the hospitality of the house was carried on; there was a staircase climbing to bedrooms on the outer side of the wall; there was a small, trickling fountain with a stucco statuette in the midst of it; there was a little boy in a white cap and apron cleaning copper vessles at a conspicuous kitchen door; there was a chattering landlady, neatly laced, arranging apricots and grapes into an artistic pyramid upon a pink plate. I looked about, and on a green bench outside of an open door labelled *Salle à Manger*, I perceived Caroline Spencer. No sooner had I looked at her than I saw that something had happened since the morning. She was leaning back on her bench, her hands were clasped in her lap, and her eyes were fixed upon the landlady, at the other side of the court, manipulating her apricots.

But I saw she was not thinking of apricots. She was staring absently, thoughtfully; as I came near her I perceived that she had been crying. I sat down on the bench beside her before she saw me; then, when she had done so, she simply turned round, without surprise, and rested her sad eyes upon me. Something very bad indeed had happened; she was completely changed.

I immediately charged her with it.

'Your cousin has been giving you bad news; you are in great distress.'

For a moment she said nothing, and I supposed that she was afraid to speak, lest her tears should come back. But presently I perceived that in the short time that had elapsed since my leaving her in the morning she had shed them all, and that she was now softly stoical and composed.

'My poor cousin is in distress,' she said at last. 'His news was bad.' Then, after a brief hesitation: 'He was in terrible want of money.'

'In want of yours, you mean?'

'Of any that he could get—honestly. Mine was the only money.'

'And he has taken yours?'

She hesitated again a moment, but her glance, meanwhile, was pleading.

'I gave him what I had.'

I have always remembered the accent of those words as the most angelic piece of human intonation I have ever listened to.

Almost with a sense of personal outrage I jumped up.

'Good heavens!' I said, 'do you call that getting it honestly?'

But I had gone too far; she blushed deeply. 'We will not speak of it,' she said.

'We *must* speak of it,' I answered, sitting down again. 'I am your friend; it seems to me you need one. What is the matter with your cousin?'

'He is in debt.'

'No doubt! But what is the special fitness of your paying his debts?'

'He has told me all his story; I am very sorry for him.'

'So am I! But I hope he will give you back your money.'

'Certainly he will; as soon as he can.'

'When will that be?'

'When he has finished his great picture.'

'My dear young lady, confound his great picture! Where is this unhappy cousin?'

She certainly hesitated now. Then—'At his dinner,' she answered.

I turned about and looked through the open door into the *salle à manger.* There alone at the end of a long table, I perceived the object of Miss Spencer's compassion—the bright young art student. He was dining too attentively to notice me at first; but in the act of setting down a well-emptied wine-glass he caught sight of my observant attitude. He paused in his repast, and with his head on one side, and his lank jaws slowly moving, fixedly returned my gaze. Then the landlady came lightly brushing by with her pyramid of apricots.

'And that nice little plate of fruit is for him?' I exclaimed.

Miss Spencer glanced at it tenderly.

'They do that so prettily!' she murmured.

I felt helpless and irritated. 'Come now, really,' I said; 'do you approve of that great long fellow accepting your funds?'

She looked away from me; I was evidently giving her pain. The case was hopeless; the great long fellow had 'interested' her.

'Excuse me if I speak of him so unceremoniously,' I said. 'But you are really too generous, and he is not quite delicate enough. He made his debts himself—he ought to pay them himself.'

'He has been foolish,' she answered; 'I know that. He has told me everything. We had a long talk this morning; the poor fellow threw himself upon my charity. He has signed notes to a large amount.'

'The more fool he!'

'He is in extreme distress; and it is not only himself. It is his poor wife.'

'Ah, he has a poor wife.'

'I didn't know it,—but he confessed everything. He married two years since, secretly.'

'Why secretly?'

Caroline Spencer glanced about her, as if she feared listeners. Then softly, in a little impressive tone—'She was a countess!'

'Are you very sure of that?'

'She has written me a most beautiful letter.'

'Asking you for money, eh?' I pursued, brutally, cynically perhaps, but irresistibly.

'Asking me for confidence and sympathy,' said Miss Spencer. 'She has been disinherited by her father. My cousin told me the story and she tells it in her own way, in the letter. It is like an old romance. Her father opposed the marriage and when he discovered that she had secretly disobeyed him he cruelly cast her off. It is really most romantic. They are the oldest family in Provence.'

I looked and listened, marvelling. It really seemed that the poor woman was enjoying the 'romance' of having a discarded countess-cousin, out of Provence, so deeply as almost to lose the sense of what the forfeiture of her money meant for her.

'My dear young lady,' I said, 'you don't want to be ruined for picturesqueness' sake?'

'I shall not be ruined. I shall come back before long to stay with them. The countess insists upon that.'

'Come back! You are going home, then?'

She sat for a moment with her eyes lowered, then with a heroic suppression of a faint tremor of the voice:

'I have no money for travelling!' she answered.

'You gave it *all* up?'

'I have kept enough to take me home.'

I gave an angry groan, and at this juncture Miss Spencer's cousin, the fortunate possessor of her precious purse, and of the hand of the Provençal countess, emerged from the little dining-room. He stood on the threshold for an instant, removing the stone from a plump apricot which he had brought away from the table; then he put the apricot into his mouth, and while he let it sojourn there, gratefully, stood looking at us, with his long legs apart and his hands dropped into the pockets of his velvet jacket. My companion got up, giving him a thin glance which I caught in its passage, and which seemed to designate a strange commixture of resignation and fascination,—a sort of perverted enthusiasm. Ugly, vulgar, pretentious, dishonest as I thought the creature, he had appealed successfully to her eager but most innocent imagination. I was profoundly disgusted, but I had no warrant absolutely to interfere. Besides, I felt that it would be vain.

The young man waved his hand with a pictorial gesture. 'Nice old court,' he observed. 'Nice mellow old place. Good tone in that brick. Nice crooked old staircase.'

Decidedly, I was too much displeased. Without responding, I gave my hand to Caroline Spencer. She looked at me an instant with her little white face and expanded eyes, and as she showed her pretty teeth I suppose she meant to smile.

'Don't be sorry for me,' she said, 'I am very sure I shall see something of Europe yet.'

I told her that I should not bid her goodbye. I should find a moment to come back the next morning. Her cousin, who had put on his sombrero again, flourished it off at me by way of a bow, with which I took my departure.

The next morning I came back to the inn, where I met in the court the landlady, more loosely laced than in the evening. On my asking for Miss Spencer,—*Partie, Monsieur,*' said the landlady. 'She went away last night at ten o'clock, with her—her—not her husband, eh?—in fine, her *Monsieur.* They went down to the American ship.' I turned away; the poor girl had been about thirteen hours in Europe.

III.

I myself, more fortunate, was there some five years longer. During this period I lost my friend Latouche, who died of a malarious fever during a tour in the Levant. One of the first things I did on my return was to go up to Grimwinter to pay a consolatory visit to his poor mother. I found her in deep affliction, and I sat with her the whole of the morning that followed my arrival (I had come in late at night), listening to her tearful descant and singing the praise of my friend. We talked of nothing else, and our conversation terminated only with the arrival of a quick little woman who drove herself up to the door in a carry-all, and whom I saw toss the reins upon the horse's back with the briskness of a startled sleeper throwing back the bedclothes. She jumped out of the carry-all and she jumped into the room. She proved to be the minister's wife and the great town-gossip, and she had evidently, in the latter capacity, a choice morsel to communicate. I was as sure of this as I was that poor Mrs. Latouche was not absolutely too bereaved to listen to her. It seemed to me discreet to retire. I said I believed I would go and take a walk before dinner.

'And, by the way,' I added, 'if you will tell me where my old friend Miss Spencer lives I will walk to her house.'

The minister's wife immediately responded. Miss Spencer lived in the fourth house beyond the Baptist church; the Baptist church was the one on the right, with that queer, green thing over the door; they called it a portico, but it looked more like an old-fashioned bedstead.

'Yes, do go and see poor Caroline,' said Mrs. Latouche. 'It will refresh her to see a strange face.'

'I should think she had had enough of strange faces!' cried the minister's wife.

'I mean, to see a visitor,' said Mrs. Latouche, amending her phrase.

'I should think she had had enough of visitors!' her companion enjoined. 'But you don't mean to stay ten years,' she added, glancing at me.

'Has she a visitor of that sort?' I inquired, perplexed.

'You will see the sort!' said the minister's wife. 'She's easily seen; she generally sits in the front yard. Only take care what you say to her, and be very sure you are polite.'

'Ah, she is so sensitive?'

The minister's wife jumped up and dropped me a courtesy—a most ironical courtesy.

'That's what she is, if you please. She's a countess!'

And pronouncing this word with the most scathing accent, the little woman seemed fairly to laugh in the countess's face. I stood a moment, staring, wondering, remembering.

'Oh, I shall be very polite!' I cried; and grasping my hat and stick, I went on my way.

I found Miss Spencer's residence without difficulty. The Baptist church was easily identified, and the small dwelling near it, of a rusty white, with a large central chimney-stack and a Virginia creeper, seemed naturally and properly the abode of a frugal old maid with a taste for the picturesque. As I approached I slackened my pace, for I had heard that some one was always sitting in the front yard, and I wished to reconnoitre. I looked cautiously over the low, white fence which separated the small garden space from the unpaved street; but I descried nothing in the way of a countess. A small, straight path led up to the crooked door-step, and on either side of it was a little grass-plot, fringed with currant-bushes. In the middle of the grass, on either side, was a large quince-tree, full of antiquity and contortions, and beneath one of the quince-trees were placed a small table and a couple of chairs. On the table lay a piece of unfinished embroidery and two or three books in bright-coloured paper covers. I went in at the gate and paused half-way along the path, scanning the place for some further token of its occupant, before whom—I could hardly have said why—I hesitated abruptly to present myself. Then I saw that the poor little house was very shabby. I felt a sudden doubt of my right to intrude, for curiosity had been my motive, and curiosity here seemed singularly indelicate. While I hesitated, a figure appeared in the open doorway and stood there looking at me. I immediately recognized Caroline Spencer, but she looked at me as if she had never seen me before. Gently, but gravely and timidly, I advanced to the doorstep and then I said, with an attempt at friendly badinage:

'I waited for you over there to come back, but you never came.'

'Waited where sir?' she asked softly, and her light-coloured eyes expanded more than before.

She was much older; she looked tired and wasted.

'Well,' I said, 'waited at Havre.'

She stared; then she recognized me. She smiled and blushed and clapsed her two hands together.

'I remember you now,' she said. 'I remember that day.'

But she stood there, neither coming out nor asking me to come in. She was embarrassed.

I too felt a little awkward. I poked my stick into the path.

'I kept looking out for you, year after year,' I said.

'You mean in Europe?' murmured Miss Spencer.

'In Europe, of course! Here, apparently, you are easy enough to find.'

She leaned her hand against the unpainted door-post, and her head fell a little to one side. She looked at me for a moment without speaking, and I thought I recognized the expression that one sees in women's eyes when tears are rising. Suddenly she stepped out upon the cracked slab of stone before the threshold and closed the door behind her. Then she began to smile intently, and I saw that her teeth were as pretty as ever. But there had been tears too.

'Have you been there ever since?' she asked almost in a whisper.

'Until three weeks ago. And you—you never came back?'

Still looking at me with her fixed smile, she put her hand behind her and opened the door again.

'I am not very polite,' she said. 'Won't you come in?'

'I am afraid I incommode you.'

'Oh no!' she answered, smiling more than ever.

And she pushed back the door, with a sign that I should enter.

I went in, following her. She led the way to a small room on the left of the narrow hall, which I supposed to be her parlour, though it was at the back of the house, and we passed the closed door of another apartment which apprently enjoyed a view of the quince trees. This one looked out upon a small wood-shed and two clucking hens. But I thought it very pretty, until I saw that its elegance was of the most frugal kind; after which, presently, I thought it prettier still, for I had never seen faded chintz and old mezzotint engravings, framed in varnished autumn leaves, disposed in so graceful a fashion. Miss Spencer sat down on a very small portion of the sofa, with her hands tightly clasped in her lap. She looked ten years older, and it would have sounded very perverse now to speak of her as pretty. But I thought her so; or at least I thought her touching. She was evidently agitated. I tried to appear not to notice it; but suddenly, in the most inconsequent fashion,—it was an irresistible memory of our little friendship at Havre,—I said to her:

'I do incommode you. You are distressed.'

She raised her two hands to her face, and for a moment kept it buried in them. Then taking them away:

'It's because you remind me——,' she said.

'I remind you, you mean, of that miserable day at Havre?'

She shook her head.

'It was not miserable. It was delightful.'

'I never was so shocked,' I rejoined, 'as when, on going back to your inn the next morning, I found you had set sail again.'

She was silent a moment; and then she said:

'Please let us not speak of that.'

'Did you come straight back here?' I asked.

'I was back here just thirty days after I had gone away.'

'And here you have remained ever since?'

'Oh, yes!' she said gently.

'When are you going to Europe again?'

This question seemed brutal; but there was something that irritated me in the softness of her resignation, and I wished to extort from her some expression of impatience.

She fixed her eyes for a moment upon a small sun-spot on the carpet; then she got up and lowered the window-blind a little to obliterate it. Presently, in the same mild voice, answering my question, she said:

'Never!'

'I hope your cousin repaid you your money.'

'I don't care for it now,' she said, looking away from me.

'You don't care for your money?'

'For going to Europe.'

'Do you mean that you would not go if you could?'

'I can't—I can't,' said Caroline Spencer. 'It is all over; I never think of it.'

'He never repaid you, then!' I exclaimed.

'Please—please,' she began.

But she stopped; she was looking towards the door. There had been a rustling and a sound of steps in the hall.

I also looked towards the door, which was open, and now admitted another person—a lady who paused just within the threshold. Behind her came a young man. The lady looked at me with a good deal of fixedness—long enough for my glance to receive a vivid impression of herself. Then she turned to Caroline Spencer, and, with a smile and a strong foreign accent:

'Excuse my interruption!' she said. 'I knew not you had company —the gentleman came in so quietly.'

With this, she directed her eyes towards me again.

She was very strange; yet my first feeling was that I had seen her before. Then I perceived that I had only seen ladies who were very much like her. But I had seen them very far away from Grimwinter, and it was an odd sensation to be seeing her here. Whither was it the sight of her seemed to transport me? To some dusky landing before a shabby Parisian *quatriéme*—to an open door revealing a mussy ante-chamber, and to Madame leaning over the banisters, while she holds a faded dressing-gown together, and bawls down to the portress to bring up her coffee. Miss Spencer's visitor was a very large woman, of middle age, with a plump, dead-white face, and hair drawn back *à la chinoise*. She had a small, penetrating eye, and what is called in French an agreeable smile. She wore an all pink cashmere dressing-gown, covered with white embroideries, and, like 'Madame,' in my momentary vision, she was holding it together in front with a bare and rounded arm, and a plump and deeply dimpled hand.

'It is only to spick about my *café*,' she said to Miss Spencer with her agreeable smile. 'I should like it served in the garden under the leetle tree.'

The young man behind her had now stepped into the room, and he also stood looking at me. He was a pretty-faced little fellow, with an air of provincial foppishness—a tiny Adonis of Grimwinter. He had a small, pointed nose, a small, pointed chin, and, as I observed, the most diminutive feet. He looked at me foolishly, with his mouth open.

'You shall have your coffee,' said Miss Spencer, who had a faint red spot in each of her cheeks.

'It is well!' said the lady in the dressing-gown. 'Find your bouk,' she added, turning to the young man.

He looked vaguely round the room.

'My grammer, d'ye mean?' he asked, with a helpless intonation.

But the large lady was looking at me curiously, and gathering in her dressing-gown with her white arm.

'Find your bouk, my friend,' she repeated.

'My poetry, d'ye mean?' said the young man, also gazing at me again.

'Never mind your bouk,' said his companion. 'Today we will talk. We will make some conversation. But we must not interrupt. Come,' and she turned away. 'Under the leetle tree,' she added, for the benfit of Miss Spencer.

Then she gave me a sort of salutation, and a '*Monsieur*!' with which she swept away again, followed by the young man.

Caroline Spencer stood there with her eyes fixed upon the ground.

'Who is that!' I asked.

'The countess, my cousin.'

'And who is the young man?'

'Her pupil, Mr. Mixter.'

This description of the relation between the two persons who had just left the room made me break into a little laugh. Miss Spencer looked at me gravely.

'She gives French lessons; she has lost her fortune.'

'I see,' I said. 'She is determined to be a burden to no one. That is very proper.'

Miss Spencer looked down on the ground again.

'I must go and get the coffee,' she said.

'Has the lady many pupils?' I asked.

'She has only Mr. Mixter. She gives her time to him.'

At this I could not laugh, though I smelt provocation. Miss Spencer was too grave.

'He pays very well,' she presently added, with simplicity. 'He is very rich. He is very kind. He takes the countess to drive.' And she was turning away.

'You are going for the countess's coffee?' I said.

'If you will excuse me a few moments?'

'Is there no one else to do it?'

She looked at me with the softest serenity.

'I keep no servants.'

'Can she not wait upon herself?'

'She is not used to that.'

'I see,' said I, as gently as possible. 'But before you go, tell me this; who is this lady?'

'I told you about her before—that day. She is the wife of my cousin, whom you saw.'

'The lady who was disowned by her family in consequence of her marriage?'

'Yes; they have never seen her again. They have cast her off.'

'And where is her husband?'

'He is dead.'

'And where is your money?'

The poor girl flinched; there was something too methodical in my questions.

'I don't know,' she said wearily.

But I continued a moment.

'On her husband's death this lady came over here?'

'Yes, she arrived one day——.'

'How long ago?'

'Two years.'

'She has been here ever since?'

'Every moment.'

'How does she like it?'

'Not at all.'

'And how do *you* like it?'

Miss Spencer laid her face in her two hands an instant, as she had done ten minutes before. Then, quickly, she went to get the countess's coffee.

I remained alone in the little parlour; I wanted to see more—to learn more. At the end of five minutes the young man whom Miss Spencer had described as the countess's pupil came in. He stood looking at me for a moment with parted lips I saw he was a very weak-eyed young man.

'She wants to know if you won't come out there?' he observed at last.

'Who wants to know?'

'The countess. That French lady.'

'She has asked you to bring me?'

'Yes, sir,' said the young man feebly, looking at my six feet of stature.

I went out with him, and we found the countess sitting under one of the little quince trees in front of the house. She was drawing a needle through the piece of embroidery which she had taken from the small table. She pointed graciously to the chair beside her. I seated myself. Mr. Mixter glanced about him, and then sat down in the grass at her feet. He gazed upward, looking with parted lips from the countess to me.

'I am sure you speak French,' said the countess, fixing her brilliant little eyes upon me.

'I do, madam, after a fashion,' I answered, in the lady's own tongue.

'*Voilà!*' she cried most expressively, 'I knew it so soon as I looked at you. You have been in my poor dear country.'

'A long time.'

'You know Paris?'

'Thoroughly, madame.' And with a certain conscious purpose I let my eyes meet her own.

She presently, hereupon, moved her own and glanced down at Mr. Mixter.

'What are we talking about?' she demanded of her attentive pupil.

He pulled his knees up, plucked at the grass with his hand, stared, blushed a little.

'You are talking French,' said Mr. Mixter.

'*La belle découverte!*' said the countess. 'Here are ten months,' she explained to me, 'that I am giving him lessons. Don't put yourself out not to say he's a fool; he won't understand you.'

'I hope your other pupils are more gratifying,' I remarked.

'I have no others. They don't know what French is in this place, they don't want to know. You may therefore imagine the pleasure it is to me to meet a person who speaks it like yourself.' I replied that my own pleasure was not less, and she went on drawing her stitches through her embroidery, with her little finger curled out. Every few moments she put her eyes close to her work, near-sightedly. I thought her a very disagreeable person; she was coarse, affected, dishonest and no more a countess than I was a caliph. 'Talk to me of Paris,' she went on. 'The very name of it gives me an emotion! How long since you were there?'

'Two months ago.'

'Happy man! Tell me something about it. What were they doing? Oh, for an hour of the boulevards!'

'They were doing about what they are always doing—amusing themselves a good deal.'

'At the theatres, eh?' sighed the countess. 'At the *cafés-concerts*—at the little tables in front of the doors? *Quelle existence!* You know I am a Parisienne, *monsieur*,' she added, '—to my finger-tips.'

'Miss Spencer was mistaken, then,' I ventured to rejoin, 'in telling me that you were a Provençale.'

She stared a moment, then she put her nose to her embroidery, which had a dingy, desultory aspect. 'Ah, I am a Provençale by birth; but I am a Parisienne by—inclination.'

'And by experience, I suppose?' I said.

She questioned me a moment with her hard little eyes.

'Oh, experience! I could talk of that if I wished. I never expected, for example, that experience had *this* in store for me.' And she pointed with her bare elbow, and with a jerk of her head, at everything that surrounded her—at the little white house, the quince tree, the rickety paling, even at Mr. Mixter.

'You are in exile!' I said smiling.

'You may imagine what it is! These two years that I have been here I have passed hours—hours! One gets used to things, and sometimes I think I have got used to this. But there are some things that are always beginning over again. For example, my coffee.'

'Do you always have coffee at this hour?' I inquired.

She tossed back her head and measured me.

'At what hour would you prefer me to have it? I must have my *demi-tasse* after breakfast.'

'Ah, you breakfast at this hour?'

'At midday—*comme cela se fait.* Here they breakfast at a quarter past seven! That ''quarter past'' is charming!'

'But you were telling me about your coffee,' I observed, sympathetically.

'My *cousine* can't believe in it; she can't understand it. She's an excellent girl; but that little cup of black coffee, with a drop of cognac, served at this hour—they exceed her comprehension. So I have to break the ice every day, and it takes the coffee the time you see to arrive. And when it arrives, *monsieur*! If I don't offer you any of it you must not take it ill. It will be because I know you have drunk it on the boulevards.'

I resented extremely this scornful treatment of poor Caroline Spencer's humble hospitality; but I said nothing, in order to say nothing uncivil. I only looked on Mr. Mixter, who had clasped his arms round his knees and was watching my companion's demonstrative graces in solemn fascination. She presently saw that I was observing him; she glanced at me with a little, bold, explanatory smile. 'You know, he adores me,' she murmured, putting her nose into her tapestry again. I expressed the promptest credence and she went on. 'He dreams of becoming my lover! Yes, it's his dream. He has read a French novel; it took him six months. But ever since that he has thought himself the hero, and me the heroine!'

Mr. Mixter had evidently not an idea that he was being talked about; he was too preoccupied with the ecstasy of contemplation. At this moment Caroline Spencer came out of the house, bearing a coffee-pot on a little tray. I noticed that on her way from the door to the table she gave me a single quick, vaguely appealing glance. I wondered what it signified; I felt that it signified a sort of half-frightened longing to know what, as a man of the world who had been in France, I thought of the countess. It made me extremely uncomfortable. I could not tell her that the countess was very possibly the runaway wife of a little *coiffeur.* I tried suddenly, on the contrary, to show a high consideration for her. But I got up; I couldn't stay longer. It vexed me to see Caroline Spencer standing there like a waiting-maid.

'You expect to remain some time at Grimwinter?' I said to the countess.

She gave a terrible shrug.

'Who knows? Perhaps for years. When one is in misery!——*Chère belle,*' she added, turning to Miss Spencer, 'you have forgotten the cognac!'

I detained Caroline Spencer as, after looking a moment in silence at the little table, she was turning away to get this missing delicacy.

I silently gave her my hand in farewell. She looked very tired, but there was a strange hint of prospective patience in her severely mild little face. I thought she was rather glad I was going. Mr. Mixter had risen to his feet and was pouring out the countess's coffee. As I went back past the Baptist church I reflected that poor Miss Spencer had been right in her presentiment that she should still see something of Europe.

Théodolinde

[First appeared in the *Lippincott's Magazine*, vol. xxi (May 1878), pp. 553-63. The tale was revised and reprinted in volume ii of *Stories Revived* (1885).]

I HAD INVITED THE EXCELLENT FELLOW TO DINNER, AND HAD begun to wonder, the stroke of half-past six having sounded, why he did not present himself. At last I stepped out upon the balcony and looked along the street in the direction from which, presumably, he would approach. A Parisian thoroughfare is always an entertaining spectacle, and I had still much of a stranger's alertness of attention. Before long, therefore, I quite forgot my unpunctual guest in my relish of the multifarious animation of the brilliant city. It was a perfect evening towards the end of April; there was a charming golden glow on the opposite housetops, which looked towards the west; there was a sort of vernal odour in the street, mingling with the emanations of the restaurant across the way, whose door now always stood open; with the delightful aroma of the chocolate-shop which occupied the ground-floor of the house in whose entresol I was lodged; and, as I fancied, with certain luscious perfumes hovering about the brilliantly-polished window of the hairdresser's establishment adjacent to the restaurant. Then there was a woman in a minutely-fluted cap selling violets in a little handcart, which she gently pushed along over the smooth asphalt, and which, as she passed, left a sensible trace in the thick mild air. All this made a thoroughly Parisian mixture, and I envied Sanguinetti the privilege of spending his life in a city in which even the humblest of one's senses was the medium of poetic impressions. There was poetry in the warm, succulent exhalations of the opposite restaurant, where, among the lighted lamps, I could see the little tables glittering with their glass and silver, the tenderly-brown rolls nestling in the petals of the folded napkins, the waiters in their snowy aprons standing in the various attitudes of imminent *empressement*, the agreeable *dame de comptoir* sitting idle for the moment and rubbing her plump white hands. To a person so inordinately fond of chocolate as myself—there was literally a pretty little box half emptied of large soft globules of the compound standing at that moment on my table, for all the world as if I had been a sweet-toothed school-girl—there was of course something very agreeable in the faint upward gusts of the establishment in my *rez-de-chaussée*. Presently, too, it appeared to me that the savours peculiar to the hairdressing-shop had assumed an extraordinary intensity, and that my right-hand nostril was in the act of being titillated by what might fairly be called the very poetry of cosmetics. Glancing that way again, I perceived the source of this rich effluvium. The hairdresser's door was open, and a person whom I took to be his wife had come to inhale upon the threshold the lighter atmosphere of the street. She stood there for some moments looking up and down, and I had time to see that she was very pretty. She wore a plain black silk dress, and one needed to know no more of millinery than most men to observe that it was admirably fitted to a charming figure. She had a little knot of pink ribbon at her throat and a bunch of violets in her rounded bosom. Her face seemed to me at once beautiful and lively—two merits that are not always united; for smiles, I have observed, are infrequent with women who are either very ugly or very pretty. Her light-brown hair was, naturally enough, dressed with consummate art, and the character of her beauty being suggestive of purity and gentleness, she looked (her black silk dress apart) like a Madonna who should have been *coiffée* in the Rue de la Paix. What a delightful person for a barber's wife! I thought; and I saw her sitting in the little front shop at the desk and taking the money with a gracious smile from the gentlemen who had been having their whiskers trimmed in the inner sanctuary. I touched my own whiskers, and straightway decided that they needed trimming. In a few moments this lovely woman stepped out upon the pavement, and strolled along in front of the shop-window on a little tour of inspection. She stood there a moment, looking at the brilliant array of brightly-capped flaçons, of ivory toilet-implements, of detached human tresses disposed in every variety of fashionable convolution: she inclined her head to one side and gently stroked her chin. I was able to perceive that even with her back turned she was hardly less pretty than when seen in front—her back had, as they say, so much *chic*. The inclination of her head denoted contentment, even complacency; and, indeed, well it might, for the window was most artistically arranged. Its principal glory was conferred by two waxen heads of lovely ladies, such as are usually seen in hairdressers' windows; and these wig-wearing puppets, which maintained a constant rotary movement, seemed to be a triumph of the modeller's art. One of the revolving ladies was dark, and the other fair, and each tossed back her head and thrust out her waxen bosom and parted her rosy lips in the most stylish manner conceivable. Several persons passing by had stopped to admire them. In a few moments a second inmate came to the door of the shop, and said a word to the barber's pretty wife. This was not the barber himself, but a young woman apparently employed in the shop. She was a nice-looking young woman enough, but she had by no means the beauty of her companion, who, to my regret, on hearing her voice, instantly went in.

After this I fell to watching something else, I forget what: I had quite forgotten Sanguinetti. I think I was looking at a gentleman and lady who had come into the resturant and placed themselves near the great sheet of plate glass which separated the interior from the street. The lady, who had the most wonderfully arched eyebrows, was evidently ordering the dinner, and I was struck with the profusion of its items. At last she began to eat her soup, with her little finger very much curled out, and then my gaze wandered towards the hairdresser's window again. This circumstance reminded me that I was really very good-natured to be waiting so placidly for that dilatory Sanguinetti. There he stood in front of the coiffeur's, staring as intently and serenely into the window as if he had the whole evening before him. I waited a few moments to give him a chance to move on, but he remained there rapt in contemplation. What in the world was he looking at? Had he spied something that could play a part in his collection? For Sanguinetti was a collector, and had a room full of old crockery and uncomfortable chairs. But he cared for nothing that was not a hundred years old, and the pretty things in the hairdresser's window all bore the stamp of the latest Parisian manufacture—were part and parcel of that modern rubbish which he so cordially despised. What, then, had so forcibly arrested his attention? Was the poor fellow thinking of buying a new chignon or a solitary pendent curl for the object of his affections? This could hardly be, for to my almost certain knowledge his affections had no object save the faded crockery and the singular chairs I have mentioned. I had, indeed, more than once thought it a pity that he should not interest himself in some attractive little woman, for he might end by marrying her; and that would be a blessing, inasmuch as she would probably take measures for his being punctual when he was asked out to dinner. I tapped on the edge of the little railing which served as my window-guard, but the noise of the street prevented this admonition from reaching his ear. He was decidedly quite too absorbed. Then I ventured to hiss at him in the manner of the Latin races—a mode of address to which I have always had a lively aversion, but which, it must be confessed, proceeding from Latin lips, reaches its destination in cases in which a nobler volume of sound will stop halfway. Still, like the warrior's widow in Tennyson's song, he neither spake nor moved. But here, suddenly, I comprehended the motive of his immobility: he was looking of course at the barber's beautiful wife, the pretty woman with the face of a Madonna and the coiffure of a duchess, whom I myself had just found so charming. This was really an excuse, and I felt disposed to allow him a few moments' grace. There was evidently an unobstructed space behind the window through which this attractive person could be perceived as she sat at her desk in some attitude of graceful diligence—adding up the items of a fine lady's little indebtedness for rouge-pots and rice-powder or braiding ever so neatly the long tresses of a *fausse natte* of the fashionable colour. I promised myself to look out for this unobstructed space the very first time I should pass.

I gave my tarrying guest another five minutes' grace, during which the lamps were lighted in the hairdresser's shop. The window now became extremely brilliant; the ivory brushes and the little silver mirrors glittered and flashed; the coloured cosmetics in the little toilet-bottles acquired an almost appetizing radiance; and the beautiful waxen ladies, tossing back their heads more than ever from their dazzling busts, seemed to sniff up the agreeable atmosphere. Of course the hairdresser's wife had become even more vividly visible, and so, evidently, Sanguinetti was finding out. He moved no more than if he himself had been a barber's block. This was all very well, but now, seriously, I was hungry, and I felt extremely disposed to fling a flower-pot at him. I had an array of these ornaments in the balcony. Just then my servant came into the room; and beckoning to this functionary I pointed out to him the gentleman at the barber's window, and bade him go down into the street and interrupt Mr. Sanguinetti's contemplations. He departed, descended, and I presently saw him cross the way. Just as he drew near my friend, however, the latter turned round abruptly and looked at his watch. Then, with an obvious sense of alarm, he moved quickly forward, but he had not gone five steps before he paused again and cast back a supreme glance at the object of his admiration. He raised his hand to his lips, and, upon my word, he looked as if he was kissing it. My servant now accosted him with a bow, and motioned towards my balcony, but Sanguinetti, without looking up, simply passed quickly across to my door. He might well be shy about looking up—kissing his hand in the street to pretty *dames de comptoir*: for a modest little man, who was supposed to care for nothing but bric-à-brac, and not to be in the least what is called 'enterprising' with women, this was certainly a very pretty jump. And the hairdresser's wife? Had she, on her side, been kissing her fingertips to him? I thought it very possible, and remembered that I had always heard that Paris is the city of gallantry.

Sanguinetti came in, blushing a good deal, and saying that he was extremely sorry to have kept me waiting.

'Oh,' I answered, 'I understand it very well. I have been watching you from my window for the last quarter of an hour.'

He smiled a little, blushing still. 'Though I have lived in Paris for fifteen years,' he said, 'you know I always look at the shops. One never knows what one may pick up.'

'You have a taste,' I said, 'for picking up pretty faces. That is certainly a very pretty one at the hairdresser's.'

Poor Sanguinetti was really very modest: my 'chaff' discomposed him, and he began to fidget and protest.

'Oh,' I went on, 'your choice does great honour to your taste. She's a very lovely creature: I admire her myself.'

He looked at me a moment with his soup-spoon poised. He was always a little afraid of me: he was sure I thought him a very flimsy fellow, with his passion for cracked teacups and scraps of old brocade. But now he seemed a trifle reassured: he would talk a little if he dared. 'You know there are two of them,' he said, 'but one is much more beautiful than the other.'

'Precisely,' I answered—'the fair one.'

'My dear friend,' murmured my guest, 'she is the most beautiful object I ever beheld.'

'That, perhaps,' I said, 'is going a little too far. But she is uncommonly handsome.'

'She is quite perfect,' Sanguinetti declared, finishing his soup. And presently he added, 'Shall I tell you what she looks like?'

'Like a fashionable angel,' I said.

'Yes,' he answered, smiling, 'or like a Madonna who should have had her hair dressed—over there.'

'My dear fellow,' I said, 'that is just the comparison I hit upon a while ago.'

'That proves the truth of it. It is a real Madonna type.'

'A little Parisianized,' I rejoined, 'about the corners of the mouth.'

'Possibly,' said Sanguinetti. 'But the mouth is her loveliest feature.'

'Could you see her well?' I inquired as I helped him to a sweetbread.

'Beautifully—especially after the gas was lighted.'

'Had you never noticed her before?'

'Never, strangely enough. But though, as I say, I am very fond of shop-windows, I confess to always having had a great prejudice against those of the hairdressers.'

'You see,' I said, 'how wrong you were.'

'No, not in general: this is an exception. The women are usually hideous. They have the most impossible complexions: they are always fearfully sallow. There is one of them in my street, three doors from my own house: you would say she was made of—' And he paused a moment for his comparison. 'You would say she was made of tallow.'

We finished our sweetbreads and, I think, talked of something else, my companion presently drawing from his pocket and exhibiting with some elation a little purchase in the antiquarian line which he had made that morning. It was a small coffee-cup of Sèvres manufacture and of the period of Louis XV., very delicately painted over with nosegays and garlands. I was far from being competent in such matters, but Sanguinetti assured me that it bore a certain little earmark which made it a precious acquisition. And he put it back into its little red morocco case, and fell a-musing with his eyes wandering towards the window. He was fond of old gimcracks and knickknacks of every order and epoch, but he had, I knew, a special tenderness for the productions of the baser period of the French monarchy. His collection of snuff-boxes and flowered screens was highly remarkable—might, I suppose, have been called celebrated. In spite of his very foreign name, he was a genuine compatriot of my own, and indeed our acquaintance had begun with our being, as very small boys, at school together. There was a tradition that Sanguinetti's grandfather had been an Italian image-vender in the days when those gentlemen might have claimed in America to be the only representatives of a care for the fine arts. In the early part of the century they were also less numerous than they have since become, and it was believed that the founder of the Transatlantic stock of the Sanguinettis had by virtue of his fine Italian eyes, his slouched hat, his earrings, his persuassive eloquence, his foreign idioms and his little tray of plaster effigies and busts been deemed a personage of sufficient importance to win the heart and hand of the daughter of a well-to-do-attorney in the State of Vermont. This lady had brought her husband a property which he had invested in some less brittle department of the Italian trade, and, prospering as people, alas! prospered in those good old days, had bequeathed, much augmented, to the father of my guest. My companion, who had several sisters, was brought up like a little gentleman, and showed symptoms even at the earliest age of his mania for refuse furniture. At school he used to collect old slate-pencils and match-boxes: I suppose he inherited the taste from his grandfather, who had perambulated the country with a tray covered with the most useless ornaments (like a magnified chess-board) upon his head. When he was twenty years old Sanguinetti lost his father and got his share of the patrimony, with which he immediately came to Europe, where he had lived these seventeen years. When I first saw him on coming to Paris, I asked him if he meant never to go back to New York, and I very well remember his answer: 'My dear fellow' (in a very mournful tone), 'what *can* you get there? The things are all second-rate, and during the Louis Quinze period, you know, our poor dear country was really—really—' And he shook his head very slowly and expressively.

I answered that there were (as I had been told) very good spinning-wheels and kitchen-settles, but he rejoined that he cared only for that which was truly elegant. He was a most simple-minded and amiable little bachelor, and would have done anything possible to oblige a friend, but he made no secret of his conviction that 'pretty things' were the only things in the world worth troubling one's self about. He was very near-sighted, and was always putting up his glass to look at something on your chimney-piece or your side-table. He had a lingering, solemn way of talking about the height of Madame de Pompadour's heels and the different shapes of old Dutch candlesticks; and though many of his fellow-country people thought him very 'affected,' he always seemed to me the least pretentious of men. He never read the newspapers for their politics, and didn't pretend to: he read them only for their lists of auction-sales. I had a great kindness for him, he seemed to me such a pure-minded mortal, sitting there in his innocent company of Dresden shepherdesses and beauties whose smiles were stippled on the lids of snuff-boxes. There is always something agreeable in a man who is a perfect example of a type; and Sanguinetti was all of one piece. He was the perfect authority upon pretty things.

He kept looking at the window, as I have said, and it required no great shrewdness to guess that his thoughts had stepped out of it and were hovering in front of the hairdresser's *étalage*. I was inclined to humour his enthusiasm, for it amused me to see a man who had hitherto found a pink-faced lady on a china plate a sufficiently substantial object of invocation, led captive by a charmer who would, as the phrase is, have something to say for herself.

'Shouldn't you have liked to have a closer view of her?' I asked with a sympathetic smile.

He glanced at me and blushed again: 'That lovely creature?'

'That lovely creature. Shouldn't you have liked to get nearer?'

'Indeed I should. That sheet of plate-glass is a great vexation.'

'But why didn't you make a pretext for going into the shop? You might have bought a tooth-brush.'

'I don't know that I should have gained much,' said Sanguinetti simply.

'You would have seen her move: her movement is charming.'

'Her movement is—the poetry of motion. But I could see that outside.'

'My dear fellow,' I urged, 'you are not enterprising enough. In your place I should get a footing in the shop.'

He fixed his clear little near-sighted eyes upon me. 'Yes, yes,' he said, 'it would certainly be delightful to be able to sit there and watch her: it would be more comfortable than standing outside.'

'*Je crois bien*! But sitting there and watching her? You go rather far.'

'I suppose I should be rather in the way. But every now and then she would turn her face towards me. And I don't know,' he added, 'but that she is as pretty behind as before.'

'You make an observation that I made myself. She has so much *chic*.'

Sanguinetti kissed his finger-tips with a movement that he had learned of his long Parisian sojourn. 'The poetry of *chic*— But I shall go further,' he presently pursued. 'I don't despair, I don't despair.' And he paused with his hands in his pockets, tilting himself back in his seat.

'You don't despair of what?'

'Of making her my own.'

I burst out laughing: 'Your own, my dear fellow! You are more enterprising than I thought. But what do you mean? I don't suppose that under the circumstances you can marry her?'

'No: under the circumstances, unfortunately, I can't. But I can have her always there.'

'Always where?'

'At home, in my room. It's just the place for her.'

'Ah, my good friend,' I rejoined, laughing, but slightly scandalized, 'that's a matter of opinion.'

'It's a matter of taste. I think it would suit her.'

A matter of taste, indeed, this question of common morality! Sanguinetti was more Parisianized than I had supposed, and I reflected that Paris was certainly a very dangerous place, since it had got the better of his inveterate propriety. But I was not too much shocked to be still a good deal amused.

'Of course I shall not go too fast,' he went on. 'I shall not be too abrupt.'

'Pray don't.'

'I shall approach the matter gradually. I shall go into the shop several times to buy certain things. First a pot of cold cream, then a piece of soap, then a bottle of glycerine. I shall go into a great many ecstasies and express no end of admiration. Meanwhile, she will slowly move around, and every now and then she will look at me. And so, little by little, I well come to the great point.'

'Perhaps you will not be listened to.'

'I will make a very handsome offer.'

'What sort of an offer do you mean?'

'I am ashamed to tell you: you will call it throwing away money.'

An offer of money! He was really very crude. Should I too come to this if I continued to live in Paris? 'Oh,' I said, 'if you think that money simply will do it—'

'Why, you don't suppose,' he exclaimed, 'that I expect to have her for nothing?' He was actually cynical, and I remained silent. 'But I shall not be happy again—at least for a long time'—he went on, 'unless I succeed. I have always dreamed of just such a woman as that; and now at last, when I behold her perfect image and embodiment, why I simply can't do without her.' He was evidently very sincere.

'You are simply in love,' I said.

He looked at me a moment, and blushed: 'Yes, I honestly believe I am. It's very absurd.'

'From some point of view or other,' I said, 'love is always absurd;' and I decided that the matter was none of my business.

We talked of other things for an hour, but before he took leave of me Sanguinetti reverted to the Beautiful Being at the hairdresser's. 'I am sure you will think me a great donkey,' he said 'for taking that —that creature so seriously;' and he nodded in the direction of the other side of the street.

'I was always taught, in Boston,' I answered, 'that it is our duty to take things seriously.'

I made a point, of course, the next day of stopping at the hairdresser's window for the purpose of obtaining another glimpse of the remarkable woman who had made such an impression upon my friend. I found, in fact, that there was a large aperture in the back of the window—it came just between the two beautiful dolls—through which it was very possible to see what was going on in a considerable part of the shop. Just then, however, the object of Sanguinetti's admiration was not within the range of vision of a passer-by, and I waited some time without her appearing. At last having improvised a purchase, I entered the aromatic precinct. To my vexation, the attendant who came forward to serve me was not the charming woman whom I had seen the evening before on the pavement, but the young person of inferior attractions who had come to the door to call her. This young person also wore a black silk dress and had a very neat figure: she was beautifully *coiffée* and very polite. But she was a very different affair from Sanguinetti's friend, and I rather grudged the five francs that I paid her for the little bottle of lavender water that I didn't want. What should I do with a bottle of lavender water? I would give it to Sanguinetti. I lingered in the shop under half a dozen pretexts, but still saw no sign of its lovelier inmate. The other young woman stood smiling and rubbing her hands, answering my questions and giving explanations with high-pitched urbanity. At last I took up my little bottle and laid my hand upon the door-knob. At that moment a velvet curtain was raised at the back of the shop, and the hairdresser's wife presented herself. She stood there a moment with the curtain lifted, looking out and smiling: on her beautiful head was poised a crisp little morning-cap. Yes, she was lovely, and I really understood Sanguinetti's sudden passion. But I could not stand there staring at her, and I had exhausted my expedients: I was obliged to withdraw. I came and stood in front of the shop, however, and presently she approached the window. She looked into it to see if it was in proper order. She was still smiling—she seemed always to be smiling—but she gave no sign of seeing me, and I felt that if there had been a dozen men standing there, she would have worn that same sweetly unconscious mask. She glanced about her a moment, and then, extending a plump little white hand, she gave a touch to the back hair of one of the waxen ladies—the right-hand one, the blonde.

A couple of hours later, rising from breakfast, I repaired to my little balcony, from which post of observation I instantly espied a figure stationed in the hairdresser's window. If I had not recognized it otherwise, the absorbed, contemplative droop of its head would at once have proved it to be Sanguinetti. 'Why does he not go inside?' I asked myself. 'He can't look at her properly out there.' At this conclusion he appeared himself to have arrived, for he suddenly straightened himself up and entered the establishment. He remained within a long time. I grew tired of waiting for him to reappear, and went back to my arm-chair to finish reading the *Débats*. I had just accomplished this somewhat arduous feat when I heard the lame tinkle of my door-bell, a few moments after which Sanguinetti was ushered in.

He really looked love-sick: he was pale and heavy-eyed. 'My too-susceptible friend,' I said, 'you are very far gone.'

'Yes,' he answered: 'I am really in love. It is too ridiculous. Please don't tell any one.'

'I shall certainly tell no one,' I declared. 'But it does not seem to me exactly ridiculous.'

He gave me a grateful stare: 'Ah, if you don't find it so, *tant mieux*,'

'Regrettable, rather: that's what I should call it.'

He gave me another stare: 'You think I can't afford it?'

'It is not so much that.'

'You think it won't look well? I will arrange it so that the harshest critic will be disarmed. This morning,' he added in a moment, 'she looks lovelier than ever.'

'Yes, I have had a glimpse of her myself,' I said. 'And you have been in the shop?'

'I have spent half an hour there. I thought it best to go straight to the point.'

'What did you say?'

'I said the simple truth—that I have an intense desire to possess her.'

'And the hairdresser's wife? how did she take it?'

'She seemed a good deal amused.'

'Amused, simply? Nothing more?'

'I think she was a little flattered.'

'I hope so.'

'Yes,' my companion rejoined, 'for, after all, her own exquisite taste is half the business.' To this proposition I cordially assented, and Sanguinetti went on: 'But, after all, too, the dear creature won't lose that in coming to me. I shall make arrangements to have her hair dressed regularly.'

'I see that you mean to do things *en prince*. Who is it that dresses her hair?'

'The coiffeur himself.'

'The husband?'

'Exactly. They say he is the best in Paris.'

'The best husband?' I asked.

'My dear fellow, be serious—the best coiffeur.'

'It will certainly be very obliging of him.'

'Of course,' said Sanguinetti, 'I shall pay him for his visits, as—if—as if—' And he paused a moment.

'As if what?'

'As if she were one of his fine ladies. His wife tells me that he goes to all the duchesses.'

'Of course,' I replied, 'that will be something. But still—'

'You mean,' said my companion, 'that I live so far away? I know that, but I will pay him his cab-fare.'

I looked at him, and—I couldn't help it—I began to laugh. I had never seen such a strange mixture of ardour and coolness.

'Ah,' he exclaimed, blushing, 'you *do* think it ridiculous?'

'Yes,' I said, 'coming to this point, I confess it makes me laugh.'

'I don't care,' Sanguinetti declared with amiable doggedness: 'I mean to keep her to myself.'

Just at this time my attention was much taken up by the arrival in Paris of some relatives who had no great talent for assimilating their habits to foreign customs, and who carried me about in their train as cicerone and interpreter. For three or four weeks I was constantly in their company, and I saw much less of Sanguinetti than I had done before. He used to appear, however, at odd moments in my rooms, being, as may be imagined, very often in the neighbourhood. I always asked him for the latest tidings of his grand passion, which had begun to glow with a fervour that made him perfectly indifferent to the judgement of others. The poor fellow was most sincerely in love.

'*Je suis tout à ma passion*,' he would say when I asked him the news. 'Until the matter is settled I can think of nothing else. I have always been so when I have wanted a thing intensely. It has become a monomania, a fixed idea; and naturally this case is not an exception.'

He was always going into the shop. 'We talk it over,' he said. 'She can't make up her mind.'

'I can imagine the difficulty.' I answered.

'She says it's a great change.'

'I can also imagine that.'

'I never see the husband,' said Sanguinetti. 'He is always away with the duchesses. But she talks it over with him. At first he wouldn't listen to it.'

'Naturally.'

'He said it would be an irreparable loss. But I am in hopes he will come round. He can get on very well with the other.'

'The other?—the little dark one? She is not nearly so pretty.'

'Of course not. But she isn't bad in her way. I really think,' said Sanguinetti, 'that he will come round. If he does not, we will do without his consent, and take the consequences. He will not be sorry, after all, to have the money.'

You may be sure that I felt plenty of surprise at the business-like tone in which Sanguinetti discussed this unscrupulous project of becoming the 'possessor' of another man's wife. There was certainly no hypocrisy about it: he had quite passed beyond the stage at which it is deemed needful to throw a sop to propriety. But I said to myself that this was doubtless the Parisian tone, and that since it had made its mark upon so perfect a little model of social orthodoxy as my estimable friend, nothing was more possible than that I too should become equally perverted. Whenever, after this, Sanguinetti came in, he had something to say at first about the lovely creature across the way. 'Have you noticed her this morning?' he would demand. 'She is really enchanting. I thought of asking leave to kiss her.'

'I wonder you should ask leave,' I answered. 'I should suppose you would do it without leave, and count upon being forgiven.'

'I am afraid of hurting her,' he said. 'And then if I should be seen from the street, it would look rather absurd.'

I could only say that he seemed to me a very odd mixture of audacity and discretion, but he went on without heeding my comments: 'You may laugh at the idea, but, upon my word, to me she is different every day: she has never the same expression. Sometimes she's a little melancholy—sometimes she's in high spirits.'

'I should say she was always smiling.'

'Superficially, yes,' said Sanguinetti. 'That's all the vulgar see. But there's something beneath it—the most delicious little pensive look. At bottom she's sad. She's weary of her position there, it's so public.'

'Yesterday she was very pale,' he would say at another time: 'I'm sure she wants rest. That constant movement can't be good for her. It's true,' he added, 'that she moves very slowly.'

'Yes,' said I, 'she seemed to me to move very slowly.'

'And so beautifully! Still, with me,' Sanguinetti went on, 'she shall be perfectly quiet: I will see how that suits her.'

'I should think,' I objected, 'that she would need a little exercise.'

He stared a moment and then accused me, as he often did, of 'making game of him.' 'There is something in your tone in saying that,' he declared; but he very shortly afterward forgot my sarcastic tendencies, and came to announce to me a change in the lady's coiffure: 'Have you noticed that she has her hair dressed differently? I don't know that I like it: it covers up her forehead. But it's beautifully done, it's entirely new, and you will see that it will set the fashion for all Paris.'

'Do they take the fashion from her?' I asked.

'Always. All the knowing people keep a note of her successive coiffures.'

'And when you have carried her off, what will the knowing people do?'

'They will go by the other, the dark one—Mademoiselle Clémentine.'

'Is that her name? And the name of your sweetheart?'

Sanguinetti looked at me an instant with his usual helplessly mistrustful little blush, and then he answered, 'Théodolinde.'

When I asked him how his suit was prospering, he usually replied that he believed it to be merely a question of time. 'We keep talking it over, and in that way, at any rate, I can see her. The poor woman can't get used to the idea.'

'I should think not.'

'She says it would change everything—that the shop would be a different place without her. She is so well known, so universally admired. I tell her that it will not be impossible to get a clever substitute; and she answers that, clever as the substitute may be, she will never have the peculiar charm of Théodolinde.'

'Ah! she herself is aware then of this peculiar charm?'

'Perfectly, and it delights her to have me talk about it.'

A part of the charm's peculiarity, I reflected, was that it was not spoiled by the absence of modesty; yet I also remembered the coiffeur's handsome wife had looked extremely modest. Sanguinetti, however, appeared bent upon ministering to her vanity: I learned that he was making her presents. 'I have given her a pair of earrings,' he announced, 'and she is wearing them now. Do notice them as you pass. They are great big amethysts, and are extremely becoming.'

I looked out for our beautiful friend the next time I left the house, but she was not visible through the hairdresser's window. Her plainer companion was waiting upon a fine lady, presumably one of the duchesses, while Madame Théodolinde herself, I supposed, was posturing before one of the mirrors in the inner apartment with Sanguinetti's big amethysts in her ears.

One day he told me that he had determined to buy her a *parure*, and he greatly wished I would come and help him to choose it. I called him an extravagant dog, but I good-naturedly consented to accompany him to the jeweller's. He led me to the Palais Royal, and there, somewhat to my surprise, introduced me into one of those dazzling little shops which wear upon their front in neat gilt letters the candid announcement, 'Imitation.' Here you may purchase any number of glittering gems for the most trifling sum, and indulge at a moderate expense a pardonable taste for splendour. And the splendour is most effective, the glitter of the counterfeit jewels most natural. It is only the sentiment of the thing, you say to yourself, that prevents you from making all your purchases of jewelry in one of these convenient establishments; though, indeed, as their proprietors very aptly remark, five thousand dollars more is a good deal to pay for sentiment. Of this expensive superstition, however, I should have expected Sanguinetti to be guilty.

'You are not going to get a real set?' I asked.

He seemed a little annoyed: 'Wouldn't you in that case blow me up for my extravagance?'

'It is highly probable. And yet a present of false jewelry! The handsomer it is, you know, the more ridiculous it is.'

'I have thought of that,' said my friend, 'and I confess I am rather ashamed of myself. I should like to give her a real set. But, you see, I want diamonds and sapphires, and a real set such as I desire would cost about twenty thousand dollars. That's a good deal for—for—' And he paused a moment.

'For a barber's wife,' I said to myself.

'Besides,' my companion added, 'she won't know the difference.' I thought he rather under-estimated her intelligence: a pretty Parisienne was, by instinct, a judge of *parures*. I remembered, however, that he had rarely spoken of this lady's intellectual qualities: he had dwelt exclusively upon her beauty and sweetness. So I stood by him while he purchased for two hundred francs a gorgeous necklace and coronet of the stones of Golconda. His passion was an odd affair altogether, and an oddity the more or the less hardly mattered. He remarked, moreover, that he had at home a curious collection of artificial gems, and that these things would be an interesting addition to his stock. 'I shall make her wear them all,' he exclaimed; and I wondered how she would like it.

He told me afterwards that his offering had been most gratefully received, that she was now wearing the wonderful necklace, and that she looked lovelier than ever.

That evening, however, I stopped before the shop to catch a glimpse, if possible, of the barber's lady thus splendidly adorned. I had seldom been fortunate enough to espy her, and on this occasion I turned away disappointed. Just as I was doing so I perceived something which suggested that she was making a fool of my amiable friend. On the radiant bosom of one of the great waxen dolls in her window glittered a necklace of brilliants which bore a striking resemblance to the article I had helped Sanguinetti to select. She had made over her lover's tribute to this rosy effigy, to whom, it must be confessed, it was very becoming.

Yet, for all this, I was out in my calculation. A week later Sanguinetti came into my rooms with a radiant countenance, and announced to me the consummation of his dream. 'She is mine! she is mine! mine only!' he cried, dropping into a chair.

'She has left the shop?' I demanded.

'Last night—at eleven o'clock. We went off in a cab.'

'You have her at home?'

'For ever and ever!' he declared ecstatically.

'My dear fellow, my compliments!'

'It was not an easy matter,' he went on. 'But I held her in my arms.'

I renewed my compliments, and said I hoped she was happy; and he declared that she was smiling more than ever. Positively! And he added that I must immediately come and see her: he was impatient to present me. Nothing, I answered, would give me greater pleasure, but meanwhile what did the husband say?

'He grumbles a bit,' said Sanguinetti, 'but I gave him five hundred francs.'

'You have got off easily,' I said; and I promised that at my first moment of leisure I would call upon my friend's new companion. I saw him three or four times before this moment arrived, and he assured me that she had made a happy man of him. 'Whenever I have greatly wanted a thing, waited for it, and at last got it, I have always been in bliss for a month afterwards,' he said. 'But I think that this time my pleasure will really last.'

'It will last as long, I hope, as she does herself' I answered.

'I am sure it will. This is the sort of thing—yes, smile away—in which I get my happiness.'

'*Vous n'êtes pas difficile*,' I rejoined.

'Of course she's perishable,' he added in a moment.

'Ah!' said I, 'you must take good care of her.'

And a day or two later, on his coming for me, I went with him to his apartment. His rooms were charming, and lined from ceiling to floor with the 'pretty things' of the occupant—tapestries and bronzes, terra-cotta medallions and precious specimens of porcelain. There were cabinets and tables charged with similar treasures: the place was a perfect little museum. Sanguinetti led me through two or three rooms, and then stopped near a window, close to which half hidden by the curtain, stood a lady, with her head turned away from us, looking out. In spite of our approach, she stood motionless until my friend went up to her and with a gallant, affectionate movement placed his arm round her waist. Hereupon she slowly turned and gazed at me with a beautiful brilliant face and large quiet eyes.

'It is a pity she creaks,' said my companion as I was making my bow. And then, as I made it, I perceived with amazement—and amusement—the cause of her creaking. She existed only from the waist upward, and the skirt of her dress was a very neat pedestal covered with red velvet. Sanguinetti gave another loving twist, and she slowly revolved again, making a little gentle squeal. She exhibited the back of her head, with its beautifully braided tresses resting upon her sloping waxen shoulders. She was the right-hand effigy of the coiffeur's window—the blonde! Her movement, as Sanguinetti had claimed, was particularly commendable, and of all his pretty things she was certainly the prettiest.

Daisy Miller: A Study

IN TWO PARTS

[First appeared in the *Cornhill Magazine*, vols. xxxvii-xxxviii (June-July 1878), pp. 678-98, 44-67. This first publication was followed by two unauthorized periodical appearances: in *Littell's Living Age*, vol. cxxxviii (6 and 27 July 1878), pp. 27-40, 226-41; and, with an added subtitle—'Americans Abroad'—coined by the journal, in the New York *Home Journal* (31 July 1878), p. 1; (7 August), p. 1; (14 August), p. 1. The tale received book status first in America where the *Cornhill* text was reprinted as No. 28 of Harper's Half-Hour Series (New York: Harper and Brothers, 1878). The first revised version came when the tale appeared in book form in England, in volume i of *Daisy Miller: A Study* (1879). This text was later reproduced in volume xiii of James's first 'Collective Edition' (1883). Using the text of 1879, James finally revised the tale for the New York Edition, where it appears in volume xviii (*Daisy Miller, Etc.*, 1909). During James's lifetime, the final text was reprinted in *The Uniform Tales of Henry James* (London, Martin Secker, 1915-20—1915).]

PART I

AT THE LITTLE TOWN OF VEVEY, IN SWITZERLAND, THERE IS A PARticularly comfortable hotel. There are, indeed, many hotels; for the entertainment of tourists is the business of the place, which, as many travellers will remember, is seated upon the edge of a remarkably blue lake—a lake that it behoves every tourist to visit. The shore of the lake presents an unbroken array of establishments of this order, of every category, from the 'grand hotel' of the newest fashion, with a chalk-white front, a hundred balconies, and a dozen flags flying from its roof, to the little Swiss *pension* of an elder day, with its name inscribed in German-looking lettering upon a pink or yellow wall, and an awkward summer-house in the angle of the garden. One of the hotels at Vevey, however, is famous, even classical, being distinguished from many of its upstart neighbours by an air both of luxury and of maturity. In this region, in the month of June, American travellers are extremely numerous; it may be said, indeed, that Vevey assumes at this period some of the characteristics of an American watering-place. There are sights and sounds which evoke a vision, an echo, of Newport and Saratoga. There is a flitting hither and thither of 'stylish' young girls, a rustling of muslin flounces, a rattle of dance-music in the morning hours, a sound of high-pitched voices at all times. You receive an impression of these things at the excellent inn of the 'Trois Couronnes', and are transported in fancy to the Ocean House or to the Congress Hall. But at the 'Trois Couronnes,' it must be added, there are other features that are much at variance with these suggestions: neat German waiters, who look like secretaries of legation; Russian princesses sitting in the garden; little Polish boys walking about, held by the hand, with their governors; a view of the snowy crest of the Dent du Midi and the picturesque towers of the Castle of Chillon.

I hardly know whether it was the analogies or the differences that were uppermost in the mind of a young American, who, two or three years ago, sat in the garden of the 'Trois Couronnes,' looking about him, rather idly, at some of the graceful objects I have mentioned. It was a beautiful summer morning, and in whatever fashion the young American looked at things, they must have seemed to him charming. He had come from Geneva the day before, by the little steamer, to see his aunt, who was staying at the hotel—Geneva having been for a long time his place of residence. But his aunt had a headache—his aunt had almost always a headache—and now she was shut up in her room, smelling camphor, so that he was at liberty to wander about. He was some seven-and-twenty years of age; when his friends spoke of him, they usually said that he was at Geneva, 'studying.' When his enemies spoke of him they said—but, after all, he had no enemies; he was an extremely amiable fellow, and universally liked. What I should say is, simply, that when certain persons spoke of him they affirmed that the reason of his spending so much time at Geneva was that he was extremely devoted to a lady who lived there—a foreign lady—a person older than himself. Very few Americans—indeed I think none—had ever seen this lady, about whom there were some singular stories. But Winterbourne had an old attachment for the little metropolis of Calvinism; he had been put to school there as a boy, and he had afterwards gone to college there—circumstances which had led to his forming a great many youthful friendships. Many of these he had kept, and they were a source of great satisfaction to him.

After knocking at his aunt's door and learning that she was indisposed, he had taken a walk about the town, and then he had come in to his breakfast. He had now finished his breakfast; but he was drinking a small cup of coffee, which had been served to him on a little table in the garden by one of the waiters who looked like an *attaché*. At last he finished his coffee and lit a cigarette. Presently a small boy came walking along the path—an urchin of nine or ten. The child, who was diminutive for his years, had an aged expression of countenance, a pale complexion, and sharp little features. He was dressed in knickerbockers, with red stockings, which displayed his poor little spindleshanks; he also wore a brilliant red cravat. He carried in his hand a long alpenstock, the sharp point of which he thrust into everything that he approached—the flower-beds, the garden-benches, the trains of the ladies' dresses. In front of Winterbourne he paused, looking at him with a pair of bright, penetrating little eyes.

'Will you give me a lump of sugar?' he asked, in a sharp, hard little voice—a voice immature, and yet, somehow, not young.

Winterbourne glanced at the small table near him, on which his coffee-service rested, and saw that several morsels remained. 'Yes, you may take one,' he answered; 'but I don't think sugar is good for little boys.'

This little boy stepped forward and carefully selected three of the coveted fragments, two of which he buried in the pocket of his knickerbockers, depositing the other as promptly in another place. He poked his alpenstock, lance fashion, into Winterbourne's bench, and tried to crack the lump of sugar with his teeth.

'Oh, blazes; it's har-r-d!' he exclaimed, pronouncing the adjective in a peculiar manner.

Winterbourne had immediately perceived that he might have the honour of claiming him as a fellow-countryman. 'Take care you don't hurt your teeth,' he said paternally.

'I haven't got any teeth to hurt. They have all come out. I have only got seven teeth. My mother counted them last night, and one came out right afterwards. She said she'd slap me if any more came out. I can't help it. It's this old Europe. It's the climate that makes them come out. In America they didn't come out. It's these hotels.'

Winterbourne was much amused. 'If you eat three lumps of sugar, your mother will certainly slap you,' he said.

'She's got to give me some candy, then,' rejoined his young interlocutor. 'I can't get any candy here—any American candy. American candy's the best candy.'

'And are American little boys the best little boys?' asked Winterbourne.

'I don't know. I'm an American boy,' said the child.

'I see you are one of the best!' laughed Winterbourne.

'Are you an American man?' pursued this vivacious infant. And then, on Winterbourne's affirmative reply—'American men are the best,' he declared.

His companion thanked him for the compliment; and the child, who had now got astride of his alpenstock, stood looking about him, while he attacked a second lump of sugar. Winterbourne wondered if he himself had been like this in his infancy, for he had been brought to Europe at about this age.

'Here comes my sister!' cried the child, in a moment. 'She's an American girl.'

Winterbourne looked along the path and saw a beautiful young lady advancing. 'American girls are the best girls,' he said, cheerfully, to his young companion.

'My sister ain't the best!' the child declared. 'She's always blowing at me.'

'I imagine that is your fault, not hers,' said Winterbourne. The young lady meanwhile had drawn near. She was dressed in white muslin, with a hundred frills and flounces, and knots of pale-coloured ribbon. She was bare-headed; but she balanced in her hand a large parasol, with a deep border of embroidery; and she was strikingly, admirably pretty. 'How pretty they are!' thought Winterbourne, straightening himself in his seat, as if he were prepared to rise.

The young lady paused in front of his bench, near the parapet of the garden, which overlooked the lake. The little boy had now converted his alpenstock into a vaulting-pole, by the aid of which he was springing about in the gravel, and kicking it up not a little.

'Randolph,' said the young lady, 'what *are* you doing?'

'I'm going up the Alps,' replied Randolph. 'This is the way!' And he gave another little jump, scattering the pebbles about Winterbourne's ears.

'That's the way they come down,' said Winterbourne.

'He's an American man!' cried Randolph, in his little hard voice.

The young lady gave no heed to this announcement, but looked straight at her brother. 'Well, I guess you had better be quiet,' she simply observed.

It seemed to Winterbourne that he had been in a manner presented. He got up and stepped slowly towards the young girl, throwing away his cigarette. 'This little boy and I have made acquaintance,' he said, with great civility. In Geneva, as he had been perfectly aware, a young man was not at liberty to speak to a young unmarried lady except under certain rarely-occurring conditions; but here at Vevey, what conditions could be better than these?—a pretty American girl coming and standing in front of you in a garden. This pretty American girl, however, on hearing Winterbourne's observation, simply glanced at him; she then turned her head and looked over the parapet, at the lake and the opposite mountains. He wondered whether he had gone too far; but he decided that he must advance farther, rather than retreat. While he was thinking of something else to say, the young lady turned to the little boy again.

'I should like to know where you got that pole,' she said.

'I bought it!' responded Randolph.

'You don't mean to say you're going to take it to Italy.'

'Yes, I am going to take it to Italy!' the child declared.

The young girl glanced over the front of her dress, and smoothed out a knot or two of ribbon. Then she rested her eyes upon the prospect again. 'Well, I guess you had better leave it somewhere,' she said, after a moment.

'Are you going to Italy?' Winterbourne inquired, in a tone of great respect.

The young lady glanced at him again. 'Yes, sir,' she replied. And she said nothing more.

'Are you—a—going over the Simplon?' Winterbourne pursued, a little embarrassed.

'I don't know,' she said. 'I suppose its some mountain. Randolph, what mountain are we going over?'

'Going where?' the child demanded.

'To Italy,' Winterbourne explained.

'I don't know,' said Randolph. 'I don't want to go to Italy. I want to go to America.'

'Oh, Italy is a beautiful place!' rejoined the young man.

'Can you get candy there?' Randolph loudly inquired.

'I hope not,' said his sister. 'I guess you have had enough candy, and mother thinks so too.'

'I haven't had any for ever so long—for a hundred weeks!' cried the boy, still jumping about.

The young lady inspected her flounces and smoothed her ribbons again; and Winterbourne presently risked an observation upon the beauty of the view. He was ceasing to be embarrassed, for he had begun to perceive that she was not in the least embarrassed herself. There had not been the slightest alteration in her charming complexion; she was evidently neither offended nor fluttered. If she looked another way when he spoke to her, and seemed not particularly to hear him, this was simply her habit, her manner. Yet, as he talked a little more, and pointed out some of the objects of interest in the view, with which she appeared quite unacquainted, she gradually gave him more of the benefit of her glance; and then he saw that this glance was perfectly direct and unshrinking. It was not, however, what would have been called an immodest glance, for the young girl's eyes were singularly honest and fresh. They were wonderfully pretty eyes; and, indeed, Winterbourne had not seen for a long time anything prettier than his fair countrywoman's various features—her complexion, her nose, her ears, her teeth. He had a great relish for feminine beauty; he was addicted to observing and analysing it; and as regards this young lady's face he made several observations. It was not at all insipid, but it was not exactly expressive; and though it was eminently delicate, Winterbourne mentally accused it—very forgivingly—of a want of finish. He thought it very possible that Master Randolph's sister was a coquette; he was sure she had a spirit of her own; but in her bright, sweet, superficial little visage there was no mockery, no irony. Before long it became obvious that she was much disposed towards conversation. She told him that they were going to Rome for the winter—she and her mother and Randolph. She asked him if he was a 'real American;' she shouldn't have taken him for one; he seemed more like a German—this was said after a little hesitation, especially when he spoke. Winterbourne, laughing, answered that he had met Germans who spoke like Americans; but that he had not, so far as he remembered, met an American who spoke like a German. Then he asked her if she should not be more comfortable in sitting upon the bench which he had just quitted. She answered that she liked standing up and walking about; but she presently sat down. She told him she was from New York State—'if you know where that is.' Winterbourne learned more about her by catching hold of her small, slippery brother and making him stand a few minutes by his side.

'Tell me your name, my boy,' he said.

'Randolph C. Miller,' said the boy, sharply. 'And I'll tell you her name;' and he levelled his alpenstock at his sister.

'You had better wait till you are asked!' said this young lady, calmly.

'I should like very much to know your name,' said Winterbourne.

'Her name is Daisy Miller!' cried the child. 'But that isn't her real name; that isn't her name on her cards.'

'It's a pity you haven't got one of my cards!' said Miss Miller.

'Her real name is Annie P. Miller,' the boy went on.

'Ask him *his* name,' said his sister, indicating Winterbourne.

But on this point Randolph seemed perfectly indifferent; he continued to supply information with regard to his own family. 'My father's name is Ezra B. Miller,' he announced. 'My father ain't in Europe; my father's in a better place than Europe.'

Winterbourne imagined for a moment that this was the manner in which the child had been taught to intimate that Mr. Miller had been removed to the sphere of celestial rewards. But Randolph immediately added, 'My father's in Schenectady. He's got a big business. My father's rich, you bet.'

'Well!' ejaculated Miss Miller, lowering her parasol and looking at the embroidered border. Winterbourne presently released the child, who departed, dragging his alpenstock along the path. 'He doesn't like Europe,' said the young girl. 'He wants to go back.'

'To Schenectady, you mean?'

'Yes; he wants to go right home. He hasn't got any boys here. There is one boy here, but he always goes round with a teacher; they won't let him play.'

'And your brother hasn't any teacher?' Winterbourne inquired.

'Mother thought of getting him one, to travel round with us. There was a lady told her of a very good teacher; an American lady—perhaps you know her—Mrs. Sanders. I think she came from Boston. She told her of this teacher, and we thought of getting him to travel round with us. But Randolph said he didn't want a teacher travelling round with us. He said he wouldn't have lessons when he was in the cars. And we *are* in the cars about half the time. There was an English lady we met in the cars—I think her name was Miss Featherstone; perhaps you know her. She wanted to know why I didn't give Randolph lessons—give him 'instruction,' she called it. I guess he could give me more instruction than I could give him. He's very smart.'

'Yes,' said Winterbourne; 'he seems very smart.'

'Mother's going to get a teacher for him as soon as we get to Italy. Can you get good teachers in Italy?'

'Very good, I should think,' said Winterbourne.

'Or else she's going to find some school. He ought to learn some more. He's only nine. He's going to college.' And in this way Miss Miller continued to converse upon the affairs of her family, and upon other topics. She sat there with her extremely pretty hands, ornamented with very brilliant rings, folded in her lap, and with her pretty eyes now resting upon those of Winterbourne, now wandering over the garden, the people who passed by, and the beautiful view. She talked to Winterbourne as if she had kown him a long time. He found it very pleasant. It was many years since he had heard a young girl talk so much. It might have been said of this unknown young lady, who had come and sat down beside him upon a bench, that she chattered. She was very quiet; she sat in a charming tranquil attitude, but her lips and her eyes were constantly moving. She had a soft, slender, agreeable voice, and her tone was decidedly sociable. She gave Winterbourne a history of her movements and intentions, and those of her mother and brother, in Europe, and enumerated, in particular, the various hotels at which they had stopped. 'That English lady, in the cars,' she said—'Miss Featherstone—asked me if we didn't all live in hotels in America. I told her I had never been in so many hotels in my life as since I came to Europe. I have never seen so many—it's nothing but hotels.' But Miss Miller did not make this remark with a querulous accent; she appeared to be in the best humour with everything. She declared that the hotels were very good, when once you got used to their ways, and that Europe was perfectly sweet. She was not disappointed—not a bit. Perhaps it was because she had heard so much about it before. She had ever so many intimate friends that had been there ever so many times. And then she had had ever so many dresses and things from Paris. Whenever she put on a Paris dress she felt as if she were in Europe.

'It was a kind of a wishing-cap,' said Winterbourne.

'Yes,' said Miss Miller, without examining this analogy; 'it always made me wish I was here. But I needn't have done that for dresses. I am sure they send all the pretty ones to America; you see the most frightful things here. The only thing I don't like,' she proceeded, 'is the society. There isn't any society; or, if there is, I don't know where it keeps itself. Do you? I suppose there is some society somewhere, but I haven't seen anything of it. I'm very fond of society, and I have always had a great deal of it. I don't mean only in Schenectady, but in New York. I used to go to New York every winter. In New York I had lots of society. Last winter I had seventeen dinners given me; and three of them were by gentlemen,' added Daisy Miller. 'I have more friends in New York than in Schenectady—more gentleman friends; and more young lady friends too,' she resumed in a moment. She paused again for an instant; she was looking at Winterbourne with all her prettiness in her lively eyes and in her light, slightly monotonous smile. 'I have always had,' she said, 'a great deal of gentlemen's society.'

Poor Winterbourne was amused, perplexed, and decidedly charmed. He had never yet heard a young girl express herself in just this fashion; never, at least, save in cases where to say such things seemed a kind of demonstrative evidence of a certain laxity of deportment. And yet was he to accuse Miss Daisy Miller of actual or potential *inconduite*, as they said at Geneva? He felt that he had lived at Geneva so long that he had lost a good deal; he had become dishabituated to the American tone. Never, indeed, since he had grown old enough to appreciate things, had he encountered a young American girl of so pronounced a type as this. Certainly she was very charming, but how deucedly sociable! Was she simply a pretty girl from New York State —were they all like that, the pretty girls who had a good deal of gentlemen's society? Or was she also a designing, an audacious, an unscrupulous young person? Winterbourne had lost his instinct in this matter, and his reason could not help him. Miss Daisy Miller looked extremely innocent. Some people had told him that, after all, American girls were exceedingly innocent; and others had told him that, after all, they were not. He was inclined to think Miss Daisy Miller was a flirt—a pretty American flirt. He had never, as yet, had any relations with young ladies of this category. He had known, here in Europe, two or three women—persons older than Miss Daisy Miller, and provided, for respectability's sake, with husbands—who were great coquettes—dangerous, terrible women, with whom one's relations were liable to take a serious turn. But this young girl was not a coquette in that sense; she was very unsophisticated; she was only a pretty American flirt. Winterbourne was almost grateful for having found the formula that applied to Miss Daisy Miller. He leaned back in his seat; he remarked to himself that she had the most charming nose he had ever seen; he wondered what were the regular conditions and limitations of one's intercourse with a pretty American flirt. It presently became apparent that he was on the way to learn.

'Have you been to that old castle?' asked the young girl, pointing with her parasol to the far-gleaming walls of the Château de Chillon.

'Yes, formerly, more than once,' said Winterbourne. 'You too, I suppose, have seen it?'

'No; we haven't been there. I want to go there dreadfully. Of course I mean to go there. I wouldn't go away from here without having seen that old castle.'

'It's a very pretty excursion,' said Winterbourne, 'and very easy to make. You can drive, you know, or you can go by the little steamer.'

'You can go in the cars,' said Miss Miller.

'Yes; you can go in the cars,' Winterbourne assented.

'Our courier says they take you right up to the castle,' the young girl continued. 'We were going last week; but my mother gave out. She suffers dreadfully from dyspepsia. She said she couldn't go. Randolph wouldn't go either; he says he doesn't think much of old castles. But I guess we'll go this week, if we can get Randolph.'

'Your brother is not interested in ancient monuments?' Winterbourne inquired, smiling.

'He says he don't care much about old castles. He's only nine. He wants to stay at the hotel. Mother's afraid to leave him alone, and the courier won't stay with him; so we haven't been to many places. But it will be too bad if we don't go up there.' And Miss Miller pointed again at the Château de Chillon.

'I should think it might be arranged,' said Winterbourne. 'Couldn't you get some one to stay—for the afternoon—with Randolph?'

Miss Miller looked at him a moment; and then, very placidly—'I wish *you* would stay with him!' she said.

Winterbourne hesitated a moment. 'I should much rather go to Chillon with you.'

'With me?' asked the young girl, with the same placidity.

She didn't rise, blushing, as a young girl at Geneva would have done; and yet Winterbourne, conscious that he had been very bold, thought it possible she was offended. 'With your mother,' he answered very respectfully.

But it seemed that both his audacity and his respect were lost upon Miss Daisy Miller. 'I guess my mother won't go after all,' she said. 'She don't like to ride round in the afternoon. But did you really mean what you said just now; that you would like to go up there?'

'Most earnestly,' Winterbourne declared.

'Then we may arrange it. If mother will stay with Randolph, I guess Eugenio will.'

'Eugenio?' the young man inquired.

'Eugenio's our courier. He doesn't like to stay with Randolph; he's the most fastidious man I ever saw. But he's a splendid courier. I guess he'll stay at home with Randolph if mother does, and then we can go to the castle.'

Winterbourne reflected for an instant as lucidly as possible—'we' could only mean Miss Daisy Miller and himself. This programme seemed almost too agreeable for credence; he felt as if he ought to kiss the young lady's hand. Possibly he would have done so—and quite spoiled the project; but at this moment another person—presumably Eugenio—appeared. A tall, handsome man, with superb whiskers, wearing a velvet morning-coat and a brilliant watch-chain, approached Miss Miller, looking sharply at her companion. 'Oh, Eugenio!' said Miss Miller, with the friendliest accent.

Eugenio had looked at Winterbourne from head to foot; he now bowed gravely to the young lady. 'I have the honour to inform Mademoiselle that luncheon is upon the table.'

Miss Miller slowly rose. 'See here, Eugenio,' she said. 'I'm going to that old castle, any way.'

'To the Château de Chillon, Mademoiselle?' the courier inquired. 'Mademoiselle has made arrangements?' he added, in a tone which struck Winterbourne as very impertinent.

Eugenio's tone apparantly threw, even to Miss Miller's own apprehension, a slightly ironical light upon the young girl's situation. She turned to Winterbourne, blushing a little—a very little. 'You won't back out?' she said.

'I shall not be happy till we go!' he protested.

'And you are staying in this hotel?' she went on. 'And you are really an American?'

ourier stood looking at Winterbourne, offensively. The nan, at least, thought his manner of looking an offence to Iiller; it conveyed an imputation that she 'picked up' acquain- s. 'I shall have the honour of presenting to you a person who w tell you all about me,' he said smiling, and referring to his aunt.

'Oh, well, we'll go some day,' said Miss Miller. And she gave him a smile and turned away. She put up her parasol and walked back to the inn beside Eugenio. Winterbourne stood looking after her; and as she moved away, drawing her muslin furbelows over the gravel, said to himself that she had the *tournure* of a princess.

He had, however, engaged to do more than proved feasible, in promising to present his aunt, Mrs. Costello, to Miss Daisy Miller. As soon as the former lady had got better of her headache he waited upon her in her apartment; and, after the proper inquiries in regard to her health, he asked her if she had observed, in the hotel, an American family—a mamma, a daughter, and a little boy.

'And a courier?' said Mrs. Costello. 'Oh, yes, I have observed them. Seen them—heard them—and kept out of their way.' Mrs. Costello was a widow with a fortune; a person of much distinction, who frequently intimated that, if she were not so dreadfully liable to sick-headaches, she would probably have left a deeper impress upon her time. She had a long pale face, a high nose, and a great deal of very striking white hair, which she wore in large puffs and *rouleaux* over the top of her head. She had two sons married in New York, and another who was now in Europe. This young man was amusing himself at Hombourg, and, though he was on his travels, was rarely perceived to visit any particular city at the moment selected by his mother for her own appearance there. Her nephew, who had come up to Vevey expressly to see her, was therefore more attentive than those who, as she said, were nearer to her. He had imbibed at Geneva the idea that one must always be attentive to one's aunt. Mrs. Costello had not seen him for many years, and she was greatly pleased with him, manifesting her approbation by initiating him into many of the secrets of that social sway which, as she gave him to understand, she exerted in the American capital. She admitted that she was very exclusive; but, if he were acquainted with New York, he would see that one had to be. And her picture of the minutely hierarchical constitution of the society of that city, which she presented to him in many different lights, was, to Winterbourne's imagination, almost oppressively striking.

He immediately perceived, from her tone, that Miss Daisy Miller's place in the social scale was low. 'I am afraid you don't approve of them,' he said.

'They are very common,' Mrs. Costello declared. 'They are the sort of Americans that one does one's duty by not—not accepting.'

'Ah, you don't accept them?' said the young man.

'I can't, my dear Frederick. I would if I could, but I can't.'

'The young girl is very pretty,' said Winterbourne, in a moment.

'Of course she's pretty. But she is very common.'

'I see what you mean of course.' said Winterbourne, after another pause.

'She has that charming look that they all have,' his aunt resumed. 'I can't think where they pick it up; and she dresses in perfection—no, you don't know how well she dresses. I can't think where they get their taste.'

'But, my dear aunt, she is not, after all, a Comanche savage.'

'She is a young lady,' said Mrs. Costello, 'who has an intimacy with her mamma's courier.'

'An intimacy with the courier?' the young man demanded.

'Oh, the mother is just as bad! They treat the courier like a familiar friend—like a gentleman. I shouldn't wonder if he dines with them. Very likely they have never seen a man with such good manners, such fine clothes, so like a gentleman. He probably corresponds to the young lady's idea of a Count. He sits with them in the garden, in the evening. I think he smokes.'

Winterbourne listened with interest to these disclosures; they helped him to make up his mind about Miss Daisy. Evidently she was rather wild. 'Well,' he said, 'I am not a courier, and yet she was very charming to me.'

'You had better have said at first,' said Mrs. Costello with dignity, 'that you had made her acquaintance.'

'We simply met in the garden, and we talked a bit.'

'*Tout bonnement*! And pray what did you say?'

'I said I should take the liberty of introducing her to my admirable aunt.'

'I am much obliged to you.'

'It was to guarantee my respectability,' said Winterbourne.

'And pray who is to guarantee hers?'

'Ah, you are cruel!' said the young man. 'She's a very nice young girl.'

'You don't say that as if you believed it,' Mrs. Costello observed.

'She is completely uncultivated,' Winterbourne went on. 'But she is wonderfully pretty, and, in short, she is very nice. To prove that I believe it, I am going to take her to the Château de Chillon.'

'You two are going off there together? I should say it proved just the contrary. How long had you known her, may I ask, when this interesting project was formed? You haven't been twenty-four hours in the house.'

'I had known her half an hour!' said Winterbourne, smiling.

'Dear me!' cried Mrs. Costello. 'What a dreadful girl!'

Her nephew was silent for some moments. 'You really think, then,' he began, earnestly, and with a desire for trustworthy information—'you really think that—.' But he paused again.

'Think what, sir?' said his aunt.

'That she is the sort of young lady who expects a man—sooner or later—to carry her off?'

'I haven't the least idea what such young ladies expect a man to do. But I really think that you had better not meddle with little American girls that are uncultivated, as you call them. You have lived too long out of the country. You will be sure to make some great mistake. You are too innocent.'

'My dear aunt, I am not so innocent,' said Winterbourne, smiling and curling his moustache.

'You are too guilty, then!'

Winterbourne continued to curl his moustache, meditatively. 'You won't let the poor girl know you then?' he asked at last.

'Is it literally true that she is going to the Château de Chillon with you?'

'I think that she fully intends it.'

'Then, my dear Frederick,' said Mrs. Costello, 'I must decline the honour of her acquaintance. I am an old woman, but I am not too old—thank Heaven—to be shocked!'

'But don't they all do these things—the young girls in America?' Winterbourne inquired.

Mrs. Costello stared a moment. 'I should like to see my granddaughters do them!' she declared, grimly.

This seemed to throw some light upon the matter, for Winterbourne remembered to have heard that his pretty cousins in New York were 'tremendous flirts.' If, therefore, Miss Daisy Miller exceeded the liberal margin allowed to these young ladies, it was probable that anything might be expected of her. Winterbourne was impatient to see her again, and he was vexed with himself that, by instinct, he should not appreciate her justly.

Though he was impatient to see her, he hardly knew what he should say to her about his anut's refusal to become acquainted with her; but he discovered, promptly enough, that with Miss Daisy Miller there was no great need of walking on tiptoe. He found her that evening in the garden, wandering about in the warm starlight, like an indolent sylph, and swinging to and fro the largest fan he had ever beheld. It was ten o'clock. He had dined with his aunt, had been sitting with her since dinner, and had just taken leave of her till the morrow. Miss Daisy Miller seemed very glad to see him; she declared it was the longest she had ever passed.

'Have you been all alone?' he asked.

'I have been walking round with mother. But mother gets tired walking round,' she answered.

'Has she gone to bed?'

'No; she doesn't like to go to bed,' said the young girl. 'She doesn't sleep—not three hours. She says she doesn't know how she lives. She's dreadfully nervous. I guess she sleeps more than she thinks. She's gone somewhere after Randolph; she wants to try to get him to go to bed. He doesn't like to go to bed.'

'Let us hope she will persuade him,' observed Winterbourne.

'She will talk to him all she can; but he doesn't like her to talk to him.' said Miss Daisy, opening her fan. 'She's going to try to get Eugenio to talk to him. But he isn't afraid of Eugenio. Eugenio's a splendid courier, but he can't make much impression on Randolph! I don't believe he'll go to bed before eleven.' It appeared that Randolph's vigil was in fact triumphantly prolonged, for Winterbourne strolled about with the young girl for some time without meeting her mother. 'I have been looking round for that lady you want to introduce me to,' his companion resumed. 'She's your aunt.' Then, on Winterbourne's admitting the fact, and expressing some curiosity as to how she had learned it, she said she had heard all about Mrs. Costello from the chambermaid. She was very quiet and very *comme il faut*; she wore white puffs; she spoke to no one, and she never dined at the *table d'hôte*. Every two days she had a headache. 'I think that's a lovely description, headache and all!' said Miss Daisy, chattering along in her thin, gay voice. 'I want to know her ever so much. I know just what *your* aunt would be; I know I should like her. She would be very exclusive. I like a lady to be exclusive; I'm dying to be exclusive myself. Well, we *are* exclusive, mother and I. We don't speak to every one—or they don't speak to us. I suppose it's about the same thing. Any way, I shall be ever so glad to know your aunt.'

Winterbourne was embarrassed. 'She would be most happy,' he said; 'but I am afraid those headaches will interfere.'

The young girl looked at him through the dusk. 'But I suppose she doesn't have a headache every day,' she said, sympathetically.

Winterbourne was silent a moment. 'She tells me she does,' he answered at last—not knowing what to say.

Miss Daisy Miller stopped and stood looking at him. Her prettiness was still visible in the darkness; she was opening and closing her enormous fan. 'She doesnt want to know me!' she said, suddenly. 'Why don't you say so? You needn't be afraid. I'm not afraid!' And she gave a little laugh.

Winterbourne fancied there was a tremor in her voice; he was touched, shocked, mortified by it. 'My dear young lady,' he protested, 'she knows no one. It's her wretched health.'

The young girl walked on a few steps, laughing still. 'You needn't be afraid,' she repeated. 'Why should she want to know me?' Then she paused again; she was close to the parapet of the garden, and in front of her was the starlit lake. There was a vague sheen upon its surface, and in the distance were dimly-seen mountain forms. Daisy Miller looked out upon the mysterious prospect, and then she gave another little laugh. 'Gracious! she *is* exclusive!' she said. Winterbourne wondered whether she was seriously wounded, and for a moment almost wished that her sense of injury might be such as to make it becoming in him to attempt to reassure and comfort her. He had a pleasant sense that she would be very approachable for consolatory purposes. He felt then, for the instant, quite ready to sacrifice his aunt, conversationally; to admit that she was a proud, rude woman, and to declare that they needn't mind her. But before he had time to commit himself to this perilous mixture of gallantry and impiety, the young lady, resuming her walk, gave an exclamation in quite another tone. 'Well; here's mother! I guess she hasn't got Randolph to go to bed.' The figure of a lady appeared, at a distance, very indistinct in the darkness, and advancing with a slow and wavering movement. Suddenly it seemed to pause.

'Are you sure it is your mother? Can you distinguish her in this thick dusk?' Winterbourne asked.

'Well!' cried Miss Daisy Miller, with a laugh, 'I guess I know my own mother. And when she has got on my shawl, too! She is always wearing my things.'

The lady in question, ceasing to advance, hovered vaguely about the spot at which she had checked her steps.

'I am afraid your mother doesn't see you,' said Winterbourne. 'Or perhaps,' he added—thinking, with Miss Miller, the joke permissible —'perhaps she feels guilty about your shawl.'

'Oh, it's a fearful old thing!' the young girl replied, serenely. 'I told her she could wear it. She won't come here, because she sees you.'

'Ah, then,' said Winterbourne, 'I had better leave you.'

'Oh, no; come on!' urged Miss Daisy Miller.

'I'm afraid your mother doesn't approve of my walking with you.'

Miss Miller gave him a serious glance. 'It isn't for me; it's for you

—that is, it's for *her.* Well; I don't know who it's for! But mother doesn't like any of my gentlemen friends. She's right down timid. She always makes a fuss if I introduce a gentleman. But I *do* introduce them—almost always. If I didn't introduce my gentlemen friends to mother,' the young girl added, in her little soft, flat monotone, 'I shouldn't think I was natural.'

'To introduce me,' said Winterbourne, 'you must know my name.' And he proceeded to pronounce it.

'Oh, dear; I can't say all that!' said his companion, with a laugh. But by this time they had come up to Mrs. Miller, who, as they drew near, walked to the parapet of the garden and leaned upon it, looking intently at the lake, and turning her back to them. 'Mother!' said the young girl, in a tone of decision. Upon this the elder lady turned round. 'Mr. Winterbourne,' said Miss Daisy Miller, introducing the young man very frankly and prettily. 'Common' she was, as Mrs. Costello had pronounced her; yet it was a wonder to Winterbourne that, with her commonness, she had a singularly delicate grace.

Her mother was a small, spare, light person, with a wandering eye, a very exiguous nose, and a large forehead, decorated with a certain amount of thin, much-frizzled hair. Like her daughter, Mrs. Miller was dressed with extreme elegance; she had enormous diamonds in her ears. So far as Winterbourne could observe, she gave him no greeting—she certainly was not looking at him. Daisy was near her, pulling her shawl straight. 'What are you doing, poking round here?' this young lady inquired; but by no means with that harshness of accent which her choice of words may imply.

'I don't know,' said her mother, turning towards the lake again.

'I shouldn't think you'd want that shawl!' Daisy exclaimed.

'Well—I do!' her mother answered, with a little laugh.

'Did you get Randolph to go to bed?' asked the young girl.

'No; I couldn't induce him,' said Mrs. Miller, very gently. 'He wants to talk to the waiter. He likes to talk to that waiter.'

'I was telling Mr. Winterbourne,' the young girl went on; and to the young man's ear her tone might have indicated that she had been uttering his name all her life.

'Oh, yes!' said Winterbourne; 'I have the pleasure of knowing your son.'

Randolph's mamma was silent; she turned her attention to the lake. But at last she spoke. 'Well, I don't see how he lives!'

'Anyhow, it isn't so bad as it was at Dover,' said Daisy Miller.

'And what occurred at Dover?' Winterbourne asked.

'He wouldn't go to bed at all. I guess he sat up all night—in the public parlour. He wasn't in bed at twelve o'clock: I know that.'

'It was half-past twelve,' declared Mrs. Miller, with mild emphasis.

'Does he sleep much during the day?' Winterbourne demanded.

'I guess he doesn't sleep much,' Daisy rejoined.

'I wish he would!' said her mother. 'It seems as if he couldn't.'

'I think he's real tiresome,' Daisy pursued.

Then, for some moments, there was silence. 'Well, Daisy Miller,' said the elder lady, presently, 'I shouldn't think you'd want to talk against your own brother!'

'Well, he *is* tiresome, mother,' said Daisy, quite without the asperity of a retort.

'He's only nine,' urged Mrs. Miller.

'Well, he wouldn't go to that castle,' said the young girl. 'I'm going there with Mr. Winterbourne.'

To this announcement, very placidly made, Daisy's mamma offered no response. Winterbourne took for granted that she deeply disapproved of the projected excursion; but he said to himself that she was a simple, easily-managed person, and that a few deferential protestations would take the edge from her displeasure. 'Yes,' he began; 'your daughter has kindly allowed me the honour of being her guide.'

Mrs. Miller's wandering eyes attached themselves, with a sort of appealing air, to Daisy, who, however, strolled a few steps farther, gently humming to herself. 'I presume you will go in the cars,' said her mother.

'Yes; or in the boat,' said Winterbourne.

'Well, of course, I don't know,' Mrs. Miller rejoined. 'I have never been to the castle.'

'It is a pity you shouldn't go,' said Winterbourne, beginning to feel reassured as to her opposition. And yet he was quite prepared to find that, as a matter of course, she meant to accompany her daughter.

'We've been thinking ever so much about going,' she pursued; 'but it seems as if we couldn't. Of course Daisy—she wants to go round. But there's a lady here—I don't know her name—she says she shouldn't think we'd want to go to see castles *here*; she should think we'd want to wait till we got to Italy. It seems as if there would be so many there,' continued Mrs. Miller, with an air of increasing confidence. 'Of course, we only want to see the principal ones. We visited several in England,' she presently added.

'Ah, yes! in England there are beautiful castles,' said Winterbourne. 'But Chillon, here, is very well worth seeing.'

'Well, if Daisy feels up to it—,' said Mrs. Miller, in a tone impregnated with a sense of the magnitude of the enterprise. 'It seems as if there was nothing she wouldn't undertake.'

'Oh, I think she'll enjoy it!' Winterbourne declared. And he desired more and more to make it a certainty that he was to hav privilege of a *tête-à-tête* with the young lady, who was still strolli along in front of them, softly vocalizing. 'You are not disposed, madam,' he inquired, 'to undertake it yourself?'

Daisy's mother looked at him, an instant, askance, and then walked forward in silence. Then—'I guess she had better go alone,' she said, simply.

Winterbourne observed to himself that this was a very different type of maternity from that of the vigilant matrons who massed themselves in the forefront of social intercourse in the dark old city at the other end of the lake. But his meditations were interrupted by hearing his name very distinctly pronounced by Mrs. Miller's unprotected daughter.

'Mr. Winterbourne!' murmured Daisy.

'Mademoiselle!' said the young man.

'Don't you want to take me out in a boat?'

'At present?' he asked.

'Of course!' said Daisy.

'Well, Annie Miller!' exclaimed her mother.

'I beg you, madam, to let her go,' said Winterbourne, ardently; for he had never yet enjoyed the sensation of guiding through the summer starlight a skiff freighted with a fresh and beautiful young girl.

'I shouldn't think she'd want to,' said her mother. 'I should think she'd rather go indoors.'

'I'm sure Mr. Winterbourne wants to take me,' Daisy declared. 'He's so awfully devoted!'

'I will row you over to Chillon, in the starlight.'

'I don't believe it!' said Daisy.

'Well!' ejaculated the elder lady again.

'You haven't spoken to me for half an hour,' her daughter went on.

'I have been having some very pleasant conversation with your mother,' said Winterbourne.

'Well; I want you to take me out in a boat!' Daisy repeated. They had all stopped, and she had turned round and was looking at Winterbourne. Her face wore a charming smile, her pretty eyes were gleaming, she was swinging her great fan about. No; it's impossible to be prettier than that, thought Winterbourne.

'There are half a dozen boats moored at that landing-place,' he said, pointing to certain steps which descended from the garden to the lake. 'If you will do me the honour to accept my arm, we will go and select one of them.'

Daisy stood there smiling; she threw back her head and gave a little, light laugh. 'I like a gentleman to be formal!' she declared.

'I assure you it's a formal offer.'

'I was bound I would make you say something,' Daisy went on.

'You see it's not very difficult,' said Winterbourne. 'But I am afraid you are chaffing me.'

'I think not, sir,' remarked Mrs. Miller, very gently.

'Do, then, let me give you a row,' he said to the young girl.

'It's quite lovely, the way you say that!' cried Daisy.

'It will be still more lovely to do it.'

'Yes, it would be lovely!' said Daisy. But she made no movement to accompany him; she only stood there laughing.

'I should think you had better find out what time it is,' interposed her mother.

'It is eleven o'clock, madam,' said a voice, with a foreign accent, out of the neighbouring darkness; and Winterbourne, turning, perceived the florid personage who was in attendance upon the two ladies. He had apparently just approached.

'Oh, Eugenio,' said Daisy, 'I am going out in a boat!'

Eugenio bowed. 'At eleven o'clock, Mademoiselle?'

'I am going with Mr. Winterbourne. This very minute.'

'Do tell her she can't,' said Mrs. Miller to the courier.

'I think you had better not go out in a boat, Mademoiselle,' Eugenio declared.

Winterbourne wished to Heaven this pretty girl were not so familiar with her courier; but he said nothing.

I suppose you don't think it's proper!' Daisy exclaimed. 'Eugenio doesn't think anything's proper.'

'I am at your service,' said Winterbourne.

'Does Mademoiselle propose to go alone?' asked Eugenio of Mrs. Miller.

'Oh, no; with this gentleman!' answered Daisy's mamma.

The courier looked for a moment at Winterbourne—the latter thought he was smiling—and then, solemnly, with a bow, 'As Mademoiselle pleases!' he said.

'Oh, I hoped you would make a fuss!' said Daisy. 'I don't care to go now.'

'I myself shall make a fuss if you don't go,' said Winterbourne.

'That's all I want—a little fuss!' And the young girl began to laugh again.

'Mr. Randolph has gone to bed!' the courier announced, frigidly.

'Oh, Daisy; now we can go!' said Mrs. Miller.

Daisy turned away from Winterbourne, looking at him, smiling, and fanning herself. 'Good-night,' she said; 'I hope you are disappointed, or disgusted, or something!'

He looked at her, taking the hand she offered him. 'I am puzzled,' he answered.

'Well; I hope it won't keep you awake!' she said, very smartly; and, under the escort of the privileged Eugenio, the two ladies passed towards the house.

Winterbourne stood looking after them; he was indeed puzzled. He lingered beside the lake for a quarter of an hour, turning over the mystery of the young girl's sudden familiarities and caprices. But the only very definite conclusion he came to was that he should enjoy deucedly 'going off' with her somewhere.

Two days afterwards he went off with her to the Castle of Chillon. He waited for her in the large hall of the hotel, where the couriers, the servants, the foreign tourists were lounging about and staring. It was not the place he should have chosen, but she had appointed it. She came tripping downstairs, buttoning her long gloves, squeezing her folded parasol against her pretty figure, dressed in the perfection of a soberly elegant travelling-costume. Winterbourne was a man of imagination and, as our ancestors used to say, sensibility; as he looked at her dress and, on the great staircase, her little rapid, confiding step, he felt as if there were something romantic going forward. He could have believed he was going to elope with her. He passed out with her among all the idle people that were assembled there; they were all looking at her very hard; she had begun to chatter as soon as she joined him. Winterbourne's preference had been that they should be conveyed to Chillon in a carriage; but she expressed a lively wish to go in the little steamer; she declared that she had a passion for steamboats. There was always such a lovely breeze upon the water, and you saw such lots of people. The sail was not long, but Winterbourne's companion found time to say a great many things. To the young man himself their little excursion was so much of an escapade—an adventure—that, even allowing for her habitual sense of freedom, he had some expectation of seeing her regard it in the same way. But it must be confessed that, in this particular, he was disappointed. Daisy Miller was extremely animated, she was in charming spirits; but she was apparently not at all excited; she was not fluttered; she avoided neither his eyes nor those of any one else; she blushed neither when she looked at him nor when she felt that people were looking at her. People continued to look at her a great deal, and Winterbourne took much satisfaction in his pretty companion's distinguished air. He had been a little afraid that she would talk loud, laugh overmuch, and even, perhaps, desire to move about the boat a d deal. But he quite forgot his fears; he sat smiling, with his eyes pon her face, while, without moving from her place, she delivered erself of a great number of original reflections. It was the most charming garrulity he had ever heard. He had assented to the idea that she was 'common,' but was she so, after all, or was he simply getting used to her commonness? Her conversation was chiefly of what metaphysicians term the objective cast; but every now and then it took a subjective turn.

'What on *earth* are you so grave about?' she suddenly demanded, fixing her agreeable eyes upon Winterbourne's.

'Am I grave?' he asked. 'I had an idea I was grinning from ear to ear.'

'You look as if you were taking me to a funeral. If that's a grin, your ears are very near together.'

'Should you like me to dance a hornpipe on the deck?'

'Pray do, and I'll carry round your hat. It will pay the expenses of our journey.'

'I never was better pleased in my life,' murmured Winterbourne.

She looked at him a moment, and then burst into a little laugh. 'I like to make you say those things! You're a queer mixture!'

In the castle, after they had landed, the subjective element decidedly prevailed. Daisy tripped about the vaulted chambers, rustled her skirts in the corkscrew staircases, flirted back with a pretty little cry and a shudder from the edge of the *oubliettes*, and turned a singularly well-shaped ear to everything Winterbourne told her about the place. But he saw that she cared very little for feudal antiquities, and that the dusky traditions of Chillon made but a slight impression upon her. They had the good fortune to have been able to walk about without other companionship than that of the custodian; and Winterbourne arranged with this functionary that they should not be hurried —that they should linger and pause wherever they chose. The custodian interpreted the bargain generously—Winterbourne, on his side, had been generous—and ended by leaving them quite to themselves. Miss Miller's observations were not remarkable for logical consistency; for anything she wanted to say she was sure to find a pretext. She found a great many pretexts in the rugged embrasures of Chillon for asking Winterbourne sudden questions about himself—his family, his previous history, his tastes, his habits, his intentions—and for supplying information upon corresponding points in her own personality. Of her own tastes, habits, and intentions Miss Miller was prepared to give the most definite, and indeed the most favourable, account.

'Well; I hope you know enough!' she said to her companion, after he had told her the history of the unhappy Bonivard. 'I never saw man that knew so much!' The history of Bonivard had evidently, as they say, gone into one ear and out of the other. But Daisy went on to say that she wished Winterbourne would travel with them and 'go round' with them; they might know something, in that case. 'Don't you want to come and teach Randolph?' she asked. Winterbourne said that nothing could possibly please him so much; but that he had unfortunately other occupations. 'Other occupations? I don't believe it!' said Miss Daisy. 'What do you mean? You are not in business.' The young man admitted that he was not in business; but he had engagements which, even within a day or two, would force him to go back to Geneva. 'Oh, bother!' she said: 'I don't believe it!' and she began to talk about something else. But a few moments later, when he was pointing out to her the pretty design of an antique fireplace, she broke out irrelevantly, 'You don't mean to say you are going back to Geneva?'

'It is a melancholy fact that I shall have to return to Geneva tomorrow.'

'Well, Mr. Winterbourne,' said Daisy; 'I think you're horrid!'

'Oh, don't say such dreadful things!' said Winterbourne—'just at the last!'

'The last!' cried the young girl; 'I call it the first. I have half a mind to leave you here and go straight back to the hotel alone.' And for the next ten minutes she did nothing but call him horrid. Poor Winterbourne was fairly bewildered; no young lady had as yet done him the honour to be so agitated by the announcement of his movements. His companion, after this, ceased to pay any attention to the curiosities of Chillon or the beauties of the lake; she opened fire upon the mysterious charmer in Geneva whom she appeared to have instantly taken it for granted that he was hurrying back to see. How did Miss Daisy Miller know that there was a charmer in Geneva? Winterbourne, who denied the existence of such a person, was quite unable to discover; and he was divided between amazement at the rapidity of her induction and amusement at the frankness of her *persiflage*. She seemed to him, in all this, an extraordinary mixture of innocence and crudity. 'Does she never allow you more than three days at a time?' asked Daisy, ironically. 'Doesn't she give you a vacation in summer? There's no one so hard worked but they can get leave to go off somewhere at this season. I suppose, if you stay another day, she'll come after you in the boat. Do wait over till Friday, and I will go down to the landing to see her arrive!' Winterbourne began to think he had been wrong to feel disappointed in the temper in which the young lady had embarked. If he had missed the personal accent, the personal accent was now making its appearance. It sounded very distinctly, at last, in her telling him she would stop 'teasing' him if he would promise her solemnly to come down to Rome in the winter.

'That's not a difficult promise to make,' said Winterbourne. 'My aunt has taken an apartment in Rome for the winter, and has already asked me to come and see her.'

'I don't want you to come for your aunt,' said Daisy; 'I want you to come for me.' And this was the only allusion that the young man was ever to hear her make to his invidious kinswoman. He declared that, at any rate, he would certainly come. After this Daisy stopped teasing. Winterbourne took a carriage, and they drove back to Vevey in the dusk; the young girl was very quiet.

In the evening Winterbourne mentioned to Mrs. Costello that he had spent the afternoon at Chillon, with Miss Daisy Miller.

'The Americans—of the courier?' asked this lady.

'Ah, happily,' said Winterbourne, 'the courier stayed at home.'

'She went with you all alone?'

'All alone.'

Mrs. Costello sniffed a little at her smelling-bottle. 'And that,' she exclaimed, 'is the young person whom you wanted me to know!'

PART II

Winterbourne, who had returned to Geneva the day after his excursion to Chillon, went to Rome towards the end of January. His aunt had been established there for several weeks, and he had received a couple of letters from her. 'Those people you were so devoted to last summer at Vevey have turned up here, courier and all,' she wrote. 'They seem to have made several acquaintances, but the courier continues to be the most *intime*. The young lady, however, is also very intimate with some third-rate Italians, with whom she rackets about in a way that makes much talk. Bring me that pretty novel of Cherbuliez's—*Paule Méré*—and don't come later than the 23rd.'

In the natural course of events, Winterbourne, on arriving in Rome, would presently have ascertained Mrs. Miller's address at the American banker's, and have gone to pay his compliments to Miss Daisy. 'After what happened at Vevey I think I may certainly call upon them,' he said to Mrs. Costello.

'If, after what happens—at Vevey and everywhere—you desire to keep up the acquaintance, you are very welcome. Of course a man may know every one. Men are welcome to the privilege!'

'Pray what is it that happens—here, for instance?' Winterbourne demanded.

'The girl goes about alone with her foreigners. As to what happ further, you must apply elsewhere for information. She has pic up half-a-dozen of the regular Roman fortune-hunters, and she takes them about to people's houses. When she comes to a party she brings with her a gentleman with a good deal of manner and a wonderful moustache.'

'And where is the mother?'

'I haven't the least idea. They are very dreadful people.'

Winterbourne meditated a moment. 'They are very ignorant—very innocent only. Depend upon it they are not bad.'

'They are hopelessly vulgar,' said Mrs. Costello. 'Whether or no being hopelessly vulgar is being "bad" is a question for the metaphysicians. They are bad enough to dislike, at any rate; and for this short life that is quite enough.'

The news that Daisy Miller was surrounded by half-a-dozen wonderful moustaches checked Winterbourne's impulse to go straightway to see her. He had perhaps not definitely flattered himself that he had made an ineffaceable impression upon her heart, but he was annoyed at hearing of a state of affairs so little in harmony with an image of a very pretty girl looking out of an old Roman window and asking herself urgently when Mr. Winterbourne would arrive. If, however, he determined to wait a little before reminding Miss Miller of his claims to her consideration, he went very soon to call upon two or three other friends. One of these friends was an American lady who had spent several winters at Geneva, where she had placed her children at school. She was a very accomplished woman, and she lived in the Via Gregoriana. Winterbourne found her in a little crimson drawing-room, on a third floor; the room was filled with southern sunshine. He had not been there ten minutes when the servant came in, announcing 'Madame Mila!' This announcement was presently followed by the entrance of little Randolph Miller, who stopped in the middle of the room and stood staring at Winterbourne. An instant later his pretty sister crossed the threshold; and then, after a considerable interval, Mrs. Miller slowly advanced.

'I know you!' said Randolph.

'I'm sure you know a great many things,' exclaimed Winterbourne, taking him by the hand. 'How is your education coming on?'

Daisy was exchanging greetings very prettily with her hostess; but when she heard Winterbourne's voice she quickly turned her head. 'Well, I declare!' she said.

'I told you I should come, you know,' Winterbourne rejoined, smiling.

'Well—I didn't believe it,' said Miss Daisy.

'I am much obliged to you,' laughed the young man.

'You might have come to see me!' said Daisy.

'I arrived only yesterday.'

'I don't believe that!' the young girl declared.

Winterbourne turned with a protesting smile to her mother; but this lady evaded his glance, and, seating herself, fixed her eyes upon her son. 'We've got a bigger place than this,' said Randolph. 'It's all gold on the walls.'

Mrs. Miller turned uneasily in her chair. 'I told you if I was to bring you, you would say something!' she murmured.

'I told *you*!' Randolph exclaimed. 'I tell *you*, sir!' he added jocosely, giving Winterbourne a thump on the knee. 'It *is* bigger, too!'

Daisy had entered upon a lively conversation with her hostess; Winterbourne judged it becoming to address a few words to her mother. 'I hope you have been well since we parted at Vevey,' he said.

Mrs. Miller now certainly looked at him—at his chin. 'Not very well, sir,' she answered.

'She's got the dyspepsia,' said Randolph. 'I've got it too. Father's got it. I've got it most!'

This announcement, instead of embarrassing Mrs. Miller, seemed to relieve her. 'I suffer from the liver,' she said. 'I think it's this climate; it's less bracing than Schenectady, especially in the winter season. I don't know whether you know we reside at Schenectady. I was saying to Daisy that I certainly hadn't found anyone like Dr. Davis, and I didn't believe I should. Oh, at Schenectady, he stands first; they think everything of him. He has so much to do, and yet there was nothing he wouldn't do for me. He said he never saw anything like my dyspepsia, but he was bound to cure it. I'm sure there was nothing he wouldn't try. He was just going to try something new when we came off. Mr. Miller wanted Daisy to see Europe herself. But I wrote to Mr. Miller that it seems as if I couldn't get on without Dr. Davis. At Schenectady he stands at the very top; and there's a great deal of sickness there, too. It affects my sleep.'

Winterbourne had a good deal of pathological gossip with Dr. Davis's patient, during which Daisy chattered unremittingly to her own companion. The young man asked Mrs. Miller how she was pleased with Rome. 'Well, I must say I am disappointed,' she answered. 'We had heard so much about it; I suppose we had heard too much. But we couldn't help that. We had been led to expect something different.'

'Ah, wait a little, and you will become very fond of it,' said Winterbourne.

'I hate it worse and worse every day!' cried Randolph.

'You are like the infant Hannibal,' said Winterbourne.

'No, I ain't!' Randolph declared, at a venture.

'You are not much like an infant,' said his mother. 'But we have seen places,' she resumed, 'that I should put a long way before Rome.' And in reply to Winterbourne's interrogation, 'There's Zurich,' she concluded; 'I think Zurich is lovely; and we hadn't heard half so much about it.'

'The best place we've seen is the City of Richmond!' said Randolph.

'He means the ship,' his mother explained. 'We crossed in that ship. Randolph had a good time on the City of Richmond.'

'It's the best place I've seen,' the child repeated. 'Only it was turned the wrong way.'

'Well, we've got to turn the right way some time,' said Mrs. Miller, with a little laugh. Winterbourne expressed the hope that her daughter at least found some gratification in Rome, and she declared that Daisy was quite carried away. 'It's on account of the society—the society's splendid. She goes round everywhere; she has made a great number of acquaintances. Of course she goes round more than I do. I must say they have been very sociable; they have taken her right in. And then she knows a great many gentlemen. Oh, she thinks there's nothing like Rome. Of course, it's a great deal pleasanter for a young lady if she knows plenty of gentlemen.'

By this time Daisy had turned her attention again to Winterbourne. 'I've been telling Mrs. Walker how mean you were!' the young girl announced.

'And what is the evidence you have offered?' asked Winterbourne, rather annoyed at Miss Miller's want of appreciation of the zeal of an admirer who on his way down to Rome had stopped neither at Bologna nor at Florence, simply because of a certain sentimental impatience. He remembered that a cynical compatriot had once told him that American women—the pretty ones, and this gave a largeness to the axiom—were at once the most exacting in the world and the least endowed with a sense of indebtedness.

'Why, you were awfully mean at Vevey,' said Daisy. 'You wouldn't do anything. You wouldn't stay there when I asked you.'

'My dearest young lady,' cried Winterbourne, with eloquence, 'have I come all the way to Rome to encounter your reproaches?'

'Just hear him say that!' said Daisy to her hostess, giving a twist to a bow on this lady's dress. 'Did you ever hear anything so quaint?'

'So quaint, my dear?' murmured Mrs. Walker, in the tone of a partisan of Winterbourne.

'Well, I don't know,' said Daisy, fingering Mrs. Walker's ribbons. 'Mrs. Walker, I want to tell you something.'

'Motherr,' interposed Randolph, with his rough ends to his words, 'I tell you you've got to go. Eugenio'll raise something!'

'I'm not afraid of Eugenio,' said Daisy, with a toss of her head. 'Look here, Mrs. Walker,' she went on, 'you know I'm coming to your party.'

'I am delighted to hear it.'

'I've got a lovely dress.'

'I am very sure of that.'

'But I want to ask a favour—permission to bring a friend.'

'I shall be happy to see any of your friends,' said Mrs. Walker, turning with a smile to Mrs. Miller.

'Oh, they are not my friends,' answered Daisy's mamma, smiling shyly, in her own fashion. 'I never spoke to them!'

'It's an intimate friend of mine—Mr. Giovanelli,' said Daisy, without a tremor in her clear little voice or a shadow on her brilliant little face.

Mrs. Walker was silent a moment she gave a rapid glance at Winterbourne. 'I shall be glad to see Mr. Giovanelli,' she then said.

'He's an Italian,' Daisy pursued, with the prettiest serenity. 'He's a great friend of mine—he's the handsomest man in the world—except Mr. Winterbourne! He knows plenty of Italians, but he wants to know some Americans. He thinks ever so much of Americans. He's tremendously clever. He's perfectly lovely!'

It was settled that this brilliant personage should be brought to Mrs. Walker's party, and then Mrs. Miller prepared to take her leave. 'I guess we'll go back to the hotel,' she said.

'You may go back to the hotel, mother, but I'm going to take a walk,' said Daisy.

'She's going to walk with Mr. Giovanelli,' Randolph proclaimed.

'I am going to the Pincio,' said Daisy, smiling.

'Alone, my dear—at this hour?' Mrs. Walker asked. The afternoon was drawing to a close—it was the hour for the throng of carriages and of contemplative pedestrians. 'I don't think it's safe, my dear,' said Mrs. Walker.

'Neither do I,' subjoined Mrs. Miller. 'You'll get the fever as sure as you live. Remember what Dr. Davis told you!'

'Give her some medicine before she goes,' said Randolph.

The company had risen to its feet; Daisy, still showing her pretty teeth, bent over and kissed her hostess. 'Mrs. Walker, you are too perfect,' she said. 'I'm not going alone; I am going to meet a friend.'

'Your friend won't keep you from getting the fever,' Mrs. Miller observed.

'Is it Mr. Giovanelli?' asked the hostess.

Winterbourne was watching the young girl; at this question his attention quickened. She stood there smiling and smoothing her bonnet ribbons; she glanced at Winterbourne. Then, while she glanced and smiled, she answered without a shade of hesitation, 'Mr. Giovanelli—the beautiful Giovanelli.'

'My dear young friend,' said Mrs. Walker, taking her hand, pleadingly, 'don't walk off to the Pincio at this hour to meet a beautiful Italian.'

'Well, he speaks English,' said Mrs. Miller.

'Gracious me!' Daisy exclaimed, 'I don't want to do anything improper. There's an easy way to settle it.' She continued to glance at Winterbourne. 'The Pincio is only a hundred yards distant, and if Mr. Winterbourne were as polite as he pretends he would offer to walk with me!'

Winterbourne's politeness hastened to affirm itself, and the young girl gave him a gracious leave to accompany her. They passed downstairs before her mother, and at the door Winterbourne perceived Mrs. Miller's carriage drawn up, with the ornamental courier whose acquaintance he had made at Vevey seated within. 'Good-bye, Eugenio!' cried Daisy, 'I'm going to take a walk.' The distance from the Via Gregoriana to the beautiful garden at the other end of the Pincian Hill is, in fact, rapidly traversed. As the day was splendid, however, and the concourse of vehicles, walkers, and loungers numerous, the young Americans found their progress much delayed. This fact was highly agreeable to Winterbourne, in spite of his consciousness of his singular situation. The slow-moving, idly-gazing Roman crowd bestowed much attention upon the extremely pretty young foreign lady who was passing through it upon his arm; and he wondered what on earth had been in Daisy's mind when she proposed to expose herself, unattended, to its appreciation. His own mission, to her sense, apparently, was to consign her to the hands of Mr. Giovanelli; but Winterbourne, at once annoyed and gratified, resolved that he would do no such thing.

'Why haven't you been to see me?' asked Daisy. 'You can't get out of that.'

'I have had the honour of telling you that I have only just stepped out of the train.'

'You must have stayed in the train a good while after it stopped!' cried the young girl, with her little lauagh. 'I suppose you were asleep. You have had time to go to see Mrs. Walker.'

'I knew Mrs. Walker—' Winterbourne began to explain.

'I know where you knew her. You knew her at Geneva. She told me so. Well, you knew me at Vevey. That's just as good. So you ought to have come.' She asked him no other question than this; she began to prattle about her own affairs. 'We've got splendid rooms at the hotel; Eugenio says they're the best rooms in Rome. We are going to stay all winter—if we don't die of the fever; and I guess we'll stay then. It's a great deal nicer than I thought; I thought it would be fearfully quiet; I was sure it would be awfully poky. I was sure we should be going round all the time with one of those dreadful old men that explain about the pictures and things. But we only had about a week of that, and now I'm enjoying myself. I know ever so many people, and they are all so charming. The society's extremely select. There are all kinds—English, and Germans, and Italians. I think I like the English best. I like their style of conversation. But there are some lovely Americans. I never saw anything so hospitable. There's something or other every day. There's not much dancing; but I must say I never thought dancing was everything. I was always fond of conversation. I guess I shall have plenty at Mrs. Walker's—her rooms are so small.' When they had passed the gate of the Pincian Gardens, Miss Miller began to wonder where Mr. Giovanelli might be. 'We had better go straight to that place in front,' she said, 'where you look at the view.'

'I certainly shall not help you to find him,' Winterbourne declared.

'Then I shall find him without you,' said Miss Daisy.

'You certainly won't leave me!' cried Winterbourne.

She burst into her little laugh. 'Are you afraid you'll get lost—or run over? But there's Giovanelli, leaning against that tree. He's staring at the women in the carriages: did you ever see anything so cool?'

Winterbourne perceived at some distance a little man standing with folded arms, nursing his cane. He had a handsome face, an artfully poised hat, a glass in one eye and a nosegay in his button-hole. Winterbourne looked at him a moment and then said, 'Do you mean to speak to that man?'

'Do I mean to speak to him? Why, you don't suppose I mean to communicate by signs?'

'Pray understand, then,' said Winterbourne, 'that I intend to remain with you.'

Daisy stopped and looked at him, without a sign of troubled consciousness in her face; with nothing but the presence of her charming eyes and her happy dimples. 'Well, she's a cool one!' thought the young man.

'I don't like the way you say that,' said Daisy. 'It's too imperio

'I beg your pardon if I say it wrong. The main point is to give y an idea of my meaning.'

The young girl looked at him more gravely, but with eyes that were prettier than ever. 'I have never allowed a gentleman to dictate to me, or to interfere with anything I do.'

'I think you have made a mistake,' said Winterbourne. 'You should sometimes listen to a gentleman—the right one.'

Daisy began to laugh again. 'I do nothing but listen to gentlemen!' she exclaimed. 'Tell me if Mr. Giovanelli is the right one?'

The gentleman with the nosegay in his bosom had now perceived our two friends, and was approaching the young girl with obsequious rapidity. He bowed to Winterbourne as well as to the latter's companion; he had a brilliant smile, an intelligent eye; Winterbourne thought him not a bad-looking fellow. But he nevertheless said to Daisy—'No, he's not the right one.'

Daisy evidently had a natural talent for performing introductions; she mentioned the name of each of her companions to the other. She strolled along with one of them on each side of her; Mr. Giovanelli, who spoke English very cleverly—Winterbourne afterwards learned that he had practised the idiom upon a great many American heiresses—addressed her a great deal of very polite nonsense; he was extremely urbane, and the young American, who said nothing, reflected upon that profundity of Italian cleverness which enables people to appear more gracious in proportion as they are more acutely disappointed. Giovanelli, of course, had counted upon something more intimate; he had not bargained for a party of three. But he kept his temper in a manner which suggested far-stretching intentions. Winterbourne flattered himself that he had taken his measure. 'He is not a gentleman,' said the young American; 'he is only a clever imitation of one. He is a music-master, or a penny-a-liner, or a third-rate artist. Damn his good looks!' Mr. Giovanelli had certainly a very pretty face; but Winterbourne felt a superior indignation at his own lovely fellow-countrywoman's not knowing the difference between a spurious gentleman and a real one. Giovanelli chattered and jested and made himself wonderfully agreeable. It was true that if he was an imitation the imitation was brilliant. 'Nevertheless,' Winterbourne said to himself, 'a nice girl ought to know!' And then he came back to the question whether this was in fact a nice girl. Would a nice girl—even allowing for her being a little American flirt—make a rendezvous with a presumably low-lived foreigner? The rendezvous in this case, indeed, had been in broad daylight, and in the most crowded corner of Rome; but was it not impossible to regard the choice of these circumstances as a proof of extreme cynicism? Singular though it may seem, Winterbourne was vexed that the young girl, in joining her *amoroso*, should not appear more impatient of his own company, and he was vexed because of his inclination. It was impossible to regard her as a perfectly well-conducted young lady; she was wanting in a certain indispensable delicacy. It would therefore simplify matters greatly to be able to treat her as the object of one of those sentiments which are called by romancers 'lawless passions.' That she should seem to wish to get rid of him would help him to think more lightly of her, and to be able to think more lightly of her would make her much less perplexing. But Daisy, on this occasion, continued to present herself as an inscrutable combination of audacity and innocence.

She had been walking some quarter of an hour, attended by her two cavaliers, and responding in a tone of very childish gaiety, as it seemed to Winterbourne, to the pretty speeches of Mr. Giovanelli, when a carriage that had detached itself from the revolving train drew up beside the path. At the same moment Winterbourne perceived that his friend Mrs. Walker—the lady whose house he had lately left—was seated in the vehicle and was beckoning to him. Leaving Miss Miller's side, he hastened to obey her summons. Mrs. Walker was flushed; she wore an excited air. 'It is really too dreadful,' she said. 'That girl must not do this sort of thing. She must not walk here with you two men. Fifty people have noticed her.'

Winterbourne raised his eyebrows. 'I think it's a pity to make too much fuss about it.'

'It's a pity to let the girl ruin herself!'

'She is very innocent,' said Winterbourne.

'She's very crazy!' cried Mrs. Walker. 'Did you ever see anything so imbecile as her mother? After you had all left me, just now, I could not sit still for thinking of it. It seemed too pitiful, not even to attempt to save her. I ordered the carriage and put on my bonnet, and came here as quickly as possible. Thank heaven, I have found you!'

'What do you propose to do with us?' asked Winterbourne, smiling.

'To ask her to get in, to drive her about here for half-an-hour, so that the world may see she is not running absolutely wild, and then to take her safely home.'

'I don't think it's a very happy thought,' said Winterbourne; 'but you can try.'

Mrs. Walker tried. The young man went in pursuit of Miss Miller, who had simply nodded and smiled at his interlocutor in the carriage, and had gone her way with her companion. Daisy, on learning that

Mrs. Walker wished to speak to her, retraced her steps with a pe good grace and with Mr. Giovanelli at her side. She declared that sh was delighted to have a chance to present this gentleman to Mrs. Walker. She immediately achieved the introduction, and declared that she had never in her life seen anything so lovely as Mrs. Walker's carriage-rug.

'I am glad you admire it,' said this lady, smiling sweetly. 'Will you get in and let me put it over you?'

'Oh, no, thank you,' said Daisy. 'I shall admire it much more as I see you driving round with it.'

'Do get in and drive with me,' said Mrs. Walker.

'That would be charming, but it's so enchanting just as I am!' and Daisy gave a brilliant glance at the gentlemen on either side of her.

'It may be enchanting, dear child, but it is not the custom here,' urged Mrs. Walker, leaning forward in her victoria with her hands devoutly clasped.

'Well, it ought to be, then!' said Daisy. 'If I didn't walk I should expire.'

'You should walk with your mother, dear,' cried the lady from Geneva, losing patience.

'With my mother dear!' exclaimed the young girl. Winterbourne saw that she scented interference. 'My mother never walked ten steps in her life. And then, you know,' she added with a laugh, 'I am more than five years old.'

'You are old enough to be more reasonable. You are old enough, dear Miss Miller, to be talked about.'

Daisy looked at Mrs. Walker, smiling intensely. 'Talked about? What do you mean?'

'Come into my carriage and I will tell you.'

Daisy turned her quickened glance again from one of the gentlemen beside her to the other. Mr. Giovanelli was bowing to and fro, rubbing down his gloves and laughing very agreeably; Winterbourne thought it a most unpleasant scene. 'I don't think I want to know what you mean,' said Daisy presently. 'I don't think I should like it.'

Winterbourne wished that Mrs. Walker would tuck in her carriage-rug and drive away; but this lady did not enjoy being defied, as she afterwards told him. 'Should you prefer being thought a very reckless girl?' she demanded.

'Gracious!' exclaimed Daisy. She looked again at Mr. Giovanelli, then she turned to Winterbourne. There was a little pink flush in her cheek; she was tremendously pretty. 'Does Mr. Winterbourne think,' she asked slowly, smiling, throwing back her head and glancing at him from head to foot, 'that—to save my reputation—I ought to get into the carriage?'

Winterbourne coloured; for an instant he hesitated greatly. It seemed so strange to hear her speak that way of her 'reputation.' But he himself, in fact, must speak in accordance with gallantry. The finest gallantry, here, was simply to tell her the truth; and the truth, for Winterbourne, as the few indications I have been able to give have made him known to the reader, was that Daisy Miller should take Mrs. Walker's advice. He looked at her exquisite prettiness; and then he said very gently, 'I think you should get into the carriage.'

Daisy gave a violent laugh. 'I never heard anything so stiff! If this is improper, Mrs. Walker,' she pursued, 'then I am all improper, and you must give me up. Good-bye; I hope you'll have a lovely ride!' and, with Mr. Giovanelli, who made a triumphantly obsequious salute, she turned away.

Mrs. Walker sat looking after her, and there were tears in Mrs. Walker's eyes. 'Get in here, sir,' she said to Winterbourne, indicating the place beside her. The young man answered that he felt bound to accompany Miss Miller; whereupon Mrs. Walker declared that if he refused her this favour she would never speak to him again. She was evidently in earnest. Winterbourne overtook Daisy and her companion and, offering the young girl his hand, told her that Mrs. Walker had made an imperious claim upon his society. He expected that in answer she would say something rather free, something to commit herself still further to that 'recklessness' from which Mrs. Walker had so charitably endeavoured to dissuade her. But she only shook his hand, hardly looking at him; while Mr. Giovanelli bade him farewell with a too-emphatic flourish of the hat.

Winterbourne was not in the best possible humour as he took his seat in Mrs. Walker's victoria. 'That was not clever of you,' he said candidly, while the vehicle mingled again with the throng of carriages.

'In such a case,' his companion answered, 'I don't wish to be clever, I wish to be *earnest*!'

'Well, your earnestness has only offended her and put her off.'

'It has happened very well,' said Mrs. Walker. 'If she is so perfectly determined to compromise herself, the sooner one knows it the better; one can act accordingly.'

'I suspect she meant no harm,' Winterbourne rejoined.

'So I thought a month ago. But she has been going too far.'

'What has she been doing?'

'Everything that is not done here. Flirting with any man she could pick up; sitting in corners with mysterious Italians; dancing all the evening with the same partners; receiving visits at eleven o'clock at night. Her mother goes away when visitors come.'

'But her brother,' said Winterbourne, laughing, 'sits up till midnight.'

'He must be edified by what he sees. I'm told that at their hotel every one is talking about her, and that a smile goes round among all the servants when a gentleman comes and asks for Miss Miller.'

'The servants be hanged!' said Winterbourne angrily. 'The poor girl's only fault,' he presently added, 'is that she is very uncultivated.'

'She is naturally indelicate,' Mrs. Walker declared. 'Take that example this morning. How long had you known her at Vevey?'

'A couple of days.'

'Fancy, then, her making it a personal matter that you should have left the place!'

Winterbourne was silent for some moments, then he said, 'I suspect, Mrs. Walker, that you and I have lived too long at Geneva!' And he added a request that she should inform him with what particular design she had made him enter her carriage.

'I wished to beg you to cease your relations with Miss Miller—not to flirt with her—to give her no further opportunity to expose herself—to let her alone, in short.'

'I'm afraid I can't do that,' said Winterbourne. 'I like her extremely.'

'All the more reason that you shouldn't help her to make a scandal.'

'There shall be nothing scandalous in my attentions to her.'

'There certainly will be in the way she takes them. But I have said what I had on my conscience,' Mrs. Walker pursued. 'If you wish to rejoin the young lady I will put you down. Here, by the way, you have a chance.'

The carriage was traversing that part of the Pincian Garden that overhangs the wall of Rome and overlooks the beautiful Villa Borghese. It is bordered by a large parapet, near which there are several seats. One of the seats, at a distance, was occupied by a gentleman and a lady, towards whom Mrs. Walker gave a toss of her head. At the same moment these persons rose and walked towards the parapet. Winterbourne had asked the coachman to stop; he now descended from the carriage. His companion looked at him a moment in silence; then, while he raised his hat, she drove majestically away. Winterbourne stood there; he had turned his eyes towards Daisy and her cavalier. They evidently saw no one; they were too deeply occupied with each other. When they reached the low garden-wall they stood a moment looking off at the great flat-topped pine-clusters of the Villa Borghese; then Giovanelli seated himself, familiarly, upon the broad ledge of the wall. The western sun in the opposite sky sent out illiant shaft through a couple of cloud-bars, whereupon Daisy's companion took her parasol out of her hands and opened it. She came a little nearer and he held the parasol over her; then, still holding it, he let it rest upon her shoulder, so that both of their heads were hidden from Winterbourne. This young man lingered a moment, then he began to walk. But he walked—not towards the couple with the parasol; towards the residence of his aunt, Mrs. Costello.

He flattered himself on the following day that there was no smiling among the servants when he, at least, asked for Mrs. Miller at her hotel. This lady and her daughter, however, were not at home; and on the next day after, repeating his visit, Winterbourne again had the misfortune not to find them. Mrs. Walker's party took place on the evening of the third day, and in spite of the frigidity of his last interview with the hostess Winterbourne was among the guests. Mrs. Walker was one of those American ladies who, while residing abroad, make a point, in their own phrase, of studying European society; and she had on this occasion collected several specimens of her diversely-born fellow-mortals to serve, as it were, as text books. When Winterbourne arrived Daisy Miller was not there, but in a few moments he saw her mother come in alone, very shyly and ruefully. Mrs. Miller's hair above her exposed-looking temples was more frizzled than ever. As she approached Mrs. Walker, Winterbourne also drew near.

'You see I've come all alone,' said poor Mrs. Miller. 'I'm so frightened; I don't know what to do; It's the first time I've ever been to a party alone—especially in this country. I wanted to bring Randolph or Eugenio, or someone, but Daisy just pushed me off by myself. I ain't used to going round alone.'

'And does not your daughter intend to favour us with her society?' demanded Mrs. Walker, impressively.

'Well, Daisy's all dressed,' said Mrs. Miller, with that accent of the dispassionate, if not of the philosophic, historian with which she always recorded the current incidents of her daughter's career. 'She got dressed on purpose before dinner. But she's got a friend of hers there; that gentleman—the Italian—that she wanted to bring. They've got going at the piano; it seems as if they couldn't leave off. Mr. Giovanelli sings splendidly. But I guess they'll come before very long,' concluded Mrs. Miller hopefully.

'I'm sorry she should come—in that way,' said Mrs. Walker.

'Well, I told her that there was no use in her getting dressed before dinner if she was going to wait three hours,' responded Daisy's mamma. 'I didn't see the use of her putting on such a dress as that to sit round with Mr. Giovanelli.'

'This is most horrible!' said Mrs. Walker, turning away and addressing herself to Winterbourne. '*Elle s'affiche.* It's her revenge for my having ventured to remonstrate with her. When she comes I shall not speak to her.'

Daisy came after eleven o'clock, but she was not, on such an occasion, a young lady to wait to be spoken to. She rustled forward in radiant loveliness, smiling and chattering, carrying a large bouquet and attended by Mr. Giovanelli. Everyone stopped talking, and turned and looked at her. She came straight to Mrs. Walker. 'I'm afraid you thought I never was coming, so I sent mother off to tell you. I wanted to make Mr. Giovanelli practise some things before he came; you know he sings beautifully, and I want you to ask him to sing. This is Mr. Giovanelli; you know I introduced him to you; he's got the most lovely voice and he knows the most charming set of songs. I made him go over them this evening, on purpose; we had the greatest time at the hotel.' Of all this Daisy delivered herself with the sweetest, brightest audibleness, looking now at her hostess and now round the room, while she gave a series of little pats, round her shoulders, to the edges of her dress. 'Is there anyone I know?' she asked.

'I think everyone knows you!' said Mrs. Walker pregnantly, and she gave a very cursory greeting to Mr. Giovanelli. This gentleman bore himself gallantly. He smiled and bowed and showed his white teeth, he curled his moustaches and rolled his eyes, and performed all the proper functions of a handsome Italian at an evening party. He sang, very prettily, half-a-dozen songs, though Mrs. Walker afterwards declared that she had been quite unable to find out who asked him. It was apparently not Daisy who had given him his orders. Daisy sat at a distance from the piano, and though she had publicly, as it were, professed a high admiration for his singing, talked, not inaudibly, while it was going on.

'It's a pity these rooms are so small; we can't dance,' she said to Winterbourne as if she had seen him five minutes before.

'I am sorry we can't dance,' Winterbourne answered; 'I don't dance.'

'Of course you don't dance; you're too stiff,' said Miss Daisy. 'I hope you enjoyed your drive with Mrs. Walker.'

'No, I didn't enjoy it; I preferred walking with you.'

'We paired off, that was much better,' said Daisy. 'But did you ever hear anything so cool as Mrs. Walker's wanting me to get into her carriage and drop poor Mr. Giovanelli, and under the pretext that it was proper? People have different ideas! It would have been most unkind; he had been talking about that walk for ten days.'

'He should not have talked about it at all,' said Winterbourne; 'he would never have proposed to a young lady of this country to walk about the streets with him.'

'About the streets?' cried Daisy, with her pretty stare. 'Where then would he have proposed to her to walk? The Pincio is not the streets, either; and I, thank goodness, am not a young lady of this country. The young ladies of this country have a dreadfully poky time of it, so far as I can learn; I don't see why I should change my habits for *them*.'

'I am afraid your habits are those of a flirt,' said Winterbourne gravely.

'Of course they are,' she cried, giving him her little smiling stare again. 'I'm a fearful, frightful flirt! Did you ever hear of a nice girl that was not? But I suppose you will tell me now that I am not a nice girl.'

'You're a very nice girl, but I wish you would flirt with me and me only,' said Winterbourne.

'Ah! thank you, thank you very much; you are the last man I should think of flirting with. As I have had the pleasure of informing you, you are too stiff.'

'You say that too often,' said Winterbourne.

Daisy gave a delighted laugh. 'If I could have the sweet hope of making you angry, I should say it again.'

'Don't do that; when I am angry I'm stiffer than ever. But if you won't flirt with me, do cease at least to flirt with your friend at the piano; they don't understand that sort of thing here.'

'I thought they understood nothing else!' exclaimed Daisy.

'Not in young unmarried women.'

'It seems to me much more proper in young unmarried women than in old married ones,' Daisy declared.

'Well,' said Winterbourne, 'when you deal with natives you must go by the custom of the place. Flirting is a purely American custom; it doesn't exist here. So when you show yourself in public with Mr. Giovanelli and without your mother—'

'Gracious! poor mother!' interposed Daisy.

'Though you may be flirting, Mr. Giovanelli is not; he means something else.'

'He isn't preaching, at any rate,' said Daisy with vivacity. 'And if you want very much to know, we are neither of us flirting, we are too good friends for that; we are very intimate friends.'

'Ah!' rejoined Winterbourne, 'if you are in love with each other it is another affair.'

She had allowed him up to this point to talk so frankly that he had no expectation of shocking her by this ejaculation; but she immediately got up, blushing visibly, and leaving him to exclaim mentally that little American flirts were the queerest creatures in the world. Mr. Giovanelli, at least,' she said, giving her interlocutor a single glance, 'never says such very disagreeable things to me.'

Winterbourne was bewildered; he stood staring. Mr. Giovanelli had finished singing; he left the piano and came over to Daisy. 'Won't you come into the other room and have some tea?' he asked, bending before her with his ornamental smile.

Daisy turned to Winterbourne, beginning to smile again. He was still more perplexed, for this inconsequent smile made nothing clear, though it seemed to prove, indeed, that she had a sweetness and softness that reverted instinctively to the pardon of offences. 'It has never occurred to Mr. Winterbourne to offer me any tea,' she said, with her little tormenting manner.

'I have offered you advice,' Winterbourne rejoined.

'I prefer weak tea!' cried Daisy, and she went off with the brilliant Giovanelli. She sat with him in the adjoining room, in the embrasure of the window, for the rest of the evening. There was an interesting performance at the piano, but neither of these young people gave heed to it. When Daisy came to take leave of Mrs. Walker, this lady conscientiously repaired the weakness of which she had been guilty at the moment of the young girl's arrival. She turned her back straight upon Miss Miller and left her to depart with what grace she might. Winterbourne was standing near the door; he saw it all. Daisy turned very pale and looked at her mother, but Mrs. Miller was humbly unconscious of any violation of the usual social forms. She appeared, indeed, to have felt an incongruous impulse to draw attention to her own striking observance of them. 'Good-night, Mrs. Walker,' she said; 'we've had a beautiful evening. You see if I let Daisy come to parties without me, I don't want her to go away without me.' Daisy turned away, looking with a pale, grave face at the circle near the door; Winterbourne saw that, for the first moment, she was too much shocked and puzzled even for indignation. He on his side was greatly touched.

'That was very cruel,' he said to Mrs. Walker.

'She never enters my drawing-room again,' replied his hostess.

Since Winterbourne was not to meet her in Mrs. Walker's drawing-room, he went as often as possible to Mrs. Miller's hotel. The ladies were rarely at home, but when he found them the devoted Giovanelli was always present. Very often the brilliant little Roman was in the drawing-room with Daisy alone, Mrs. Miller being apparently constantly of the opinion that discretion is the better part of surveillance. Winterbourne noted, at first with surprise, that Daisy on these occasions was never embarrassed or annoyed by his own entrance; but he very presently began to feel that she had no more surprises for him; the unexpected in her behaviour was the only thing to expect. She showed no displeasure at her *tête-à-tête* with Giovanelli being interrupted; she could chatter as freshly and freely with two gentlemen as with one; there was always, in her conversation, the same odd mixture of audacity and puerility. Winterbourne remarked to himself that if she was seriously interested in Giovanelli it was very singular that she should not take more trouble to preserve the sanctity of their interviews, and he liked her the more for her innocent-looking indifference and her apparently inexhaustible good humour. He could hardly have said why, but she seemed to him a girl who would never be jealous. At the risk of exciting a somewhat derisive smile on the reader's part, I may affirm that with regard to the women who had hitherto interested him, it very often seemed to Winterbourne among the possibilities that, given certain contingencies, he should be afraid—literally afraid-of these ladies; he had a pleasant sense that he should never be afraid of Daisy Miller. It must be added that this sentiment was not altogether flattering to Daisy; it was part of his conviction, or rather of his apprehension, that she would prove a very light young person.

But she was evidently very much interested in Giovanelli. She looked at him whenever he spoke; she was perpetually telling him to do this and to do that; she was constantly 'chaffing' and abusing him. She appeared completely to have forgotten that Winterbourne had said anything to displease her at Mrs. Walker's little party. One Sunday afternoon, having gone to St. Peter's with his aunt, Winterbourne perceived Daisy strolling about the great church in company with the inevitable Giovanelli. Presently he pointed out the young girl and her cavalier to Mrs. Costello. This lady looked at them a moment through her eyeglass, and then she said:

'That's what makes you so pensive in these days, eh?'

'I had not the least idea I was pensive,' said the young man.

'You are very much pre-occupied, you are thinking of something.'

'And what is it,' he asked, 'that you accuse me of thinking of?'

'Of that young lady's—Miss Baker's, Miss Chandler's—what's her name? Miss Miller's intrigue with that little barber's block.'

'Do you call it an intrigue,' Winterbourne asked—'an affair that goes on with such peculiar publicity?'

'That's their folly,' said Mrs. Costello, 'it's not their merit.'

'No,' rejoined Winterbourne, with something of that pensiveness to which his aunt had alluded. 'I don't believe that there is anything to be called an intrigue.'

'I have heard a dozen people speak of it; they say she is quite carried away by him.'

'They are certainly very intimate,' said Winterbourne.

Mrs. Costello inspected the young couple again with her optical instrument. 'He is very handsome. One easily sees how it is. She thinks him the most elegant man in the world, the finest gentleman. She has never seen anything like him; he is better even than the courier. It was the courier probably who introduced him, and if he succeeds in marrying the young lady, the courier will come in for a magnificent commission.'

'I don't believe she thinks of marrying him,' said Winterbourne, 'and I don't believe he hopes to marry her.'

'You may be very sure she thinks of nothing. She goes on from day to day, from hour to hour, as they did in the Golden Age. I can imagine nothing more vulgar. And at the same time,' added Mrs. Costello, 'depend upon it that she may tell you any moment that she is "engaged." '

'I think that is more than Giovanelli expects,' said Winterbourne.

'Who is Giovanelli?'

'The little Italian. I have asked questions about him and learned something. He is apparently a perfectly respectable little man. I believe he is in a small way, a *cavaliere avvocato*. But he doesn't move in what are called the first circles. I think it is really not absolutely impossible that the courier introduced him. He is evidently immensley charmed with Miss Miller. If she thinks him the finest gentleman in the world, he, on his side, has never found himself in personal contact with such splendour, such opulence, such expensiveness, as this young lady's. And then she must seem to him wonderfully pretty and interesting. I rather doubt that he dreams of marrying her. That must appear to him too impossible a piece of luck. He has nothing but his handsome face to offer, and there is a substantial Mr. Miller in that mysterious land of dollars. Giovanelli knows that he hasn't a title to offer. If he were only a count or a *marchese*! He must wonder at his luck at the way they have taken him up.'

'He accounts for it by his handsome face, and thinks Miss Miller a young lady *qui se passe ses fantaisies*!' said Mrs. Costello.

'It is very true,' Winterbourne pursued, 'that Daisy and her mamma have not yet risen to that stage of—what shall I call it?—of culture, at which the idea of catching a count or a *marchese* begins. I believe that they are intellectually incapable of that conception.'

'Ah! but the *avvocato* can't believe it,' said Mrs. Costello.

Of the observation excited by Daisy's 'intrigue,' Winterbourne gathered that day at St. Peter's sufficient evidence. A dozen of the

American colonists in Rome came to talk with Mrs. Costello, who sat on a little portable stool at the base of one of the great pilasters. The vesper service was going forward in splendid chants and organ-tones in the adjacent choir, and meanwhile, between Mrs. Costello and her friends, there was a great deal said about poor little Miss Miller's going really 'too far.' Winterbourne was not pleased with what he heard; but when, coming out upon the great steps of the church, he saw Daisy, who had emerged before him, get into an open cab with her accomplice and roll away through the cynical streets of Rome, he could not deny to himself that she was going very far indeed. He felt very sorry for her—not exactly that he believed that she had completely lost her head, but because it was painful to hear so much that was pretty, and undefended, and natural, assigned to a vulgar place among the categories of disorder. He made an attempt after this to give a hint to Mrs. Miller. He met one day in the Corso a friend—a tourist like himself—who had just come out of the Doria Palace, where he had been walking through the beautiful gallery. His friend talked for a moment about the superb portrait of Innocent X. by Velasquez, which hangs in one of the cabinets of the palace, and then said, 'And in the same cabinet, by the way, I had the pleasure of contemplating a picture of a different kind—that pretty American girl whom you pointed out to me last week.' In answer to Winterbourne's inquiries, his friend narrated that the pretty American girl—prettier than ever—was seated with a companion in the secluded nook in which the great papal portrait was enshrined.

'Who was her companion?' asked Winterbourne.

'A little Italian with a bouquet in his button hole. The girl is delightfully pretty, but I thought I understood from you the other day that she was a young lady *du meilleur monde.*'

'So she is!' answered Winterbourne; and having assured himself that his informant had seen Daisy and her companion but five minutes before, he jumped into a cab and went to call on Mrs. Miller. She was at home; but she apologized to him for receiving him in Daisy's absence.

'She's gone out somewhere with Mr. Giovanelli,' said Mrs. Miller. 'She's always going round with Mr. Giovanelli.'

'I have noticed that they are very intimate,' Winterbourne observed.

'Oh! it seems as if they couldn't live without each other!' said Mrs. Miller. 'Well, he's a real gentleman anyhow. I keep telling Daisy she's engaged!'

'And what does Daisy say?'

'Oh, she says she isn't engaged. But she might as well be!' this impartial parent resumed. 'She goes on as if she was. But I've made Mr. Giovanelli promise to tell me, if *she* doesn't. I should want to write to Mr. Miller about it—shouldn't you?'

Winterbourne replied that he certainly should; and the state of mind Daisy's mamma struck him as so unprecedented in the annals of parental vigilance that he gave up as utterly irrelevant the attempt to place her upon her guard.

After this Daisy was never at home, and Winterbourne ceased to meet her at the houses of their common acquaintance, because, as he perceived, these people had quite made up their minds that she was going too far. They ceased to invite her, and they intimated that they desired to express to observant Europeans the great truth that, though Miss Daisy Miller was a young American lady, her behaviour was not representative—was regarded by her compatriots as abnormal. Winterbourne wondered how she felt about all the cold shoulders that were turned towards her, and sometimes it annoyed him to suspect that she did not feel at all. He said to himself that she was too light and childish, too uncultivated and unreasoning, too provincial, to have reflected upon her ostracism or even to have perceived it. Then at other moments he believed that she carried about in her elegant and irresponsible little organism a defiant, passionate, perfectly observant consciousness of the impression she produced. He asked himself whether Daisy's defiance came from the consciousness of innocence or from her being, essentially, a young person of the reckless class. It must be admitted that holding oneself to a belief in Daisy's 'innocence' came to seem to Winterbourne more and more a matter of fine-spun gallantry. As I have already had occasion to relate, he was angry at finding himself reduced to chopping logic about this young lady; he was vexed at his want of instinctive certitude as to how far her eccentricities were generic, national, and how far they were personal. From either view of them he had somehow missed her, and now it was too late. She was 'carried away' by Mr. Giovanelli.

A few days after his brief interview with her mother, he encountered her in that beautiful abode of flowering desolation known as the Palace of the Cæsars. The early Roman spring had filled the air with bloom and perfume, and the rugged surface of the Palatine was muffled with tender verdure. Daisy was strolling along the top of one of those great mounds of ruin that are embanked with mossy marble and paved with monumental inscriptions. It seemed to him that Rome had never been so lovely as just then. He stood looking off at the enchanting harmony of line and colour that remotely encircles the city, inhaling the softly humid odours and feeling the freshness of the year and the antiquity of the place reaffirm themselves in mysterious interfusion. It seemed to him also that Daisy had never looked so pretty; but this had been an observation of his whenever he met her. Giovanelli was at her side, and Giovanelli, too, wore an aspect of even unwonted brilliancy.

'Well,' said Daisy, 'I should think you would be lonesome!'

'Lonesome?' asked Winterbourne.

'You are always going round by yourself. Can't you get anyone to walk with you?'

'I am not so fortunate,' said Winterbourne, 'as your companion.'

Giovanelli, from the first, had treated Winterbourne with distinguished politeness; he listened with a deferential air to his remarks; he laughed, punctiliously, at his pleasantries; he seemed disposed to testify to his belief that Winterbourne was a superior young man. He carried himself in no degree like a jealous wooer; he had obviously a great deal of tact; he had no objection to your expecting a little humility of him. It even seemed to Winterbourne at times that Giovanelli would find a certain mental relief in being able to have a private understanding with him—to say to him, as an intelligent man, that, bless you, *he* knew how extraordinary was this young lady, and didn't flatter himself with delusive—or at least *too* delusive—hopes of matrimony and dollars. On this occasion he strolled away from his companion to pluck a sprig of almond-blossom, which he carefully arranged in his button-hole.

'I know why you say that,' said Daisy, watching Giovanelli. 'Because you think I go round too much with *him*!' And she nodded at her attendant.

'Every one thinks so—if you care to know,' said Winterbourne.

'Of course I care to know!' Daisy exclaimed seriously. 'But I don't believe it. They are only pretending to be shocked. They don't really care a straw what I do. Besides, I don't go round so much.'

'I think you will find they do care. They will show it—disagreeably.'

Daisy looked at him a moment. 'How—disagreeably?'

'Haven't you noticed anything?' Winterbourne asked.

'I have noticed you. But I noticed you were as stiff as an umbrella the first time I saw you.'

'You will find I am not so stiff as several others,' said Winterbourne, smiling.

'How shall I find it?'

'By going to see the others.'

'What will they do to me?'

'They will give you the cold shoulder. Do you know what th means?'

Daisy was looking at him intently; she began to colour. 'Do you mean as Mrs. Walker did the other night?'

'Exactly!' said Winterbourne.

She looked away at Giovanelli, who was decorating himself with his almond-blossom. Then looking back at Winterbourne—'I shouldn't think you would let people be so unkind!' she said.

'How can I help it?' he asked.

'I should think you would say something.'

'I do say something;' and he paused a moment. 'I say that your mother tells me that she believes you are engaged.'

'Well, she does,' said Daisy very simply.

Winterbourne began to laugh. 'And does Randolph believe it?' he asked.

'I guess Randolph doesn't believe anything,' said Daisy. Randolph's scepticism excited Winterbourne to further hilarity, and he observed Giovanelli was coming back to them. Daisy, observing it too, addressed herself again to her countryman. 'Since you have mentioned it,' she said, 'I *am* engaged.' . . . Winterbourne looked at her; he had stopped laughing. 'You don't believe it!' she added.

He was silent a moment; and then, 'Yes, I believe it!' he said.

'Oh, no, you don't,' she answered. 'Well, then—I am not!'

The young girl and her cicerone were on their way to the gate of the enclosure, so that Winterbourne, who had but lately entered, presently took leave of them. A week afterwards he went to dine at a beautiful villa on the Cælian Hill, and, on arriving, dismissed his hired vehicle. The evening was charming, and he promised himself the satisfaction of walking home beneath the Arch of Constantine and past the vaguely-lighted monuments of the Forum. There was a waning moon in the sky, and her radiance was not brilliant, but she was veiled in a thin cloud-curtain which seemed to diffuse and equalize it. When, on his return from the villa (it was eleven o'clock), Winterbourne approached the dusky circle of the Colosseum, it recurred to him, as a lover of the picturesque, that the interior, in the pale moonshine, would be well worth a glance. He turned aside and walked to one of the empty arches, near which, as he observed, an open carriage—one of the little Roman street-cabs—was stationed. Then he passed in, among the cavernous shadows of the great structure, and emerged upon the clear and silent arena. The place had never seemed to him more impressive. One-half of the gigantic circus was in deep shade; the other was sleeping in the luminous dusk. As he stood there he began to murmur Byron's famous lines, out of *Manfred*; but before he had finished his quotation he remembered that if nocturnal meditations in the Colosseum are recommended by the poets, they are deprecated by the doctors. The historic atmosphere was there, certainly; but the historic atmosphere, scientifically considered, was no better than a villainous miasma. Winterbourne walked to the middle of the arena, to take a more general glance, intending thereafter to make a hasty retreat. The great cross in the centre was covered with shadow; it was only as he drew near it that he made it out distinctly. Then he saw that two persons were stationed upon the low steps which formed its base. One of these was a woman, seated; her companion was standing in front of her.

Presently the sound of the woman's voice came to him distinctly in the warm night-air. 'Well, he looks at us as one of the old lions or tigers may have looked at the Christian martyrs!' These were the words he heard, in the familiar accent of Miss Daisy Miller.

'Let us hope he is not very hungry,' responded the ingenious Giovanelli. 'He will have to take me first; you will serve for dessert!'

Winterbourne stopped, with a sort of horror; and, it must be added, with a sort of relief. It was as if a sudden illumination had been flashed upon the ambiguity of Daisy's behaviour and the riddle had become easy to read. She was a young lady whom a gentleman need no longer be at pains to respect. He stood there looking at her—looking at her companion, and not reflecting that though he saw them vaguely, he himself must have been more brightly visible. He felt angry with himself that he had bothered so much about the right way of regarding Miss Daisy Miller. Then, as he was going to advance again, he checked himself; not from the fear that he was doing her injustice, but from a sense of the danger of appearing unbecomingly exhilarated by this sudden revulsion from cautious criticism. He turned away towards the entrance of the place; but as he did so he heard Daisy speak again.

'Why, it was Mr. Winterbourne! He saw me—and he cuts me!'

What a clever little reprobate she was, and how smartly she played at injured innocence! But he wouldn't cut her. Winterbourne came forward again, and went towards the great cross. Daisy had got up; Giovanelli lifted his hat. Winterbourne had now begun to think simply of the craziness, from a sanitary point of view, of a delicate young girl lounging away the evening in this nest of malaria. What if she *were* a clever little reprobate? that was no reason for her dying of the *perniciosa*. 'How long have you been here?' he asked, almost brutally.

Daisy, lovely in the flattering moonlight, looked at him a moment. Then—'All the evening,' she answered gently. . . . 'I never saw anything so pretty.'

'I am afraid,' said Winterbourne, 'that you will not think Roman fever very pretty. This is the way people catch it. I wonder,' he added, turning to Giovanelli, 'that you, a native Roman, should countenance such a terrible indiscretion.'

'Ah,' said the handsome native, 'for myself, I am not afraid.'

'Neither am I—for you! I am speaking for this young lady.'

Giovanelli lifted his well-shaped eyebrows and showed his brilliant teeth. But he took Winterbourne's rebuke with docility. 'I told the Signorina it was a grave indiscretion; but when was the Signorina ever prudent?'

'I never was sick, and I don't mean to be!' the Signoria declared. 'I don't look like much, but I'm healthy! I was bound to see the Colosseum by moonlight; I shouldn't have wanted to go home without that; and we have had the most beautiful time, haven't we, Mr. Giovanelli? If there has been any danger, Eugenio can give me some pills. He has got some splendid pills.'

'I should advise you,' said Winterbourne, 'to drive home as fast as possible and take one!'

'What you say is very wise,' Giovanelli rejoined. 'I will go and make sure the carriage is at hand.' And he went forward rapidly.

Daisy followed with Winterbourne. He kept looking at her; she seemed not in the least embarrassed. Winterbourne said nothing; Daisy chattered about the beauty of the place. 'Well, I *have* seen the Colosseum by moonlight!' she exclaimed. 'That's one good thing.' Then, noticing Winterbourne's silence, she asked him why he didn't speak. He made no answer; he only began to laugh. They passed under one of the dark archways; Giovanelli was in front with the carriage. Here Daisy stopped a moment, looking at the young American. '*Did* you believe I was engaged the other day?' she asked.

'It doesn't matter what I believed the other day,' said Winterbourne, still laughing.

'Well, what do you believe now?'

'I believe that it makes very little difference whether you are engaged or not!'

He felt the young girl's pretty eyes fixed upon him through the thick gloom of the archway; she was apparently going to answer. But Giovanelli hurried her forward. 'Quick, quick,' he said; 'if we get in by midnight we are quite safe.'

Daisy took her seat in the carriage, and the fortunate Italian placed himself beside her. 'Don't forget Eugenio's pills!' said Winterbourne, as he lifted his hat.

'I don't care,' said Daisy, in a little strange tone, 'whether I have Roman fever or not!' Upon this the cab-driver cracked his whip, and they rolled away over the desultory patches of the antique pavement.

Winterbourne—to do him justice, as it were—mentioned to no one that he had encountered Miss Miller, at midnight, in the Colosseum with a gentleman; but nevertheless, a couple of days later, the fact of her having been there under these circumstances was known to every member of the little American circle, and commented accordingly. Winterbourne reflected that they had of course known it at the hotel, and that, after Daisy's return, there had been an exchange of remarks between the porter and the cab-driver. But the young man was conscious at the same moment that it had ceased to be a matter of serious regret to him that the little American flirt should be 'talked about' by low-minded menials. These people, a day or two later, had serious information to give: the little American flirt was alarmingly ill. Winterbourne, when the rumour came to him, immediately went to the hotel for more news. He found that two or three charitable friends had preceded him, and that they were being entertained in Mrs. Miller's salon by Randolph.

'It's going round at night,' said Randolph—'that's what made her sick. She's always going round at night. I shouldn't think she'd want to—it's so plaguey dark. You can't see anything here at night, except when there's a moon. In America there's always a moon!' Mrs. Miller was invisible; she was now, at least, giving her daughter the advantage of her society. It was evident that Daisy was dangerously ill.

Winterbourne went often to ask for news of her, and once he saw Mrs. Miller, who, though deeply alarmed, was—rather to his surprise—perfectly composed, and, as it appeared, a most efficient and judicious nurse. She talked a good deal about Dr. Davis, but Winterbourne paid her the compliment of saying to himself that she was not, after all, such a monstrous goose. 'Daisy spoke of you the other day,' she said to him. 'Half the time she doesn't know what she's saying, but that time I think she did. She gave me a message; she told me to tell you. She told me to tell you that she never was engaged to that handsome Italian. I am sure I am very glad; Mr. Giovanelli hasn't been near us since she was taken ill. I thought he was so much of a gentleman; but I don't call that very polite! A lady told me that he was afraid I was angry with him for taking Daisy round at night. Well, so I am; but I suppose he knows I'm a lady. I would scorn to scold him. Any way, she says she's not engaged. I don't know why she wanted you to know; but she said to me three times—"Mind you tell Mr. Winterbourne." And then she told me to ask if you remembered the time you went to the castle, in Switzerland. But I said I wouldn't give any such messages as that. Only, if she is not engaged, I'm sure I'm glad to know it.'

But, as Winterbourne had said, it mattered very little. A week after this the poor girl died; it had been a terrible case of the fever. Daisy's grave was in the little Protestant cemetery, in an angle of the wall of imperial Rome, beneath the cypresses and the thick spring-flowers. Winterbourne stood there beside it, with a number of other mourners; a number larger than the scandal excited by the young lady's career would have led you to expect. Near him stood Giovanelli, who came nearer still before Winterbourne turned away. Giovanelli was very pale; on this occasion he had no flower in his button-hole; he seemed to wish to say something. At last he said, 'She was the most beautiful young lady I ever saw, and the most amiable.' And then he added in a moment, 'And she was the most innocent.'

Winterbourne looked at him, and presently repeated his words, 'And the most innocent?'

'The most innocent!'

Winterbourne felt sore and angry. 'Why the devil,' he asked 'did you take her to that fatal place?'

Mr. Giovanelli's urbanity was apparently imperturbable. He looked on the ground a moment, and then he said, 'For myself, I had no fear; and she wanted to go.'

'That was no reason!' Winterbourne declared.

The subtle Roman again dropped his eyes. 'If she had lived, I should have got nothing. She would never have married me, I am sure.'

'She would never have married you?'

'For a moment I hoped so. But no. I am sure.'

Winterbourne listened to him; he stood staring at the raw protuberance among the April daisies. When he turned away again Mr. Giovanelli, with his light slow step, had retired.

Winterbourne almost immediately left Rome; but the following summer he again met his aunt, Mrs. Costello, at Vevey. Mrs. Costello was fond of Vevey. In the interval Winterbourne had often thought of Daisy Miller and her mystifying manners. One day he spoke of her to his aunt—said it was on his conscience that he had done her injustice.

'I am sure I don't know,' said Mrs. Costello. 'How did your injustice affect her?'

'She sent me a message before her death which I didn't understand at the time. But I have understood it since. She would have appreciated one's esteem.'

'Is that a modest way,' asked Mrs. Costello, 'of saying that she would have reciprocated one's affection?'

Winterbourne offered no answer to this question; but he presently said, 'You were right in that remark that you made last summer. I was booked to make a mistake. I have lived too long in foreign parts.'

Nevertheless, he went back to live at Geneva, whence there continue to come the most contradictory accounts of his motives of sojourn: a report that he is 'studying' hard—an intimation that he is much interested in a very clever foreign lady.

Longstaff's Marriage

[First appeared in the *Scribner's Monthly*, vol. xvi (August 1878), pp. 537-50. The tale was revised and reprinted in volume i of *The Madonna of the Future* (1879). The text of 1879 was later reproduced in volume xiii of James's first 'Collective Edition' (1883).]

FORTY YEARS AGO THAT TRADITIONAL AND ANECDOTICAL LIBERTY of young American women, which is notoriously the envy of their foreign sisters, was not so firmly established as at the present hour; yet it was sufficiently recognized to make it no scandal that so pretty a girl as Diana Belfield should start for the grand tour of Europe under no more imposing protection than that of her cousin and intimate friend, Miss Agatha Gosling. She had, from the European point of view, beauty enough to make her enterprise perilous—the beauty foreshadowed in her name, which might have been given her in prevision of her tall, light figure, her nobly poised head, weighted with a coronal of auburn braids, her frank quick glance and her rapid gliding step. She used often to walk about with a big dog who had the habit of bounding at her side and tossing his head against her outstretched hand; and she had, moreover, a trick of carrying her long parasol always folded, for she was not afraid of the sunshine, across her shoulder, in the fashion of a soldier's musket on a march. Thus equipped, she looked wonderfully like that charming antique statue of the goddess of the chase which we encounter in various replicas in half the museums of the world. You half expected to see a sandal-shod foot peep out beneath her fluttering robe. It was with this tread of the wakeful huntress that she stepped upon the old sailing-vessel which was to bear her to the lands she had dreamed of. Behind her, with a great many shawls and satchels, came her little kinswoman, with quite another *démarche*. Agatha Gosling was not a beauty but she was the most judicious and most devoted of companions. These two persons had come together on the death of Diana's mother and the taking possession by the young lady of her patrimony. The first use she made of her inheritance was to divide it with Agatha, who had not a penny of her own; the next was to purchase a letter of credit upon a European banker. The cousins had contracted a classical friendship,—they had determined to be sufficient to each other, like the Ladies of Llangollen. Only, though their friendship was exclusive, their Llangollen was to be comprehensive. They would tread the pavements of historic cities and stand in the coloured light-shafts of Gothic cathedrals, wander on tinkling mules through mountain-gorges and sit among dark-eyed peasants by southern seas. It may seem singular that a beautiful girl with a pretty fortune should have been left to seek the supreme satisfaction of life in friendship tempered by sight-seeing; but Diana herself considered this pastime no beggarly alternative. Though she never told it herself, her biographer may do so; she had had, in vulgar parlance, a hundred offers. To say that she had declined them is to say too little; she had really scorned them. They had come from honourable and amiable men, and it was not her suitors in themselves that she disrelished; it was simply the idea of marrying. She found it insupportable: a fact which completes her analogy with the mythic divinity to whom I have likened her. She was passionately single, fiercely virginal; and in the straight-glancing grey eye which provoked men to admire, there was a certain silvery ray which forbade them to hope. The fabled Diana took a fancy to a beautiful shepherd, but the real one had not yet found, sleeping or waking, her Endymion.

Thanks to this defensive eyebeam, the dangerous side of our heroine's enterprise was slow to define itself; thanks, too, to the exquisite decency of her companion. Agatha Gosling had an almost Quakerish purity and dignity; a bristling dragon could not have been a better safeguard than this glossy, grey-breasted dove. Money, too, is a protection, and Diana had enough to purchase privacy. She travelled extensively, and saw all the churches and pictures, the castles and cottages included in the list which had been drawn up by the two friends in evening talks, at home, between two wax candles. In the evening they used to read aloud to each other from 'Corinne' and 'Childe Harold,' and they kept a diary in common, at which they 'collaborated,' like French playwrights, and which was studded with quotations from the authors I have mentioned. This lasted a year, at the end of which they found themselves a trifle weary. A snug posting-carriage was a delightful habitation, but looking at miles of pictures was very fatiguing to the back. Buying souvenirs and trinkets under foreign arcades was a most absorbing occupation; but inns were dreadfully apt to be draughty, and bottles of hot water, for application to the feet, had a disagreeable way of growing lukewarm. For these and other reasons our heroines determined to take a winter's rest, and for this purpose they betook themselves to the charming town of Nice, which was then but in the infancy of its fame. It was simply one of the hundred hamlets of the Riviera,—a place where the blue waves broke on an almost empty strand, and the olive-trees sprouted at the doors of the inns. In those days Nice was Italian, and the 'Promenade des Anglais' existed only in an embryonic form. Exist, however, it did, practically, and British invalids, in moderate numbers, might have been seen taking the January sunshine beneath London umbrellas, before the many-twinkling sea. Our young Americans quietly took their place in this harmless society. They drove along the coast, through the strange, dark, huddled fishing-villages, and they rode on donkeys among the bosky hills. They painted in water-colours and hired a piano; they subscribed to the circulating library and took lessons in the language of Silvio Pellico from an old lady with very fine eyes, who wore an enormous brooch of cracked malachite, and gave herself out as the widow of a Roman exile.

They used to go and sit by the sea, each provided with a volume from the circulating library; but they never did much with their books. The sunshine made the page too dazzling, and the people who strolled up and down before them were more entertaining than the ladies and gentlemen in the novels. They looked at them constantly from under their umbrellas; they learned to know them all by sight. Many of their fellow-visitors were invalids,—mild, slow-moving consumptives. But that women enjoy the exercise of pity, I should have said that these pale promenaders were a saddening spectacle. In several of them, however, our friends took a personal interest; they watched them from day to day; they noticed their changing colour; they had their ideas about who was getting better and who was getting worse. They did little, however, in the way of making acquaintances,—partly because consumptive people are no great talkers, and partly because this was also Diana's disposition. She said to her friend that they had not come to Europe to pay morning-calls; they had left their best bonnets and card-cases behind them. At the bottom of her reserve was the apprehension that she should be 'admired;' which was not fatuity, but simply an inference based upon uncomfortable experience. She had seen in Europe, for the first time, certain horrid men, —polished adventurers, with offensive looks and mercenary thoughts; and she had a wholesome fear that one of these gentlemen might approach her through some accidental breach in her reserve. Agatha Gosling, who had neither in reminiscence nor in prospect the same reasons for being on the defensive, would have been glad to extend the circle of her intimacy, and would even have consented to put on a best bonnet for the purpose. But she had to content herself with an occasional murmur of small talk, on a bench before the sea, with two or three English ladies of the botanizing class; jovial little spinsters who wore stout boots, gauntlets, and 'uglies,' and in pursuit of wayside flowers scrambled into places where the first-mentioned articles were uncompromisingly visible. For the rest, Agatha contented herself with spinning suppositions about the people she never spoke to. She framed a great deal of hypothetic gossip, invented theories and explanations,—generally of the most charitable quality. Her companion took no part in these harmless devisings, except to listen to them with an indolent smile. She seldom honoured her fellow-mortals with finding apologies for them, and if they wished her to read their history, they must write it out in the largest letters.

There was one person at Nice upon whose biography, if it had been laid before her in this fashion, she probably would have bestowed a certain amount of attention. Agatha had noticed the gentleman first; or Agatha, at least, had first spoken of him. He was young and he looked interesting; Agatha had indulged in a good deal of wondering as to whether or no be belonged to the invalid category. She preferred to believe that one of his lungs was 'affected'; it certainly made him more interesting. He used to stroll about by himself and sit for a long time in the sun, with a book peeping out of his pocket. This book he never opened; he was always staring at the sea. I say always, but my phrase demands an immediate modification; he looked at the sea whenever he was not looking at Diana Belfield. He was tall and fair, slight, and as Agatha Gosling said, aristocratic-looking. He dressed with a certain careless elegance, which Agatha deemed picturesque; she declared one day that he reminded her of a love-sick prince. She learned eventually from one of the botanizing spinsters that he was not a prince, that he was simply an English gentleman, Mr. Reginald Longstaff. There remained the possibility that he was love-sick; but this point could not be so easily settled. Agatha's informant had assured her, however, that if they were not princes, the Longstaffs, who came from a part of the country in which she had visited, and owned great estates there, had a pedigree which many princes might envy. It was one of the oldest and the best of English names; they were one of the innumerable untitled country families who held their heads as high as the highest. This poor Mr. Longstaff was a beautiful specimen of a young English gentleman; he looked so gentle, yet so brave; so modest, yet so cultivated! The ladies spoke of him habitually as 'poor' Mr. Longstaff, for they now took for granted there was something the matter with him. At last Agatha Gosling discovered what it was, and made a solemn proclamation of the same. The matter with poor Mr. Longstaff was simply that he was in love with Diana! It was certainly natural to suppose he was in love with some one, and, as Agatha said, it could not possibly be with herself. Mr. Longstaff was pale, with crumpled locks; he never spoke to any one; he was evidently preoccupied, and this mild, candid face was a sufficient proof that the weight on his heart was not a bad conscience. What could it be, then, but an unrequited passion? It was, however, equally pertinent to inquire why Mr. Longstaff took no steps to bring about a requital.

'Why in the world does he not ask to be introduced to you?' Agatha Gosling demanded of her companion.

Diana replied, quite without eagerness, that it was plainly because he had nothing to say to her, and she declared with a trifle more emphasis that she was incapable of furnishing him a topic of conversation. She added that she thought they had gossipped enough about the poor man, and that if by any chance he should have the bad taste to speak to them, she should certainly go away and leave him alone with Miss Gosling. It is true, however, that at an earlier period, she had let fall the remark that he was quite the most 'distinguished' person at Nice; and afterwards, though she was never the first to allude to him, she had more than once let her companion pursue the theme for some time without reminding her of its futility. The one person to whom Mr. Longstaff was observed to speak was an elderly man of foreign aspect who approached him occasionally in the most deferential manner, and whom Agatha Gosling supposed to be his servant. This individual was apparently an Italian; he had an obsequious attitude, a pair of grizzled whiskers, an insinuating smile. He seemed to come to Mr. Longstaff for orders; presently he went away to execute them, and Agatha noticed that on retiring, he always managed to pass in front of her companion, on whom he fixed his respectful but penetrating gaze. 'He knows the secret,' she always said, with gentle jocoseness; 'he knows what is the matter with his master and he wants to see whether he approves of you. Old servants never want their masters to marry, and I think this worthy man is rather afraid of you. At any rate, the way he stares at you tells the whole story.'

'Every one stares at me!' said Diana wearily. 'A cat may look at a king.'

As the weeks went by, Agatha Gosling quite made up her mind that it *was* Mr. Longstaff's lungs. The poor young man's invalid character was now most apparent; he could hardly hold up his head or drag one foot after the other; his servant was always near him to give him an arm or to hand him an extra overcoat. No one, indeed, knew, with certainty, that he was consumptive; but Agatha agreed with the lady who had given the information about his pedigree, that this fact was in itself extremely suspicious; for, as the little Englishwoman forcibly remarked, unless he were ill, why should he make such a mystery of it? Consumption declaring itself in a young man of family and fortune was particularly sad; such people had often diplomatic reasons for pretending to enjoy excellent health. It kept the legacy-hunters and the hungry next-of-kin from worrying them to death. Agatha observed that this poor gentleman's last hours seemed likely to be only too lonely. She felt very much like offering to nurse him; for, being no relation, he could not accuse her of mercenary motives. From time to time he got up from the bench where he habitually sat, and strolled slowly past the two friends. Every time that he came near them, Agatha had a singular feeling,—a conviction that now he was really going to speak to them, in tones of the most solemn courtesy. She could not fancy him speaking otherwise. He began, at a distance, by fixing his grave, soft eyes on Diana, and, as he advanced, you would have said that he was coming straight up to her with some tremulous compliment. But as he drew nearer, his intentness seemed to falter; he strolled more slowly, he looked away at the sea, and he passed in front of her without having the courage to let his eyes rest upon her. Then he passed back again in the same fashion, sank down upon his bench, fatigued apparently by his aimless stroll, and fell into a melancholy reverie. To enumerate these small incidents in his deportment is to give it a melodramatic cast which it was far from possessing; something in his manner saved it from the shadow of impertinence, and it may be affirmed that not a single idler on the sunny shore suspected his speechless 'attentions.'

'I wonder why it doesn't annoy us more that he should look at us so much,' said Agatha Gosling, one day.

'That who should look at us?' asked Diana, not at all affectedly.

Agatha fixed her eyes for a moment on her friend, and then said gently:

'Mr. Longstaff. Now, don't say "Who is Mr. Longstaff?" ' she added.

'I have got to learn, really,' said Diana, 'that the person you appear to mean, does look at us. I have never caught him in the act.'

'That is because whenever you turn your eyes towards him he looks away. He is afraid to meet them. But I see him.'

These words were exchanged one day as the two friends sat as usual before the twinkling sea; and, beyond them, as usual, lounged Reginald Longstaff. Diana bent her head faintly forward and glanced towards him. He was looking full at her and their eyes met, apparently for the first time. Diana dropped her own upon her book again, and then, after a silence of some moments, 'It does annoy me,' she said. Presently she added that she would go home and write a letter, and, though she had never taken a step in Europe without having Agatha by her side, Miss Gosling now allowed her to depart unattended. 'You won't mind going alone?' Agatha had asked. 'It is but three minutes, you know.'

Diana replied that she preferred to go alone, and she moved away, with her parasol over her shoulder.

Agatha Gosling had a particular reason for this rupture of their maidenly custom. She felt a strong conviction that if she were left alone, Mr. Longstaff would come and speak to her and say something very important, and she deferred to this conviction without the sense of doing anything immodest. There was something solemn about it; it was a sort of presentiment; but it did not frighten her; it only made her feel very kind and appreciative. It is true that when at the end of ten minutes (they had seemed rather long), she saw him rise from his seat and slowly come towards her, she was conscious of a certain trepidation. Mr. Longstaff drew near; at last, he was close to her; he stopped and stood looking at her. She had averted her head, so as not to appear to expect him; but now she looked round again, and he very gravely lifted his hat.

'May I take the liberty of sitting down?' he asked.

Agatha bowed in silence, and, to make room for him, moved a blue shawl of Diana's, which was lying on the bench; he slowly sank into the place and then said very gently:

'I have ventured to speak to you, because I have something particular to say.' His voice trembled and he was extremely pale. His eyes, which Agatha thought very handsome, had a remarkable expression.

'I am afraid you are ill,' she said, with great kindness. 'I have often noticed you and pitied you.'

'I thought you did, a little,' the young man answered. 'That is why I made up my mind to speak to you.'

'You are getting worse,' said Agatha, softly.

'Yes, I am getting worse; I am dying. I am perfectly conscious of it; I have no illusions. I am weaker every day; I shall last but a few weeks.' This was said very simply; sadly but not lugubriously.

But Agatha felt almost awe-stricken; there stirred in her heart a delicate sense of sisterhood with this beautiful young man who sat there and talked thus submissively of death.

'Can nothing be done?' she said.

He shook his head and smiled a little. 'Nothing but to try and get what pleasure I can from this little remnant of life.'

Though he smiled she felt that he was very serious; that he was, indeed, deeply agitated, and trying to master his emotion.

'I am afraid you get very little pleasure,' Agatha rejoined. 'You seem entirely alone.'

'I am entirely alone. I have no family,—no near relations. I am absolutely alone.'

Agatha rested her eyes on him compassionately, and then—

'You ought to have spoken to *us*,' she said.

He sat looking at her; he had taken off his hat; he was slowly passing his hand over his forehead. 'You see I do—at last!'

'You wanted to before?'

'Very often.'

'I thought so!' said Agatha, with a candour which was in itself a dignity.

'But I couldn't,' said Mr. Longstaff. 'I never saw you alone.'

Before she knew it Agatha was blushing a little; for, to the ear, simply, his words implied that it was to her only he would appeal for the pleasure he had coveted. But the next instant she had become conscious that what he meant was simply that he admired her companion so much that he was afraid of her, and that, daring to speak to herself, he thought her a much smaller and less interesting personage. Her blush immediately faded; for there was no resentment to keep the colour in her cheek; and there was no resentment still when she perceived that, though her neighbour was looking straight at her, with his inspired, expanded eyes, he was thinking too much of Diana to have noticed this little play of confusion.

'Yes, it's very true,' she said. 'It is the first time my friend has left me.'

'She is very beautiful,' said Mr. Longstaff.

'Very beautiful,—and as good as she is beautiful.'

'Yes, yes,' he rejoined, solemnly. 'I am sure of that. I *know* it!'

'I know it even better than you,' said Agatha, smiling a little.

'Then you will have all the more patience with what I want to say to you. It is very strange; it will make you think, at first, that I am perhaps out of my mind. But I am not; I am thoroughly reasonable. You will see.' Then he paused a moment; his voice had begun to tremble again.

'I know what you are going to say,' said Agatha, very gently. 'You are in love with my friend.'

Mr. Longstaff gave her a look of devoted gratitude; he lifted up the edge of the blue shawl, which he had often seen Diana wear, and pressed it to his lips.

'I am extremely grateful!' he exclaimed. You don't think me crazy, then?'

'If you are crazy, there have been a great many madmen!' said Agatha.

'Of course there have been a great many. I have said that to myself, and it has helped me. They have gained nothing but the pleasure of their love, and I therefore, in gaining nothing and having nothing, am not worse off than the rest. But they had more than I, didn't they? You see I have had absolutely nothing,—not even a glance,' he went on. 'I have never even seen her look at me. I have not only never spoken to her, but I have never been near enough to speak to her. This is all I have ever had,—to lay my hand on something she has worn! and yet for the past month I have thought of her night and day. Sitting over there, a hundred rods away, simply because she was sitting in this place, in the same sunshine, looking out on the same sea: that was happiness enough for me. I am dying, but for the last five weeks that has kept me alive. It was for that I got up every day and came out here; but for that, I should have stayed at home and never have got up again. I have never sought to be presented to her, because I didn't wish to trouble her for nothing. It seemed to me it would be an impertinence to tell her of my admiration. I have nothing to offer her,—I am but the shadow of a living man, and if I were to say to her, "Madam, I love you," she could only answer, "Well, sir, what then?" Nothing—nothing! To speak to her of what I felt seemed only to open the lid of a grave in her face. It was more delicate not to do that; so I kept my distance and said nothing. Even this, as I say, has been a happiness, but it has been a happiness that has tired me out. This is the last of it. I must give up and make an end!' And he stopped, panting a little and apparently exhausted with his eloquence.

Agatha had always heard of love at first sight; she had read of it in poems and romances, but she had never been so near to it as this. It seemed to her most beautiful, and she believed in it devoutly. It made Mr. Longstaff brilliantly interesting; it cast a glory over the details of his face and person, and the pleading inflections of his voice. The little English ladies had been right; he was certainly a perfect gentleman. She could trust him.

'Perhaps if you stay at home awhile you will get better,' she said soothingly.

Her tone seemed to him such an indication that she accepted the propriety and naturalness of his passion that he put out his hand and for an instant laid it on her own.

'I knew you were reasonable—I knew I could talk to you. But I shall not get well. All the great doctors say so, and I believe them. If the passionate desire to get well for a particular purpose could work a miracle and cure a mortal disease, I should have seen the miracle two months ago. To get well and have a right to speak to your friend —that was my passionate desire. But I am worse than ever; I am very weak and I shall not be able to come out any more. It seemed to me today that I should never see you again, and yet I wanted so much to be able to tell you this! It made me very unhappy. What a wonderful chance it is that she went away! I must be grateful; if heaven doesn't grant my great prayers it grants my small ones. I beg you to render me this service. Tell her what I have told you. Not now—not till I am gone. Don't trouble her with it while I am in life. Please promise me that. But when I am dead it will seem less importunate, because then you can speak of me in the past. It will be like a story. My servant will come and tell you. Then say to her—"You were his last thought, and it was his last wish that you should know it." ' He slowly got up and put out his hand; his servant, who had been standing at a distance, came forward with obsequious solemnity, as if it were part of his duty to adapt his deportment to the tone of his master's conversation. Agatha Gosling took the young man's hand and he stood and looked at her a moment longer. She too had risen to her feet; she was much impressed.

'You wont tell her until *after*—?' he said pleadingly. She shook her head. 'And then you will tell her, faithfully?' She nodded, he pressed her hand, and then, having raised his hat, he took his servant's arm and slowly moved away.

Agatha kept her word; she said nothing to Diana about her interview. The young Americans came out and sat upon the shore the next day, and the next, and the next, and Agatha watched intently for Mr. Longstaff's reappearance. But she watched in vain; day after day he was absent, and his absence confirmed his sad prediction. She thought all this a wonderful thing to happen to a woman, and as she glanced askance at her beautiful companion, she was almost irritated at seeing her sit there so careless and serene, while a poor young man was dying, as one might say, of love for her. At moments she wondered whether, in spite of her promise, it was not her Christian duty to tell Diana his story and give her the chance to go to him. But it occurred to Agatha, who knew very well that her companion had a certain stately pride in which she herself was lacking, that even if she were told of his condition Diana might decline to do anything; and this she felt to be a most painful contingency. Besides, she had promised, and she always kept her promises. But her thoughts were constantly with Mr. Longstaff, and the romance of the affair. This made her melancholy and she talked much less than usual. Suddenly she was aroused from a reverie by hearing Diana express a careless curiosity as to what had become of the solitary young man who used to sit on the neighbouring bench and do them the honour to stare at them.

For almost the first time in her life, Agatha Gosling deliberately dissembled.

'He has either gone away, or he has taken to his bed. I believe he is dying alone, in some wretched mercenary lodging.'

'I prefer to believe something more cheerful,' said Diana. 'I believe he is gone to Paris and is eating a beautiful dinner at the Trois Frères Provençaux.'

Agatha for a moment said nothing; and then—

'I don't think you care what becomes of him,' she ventured to observe.

'My dear child, why should I care?' Diana demanded.

And Agatha Gosling was forced to admit that there really was no particular reason. But the event contradicted her. Three days afterward she took a long drive with her friend, from which they returned only as dusk was closing in. As they descended from the carriage at the door of their lodging she observed a figure standing in the street, slightly apart, which even in the early darkness had an air of familiarity. A second glance assured her that Mr. Longstaff's servant was hovering there in the hope of catching her attention. She immediately determined to give him a liberal measure of it. Diana left the vehicle and passed into the house, while the coachman fortunately asked for orders for the morrow. Agatha briefly gave such as were necessary, and then, before going in, turned to the hovering figure. It approached on tiptoe, hat in hand, and shaking its head very sadly. The old man wore an air of animated affliction which indicated that Mr. Longstaff was a generous master, and he proceeded to address Miss Gosling in that macaronic French which is usually at the command of Italian domestics who have seen the world.

'I stole away from my dear gentleman's bedside on purpose to have ten words with you. The old woman at the fruit-stall opposite told me that you had gone to drive, so I waited; but it seemed to me a thousand years till you returned!'

'But you have not left your master alone?' said Agatha.

'He has two Sisters of Charity—heaven reward them! They watch with him night and day. He is very low, *pauvre cher homme*!' And the old man looked at his interlocutress with that clear, human, sympathetic glance with which Italians of all classes bridge over the social gulf. Agatha felt that he knew his master's secret, and that she might discuss it with him freely.

'Is he dying?' she asked.

'That's the question, dear lady! He is very low. The doctors have given him up; but the doctors don't know his malady. They have felt his dear body all over, they have sounded his lungs, and looked at his tongue and counted his pulse; they know what he eats and drinks—it's soon told! But they haven't seen his *mind*, dear lady. I have; and so far I'm a better doctor than they. I know his secret—I know that he loves the beautiful girl above!' and the old man pointed to the upper windows of the house.

'Has your master taken you into his confidence?' Agatha demanded.

He hesitated a moment; then shaking his head a little and laying his hand on his heart—

'Ah, dear lady,' he said, 'the point is whether I have taken him into mine. I have not, I confess; he is too far gone. But I have determined to be his doctor and to try a remedy the others have never thought of. Will you help me?'

'If I can,' said Agatha. 'What is your remedy?'

The old man pointed to the upper windows of the house again.

'Your lovely friend! Bring her to his bedside.'

'If he is dying,' said Agatha, 'how would that help him?'

'He's dying for want of it. That's my idea at least, and I think it's worth trying. If a young man loves a beautiful woman, and, having never so much as touched the tip of her glove, falls into a mortal illness and wastes away, it requires no great wit to see that his illness doesn't come from his having indulged himself too grossly. It comes rather from the opposite cause! If he sinks when she's away, perhaps he'll come up when she's there. At any rate, that's my theory; and any theory is good that will save a dying man. Let the Diana come and stand a moment by his bed, and lay her hand upon his. We shall see what happens. If he gets well, it's worth while; if he doesn't, there is no harm done. A young lady risks nothing in going to see a poor gentleman who lies in a stupor between two holy women.'

Agatha was much impressed with this picturesque reasoning, but she answered that it was quite impossible that her beautiful friend should go upon this pious errand without a special invitation from Mr. Longstaff. Even should he beg Diana to come to him Agatha was by no means sure her companion would go; but it was very certain she would not take such an extraordinary step at the mere suggestion of a servant.

'But you, dear lady, have the happiness not to be a servant,' the old man rejoined. 'Let the suggestion be yours.'

'From me it could come with no force, for what am I supposed to know about your poor master?'

'You have not told the Diana what he told you the other day?'

Agatha answered this question by another question.

'Did he tell you what he had told me?'

The old man tapped his forehead an instant and smiled.

'A good servant, you know, dear lady, needs never to be told things! If you have not repeated my master's words to your beautiful friend, I beg you most earnestly to do so. I am afraid she is rather cold.'

Agatha glanced a moment at the upper windows and then she gave a silent nod. She wondered greatly to find herself discussing Diana's character with this aged menial; but the situation was so strange and romantic that one's old landmarks of propriety were quite obliterated, and it seemed natural that a *valet de chambre* should be as frank and familiar as a servant in an old-fashioned comedy.

'If it is necessary that my dear master shall send for the young lady,' Mr. Longstaff's domestic resumed, 'I think I can promise you that he will. Let me urge you meanwhile, to talk to her! If she is cold, melt her down. Prepare her to find him very interesting. If you could see him, poor gentleman, lying there as still and handsome as if he were his own monument in a *campo santo*, I think he would interest you.'

This seemed to Agatha a very touching image, but she came to a sense that her interview with Mr. Longstaff's representative, now unduly prolonged, was assuming a nocturnal character. She abruptly brought it to a close, after having assured her interlocutor that she would reflect upon what he had told her, and she rejoined her companion in the deepest agitation. Late that evening her agitation broke out. She went into Diana's room, where she found this young lady standing white-robed before her mirror, with her auburn tresses rippling down to her knees; and then, taking her two hands, she told the story of the young Englishman's passion, told of his coming to talk to her that day that Diana had left her alone on the bench by the sea, and of his venerable valet having, a couple of hours before, sought speech of her on the same subject. Diana listened, at first with a rosy flush, and then with a cold, an almost cruel, frown.

'Take pity upon him,' said Agatha Gosling,—'take pity upon him and go and see him.'

'I don't understand,' said her companion, 'and it seems to me very disagreeable. What is Mr. Longstaff to me?' But before they separated, Agatha had persuaded her to say that if a message really should come from the young man's death-bed, she would not refuse him the light of her presence.

The message really came, brought of course by the invalid's zealous chamberlain. He reappeared on the morrow, announcing that his master very humbly begged for the honour of ten minutes' conversation with the two ladies. They consented to follow him, and he led the way to Mr. Longstaff's apartments. Diana still wore her cloudy brow, but it made her look terribly handsome. Under the old man's guidance they passed through a low green door in a yellow wall, across a tangled garden full of orange-trees and winter roses, and into a white-wainscoted saloon, where they were presently left alone before a great classic, Empire clock, perched upon a frigid southern chimney-place. They waited, however, but a few moments; the door of the adjoining room opened and the Sisters of Charity, in white-winged hoods and with their hands thrust into the loose sleeves of the opposite arm, came forth and stood with downcast eyes on either side of the threshold. Then the old servant appeared between them and beckoned to the two young girls to advance. The latter complied with a certain hesitation, and he led them into the chamber of the dying man. Here, pointing to the bed, he silently left them and withdrew; not closing, however, the door of communication of the saloon, where he took up his station with the Sisters of Charity.

Diana and her companion stood together in the middle of the darker room, waiting for an invitation to approach their summoner. He lay in his bed, propped up on pillows, with his arms outside the counterpane. For a moment he simply gazed at them; he was as white as the sheet that covered him, and he certainly looked like a dying man. But he had the strength to bend forward and to speak in a soft, distinct voice.

'Would you be so kind,' said Mr. Longstaff, 'as to come nearer?'

Agatha Gosling gently pushed her friend forward, but she followed her to the bedside. Diana stood there, her frown had melted away; and the young man sank back upon his pillows and looked at her. A faint colour came into his face, and he clasped his two hands together on his breast. For some moments he simply gazed at the beautiful girl before him. It was an awkward situation for her, and Agatha expected her at any moment to turn away in disgust. But, slowly, her look of proud compulsion of mechanical compliance, was exchanged for something more patient and pitying. The young Englishman's face expressed a kind of spiritual ecstasy which, it was impossible not to feel, gave a peculiar sanctity to the occasion.

'It was very generous of you to come,' he said at last. 'I hardly ventured to hope you would. I suppose you know—I suppose your friend, who listened to me so kindly, has told you.'

'Yes, she knows,' murmured Agatha—'she knows.'

'I did not intend you should know until after my death,' he went on; 'but,'—and he paused a moment and shook his clasped hands together,—'I couldn't wait! And when I felt that I couldn't wait, a new idea, a new desire, came into my mind.' He was silent again for an instant, still looking with worshipful entreaty at Diana. The colour in his face deepened. 'It is something that you may do for me. You will think it a most extraordinary request; but, in my position, a man grows bold. Dear lady, will you marry me?'

'Oh, dear!' cried Agatha Gosling, just audibly. Her companion said nothing. Her attitude seemed to say that in this remarkable situation, one thing was no more surprising than another. But she paid Mr. Longstaff's proposal the respect of slowly seating herself in a chair which had been placed near his bed; here she rested in maidenly majesty, with her eyes fixed on the ground.

'It will help me to die happy, since die I must!' the young man continued. 'It will enable me to do something for you—the only thing I can do. I have property,—lands, houses, a great many beautiful things,—things I have loved, and am very sorry to be leaving behind me. Lying here helpless and hopeless through so many days, the thought has come to me of what a bliss it would be to know that they would rest in your hands. If you were my wife, they would rest there safely. You might be spared much annoyance; and it is not only that. It is a fancy I have beyond that. It would be the feeling of it! I am fond of life. I don't want to die; but since I must die, it would be a happiness to have got just this out of life—this joining of our hands before a priest. You could go away then. For you it would make no change—it would be no burden. But I should have a few hours in which to lie and think of my happiness.'

There was something in the young man's tone so simple and sincere, so tender and urgent, that Agatha Gosling was touched to tears. She turned away to hide them, and went on tiptoe to the window, where she wept silently. Diana apparently was not unmoved. She raised her eyes, and let them rest kindly on those of Mr. Longstaff, who continued softly to urge his proposal. 'It would be a great charity,' he said, 'a great condescension; and it can produce no consequence to you that you could regret. It can only give you a larger liberty. You know very little about me, but I have a feeling that, so far as belief goes, you can believe me, and that is all I ask of you. I don't ask you to love me,—that takes time. It is something I cannot pretend to. It is only to consent to the form, the ceremony. I have seen the English clergyman; he says he will perform it. He will tell you, besides, all about me,—that I am an English gentleman, and that the name I offer you is one of the best in the world.'

It was strange to hear a dying man lie there and argue his point in this categorical fashion; but now, apparently, his argument was finished. There was a deep silence, and Agatha thought it would be delicate on her own part to retire. She moved quietly into the adjoining room, where the two Sisters of Charity still stood with their hands in their sleeves, and the old Italian *valet* was taking snuff with a melancholy gesture, like a perplexed diplomatist. Agatha turned her back to these people, and, approaching a window again, stood looking out into the garden upon the orange-trees and the winter roses. It seemed to her that she had been listening to the most beautiful, most romantic, and most eloquent of declarations. How could Diana be insensible to it? She earnestly hoped her companion would consent to the solemn and interesting ceremony proposed by Mr. Longstaff, and though her delicacy had prompted her to withdraw, it permitted her to listen eagerly to what Diana would say. Then (as she heard nothing) it was eclipsed by the desire to go back and whisper, with a sympathetic kiss, a word of counsel. She glanced round again at the Sisters of Charity, who appeared to have perceived that the moment was one of suspense. One of them detached herself, and, as Agatha returned, followed her a few steps into the room. Diana had got up from her chair. She was looking about her uneasily. She grasped at Agatha's hand. Reginald Longstaff lay there with his wasted face and his brilliant eyes, looking at them both. Agatha took her friend's two hands in both her own.

'It is very little to do, dearest,' she murmured, 'and it will make him very happy.'

The young man appeared to have heard her, and he repeated her words in a tone of intense entreaty.

'It is very little to do, dearest.'

Diana looked round at him an instant. Then, for an instant, she covered her face with her two hands. Removing them, but holding them still against her cheeks, she looked at her companion with eyes that Agatha always remembered—eyes through which a thin gleam of mockery flashed from the seriousness of her face.

'Suppose, after all, he should get well?' she murmured.

Longstaff heard it; he gave a long, soft moan, and turned away. The Sister immediately approached his bed, on the other side, dropped on her knees and bent over him, while he leaned his head against the great white cape along which her crucifix depended. Diana stood a moment longer, looking at him; then, gathering her shawl together with a great dignity, she slowly walked out of the room. Agatha could do nothing but follow her. The old Italian, holding the door open for them to pass out, made them an exaggerated obeisance.

In the garden Diana paused, with a flush in her cheek, and said,

'If he could die with it, he could die without it!' But beyond the garden gate, in the empty sunny street, she suddenly burst into tears.

Agatha made no reproaches, no comments; but her companion,

during the rest of the day, spoke of Mr. Longstaff several times with an almost passionate indignation. She pronounced his conduct indelicate, egotistic, impertinent; she declared that she had found the scene most revolting. Agatha, for the moment, remained silent, but the next day she attempted to suggest something in apology for the poor young man. Then Diana, with great emphasis, begged her to be so good as never to mention his name again; and she added that he had put her completely out of humour with Nice, from which place they would immediately take their departure. This they did without delay; they began to travel again. Agatha heard no more of Reginald Longstaff; the English ladies who had been her original source of information with regard to him had now left Nice; otherwise she would have written to them for news. That is, she would have thought of writing to them; I suspect that, on the whole, she would have denied herself this satisfaction, on the ground of loyalty to her friend. Agatha, at any rate, could only drop a tear, at solitary hours, upon the young man's unanswered prayer and early death. It must be confessed, however, that sometimes, as the weeks elapsed, a certain faint displeasure mingled itself with her sympathy—a wish that, roughly speaking, poor Mr. Longstaff had left them alone. Since that strange interview at his bedside things had not gone well; the charm of their earlier contentment seemed broken. Agatha said to herself that, really, if she were superstitious, she might fancy that Diana's conduct on this occasion had brought them under an evil charm. It was no superstition, certainly, to think that this young lady had lost a certain evenness of temper. She was impatient, absent-minded, indifferent, capricious. She expressed unaccountable opinions and proposed unnatural plans. It is true that disagreeable things were constantly happening to them—things which would have taxed the most unruffled spirit. Their post-horses broke down, their postilions were impertinent, their luggage went astray, their servants betrayed them. The heavens themselves seemed to join in the conspiracy, and for days together were dark and ungenerous, treating them only to wailing winds and watery clouds. It was, in a large measure, in the light of after years that Agatha judged this period, but even at the time she felt it to be depressing, uncomfortable, unnatural. Diana apparently shared this feeling, though she never openly avowed it. She took refuge in a kind of haughty silence, and whenever a new *contretemps* came to her knowledge, she simply greeted it with a bitter smile which Agatha always interpreted as an ironical reflection on poor, fantastic, obtrusive Mr. Longstaff, who, through some mysterious action upon the machinery of nature, had turned the tide of their fortunes. At the end of the summer, suddenly, Diana proposed they should go home, in the tone of a person who gives up a hopeless struggle. Agatha assented, and the two ladies returned to America, much to the relief of Miss Gosling, who had an uncomfortable sense that there was something unexpressed and unregulated between them, which gave their conversation a resemblance to a sultry morning. But at home they separated very tenderly, for Agatha had to go and devote herself to her nearer kinsfolk in the country. These good people after her long absence were exacting, so that for two years she saw nothing of her late companion.

She often, however, heard from her, and Diana figured in the town gossip that was occasionally wafted to her rural home. She sometimes figured strangely—as a rattling coquette, who carried on flirtations by the hundred and broke hearts by the dozen. This had not been Diana's former character and Agatha found matter for meditation in the change. But the young lady's own letters said little of her admirers and displayed no trophies. They came very fitfully—sometimes at the rate of a dozen a month and sometimes not at all; but they were usually of a serious and abstract cast and contained the author's opinions upon life, death, religion and immortality. Mistress of her actions and of a pretty fortune, it might have been expected that news would come in trustworthy form of Diana's at last accepting one of her rumoured lovers. Such news in fact came, and it was apparently trustworthy, inasmuch as it proceeded from the young lady herself. She wrote to Agatha that she was to be married, and Agatha immediately congratulated her upon her happiness. Then Diana wrote back that though she was to be married she was not at all happy; and she shortly afterwards added that she had broken off her projected union and that her felicity was smaller than ever. Poor Agatha was sorely perplexed and found it a comfort that a month after this her friend should have sent her a peremptory summons to come to her. She immediately obeyed. Arriving, after a long journey, at the dwelling of her young hostess, she saw Diana at the farther end of the drawing-room, with her back turned, looking out of the window. She was evidently watching for Agatha, but Miss Gosling had come in, by accident, through a private entrance which was not visible from the window. She gently approached her friend and then Diana turned. She had her two hands laid upon her cheeks and her eyes were sad; her face and attitude suggested something that Agatha had seen before and kept the memory of. While she kissed her Agatha remembered that it was just so she had stood for that last moment before poor Mr. Longstaff.

'Will you come abroad with me again?' Diana asked. 'I am very ill.'

'Dearest, what is the matter?' said Agatha.

'I don't know; I believe I am dying. They tell me this place is bad for me; that I must have another climate; that I must move about. Will you take care of me; I shall be very easy to take care of now.'

Agatha, for all answer, embraced her afresh, and as soon after this as possible the two friends embarked again for Europe. Miss Gosling had lent herself the more freely to this scheme as her companion's appearance seemed a striking confirmation of her words. Not, indeed, that she looked as if she were dying, but in the two years that had elapsed since their separation she had wasted and faded. She looked more than two years older and the brilliancy of her beauty was dimmed. She was pale and languid, and she moved more slowly than when she seemed a goddess treading the forest leaves. The beautiful statue had grown human and taken on some of the imperfections of humanity. And yet the doctors by no means affirmed that she had a mortal malady, and when one of them was asked by an inquisitive matron why he had recommended this young lady to cross the seas, he replied with a smile that it was a principle in his system to prescribe the remedies that his patients acutely desired.

At present the fair travellers had no misadventures. The broken charm had removed itself; the heavens smiled upon them and their postilions treated them like princesses. Diana, too, had completely recovered her native placidity; she was the gentlest, the most docile, the most reasonable of women. She was silent and subdued as was natural in an invalid; though in one important particular her demeanour was certainly at variance with the idea of debility. She relished movement much more than rest, and constant change of place became the law of her days. She wished to see all the places that she had not seen before, and all the old ones over again.

'If I am really dying,' she said, smiling softly, 'I must leave my farewell cards everywhere.' So she lived in a great open carriage, leaning back in it and looking, right and left, at everything she passed. On her former journey to Europe she had seen but little of England, and now she would visit the whole of this famous island. So she rolled for weeks through the beautiful English landscape, past meadows and hedge-rows, over the avenues of great estates and under the walls of castles and abbeys. For the English parks and manors, the 'Halls' and 'Courts,' she had an especial admiration, and into the grounds of such as were open to appreciative tourists she made a point of penetrating. Here she stayed her carriage beneath the oaks and beeches, and sat for an hour at a time listening to nightingales and watching browsing deer. She never failed to visit a residence that lay on her road, and as soon as she arrived at a place she inquired punctiliously whether there were any fine country-seats in the neighbourhood. In this fashion she spent a whole summer. Through the autumn she continued to wander restlessly; she visited, on the Continent, a hundred watering-places and travellers' resorts. The beginning of the winter found her in Rome, where she confessed to extreme fatigue and determined to seek repose.

'I am weary, weary,' she said to her companion. 'I didn't know how weary I was. I feel like sinking down in this City of Rest, and resting forever.'

She took a lodging in an old palace, where her chamber was hung with ancient tapestries, and her drawing-room decorated with the arms of a pope. Here, giving way to her fatigue, she ceased to wander. The only thing she did was to go every day to St. Peter's. She went nowhere else. She sat at her window all day with a big book in her lap, which she never read, looking out into a Roman garden at a fountain plashing into a weedy alcove, and half a dozen nymphs in mottled marble. Sometimes she told her companion that she was happier this way than she had ever been,—in this way, and in going to St. Peter's. In the great church she often spent the whole afternoon. She had a servant behind her, carrying a stool. He placed her stool against a marble pilaster, and she sat there for a long time, looking up into the airy hollow of the dome and over the peopled pavement. She noticed every one who passed her, but Agatha, lingering beside her, felt less at liberty, she hardly knew why, to murmur a sportive commentary on the people about them than she had felt when they sat upon the shore at Nice.

One day Agatha left her and strolled about the church by herself. The ecclesiastical life of Rome had not shrunken to its present smallness, and in one corner or another of St. Peter's, there was always some point of worship. Agatha found entertainment, and was absent for half an hour. When she came back, she found her companion's place deserted, and she sat down on the empty stool to await her reappearance. Some time elapsed and she wandered away in quest of her. She found her at last, near one of the side-alters; but she was not alone. A gentleman stood before her whom she appeared just to have encountered. Her face was very pale, and its expression led Agatha to look straightway at the stranger. Then she saw he was no stranger; he was Reginald Longstaff! He, too, evidently had been much startled, but he was already recovering himself. He stood very gravely an instant longer; then he silently bowed to the two ladies and turned away.

Agatha felt at first as if she had seen a ghost; but the impression was immediately corrected by the fact that Mr. Longstaff's aspect was very much less ghostly than it had been in life. He looked like a strong man; he held himself upright and had a flush of colour. What Agatha saw in Diana's face was not surprise; it was a pale radiance which she waited a moment to give a name to. Diana put out her hand and laid it in her arm, and her touch helped Agatha to know what it was that her face expressed. Then she felt too that this knowledge itself was not a surprise; she seemed to have been waiting for it. She looked at her friend again and Diana was beautiful. Diana blushed and became more beautiful yet. Agatha led her back to her seat near the marble pilaster.

'So you were right,' Agatha said presently. 'He would, after all, have got well.'

Diana would not sit down; she motioned to her servant to bring away the stool, and continued to move towards the door. She said nothing until she stood without, in the great square of the colonnades and fountains. Then she spoke:

'I am right now, but I was wrong then. He got well because I refused him. I gave him a hurt that cured him.'

That evening, beneth the Roman lamps, in the great drawing-room of the arms of the pope, a remarkable conversation took place between the two friends. Diana wept and hid her face; but her tears and her shame were gratuitous. Agatha felt, as I have said, that she had already guessed all the unexplained, and it was needless for her companion to tell her that three weeks after she had refused Reginald Longstaff she insanely loved him. It was needless that Diana should confess that his image had never been out of her mind, that she believed he was still among the living, and that she had come back to Europe with a desperate hope of meeting him. It was in this hope that she had wandered from town to town, and noticed all the passers; and it was in this hope that she had lingered in so many English parks. She knew her love was very strange; she could only say it had consumed her. It had all come upon her afterward,—in retrospect, in meditation. Or rather, she supposed, it had been there always since she first saw him, and the revulsion from displeasure to pity, after she left his bedside, had brought it out. And with it came the faith that he had indeed got well, both of his malady and of his own passion. This was her punishment! And then she spoke with a divine simplicity which Agatha, weeping a little too, wished that, if this possibility were a fact, the young man might have heard. 'I am so glad he is well and strong. And that he looks so handsome and so good!' And she presently added, 'Of course he has got well only to hate me. He wishes never to see me again. Very good. I have had my wish; I have seen him once more. That was what I wanted and I can die content.'

It seemed in fact, as if she were going to die. She went no more to St. Peter's, and exposed herself to no more encounters with Mr. Longstaff. She sat at her window and looked out at the mottled dryads and the cypresses, or wandered about her quarter of the palace with a vaguely smiling resignation. Agatha watched her with a sadness that was less submissive. This too was something that she had heard of, that she had read of in poetry and fable, but that she had never supposed she should see;—her companion was dying of love! Agatha pondered many things and resolved upon several. The first of these latter was sending for the doctor. This personage came, and Diana let him look at her through his spectacles, and hold her white wrist. He announced that she was ill, and she smiled and said she knew it; and then he gave her a little phial of gold-coloured fluid, which he bade her to drink. He recommended her to remain in Rome, as the climate exactly suited her complaint. Agatha's second desire was to see Mr. Longstaff, who had appealed to her, she reflected, in the day of his own tribulation, and whom she therefore had a right to approach at present. She disbelieved, too, that the passion which led him to take that extraordinary step at Nice was extinct; such passions as that never died. If he had made no further attempt to see Diana it was because he believed that she was still as cold as when she turned away from his death-bed. It must be added, moreover, that Agatha felt a lawful curiosity to learn how from that death-bed he had risen again into blooming manhood.

On this last point, all elucidation left something unexplained. Agatha went to St. Peter's, feeling sure, that sooner or later she should encounter him there. At the end of a week she perceived him, and seeing her, he immediately came and spoke to her. As Diana had said, he was now extremely handsome, and he looked particularly good. He was a blooming, gallant, quiet, young English gentleman. He seemed much embarrassed, but his manner to Agatha expressed the highest consideration.

'You must think me a dreadful imposter,' he said, very gravely. 'But I *was* dying,—or I believed I was.'

'And by what miracle did you recover?'

He was silent a moment, and then he said:

'I suppose it was by the miracle of wounded pride!' Then she noticed that he asked nothing about Diana; and presently she felt that he knew she was thinking of this. 'The strangest part of it,' he added, 'was that when I came back to strength, what had gone before had become as a simple dream. And what happened to me here the other day,' he went on, 'failed to make it a reality again!'

Agatha looked at him a moment in silence, and saw again that he was handsome and kind; and then dropping a sigh over the wonderful mystery of things, she turned sadly away. That evening, Diana said to her:

'I know that you have seen him!'

Agatha came to her and kissed her.

'And I am nothing to him now?'

'My own dearest—' murmured Agatha.

Diana had drunk the little phial of gold-coloured liquid; but after this, she ceased to wander about the palace; she never left her room. The old doctor was with her constantly now, and he continued to say that the air of Rome was very good for her complaint. Agatha watched her in helpless sadness; she saw her fading and sinking, and yet she was unable to comfort her. She tried it once in saying hard things about Mr. Longstaff, in pointing out that he had not been honourable, rising herein to a sublime hypocrisy, for, on that last occasion at St. Peter's, the poor girl had felt a renewed personal admiration,—the quickening of a private flame; she saw nothing but his good looks and his kind manner.

'What did he want—what did he mean, after all?' she ingenuously murmured, leaning over Diana's sofa. 'Why should he have been wounded at what you said? It would have been part of the bargain that he should not get well. Did he mean to take an unfair advantage—to make you his wife under false pretences? When you put your finger on the weak spot, why should he resent it? No, it was not honourable.'

Diana smiled sadly; she had no false shame now, and she spoke of this thing as if it concerned another person.

'He would have counted on my forgiving him!' she said. A little while after this, she began to sink more rapidly. Then she called her friend to her, and said simply: 'Send for him!' And as Agatha looked perplexed and distressed, she added, 'I know he is still in Rome.'

Agatha at first was at a lost where to find him, but among the benefits of the papal dispensation, was the fact that the pontifical police could instantly help you to lay your hand upon any sojourner in the Eternal City. Mr. Longstaff had a passport in detention by the government, and this document formed a basis of instruction to the servant whom Agatha sent to investigate the authorities. The servant came back with the news that he had seen the distinguished stranger, who would wait upon the ladies at the hour they had proposed. When this hour came and Mr. Longstaff was announced, Diana said to her companion that she must remain with her. It was an afternoon in spring; the high windows into the palace garden were open, and the room was filled with great sheaves and stacks of the abundant Roman flowers. Diana sat in a deep arm-chair.

It was certinly a difficult position for Reginald Longstaff. He stopped on the threshold and looked awhile at the woman to whom he had made his extraordinary offer; then, pale and agitated, he advanced rapidly towards her. He was evidently shocked at the state in which he found her; he took her hand, and, bending over it, raised it to his lips. She fixed her eyes on him a little, and she smiled a little.

'It is I who am dying, now,' she said. 'And now I want to ask something of *you*—to ask what you asked of me.'

He stared, and a deep flush of colour came into his face; he hesitated for an appreciable moment. Then lowering his head with a movement of assent he kissed her hand again.

'Come back to-morrow,' she said; 'that is all I ask of you.'

He looked at her again for a while in silence; then he abruptly turned and left her; She sent for the English clergyman and told him that she was a dying woman, and that she wanted the marriage service read beside her couch. The clergyman, too, looked at her, marvelling; but he consented to humour so tenderly romantic a whim and made an appointment for the afternoon of the morrow. Diana was very tranquil. She sat motionless, with her hands clasped and her eyes closed. Agatha wandered about, arranging and re-arranging the flowers. On the morrow she encountered Mr. Longstaff in one of the outer rooms. He had come before his time. She made this objection to his being admitted; but he answered that he knew he was early and had come with intention; he wished to spend the intervening hour with his prospective bride. So he went in and sat down by her couch again, and Agatha, leaving them alone, never knew what passed between them. At the end of the hour the clergyman arrived, and read the marriage service to them, pronouncing the nuptial blessing, while Agatha stood by as witness. Mr. Longstaff went through all this with a solemn, inscrutable face, and Agatha, observing him, said to herself that one must at least do him the justice to admit that he was performing punctiliously whbat honour demanded. When the clergyman had gone he asked Diana when he might see her again.

'Never!' she said, with her strange smile. And she added—'I shall not live long now.

He kissed her face, but he was obliged to leave her. He gave Agatha an anxious look as if he wished to say something to her, but she preferred not to listen to him. After this Diana sank rapidly. The next day Reginald Longstaff came back and insisted upon seeing Agatha.

'Why should she die?' he asked. 'I want her to live.'

'Have you forgiven her?' said Agatha.

'She saved me!' he cried.

Diana consented to see him once more; there were two doctors in attendance now, and they also had consented. He knelt down beside her bed and asked her to live. But she feebly shook her head.

'It would be wrong of me,' she said.

Later, when he came back once more, Agatha told him she was gone. He stood wondering, with tears in his eyes.

'I don't understand,' he said. 'Did she love me or not?'

'She loved you,' said Agatha, 'more than she believed you could now love her; and it seemed to her that, when she had had her moment of happiness, to leave you at liberty was the tenderest way she could show it!'

An International Episode

IN TWO PARTS

[First appeared in the *Cornhill Magazine*, vols. xxxviii-xxxix (December 1878-January 1879), pp. 687-713, 61-90. Its first book publication was in America where it appeared as No. 91 of Harper's Half-Hour Series (New York: Harper and Brothers, 1879). The text there follows the *Cornhill* version. For the first English book edition, however, the tale was revised and reprinted in volume ii of *Daisy Miller: A Study* (1879). Although otherwise this revision is very slight, James added one completely new scene to the text of 1879. The 1879 text was later reproduced in volume xii of James's first 'Collective Edition' (1883). Using the text of 1879, James finally revised the tale for the New York Edition where it appears in volume xiv (*Lady Barbarina, Etc.*, 1908).]

PART I

FOUR YEARS AGO—IN 1874—TWO YOUNG ENGLISHMEN HAD OCCAsion to go to the United States. They crossed the ocean at midsummer, and, arriving in New York on the first day of August, were much struck with the fervid temperature of that city. Disembarking upon the wharf, they climbed into one of those huge high-hung coaches which convey passengers to the hotels, and with a great deal of bouncing and bumping, took their course through Broadway. The midsummer aspect of New York is not perhaps the most favourable one; still, it is not without its picturesque and even brilliant side. Nothing could well resemble less a typical English street than the interminable avenue, rich in incongruities, through which our two travellers advanced—looking out on each side of them at the comfortable animation of the sidewalks, the high-coloured, heterogeneous architecture, the huge white marble façades, glittering in the strong, crude light, and bedizened with gilded lettering, the multifarious awnings, banners, and streamers, the extraordinary number of omnibuses, horse-cars, and other democratic vehicles, the vendors of cooling fluids, the white trousers and big straw-hats of the policemen, the tripping gait of the modish young persons on the pavement, the general brightness, newness, juvenility, both of people and things. The young men had exchanged few observations; but in crossing Union Square, in front of the monument to Washington—in the very shadow, indeed, projected by the image of the *pater patriæ*—one of them remarked to the other, 'It seems a rum-looking place.'

'Ah, very odd, very odd,' said the other, who was the clever man of the two.

'Pity it's so beastly hot,' resumed the first speaker, after a pause.

'You know we are in a low latitude,' said his friend.

'I daresay,' remarked the other.

'I wonder,' said the second speaker, presently, 'if they can give one a bath.'

'I daresay not,' rejoined the other.

'Oh, I say!' cried his comrade.

This animated discussion was checked by their arrival at the hotel, which had been recommended to them by an American gentleman whose acquaintance they made—with whom, indeed, they became very intimate—on the steamer, and who had proposed to accompany them to the inn and introduce them, in a friendly way, to the proprietor. This plan, however, had been defeated by their friend's finding that his 'partner' was awaiting him on the wharf, and that his commercial associate desired him instantly to come and give his attention to certain telegrams received from St. Louis. But the two Englishmen, with nothing but their national prestige and personal graces to recommend them, were very well received at the hotel, which had an air of capacious hospitality. They found that a bath was not unattainable, and were indeed struck with the facilities for prolonged and reiterated immersion with which their apartment was supplied. After bathing a good deal—more indeed than they had ever done before on a single occasion—they made their way into the dining-room of the hotel, which was a spacious restaurant, with a fountain in the middle, a great many tall plants in ornamental tubs, and an array of French waiters. The first dinner on land, after a sea voyage, is under any circumstances a delightful occasion, and there was something particularly agreeable in the circumstances in which our young Englishmen found themselves. They were extremely good-natured young men; they were more observant than they appeared; in a sort of inarticulate, accidentally dissimulative fashion, they were highly appreciative. This was perhaps especially the case with the elder, who was also, as I have said, the man of talent. They sat down at a little table which was a very different affair from the great clattering see-saw in the saloon of the steamer. The wide doors and windows of the restaurant stood open, beneath large awnings, to a wide pavement, where there were other plants in tubs, and rows of spreading trees, and beyond which there was a large shady square, without any palings and with marble-paved walks. And above the vivid verdure rose other façades of white marble and of pale chocolate-coloured stone, squaring themselves against the deep blue sky. Here, outside, in the light and the shade and the heat, there was a great tinkling of the bells of innumerable street-cars, and a constant strolling and shuffling and rustling of many pedestrians, a large proportion of whom were young women in Pompadour-looking dresses. Within, the place was cool and vaguely-lighted; with the plash of water, the odour of flowers and the flitting of French waiters, as I have said, upon soundless carpets.

'It's rather like Paris, you know,' said the younger of our two travellers.

'It's like Paris—only more so,' his companion rejoined.

'I suppose it's the French waiters,' said the first speaker. 'Why don't they have French waiters in London?'

'Fancy a French waiter at a club,' said his friend.

The young Englishman stared a little, as if he could not fancy it. 'In Paris I'm very apt to dine at a place where there's an English waiter. Don't you know, what's-his-name's, close to the thingumbob? They always set an English waiter at me. I suppose they think I can't speak French.'

'Well, you can't.' And the elder of the young Englishmen unfolded his napkin.

His companion took no notice whatever of this declaration. 'I say,' he resumed, in a moment, 'I suppose we must learn to speak American. I suppose we must take lessons.'

'I can't understand them,' said the clever man.

'What the deuce is *he* saying?' asked his comrade, appealing from the French waiter.

'He is recommending some soft-shell crabs,' said the clever man.

And so, in desultory observation of the idiosyncrasies of the new society in which they found themselves, the young Englishmen proceeded to dine—going in largely, as the phrase is, for cooling draughts and dishes, of which their attendant offered them a very long list. After dinner they went out and slowly walked about the neighbouring streets. The early dusk of waning summer was coming on, but the heat was still very great. The pavements were hot even to the stout boot-soles of the British travellers, and the trees along the kerb-stone emitted strange exotic odours. The young men wandered through the adjoining square—that queer place without palings, and with marble walks arranged in black and white lozenges. There were a great many benches, crowded with shabby-looking people, and the travellers remarked, very justly, that it was not much like Belgrave Square. On one side was an enormous hotel, lifting up into the hot darkness an immense array of open, brightly-lighted windows. At the base of this populous structure was an eternal jangle of horse-cars, and all round it, in the upper dusk, was a sinister hum of mosquitoes. The ground-floor of the hotel seemed to be a huge transparent cage, flinging a wide glare of gaslight into the street, of which it formed a sort of public adjunct, absorbing and emitting the passers-by promiscuously. The young Englishmen went in with everyone else, from curiosity, and saw a couple of hundred men sitting on divans along a great marble-paved corridor, with their legs stretched out, together with several dozen more standing in a *queue*, as at the ticket-office of a railway station, before a brillantly illuminated counter, of vast extent. These latter persons, who carried portmanteaux in their hands, had a dejected, exhausted look; their garments were not very fresh, and they seemed to be rendering some mysterious tribute to a magnificent young man with a waxed moustache and a shirt front adorned with diamond buttons, who every now and then dropped an absent glance over their multitudinous patience. They were American citizens doing homage to an hotel-clerk.

By bed time—in their impatience to taste of a terrestrial couch again our seafarers went to bed early—it was still insufferably hot, and the buzz of the mosquitoes at the open windows might have passed for an audible crepitation of the temperature. 'We can't stand this, you know,' the young Englishmen said to each other; and they tossed about all night more boisterously than they had tossed upon the Atlantic billows. On the morrow, their first thought was that they would re-embark that day for England; and then it occured to them that they might find an asylum nearer at hand. The cave of Æolus became their ideal of comfort, and they wondered where the Americans went when they wished to cool off. They had not the least idea, and they determined to apply for information to Mr. J. L. Westgate. This was the name inscribed in a bold hand on the back of a letter carefully preserved in the pocket-book of our junior traveller. Beneath the address, in the left-hand corner of the envelope, were the words, 'Introducing Lord Lambeth and Percy Beaumont, Esq.' The letter had been given to the two Englishmen by a good friend of theirs in London, who had been in America two years previously and had singled out Mr. J. L. Westgate from the many friends he had left there as the consignee, as it were, of his compatriots. 'He is a capital fellow,' the Englishman in London had said, 'and he has got an awfully pretty wife. He's tremendously hospitable—he will do everything in the world for you; and as he knows everyone over there, it is quite needless I should give you any other introduction. He will make you see every one; trust to him for putting you into circulation.

He has got a tremendously pretty wife.' It was natural that in the hour of tribulation Lord Lambeth and Mr. Percy Beaumont should have bethought themselves of a gentleman whose attractions had been thus vividly depicted; all the more so that he lived in the Fifth Avenue and that the Fifth Avenue, as they had ascertained the night before, was contiguous to their hotel. 'Ten to one he'll be out of town,' said Percy Beaumont; 'but we can at least find out where he has gone, and we can immediately start in pursuit. He can't possibly have gone to a hotter place, you know.'

'Oh, there's only one hotter place,' said Lord Lambeth, 'and I hope he hasn't gone there.'

They strolled along the shady side of the street to the number indicated upon the precious letter. The house presented an imposing chocolate-coloured expanse, relieved by facings and window-cornices of florid sculpture, and by a couple of dusty rose-trees, which clambered over the balconies and the portico. This last-mentioned feature was approached by a monumental flight of steps.

'Rather better than a London house,' said Lord Lambeth, looking down from this altitude, after they had rung the bell.

'It depends upon what London house you mean,' replied his companion. 'You have a tremendous chance to get wet between the house-door and your carriage.'

'Well,' said Lord Lambeth, glancing at the burning heavens, 'I "guess" it doesn't rain so much here!'

The door was opened by a long negro in a white jacket, who grinned familiarly when Lord Lambeth asked for Mr. Westgate.

'He ain't at home, sir; he's down town at his o'fice.'

'Oh, at his office?' said the visitors. 'And when will he be at home?'

'Well, sir, when he goes out dis way in de mo'ning, he ain't liable to come home all day.'

This was discouraging; but the address of Mr. Westgate's office was freely imparted by the intelligent black, and was taken down by Percy Beaumont in his pocket-book. The two gentlemen then returned, languidly, to their hotel, and sent for a hackney-coach; and in this commodious vehicle they rolled comfortably down town. They measured the whole length of Broadway again, and found it a path of fire; and then, deflecting to the left, they were deposited by their conductor before a fresh, light, ornamental structure, ten stories high, in a street crowded with keen-faced, light-limbed young men, who were running about very quickly and stopping each other eagerly at corners and in doorways. Passing into this brilliant building, they were introduced by one of the keen-faced young men—he was a charming fellow, in wonderful cream-coloured garments and a hat with a blue ribbon, who had evidently perceived them to be aliens and helpless—to a very snug hydraulic elevator, in which they took their place with many other persons, and which, shooting upward in its vertical socket, presently projected them into the seventh horizontal compartment of the edifice. Here, after brief delay, they found themselves face to face with the friend of their friend in London. His office was composed of several different rooms, and they waited very silently in one of them after they had sent in their letter and their cards. The letter was not one which it would take Mr. Westgate very long to read, but he came out to speak to them more instantly than they could have expected; he had evidently jumped up from his work. He was a tall, lean personage, and was dressed all in fresh white linen; he had a thin, sharp, familiar face, with an expression that was at one and the same time sociable and business-like, a quick, intelligent eye, and a large brown moustache, which concealed his mouth and made his chin, beneath it, look small. Lord Lambeth thought he looked tremendously clever.

'How do you do, Lord Lambeth—how do you do sir?' he said, holding the open letter in his hand. 'I'm very glad to see you—I hope you're very well. You had better come in here—I think it's cooler;' and he led the way into another room, where there were law-books and papers, and windows wide open beneath striped awnings. Just opposite one of the windows, on a line with his eyes, Lord Lambeth observed the weather-vane of a church steeple. The uproar of the street sounded infinitely far below, and Lord Lambeth felt very high in the air. 'I say it's cooler,' pursued their host, 'but everything is relative. How do you stand the heat?'

'I can't say we like it,' said Lord Lambeth; 'but Beaumont likes it better than I.'

'Well, it won't last,' Mr. Westgate very cheerfully declared; 'nothing unpleasant lasts over here. It was very hot when Captain Littledale was here; he did nothing but drink sherry-cobblers. He expresses some doubt in his letter whether I will remember him—as if I didn't remember making six sherry-cobblers for him one day, in about twenty minutes. I hope you left him well; two years having elapsed since then.'

'Oh, yes, he's all right,' said Lord Lambeth.

'I am always very glad to see your countrymen,' Mr. Westgate pursued. 'I thought it would be time some of you should be coming along. A friend of mine was saying to me only a day or two ago, "It's time for the water-melons and the Englishmen." '

'The Englishmen and the water-melons just now are about the

same thing,' Percy Beaumont observed, wiping his dripping forehead.

'Ah, well, we'll put you on ice, as we do the melons. You must go down to Newport.'

'We'll go anywhere!' said Lord Lambeth.

'Yes, you want to go to Newport—that's what you want to do,' Mr. Westgate affirmed. 'But let's see—when did you get here?'

'Only yesterday,' said Percy Beaumont.

'Ah, yes, by the "Russia." Where are you staying?'

'At the "Hanover," I think they call it.'

'Pretty comfortable?' inquired Mr. Westgate.

'It seems a capital place, but I can't say we like the gnats,' said Lord Lambeth.

Mr. Westgate stared and laughed. 'Oh, no, of course you don't like the gnats. We shall expect you to like a good many things over here, but we shan't insist upon your liking the gnats; though certainly you'll admit that, as gnats, they are fine, eh? But you oughtn't to remain in the city.'

'So we think,' said Lord Lambeth. 'If you would kindly suggest something——'

'Suggest something, my dear sir?'—and Mr. Westgate looked at him, narrowing his eyelids. 'Open your mouth and shut your eyes! Leave it to me, and I'll put you through. It's a matter of national pride with me that all Englishmen should have a good time; and, as I have had considerable practice, I have learned to minister to their wants. I find they generally want the right thing. So just please to consider yourselves my property; and if anyone should try to appropriate you, please to say, "Hands off; too late for the market." But let's see,' continued the American, in his slow, humorous voice, with a distinctness of utterance which appeared to his visitors to be part of a humorous intention—a strangely leisurely, speculative voice for a man evidently so busy and, as they felt, so professional—'let's see; are you going to make something of a stay, Lord Lambeth?'

'Oh dear no,' said the young Englishman; 'my cousin was coming over on some business, so I just came across, at an hour's notice, for the lark.'

'Is it your first visit to the United States?'

'Oh dear, yes.'

'I was obliged to come on some business,' said Percy Beaumont 'and I brought Lambeth along.'

'And *you* have been here before, sir?'

'Never—never.'

'I thought, from your referring to business ——' said Mr. Westgate.

'Oh, you see I'm by way of being a barrister,' Percy Beaumont answered. 'I know some people that think of bringing a suit against one of your railways, and they asked me to come over and take measures accordingly.'

Mr. Westgate gave one of his slow, keen looks again. 'What's your railroad?' he asked.

'The Tennessee Central.'

The American tilted back his chair a little, and poised it an instant. 'Well, I'm sorry you want to attack one of our institutions,' he said smiling. 'But I guess you had better enjoy yourself *first*!'

'I'm certainly rather afraid I can't work in this weather,' the young barrister confessed.

'Leave that to the natives,' said Mr. Westgate. 'Leave the Tennessee Central to me, Mr. Beaumont. Some day we'll talk it over, and I guess I can make it square. But I didn't know you Englishmen ever did any work, in the upper classes.'

'Oh, we do a lot of work; don't we, Lambeth?' asked Percy Beaumont.

'I must certainly be at home by the 19th of September,' said the younger Englishman, irrelevantly, but gently.

'For the shooting, eh? or is it the hunting—or the fishing?' inquired his entertainer.

'Oh, I must be in Scotland,' said Lord Lambeth, blushing a little.

'Well then,' rejoined Mr. Westgate, 'you had better amuse yourself first, also. You must go down and see Mrs. Westgate.'

'We should be so happy—if you would kindly tell us the train,' said Percy Beaumont.

'It isn't a train—it's a boat.'

'Oh, I see. And what is the name of—a—the—a—town?'

'It isn't a town,' said Mr. Westgate, laughing. 'It's a—well, what shall I call it? It's a watering-place. In short, it's Newport. You'll see what it is. It's cool; that's the principal thing. You will greatly oblige me by going down there and putting yourself into the hands of Mrs. Westgate. It isn't perhaps for me to say it; but you couldn't be in better hands. Also in those of her sister, who is staying with her. She is very fond of Englishmen. She thinks there is nothing like them.'

'Mrs. Westgate or—a—her sister?' asked Percy Beaumont, modestly, yet in the tone of an inquiring traveller.

'Oh, I mean my wife,' said Mr. Westgate. 'I don't suppose my sister-in-law knows much about them. She has always led a very quiet life; she has lived in Boston.'

Percy Beaumont listened with interest. 'That, I believe,' he said, 'is the most—a—intellectual town?'

'I believe it is very intellectual. I don't go there much,' responded his host.

'I say, we ought to go there,' said Lord Lambeth to his companion.

'Oh, Lord Lambeth, wait till the great heat is over!' Mr. Westgate interposed. 'Boston in this weather would be very trying; it's not the temperature for intellectual exertion. At Boston, you know, you have to pass an examination at the city limits; and when you come away they give you a kind of degree.'

Lord Lambeth stared, blushing a little; and Percy Beaumont stared a little also—but only with his fine natural complexion; glancing aside after a moment to see that his companion was not looking too credulous, for he had heard a great deal of American humour. 'I daresay it is very jolly,' said the younger gentleman.

'I daresay it is,' said Mr. Westgate. 'Only I must impress upon you that at present—tomorrow morning, at an early hour—you will be expected at Newport. We have a house there; half the people in New York go there for the summer. I am not sure that at this very moment my wife can take you in; she has got a lot of people staying with her; I don't know who they all are; only she may have no room. But you can begin with the hotel, and meanwhile you can live at my house. In that way—simply sleeping at the hotel—you will find it tolerable. For the rest, you must make yourself at home at my place. You musn't be shy, you know; if you are only here for a month that will be a great waste of time. Mrs. Westgate won't neglect you, and you had better not try to resist her. I know something about that. I expect you'll find some pretty girls on the premises. I shall write to my wife by this afternoon's mail, and tomorrow morning she and Miss Alden will look out for you. Just walk right in and make yourself comfortable. Your steamer leaves from this part of the city, and I will immediately send out and get you a cabin. Then, at half-past four o'clock, just call for me here, and I will go with you and put you on board. It's a big boat; you might get lost. A few days hence, at the end of the week, I will come down to Newport, and see how you are getting on.'

The two young Englishmen inaugurated the policy of not resisting Mrs. Westgate by submitting, with great docility and thankfulness, to her husband. He was evidently a very good fellow, and he made an impression upon his visitors; his hospitality seemed to recommend itself, consciously—with a friendly wink, as it were—as if it hinted, judicially, that you could not possibly make a better bargain. Lord Lambeth and his cousin left their entertainer to his labours and returned to their hotel, where they spent three or four hours in their respective shower-baths. Percy Beaumont had suggested that they ought to see something of the town; but 'Oh, damn the town!' his noble kinsman had rejoined. They returned to Mr. Westgate's office in a carriage, with their luggage, very punctually; but it must be reluctantly recorded that, this time, he kept them waiting so long that they felt themselves missing the steamer and were deterred only by an amiable modestly from dispensing with his attendance and starting on a hasty scramble to the wharf. But when at last he appeared, and the carriage plunged into the purlieus of Broadway, they jolted and jostled to such good purpose that they reached the huge white vessel while the bell for departure was still ringing and the absorption of passengers still active. It was indeed, as Mr. Westgate had said, a big boat, and his leadership in the innumerable and interminable corridors and cabins, with which he seemed perfectly acquainted, and of which anyone and everyone appeared to have the *entrée*, was very grateful to the slightly bewildered voyagers. He showed them their state-room—a spacious apartment, embellished with gas-lamps, mirrors *en pied* and sculptured furniture—and then, long after they had been intimately convinced that the steamer was in motion and launched upon the unknown stream that they were about to navigate, he bade them a sociable farewell.

'Well, good-bye, Lord Lambeth,' he said 'Good-bye, Mr. Percy Beaumont; I hope you'll have a good time. Just let them do what they want with you. I'll come down by-and-by and look after you.'

The young Englishmen emerged from their cabin and amused themselves with wandering about the immense labyrinthine steamer, which struck them as an extraordinary mixture of a ship and an hotel. It was densely crowded with passengers, the larger number of whom appeared to be ladies and very young children; and in the big saloons, ornamented in white and gold, which followed each other in surprising succession, beneath the swinging gas-light, and among the small side-passages where the negro domestics of both sexes assembled with an air of philosophic leisure, everyone was moving to and fro and exchanging loud and familiar observations. Eventually, at the instance of a discriminating black, our young men went and had some 'supper,' in a wonderful place arranged like a theatre, where, in a gilded gallery, upon which little boxes appeared to open, a large orchestra was playing operatic selections, and, below, people were handing about bills of fare, as if they had been programmes. All this was sufficiently curious; but the agreeable thing later, was to sit out on one of the great white decks of the steamer, in the warm breezy darkness, and, in the vague starlight, to make out the line of low, mysterious coast. The young Englishmen tried American cigars—those of Mr. Westgate—and talked together as they usually talked, with many odd silences, lapses of logic and incongruities of transition; like people who have grown old together, and learned to supply each other's missing phrases; or, more especially, like people thoroughly conscious of a common point of view, so that a style of conversation superficially lacking in finish might suffice for reference to a fund of associations in the light of which everything was all right.

'We really seem to be going out to sea,' Percy Beaumont observed. 'Upon my word, we are going back to England. He has shipped us off again. I call that "real mean." '

'I suppose it's all right,' said Lord Lambeth. 'I want to see those pretty girls at Newport. You know he told us the place was an island; and aren't all islands in the sea?'

'Well,' resumed the elder traveller after a while, 'if his house is as good as his cigars, we shall do very well.'

'He seems a very good fellow,' said Lord Lambeth, as if this idea had just occurred to him.

'I say, we had better remain at the inn,' rejoined his companion, presently. 'I don't think I like the way he spoke of his house. I don't like stopping in the house with such a tremendous lot of women.'

'Oh, I don't mind,' said Lord Lambeth. And then they smoked awhile in silence. 'Fancy his thinking we do no work in England!' the young man resumed.

'I daresay he didn't really think so,' said Percy Beaumont.

'Well, I guess they don't know much about England over here!' declared Lord Lambeth, humorously. And then there was another long pause. 'He was devilish civil,' observed the young nobleman.

'Nothing, certainly, could have been more civil,' rejoined his companion.

'Littledale said his wife was great fun,' said Lord Lambeth.

'Whose wife—Littledale's?'

'This American's—Mrs. Westgate. What's his name? J.L.'

Beaumont was silent a moment. 'What was fun to Littledale,' he said at last,rather sententiously, 'may be death to us.'

'What do you mean by that?' asked his kinsman. 'I am as good a man as Littledale.'

'My dear boy, I hope you won't begin to flirt,' said Percy Beaumont.

'I don't care. I daresay I shan't begin.'

'With a married woman, if she's bent upon it, it's all very well,' Beaumont expounded. 'But our friend mentioned a young lady—a sister, a sister-in-law. For God's sake, don't get entangled with her.'

'How do you mean, entangled?'

'Depend upon it she will try to hook you.'

'Oh, bother!' said Lord Lambeth.

'American girls are very clever,' urged his companion.

'So much the better,' the young man declared.

'I fancy they are always up to some game of that sort,' Beaumont continued.

'They can't be worse than they are in England,' said Lord Lambeth, judicially.

'Ah, but in England,' replied Beaumont, 'you have got your natural protectors. You have got your mother and sisters.'

'My mother and sisters—' began the young nobleman, with a certain energy. But he stopped in time, puffing at his cigar.

'Your mother spoke to me about it, with tears in her eyes,' said Percy Beaumont. 'She said she felt very nervous. I promised to keep you out of mischief.'

'You had better take care of yourself,' said the object of maternal and ducal solicitude.

'Ah,' rejoined the young barrister, 'I haven't the expectation of a hundred thousand a year—not to mention other attractions.'

'Well,' said Lord Lambeth, 'don't cry out before you're hurt!'

It was certainly very much cooler at Newport, where our travellers found themselves assigned to a couple of diminutive bed-rooms in a far-away angle of an immense hotel. They had gone ashore in the early summer twilight, and had very promptly put themselves to bed; thanks to which circumstance and to their having, during the previous hours, in the commodious cabin, slept the sleep of youth and health, they began to feel, towards eleven o'clock, very alert and inquisitive. They looked out of their windows across a row of small green fields, bordered with low stone walls, of rude construction, and saw a deep blue ocean lying beneath a deep blue sky and flecked now and then with scintillating patches of foam. A strong, fresh breeze came in through the curtainless casements and prompted our young men to observe, generously, that it didn't seem half a bad climate. They made other observations after they had emerged from their rooms in pursuit of breakfast—a meal of which they partook in a huge bare hall, where a hundred negroes, in white jackets, were shuffling about upon an uncarpeted floor; where the flies were superabundant and the tables and dishes covered over with a strange, voluminous integument of coarse blue gauze; and where several little boys and girls, who had risen late, were seated in fastidious solitude at the morning repast. These young persons had not the morning paper before them, but they were engaged in languid perusal of the bill of fare.

This latter document was a great puzzle to our friends, who, on reflecting that its bewildering categories had relation to breakfast alone, had an uneasy prevision of an encyclopaedic dinner-list. They found a great deal of entertainment at the hotel, an enormous wooden structure, for the erection of which it seemed to them that the virgin forests of the West must have been terribly deflowered. It was perforated from end to end with immense bare corridors, through which a strong draught was blowing—bearing along wonderful figures of ladies in white morning-dresses and clouds of Valenciennes lace, who seemed to float down the long vistas with expanded furbelows, like angels spreading their wings. In front was a gigantic verandah, upon which an army might have encamped—a vast wooden terrace, with a roof as lofty as the nave of a cathedral. Here our young Englishmen enjoyed, as they supposed, a glimpse of American society, which was distributed over the measureless expanse in a variety of sedentary attitudes, and appeared to consist largely of pretty young girls, dressed as if for a *fête champêtre*, swaying to and fro in rocking-chairs, fanning themselves with large straw fans, and enjoying an enviable exemption from social cares. Lord Lambeth had a theory, which it might be interesting to trace to its origin, that it would be not only agreeable, but easily possible, to enter into relations with one of these young ladies; and his companion found occasion to check the young nobleman's colloquial impulses.

'You had better take care,' said Percy Beaumont, 'or you will have an offended father or brother pulling out a bowie-knife.'

'I assure you it is all right,' Lord Lambeth replied. 'You know the Americans come to these big hotels to make acquaintances.'

'I know nothing about it, and neither do you,' said his kinsman, who, like a clever man, had begun to perceive that the observation of American society demanded a readjustment of one's standard.

'Hang it, then, let's find out!' cried Lord Lambeth with some impatience. 'You know, I don't want to miss anything.'

'We will find out,' said Percy Beaumont, very reasonably. 'We will go and see Mrs. Westgate and make all the proper inquiries.'

And so the two inquiring Englishmen, who had this lady's address inscribed in her husband's hand upon a card, descended from the verandah of the big hotel and took their way, according to direction, along a large straight road, past a series of fresh-looking villas, embosomed in shrubs and flowers and enclosed in an ingenious variety of wooden palings. The morning was brilliant and cool, the villas were smart and snug, and the walk of the young travellers was very entertaining. Everything looked as if it had received a coat of fresh paint the day before—the red roofs, the green shutters, the clean, bright browns and buffs of the house-fronts. The flower-beds on the little lawns seemed to sparkle in the radiant air, and the gravel in the short carriage-sweeps to flash and twinkle. Along the road came a hundred little basket-phaetons, in which, almost always, a couple of ladies were sitting—ladies in white dresses and long white gloves, holding the reins and looking at the two Englishmen, whose nationality was not elusive, through thick blue veils, tied tightly about their faces as if to guard their complexions. At last the young men came within sight of the sea again, and then, having interrogated a gardener over the paling of a villa, they turned into an open gate. Here they found themselves face to face with the ocean and with a very picturesque structure, resembling a magnified *chalet*, which was perched upon a green embankment just above it. The house had a verandah of extraordinary width all around it, and a great many doors and windows standing open to the verandah. These various apertures had, in common, such an accessible, hospitable air, such a breezy flutter, within, of light curtains, such expansive thresholds and reassuring interiors, that our friends hardly knew which was the regular entrance, and, after hesitating a moment, presented themselves at one of the windows. The room within was dark, but in a moment a graceful figure vaguely shaped itself in the rich-looking gloom, and a lady came to meet them. Then they saw that she had been seated at a table, writing, and that she had heard them and had got up. She stepped out into the light; she wore a frank, charming smile, with which she held out her hand to Percy Beaumont.

'Oh, you must be Lord Lambeth and Mr. Beaumont,' she said. 'I have heard from my husband that you would come. I am extremely glad to see you.' And she shook hands with each of her visitors. Her visitors were a little shy, but they had very good manners; they responded with smiles and exclamations, and they apologized for not knowing the front door. The lady rejoined, with vivacity, that when she wanted to see people very much she did not insist upon those distinctions, and that Mr. Westgate had written to her of his English friends in terms that made her really anxious. 'He said you were so terribly prostrated,' said Mrs. Westgate.

'Oh, you mean by the heat?' replied Percy Beaumont. 'We were rather knocked up, but we feel wonderfully better. We had such a jolly—a—voyage down here. It's so very good of you to mind.'

'Yes, it's so very kind of you,' murmured Lord Lambeth.

Mrs. Westgate stood smiling; she was extremely pretty. 'Well, I did mind,' she said; 'and I thought of sending for you this morning, to the Ocean House. I am very glad you are better, and I am charmed you have arrived. You must come round to the other side of the piazza.' And she led the way, with a light, smooth step, looking back at the young men and smiling.

The other side of the piazza was, as Lord Lambeth presently remarked, a very jolly place. It was of the most liberal proportions, and with awnings, its fanciful chairs, its cushions and rugs, its view of the ocean, close at hand, tumbling along the base of the low cliffs whose level tops intervened in lawnlike smoothness, it formed a charming complement to the drawing-room. As such it was in course of use at the present moment; it was occupied by a social circle. There were several ladies and two or three gentlemen, to whom Mrs. Westgate proceeded to introduce the distinguished strangers. She mentioned a great many names, very freely and distinctly; the young Englishmen, shuffling about and bowing, were rather bewildered. But at last they were provided with chairs—low, wicker chairs, gilded and tied with a great many ribbons—and one of the ladies (a very young person, with a little snub nose and several dimples) offered Percy Beaumont a fan. The fan was also adorned with pink love-knots; but Percy Beaumont declined it, although he was very hot. Presently, however, it became cooler; the breeze from the sea was delicious, the view was charming, and the people sitting there looked exceedingly fresh and comfortable. Several of the ladies seemed to be young girls, and the gentlemen were slim, fair youths, such as our friends had seen the day before in New York. The ladies were working upon bands of tapestry, and one of the young men had an open book in his lap. Beaumont afterwards learned from one of the ladies that this young man had been reading aloud—that he was from Boston and was very fond of reading aloud. Beaumont said it was a great pity that they had interrupted him; he should like so much (from all he had heard) to hear a Bostonian read. Couldn't the young man be induced to go on?

'Oh no,' said his informant, very freely; 'he wouldn't be able to get the young ladies to attend to him now.'

There was something very friendly, Beaumont perceived, in the attitude of the company; they looked at the young Englishmen with an air of animated sympathy and interest; they smiled, brightly and unanimously, at everything either of the visitors said. Lord Lambeth and his companion felt that they were being made very welcome. Mrs. Westgate seated herself between them, and, talking a great deal to each, they had occasion to observe that she was as pretty as their friend Littledale had promised. She was thirty years old, with the eyes and the smile of a girl of seventeen, and she was extremely light and graceful, elegant, exquisite. Mrs. Westgate was extremely spontaneous. She was very frank and demonstrative, and appeared always

—while she looked at you delightedly, with her beautiful young eyes, —to be making sudden confessions and concessions, after momentary hesitations.

'We shall expect to see a great deal of you,' she said to Lord Lambeth, with a kind of joyous earnestness. 'We are very fond of Englishmen here; that is, there are a great many we have been fond of. After a day or two you must come and stay with us; we hope you will stay a long time. Newport's a very nice place when you come really to know it, when you know plenty of people. Of course, you and Mr. Beaumont will have no difficulty about that. Englishmen are very well received here; there are almost always two or three of them about. I think they always like it, and I must say I should think they would. They receive ever so much attention. I must say I think they sometimes get spoiled; but I am sure you and Mr. Beaumont are proof against that. My husband tells me you are a friend of Captain Littledale; he was such a charming man. He made himself most agreeable here, and I am sure I wonder he didn't stay. It couldn't have been pleasanter for him in his own country. Though I suppose it is very pleasant in England, for English people. I don't know myself; I have been there very little. I have been a great deal abroad, but I am always on the Continent. I must say I'm extremely fond of Paris; you know we Americans always are; we go there when we die. Did you ever hear that before? that was said by a great wit, I mean the good Americans; but we are all good; you'll see that for yourself. All I know of England is London, and all I know of London is that place—on that little corner, you know, where you buy jackets—jackets with that coarse braid and those big buttons. They make very good jackets in London, I will do you the justice to say that. And some people like the hats; but about the hats I was always a heretic; I always got my hats in Paris. You can't wear an English hat—at least, I never could—unless you dress your hair *à l'Anglaise*; and I must say that is a talent I have never possessed. In Paris they will make things to suit your peculiarities; but in England I think you like much more to have—how shall I say it?—one thing for everybody. I mean as regards dress. I don't know about other things; but I have always supposed that in other things everything was different. I mean according to the people—according to the classes, and all that. I am afraid you will think that I don't take a very favourable view; but you know you can't take a very favourable view in Dover Street, in the month of November. That has always been my fate. Do you know Jones's Hotel in Dover Street? That's all I know of England. Of course, every one admits that the English hotels are your weak point. There was always the most frightful fog; I couldn't see to try my things on.

When I got over to America—into the light—I usually found they were twice too big. The next time I mean to go in the season; I think I shall go next year. I want very much to take my sister; she has never been to England. I don't know whether you know what I mean by saying that the Englishmen who come here sometimes get spoiled. I mean that they take things as a matter of course—things that are done for them. Now, naturally, they are only a matter of course when the Englishmen are very nice. But, of course, they are almost always very nice. Of course, this isn't nearly such an interesting country as England; there are not nearly so many things to see, and we haven't your country life. I have never seen anything of your country life; when I am in Europe I am always on the Continent. But I have heard a great deal about it; I know that when you are among yourselves in the country you have the most beautiful time. Of course, we have nothing of that sort, we have nothing on that scale. I don't apologize, Lord Lambeth; some Americans are always apologizing; you must have noticed that. We have the reputation of always boasting and bragging and waving the American flag; but I must say that what strikes me is that we are perpetually making excuses and trying to smooth things over. The American flag has quite gone out of fashion; it's very carefully folded up, like an old tablecloth. Why should we apologize? The English never apologize—do they? No, I must say I never apologize. You must take us as we come—with all our imperfections on our heads. Of course we haven't your country life, and your old ruins, and your great estates, and your leisure-class, and all that. But if we haven't, I should think you might find it a pleasant change—I think any country is pleasant where they have pleasant manners. Captain Littledale told me he had never seen such pleasant manners as at Newport; and he had been a great deal in European society. Hadn't he been in the diplomatic service? He told me the dream of his life was to get appointed to a diplomatic post in Washington. But he doesn't seem to have succeeded. I suppose that in England promotion—and all that sort of thing—is fearfully slow. With us, you know, it's a great deal too fast. You see I admit our drawbacks. But I must confess I think Newport is an ideal place. I don't know anything like it anywhere. Captain Littledale told me he didn't know anything like it anywhere. It's entirely different from most watering-places; it's a most charming life. I must say I think that when one goes to a foreign country, one ought to enjoy the differences. Of course there are differences; otherwise what did one come abroad for? Look for your pleasure in the differences, Lord Lambeth; that's the way to do it; and then I am sure you will find American society—at least Newport society—most charming and most interesting. I wish very much my husband were here; but he's dreadfully confined to New York. I suppose you think that is very strange—for a gentleman. But you see we haven't any leisure-class.'

Mrs. Westgate's discourse, delivered in a soft, sweet voice, flowed on like a miniature torrent and was interrupted by a hundred little smiles, glances, and gestures, which might have figured the irregularities and obstructions of such a stream. Lord Lambeth listened to her with, it must be confessed, a rather ineffectual attention, although he indulged in a good many little murmurs and ejaculations of assent and deprecation. He had no great faculty for apprehending generalizations. There were some three or four indeed which, in the play of his own intelligence, he had originated, and which had seemed convenient at the moment; but at the present time he could hardly have been said to follow Mrs. Westgate as she darted gracefully about in the sea of speculation. Fortunately she asked for no especial rejoinder, for she looked about at the rest of the company as well, and smiled at Percy Beaumont, on the other side of her, as if he too must understand her and agree with her. He was rather more successful than his companion; for besides being, as we know, cleverer, his attention was not vaguely distracted by the close vicinity to a remarkably interesting young girl, with dark hair and blue eyes. This was the case with Lord Lambeth, to whom it occurred after a while that the young girl with blue eyes and dark hair was the pretty sister of whom Mrs. Westgate had spoken. She presently turned to him with a remark which established her identity.

'It's a great pity you couldn't have brought my brother-in-law with you. It's a great shame he should be in New York in these days.'

'Oh yes; it's so very hot,' said Lord Lambeth.

'It must be dreadful,' said the young girl.

'I daresay he is very busy,' Lord Lambeth observed.

'The gentlemen in America work too much,' the young girl went on.

'Oh, do they? I daresay they like it,' said her interlocutor.

'I don't like it. One never sees them.'

'Don't you, really?' asked Lord Lambeth. 'I shouldn't have fancied that.'

'Have you come to study American manners?' asked the young girl.

'Oh, I don't know. I just came over for a lark. I haven't got long.' Here there was a pause, and Lord Lambeth began again. 'But Mr. Westgate will come down here, will not he?'

'I certainly hope he will. He must help to entertain you and Mr. Beaumont.'

Lord Lambeth looked at her a little with his handsome brown eyes. 'Do you suppose he would have come down with us, if we had urged him?'

Mr. Westgate's sister-in-law was silent a moment, and then—'I daresay he would,' she answered.

'Really!' said the young Englishman. 'He was immensely civil to Beaumont and me,' he added.

'He is a dear good fellow,' the young lady rejoined. 'And he is a perfect husband. But all Americans are that,' she continued, smiling.

'Really!' Lord Lambeth exclaimed again; and wondered whether all American ladies had such a passion for generalizing as these two.

He sat there a good while: there was a deal of talk; it was all very friendly and lively and jolly. Everyone present, sooner or later, said something to him, and seemed to make a particular point of addressing him by name. Two or three other persons came in, and there was a shifting of seats and changing of places; the gentlemen all entered into intimate conversation with the two Englishmen, made them urgent offers of hospitality and hoped they might frequently be of service to them. They were afraid Lord Lambeth and Mr. Beaumont were not very comfortable at their hotel—that it was not, as one of them said, 'so private as those dear little English inns of yours.' This last gentleman went on to say that unfortunately, as yet, perhaps, privacy was not quite so easily obtained in America as might be desired; still, he continued, you could generally get it by paying for it; in fact, you could get everything in America nowadays by paying for it. American life was certainly growing a great deal more private; it was growing very much like England. Everything at Newport, for instance, was thoroughly private; Lord Lambeth would probably be struck with that. It was also represented to the strangers that it mattered very little whether their hotel was agreeable, as everyone would want them to make visits; they would stay with other people, and, in any case, they would be a great deal at Mrs. Westgate's. They would find that very charming; it was the pleasantest house in Newport. It was a pity Mr. Westgate was always away; he was a man of the highest ability—very acute, very acute. He worked like a horse and he left his wife—well, to do about as she liked. He liked her to enjoy herself, and she seemed to know how. She was extremely brilliant, and a splendid talker. Some people preferred her sister; but Miss Alden was very different; she was in a different style altogether. Some people even thought her prettier, and, certainly, she was not so sharp. She was more in the Boston style; she had lived a great deal in Boston and she was very highly educated. Boston girls, it was propounded, were more like English young ladies.

Lord Lambeth had presently a chance to test the truth of this proposition; for on the company rising in compliance with a suggestion from their hostess that they should walk down to the rocks and look at the sea, the young Englishman again found himself, as they strolled across the grass, in proximity to Mrs. Westgate's sister. Though she was but a girl of twenty, she appeared to feel the obligation to exert an active hospitality; and this was perhaps the more to be noticed as she seemed by nature a reserved and retiring person, and had little of her sister's fraternizing quality. She was perhaps rather too thin, and she was a little pale; but as she moved slowly over the grass, with her arms hanging at her sides, looking gravely for a moment at the sea and then brightly, for all her gravity, at him, Lord Lambeth thought her at least as pretty as Mrs. Westgate and reflected that if this was the Boston style the Boston style was very charming. He thought she looked very clever; he could imagine that she was highly educated; but at the same time she seemed gentle and graceful. For all her cleverness, however, he felt that she had to think a little what to say; she didn't say the first thing that came into her head; he had come from a different part of the world and from a different society, and she was trying to adapt her conversation. The others were scattering themselves near the rocks; Mrs. Westgate had charge of Percy Beaumont.

'Very jolly place, isn't it?' said Lord Lambeth. 'It's a very jolly place to sit.'

'Very charming,' said the young girl; 'I often sit here; there are all kinds of cosy corners—as if they had been made on purpose.'

'Ah! I suppose you have had some of them made,' said the young man.

Miss Alden looked at him a moment. 'Oh no, we have had nothing made. It's pure nature.'

'I should think you would have a few little benches—rustic seats and that sort of thing. It might be so jolly to sit here, you know,' Lord Lambeth went on.

'I am afraid we haven't so many of those things as you,' said the young girl, thoughtfully.

'I daresay you go in for pure nature, as you were saying. Nature, over here, must be so grand, you know.' And Lord Lambeth looked about him.

The little coast-line hereabouts was very pretty, but it was not at all grand; and Miss Alden appeared to rise to a perception of this fact. 'I am afraid it seems to you very rough,' she said. 'It's not like the coast scenery in Kingsley's novels.'

'Ah, the novels always overdo it, you know,' Lord Lambeth rejoined. 'You must not go by the novels.'

They were wandering about a little on the rocks, and they stopped and looked down into a narrow chasm where the rising tide made a curious bellowing sound. It was loud enough to prevent their hearing each other, and they stood there for some moments in silence. The young girl looked at her companion, observing him attentively, but covertly, as women, even when very young, know how to do. Lord Lambeth repaid observation; tall, straight, and strong, he was handsome as certain young Englishmen, and certain young Englishmen almost alone, are handsome; with a perfect finish of feature and a look of intellectual repose and gentle good temper which seemed somehow to be consequent upon his well-cut nose and chin. And to speak of Lord Lambeth's expression of intellectual repose is not simply a civil way of saying that he looked stupid. He was evidently not a young man of an irritable imagination; he was not, as he would himself have said, tremendously clever; but, though there was a kind of appealing dullness in his eye, he looked thoroughly reasonable and competent, and his appearance proclaimed that to be a nobleman, an athlete, and an excellent fellow, was a sufficiently brilliant combination of qualities. The young girl beside him, it may be attested without further delay, thought him the handsomest young man she had ever seen; and Bessie Alden's imagination, unlike that of her companion, was irritable. He, however, was also making up his mind that she was uncommonly pretty.

'I daresay it's very gay here—that you have lots of balls and parties,' he said; for, if he was not tremendously clever, he rather prided himself on having, with women, a sufficiency of conversation.

'Oh yes, there is a great deal going on,' Bessie Alden replied. 'There are not so many balls, but there are a good many other things. You will see for yourself; we live rather in the midst of it.'

'It's very kind of you to say that. But I thought you Americans were always dancing.'

'I suppose we dance a good deal; but I have never seen much of it. We don't do it much, at any rate, in summer. And I am sure,' said Bessie Alden, 'that we don't have so many balls as you have in England.'

'Really!' exclaimed Lord Lambeth. 'Ah, in England it all depends, you know.'

'You will not think much of our gaieties,' said the young girl, looking at him with a little mixture of interrogation and decision which was peculiar to her. The interrogation seemed earnest and the decision seemed arch; but the mixture, at any rate, was charming.

'Those things, with us, are much less splendid than in England.'

'I fancy you don't mean that,' said Lord Lambeth, laughing.

'I assure you I mean everything I say,' the young girl declared. 'Certainly, from what I have read about English society, it is very different.'

'Ah, well, you know,' said her companion, 'those things are often described by fellows who know nothing about them. You mustn't mind what you read.'

'Oh, I *shall* mind what I read!' Bessie Alden rejoined. 'When I read Thackeray and George Eliot, how can I help minding them?'

'Ah, well, Thackeray—and George Eliot,' said the young nobleman; 'I haven't read much of them.'

'Don't you suppose they know about society?' asked Bessie Alden.

'Oh, I daresay they know; they were so very clever. But these fashionable novels,' said Lord Lambeth, 'they are awful rot, you know.'

His companion looked at him a moment with her dark blue eyes, and then she looked down in the chasm where the water was tumbling about. 'Do you mean Mrs. Gore, for instance?' she said presently, raising her eyes.

'I am afraid I haven't read that either,' was the young man's rejoinder, laughing a little and blushing. 'I am afraid you'll think I am not very intellectual.'

'Reading Mrs. Gore is no proof of intellect. But I like reading everything about English life—even poor books. I am so curious about it.'

'Aren't ladies always curious?' asked the young man, jestingly.

But Bessie Alden appeared to desire to answer his question seriously. 'I don't think so—I don't think we are enough so—that we care about many things. So it's all the more of a compliment,' she added, 'that I should want to know so much about England.'

The logic here seemed a little close; but Lord Lambeth, made conscious of a compliment, found his natural modesty just at hand. 'I am sure you know a great deal more than I do.'

'I really think I know a great deal—for a person who has never been there.'

'Have you really never been there?' cried Lord Lambeth. 'Fancy!'

'Never—except in imagination,' said the young girl.

'Fancy!' repeated her companion. 'But I daresay you'll go soon, won't you?'

'It's the dream of my life!' declared Bessie Alden, smiling.

'But your sister seems to know a tremendous lot about London,' Lord Lambeth went on.

The young girl was silent a moment. 'My sister and I are two very different persons,' she presently said. 'She has been a great deal in Europe. She has been in England several times. She has known a great many English people.'

'But you must have known some, too,' said Lord Lambeth.

'I don't think that I have ever spoken to one before. You are the first Englishman that—to my knowledge—I have ever talked with.'

Bessie Alden made this statement with a certain gravity—almost, as it seemed to Lord Lambeth, an impressiveness. Attempts at impressiveness always made him feel awkward, and he now began to laugh and swing his stick. 'Ah, you would have been sure to know!' he said. And then he added, after an instant—'I'm sorry I am not a better specimen.'

The young girl looked away; but she smiled, laying aside her impressiveness. 'You must remember that you are only a beginning,' she said. Then she retraced her steps, leading the way back to the lawn, where they saw Mrs. Westgate come towards them with Percy Beaumont still at her side. 'Perhaps I shall go to England next year,' Miss Alden continued; 'I want to, immensely. My sister is going to Europe, and she has asked me to go with her. If we go, I shall make her stay as long as possible in London.'

'Ah, you must come in July,' said Lord Lambeth. 'That's the time when there is most going on.'

'I don't think I can wait till July,' the young girl rejoined. 'By the first of May I shall be very impatient.' They had gone further, and Mrs. Westgate and her companion were near them. 'Kitty,' said Miss Alden, 'I have given out that we are going to London next May. So please to conduct yourself accordingly.'

Percy Beaumont wore a somewhat animated—even a slightly irritated—air. He was by no means so handsome a man as his cousin, although in his cousin's absence he might have passed for a striking specimen of the tall, muscular, fair-bearded, clear-eyed Englishman. Just now Beaumont's clear eyes, which were small and of a pale grey colour, had a rather troubled light, and, after glancing at Bessie Alden while she spoke, he rested them upon his kinsman. Mrs. Westgate meanwhile, with her superfluously pretty gaze, looked at every one alike.

'You had better wait till the time comes,' she said to her sister. 'Perhaps next May you won't care so much about London. Mr. Beaumont and I,' she went on, smiling at her companion, 'have had a tremendous discussion. We don't agree about anything. It's perfectly delightful.'

'Oh, I say, Percy!' exclaimed Lord Lambeth.

'I disagree,' said Beaumont, stroking down his back hair, 'even to the point of not thinking it delightful.'

'Oh, I say!' cried Lord Lambeth again.

'I don't see anything delightful in my disagreeing with Mrs. Westgate,' said Percy Beaumont.

'Well, I do!' Mrs. Westgate declared; and she turned to her sister. 'You know you have to go to town. The phaeton is there. You had better take Lord Lambeth.'

At this point Percy Beaumont certainly looked straight at his kinsman; he tried to catch his eye. But Lord Lambeth would not look at him; his own eyes were better occupied. 'I shall be very happy,' cried Bessie Alden. 'I am only going to some shops. But I will drive you about and show you the place.'

'An American woman who respects herself,' said Mrs. Westgate, turning to Beaumont with her bright expository air, 'must buy something every day of her life. If she cannot do it herself, she must send out some member of her family for the purpose. So Bessie goes forth to fulfil my mission.'

The young girl had walked away, with Lord Lambeth by her side, to whom she was talking still; and Percy Beaumont watched them as they passed towards the house. 'She fulfils her own mission,' he presently said; 'that of being a very attractive young lady.'

'I don't know that I should say very attractive,' Mrs. Westgate rejoined. 'She is not so much that as she is charming when you really know her. She is very shy.'

'Oh indeed?' said Percy Beaumont.

'Extremely shy,' Mrs. Westgate repeated. 'But she is a dear good girl; she is a charming species of girl. She is not in the least a flirt; that isn't at all her line; she doesn't know the alphabet of that sort of thing. She is very simple—very serious. She has lived a great deal in Boston, with another sister of mine—the eldest of us—who married a Bostonian. She is very cultivated, not at all like me—I am not in the least cultivated. She has studied immensely and read everything; she is what they call in Boston "thoughtful." '

'A rum sort of girl for Lambeth to get hold of!' his lordship's kinsman privately reflected.

'I really believe,' Mrs. Westgate continued, 'that the most charming girl in the world is a Boston superstructure upon a New York *fond*; or perhaps a New York superstructure upon a Boston *fond*. At any rate it's the mixture,' said Mrs. Westgate, who continued to give Percy Beaumont a great deal of information.

Lord Lambeth got into a little basket-phaeton with Bessie Alden, and she drove him down the long avenue, whose extent he had measured on foot a couple of hours before, into the ancient town, as it was called in that part of the world, of Newport. The ancient town was a curious affair—a collection of fresh-looking little wooden houses, painted white, scattered over a hill-side and clustered about a long, straight street, paved with enormous cobble-stones. There were plenty of shops—a large proportion of which appeared to be those of fruit-vendors, with piles of huge water-melons and pumpkins stacked in front of them; and, drawn up before the shops, or bumping about on the cobble-stones, were innumerable other basket-phaetons freighted with ladies of high fashion, who greeted each other from vehicle to vehicle and conversed on the edge of the pavement in a manner that struck Lord Lambeth as demonstrative—with a great many 'Oh, my dears,' and little quick exclamations and caresses. His companion went into seventeen shops—he amused himself with counting them—and accumulated, at the bottom of the phaeton, a pile of bundles that hardly left the young Englishman a place for his feet. As she had no groom nor footman, he sat in the phaeton to hold the ponies; where, although he was not a particularly acute observer, he saw much to entertain him—especially the ladies just mentioned, who wandered up and down with the appearance of a kind of aimless intentness, as if they were looking for something to buy, and who, tripping in and out of their vehicles, displayed remarkably pretty feet. It all seemed to Lord Lambeth very odd, and bright, and gay. Of course, before they got back to the villa, he had had a great deal of desultory conversation with Bessie Alden.

The young Englishmen spent the whole of that day and the whole of many successive days in what the French call the *intimité* of their new friends. They agreed that it was extremely jolly—that they had never known anything more agreeable. It is not proposed to narrate minutely the incidents of their sojourn on this charming shore; though if it were convenient I might present a record of impressions none the less delectable that they were not exhaustively analysed. Many of them still linger in the minds of our travellers, attended by a train of harmonious images—images of brilliant mornings on lawns and piazzas that overlooked the sea; of innumerable pretty girls; of infinite lounging and talking and laughing and flirting and lunching and dining; of universal friendliness and frankness; of occasions on which they knew everyone and everything and had an extraordinary sense of ease; of drives and rides in the late afternoon, over gleaming beaches, on long sea-roads, beneath a sky lighted up by marvellous sunsets; of suppers, on the return, informal, irregular, agreeable; of evenings at open windows or on the perpetual verandahs, in the summer starlight, above the warm Atlantic. The young Englishmen were introduced to everybody, entertained by everybody, intimate with everybody. At the end of three days they had removed their luggage from the hotel, and had gone to stay with Mrs. Westgate—a step to which Percy Beaumont at first offered some conscientious opposition. I call his opposition conscientious because it was founded upon some talk that he had had, on the second day, with Bessie Alden. He had indeed had a good deal of talk with her, for she was not literally always in conversation with Lord Lambeth. He had meditated upon Mrs. Westgate's account of her sister, and he discovered, for himself, that the young lady was clever and appeared to have read a great deal. She seemed very nice, though he could not make out that, as Mrs. Westgate had said, she was shy. If she was shy she carried it off very well.

'Mr. Beaumont,' she had said, 'please tell me something about Lord Lambeth's family. How would you say it in England?—his position.'

'His position?' Percy Beaumont repeated.

'His rank—or whatever you call it. Unfortunately we haven't got a "Peerage," like the people in Thackeray.'

'That's a great pity,' said Beaumont. 'You would find it all set forth there so much better than I can do it.'

'He is a Peer, then?'

'Oh yes, he is a Peer.'

'And has he any other title than Lord Lambeth?'

'His title is the Marquis of Lambeth,' said Beaumont; and then he was silent; Bessie Alden appeared to be looking at him with interest. 'He is the son of the Duke of Bayswater,' he added, presently.

'The eldest son?'

'The only son.'

'And are his parents living?'

'Oh yes; if his father were not living he would be a duke.'

'So that when his father dies,' pursued Bessie Alden, with more simplicity than might have been expected in a clever girl, 'he will become Duke of Bayswater?'

'Of course,' said Percy Beaumont. 'But his father is in excellent health.'

'And his mother?'

Beaumont smiled a little. 'The Duchess is uncommonly robust.'

'And has he any sisters?'

'Yes, there are two.'

'And what are they called?'

'One of them is married. She is the Countess of Pimlico.'

'And the other?'

'The other is unmarried; she is plain Lady Julia.'

Bessie Alden looked at him a moment. 'Is she very plain?'

Beaumont began to laugh again. 'You would not find her so handsome as her brother,' he said; and it was after this that he attempted to dissuade the heir of the Duke of Bayswater from accepting Mrs. Westgate's invitation. 'Depend upon it,' he said, 'that girl means to try for you.'

'It seems to me you are doing your best to make a fool of me,' the modest nobleman answered.

'She has been asking me,' said Beaumont, 'all about your people and your possessions.'

'I am sure it is very good of her!' Lord Lambeth rejoined.

'Well, then,' observed his companion, 'if you go, you go with your eyes open.'

'Damn my eyes!' exclaimed Lord Lambeth. 'If one is to be a dozen times a day at the house, it is a great deal more convenient to sleep there. I am sick of travelling up and down this beastly Avenue.'

Since he had determined to go, Percy Beaumont would of course have been very sorry to allow him to go alone; he was a man of conscience, and he remembered his promise to the Duchess. It was obviously the memory of this promise that made him say to his companion a couple of days later, that he rather wondered he should be so fond of that girl.

'In the first place, how do you know how fond I am of her? asked Lord Lambeth. 'And in the second place why shouldn't I be fond of her?'

'I shouldn't think she would be in your line.'

'What do you call my "line?" You don't set her down as "fast?" '

'Exactly so. Mrs. Westgate tells me that there is no such thing as the "fast girl" in America; that it's an English invention, and that the term has no meaning here.'

'All the better. It's an animal I detest.'

'You prefer a blue-stocking.'

'Is that what you call Miss Alden?'

'Her sister tells me,' said Percy Beaumont, 'that she is tremendously literary.'

'I don't know anything about that. She is certainly very clever.'

'Well,' said Beaumont, 'I should have supposed you would have found that sort of thing awfully slow.'

'In point of fact,' Lord Lambeth rejoined, 'I find it uncommonly lively.'

After this, Percy Beaumont held his tongue; but on August 10th he wrote to the Duchess of Bayswater. He was, as I have said, a man of conscience, and he had a strong, incorruptible sense of the proprieties of life. His kinsman, meanwhile, was having a great deal of talk with Bessie Alden—on the red sea-rocks beyond the lawn; in the course of long island rides, with a slow return in the glowing twilight; on the deep verandah, late in the evening. Lord Lambeth, who had stayed at many houses, had never stayed at a house in which it was possible for a young man to converse so frequently with a young lady. This young lady no longer applied to Percy Beaumont for information concerning his lordship. She addressed herself directly to the young nobleman. She asked him a great many questions, some of which bored him a little; for he took no pleasure in talking about himself.

'Lord Lambeth,' said Bessie Alden, 'are you an hereditary legislator?'

'Oh, I say,' cried Lord Lambeth, 'don't make me call myself such names as that.'

'But you are a member of Parliament,' said the young girl.

'I don't like the sound of that, either.'

'Doesn't your father sit in the House of Lords?' Bessie Alden went on.

'Very seldom,' said Lord Lambeth.

'Is it an important position?' she asked.

'Oh dear no,' said Lord Lambeth.

'I should think it would be very grand,' said Bessie Alden, 'to possess, simply by an accident of birth, the right to make laws for a great nation.'

'Ah, but one doesn't make laws. It's a great humbug.'

'I don't believe that,' the young girl declared. 'It must be a great privilege, and I should think that if one thought of it in the right way —from a high point of view—it would be very inspiring.'

'The less one thinks of it the better,' Lord Lambeth affirmed.

'I think it's tremendous,' said Bessie Alden; and on another occasion she asked him if he had any tenantry. Hereupon it was that, as I have said, he was a little bored.

'Do you want to buy up their leases?' he asked.

'Well—have you got any livings?' she demanded.

'Oh, I say!' he cried. 'Have you got a clergyman that is looking out?' But she made him tell her that he had a Castle; he confessed to but one. It was the place in which he had been born and brought up, and, as he had an old-time liking for it, he was beguiled into describing it a little and saying it was really very jolly. Bessie Alden listened with great interest, and declared that she would give the world to see such a place. Whereupon—'It would be awfully kind of you to come and stay there,' said Lord Lambeth. He took a vague satisfaction in the circumstance that Percy Beaumont had not heard him make the remark I have just recorded.

Mr. Westgate, all this time, had not, as they said at Newport, 'come on.' His wife more than once announced that she expected him on the morrow; but on the morrow she wandered about a little, with a telegram in her jewelled fingers, declaring it was very tiresome that his business detained him in New York; that he could only hope the Englishmen were having a good time. 'I must say,' said Mrs. Westgate, 'that it is no thanks to him if you are!' And she went on to explain, while she continued that slow-paced promenade which enabled her well-adjusted skirts to display themselves so advantageously, that unfortunately in America there was no leisure-class. It was Lord Lambeth's theory, freely propounded when the young men were together, that Percy Beaumont was having a very good time with Mrs. Westgate, and that under the pretext of meeting for the purpose of animated discussion, they were indulging in practices that imparted a shade of hypocrisy to the lady's regret for her husband's absence.

'I assure you we are always discussing and differing,' said Percy Beaumont. 'She is awfully argumentative. American ladies certainly don't mind contradicting you. Upon my word I don't think I was ever treated so by a woman before. She's so devilish positive.'

Mrs. Westgate's positive quality, however, evidently had its attractions; for Beaumont was constantly at his hostess's side. He detached himself one day to the extent of going to New York to talk over the Tennessee Central with Mr. Westgate; but he was absent only forty-eight hours, during which, with Mr. Westgate's assistance, he completely settled this piece of business. 'They certainly do things quickly in New York,' he observed to his cousin; and he added that Mr. Westgate had seemed very uneasy lest his wife should miss her visitor—he had been in such an awful hurry to send him back to her. 'I'm afraid you'll never come up to an American husband—if that's what the wives expect,' he said to Lord Lambeth.

Mrs. Westgate, however, was not to enjoy much longer the entertainment with which an indulgent husband had desired to keep her provided. On August 21st Lord Lambeth received a telegram from his mother, requesting him to return immediately to England; his father had been taken ill, and it was his filial duty to come to him.

The young Englishman was visibly annoyed. 'What the deuce does it mean?' he asked of his kinsman. 'What am I to do?'

Percy Beaumont was annoyed as well; he had deemed it his duty, as I have narrated, to write to the Duchess, but he had not expected that this distinguished woman would act so promptly upon his hint.

'It means,' he said, 'that your father is laid up. I don't suppose it's anything serious; but you have no option. Take the first steamer; but don't be alarmed.'

Lord Lambeth made his farewells; but the few last words that he exchanged with Bessie Alden are the only ones that have a place in our record. 'Of course I needn't assure you,' he said, 'that if you should come to England next year, I expect to be the first person that you inform of it.'

Bessie Alden looked at him a little and she smiled. 'Oh, if we come to London,' she answered, 'I should think you would hear of it.'

Percy Beaumont returned with his cousin, and his sense of duty compelled him, one windless afternoon, in mid-Atlantic, to say to Lord Lambeth that he suspected that the Duchess's telegram was in part the result of something he himself had written to her. 'I wrote to her—as I explicitly notified you I had promised to do—that you were extremely interested in a little American girl.'

Lord Lambeth was extremely angry, and he indulged for some moments in the simple language of indignation. But I have said that he was a reasonable young man, and I can give no better proof of it than the fact that he remarked to his companion at the end of half an hour—'You were quite right after all. I am very much interested in her. Only, to be fair,' he added, 'you should have told my mother also that she is not—seriously—interested in me.'

Percy Beaumont gave a little laugh. 'There is nothing so charming as modesty in a young man in your position. That speech is a capital proof that you are sweet on her.'

'She is not interested—she is not!' Lord Lambeth repeated.

'My dear fellow,' said his companion, 'you are very far gone.'

PART II

In point of fact, as Percy Beaumont would have said, Mrs. Westgate disembarked on the 18th of May on the British coast. She was accompanied by her sister, but she was not attended by any other member of her family. To the deprivation of her husband's society Mrs Westgate was, however, habituated; she had made half-a-dozen journeys to Europe without him, and she now accounted for his absence, to interrogative friends on this side of the Atlantic, by allusion to the regretable but conspicuous fact that in America there was no leisure-class. The two ladies came up to London and alighted at Jones's Hotel, where Mrs. Westgate, who had made on former occasions the most agreeable impression at this establishment, received an obsequious greeting. Bessie Alden had felt much excited about coming to England; she had expected the 'associations' would be very charming, that it would be an infinite pleasure to rest her eyes upon the things she had read about in the poets and historians. She was very fond of the poets and historians, of the picturesque, of the past, of retrospect, of mementoes and reverberations of greatness; so that on coming into the great English world, where strangeness and familiarity would go hand in hand, she was prepared for a multitude of fresh emotions. They began very promptly—these tender, fluttering sensations; they began with the sight of the beautiful English landscape, whose dark richness was quickened and brightened by the season; with the carpeted fields and flowering hedgerows, as she looked at them from the window of the train; with the spires of the rural churches, peeping above the rook-haunted tree-tops; with the oak-studded parks, the ancient homes, the cloudy light, the speech, the manners, the thousand differences. Mrs. Westgate's impressions had of course much less novelty and keenness, and she gave but a wandering attention to her sister's ejaculations and rhapsodies.

'You know my enjoyment of England is not so intellectual as Bessie's,' she said to several of her friends in the course of her visit to this country. 'And yet if it is not intellectual, I can't say it is physical. I don't think I can quite say what it is, my enjoyment of England.' When once it was settled that the two ladies should come abroad and should spend a few weeks in England on their way to the Continent, they of course exchanged a good many allusions to their London acquaintance.

'It will certainly be much nicer having friends there,' Bessie Alden had said one day, as she sat on the sunny deck of the steamer, at her sister's feet, on a large blue rug.

'Whom do you mean by friends?' Mrs. Westgate asked.

'All those English gentlemen whom you have known and entertained. Captain Littledale, for instance. And Lord Lambeth and Mr. Beaumont,' added Bessie Alden.

'Do you expect them to give us a very grand reception?'

Bessie reflected a moment; she was addicted, as we know, to reflection. 'Well, yes.'

'My poor sweet child!' murmured her sister.

'What have I said that is so silly?' asked Bessie.

'You are a little too simple; just a little. It is very becoming, but it pleases people at your expense.'

'I am certainly too simple to understand you.' said Bessie.

'Shall I tell you a story?' asked her sister.

'If you would be so good. That is what they do to amuse simple people.'

Mrs. Westgate consulted her memory, while her companion sat gazing at the shining sea. 'Did you ever hear of the Duke of Green-Erin?'

'I think not,' said Bessie.

'Well, it's no matter,' her sister went on.

'It's a proof of my simplicity.'

'My story is meant to illustrate that of some other people,' said Mrs. Westgate. 'The Duke of Green-Erin is what they call in England a great swell; and some five years ago he came to America. He spent most of his time in New York, and in New York he spent his days and his nights at the Butterworths'. You have heard, at least of the Butterworths. *Bien.* They did everything in the world for him—they turned themselves inside out. They gave him a dozen dinner parties and balls, and were the means of his being invited to fifty more. At first he used to come into Mrs. Butterworth's box at the opera in a tweed travelling suit; but some one stopped that. At any rate, he had a beautiful time, and they parted the best friends in the world. Two years elapse, and the Butterworths come abroad and go to London. The first thing they see in all the papers—in England those things are in the most prominent place—is that the Duke of Green-Erin has arrived in town for the Season. They wait a little, and then Mr. Butterworth—as polite as ever—goes and leaves a card. They wait a little more; the visit is not returned; they wait three weeks—*silence de mort*—the Duke gives no sign. The Butterworths see a lot of other people, put down the Duke of Green-Erin as a rude, ungrateful man, and forget all about him. One fine day they go to Ascot Races, and there they meet him face to face. He stares a moment and then comes up to Mr. Butterworth, taking something from his pocket-book—something which proves to be a banknote. "I'm glad to see you, Mr. Butterworth," he says, "so that I can pay you that ten pounds I lost to you in New York. I saw the other day you remembered our bet; here are the ten pounds, Mr. Butterworth. Good-bye, Mr. Butterworth." And off he goes, and that's the last they see of the Duke of Green-Erin.'

'Is that your story?' asked Bessie Alden.

'Don't you think it's interesting?' her sister replied.

'I don't believe it,' said the young girl.

'Ah!' cried Mrs. Westgate, 'you are not so simple after all. Believe it or not, as you please; there is no smoke without fire.'

'Is that the way,' asked Bessie after a moment, 'that you expect your friends to treat you?'

'I defy them to treat me very ill, because I shall not give them the opportunity. With the best will in the world, in that case, they can't be very offensive.'

Bessie Alden was silent a moment. 'I don't see what makes you talk that way,' she said. 'The English are a great people.'

'Exactly; and that is just the way they have grown great—by dropping you when you have ceased to be useful. People say they are not clever; but I think they are very clever.'

'You know you have liked them—all the Englishmen you have seen,' said Bessie.

'They have liked me,' her sister rejoined; 'it would be more correct to say that. And of course one likes that.'

Bessie Alden resumed for some moments her studies in sea-green. 'Well,' she said, 'whether they like me or not, I mean to like them. And happily,' she added, 'Lord Lambeth does not owe me ten pounds.'

During the first few days after their arrival at Jones's Hotel our charming Americans were much occupied with what they would have called looking about them. They found occasion to make a large number of purchases, and their opportunities for conversation were such only as were offered by the deferential London shopmen. Bessie Alden, even in driving from the station, took an immense fancy to the British metropolis, and, at the risk of exhibiting her as a young woman of vulgar tastes, it must be recorded that for a considerable period she desired no higher pleasure than to drive about the crowded streets in a Hansom cab. To her attentive eyes they were full of a strange picturesque life, and it is at least beneath the dignity of our historic muse to enumerate the trivial objects and incidents which this simple young lady from Boston found so entertaining. It may be freely mentioned, however, that whenever, after a round of visits in Bond Street and Regent Street, she was about to return with her sister to Jones's Hotel, she made an earnest request that they should be driven home by way of Westminster Abbey. She had begun by asking whether it would not be possible to take the Tower on the way to their lodgings; but it happened that at a more primitive stage of her culture Mrs. Westgate had paid a visit to this venerable monument, which she spoke of ever afterwards vaguely as a dreadful disappointment; so that she expressed the liveliest disapproval of any attempt to combine historical researches with the purchase of hair-brushes and note-paper. The most she would consent to do in this line was to spend half-an-hour at Madame Tussaud's, where she saw several dusty wax effigies of members of the Royal Family. She told Bessie that if she wished to go to the Tower she must get some one else to take her.

Bessie expressed hereupon an earnest disposition to go alone; but upon this proposal as well Mrs. Westgate sprinkled cold water.

'Remember,' she said, 'that you are not in your innocent little Boston. It is not a question of walking up and down Beacon Street.' Then she went on to explain that there were two classes of American girls in Europe—those that walked about alone and those that did not. 'You happen to belong, my dear,' she said to her sister, 'to the class that does not.'

'It is only,' answered Bessie, laughing, 'because you happen to prevent me.' And she devoted much private meditation to this question of effecting a visit to the Tower of London.

Suddenly it seemed as if the problem might be solved; the two ladies at Jones's Hotel received a visit from Willie Woodley. Such was the social appellation of a young American who had sailed from New York a few days after their own departure, and who, having the privilege of intimacy with them in that city, had lost no time, on his arrival in London, in coming to pay them his respects. He had, in fact, gone to see them directly after going to see his tailor, than which there can be no greater exhibition of promptitude on the part of a young American who has just alighted at the Charing Cross Hotel. He was a slim, pale youth, of the most amiable disposition, famous for the skill with which he led the 'German' in New York. Indeed, by the young ladies who habitually figured in this Terpsichorean revel he was believed to be 'the best dancer in the world;' it was in these terms that he was always spoken of, and that his identity was indicated. He was the gentlest, softest young man it was possible to meet; he was beautifully dressed—'in the English style'—and he knew an immense deal about London. He had been at Newport during the previous summer, at the time of our young Englishmen's visit, and he took extreme pleasure in the society of Bessie Alden, whom he always addressed as 'Miss Bessie.' She immediately arranged with him, in the presence of her sister, that he should conduct her to the scene of Anne Boleyn's execution.

'You may do as you please,' said Mrs. Westgate. 'Only—if you desire the information—it is not the custom here for young ladies to knock about London with young men.'

'Miss Bessie has waltzed with me so often,' observed Willie Woodley; 'she can surely go out with me in a Hansom.'

'I consider waltzing,' said Mrs. Westgate, 'the most innocent pleasure of our time.'

'It's a compliment to our time!' exclaimed the young man, with a little laugh, in spite of himself.

'I don't see why I should regard what is done here,' said Bessie

Alden. 'Why should I suffer the restrictions of a society of which I enjoy none of the privileges?'

'That's very good—very good,' murmured Willie Woodley.

'Oh, go to the Tower, and feel the axe, if you like!' said Mrs. Westgate. 'I consent to your going with Mr. Woodley; but I should not let you go with an Englishman.'

'Miss Bessie wouldn't care to go with an Englishman!' Mr. Woodley declared, with a faint asperity that was, perhaps, not unnatural in a young man who, dressing in the manner that I have indicated, and knowing a great deal, as I have said, about London, saw no reason for drawing these sharp distinctions. He agreed upon a day with Miss Bessie—a day of that same week.

An ingenious mind might, perhaps, trace a connection between the young girl's allusion to her destitution of social privileges and a question she asked on the morrow as she sat with her sister at lunch.

'Don't you mean to write to—to any one?' said Bessie.

'I wrote this morning to Captain Littledale,' Mrs. Westgate replied.

'But Mr. Woodley said that Captain Littledale had gone to India.'

'He said he thought he had heard so; he knew nothing about it.'

For a moment Bessie Alden said nothing more; then, at last, 'And don't you intend to write to—to Mr. Beaumont?' she inquired.

'You mean to Lord Lambeth,' said her sister.

'I said Mr. Beaumont because he was so good a friend of yours.'

Mrs. Westgate looked at the young girl with sisterly candour. 'I don't care two straws for Mr. Beaumont.'

'You were certainly very nice to him.'

'I am nice to every one,' said Mrs. Westgate, simply.

'To every one but me,' rejoined Bessie, smiling.

Her sister continued to look at her; then, at last, 'Are you in love with Lord Lambeth?' she asked.

The young girl stared a moment, and the question was apparently too humorous even to make her blush. 'Not that I know of,' she answered.

'Because if you are,' Mrs. Westgate went on, 'I shall certainly not send for him.'

'That proves what I said,' declared Bessie, smiling—'that you are not nice to me.'

'It would be a poor service, my dear child,' said her sister.

'In what sense? There is nothing against Lord Lambeth, that I know of.'

Mrs. Westgate was silent a moment. 'You *are* in love with him then?'

Bessie stared again; but this time she blushed a little. 'Ah! if you won't be serious,' she answered, 'we will not mention him again.'

For some moments Lord Lambeth was not mentioned again, and it was Mrs. Westgate who, at the end of this period, reverted to him. 'Of course I will let him know we are here; because I think he would be hurt—justly enough—if we should go away without seeing him. It is fair to give him a chance to come and thank me for the kindness we showed him. But I don't want to seem eager.'

'Neither do I,' said Bessie, with a little laugh.

'Though I confess,' added her sister, 'that I am curious to see how he will behave.'

'He behaved very well at Newport.'

'Newport is not London. At Newport he could do as he liked; but here it is another affair. He has to have an eye to consequences.'

'If he had more freedom, then, at Newport,' argued Bessie, 'it is the more to his credit that he behaved well; and if he has to be so careful here, it is possible he will behave even better.'

'Better—better,' repeated her sister. 'My dear child, what is your point of view?'

'How do you mean—my point of view?'

'Don't you care for Lord Lambeth—a little?'

This time Bessie Alden was displeased; she slowly got up from table, turning her face away from her sister. 'You will oblige me by not talking so,' she said.

Mrs. Westgate sat watching her for some moments as she moved slowly about the room and went and stood at the window. 'I will write to him this afternoon,' she said at last.

'Do as you please!' Bessie answered; and presently she turned round. 'I am not afraid to say that I like Lord Lambeth. I like him very much.'

'He is not clever,' Mrs. Westgate declared.

'Well, there have been clever people whom I have disliked,' said Bessie Alden; 'so that I suppose I may like a stupid one. Besides, Lord Lambeth is not stupid.'

'Not so stupid as he looks!' exclaimed her sister, smiling.

'If I were in love with Lord Lambeth, as you said just now, it would be bad policy on your part to abuse him.'

'My dear child, don't give me lessons in policy!' cried Mrs. Westgate. 'The policy I mean to follow is very deep.'

The young girl began to walk about the room again; then she stopped before her sister. 'I have never heard in the course of five minutes,' she said, 'so many hints and innuendoes. I wish you would tell me in plain English what you mean.'

'I mean that you may be much annoyed.'

'That is still only a hint,' said Bessie.

Her sister looked at her, hesitating an instant. 'It will be said of you that you have come after Lord Lambeth—that you followed him.'

Bessie Alden threw back her pretty head like a startled hind, and a look flashed into her face that made Mrs. Westgate rise from her chair. 'Who says such things as that?' she demanded.

'People here.'

'I don't believe it,' said Bessie.

'You have a very convenient faculty of doubt. But my policy will be, as I say, very deep. I shall leave you to find out this kind of thing for yourself.'

Bessie fixed her eyes upon her sister, and Mrs. Westgate thought for a moment there were tears in them. 'Do they talk that way here?' she asked.

'You will see. I shall leave you alone.'

'Don't leave me alone,' said Bessie Alden. 'Take me away.'

'No; I want to see what you make of it,' her sister continued.

'I don't understand.'

'You will understand after Lord Lambeth has come,' said Mrs. Westgate, with a little laugh.

The two ladies had arranged that on this afternoon Willie Woodley should go with them to Hyde Park, where Bessie Alden expected to derive much entertainment from sitting on a little green chair, under the great trees, beside Rotton Row. The want of a suitable escort had hitherto rendered this pleasure inaccessible; but no escort, now, for such an expedition, could have been more suitable than their devoted young countryman, whose mission in life, it might almost be said, was to find chairs for ladies, and who appeared on the stroke of half-past five with a white camellia in his button-hole.

'I have written to Lord Lambeth, my dear,' said Mrs. Westgate to her sister, on coming into the room where Bessie Alden, drawing on her long grey gloves, was entertaining their visitor.

Bessie said nothing, but Willie Woodley exclaimed that his lordship was in town; he had seen his name in the *Morning Post*.

'Do you read the *Morning Post*?' asked Mrs. Westgate.

'Oh yes; it's great fun,' Willie Woodley affirmed.

'I want so to see it,' said Bessie, 'there is so much about it in Thackeray.'

'I will send it to you every morning,' said Willie Woodley.

He found them what Bessie Alden thought excellent places, under the great trees, beside the famous avenue whose humours had been made familiar to the young girl's childhood by the pictures in *Punch*.

The day was bright and warm, and the crowd of riders and spectators, and the great procession of carriages, were proportionately dense and brilliant. The scene bore the stamp of the London Season at its height, and Bessie Alden found more entertainment in it than she was able to express to her companions. She sat silent, under her parasol, and her imagination, according to its wont, let itself loose into the great changing assemblage of striking and suggestive figures. They stirred up a host of old impressions and preconceptions, and she found herself fitting a history to this person and a theory to that, and making a place for them all in her little private museum of types. But if she said little, her sister on one side and Willie Woodley on the other expressed themselves in lively alternation.

'Look at that green dress with blue flounces,' said Mrs. Westgate. '*Quelle toilette*!'

'That's the Marquis of Blackborough,' said the young man—'the one in the white coat. I heard him speak the other night in the House of Lords; it was something about ramrods; he called them *wamwods*. He's an awful swell.'

'Did you ever see anything like the way they are pinned back?' Mrs. Westgate resumed. 'They never know where to stop.'

'They do nothing but stop,' said Willie Woodley. 'It prevents them from walking. Here comes a great celebrity—Lady Beatrice Bellevue. She's awfully fast; see what little steps she takes.'

'Well my dear,' Mrs. Westgate pursued, 'I hope you are getting some ideas for your *couturière*?'

'I am getting plenty of ideas,' said Bessie, 'but I don't know that my *couturière* would appreciate them.'

Willie Woodley presently perceived a friend on horseback, who drove up beside the barrier of the Row and beckoned to him. He went forward and the crowd of pedestrians closed about him, so that for some ten minutes he was hidden from sight. At last he reappeared, bringing a gentleman with him—a gentleman whom Bessie at first supposed to be his friend dismounted. But at a second glance she found herself looking at Lord Lambeth, who was shaking hands with her sister.

'I found him over there,' said Willie Woodley, 'and I told him you were here.'

And then Lord Lambeth, touching his hat a little, shook hands with Bessie. 'Fancy your being here!' he said. He was blushing and smiling; he looked very handsome, and he had a kind of splendour that he had not had in America. Bessie Alden's imagination, as we know, was just then in exercise; so that the tall young Englishman, as he stood there looking down at her, had the benefit of it. 'He is handsomer and more splendid than anything I have ever seen,' she said to herself. And then she remembered that he was a Marquis, and she thought he looked like a Marquis.

'I say, you know,' he cried, 'you ought to have let a man know you were here!

'I wrote to you an hour ago,' said Mrs. Westgate.

'Doesn't all the world know it?' asked Bessie, smiling.

'I assure you I didn't know it!' cried Lord Lambeth. 'Upon my honour I hadn't heard of it. Ask Woodley now; had I, Woodley?'

'Well, I think you are rather a humbug,' said Willie Woodley.

'You don't believe that—do you, Miss Alden?' asked his lordship. 'You don't believe I'm a humbug, eh?'

'No,' said Bessie, 'I don't.'

'You are too tall to stand up, Lord Lambeth,' Mrs. Westgate observed. 'You are only tolerable when you sit down. Be so good as to get a chair.'

He found a chair and placed it sidewise, close to the two ladies. 'If I hadn't met Woodley I should never have found you,' he went on. 'Should I, Woodley?'

'Well, I guess not,' said the young American.

'Not even with my letter?' asked Mrs. Westgate.

'Ah, well, I haven't got your letter yet; I suppose I shall get it this evening. It was awfully kind of you to write.'

'So I said to Bessie,' observed Mrs. Westgate.

'Did she say so, Miss Alden?' Lord Lambeth inquired. 'I daresay you have been here a month.'

'We have been here three,' said Mrs. Westgate.

'Have you been here three months?' the young man asked again of Bessie.

'It seems a long time,' Bessie answered.

'I say, after that you had better not call me a humbug!' cried Lord Lambeth. 'I have only been in town three weeks; but you must have been hiding away—I haven't seen you anywhere.'

'Where should you have seen us—where should we have gone?' asked Mrs. Westgate.

'You should have gone to Hurlingham,' said Willie Woodley.

'No, let Lord Lambeth tell us,' Mrs. Westgate insisted.

'There are plenty of places to go to,' said Lord Lambeth—'each one stupider than the other. I mean people's houses; they send you cards.'

'No one has send us cards,' said Bessie.

'We are very quiet,' her sister declared. 'We are here as travellers.'

'We have been to Madame Tussaud's,' Bessie pursued.

'Oh, I say!' cried Lord Lambeth.

'We thought we should find your image there,' said Mrs. Westgate—'yours and Mr. Beaumont's.'

'In the Chamber of Horrors?' laughed the young man.

'It did duty very well for a party,' said Mrs. Westgate. 'All the women were *décolletées*, and many of the figures looked as if they could speak if they tried.'

'Upon my word,' Lord Lambeth rejoined, 'you see people at London parties that look as if they couldn't speak if they tried.'

'Do you think Mr. Woodley could find us Mr. Beaumont?' asked Mrs. Westgate.

Lord Lambeth stared and looked round him. 'I daresay he could. Beaumont often comes here. Don't you think you could find him, Woodley? Make a dive into the crowd.'

'Thank you; I have had enough diving,' said Willie Woodley. 'I will wait till Mr. Beaumont comes to the surface.'

'I will bring him to see you,' said Lord Lambeth; 'where are you staying?'

'You will find the address in my letter—Jones's Hotel.'

'Oh, one of those places just out of Piccadilly? Beastly hole, isn't it?' Lord Lambeth inquired.

'I believe it's the best hotel in London,' said Mrs. Westgate.

'But they give you awful rubbish to eat, don't they?' his lordship went on.

'Yes,' said Mrs. Westgate.

'I always feel so sorry for the people that come up to town and go to live in those places,' continued the young man. 'They eat nothing but filth.'

'Oh, I say!' cried Willie Woodley.

'Well, how do you like London, Miss Alden?' Lord Lambeth asked, unperturbed by this ejaculation.

'I think it's grand,' said Bessie Alden.

'My sister likes it, in spite of the "filth"!' Mrs. Westgate exclaimed.

'I hope you are going to stay a long time.'

'As long as I can,' said Bessie.

'And where is Mr. Westgate?' asked Lord Lambeth of this gentleman's wife.

'He's where he always is—in that tiresome New York.'

'He must be tremendously clever,' said the young man.

'I suppose he is,' said Mrs. Westgate.

Lord Lambeth sat for nearly an hour with his American friends; but it is not our purpose to relate their conversation in full. He addressed a great many remarks to Bessie Alden, and finally turned towards her altogether, while Willie Woodley entertained Mrs. Westgate. Bessie herself said very little; she was on her guard, thinking of what her sister had said to her at lunch. Little by little, however, she interested herself in Lord Lambeth again, as she had done at Newport; only it seemed to her that here he might become more interesting. He would be an unconcious part of the antiquity, the impressiveness, the picturesqueness of England; and poor Bessie Alden, like many a Yankee maiden, was terribly at the mercy of picturesqueness.

'I have often wished I were at Newport again,' said the young man. 'Those days I spent at your sister's were awfully jolly.'

'We enjoyed them very much; I hope your father is better.'

'Oh dear, yes. When I got to England, he was out grouse-shooting. It was what you call in America a gigantic fraud. My mother had got nervous. My three weeks at Newport seemed like a happy dream.'

'America certainly is very different from England,' said Bessie.

'I hope you like England better, eh?' Lord Lambeth rejoined, almost persuasively.

'No Englishman can ask that seriously of a person of another country.'

Her companion looked at her for a moment. 'You mean it's a matter of course?'

'If I were English,' said Bessie, 'it would certainly seem to me a matter of course that every one should be a good patriot.'

'Oh dear, yes; patriotism is everything,' said Lord Lambeth, not quite following, but very contented. 'Now, what are you going to do here?'

'On Thursday I am going to the Tower.'

'The Tower?'

'The Tower of London. Did you never hear of it?'

'Oh yes, I have been there,' said Lord Lambeth. 'I was taken there by my governess, when I was six years old. It's a rum idea, your going there.'

'Do give me a few more rum ideas,' said Bessie. 'I want to see everything of that sort. I am going to Hampton Court, and to Windsor, and to the Dulwich Gallery.'

Lord Lambeth seemed greatly amused. 'I wonder you don't go to the Rosherville Gardens.'

'Are they interesting?' asked Bessie.

'Oh, wonderful!'

'Are they very old? That's all I care for,' said Bessie.

'They are tremendously old; they are all falling to ruins.'

'I think there is nothing so charming as an old ruinous garden,' said the young girl. 'We must certainly go there.'

Lord Lambeth broke out into merriment. 'I say, Woodley,' he cried, 'here's Miss Alden wants to go to the Rosherville Gardens!'

Willie Woodley looked a little blank; he was caught in the fact of ignorance of an apparently conspicuous feature of London life. But in a moment he turned it off. 'Very well,' he said, 'I'll write for a permit.'

Lord Lambeth's exhilaration increased. ''Gad, I believe you Americans would go anywhere,' he cried.

'We wish to go to Parliament,' said Bessie. 'That's one of the first things.'

'Oh, it would bore you to death!' cried the young man.

'We wish to hear you speak.'

'I never speak—except to young ladies,' said Lord Lambeth, smiling.

Bessie Alden looked at him awhile; smiling, too, in the shadow of her parasol. 'You are very strange,' she murmured. 'I don't think I approve of you.'

'Ah, now, don't be severe, Miss Alden!' said Lord Lambeth, smiling still more. 'Please don't be severe. I want you to like me—awfully.'

'To like you awfully? You must not laugh at me, then, when I make mistakes. I consider it my right—as a free-born American—to make as many mistakes as I choose.'

'Upon my word, I didn't laugh at you,' said Lord Lambeth.

'And not only that,' Bessie went on; 'but I hold that all my mistakes shall be set down to my credit. You must think the better of me for them.'

'I can't think better of you than I do,' the young man declared.

Bessie Alden looked at him a moment again. 'You certainly speak very well to young ladies. But why don't you address the House?—isn't that what they call it?'

'Because I have nothing to say,' said Lord Lambeth.

'Haven't you a great position?' asked Bessie Alden.

He looked a moment at the back of his glove. 'I'll set that down,' he said, 'as one of your mistakes—to your credit.' And, as if he disliked talking about his position, he changed the subject. 'I wish you would let me go with you to the Tower, and to Hampton Court, and to all those other places.'

'We shall be most happy,' said Bessie.

'And of course I shall be delighted to show you the House of Lords—some day that suits you. There are a lot of things I want to do for you. I want to make you have a good time. And I should like very much to present some of my friends to you, if it wouldn't bore you. Then it would be awfully kind of you to come down to Branches.'

'We are much obliged to you, Lord Lambeth,' said Bessie. 'What is Branches?'

'It's a house in the country. I think you might like it.'

Willie Woodley and Mrs. Westgate, at this moment, were sitting in silence, and the young man's ear caught these last words of Lord Lambeth's. 'He's inviting Miss Bessie to one of his castles,' he murmured to his companion.

Mrs. Westgate, foreseeing what she mentally called 'complications,' immediately got up; and the two ladies, taking leave of Lord Lambeth, returned, under Mr. Woodley's conduct, to Jones's Hotel.

Lord Lambeth came to see them on the morrow, bringing Percy Beaumont with him—the latter having instantly declared his intention of neglecting none of the usual offices of civility. This declaration, however, when his kinsman informed him of the advent of their American friends, had been preceded by another remark.

'Here they are, then, and you are in for it.'

'What am I in for?' demanded Lord Lambeth.

'I will let your mother give it a name. With all respect to whom,' added Percy Beaumont, 'I must decline on this occasion to do any more police duty. Her Grace must look after you herself.'

'I will give her a chance,' said her Grace's son, a trifle grimly. 'I shall make her go and see them.'

'She won't do it, my boy.'

'We'll see if she doesn't,' said Lord Lambeth.

But if Percy Beaumont took a sombre view of the arrival of the two ladies at Jones's Hotel, he was sufficiently a man of the world to offer them a smiling countenance. He fell into animated conversation—conversation, at least, that was animated on her side—with Mrs. Westgate, while his conpanion made himself agreeable to the younger lady. Mrs. Westgate began confessing and protesting, declaring and expounding.

'I must say London is a great deal brighter and prettier just now than it was when I was here last—in the month of November. There is evidently a great deal going on, and you seem to have a good many flowers. I have no doubt it is very charming for all you people, and that you amuse yourselves immensely. It is very good of you to let Bessie and me come and sit and look at you. I suppose you will think I am very satirical, but I must confess that that's the feeling I have in London.'

'I am afraid I don't quite understand to what feeling you allude,' said Percy Beaumont.

'The feeling that it's all very well for you English people. Everything is beautifully arranged for you.'

'It seems to me it is very well for some Americans, sometimes,' rejoined Beaumont.

'For some of them, yes—if they like to be patronized. But I must say I don't like to be patronized. I may be very eccentric, and undisciplined, and outrageous; but I confess I never was fond of patronage. I like to associate with people on the same terms as I do in my own country; that's a peculiar taste that I have. But here people seem to expect something else—Heaven knows what! I am afraid you will think I am very ungrateful, for I certainly have received a great deal of attention. The last time I was here, a lady sent me a message that I was at liberty to come and see her.'

'Dear me, I hope you didn't go, observed Percy Beaumont.

'You are deliciously *naïf*, I must say that for you!' Mrs. Westgate exclaimed. 'It must be a great advantage to you here in London. I suppose that if I myself had a little more *naïveté*, I should enjoy it more. I should be content to sit on a chair in the Park, and see the people pass, and be told that this is the Duchess of Suffolk, and that is the Lord Chamberlain, and that I must be thankful for the privilege of beholding them. I daresay it is very wicked and critical of me to ask for anything else. But I was always critical, and I freely confess to the sin of being fastidious. I am told there is some remarkably superior second-rate society provided here for strangers. *Merci*! I don't want any superior second-rate society. I want the society that I have been accustomed to.'

'I hope you don't call Lambeth and me second-rate,' Beaumont interposed.

'Oh, I am accustomed to you!' said Mrs. Westgate. 'Do you know that you English sometimes make the most wonderful speeches? The first time I came to London, I went out to dine—as I told you, I have received a great deal of attention. After dinner, in the drawing-room, I had some conversation with an old lady; I assure you I had. I forget what we talked about; but she presently said, in allusion to something we were discussing, "Oh, you know, the aristocracy do so-and-so; but in one's own class of life it is very different." In one's own class of life! What is a poor unprotected American woman to do in a country where she is liable to have that sort of thing said to her?'

'You seem to get hold of some very queer old ladies; I compliment you on your acquaintance!' Percy Beaumont exclaimed. 'If you are trying to bring me to admit that London is an odious place, you'll not succeed. I'm extremely fond of it, and I think it the jolliest place in world.'

'*Pour vous autres.* I never said the contrary,' Mrs. Westgate retorted. I make use of this expression because both interlocutors had begun to raise their voices. Percy Beaumont naturally did not like to hear his country abused, and Mrs. Westgate, no less naturally, did not like a stubborn debater.

'Hallo!' said Lord Lambeth; 'what are they up to now?' And he came away from the window, where he had been standing with Bessie Alden.

'I quite agree with a very clever countrywoman of mine,' Mrs. Westgate continued, with charming ardour, though with imperfect relevancy. She smiled at the two gentlemen for a moment with terrible brightnes, as if to toss at their feet—upon their native heath—the gauntlet of defiance. 'For me, there are only two social positions worth speaking of—that of an American lady and that of the Emperor of Russia.'

'And what do you do with the American gentlemen?' asked Lord Lambeth.

'She leaves them in America!' said Percy Beaumont.

On departure of their visitors, Bessie Alden told her sister that Lord Lambeth would come the next day, to go with them to the Tower, and that he had kindly offered to bring his 'trap,' and drive them thither. Mrs. Westgate listened in silence to this communication, and for some time afterwards she said nothing. But at last, 'If you had not requested me the other day not to mention it,' she began, 'there is something I should venture to ask you.' Bessie frowned a little; her dark blue eyes were more dark than blue. But her sister went on. 'As it is, I will take the risk. You are not in love with Lord Lambeth: I believe it, perfectly. Very good. But is there, by chance, any danger of your becoming so? It's a very simple question; don't take offence. I have a particular reason,' said Mrs. Westgate, 'for wanting to know.'

Bessie Alden for some moments said nothing; she only looked displeased. 'No; there is no danger,' she answered at last, curtly.

'Then I should like to frighten them,' declared Mrs. Westgate, clasping her jewelled hands.

'To frighten whom?'

'All these people; Lord Lambeth's family and friends.'

'How should you frighten them?' asked the young girl.

'It wouldn't be I—it would be you. It would frighten them to think that you should absorb his lordship's young affections.'

Bessie Alden, with her clear eyes still overshadowed by her dark brows, continued to interrogate. 'Why should that frighten them?'

Mrs. Westgate poised her answer with a smile before delivering it. 'Because they think you are not good enough. You are a charming girl, beautiful and amiable, intelligent and clever, and as *bien-élevée* as it is possible to be; but you are not a fit match for Lord Lambeth.'

Bessie Alden was decidedly disgusted. 'Where do you get such extraordinary ideas?' she asked. 'You have said some such strange things lately. My dear Kitty, where do you collect them?'

Kitty was evidently enamoured of her idea. 'Yes, it would put them on pins and needles, and it wouldn't hurt you. Mr. Beaumont is already most uneasy; I could soon see that.'

The young girl meditated a moment. 'Do you mean that they spy upon him—that they interfere with him?'

'I don't know what power they have to interfere, but I know that a British mamma may worry her son's life out.'

It has been intimated that, as regards certain disagreeable things, Bessie Alden had a fund of scepticism. She abstained on the present occasion from expressing disbelief, for she wished not to irritate her sister. But she said to herself that Kitty had been misinformed—that this was a traveller's tale. Though she was a girl of a lively imagination, there could in the nature of things be, to her sense, no reality in the idea of her belonging to a vulgar category. What she said aloud was—'I must say that in that case I am very sorry for Lord Lambeth.'

Mrs. Westgate, more and more exhilarated by her scheme, was smiling at her again. 'If I could only believe it was safe!' she exclaimed. 'When you begin to pity him, I, on my side, am afraid.'

'Afraid of what?'

'Of your pitying him too much.'

Bessie Alden turned away impatiently; but at the end of a minute she turned back. 'What if I should pity him too much?' she asked.

Mrs. Westgate hereupon turned away, but after a moment's reflection she also faced her sister again. 'It would come, after all, to the same thing,' she said.

Lord Lambeth came the next day with his trap, and the two ladies, attended by Willie Woodley, placed themselves under his guidance and were conveyed eastward, through some of the duskier portions of the metropolis, to the great turreted dungeon which overlooks the London shipping. They all descended from their vehicle and entered the famous enclosure; and they secured the services of a venerable beefeater, who, though there were many other claimants for legendary information, made a fine exclusive party of them and marched them through courts and corridors, through armouries and prisons. He delivered his usual peripatetic discourse, and they stopped and stared, and peeped and stooped, according to the official admonitions. Bessie Alden asked the old man in the crimson doublet a great many questions; she thought it a most fascinating place. Lord Lambeth was in high good-humour; he was constantly laughing; he enjoyed what he would have called the lark. Willie Woodley kept looking at the ceilings and tapping the walls with the knuckle of a pearl-grey glove; and Mrs. Westgate, asking at frequent intervals to be allowed to sit down and wait till they came back, was as frequently informed that they would never come back. To a great many of Bessie's questions—chiefly on collateral points of English history—the ancient warder was naturally unable to reply; whereupon she always appealed to Lord Lambeth. But his lordship was very ignorant. He declared that he knew nothing about that sort of thing, and he seemed greatly diverted at being treated as an authority.

'You can't expect every one to know as much as you,' he said.

'I should expect you to know a great deal more,' declared Bessie Alden.

'Women always know more than men about names and dates, and that sort of thing,' Lord Lambeth rejoined. 'There was Lady Jane Grey we have just been hearing about, who went in for Latin and Greek, and all the learning of her age.'

'*You* have no right to be ignorant, at all events,' said Bessie.

'Why haven't I as good a right as any one else?'

'Because you have lived in the midst of all these things.'

'What things do you mean? Axes, and blocks, and thumb-screws?'

'All these historical things. You belong to an historical family.'

'Bessie is really too historical,' said Mrs. Westgate, catching a word of this dialogue.

'Yes, you are too historical,' said Lord Lambeth, laughing, but thankful for a formula. 'Upon my honour, you are too historical!'

He went with the ladies a couple of days later to Hampton Court, Willie Woodley being also of the party. The afternoon was charming, the famous horse-chestnuts were in blossom, and Lord Lambeth, who quite entered into the spirit of the cockney excursionist, declared that it was a jolly old place. Bessie Alden was in ecstasies; she went about murmuring and exclaiming.

'It's too lovely,' said the young girl, 'it's too enchanting; it's too exactly what it ought to be!'

At Hampton Court the little flocks of visitors are not provided with an official bell-wether, but are left to browse at discretion upon the local antiquities. It happened in this manner that, in default of another informant, Bessie Alden, who on doubtful questions was able to suggest a great many alternatives, found herself again applying for intellectual assistance to Lord Lambeth. But he again assured her that he was utterly helpless in such matters—that his education had been sadly neglected.

'And I am sorry it makes you unhappy,' he added in a moment.

'You are very disappointing, Lord Lambeth,' she said.

'Ah, now, don't say that!' he cried. 'That's the worst thing you could possibly say.'

'No,' she rejoined; 'it is not so bad as to say that I had expected nothing of you.'

'I don't know. Give me a notion of the sort of thing you expected.'

'Well,' said Bessie Alden, 'that you would be more what I should like to be—what I should try to be—in your place.'

'Ah, my place!' exclaimed Lord Lambeth; 'you are always talking about my place!'

The young girl looked at him; he thought she coloured a little; and for a moment she made no rejoinder.

'Does it strike you that I am always talking about your place?' she asked.

'I am sure you do it a great honour,' he said, fearing he had been uncivil.

'I have often thought about it,' she went on after a moment. 'I have often thought about your being an hereditary legislator. An hereditary legislator ought to know a great many things.'

'Not if he doesn't legislate.'

'But you do legislate; it's absurd your saying you don't. You are very much looked up to here—I am assured of that.'

'I don't know that I ever noticed it.'

'It is because you are used to it, then. You ought to fill the place.'

'How do you mean, to fill it?' asked Lord Lambeth.

'You ought to be very clever and brilliant, and to know almost everything.'

Lord Lambeth looked at her a moment. 'Shall I tell you something?' he asked. 'A young man in my position, as you call it——'

'I didn't invent the term,' interposed Bessie Alden. 'I have seen it in a great many books.'

'Hang it, you are always at your books! A fellow in my position, then, does very well, whatever he does. That's about what I mean to say.'

'Well, if your own people are content with you,' said Bessie Alden, laughing, 'it is not for me to complain. But I shall always think that, properly, you should have been a great mind—a great character.'

'Ah, that's very theoretic!' Lord Lambeth declared. 'Depend upon it, that's a Yankee prejudice.'

'Happy the country,' said Bessie Alden, 'where even people's prejudices are so elevated!'

'Well, after all,' observed Lord Lambeth, 'I don't know that I am such a fool as you are trying to make me out.'

'I said nothing so rude as that; but I must repeat that you are disappointing.'

'My dear Miss Alden,' exclaimed the young man, 'I am the best fellow in the world!'

'Ah, if it were not for that!' said Bessie Alden, with a smile.

Mrs. Westgate had a good many more friends in London than she pretended, and before long she had renewed acquaintance with most of them. Their hospitality was extreme, so that, one thing leading to another, she began, as the phrase is, to go out. Bessie Alden, in this way, saw something of what she found it a great satisfaction to call to herself English society. She went to balls and danced, she went to dinners and talked, she went to concerts and listened (at concerts Bessie always listened), she went to exhibitions and wondered. Her enjoyment was keen and her curiosity insatiable, and, grateful in general for all her opportunities, she especially prized the privilege of meeting certain celebrated persons—authors and artists, philosophers and statesmen—of whose renown she had been a humble and distant beholder, and who now, as a part of the habitual furniture of London drawing-rooms, struck her as stars fallen from the firmament and become palpable—revealing also, sometimes, on contact, qualities not to have been predicted of sidereal bodies. Bessie, who knew so many of her contemporaries by reputation, had a good many personal disappointments; but, on the other hand, she had innumerable satisfactions and enthusiasms, and she communicated the emotions of either class to a dear friend, of her own sex, in Boston, with whom she was in voluminous correspondence. Some of her reflections, indeed, she attempted to impart to Lord Lambeth, who came almost every day to Jones's Hotel, and whom Mrs. Westgate admitted to be really devoted. Captain Littledale, it appeared, had gone to India; and of several others of Mrs. Westgate's ex-pensioners—gentlemen who, as she said, had made, in New York, a club-house of her drawing-room—no tidings were to be obtained; but Lord Lambeth was certainly attentive enough to make up for the accidental absences, the short memories, all the other irregularities, of every one else. He drove them in the Park, he took them to visit private collections of pictures, and, having a house of his own, invited them to dinner. Mrs. Westgate, following the fashion of many of her compatriots, caused herself and her sister to be presented at the English Court by her diplomatic representative—for it was in this manner that she alluded to the American Minister to England, inquiring what on earth he was put there for, if not to make the proper arrangements for one's going to a Drawing Room.

Lord Lambeth declared that he hated Drawing Rooms, but he participated in the ceremony on the day on which the two ladies at Jones's Hotel repaired to Buckingham Palace in a remarkable coach which his lordship had sent to fetch them. He had on a gorgeous uniform, and Bessie Alden was particularly struck with his appearance—especially when on her asking him, rather foolishly as she felt, if he were a loyal subject, he replied that he was a loyal subject to *her*. This declaration was emphasized by his dancing with her at a royal ball to which the two ladies afterwards went, and was not impaired by the fact that she thought he danced very ill. He seemed to her wonderfully kind; she asked herself, with growing vivacity, why he should be so kind. It was his disposition—that seemed the natural answer. She had told her sister that she liked him very much, and now that she liked him more she wondered why. She liked him for his disposition; to this question as well that seemed the natural answer. When once the impressions of London life began to crowd thickly upon her she completely forgot her sister's warning about the cynicism of public opinion. It had given her great pain at the moment; but there was no particular reason why she should remember it; it corresponded too little with any sensible reality; and it was disagreeable to Bessie to remember disagreeable things. So she was not haunted with the sense of a vulgar imputation. She was not in love with Lord Lambeth—she assured herself of that. It will immediately be observed that when such assurances become necessary the state of a young lady's affections is already ambiguous; and indeed Bessie Alden made no attempt to dissimulate—to herself, of course—a certain tenderness that she felt for the young nobleman. She said to herself that she liked the type to which he belonged—the simple, candid, manly, healthy English temperament. She spoke to herself of him as women speak of young men they like—alluded to his bravery (which she had never in the least seen tested), to his honesty and gentlemanliness; and was not silent upon the subject of his good looks. She was perfectly conscious, moreover, that she liked to think of his more adventitious merits—that her imagination was excited and gratified by the sight of a handsome young man endowed with such large opportunities—opportunities she hardly knew for what, but, as she supposed, for doing great things—for setting an example, for exerting an influence, for conferring happiness, for encouraging the arts. She had a kind of ideal of conduct for a young man who should find himself in this magnificent position, and she tried to adapt it to Lord Lambeth's deportment, as you might attempt to fit a silhouette in cut paper upon a shadow projected upon a wall. But Bessie Alden's silhouette refused to coincide with his lordship's image; and this want of harmony sometimes vexed her more than she thought reasonable. When he was absent it was of course less striking—then he seemed to her a sufficiently graceful combination of high responsibilities and amiable qualities. But when he sat there within sight, laughing and talking with his customary good humour and simplicity, she measured it more accurately, and she felt acutely that if Lord Lambeth's position was heroic, there was but little of the hero in the young man himself. Then her imagination wandered away from him—very far away; for it was an incontestable fact that at such moments he seemed distinctly dull. I am afraid that while Bessie's imagination was thus invidiously roaming, she cannot have been herself a very lively companion; but it may well have been that these occasional fits of indifference seemed to Lord Lambeth a part of the young girl's personal charm. It had been a part of this charm from the first that he felt that she judged him and measured him more freely and irresponsibly—more at her ease and her leisure, as it were—than several young ladies with whom he had been on the whole about as intimate. To feel this, and yet to feel that she also liked him, was very agreeable to Lord Lambeth. He fancied he had compassed that gratification so desirable to young men of title and fortune—being liked for himself. It is true that a cynical counsellor might have whispered to him, 'Liked for yourself? Yes; but not so very much!' He had, at any rate, the constant hope of being liked more.

It may seem, perhaps, a trifle singular—but it is nevertheless true—that Bessie Alden, when he struck her as dull, devoted some time, on grounds of conscience, to trying to like him more. I say on grounds of conscience, because she felt that he had been extremely 'nice' to her sister, and because she reflected that it was no more than fair that she should think as well of him as he thought of her. This effort was possibly sometimes not so successful as it might have been, for the result of it was occasionally a vague irritation, which expressed itself in hostile criticism of several British institutions. Bessie Alden went to some entertainments at which she met Lord Lambeth; but she went to others at which his lordship was neither actually nor potentially present; and it was chiefly on these latter occasions that she encountered those literary and artistic celebrities of whom mention has been made. After a while she reduced the matter to a principle. If Lord Lambeth should appear anywhere, it was a symbol that there would be no poets and philosphers; and in consequence—for it was almost a strict consequence—she used to enumerate to the young man these objects of her admiration.

'You seem to be awfully fond of those sort of people,' said Lord Lambeth one day, as if the idea had just occurred to him.

'They are the people in England I am most curious to see,' Bessie Alden replied.

'I suppose that's because you have read so much,' said Lord Lambeth, gallantly.

'I have not read so much. It is because we think so much of them at home.'

'Oh, I see!' observed the young nobleman. 'In Boston.'

'Not only in Boston; everywhere,' said Bessie. 'We hold them in great honour; they go to the best dinner parties.'

'I daresay you are right. I can't say I know many of them.'

'It's a pity you don't,' Bessie Alden declared. 'It would do you good.'

'I daresay it would,' said Lord Lambeth, very humbly. 'But I must say I don't like the looks of some of them.'

'Neither do I—of some of them. But there are all kinds, and many of them are charming.'

'I have talked with two or three of them,' the young man went on, 'and I thought they had a kind of fawning manner.'

'Why should they fawn?' Bessie Alden demanded.

'I'm sure I don't know. Why, indeed?'

'Perhaps you only thought so,' said Bessie.

'Well, of course,' rejoined her companion, 'that's a kind of thing that can't be proved.'

'In America they don't fawn,' said Bessie.

'Ah! well, then, they must be better company.'

Bessie was silent a moment. 'That is one of the things I don't like about England,' she said; 'your keeping the distinguished people apart.'

'How do you mean, apart?'

'Why, letting them come only to certain places. You never see them.'

Lord Lambeth looked at her a moment. 'What people do you mean?'

'The eminent people—the authors and artists—the clever people.'

'Oh, there are other eminent people besides those!' said Lord Lambeth.

'Well, you certainly keep them apart,' repeated the young girl.

'And there are other clever people,' added Lord Lambeth, simply.

Bessie Alden looked at him, and she gave a light laugh. 'Not many,' she said.

On another occasion—just after a dinner party—she told him that there was something else in England she did not like.

'Oh, I say!' he cried; 'haven't you abused us enough?'

'I have never abused you at all,' said Bessie; 'but I don't like your *precedence*.'

'It isn't my precedence!' Lord Lambeth declared, laughing.

'Yes, it is yours—just exactly yours; and I think it's odious,' said Bessie.

'I never saw such a young lady for discussing things! Has some one had the impudence to go before you?' asked his lordship.

'It is not the going before me that I object to,' said Bessie; 'it is their thinking that they have a right to do it—a right that I cannot recognize.'

'I never saw such a young lady as you are for not "recognizing." I have no doubt the thing is beastly, but it saves a lot of trouble.'

'It makes a lot of trouble. It's horrid!' said Bessie.

'But how would you have the first people go?' asked Lord Lambeth. 'They can't go last.'

'Whom do you mean by the first people?'

'Ah, if you mean to question first principles!' said Lord Lambeth.

'If those are your first principles, no wonder some of your arrangements are horrid,' observed Bessie Alden, with a very pretty ferocity. 'I am a young girl, so of course I go last; but imagine what Kitty must feel on being informed that she is not at liberty to budge until certain other ladies have passed out!'

'Oh, I say, she is not "informed!"' cried Lord Lambeth. 'No one would do such a thing as that.'

'She is made to feel it,' the young girl insisted—'as if they were afraid she would make a rush for the door. No, you have a lovely country,' said Bessie Alden, 'but your precedence is horrid.'

'I certainly shouldn't think your sister would like it,' rejoined Lord Lambeth, with even exaggerated gravity. But Bessie Alden could induce him to enter no formal protest against this repulsive custom, which he seemed to think an extreme convenience.

Percy Beaumont all this time had been a very much less frequent visitor at Jones's Hotel than his noble kinsman; he had in fact called but twice upon the two American ladies. Lord Lambeth, who often saw him, reproached him with his neglect, and declared that, although Mrs. Westgate had said nothing about it, he was sure that she was secretly wounded by it. 'She suffers too much to speak,' said Lord Lambeth.

'That's all gammon,' said Percy Beaumont; 'there's a limit to what people can suffer!' And, though sending no apologies to Jones's Hotel, he undertook in a manner to explain his absence. 'You are always there,' he said; 'and that's reason enough for my not going.'

'I don't see why. There is enough for both of us.'

'I don't care to be a witness of your—your reckless passion,' said Percy Beaumont.

Lord Lambeth looked at him with a cold eye, and for a moment said nothing. 'It's not so obvious as you might suppose,' he rejoined, dryly, 'considering what a demonstrative beggar I am.'

'I don't want to know anything about it—nothing whatever,' said Beaumont. 'Your mother asks me every time she sees me whether I believe you are really lost—and Lady Pimlico does the same. I prefer to be able to answer that I know nothing about it—that I never go there. I stay away for consistency's sake. As I said the other day, they must look after you themselves.'

'You are devilish considerate,' said Lord Lambeth. 'They never question me.'

'They are afraid of you. They are afraid of irritating you and making you worse. So they go to work very cautiously, and, somewhere or other, they get their information. They know a great deal about you. They know that you have been with those ladies to the dome of St. Paul's and—where was the other place?—to the Thames Tunnel.'

'If all their knowledge is as accurate as that, it must be very valuable,' said Lord Lambeth.

'Well, at any rate, they know that you have been visiting the "sights of the metropolis." They think—very naturally, as it seems to me—that when you take to visiting the sights of the metropolis with a little American girl, there is serious cause for alarm.' Lord Lambeth responded to this intimation by scornful laughter, and his companion continued, after a pause: 'I said just now I didn't want to know anything about the affair; but I will confess that I am curious to learn whether you propose to marry Miss Bessie Alden.'

On this point Lord Lambeth gave his interlocutor no immediate satisfaction; he was musing, with a frown. 'By Jove,' he said, 'they go rather too far. They *shall* find me dangerous—I promise them.'

Percy Beaumont began to laugh. 'You don't redeem your promises. You said the other day you would make your mother call.'

Lord Lambeth continued to meditate. 'I asked her to call,' he said simply.

'And she declined?'

'Yes, but she shall do it yet.'

'Upon my word,' said Percy Beaumont, 'if she gets much more frightened I believe she will.' Lord Lambeth looked at him, and he went on. 'She will go to the girl herself.'

'How do you mean, she will go to her?'

'She will beg her off, or she will bribe her. She will take strong measures.'

Lord Lambeth turned away in silence, and his companion watched him take twenty steps and then slowly return. 'I have invited Mrs. Westgate and Miss Alden to Branches,' he said, 'and this evening I shall name a day.'

'And shall you invite your mother and your sisters to meet them?'

'Explicitly!'

'That will set the Duchess off,' said Percy Beaumont. 'I suspect she will come.'

'She may do as she pleases.'

Beaumont looked at Lord Lambeth. 'You do really propose to marry the little sister, then?'

'I like the way you talk about it!' cried the young man. 'She won't gobble me down; don't be afraid.'

'She won't leave you on your knees,' said Percy Beaumont. 'What *is* the inducement?'

'You talk about proposing—wait till I *have* proposed,' Lord Lambeth went on.

'That's right, my dear fellow; think about it,' said Percy Beaumont.

'She's a charming girl,' pursued his lordship.

'Oh course she's a charming girl. I don't know a girl more charming, intrinsically. But there are other charming girls nearer home.'

'I like her spirit,' observed Lord Lambeth, almost as if he were trying to torment his cousin.

'What's the peculiarity of her spirit?'

'She's not afraid, and she says things out, and she thinks herself as good as any one. She is the only girl I have ever seen that was not dying to marry me.'

'How do you know that, if you haven't asked her?'

'I don't know how; but I know it.'

'I am sure she asked me questions enough about your property and your titles,' said Beaumont.

'She has asked me questions, too; no end of them,' Lord Lambeth admitted. 'But she asked for information, don't you know.'

'Information? Ay, I'll warrant she wanted it. Depend upon it that she is dying to marry you just as much and just as little as all the rest of them.'

'I shouldn't like her to refuse me—I shouldn't like that.'

'If the thing would be so disagreeable, then, both to you and to her, in Heaven's name leave it alone,' said Percy Beaumont.

Mrs. Westgate, on her side, had plenty to say to her sister about the rarity of Mr. Beaumont's visits and the non-appearance of the Duchess of Bayswater. She professed, however, to derive more satisfaction from this latter circumstance than she could have done from the most lavish attentions on the part of this great lady. 'It is most marked,' she said, 'most marked. It is a delicious proof that we have made them miserable. The day we dined with Lord Lambeth I was really sorry for the poor fellow.' It will have been gathered that the entertainment offered by Lord Lambeth to his American friends had not been graced by the presence of his anxious mother. He had invited several choice spirits to meet them; but the ladies of his immediate family were to Mrs. Westgate's sense—a sense, possibly, morbidly acute—conspicuous by their absence.

'I don't want to express myself in a manner that you dislike,' said Bessie Alden; 'But I don't know why you should have so many theories about Lord Lambeth's poor mother. You know a great many young men in New York without knowing their mothers.'

Mrs. Westgate looked at her sister, and then turned away. 'My dear Bessie, you are superb!' she said.

'One thing is certain,' the young girl continued. 'If I believed I were a cause of annoyance—however unwitting—to Lord Lambeth's family, I should insist—'

'Insist upon my leaving England,' said Mrs. Westgate.

'No, not that. I want to go to the National Gallery again; I want to see Stratford-on-Avon and Canterbury Cathedral. But I should insist upon his coming to see us no more.'

'That would be very modest and very pretty of you—but you wouldn't do it now.'

'Why do you say "now"?' asked Bessie Alden. 'Have I ceased to be modest?'

'You care for him too much. A month ago, when you said you didn't, I believe it was quite true. But at present, my dear child,' said Mrs. Westgate, 'you wouldn't find it quite so simple a matter never to see Lord Lambeth again. I have seen it coming on.'

'You are mistaken,' said Bessie. 'You don't understand.'

'My dear child, don't be perverse,' rejoined her sister.

'I know him better, certainly, if you mean that,' said Bessie. 'And I like him very much. But I don't like him enough to make trouble for him with his family. However, I don't believe in that.'

'I like the way you say "however!" ' Mrs. Westgate exclaimed. 'Come, you would not marry him?'

'Oh no,' said the young girl.

Mrs. Westgate, for a moment, seemed vexed. 'Why not, pray?' she demanded.

'Because I don't care to,' said Bessie Alden.

The morning after Lord Lambeth had had, with Percy Beaumont, that exchange of ideas which has just been narrated, the ladies at Jones's Hotel received from his lordship a written invitation to pay their projected visit to Branches Castle on the following Tuesday. 'I think I have made up a very pleasant party,' the young nobleman said. 'Several people whom you know, and my mother and sisters, who have so long been regrettably prevented from making your acquaintance.' Bessie Alden lost no time in calling her sister's attention to the injustice she had done to the Duchess of Bayswater, whose hostility was now proved to be a vain illusion.

'Wait till you see if she comes,' said Mrs. Westgate. 'And if she is to meet us at her son's house the obligation was all the greater for her to call upon us.'

Bessie had not to wait long, and it appeared that Lord Lambeth's mother now accepted Mrs. Westgate's view of her duties. On the morrow, early in the afternoon, two cards were brought to the apartment of the American ladies—one of them bearing the name of the Duchess of Bayswater, and the other that of the Countess of Pimlico. Mrs. Westgate glanced at the clock. 'It is not yet four,' she said; 'they have come early; they wish to see us. We will receive them.' And she gave orders that her visitors should be admitted. A few moments later they were introduced, and there was a solemn exchange of amenities. The Duchess was a large lady, with a fine fresh colour; the Countess of Pimlico was very pretty and elegant.

The Duchess looked about her as she sat down—looked not especially at Mrs. Westgate. 'I daresay my son has told you that I have been wanting to come and see you,' she observed.

'You are very kind,' said Mrs. Westgate, vaguely—her conscience not allowing her to assent to this proposition—and indeed not permitting her to enunciate her own with any appreciable emphasis.

'He says you were so kind to him in America,' said the Duchess.

'We are very glad,' Mrs. Westgate replied, 'to have been able to make him a little more—a little less—a little more comfortable.'

'I think he stayed at your house,' remarked the Duchess of Bayswater, looking at Bessie Alden.

'A very short time,' said Mrs. Westgate.

'Oh!' said the Duchess; and she continued to look at Bessie, who was engaged in conversation with her daughter.

'Do you like London?' Lady Pimlico had asked of Bessie, after looking at her a good deal—at her face and her hands, her dress and her hair.

'Very much indeed,' said Bessie.

'Do you like this hotel?'

'It is very comfortable,' said Bessie.

'Do you like stopping at hotels?' inquired Lady Pimlico, after a pause.

'I am very fond of travelling,' Bessie answered, 'and I suppose hotels are a necessary part of it. But they are not the part I am fondest of.'

'Oh, I hate travelling!' said the Countess of Pimlico, and transferred her attention to Mrs. Westgate.

'My son tells me you are going to Branches,' the Duchess presently resumed.

'Lord Lambeth has been so good as to ask us,' said Mrs. Westgate, who perceived that her visitor had now begun to look at her, and who had her customary happy consciousness of a distinguished appearance. The only mitigation of her felicity on this point was that, having inspected her visitor's own costume, she said to herself, 'She won't know how well I am dressed!'

'He has asked me to go, but I am not sure I shall be able,' murmured the Duchess.

'He had offered us the p— the prospect of meeting you,' said Mrs. Westgate.

'I hate the country at this season,' responded the Duchess.

Mrs. Westgate gave a little shrug. 'I think it is pleasanter than London.'

But the Duchess's eyes were absent again; she was looking very fixedly at Bessie. In a moment she slowly rose, walked to a chair that stood empty at the young girl's right hand, and silently seated herself. As she was a majestic, voluminous woman, this little transaction had, inevitably, an air of somewhat impressive intention. It diffused a certain awkwardness, which Lady Pimlico, as a sympathetic daughter, perhaps desired to rectify in turning to Mrs. Westgate.

'I daresay you go out a great deal,' she observed.

'No, very little. We are strangers, and we didn't come here for society.'

'I see,' said Lady Pimlico. 'It's rather nice in town just now.'

'It's charming,' said Mrs. Westgate. 'But we only go to see a few people—whom we like.'

'Of course one can't like every one,' said Lady Pimlico.

'It depends upon one's society,' Mrs. Westgate rejoined.

The Duchess, meanwhile, had addressed herself to Bessie. 'My son tells me the young ladies in America are so clever.'

'I am glad they made so good an impression on him,' said Bessie, smiling.

The Duchess was not smiling; her large fresh face was very tranquil. 'He is very susceptible,' she said. 'He thinks every one clever, and sometimes they are.'

'Sometimes,' Bessie assented, smiling still.

The Duchess looked at her a little and then went on—'Lambeth is very susceptible, but he is very volatile, too.'

'Volatile?' asked Bessie.

'He is very inconstant. It won't do to depend on him.'

'Ah!' said Bessie; 'I don't recognize that description. We have depended on him greatly—my sister and I—and he has never disappointed us.'

'He will disappoint you yet,' said the Duchess.

Bessie gave a little laugh, as if she were amused at the Duchess's persistency. 'I suppose it will depend on what we expect of him.'

'The less you expect the better,' Lord Lambeth's mother declared.

'Well,' said Bessie, 'we expect nothing unreasonable.'

The Duchess, for a moment, was silent, though she appeared to have more to say. 'Lambeth says he has seen so much of you,' she presently began.

'He has been to see us very often—he has been very kind,' said Bessie Alden.

'I dare say you are used to that. I am told there is a great deal of that in America.'

'A great deal of kindness?' the young girl inquired, smiling.

'Is that what you call it? I know you have different expressions.'

'We certainly don't always understand each other,' said Mrs. Westgate, the termination of whose interview with Lady Pimlico allowed her to give her attention to their elder visitor.

'I am speaking of the young men calling so much upon the young ladies,' the Duchess explained.

'But surely in England,' said Mrs. Westgate, 'the young ladies don't call upon the young men?'

'Some of them do—almost!' Lady Pimlico declared. 'When the young men are a great *parti*.'

'Bessie, you must make a note of that,' said Mrs. Westgate. 'My sister,' she added, 'is a model traveller. She writes down all the curious facts she hears, in a little book she keeps for the purpose.'

The Duchess was a little flushed; she looked all about the room, while her daughter turned to Bessie. 'My brother told us you were wonderfully clever,' said Lady Pimlico.

'He should have said my sister,' Bessie answered—'when she says such things as that.'

'Shall you be long at Branches?' the Duchess asked, abruptly, of the young girl.

'Lord Lambeth has asked us for three days,' said Bessie.

'I shall go,' the Duchess declared, 'and my daughter too.'

'That will be charming!' Bessie rejoined.

'Delightful!' murmured Mrs. Westgate.

'I shall expect to see a great deal of you,' the Duchess continued. 'When I go to Branches I monopolize my son's guests.'

'They must be most happy,' said Mrs. Westgate, very graciously.

'I want immensely to see it—to see the Castle,' said Bessie to the Duchess. 'I have never seen one—in England at least; and you know we have none in America.'

'Ah! you are fond of castles?' inquired her Grace.

'Immensely!' replied the young girl. 'It has been the dream of my life to live in one.'

The Duchess looked at her a moment, as if she hardly knew how to take this assurance, which, from her Grace's point of view, was either very artless or very audacious. 'Well,' she said, rising, 'I will show you Branches myself.' And upon this the two great ladies took their departure.

'What did they mean by it?' asked Mrs. Westgate, when they were gone.

'They meant to be polite,' said Bessie, 'because we are going to meet them.'

'It is too late to be polite,' Mrs. Westgate replied, almost grimly. 'They meant to overawe us by their fine manners and their grandeur, and to make you *lâcher prise.*'

'*Lâcher prise*? What strange things you say!' murmured Bessie Alden.

'They meant to snub us, so that we shouldn't dare to go to Branches,' Mrs. Westgate continued.

'On the contrary,' said Bessie, 'the Duchess offered to show me the place herself.'

'Yes, you may depend upon it she won't let you out of her sight. She will show you the place from morning to night.'

'You have a theory for everything,' said Bessie.

'And you apparently have none for anything.'

'I saw no attempt to "overawe" us,' said the young girl. 'Their manners were not fine.'

'They were not even good!' Mrs. Westgate declared.

Bessie was silent awhile, but in a few moments she observed that she had a very good theory. 'They came to look at me,' she said, as if this had been a very ingenious hypothesis. Mrs. Westgate did it justice; she greeted it with a smile and pronounced it most brilliant, while, in reality, she felt that the young girl's scepticism, or her charity, or, as she had sometimes called it, appropriately, her idealism, was proof against irony. Bessie, however, remained meditative all the rest of that day and well on into the morrow.

On the morrow, before lunch, Mrs. Westgate had occasion to go out for half an hour, and left her sister writing a letter. When she came back she met Lord Lambeth at the door of the hotel, coming away. She thought he looked slightly embarrassed; he was certainly very grave. 'I am sorry to have missed you. Won't you come back?' she asked.

'No,' said the young man, 'I can't. I have seen your sister. I can never come back.' Then he looked at her a moment, and took her hand. 'Good-bye Mrs. Westgate,' he said. 'You have been very kind to me.' And with what she thought a strange, sad look in his handsome young face, he turned away.

She went in and she found Bessie still writing her letter; that is, Mrs. Westgate perceived she was sitting at the table with the pen in her hand and not writing. 'Lord Lambeth has been here,' said the elder lady at last.

Then Bessie got up and showed her a pale, serious face. She bent this face upon her sister for some time, confessing silently and, a little, pleading. 'I told him,' she said at last, 'that we could not go to Branches.'

Mrs. Westgate displayed just a spark of irritation. 'He might have waited,' she said with a smile, 'till one had seen the Castle.' Later, an hour afterwards, she said, 'Dear Bessie, I wish you might have accepted him.'

'I couldn't,' said Bessie gently.

'He is an excellent fellow,' said Mrs. Westgate.

'I couldn't,' Bessie repeated.

'If it is only,' her sister added, 'because those women will think that they succeeded—that they paralysed us!'

Bessie Alden turned away; but presently she added, 'They were interesting; I should have liked to see them again.'

'So should I!' cried Mrs. Westgate, significantly.

'And I should have liked to see the Castle,' said Bessie. 'But now we must leave England,' she added.

'Her sister looked at her. 'You will not wait to go to the National Gallery?'

'Not now.'

'Nor to Canterbury Cathedral?'

Bessie reflected a moment. 'We can stop there on our way to Paris,' she said.

Lord Lambeth did not tell Percy Beaumont that the contingency he was not prepared at all to like had occurred; but Percy Beaumont, on hearing that the two ladies had left London, wondered with some intensity what had happened; wondered, that is, until the Duchess of Bayswater came, a little, to his assistance. The two ladies went to Paris, and Mrs. Westgate beguiled the journey to that city by repeating several times, 'That's what I regret; they will think they petrified us.' But Bessie Alden seemed to regret nothing.

The Pension Beaurepas

[First appeared in the *Atlantic Monthly*, vol. xliii (April 1879), pp. 460-88. The tale was revised and reprinted in volume ii of a selection of three works entitled *Washington Square, Etc.* (1881). The first American edition of the tale was published two years later in a selection of three works entitled *The Siege of London, Etc.* (1883). The text there follows the original magazine version. The same year the revised text of 1881 was reprinted in volume xii of James's first 'Collective Edition' (1883). Using the 1881 text, James finally revised the tale for the New York Edition where it appears in volume xiv (*Lady Barbarina, Etc.*, 1908).]

I.

I WAS NOT RICH—ON THE CONTRARY; AND I HAD BEEN TOLD THE Pension Beaurepas was cheap. I had moreover been told that a boarding-house is a capital place for the study of human nature. I had a fancy for a literary career, and a friend of mine had said to me, 'If you mean to write you ought to go and live in a boarding-house; there is no other such place to pick up material.' I had read something of this kind in a letter addressed by Stendhal to his siter: 'I have a passionate desire to know human nature, and have a great mind to live in a boarding-house, where people cannot conceal their real characters.' I was an admirer of the *Chartreuse de Parme*, and it appeared to me that one could not do better than follow in the footsteps of its author. I remember, too, the magnificent boarding-house in Balzac's *Père Goriot,*—the '*pension bourgeoise des deux sexes et autres*,' kept by Madame Vauquer, *née* De Conflans. Magnificent, I mean, as a piece of portraiture; the establishment, as an establishment, was certainly sordid enough, and I hoped for better things from the Pension Beaurepas. This institution was one of the most esteemed in Geneva, and, standing in a little garden of its own, not far from the lake, had a very homely, comfortable, sociable aspect. The regular entrance was, as one might say, at the back, which looked upon the street, or rather upon a little *place*, adorned like every place in Geneva, great or small, with a fountain. This fact was not prepossessing, for on crossing the threshold you found yourself more or less in the kitchen, encompassed with culinary odours. This, however, was no great matter, for at the Pension Beaurepas there was no attempt at gentility or at concealment of the domestic machinery. The latter was of a very simple sort. Madame Beaurepas was an excellent little old woman,—she was very far advanced in life, and had been keeping a pension for forty years,—whose only faults were that she was slightly deaf, that she was fond of a surreptitious pinch of snuff, and that, at the age of seventy-three, she wore flowers in her cap. There was a tradition in the house that she was not so deaf as she pretended; that she feigned this infirmity in order to possess herself of the secrets of her lodgers. But I never subscribed to this theory; I am convinced that Madame Beaurepas had outlived the period of indiscreet curiosity. She was a philosopher, on a matter-of-fact basis; she had been having lodgers for forty years, and all that she asked of them was that they should pay their bills, make use of the door-mat, and fold their napkins. She cared very little for their secrets. '*J'en ai vus de toutes les couleurs*,' she said to me. She had quite ceased to care for individuals; she cared only for types, for categories. Her large observation had made her acquainted with a great number, and her mind was a complete collection of 'heads.' She flattered herself that she knew at a glance where to pigeon-hole a new-comer, and if she made any mistakes her deportment never betrayed them. I think that, as regards individuals, she had neither likes not dislikes; but she was capable of expressing esteem or contempt for a species. She had her own ways, I suppose, of manifesting her approval, but her manner of indicating the reverse was simple and unvarying. '*Je trouve que c'est déplacé*!'—this exhausted her view of the matter. If one of her inmates had put arsenic into the *pot-au-feu*, I believe Madame Beaurepas would have contented herself with remarking that the proceeding was misplaced. The line of misconduct to which she most objected was an undue assumption of gentility; she had no patience with boarders who gave themselves airs. 'When people come *chez moi*, it is not to cut a figure in the world; I have never had that illusion,' I remember hearing her say; 'and when you pay seven francs a day, *tout compris*, it comprises everything but the right to look down upon the others. But there are people who, the less they pay, the more they take themselves *au sérieux*. My most difficult boarders have always been those who have had the little rooms.'

Madame Beaurepas had a niece, a young woman of some forty odd years; and the two ladies, with the assistance of a couple of thick-waisted, red-armed peasant women, kept the house going. If on your exits and entrances you peeped into the kitchen, it made very little difference; for Célestine, the cook, had no pretension to be an invisible functionary or to deal in occult methods. She was always at your service, with a grateful grin: she blacked your boots; she trudged off to fetch a cab; she would have carried your baggage, if you had allowed her, on her broad little back. She was always tramping in and out, between her kitchen and the fountain in the place, where it often seemed to me that a large part of the preparation for our dinner went forward,—the wringing out of towels and table-cloths, the washing of potatoes and cabbages, the scouring of saucepans and cleansing of water-bottles. You enjoyed, from the door-step, a perpetual back view of Célestine and of her large, loose, woollen ankles, as she craned, from the waist, over into the fountain and dabbled in her various utensils. This sounds as if life went on in a very make-shift fashion at the Pension Beaurepas,—as if the tone of the establishment were sordid. But such was not at all the case. We were simply very *bourgeois*; we practised the good old Genevese principle of not sacrificing to appearances. This is an excellent principle—when you have the reality. We had the reality at the Pension Beaurepas: we had it in the shape of soft, short beds, equipped with fluffy *duvets*; of admirable coffee, served to us in the morning by Célestine in person, as we lay recumbent on these downy couches; of copious, wholesome, succulent dinners, conformable to the best provincial traditions. For myself, I thought the Pension Beaurepas picturesque, and this, with me, at that time was a great word. I was young and ingenuous; I had just come from America. I wished to perfect myself in the French tongue, and I innocently believed that French tongues might be found in Swiss mouths. I used to go to lectures at the Academy, and come home with a violent appetite. I always enjoyed my morning walk across the long bridge (there was only one, just there, in those days) which spans the deep blue outgush of the lake, and up the dark, steep streets of the old Calvinistic city. The garden faced this way, towards the lake and the old town; and this was the pleasantest approach to the house. There was a high wall, with a double gate in the middle, flanked by a couple of ancient massive posts; the big rusty *grille* contained some old-fashioned iron-work. The garden was rather mouldy and weedy, tangled and untended, but it contained a little thin-flowing fountain, several green benches, a rickety little table of the same complexion, and three orange-trees, in tubs, which were deposited as effectively as possible in front of the windows of the *salon*.

II.

As commonly happens in boarding-houses, the rustle of petticoats was, at the Pension Beaurepas, the most familiar form of the human tread. There was the usual allotment of economical widows and old maids, and to maintain the balance of the sexes there were only an old Frenchman and a young American. It hardly made the matter easier that the old Frenchman came from Lausanne. He was a native of that estimable town, but he had once spent six months in Paris, he had tasted of the tree of knowledge; he had got beyond Lausanne, whose resources he pronounced inadequate. Lausanne, as he said, '*manquait d'agréments.*' When obliged, for reasons which he never specified, to bring his residence in Paris to a close, he had fallen back on Geneva; he had broken his fall at the Pension Beaurepas. Geneva was, after all, more like Paris, and at a Genevese boarding-house there were sure to be plenty of Americans with whom one could talk about the French metropolis. M. Pigeonneau was a little lean man, with a large, narrow nose, who sat a great deal in the garden, reading with the aid of a large magnifying glass a volume from the *cabinet de lecture.*

One day, a fortnight after my arrival at the Pension Beaurepas, I came back rather earlier than usual from my academic session; it wanted half an hour of the midday breakfast. I went into the salon with the design of possessing myself of the day's *Galignani* before one of the little English old maids should have removed it to her virginal bower,—a privilege to which Madame Beaurepas frequently alluded as one of the attractions of the establishment. In the salon I found a new-comer, a tall gentleman in a high black hat, whom I immediately recognized as a compatriot. I had often seen him, or his equivalent, in the hotel parlours of my native land. He apparently supposed himself to be at the present moment in a hotel parlour; his hat was on his head, or, rather, half off it,—pushed back from his forehead, and rather suspended than poised. He stood before a table on which old newspapers were scattered, one of which he had taken up and, with his eye-glass on his nose, was holding out at arm's-length. It was that honourable but extremely diminutive sheet, the *Journal de Genève*, a newspaper of about the size of a pocket-handkerchief. As I drew near, looking for my *Galignani*, the tall gentleman gave me, over the top of his eye-glass, a somewhat solemn stare. Presently, however, before I had time to lay my hand on the object of my search, he silently offered me the *Journal de Genève.*

'It appears,' he said, 'to be the paper of the country.'

'Yes,' I answered, 'I believe it's the best.'

He gazed at it again, still holding it at arm's-length, as if it had been a looking-glass. 'Well,' he said, 'I suppose it's natural a small country should have small papers. You could wrap it up, mountains and all, in one of our dailies!'

I found my *Galignani* and went off with it into the garden, where I seated myself on a bench in the shade. Presently I saw the tall gentleman in the hat appear in one of the open windows of the salon, and stand there with his hands in his pockets and his legs a little apart.

He looked very much bored, and—I don't know why—I immediately began to feel sorry for him. He was not at all a picturesque personage; he looked like a jaded, faded man of business. But after a little he came into the garden and began to stroll about; and then his restless, unoccupied carriage, and the vague, unacquainted manner in which his eyes wandered over the place, seemed to make it proper that, as an older resident, I should exercise a certain hospitality. I said something to him, and he came and sat down beside me on my bench, clasping one of his long knees in his hands.

'When is it this big breakfast of theirs comes off?' he inquired. 'That's what I call it,—the little breakfast and the big breakfast. I never thought I should live to see the time when I should care to eat two breakfasts. But a man's glad to do anything, over here.'

'For myself,' I observed, 'I find plenty to do.'

He turned his head and glanced at me with a dry, deliberate, kind-looking eye. 'You're getting used to the life, are you?'

'I like the life very much,' I answered, laughing.

'How long have you tried it?'

'Do you mean in this place?'

'Well, I mean anywhere. It seems to me pretty much the same all over.'

'I have been in this house only a fortnight,' I said.

'Well, what should you say, from what you have seen?' my companion asked.

'Oh,' said I, 'you can see all there is immediately. It's very simple.'

'Sweet simplicity, eh? I'm afraid my two ladies will find it too simple.'

'Everything is very good,' I went on. 'And Madame Beaurepas is a charming old woman. And then it's very cheap.'

'Cheap, is it?' my friend repeated meditatively.

'Doesn't it strike you so?' I asked. I thought it very possible he had not inquired the terms. But he appeared not to have heard me; he sat there, clasping his knee and blinking, in a contemplative manner, at the sunshine.

'Are you from the United States, sir?' he presently demanded, turning his head again.

'Yes, sir,' I replied, and I mentioned the place of my nativity.

'I presumed,' he said, 'that you were American, or English. I'm from the United States myself; from New York city. Many of our people here?'

'Not so many as, I believe, there have sometimes been. There are two or three ladies.'

'Well,' my interlocutor declared, 'I am very fond of ladies' society. I think when it's nice there's nothing comes up to it. I've got two ladies here myself; I must make you acquainted with them.'

I rejoined that I should be delighted, and I inquired of my friend whether he had been long in Europe.

'Well, it seems precious long,' he said, 'but my time's not up yet. We have been here fourteen weeks and a half.'

'Are you travelling for pleasure?' I asked.

My companion turned his head again and looked at me,—looked at me so long in silence that I at last also turned and met his eyes.

'No, sir,' he said, presently. 'No, sir,' he repeated, after a considerable interval.

'Excuse me,' said I, for there was something so solemn in his tone that I feared I had been indiscreet.

He took no notice of my ejaculation; he simply continued to look at me. 'I'm travelling,' he said, at last, 'to please the doctors. They seemed to think they would like it.'

'Ah, they sent you abroad for your health.'

'They sent me abroad because they were so confoundedly puzzled they didn't know what else to do.'

'That's often the best thing,' I ventured to remark.

'It was a confession of weakness; they wanted me to stop plaguing them. They didn't know enough to cure me, and that's the way they thought they would get out of it. I wanted to be cured,—I didn't want to be transported. I hadn't done any harm.'

I assented to the general proposition of the inefficiency of doctors, and asked my companion if he had been seriously ill.

'I didn't sleep,' he said, after some delay.

'Ah, that's very annoying. I suppose you were overworked.'

'I didn't eat; I took no interest in my food.'

'Well, I hope you both eat and sleep now,' I said.

'I couldn't hold a pen,' my neighbour went on. 'I couldn't sit still. I couldn't walk from my house to the cars,—and it's only a little way. I lost my interest in business.'

'You needed a holiday,' I observed.

'That's what the doctors said. It wasn't so very smart of them. I had been paying strict attention to business for twenty-three years.'

'In all that time you have never had a holiday?' I exclaimed, with horror.

My companion waited a little. 'Sundays,' he said at last.

'No wonder, then, you were out of sorts.'

'Well, sir,' said my friend, 'I shouldn't have been where I was three years ago if I had spent my time travelling round Europe. I was in a very advantageous position. I did a very large business. I was considerably interested in lumber.' He paused, turned his head, and looked at me a moment. 'Have you any business interests yourself?' I answered that I had none, and he went on again, slowly, softly, deliberately. 'Well, sir, perhaps you are not aware that business in the United States is not what it was a short time since. Business interests are very insecure. There seems to be a general falling-off. Different parties offer different explanations of the fact, but so far as I am aware none of their observations have set things going again.' I ingeniously intimated that if business was dull it was a good time for coming away; whereupon my neighbour threw back his head and stretched his legs a while. 'Well, sir, that's one view of the matter, certainly. There's something to be said for that. These things should be looked at all round. That's the ground my wife took. That's the ground,' he added in a moment, 'that a lady would naturally take,' and he gave a little dry laugh.

'You think it's slightly illogical,' I remarked.

'Well, sir, the ground I took was that the worse a man's business is, the more it requires looking after. I shouldn't want to go out to take a walk—not even to go to church—if my house was on fire. My firm is not doing the business it was; it's like a sick child; it wants nursing. What I wanted the doctors to do was to fix me up, so that I could go on at home. I'd have taken anything they'd have given me, and as many times a day. I wanted to be right there; I had my reasons; I have them still. But I came off, all the same,' said my friend, with a melancholy smile.

I was a great deal younger than he, but there was something so simple and communicative in his tone, so expressive of a desire to fraternize, and so exempt from any theory of human differences, that I quite forgot his seniority, and found myself offering him paternal advice. 'Don't think about all that,' said I. 'Simply enjoy yourself, amuse yourself, get well. Travel about and see Europe. At the end of a year, by the time you are ready to go home, things will have improved over there, and you will be quite well and happy.'

My friend laid his hand on my knee; he looked at me for some moments, and I thought he was going to say, 'You are very young!' But he said presently, '*You* have got used to Europe, any way!'

III.

At breakfast I encountered his ladies,—his wife and daughter. They were placed, however, at a distance from me, and it was not until the *pensionnaires* had dispersed, and some of them, according to custom, had come out into the garden, that he had an opportunity of making me acquainted with them.

'Will you allow me to introduce you to my daughter?' he said, moved apparently by a paternal inclination to provide this young lady with social diversion. She was standing, with her mother, in one of the paths, looking about, with no great complacency, as I imagined, at the homely characteristics of the place, and old M. Pigeonneau was hovering near, hesitating apparently between the desire to be urbane and the absence of a pretext. 'Mrs. Ruck,—Miss Sophy Ruck,' said my friend, leading me up.

Mrs. Ruck was a large, plump, light-coloured person, with a smooth, fair face, a somnolent eye, and an elaborate coiffure. Miss Sophy was a girl of one and twenty, very small and very pretty,—what I suppose would have been called a lively brunette. Both of these ladies were attired in black silk dresses, very much trimmed; they had an air of the highest elegance.

'Do you think highly of this pension?' inquired Mrs. Ruck, after a few preliminaries.

'It's a little rough, but it seems to me comfortable,' I answered.

'Does it take a high rank in Geneva?' Mrs. Ruck pursued.

'I imagine it enjoys a very fair fame,' I said, smiling.

'I should never dream of comparing it to a New York boarding-house,' said Mrs. Ruck.

'It's quite a different style,' her daughter observed. Miss Ruck had folded her arms; she was holding her elbows with a pair of white little hands, and she was tapping the ground with a pretty little foot.

'We hardly expected to come to a pension,' said Mrs. Ruck. 'But we thought we would try; we had heard so much about Swiss pensions. I was saying to Mr. Ruck that I wondered whether this was a favourable specimen. I was afraid we might have made a mistake.'

'We knew some people who had been here; they thought everything of Madame Beaurepas,' said Miss Sophy. 'They said she was a real friend.'

'Mr. and Mrs. Parker,—perhaps you have heard her speak of them,' Mrs. Ruck pursued.

'Madame Beaurepas has had a great many Americans; she is very fond of Americans,' I replied.

'Well, I must say I should think she would be, if she compares them with some others.'

'Mother is always comparing,' observed Miss Ruck.

'Of course I am always comparing,' rejoined the elder lady. 'I never had a chance till now; I never knew my privileges. Give me an

American!' And Mrs. Ruck indulged in a little laugh.

'Well, I must say there are some things I like over here,' said Miss Sophy, with courage. And indeed I could see that she was a young woman of great decision.

'You like the shops,—that's what you like,' her father affirmed.

The young lady addressed herself to me, without heeding this remark: 'I suppose you feel quite at home here.'

'Oh, he likes it; he has got used to the life!' exclaimed Mr. Ruck.

'I wish you'd teach Mr. Ruck,' said his wife. 'It seems as if he couldn't get used to anything.'

'I'm used to you, my dear,' the husband retorted, giving me a humourous look.

'He's intensely restless,' continued Mrs. Ruck. 'That's what made me want to come to a pension. I thought he would settle down more.'

'I don't think I *am* used to you, after all,' said her husband.

In view of a possible exchange of conjugal *repartee* I took refuge in conversation with Miss Ruck, who seemed perfectly able to play her part in any colloquy. I learned from this young lady that, with her parents, after visiting the British islands, she had been spending a month in Paris, and that she thought she should have died when she left that city. 'I hung out of the carriage, when we left the hotel,' said Miss Rusk; 'I assure you I did. And mother did, too.'

'Out of the other window, I hope,' said I.

'Yes, one out of each window,' she replied, promptly. 'Father had hard work, I can tell you. We hadn't half finished; there were ever so many places we wanted to go to.'

'Your father insisted on coming away?'

'Yes; after we had been there about a month he said he had enough. He's fearfully restless; he's very much out of health. Mother and I said to him that if he was restless in Paris he needn't hope for peace anywhere. We don't mean to leave him alone till he takes us back.' There was an air of keen resolution in Miss Ruck's pretty face, of lucid apprehension of desirable ends, which made me, as she pronounced these words, direct a glance of covert compassion towards her poor recalcitrant father. He had walked away a little with his wife, and I saw only his back and his stooping, patient-looking shoulders, whose air of acute resignation was thrown into relief by the voluminous tranquillity of Mrs. Ruck. 'He will have to take us back in September, any way,' the young girl pursued; 'he will have to take us back to get some things we have ordered.'

'Have you ordered a great many things?' I asked, jocosely.

'Well, I guess we have ordered *some*. Of course we wanted to take advantage of being in Paris,—ladies always do. We have left the principle things till we go back. Of course that is the principal interest for ladies. Mother said she should feel so shabby, if she just passed through. We have promised all the people to be back in September, and I never broke a promise yet. So Mr. Ruck has got to make his plans accordingly.'

'And what are his plans?'

'I don't know; he doesn't seem able to make any. His great idea was to get to Geneva; but now that he has got here he doesn't seem to care. It's the effect of ill health. He used to be so bright; but now he is quite subdued. It's about time he should improve, any way. We went out last night to look at the jewellers' windows,—in that street behind the hotel. I had always heard of those jewellers' windows. We saw some lovely things, but it didn't seem to rouse father. He'll get tired of Geneva sooner than he did of Paris.'

'Ah,' said I, 'there are finer things here than the jewellers' windows. We are very near some of the most beautiful scenery in Europe.'

'I suppose you mean the mountains. Well, we have seen plenty of mountains at home. We used to go to the mountains every summer. We are familiar enough with the mountains. Aren't we, mother?' the young lady demanded, appealing to Mrs. Ruck, who, with her husband, had drawn near again.

'Aren't we what?' inquired the elder lady.

'Aren't we familiar with the mountains?'

'Well, I hope so,' said Mrs. Ruck.

Mr. Ruck, with his hands in his pockets, gave me a sociable wink. 'There's nothing much you can tell them!' he said.

The two ladies stood face to face a few moments, surveying each other's garments. 'Don't you want to go out?' the young girl at last inquired of her mother.

'Well, I think we had better; we have got to go up to that place.'

'To what place?' asked Mr. Ruck.

'To that jeweller's,—to that big one.'

'They all seemed big enough; they were too big!' And Mr. Ruck gave me another wink.

'That one where we saw the blue cross,' said his daughter.

'Oh, come, what do you want of that blue cross?' poor Mr. Ruck demanded.

'She wants to hang it on a black velvet ribbon and tie it round her neck,' said his wife.

'A black velvet ribbon? No, I thank you!' cried the young lady. 'Do you suppose I would wear that cross on a black velvet ribbon? On a nice little gold chain, if you please,—a little narrow gold chain, like an old-fashioned watch-chain. That's the proper thing for that blue cross. I know the sort of chain I mean; I'm going to look for one. When I want a thing,' said Miss Ruck, with decision, 'I can generally find it.'

'Look here, Sophy,' her father urged, 'you don't want that blue cross.'

'I do want it,—I happen to want it.' And Sophy glanced at me with a little laugh.

Her laugh, which in itself was pretty, suggested that there were various relations in which one might stand to Miss Ruck; but I think I was conscious of a certain satisfaction in not occupying the paternal one. 'Don't worry the poor child,' said her mother.

'Come on, mother,' said Miss Ruck.

'We are going to look about a little,' explained the elder lady to me, by way of taking leave.

'I know what that means,' remarked Mr. Ruck, as his companions moved away. He stood looking at them a moment, while he raised his hand to his head, behind, and stood rubbing it a little, with a movement that displaced his hat. (I may remark in parenthesis that I never saw a hat more easily displaced than Mr. Ruck's.) I supposed he was going to say something querulous, but I was mistaken. Mr. Ruck was unhappy, but he was very good-natured. 'Well, they want to pick up something,' he said. 'That's the principal interest, for ladies.'

IV.

Mr. Ruck distinguished me, as the French say. He honoured me with his esteem, and, as the days elapsed, with a large portion of his confidence. Sometimes he bored me a little, for the tone of his conversation was not cheerful, tending as it did almost exclusively to a melancholy dirge over the financial prostration of our common country. 'No, sir, business in the United States is not what it once was,' he found occasions to remark several times a day. 'There's not the same spring,—there's not the same hopeful feeling. You can see it in all departments.' He used to sit by the hour in the little garden of the pension, with a roll of American newspapers in his lap and his high hat pushed back, swinging one of his long legs and reading the *New York Herald*. He paid a daily visit to the American banker's, on the other side of the Rhône, and remained there a long time, turning over the old papers on the green velvet table in the middle of the Salon des Étrangers and fraternizing with chance compatriots. But in spite of these diversions his time hung heavily upon his hands. I used sometimes to propose to him to take a walk; but he had a mortal horror of pedestrianism, and regarded my own taste for it as a morbid form of activity. 'You'll kill yourself, if you don't look out,' he said, 'walking all over the country. I don't want to walk round that way; I ain't a postman!' Briefly speaking, Mr. Ruck had few resources. His wife and daughter, on the other hand, it was to be supposed, were possessed of a good many that could not be apparent to an unobtrusive young man. They also sat a great deal in the garden or in the salon, side by side, with folded hands, contemplating material objects, and were remarkably independent of most of the usual feminine aids to idleness,—light literature, tapestry, the use of the piano. They were, however, much fonder of locomotion than their companion, and I often met them in the Rue du Rhône and on the quays, loitering in front of the jewellers' windows. They might have had a cavalier in the person of old M. Pigeonneau, who professed a high appreciation of their charms, but who, owing to the absence of a common idiom, was deprived of the pleasures of intimacy. He knew no English, and Mrs. Ruck and her daughter had, as it seemed, an incurable mistrust of the beautiful tongue which, as the old man endeavoured to impress upon them, was preeminently the language of conversation.

'They have a *tournure de princesse*,—a *distinction supreme*,' he said to me. 'One is surprised to find them in a little pension, at seven francs a day.'

'Oh, they don't come for economy,' I answered. 'They must be rich.'

'They don't come for my *beaux yeux*,—for mine,' said M. Pigeonneau, sadly. 'Perhaps it's for yours, young man. *Je vous recommande la mère.*'

I reflected a moment. 'They came on account of Mr. Ruck,—because at hotels he's so restless.'

M. Pigeonneau gave me a knowing nod. 'Of course he is, with such a wife as that!—a *femme superbe*. Madame Ruck is preserved in perfection,—a miraculous *fraîcheur*. I like those large, fair, quiet women; they are often, *dans l'intimité*, the most agreeable. I'll warrant you that at heart Madame Ruck is a finished coquette.'

'I rather doubt it,' I said.

'You suppose her cold? *Ne vous y fiez pas*!'

'It is a matter in which I have nothing at stake.'

'You young Americans are droll,' said M. Pigeonneau; 'you never have anything at stake! But the little one, for example; I'll warrant you she's not cold. She is admirably made.'

'She is very pretty.'

' "She is very pretty!" *Vous dites cela d'un ton*! When you pay compliments to Mademoiselle Ruck, I hope that's not the way you do it.'

'I don't pay compliments to Mademoiselle Ruck.'

'Ah, decidedly,' said M. Pigeonneau, 'you young Americans are droll!'

I should have suspected that these two ladies would not especially commend themselves to Madame Beaurepas; that as a *maîtresse de salon*, which she in some degree aspired to be, she would have found them wanting in a certain flexibility of deportment. But I should have gone quite wrong; Madame Beaurepas had no fault at all to find with her new pensionnaires. 'I have no observation whatever to make about them,' she said to me one evening. 'I see nothing in those ladies which is at all *déplacé*. They don't complain of anything; they don't meddle; they take what's given them; they leave me tranquil. The Americans are often like that. Often, but not always,' Madame Beaurepas pursued. 'We are to have a specimen tomorrow of a very different sort.'

'An American?' I inquired.

'Two *Américaines*,—a mother and a daughter. There are Americans and Americans: when you are *difficiles*, you are more so than any one, and when you have pretensions—ah, *par exemple*, it's serious. I foresee that with this little lady everything will be serious, beginning with her *café au lait*. She has been staying at the Pension Bonrepos,—my concurrent, you know, further up the street; but she is coming away because the coffee is bad. She holds to her coffee, it appears. I don't know what liquid Madam Bonrepos may have invented, but we will do the best we can for her. Only, I know she will make me *des histoires* about something else. She will demand a new lamp for the salon; *vous allez voir cela*. She wishes to pay but eleven francs a day for herself and her daughter, *tout compris*; and for their eleven francs they expect to be lodged like princesses. But she is very "lady-like,'—isn't that what you call it in English? Oh, *pour cela*, she is lady-like!'

I caught a glimpse on the morrow of this lady-like person, who was arriving at her new residence as I came in from a walk. She had come in a cab, with her daughter and her luggage; and, with an air of perfect softness and serenity, she was disputing the fare as she stood among her boxes, on the steps. She addressed her cabman in a very English accent, but with extreme precision and correctness: 'I wish to be perfectly reasonable, but I don't wish to encourage you in exorbitant demands. With a franc and a half you are sufficiently paid. It is not the custom at Geneva to give a *pour-boire* for so short a drive. I have made inquiries, and I find it is not the custom, even in the best families. I am a stranger, yes, but I always adopt the custom of the native families. I think it my duty towards the natives.'

'But I am a native, too, *moi*!' said the cabman, with an angry laugh.

'You seem to speak with a German accent,' continued the lady. 'You are probably from Basel. A franc and a half is sufficient. I see you have left behind the little red bag which I asked you to hold between your knees; you will please to go back to the other house and get it. Very well, if you are impolite I will make a complaint of you tomorrow at the administration. Aurora, you will find a pencil in the outer pocket of my embroided satchel; please to write down his number,—87; do you see it distinctly?—in case we should forget it.'

The young lady addressed as 'Aurora'—a slight, fair girl, holding a large parcel of umbrellas—stood at hand while this allocution went forward, but she apparently gave no heed to it. She stood looking about her, in a listless manner, at the front of the house, at the corridor, at Célestine tucking up her apron in the door-way, at me as I passed in amid the disseminated luggage; her mother's parsimonious attitude seeming to produce in Miss Aurora neither sympathy nor embarrassment. At dinner the two ladies were placed on the same side of the table as myself, below Mrs. Ruck and her daughter, my own position being on the right of Mr. Ruck. I had therefore little observaton of Mrs. Church,—such I learned to be her name,—but I occasionally heard her soft, distinct voice.

'White wine, if you please; we prefer white wine. There is none on the table? Then you will please to get some, and to remember to place a bottle of it always here, between my daughter and myself.'

'That lady seems to know what she wants,' said Mr. Ruck, 'and she speaks so I can understand her. I can't understand every one, over here. I should like to make that lady's acquaintance. Perhaps she knows what *I* want, too; it seems hard to find out. But I don't want any of their sour white wine; that's one of the things I don't want. I expect she'll be an addition to the pension.'

Mr. Ruck made the acquaintance of Mrs. Church that evening in the parlour, being presented to her by his wife, who presumed on the rights conferred upon herself by the mutual proximity, at table, of the two ladies. I suspected that in Mrs. Church's view Mrs. Ruck presumed too far. The fugitive from the Pension Bonrepos, as M. Pigeonneau called her, was a little fresh, plump, comely woman, looking less than her age, with a round, bright, serious face. She was very simply and frugally dressed, not at all in the manner of Mr. Ruck's companions, and she had an air of quiet distinction which was an excellent defensive weapon. She exhibited a polite disposition to listen to what Mr. Ruck might have to say, but her manner was equivalent to an intimation that what she valued least in boarding-house life was its social opportunities. She had placed herself near a lamp, after carefully screwing it and turning it up, and she had opened in her lap, with the assistance of a large embroidered marker, an octavo volume which I perceived to be in German. To Mrs. Ruck and her daughter she was evidently a puzzle, with her economical attire and her expensive culture. The two younger ladies, however, had begun to fraternize very freely, and Miss Ruck presently went wandering out of the room with her arm round the waist of Miss Church. It was a very warm evening; the long windows of the salon stood wide open into the garden, and, inspired by the balmy darkness, M. Pigeonneau and Mademoiselle Beaurepas, a most obliging little woman, who lisped and always wore a huge cravat, declared they would organize a *fête*. They engaged in this undertaking, and the fête developed itself, consisting of half a dozen red paper lanterns, hung about on the trees, and of several glasses of *sirop*, carried on a tray by the stout-armed Célestine. As the festival deepened to its climax I went out into the garden, where M. Pigeonneau was master of ceremonies.

'But where are those charming young ladies,' he cried, 'Miss Ruck and the new-comer, *l'aimable transfuge?* Their absence has been remarked, and they are wanting to the brilliancy of the occasion. *Voyez*, I have selected a glass of syrup—a generous glass—for Mademoiselle Ruck, and I advise you, my young friend, if you wish to make a good impression, to put aside one which you may offer to the other young lady. What is her name? Miss Church. I see; it's a singular name. There is a church in which I would willingly worship!'

Mr. Ruck presently came out of the salon, having concluded his interview with Mrs. Church. Through the open window I saw the latter lady sitting under the lamp with her German octavo, while Mrs. Ruck, established, empty-handed, in an arm-chair near her, gazed at her with an air of fascination.

'Well, I told you she would know what I want,' said Mr. Ruck. 'She says I want to go up to Appenzell, wherever that is; that I want to drink whey and live in a high latitude—what did she call it?—a high altitude. She seemed to think we ought to leave for Appenzell to-morrow; she'd got it all fixed. She says this ain't a high enough lat—a high enough altitude. And she says I mustn't go too high, either; that would be just as bad; she seems to know just the right figure. She says she'll give me a list of the hotels where we must stop, on the way to Appenzell. I asked her if she didn't want to go with us, but she says she'd rather sit still and read. I expect she's a big reader.'

The daughter of this accomplished woman now reappeared, in

company with Miss Ruck, with whom she had been strolling through the outlying parts of the garden.

'Well,' said Miss Ruck, glancing at the red paper lanterns, 'are they trying to stick the flower-pots into the trees?'

'It's an illumination in honour of our arrival,' the other young girl rejoined. 'It's a triumph over Madame Bonrepos.'

'Meanwhile, at the Pension Bonrepos,' I ventured to suggest, 'they have put out their lights; they are sitting in darkness, lamenting your departure.'

She looked at me, smiling; she was standing in the light that came from the house. M. Pigeonneau, meanwhile, who had been awaiting his chance, advanced to Miss Ruck with his glass of syrup. 'I have kept it for you, mademoiselle,' he said; 'I have jealously guarded it. It is very delicious!'

Miss Ruck looked at him and his syrup, without making any motion to take the glass. 'Well, I guess it's sour,' she said in a moment, and she gave a little shake of her head.

M. Pigeonneau stood staring, with his syrup in his hand; then he slowly turned away. He looked about at the rest of us, as if to appeal from Miss Ruck's insensibility, and went to deposit his rejected tribute on a bench.

'Won't you give it to me?' asked Miss Church, in faultless French. '*J'adore le sirop, moi.*'

M. Pigeonneau came back with alacrity, and presented the glass with a very low bow. 'I adore good manners,' murmured the old man.

This incident caused me to look at Miss Church with quickened interest. She was not strikingly pretty, but in her charming, irregular face there was something brilliant and ardent. Like her mother, she was very simply dressed.

'She wants to go to America, and her mother won't let her,' said Miss Sophy to me, explaining her companion's situation.

'I am very sorry—for America,' I answered, laughing.

'Well, I don't want to say anything against your mother, but I think it's shameful,' Miss Ruck pursued.

'Mamma has very good reasons; she will tell you them all.'

'Well, I'm sure I don't want to hear them,' said Miss Ruck. 'You have got a right to go to your own country; every one has a right to go to their own country.'

'Mamma is not very patriotic,' said Aurora Church, smiling.

'Well, I call that dreadful,' her companion declared. 'I have heard that there are some Americans like that, but I never believed it.'

'There are all sorts of Americans,' I said, laughing.

'Aurora's one of the right sort,' rejoined Miss Ruck, who had apparently become very intimate with her new friend.

'Are you very patriotic?' I asked of the young girl.

'She's right down homesick,' said Miss Sophy; 'She's dying to go. If I were you my mother would have to take me.'

'Mamma is going to take me to Dresden.'

'Well, I declare I never heard of anything so dreadful!' cried Miss Ruck. 'It's like something in a story.'

'I never heard there was anything very dreadful in Dresden,' I interposed.

Miss Ruck looked at me a moment. 'Well, I don't believe *you* are a good American,' she replied, 'and I never supposed you were. You had better go in there and talk to Mrs. Church.'

'Dresden is really very nice, isn't it?' I asked of her companion.

'It isn't nice if you happen to prefer New York,' said Miss Sophy. 'Miss Church prefers New York. Tell him you are dying to see New York; it will make him angry,' she went on.

'I have no desire to make him angry,' said Aurora, smiling.

'It is only Miss Ruck who can do that,' I rejoined. 'Have you been a long time in Europe?'

'Always.'

'I call that wicked!' Miss Sophy declared.

'You might be in a worse place,' I continued. 'I find Europe very interesting.'

Miss Ruck gave a little laugh. 'I was saying that you wanted to pass for a European.'

'Yes, I want to pass for a Dalmatian.'

Miss Ruck looked at me a moment. 'Well, you had better not come home,' she said. 'No one will speak to you.'

'Were you born in these countries?' I asked of her companion.

'Oh, no; I came to Europe when I was a small child. But I remember America a little, and it seems delightful.'

'Wait till you see it again. It's just too lovely,' said Miss Sophy.

'It's the grandest country in the world,' I added.

Miss Ruck began to toss her head. 'Come away, my dear,' she said. 'If there's a creature I despise it's a man that tries to say funny things about his own country.'

'Don't you think one can be tired of Europe?' Aurora asked, lingering.

'Possibly,—after many years.'

'Father was tired of it after three weeks,' said Miss Ruck.

'I have been here sixteen years,' her friend went on, looking at me with a charming intentness, as if she had a purpose in speaking. 'It used to be for my education. I don't know what it's for now.'

'She's beautifully educated,' said Miss Ruck. 'She knows four languages.'

'I am not very sure that I know English.'

'You should go to Boston!' cried Miss Sophy. 'They speak splendidly in Boston.'

'*C'est mon rêve*,' said Aurora, still looking at me.

'Have you been all over Europe,' I asked,—'in all the different countries?'

She hesitated a moment. 'Everywhere that there's a pension. Mamma is devoted to pensions. We have lived, at one time or another, in every pension in Europe.'

'Well, I should think you had seen about enough,' said Miss Ruck.

'It's a delightful way of seeing Europe,' Aurora rejoined, with her brilliant smile. 'You may imagine how it has attached me to the different countries. I have such charming souvenirs! There is a pension awaiting us now at Dresden,—eight francs a day, without wine. That's rather dear. Mamma means to make them give us wine. Mamma is a great authority on pensions; she is known, that way, all over Europe. Last winter we were in Italy, and she discovered one at Piacenza,—four francs a day. We made economies.'

'Your mother doesn't seem to mingle much,' observed Miss Ruck, glancing through the window at the scholastic attitude of Mrs. Church.

'No, she doesn't mingle, except in the native society. Though she lives in pensions, she detests them.'

'Why does she live in them, then?' asked Miss Sophy, rather resentfully.

'Oh, because we are so poor; it's the cheapest way to live. We have tried having a cook, but the cook always steals. Mamma used to set me to watch her; that's the way I passed my *jeunesse*,—my *belle jeunesse*. We are frightfully poor,' the young girl went on, with the same strange frankness,—a curious mixture of girlish grace and conscious cynicism. '*Nous n'avons pas le sou*. That's one of the reasons we don't go back to America; mamma says we can't afford to live there.'

'Well, any one can see that you're an American girl,' Miss Ruck remarked, in a consolatory manner. 'I can tell an American girl a mile off. You've got the American style.'

'I'm afraid I haven't the American *toilette*,' said Aurora, looking at the other's superior splendour.

'Well, your dress was cut in France; any one can see that.'

'Yes,' said Aurora, with a laugh, 'my dress was cut in France,—at Avranches.'

'Well, you've got a lovely figure, any way,' pursued her companion.

'Ah,' said the young girl, 'at Avranches, too, my figure was admired.' And she looked at me askance, with a certain coquetry. But I was an innocent youth, and I only looked back at her, wondering. She was a great deal nicer than Miss Ruck, and yet Miss Ruck would not have said that. 'I try to be like an American girl,' she continued; 'I do my best, though mamma doesn't at all encourage it. I am very patriotic. I try to copy them, though mamma has brought me up *à la français*; that is, as much as one can in pensions. For instance, I have never been out of the house without mamma; oh, never, never. But sometimes I despair; American girls are so wonderfully frank. I can't be frank, like that. I am always afraid. But I do what I can, as you see. *Excusez du peu*!'

I thought this young lady at least as outspoken as most of her unexpatriated sisters; there was something almost comical in her despondency. But she had by no means caught, as it seemed to me, the American tone. Whatever her tone was, however, it had a fascination; it was a singular mixture of refinement and audacity.

The young ladies began to stroll about the garden again, and I enjoyed their society until M. Pigeonneau's festival came to an end.

V.

Mr. Ruck did not take his departure for Appenzell on the morrow, in spite of the eagerness to witness such an event which he had attributed to Mrs. Church. He continued, on the contrary, for many days after, to hang about the garden, to wander up to the banker's and back again, to engage in desultory conversation with his fellow-boarders, and to endeavour to assuage his constitutional restlessness by perusal of the American journals. But on the morrow I had the honour of making Mrs. Church's acquaintance. She came into the salon, after the midday breakfast, with her German octavo under her arm, and she appealed to me for assistance in selecting a quiet corner.

'Would you very kindly,' she said, 'move that large *fauteuil* a little more this way? Not the largest; the one with the little cushion. The *fauteuils* here are very insufficient; I must ask Madame Beaurepas for another. Thank you; a little more to the left, please; that will do. Are you particularly engaged?' she inquired, after she had seated herself. 'If not, I should like to have some conversation with you. It is some time since I have met a young American of your—what shall

I call it?—your affiliations. I have learned your name from Madame Beaurepas; I think I used to know some of your people. I don't know what has become of all my friends. I used to have a charming little circle at home, but now I meet no one I know. Don't you think there is a great difference between the people one meets and the people one would like to meet? Fortunately, sometimes,' added my interlocutress graciously, 'it's quite the same. I suppose you are a specimen, a favourable specimen,' she went on, 'of young America. Tell me, now, what is young America thinking of in these days of ours? What are its feelings, its opinions, its aspirations? What is its *ideal*?' I had seated myself near Mrs. Church and she had pointed this interrogation with the gaze of her bright little eyes. I felt it embarrassing to be treated as a favourable specimen of young America, and to be summoned to enunciate the mysterious formulas to which she alluded. Observing my hesitation, Mrs. Church clasped her hands on the open page of her book and gave an intense, melancholy smile. '*Has* it an ideal?' she softly asked. 'Well, we must talk of this,' she went on, without insisting. 'Speak, for the present, for yourself simply. Have you come to Europe with any special design?'

'Nothing to boast of,' I said. 'I am studying a little.'

'Ah, I am glad to hear that. You are gathering up a little European culture; that's what we lack, you know, at home. No individual can do much, of course. But you must not be discouraged; every little counts.'

'I see that you, at least, are doing your part,' I rejoined gallantly, dropping my eyes on my companion's learned volume.

'Yes, I frankly admit that I am fond of study. There is no one, after all, like the Germans. That is, for facts. For opinions I by no means always go with them. I form my opinions myself. I am sorry to say, however,' Mrs. Church continued, 'that I can hardly pretend to diffuse my acquisitions. I am afraid I am sadly selfish; I do little to irrigate the soil. I belong—I frankly confess it—to the class of absentees.'

'I had the pleasure, last evening,' I said, 'of making the acquaintance of your daughter. She told me you had been a long time in Europe.'

Mrs. Church smiled benignantly. 'Can one ever be too long? We shall never leave it.'

'Your daughter won't like that,' I said, smiling too.

'Has she been taking you into her confidence? She is a more sensible young lady than she sometimes appears. I have taken great pains with her; she is really—I may be permitted to say it—superbly educated.'

'She seemed to me a very charming girl,' I rejoined; 'And I learned that she speaks four languages.'

'It is not only that,' said Mrs. Church, in a tone which suggested that this might be a very superficial species of culture. 'She has made what we call *de fortes études*,—such as I suppose you are making now. She is familiar with the results of modern science; she keeps pace with the new historical school.'

'Ah,' said I, 'she has gone much further than I!'

'You doubtless think I exaggerate, and you force me, therefore, to mention the fact that I am able to speak of such matters with a certain intelligence.'

'That is very evident,' I said. 'But your daughter thinks you ought to take her home.' I began to fear, as soon as I had uttered these words, that they savoured of treachery to the young lady, but I was reassured by seeing that they produced on her mother's placid countenance no symptom whatever of irritation.

'My daughter has her little theories,' Mrs. Church observed; 'she has, I may say, her illusions. And what wonder! What would youth be without its illusions? Aurora has a theory that she would be happier in New York, in Boston, in Philadelphia, than in one of the charming old cities in which our lot is cast. But she is mistaken, that's all. We must allow our children their illusions, must we not? But we must watch over them.'

Although she herself seemed proof against discomposure, I found something vaguely irritating in her soft, sweet positiveness.

'American cities,' I said, 'are the paradise of young girls.'

'Do you mean,' asked Mrs. Church, 'that the young girls who come from those places are angels?'

'Yes,' I said, resolutely.

'This young lady—what is her odd name?—with whom my daughter has formed a somewhat precipitate acquaintance: is Miss Ruck an angel? But I won't force you to say anything uncivil. It would be too cruel to make a single exception.'

'Well,' said I, 'at any rate, in America young girls have an easier lot. They have much more liberty.'

My companion laid her hand for an instant on my arm. 'My dear young friend, I know America, I know the conditions of life there, so well. There is perhaps no subject on which I have reflected more than on our national idiosyncrasies.'

'I am afraid you don't approve of them,' said I, a little brutally.

Brutal indeed my proposition was, for Mrs. Church was not prepared to assent to it in this rough shape. She dropped her eyes on her book, with an air of acute meditation. Then, raising them, 'We are very crude,' she softly observed,—'we are very crude.' Lest even this delicately-uttered statement should seem to savour of the vice that she deprecated, she went on to explain: 'There are two classes of minds, you know,—those that hold back, and those that push forward. My daughter and I are not pushers; we move with little steps. We like the old, trodden paths; we like the old, old world.'

'Ah,' said I, 'you know what you like; there is a great virtue in that.'

'Yes, we like Europe; we prefer it. We like the opportunities of Europe; we like the *rest.* There is so much in that, you know. The world seems to me to be hurrying, pressing forward so fiercely, without knowing where it is going. "Whither?" I often ask, in my little quiet way. But I have yet to learn that any one can tell me.'

'You're a great conservative,' I observed, while I wondered whether I myself could answer this inquiry.

Mrs. Church gave me a smile which was equivalent to a confession. 'I wish to retain a *little*,—just a little. Surely, we have done so much, we might rest a while; we might pause. That is all my feeling,—just to stop a little, to wait! I have seen so many changes. I wish to draw in, to draw in,—to hold back, to hold back.'

'You shouldn't hold your daughter back!' I answered, laughing and getting up. I got up, not by way of terminating our colloquy, for I perceived Mrs. Church's exposition of her views to be by no means complete, but in order to offer a chair to Miss Aurora, who at this moment drew near. She thanked me and remained standing, but without at first, as I noticed, meeting her mother's eye.

'You have been engaged with your new acquaintance, my dear?' this lady inquired.

'Yes, mamma dear,' said the young girl gently.

'Do you find her very edifying?'

Aurora was silent a moment; then she looked at her mother. 'I don't know, mamma; she is very fresh.'

I ventured to indulge in a respectful laugh. 'Your mother has another word for that. But I must not,' I added, 'be crude.'

'*Ah, vous m'en voulez*?' inquired Mrs. Church. 'And yet I can't pretend I said it in jest. I feel it too much. We have been having a little social discussion,' she said to her daughter. 'There is still so much to be said! And I wish,' she continued, turning to me, 'that I could give you our point of view! Don't you wish, Aurora, that we could give him our point of view?

'Yes, mamma,' said Aurora.

'We consider ourselves very fortunate in our point of view, don't we dearest?' mamma demanded.

'Very fortunate indeed, mamma.'

'You see we have acquired an insight into European life,' the elder lady pursued. 'We have our place at many a European fireside. We find so much to esteem,—so much to enjoy. Do we not, my daughter?'

'So very much, mamma,' the yound girl went on, with a sort of inscrutable submissiveness. I wondered at it, it offered so strange a contrast to the mocking freedom of her tone the night before; but while I wondered, I was careful not to let my perplexity take precedence of my good manners.

'I don't know what you ladies may have found at European firesides,' I said, 'but there can be very little doubt what you have left there.'

Mrs. Church got up to acknowledge my compliment. 'We have spent some charming hours. And that reminds me that we have just now such an occasion in prospect. We are to call upon some Genevese friends,—the family of the Pasteur Galopin. They are to go with us to the old library at the Hôtel de Ville, where there are some very interesting documents of the period of the Reformation; we are promised a glimpse of some manuscripts of poor Servetus, the antagonist and victim, you know, of Calvin. Here, of course, one can only speak of Calvin under one's breath, but some day, when we are more private,' and Mrs. Church looked around the room, 'I will give you my view of him. I think it has a touch of originality. Aurora is familiar with, are you not, my daughter, familiar with my view of Calvin?'

'Yes, mamma,' said Aurora, with docility, while the two ladies went to prepare for their visit to the Pasteur Galopin.

VI.

'She has demanded a new lamp; I told you she would!' This communication was made me by Madame Beaurepas a couple of days later. 'And she has asked for a new *tapis de lit*, and she has requested me to provide Célestine with a pair of light shoes. I told her that, as a general thing, cooks are not shod with satin. That poor Célestine!'

'Mrs. Church may be exacting,' I said, 'but she is a clever little woman.'

'A lady who pays but five francs and a half shouldn't be too clever. *C'est déplacé*. I don't like the type.'

'What type do you call Mrs. Church's?'

'*Mon Dieu*,' said Madame Beaurepas, '*c'est une de ces mamans comme vous en avez, qui promènent leur fille.*'

'She is trying to marry her daughter? I don't think she's of that sort.'

But Madame Beaurepas shrewdly held to her idea. 'She is trying it in her own way; she does it very quietly. She doesn't want an American; she wants a foreigner. And she wants a *mari sérieux*. But she is travelling over Europe in search of one. She would like a magistrate.'

'A magistrate?'

'A *gros bonnet* of some kind; a professor or a deputy.'

'I am very sorry for the poor girl,' I said laughing.

'You needn't pity her too much; she's a sly thing.'

'Ah, for that, no!' I exclaimed. 'She's a charming girl.'

Madame Beaurepas gave an elderly grin. 'She has hooked you, eh? But the mother won't have you.'

I developed my idea, without heeding this insinuation. 'She's a charming girl, but she is a little odd. It's a necessity of her position. She is less submissive to her mother than she has to pretend to be. That's in self-defence; it's to make her life possible.'

'She wishes to get away from her mother,' continued Madame Beaurepas. 'She wishes to *courir les champs*.'

'She wishes to go to America, her native country.'

'Precisely. And she will certainly go.'

'I hope so!' I rejoined.

'Some fine morning—or evening—she will go off with a young man; probably with a young American.'

'*Allons donc*!' said I, with disgust.

'That will be quite America enough,' pursued my cynical hostess. 'I have kept a boarding-house for forty years. I have seen that type.'

'Have such things as that happened *chez vous*?' I asked.

'Everything has happened *chez moi*. But nothing has happened more than once. Therefore this won't happen here. It will be at the next place they go to, or the next. Besides, here there is no young American *pour la partie*,—none except you, monsieur. You are susceptible, but you are too reasonable.'

'It's lucky for you I am reasonable,' I answered. 'It's thanks to that fact that you escape a scolding.'

One morning, about this time, instead of coming back to breakfast at the pension, after my lectures at the Academy, I went to partake of this meal with a fellow-student, at an ancient eating-house in the collegiate quarter. On separating from my friend, I took my way along that charming public walk known in Geneva as the Treille, a shady terrace, of immense elevation, overhanging a portion of the lower town. There are spreading trees and well-worn benches, and over the tiles and chimneys of the *ville basse* there is a view of the snow-crested Alps. On the other side, as you turn your back to the view, the promenade is overlooked by a row of tall, sober-faced *hôtels*, the dwellings of the local aristocracy. I was very fond of the place, and often resorted to it to stimulate my sense of the picturesque. Presently, as I lingered there on this occasion, I became aware that a gentleman was seated not far from where I stood, with his back to the Alpine chain, which this morning was brilliant and distinct, and a newspaper, unfolded, in his lap. He was not reading, however; he was staring before him in gloomy contemplation. I don't know whether I recognized first the newspaper or its proprietor; one, in either case, would have helped me to identify the other. One was the *New York Herald*; the other, of course, was Mr. Ruck. As I drew nearer, he transferred his eyes from the stony, high-featured masks of the grey old houses on the other side of the terrace, and I knew by the expression of his face just how he had been feeling about these distinguished abodes. He had made up his mind that their proprietors were a dusky, narrow-minded, unsociable company, plunging their roots into a superfluous past. I endeavoured, therefore, as I sat down beside him, to suggest something more delectable.

'That's a beautiful view of the Alps,' I observed.

'Yes,' said Mr. Ruck, without moving, 'I've examined it. Fine thing, in its way,—fine thing. Beauties of nature,—that sort of thing. We came up on purpose to look at it.'

'Your ladies, then, have been with you?'

'Yes; they're just walking round. They're awfully restless. They keep saying I'm restless, but I'm as quiet as a sleeping child to them. It takes,' he added in a moment, dryly, 'the form of shopping.'

'Are they shopping now?'

'Well, if they ain't, they're trying to. They told me to sit here a while, and they'd just walk round. I generally know what that means. But that's the principal interest for ladies,' he added, retracting his irony. 'We thought we'd come up here and see the cathedral; Mrs. Church seemed to think it a dead loss that we shouldn't see the cathedral, especially as we hadn't seen many yet. And I had to come up to the banker's any way. Well, we certainly saw the cathedral. I don't know as we are any the better for it, and I don't know as I should know it again. But we saw it, any way. I don't know as I should want to go there regularly; but I suppose it will give us, in conversation, a kind of hold on Mrs. Church, eh? I guess we want something of that kind. Well,' Mr. Ruck continued, 'I stopped in at the banker's to see if there wasn't something, and they handed me out a Herald.'

'I hope the *Herald* is full of good news,' I said.

'Can't say it is. D—d bad news.'

'Political,' I inquired, 'or commercial?'

'Oh, hang politics! It's business, sir. There ain't any business. It's all gone to'—and Mr. Ruck became profane. 'Nine failures in one day. What do you say to that?'

'I hope they haven't injured you,' I said.

'Well, they haven't helped me much. So many houses on fire, that's all. If they happen to take place in your own street, they don't increase the value of your property. When mine catches, I suppose they'll write and tell me,—one of these days, when they've got nothing else to do. I didn't get a blessed letter this morning; I suppose they think I'm having such a good time over here it's a pity to disturb me. If I could attend to business for about half an hour, I'd find out something. But I can't and it's no use talking. The state of my health was never so unsatisfactory as it was about five o'clock this morning.'

'I am very sorry to hear that,' I said, 'and I recommend you strongly not to think of business.'

'I don't,' Mr. Ruck replied. 'I'm thinking of cathedrals; I'm thinking of the beauties of nature. Come,' he went on, turning round on the bench and leaning his elbow on the parapet, 'I'll think of those mountains over there; they *are* pretty, certainly. Can't you get over there?'

'Over where?'

'Over to those hills. Don't they run a train right up?'

'You can go to Chamouni,' I said. 'You can go to Grindelwald and Zermatt and fifty other places. You can't go by rail, but you can drive.'

'All right, we'll drive,—and not in a one-horse concern, either. Yes, Chamouni is one of the places we put down. I hope there are a few nice shops in Chamouni.' Mr. Ruck spoke with a certain quickened emphasis, and in a tone more explicitly humourous than he commonly employed. I thought he was excited, and yet he had not the appearance of excitement. He looked like a man who has simply taken, in the face of disaster, a sudden, somewhat imaginative, resolution not to 'worry.' He presently twisted himself about on his bench again and began to watch for his companions. 'Well, they *are* walking round,' he resumed; 'I guess they've hit on something, somewhere. And they've got a carriage waiting outside of that archway, too. They seem to do a big business in archways here, don't they? They like to have a carriage, to carry home the things,—those ladies of mine. Then they're sure they've got them.' The ladies, after this, to do them justice, were not very long in appearing. They came towards us, from under the archway to which Mr. Ruck had somewhat invidiously alluded, slowly and with a rather exhausted step and expression. My companion looked at them a moment, as they advanced. 'They're tired,' he said, softly. 'When they're tired, like that, it's very expensive.'

'Well,' said Mrs. Ruck, 'I'm glad you've had some company.' Her husband looked at her, in silence, through narrowed eyelids, and I suspected that this gracious observation on the lady's part was prompted by a restless conscience.

Miss Sophy glanced at me with her little straightforward air of defiance. 'It would have been more proper if *we* had had the company. Why didn't you come after us, instead of sitting there?' she asked of Mr. Ruck's companion.

'I was told by your father,' I explained, 'that you were engaged in sacred rites.' Miss Ruck was not gracious, though I doubt whether it was because her conscience was better than her mother's.

'Well, for a gentleman there is nothing so sacred as ladies' society,' replied Miss Ruck, in the manner of a person accustomed to giving neat retorts.

'I suppose you refer to the cathedral,' said her mother. 'Well, I must say, we didn't go back there. I don't know what it may be of a Sunday, but it gave me a chill.'

'We discovered the loveliest little lace-shop,' observed the young girl, with a serenity that was superior to bravado.

Her father looked at her a while; then turned about again, leaning on the parapet, and gazed away at the 'hills.' 'Well, it was certainly cheap.' said Mrs. Ruck, also contemplating the Alps.

'We are going to Chamouni.' said her husband. 'You haven't any occasion for lace at Chamouni.'

'Well, I'm glad to hear you have decided to go somewhere,' rejoined his wife. 'I don't want to be a fixture at a boarding-house.'

'You can wear lace anywhere,' said Miss Ruck, 'if you put it on right. That's the great thing, with lace. I don't think they know how to wear lace in Europe. I know how I mean to wear mine; but I mean to keep it till I get home.'

Her father transferred his melancholy gaze to her elaborately appointed little person; there was a great deal of very new-looking detail in Miss Ruck's appearance. Then, in a tone of voice quite out of consonance with his facial despondency, 'Have you purchased a great deal?' he inquired.

'I have purchased enough for you to make a fuss about.'

'He can't make a fuss about that,' said Mrs. Ruck.

'Well, you'll see!' declared the young girl, with a little sharp laugh.

But her father went on, in the same tone: 'Have you got it in your pocket? Why don't you put it on,—why don't you hang it round you?'

'I'll hang it round *you*, if you don't look out!' cried Miss Sophy.

'Don't you want to show it to this gentleman?' Mr. Ruck continued.

'Mercy, how you do talk about that lace!' said his wife.

'Well, I want to be lively. There's every reason for it; we're going to Chamouni.'

'You're restless; that's what's the matter with you.' And Mrs. Ruck got up.

'No, I ain't,' said her husband. 'I never felt so quiet; I feel as peaceful as a little child.'

Mrs. Ruck, who had no sense whatever of humour, looked at her daughter and at me. 'Well, I hope you'll improve,' she said.

'Send in the bills,' Mr. Ruck went on, rising to his feet. 'Don't hesitate, Sophy. I don't care what you do now. In for a penny, in for a pound.'

Miss Ruck joined her mother, with a little toss of her head, and we followed the ladies to the carriage. 'In your place,' said Miss Sophy to her father, I wouldn't talk so much about pennies and pounds before strangers.'

Poor Mr. Ruck appeared to feel the force of this observation, which, in the consciousness of a man who had never been 'mean,' could hardly fail to strike a responsive chord. He coloured a little, and he was silent; his companions got into their vehicle, the front seat of which was adorned with a large parcel. Mr. Ruck gave the parcel a little poke with his umbrella, and then, turning to me with a rather grimly penitential smile, 'After all,' he said, 'for the ladies that's the principal interest.'

VII.

Old M. Pigeonneau had more than once proposed to me to take a walk, but I had hitherto been unable to respond to so alluring an invitation. It befell, however, one afternoon, that I perceived him going forth upon a desultory stroll, with a certain lonesomeness of demeanour that attracted my sympathy. I hastily overtook him, and passed my hand into his venerable arm, a proceeding which produced in the good old man so jovial a sense of comradeship that he ardently proposed we should bend our steps to the English Garden; no locality less festive was worthy of the occasion. To the English Garden, accordingly, we went; it lay beyond the bridge, beside the lake. It was very pretty and very animated; there was a band playing in the middle, and a considerable number of persons sitting under the small trees, on benches and little chairs, or strolling beside the blue water. We joined the strollers, we observed our companions, and conversed on obvious topics. Some of these last, of course, were the pretty women who embellished the scene, and who, in the light of M. Pigeonneau's comprehensive criticism, appeared surprisingly numerous. He seemed bent upon our making up our minds which was the prettiest, and as this was an innocent game I consented to play at it.

Suddenly M. Pigeonneau stopped, pressing my arm with the liveliest emotion. '*La voilà, la voilà*, the prettiest!' he quickly murmured, 'coming towards us, in a blue dress, with the other.' It was at the other I was looking, for the other, to my surprise, was our interesting fellow-pensioner, the daughter of a vigilant mother. M. Pigeonneau, meanwhile, had redoubled his exclamations; he had recognized Miss Sophy Ruck. '*Oh, la belle rencontre, nos aimables convives*; the prettiest girl in the world, in effect!'

We immediately greeted and joined the young ladies, who, like ourselves, were walking arm in arm and enjoying the scene.

'I was citing you with admiration to my friend, even before I had recognized you,' said M. Pigeonneau to Miss Ruck.

'I don't believe in French compliments,' remarked this young lady, presenting her back to the smiling old man.

'Are you and Miss Ruck walking alone?' I asked of her companion. 'You had better accept of M. Pigeonneau's gallant protection, and of mine.'

Aurora Church had taken her hand out of Miss Ruck's arm; she looked at me, smiling, with her head a little inclined, while, upon her shoulder, she made her open parasol revolve. 'Which is most improper,—to walk alone or to walk with gentlemen? I wish to do what is most improper.'

'What mysterious logic governs your conduct?' I inquired.

'He thinks you can't understand him when he talks like that,' said Miss Ruck. 'But I do understand you, always!'

'So I have always ventured to hope, my dear Miss Ruck.'

'Well, if I didn't, it wouldn't be much loss,' rejoined this young lady.

'*Allons, en marche*!' cried M. Pigeonneau, smiling still, and undiscouraged by her inhumanity. 'Let us make together the tour of the garden.' And he imposed his society upon Miss Ruck with a respectful, elderly grace, which was evidently unable to see anything in reluctance but modesty, and was sublimely conscious of a mission to place modesty at its ease. This ill-assorted couple walked in front, while Aurora Church and I strolled along together.

'I am sure this is more improper,' said my companion; 'this is delightfully improper. I don't say that as a compliment to you,' she added. 'I would say it to any man, no matter how stupid.'

'Oh, I am very stupid,' I answered, 'but this doesn't seem to me wrong.'

'Not for you, no; only for me. There is nothing that a man can do that is wrong, is there? *En morale*, you know, I mean. Ah, yes, he can steal; but I think there is nothing else, is there?'

'I don't know. One doesn't know those things until after one has done them. Then one is enlightened.'

'And you mean that you have never been enlightened? You make yourself out very good.'

'That is better than making one's self out bad, as you do.'

The young girl glanced at me a moment, and then, with her charming smile, 'That's one of the consequences of a false position.'

'Is your position false?' I inquired, smiling too at this large formula.

'Actually so.'

'In what way?'

'Oh, in every way. For instance, I have to pretend to be a *jeune fille*. I am not a *jeune fille*; no American girl is a *jeune fille*; an American girl is an intelligent, responsible creature. I have to pretend to be very innocent, but I am not very innocent.'

'You don't pretend to be very innocent; you pretend to be—what shall I call it?—very wise.'

'That's no pretence. I am wise.'

'You are not an American girl,' I ventured to observe.

My companion almost stopped, looking at me; there was a little flush in her cheek. '*Voilà*! she said. 'There's my false position. I want to be an American girl, and I'm not.'

'Do you want me to tell you?' I went on. 'An American girl wouldn't talk as you are talking now.'

'Please tell me,' said Aurora Church, with expressive eagerness. 'How would she talk?'

'I can't tell you all the things an American girl would say, but I think I can tell you the things she wouldn't say. She wouldn't reason out her conduct, as you seem to me to do.'

Aurora gave me the most flattering attention. 'I see. She would be simpler. To do very simply things that are not at all simple,—that is the American girl!'

I permitted myself a small explosion of hilarity. 'I don't know whether you are a French girl, or what you are,' I said, 'but you are very witty.'

'Ah, you mean that I strike false notes!' cried Aurora Church, sadly. 'That's just what I want to avoid. I wish you would always tell me.'

The conversational union between Miss Ruck and her neighbour, in front of us, had evidently not become a close one. The young lady suddenly turned round to us with a question: 'Don't you want some ice-cream?'

'*She* doesn't strike false notes,' I murmured.

There was a kind of pavilion or kiosk, which served as a *café*, and at which the delicacies procurable at such an establishment were dispensed. Miss Ruck pointed to the little green tables and chairs which were set out on the gravel; M. Pigeonneau, fluttering with a sense of dissipation, seconded the proposal, and we presently sat down and gave our order to a nimble attendant. I managed again to place myself next to Aurora Church; our companions were on the other side of the table.

My neighbour was delighted with our situation. 'This is best of all,' she said. 'I never believed I should come to a café with two strange men! Now, you can't persuade me this isn't wrong.'

'To make it wrong we ought to see your mother coming down the path.'

'Ah, my mother makes everything wrong,' said the young girl, attacking with a little spoon in the shape of a spade the apex of a pink ice. And then she returned to her idea of a moment before: 'You must promise to tell me—to warn me in some way—whenever I strike a false note. You must give a little cough, like that,—ahem!'

'You will keep me very busy, and people will think I am in a consumption.'

'*Voyons*,' she continued, 'why have you never talked to me more? Is that a false note? Why haven't you been "attentive"? That's what American girls call it; that's what Miss Ruck calls it.'

I assured myself that our companions were out of ear-shot, and that Miss Ruck was much occupied with a large vanilla cream. 'Because you are always entwined with that young lady. There is no getting near you.'

Aurora looked at her friend while the latter devoted herself to her ice. 'You wonder why I like her so much, I suppose. So does mamma; *elle s'y perd.* I don't like her, particularly; *je n'en suis pas folle.* But she gives me information; she tells me about America. Mamma has always tried to prevent my knowing anything about it, and I am all the more curious. And then Miss Ruck is very fresh.'

'I may not be so fresh as Miss Ruck,' I said, 'but in future, when you want information, I recommend you to come to me for it.'

'Our friend offers to take me to America; she invites me to go back with her, to stay with her. You couldn't do that, could you?' And the young girl looked at me a moment. '*Bon*, a false note! I can see it by your face; you remind me of a *mâitre de piano*.'

'You overdo the character,—the poor American girl,' I said. 'Are you going to stay with that delightful family?'

'I will go and stay with any one that will take me or ask me. It's a real *nostalgie*. She says that in New York—in Thirty-Seventh Street—I should have the most lovely time.'

'I have no doubt you would enjoy it.'

'Absolute liberty, to begin with.'

'It seems to me you have a certain liberty here,' I rejoined.

'Ah, *this*? Oh, I shall pay for this. I shall be punished by mamma, and I shall be lectured by Madame Galopin.'

'The wife of the pasteur?'

'His *digne épouse*. Madame Galopin, for mamma, is the incarnation of European opinion. That's what vexes me with mamma, her thinking so much of people like Madame Galopin. Going to see Madame Galopin,—mamma calls that being in European society. European society! I'm so sick of that expression; I have heard it since I was six years old. Who is Madame Galopin,—who thinks anything of her here? She is nobody; she is perfectly third-rate. If I like America better than mamma, I also know Europe better.'

'But your mother, certainly,' I objected, a trifle timidly, for my young lady was excited, and had a charming little passion in her eye,—'your mother has a great many social relations all over the continent.'

'She thinks so, but half the people don't care for us. They are not so good as we, and they know it,—I'll do them that justice,—and they wonder why we should care for them. When we are polite to them, they think the less of us; there are plenty of people like that. Mamma thinks so much of them simply because they are foreigners. If I could tell you all the dull, stupid, second-rate people I have had to talk to, for no better reason than that they were *de leur pays*!—Germans, French, Italians, Turks, everything. When I complain, mamma always says that at any rate it's practice in the language. And she makes so much of the English, too; I don't know what that's practice in.'

Before I had time to suggest an hypothesis, as regards this latter point, I saw something that made me rise, with a certain solemnity, from my chair. This was nothing less than the neat little figure of

Mrs. Church—a perfect model of the *femme comme il faut*—approaching our table with an impatient step, and followed most unexpectedly in her advance by the preeminent form of Mr. Ruck. She had evidently come in quest of her daughter, and if she had commanded this gentleman's attendance it had been on no softer ground than that of his unenvied paternity to her guilty child's accomplice. My movement had given the alarm, and Aurora Church and M. Pigeonneau got up; Miss Ruck alone did not, in the local phrase, derange herself. Mrs. Church, beneath her modest little bonnet, looked very serious, but not at all fluttered; she came straight to her daughter, who received her with a smile, and then she looked all round at the rest of us, very fixedly and tranquilly, without bowing. I must do both these ladies the justice to mention that neither of them made the least little 'scene.'

'I have come for you, dearest,' said the mother.

'Yes, dear mamma.'

'Come for you—come for you,' Mrs. Church repeated, looking down at the relics of our little feast. 'I was obliged to ask Mr. Ruck's assistance. I was puzzled; I thought a long time.'

'Well, Mrs. Church, I was glad to see you puzzled once in your life!' said Mr. Ruck, with friendly jocosity. 'But you came pretty straight, for all that. I had hard work to keep up with you.'

'We will take a cab, Aurora,' Mrs. Church went on, without heeding this pleasantry,—'a closed one. Come, my daughter.'

'Yes, dear mamma.' The young girl was blushing, yet she was still smiling; she looked round at us all, and, as her eyes met mine, I thought she was beautiful. 'Good-bye,' she said to us. 'I have had a *lovely time.*'

'We must not linger,' said her mother; 'it is five o'clock. We are to dine, you know, with Madame Galopin.'

'I had quite forgotten,' Aurora declared. 'That will be charming.'

'Do you want me to assist you to carry her back, ma'am?' asked Mr. Ruck.

Mrs. Church hesitated a moment, with her serene little gaze. 'Do you prefer, then, to leave your daughter to finish the evening with these gentlemen?'

Mr. Ruck pushed back his hat and scratched the top of his head. 'Well, I don't know. How would you like that, Sophy?'

'Well, I never!' exclaimed Sophy, as Mrs. Church marched off with her daughter.

VIII.

I had half expected that Mrs. Church would make me feel the weight of her disapproval of my own share in that little act of revelry in the English Garden. But she maintained her claim to being a highly reasonable woman; I could not but admire the justice of this pretension by recognizing my irresponsibility. I had taken her daughter as I found her, which was, according to Mrs. Church's view, in a very equivocal position. The natural instinct of a young man, in such a situation, is not to protest, but to profit; and it was clear to Mrs. Church that I had had nothing to do with Miss Aurora's appearing in public under the insufficient chaperonage of Miss Ruck. Besides, she liked to converse, and she apparently did me the honour to believe that of all the members of the Pension Beaurepas I had the most cultivated understanding. I found her in the salon a couple of evenings after the incident I have just narrated, and I approached her with a view of making my peace with her, if this should prove necessary. But Mrs. Church was as gracious as I could have desired; she put her marker into her book, and folded her plump little hands on the cover. She made no specific allusion to the English Garden; she embarked, rather, upon those general considerations in which her refined intellect was so much at home.

'Always at your studies, Mrs. Church,' I ventured to observe.

'*Que voulez-vous*? To say studies is to say too much; one doesn't study in the parlours of a boarding-house. But I do what I can; I have always done what I can. That is all I have ever claimed.'

'No one can do more, and you seem to have done a great deal.'

'Do you know my secret?' she asked, with an air of brightening confidence. And she paused a moment before she imparted her secret: 'To care only for the *best*! To do the best, to know the best,—to have, to desire, to recognize, only the best. That's what I have always done, in my quiet little way. I have gone through Europe on my devoted little errand, seeking, seeing, heeding, only the best. And it has not been for myself alone; it has been for my daughter. My daughter has had the best. We are not rich, but I can say that.'

'She has had you, madam,' I rejoined finely.

'Certainly; such as I am, I have been devoted. We have got something everywhere; a little here, a little there. That's the real secret,—to get something everywhere; you always can if you *are* devoted. Sometimes it has been a little music, sometimes a little deeper insight into the history of art; every little counts, you know. Sometimes it has been just a glimpse, a view, a lovely landscape, an impression. We have always been on the lookout. Sometimes it has been a valued friendship, a delightful social tie.'

'Here comes the ''European society,'' the poor daughter's bugbear,' I said to myself. 'Certainly,' I remarked aloud,—I admit, rather perversely,—'if you have lived a great deal in pensions, you must have got acquainted with lots of people.'

Mrs. Church dropped her eyes a moment, and then, with considerable gravity, 'I think the European pension system in many respects remarkable, and in some satisfactory. But of the friendships that we have formed, few have been contracted in establishments of this kind.'

'I am sorry to hear that!' I said, laughing.

'I don't say it for you, though I might say it for some others. We have been interested in European *homes*.'

'Oh, I see.'

'We have the *entrée* of the old Genevese society. I like its tone. I prefer it to that of Mr. Ruck,' added Mrs. Church, calmly; 'to that of Mrs. Ruck and Miss Ruck,—of Miss Ruck, especially.'

'Ah, the poor Rucks haven't any tone at all,' I said. 'Don't take them more seriously than they take themselves.'

'Tell me this,' my companion rejoined: 'are they fair examples?'

'Examples of what?'

'Of our American tendencies.'

' ''Tendencies'' is a big word, dear lady; tendencies are difficult to calculate. And you shouldn't abuse those good Rucks, who have been very kind to your daughter. They have invited her to go and stay with them in Thirty-Seventh Street.'

'Aurora has told me. It might be very serious.'

'It might be very droll,' I said.

'To me,' declared Mrs. Church, 'it is simply terrible. I think we shall have to leave the Pension Beaurepas. I shall go back to Madame Bonrepos.'

'On account of the Rucks?' I asked.

'Pray, why don't they go themselves? I have given them some excellent addresses,—written down the very hours of the trains. They were going to Appenzell: I thought it was arranged.'

'They talk of Chamouni now,' I said; 'but they are very helpless and undecided.'

'I will give them some Chamouni addresses. Mrs. Ruck will send a *chaise à porteurs*; I will give her the name of a man who lets them lower than you get them at the hotels. After that they *must* go.'

'Well, I doubt,' I observed, 'whether Mr. Ruck will ever really be seen on the Mer de Glace,—in a high hat. He's not like you; he doesn't value his European privileges. He takes no interest. He regrets Wall Street, acutely. As his wife says, he is very restless, but he has no curiosity about Chamouni. So you must not depend too much on the effect of your addresses.'

'Is it a frequent type?' asked Mrs. Church, with an air of self-control.

'I am afraid so. Mr. Ruck is a broken-down man of business. He is broken down in health, and I suspect he is broken down in fortune. He has spent his whole life in buying and selling; he knows how to do nothing else. His wife and daughter have spent their lives, not in selling, but in buying; and they, on their side, know how to do nothing else. To get something in a shop that they can put on their backs,—that is their one idea; they haven't another in their heads. Of course they spend no end of money, and they do it with an implacable persistence, with a mixture of audacity and of cunning. They do it in his teeth and they do it behind his back; the mother protects the daughter, and the daughter eggs on the mother. Between them, they are bleeding him to death.'

'Ah, what a picture!' murmured Mrs. Church. 'I am afraid they are very—uncultivated.'

'I share your fears. They are perfectly ignorant; they have no resources. The vision of fine clothes occupies their whole imagination. They have not an idea—even a worse one—to compete with it. Poor Mr. Ruck, who is extremely good-natured and soft, seems to me a really tragic figure. He is getting bad news every day from home; his business is going to the dogs. He is unable to stop it; he has to stand and watch his fortunes ebb. He has been used to doing things in a big way, and he feels "mean" if he makes a fuss about bills. So the ladies keep sending them in.'

'But haven't they common sense? Don't they know they are ruining themselves?'

'They don't believe it. The duty of an American husband and father is to keep them going. If he asks them how, that's his own affair. So, by way of not being mean, of being a good American husband and father, poor Ruck stands staring at bankruptcy.'

Mrs. Church looked at me a moment, in quickened meditation. 'Why, if Aurora were to go to stay with them, she might not even be properly fed!'

'I don't, on the whole, recommend,' I said, laughing, 'that your daughter should pay a visit to Thirty-Seventh Street.'

'Why should I be subjected to such trials,—so sadly *éprouvée*? Why should a daughter of mine like that dreadful girl?'

'*Does* she like her?'

'Pray, do you mean,' asked my companion, softly, 'that Aurora is a hypocrite?'

I hesitated a moment. 'A little, since you ask me. I think you have forced her to be.'

Mrs. Church answered this possibly presumptuous charge with a tranquil, candid exultation: 'I never force my daughter!'

'She is nevertheless in a false position,' I rejoined. 'She hungers and thirsts to go back to her own country; she wants to "come out" in New York, which is certainly, socially speaking, the El Dorado of young ladies. She likes any one, for the moment, who will talk to her of that, and serve as a connecting link with her native shores. Miss Ruck performs this agreeable office.'

'Your idea is, then, that if she were to go with Miss Ruck to America she would drop her afterwards.'

I complimented Mrs. Church upon her logical mind, but I repudiated this cynical supposition. 'I can't imagine her—when it should come to the point—embarking with the *famille* Ruck. But I wish she might go, nevertheless.'

Mrs. Church shook her head serenely, and smiled at my inappropriate zeal. 'I trust my poor child may never be guilty of so fatal a mistake. She is completely in error; she is wholly unadapted to the peculiar conditions of American life. It would not please her. She would not sympathize. My daughter's ideal is not the ideal of the class of young women to which Miss Ruck belongs. I fear they are very numerous; they give the tone,—they give the tone.'

'It is you that are mistaken,' I said; 'go home for six months and see.'

'I have not, unfortunately, the means to make costly experiments. My daughter has had great advantages,—rare advantages,—and I should be very sorry to believe that *au fond* she does not appreciate them. One thing is certain: I must remove her from this pernicious influence. We must part company with this deplorable family. If Mr. Ruck and his ladies cannot be induced to go to Chamouni,—a journey that no traveller with the smallest self-respect would omit,—my daughter and I shall be obliged to retire. We shall go to Dresden.'

'To Dresden?'

'The capital of Saxony. I had arranged to go there for the autumn, but it will be simpler to go immediately. There are several works in the gallery with which my daughter has not, I think, sufficiently familiarized herself; it is especially strong in the seventeenth-century schools.'

As my companion offered me this information I perceived Mr. Ruck come lounging in, with his hands in his pockets and his elbows making acute angles. He had his usual anomalous appearance of both seeking and avoiding society, and he wandered obliquely towards Mrs. Church, whose last words he had overheard. 'The seventeenth-century schools,' he said, slowly, as if he were weighing some very small object in a very large pair of scales. 'Now, do you suppose they *had* schools at that period?'

Mrs. Church rose with a good deal of precision, making no answer to this incongruous jest. She clasped her large volume to her neat little bosom, and she fixed a gentle, serious eye upon Mr. Ruck.

'I had a letter this morning from Chamouni,' she said.

'Well,' replied Mr. Ruck, 'I suppose you've got friends all over.'

'I have friends at Chamouni, but they are leaving. To their great regret.' I had got up, too; I listened to this statement, and I wondered. I am almost ashamed to mention the subject of my agitation. I asked myself whether this was a sudden improvisation consecrated by maternal devotion; but this point has never been elucidated. 'They are giving up some charming rooms; perhaps you would like them. I should suggest your telegraphing. The weather is glorious,' continued Mrs. Church, 'and the highest peaks are now perceived with extraordinary distinctness.'

Mr. Ruck listened, as he always listened, respectfully. 'Well,' he said, 'I don't know as I want to go up Mount Blank. That's the principal attraction, isn't it?'

'There are many others. I thought I would offer you an—an exceptional opportunity.'

'Well,' said Mr. Ruck, 'you're right down friendly. But I seem to have more opportunities than I know what to do with. I don't seem able to take hold.'

'It only needs a little decision,' remarked Mrs. Church, with an air which was an admirable example of this virtue. 'I wish you good night, sir.' And she moved noiselessly away.

Mr. Ruck, with his long legs apart, stood staring after her; then he transferred his perfectly quiet eyes to me. 'Does she own a hotel over there?' he asked. 'Has she got any stock in Mount Blank?'

IX.

The next day Madam Beaurepas handed me, with her own elderly fingers, a missive which proved to be a telegram. After glancing at it, I informed her that it was apparently a signal for my departure; my brother had arrived in England, and proposed to me to meet him there; he had come on business and was to spend but three weeks in Europe. 'But my house empties itself!' cried the old woman. 'The *famille* Ruck talks of leaving me, and Madame Church *nous fait la révérence.*'

'Mrs. Church is going away?'

'She is packing her trunk; she is a very extraordinary person. Do you know what she asked me this morning? To invent some combination by which the *famille* Ruck should move away. I informed her that I was not an inventor. That poor *famille* Ruck! "Oblige me by getting rid of them," said Madame Church, as she would have asked Célestine to remove a dish of cabbage. She speaks as if the world were made for Madame Church. I intimated to her that if she objected to the company there was a very simple remedy: and at present *elle fait ses paquets.*'

'She really asked you,' I said, 'to get the Rucks out of the house?'

'She asked me to tell them that their rooms had been let, three months ago, to another family. She has an *aplomb*!'

Mrs. Church's aplomb caused me considerable diversion; I am not sure that it was not, in some degree, to laugh over it at my leisure that I went out into the garden that evening to smoke a cigar. The night was dark and not particularly balmy, and most of my fellow-pensioners, after dinner, had remained in-doors. A long straight walk conducted from the door of the house to the ancient grille that I have described, and I stood here for some time, looking through the iron bars at the silent, empty streets. The prospect was not entertaining, and I presently turned away. At this moment I saw, in the distance, the door of the house open and throw a shaft of lamp-light into the darkness. Into the lamp-light there stepped a female figure, who presently closed the door behind her. She disappeared in the dusk of the garden and I had seen her but for an instant, but I remained under the impression that Aurora Church, on the eve of her departure, had come out for a meditative stroll.

I lingered near the gate, keeping the red tip of my cigar turned towards the house, and before long a young lady emerged from among the shadows of the trees and encountered the light of a lamp that stood just outside the gate. It was in fact Aurora Church, but she seemed more bent upon conversation than upon meditation. She stood a moment looking at me, and then she said,—

'Ought I to retire,—to return to the house?'

'If you ought, I should be very sorry to tell you so,' I answered.

'But we are all alone; there is no one else in the garden.'

'It is not the first time that I have been alone with a young lady.

I am not at all terrified.'

'Ah, but I?' said the young girl. 'I have never been alone'—Then, quickly, she interrupted herself: 'Good, there's another false note!'

'Yes, I am obliged to admit that one is very false.'

She stood looking at me. 'I am going away tomorrow; after that there will be no one to tell me.'

'That will matter little,' I presently replied. 'Telling you will do no good.'

'Ah, why do you say that?' murmured Aurora Church.

I said it partly because it was true; but I said it for other reasons, as well, which it was hard to define. Standing there bare-headed, in the night air, in the vague light, this young lady looked extremely interesting; and the interest of her appearance was not diminished by a suspicion on my own part that she had come into the garden knowing me to be there. I thought her a charming girl, and I felt very sorry for her; but, as I looked at her, those reflections made to me by Madame Beaurepas on her disposition recurred to me with a certain force. I had professed a contempt for them at the time, but it now came into my head that perhaps this unfortunately situated, this insidiously mutinous, young creature was looking out for a preserver. She was certainly not a girl to throw herself at a man's head, but it was possible that in her intense—her almost morbid—desire to put into effect an ideal which was perhaps after all charged with as many fallacies as her mother affirmed, she might do something reckless and irregular,—something in which a sympathetic compatriot, as yet unknown, might find his profit. The image, unshaped though it was, of this sympathetic compatriot filled me with a sort of envy. For some moments I was silent, conscious of these things, and then I answered her question: 'Because some things—some differences—are felt, not learned. To you liberty is not natural; you are like a person who has bought a repeater, and, in his satisfaction, is constantly making it sound. To a real American girl her liberty is a very vulgarly-ticking old clock.'

'Ah, you mean, then,' said the poor girl, 'that my mother has ruined me?'

'Ruined you?'

'She has so perverted my mind that when I try to be natural I am necessarily immodest.'

'That again is a false note,' I said, laughing.

She turned away. 'I think you are cruel.'

'By no means,' I declared; 'because, for my own taste, I prefer you as—as'—

I hesitated, and she turned back. 'As what?'

'As you are.'

She looked at me a while again, and then she said, in a little reasoning voice that reminded me of her mother's, only that it was conscious and studied, 'I was not aware that I am under any particular obligation to please you!' And then she gave a little laugh, quite at variance with her voice.

'Oh, there is no obligation,' I said, 'but one has preferences. I am very sorry you are going away.'

'What does it matter to you? You are going yourself.'

'As I am going in a different direction, that makes all the greater separation.'

She answered nothing; she stood looking through the bars of the tall gate at the empty, dusky street. 'This grille is like a cage,' she said at last.

'Fortunately, it is a cage that will open.' And I laid my hand on the lock.

'Don't open it,' and she pressed the gate back. 'If you should open it I would go out—and never return.'

'Where should you go?'

'To America.'

'Straight away?'

'Somehow or other. I would go to the American consul. I would beg him to give me money,—to help me.'

I received this assertion without a smile; I was not in a smiling humour. On the contrary, I felt singularly excited, and I kept my hand on the lock of the gate. I believed (or I thought I believed) what my companion said, and I had—absurd as it may appear—an irritated vision of her throwing herself upon the consular sympathy. It seemed to me, for a moment, that to pass out of that gate with this yearning, straining young creature would be to pass into some mysterious felicity. If I were only a hero of romance, I would offer, myself, to take her to America.

In a moment more, perhaps, I should have persuaded myself that I was one, but at this juncture I heard a sound that was not romantic. It proved to be the very realistic tread of Célestine, the cook, who stood grinning at us as we turned about from our colloquy.

'I ask *bien pardon*,' said Célestine. 'The mother of mademoiselle desires that mademoiselle should come in immediately. M. le Pasteur Galopin has come to make his *adieux* to *ces dames*.'

Aurora gave me only one glance, but it was a touching one. Then she slowly departed with Célestine.

The next morning, on coming into the garden, I found that Mrs. Church and her daughter had departed. I was informed of this fact by old M. Pigeonneau, who sat there under a tree, having his coffee at a little green table.

'I have nothing to envy you,' he said; 'I had the last glimpse of that charming Miss Aurora.'

'I had a very late glimpse,' I answered, 'and it was all I could possibly desire.'

'I have always noticed,' rejoined M. Pigeonneau, 'that your desires are more moderate than mine. *Que voulez-vous*? I am of the old school. *Je crois que la race se perd.* I regret the departure of that young girl: she had an enchanting smile. *Ce sera une femme d'esprit.* For the mother, I can console myself. I am not sure that *she* was a *femme d'esprit*, though she wished to pass for one. Round, rosy, *potelée*, she yet had not the temperament of her appearance; she was a *femme austère.* I have often noticed that contradiction in American ladies. You see a plump little woman, with a speaking eye and the contour and complexion of a ripe peach, and if you venture to conduct yourself in the smallest degree in accordance with these *indices*, you discover a species of Methodist,—of what do you call it?—of Quakeress. On the other hand, you encounter a tall, lean, angular person, without colour, without grace, all elbows and knees, and you find it's a nature of the tropics! The women of duty look like coquettes, and the others look like alpenstocks! However, we have still the handsome Madame Ruck,—a real *femme de Rubens, celle-là.* It is very true that to talk to her one must know the Flemish tongue!'

I had determined, in accordance with my brother's telegram, to go away in the afternoon; so that, having various duties to perform, I left M. Pigeonneau to his international comparison. Among other things, I went in the course of the morning to the banker's, to draw money for my journey, and there I found Mr. Ruck, with a pile of crumpled letters in his lap, his chair tipped back and his eyes gloomily fixed on the fringe of the green plush table-cloth. I timidly expressed the hope that he had got better news from home, whereupon he gave me a look in which, considering his provocation, the absence of irritation was conspicuous.

He took up his letters in his large hand, and crushing them together held it out to me. 'That epistolary matter,' he said, 'is worth about five cents. But I guess,' he added, rising, 'I have taken it in by this time.' When I had drawn my money, I asked him to come and breakfast with me at the little *brasserie*, much favoured by students, to which I used to resort in the old town. 'I couldn't eat, sir,' he said, 'I couldn't eat. Bad news takes away the appetite. But I guess I'll go with you, so that I needn't go to table down there at the pension. The old woman down there is always accusing me of turning up my nose at her food. Well, I guess I shan't turn up my nose at anything now.'

We went to the little brasserie, where poor Mr. Ruck made the lightest possible breakfast. But if he ate very little, he talked a great deal; he talked about business, going into a hundred details in which I was quite unable to follow him. His talk was not angry or bitter; it was a long, meditative, melancholy monologue; if it had been a trifle less incoherent, I should almost have called it philosophic. I was very sorry for him; I wanted to do something for him, but the only thing I could do was, when we had breakfasted, to see him safely back to the Pension Beaurepas. We went across the Treille and down the Corraterie, out of which we turned into the Rue du Rhône. In this latter street, as all the world knows, are many of those brilliant jewellers' shops for which Geneva is famous. I always admired their glittering windows, and never passed them without a lingering glance. Even on this occasion, preoccupied as I was with my impending departure and with my companion's troubles, I suffered my eyes to wander along the precious tiers that flashed and twinkled behind the huge, clear plates of glass. Thanks to this inveterate habit, I made a discovery. In the largest and most brilliant of these establishments I perceived two ladies, seated before the counter with an air of absorption which sufficiently proclaimed their identity. I hoped my companion would not see them, but as we came abreast of the door, a little beyond, we found it open to the warm summer air. Mr. Ruck happened to glance in, and he immediately recognized his wife and daughter. He slowly stopped, looking at them; I wondered what he would do. The salesman was holding up a bracelet before them, on its velvet cushion, and flashing it about in an irresistible manner.

Mr. Ruck said nothing, but he presently went in, and I did the same.

'It will be an opportunity,' I remarked, as cheerfully as possible, 'for me to bid good-bye to the ladies.'

They turned round when Mr. Ruck came in, and looked at him without confusion. 'Well, you had better go home to breakfast,' remarked his wife. Miss Sophy made no remark, but she took the bracelet from the attendant and gazed at it very fixedly. Mr. Ruck seated himself on an empty stool and looked round the shop.

'Well, you have been here before,' said his wife; 'you were here the first day we came.'

Miss Ruck extended the precious object in her hands towards me. 'Don't you think that's sweet?' she inquired.

I looked at it a moment. 'No, I think it's ugly.'

She glanced at me a moment, incredulous. 'Well, I don't believe you have any taste.'

'Why, sir, it's just lovely,' said Mrs. Ruck.

'You'll see it some day on me, any way,' her daughter declared.

'No, he won't,' said Mr. Ruck quietly.

'It will be his own fault, then,' Miss Sophy observed.

'Well, if we are going to Chamouni we want to get something here,' said Mrs. Ruck. 'We may not have another chance.'

Mr. Ruck was still looking round the shop, whistling in a very low tone. 'We ain't going to Chamouni. We are going to New York city, straight.'

'Well, I'm glad to hear that,' said Mrs. Ruck. 'Don't you suppose we want to take something home?'

'If we are going straight back I must have that bracelet,' her daughter declared. 'Only I don't want a velvet case; I want a satin case.'

'I must bid you good-bye,' I said to the ladies. 'I am leaving Geneva in an hour or two.'

'Take a good look at that bracelet, so you'll know it when you see it,' said Miss Sophy.

'She's bound to have something,' remarked her mother, almost proudly.

Mr. Ruck was still looking round the shop; he was still whistling a little. 'I am afraid he is not at all well,' I said, softly, to his wife.

She twisted her head a little, and glanced at him.

'Well, I wish he'd improve!' she exclaimed.

'A satin case, and a nice one!' said Miss Ruck to the shopman.

I bade Mr. Ruck good-bye. 'Don't wait for me,' he said, sitting there on his stool, and not meeting my eye. 'I've got to see this thing through.'

I went back to the Pension Beaurepas, and when, an hour later, I left it with my luggage, the family had not returned.

The Diary of a Man of Fifty

[First appeared, simultaneously, in *Macmillan's Magazine* vol. xl (July 1879), pp. 205-23; and, in America, in *Harper's New Monthly Magazine*, vol. lix (July 1879), pp. 282-97. With one single-word substantive alteration, the tale was reprinted in volume ii of *The Madonna of the Future* (1879). A year later, the original magazine text was reproduced as No. 135 of Harper's Half-Hour Series (New York, Harper and Brothers, 1880).]

FLORENCE, *APRIL 5TH*, 1874.—THEY TOLD ME I SHOULD FIND ITALY greatly changed; and in seven and twenty years there is room for changes. But to me everything is so perfectly the same that I seem to be living my youth over again; all the forgotten impressions of that enchanting time come back to me. At the moment they were powerful enough; but they afterwards faded away. What in the world became of them? What ever becomes of such things, in the long intervals of consciousness? Where do they hide themselves away? in what unvisited cupboards and crannies of our being do they preserve themselves? They are like the lines of a letter written in sympathetic ink; hold the letter to the fire for a while and the grateful warmth brings out the invisible words. It is the warmth of this yellow sun of Florence that has been restoring the text of my own young romance; the thing has been lying before me today as a clear, fresh page. There have been moments during the last ten years when I have felt so portentously old, so fagged and finished, that I should have taken as a very bad joke any intimation that this present sense of juvenility was still in store for me. It won't last, at any rate; so I had better make the best of it. But I confess it surprises me. I have led too serious a life; but that perhaps, after all, preserves one's youth. At all events, I have travelled too far, I have worked too hard, I have lived in brutal climates and associated with tiresome people. When a man has reached his fifty-second year without being, materially, the worse for wear—when he has fair health, a fair fortune, a tidy conscience and a complete exemption from embarrassing relatives—I suppose he is bound, in delicacy, to write himself happy. But I confess I shirk this obligation. I have not been miserable; I won't go so far as to say that —or at least as to write it. But happiness—positive happiness—would have been something different. I don't know that it would have been better, by all measurements—that it would have left me better off at the present time. But it certainly would have made this difference—

that I should not have been reduced, in pursuit of pleasant images, to disinter a buried episode of more than a quarter of a century ago. I should have found entertainment more—what shall I call it?—more contemporaneous. I should have had a wife and children, and I should not be in the way of making, as the French say, infidelities to the present. Of course it's a great gain to have had an escape, not to have committed an act of thumping folly; and I suppose that, whatever serious step one might have taken at twenty-five, after a struggle, and with a violent effort, and however one's conduct might appear to be justified by events, there would always remain a certain element of regret; a certain sense of loss lurking in the sense of gain; a tendency to wonder, rather wishfully, what *might* have been. What might have been, in this case, would, without doubt, have been very sad, and what has been has been very cheerful and comfortable; but there are nevertheless two or three questions I might ask myself. Why, for instance, have I never married—why have I never been able to care for any woman as I cared for that one? Ah, why are the mountains blue and why is the sunshine warm? Happiness mitigated by impertinent conjectures—that's about my ticket.

6*th*.—I knew it wouldn't last; it's already passing away. But I have spent a delightful day; I have been strolling all over the place. Everything reminds me of something else, and yet of itself at the same time; my imagination makes a great circuit and comes back to the starting-point. There is that well-remembered odour of spring in the air, and the flowers, as they used to be, are gathered into great sheaves and stacks, all along the rugged base of the Strozzi Palace. I wandered for an hour in the Boboli Gardens; we went there several times together. I remembered all those days individually; they seem to me as yesterday. I found the corner where she always chose to sit—the bench of sun-warmed marble, in front of the screen of ilex, with that exuberant statue of Pomona just beside it. The place is exactly the same, except that poor Pomona has lost one of her tapering fingers. I sat there for half-an-hour, and it was strange how near to me she seemed. The place was perfectly empty—that is, it was filled with *her*. I closed my eyes and listened; I could almost hear the rustle of her dress on the gravel. Why do we make such an ado about death? What is it after all but a sort of refinement of life? She died ten years ago, and yet, as I sat there in the evening stillness, she was a palpable, audible presence. I went afterwards into the gallery of the palace, and wandered for an hour from room to room. The same great pictures hung in the same places and the same dark frescoes arched above them. Twice, of old, I went there with her; she had a great understanding of art. She understood all sorts of things. Before the

Madonna of the Chair I stood a long time. The face is not a particle like hers, and yet it reminded me of her. But everything does that. We stood and looked at it together once for half-an-hour; I remember perfectly what she said.

8*th.*—Yesterday I felt blue—blue and bored; and when I got up this morning I had half a mind to leave Florence. But I went out into the street, beside the Arno, and looked up and down—looked at the yellow river and the violet hills, and then decided to remain,—or rather, I decided nothing. I simply stood gazing at the beauty of Florence, and before I had gazed my fill I was in good humour again, and it was too late to start for Rome. I strolled along the quay, where something presently happened that rewarded me for staying. I stopped in front of a little jeweller's shop, where a great many objects in mosaic were exposed in the window; I stood there for some minutes —I don't know why, for I have no taste for mosaic. In a moment a little girl came and stood beside me—a little girl with a frowsy Italian head, carrying a basket. I turned away, but, as I turned, my eyes happened to fall on her basket. It was covered with a napkin, and on the napkin was pinned a piece of paper, inscribed with an address. This address caught my glance—there was a name on it I knew. It was very legibly written—evidently by a scribe who had made up in zeal what was lacking in skill. *Contessa Salvi-Scarabelli, Via Ghibellina*— so ran the superscription: I looked at it for some moments; it caused me a sudden emotion. Presently the little girl, becoming aware of my attention, glanced up at me, wondering, with a pair of timid brown eyes.

'Are you carrying your basket to the Countess Salvi?' I asked.

The child stared at me. 'To the Countess Scarabelli.'

'Do you know the Countess?'

'Know her?' murmured the child, with an air of small dismay.

'I mean, have you seen her?'

'Yes, I have seen her.' And then, in a moment, with a sudden soft smile—'*E bella*!' said the little girl. She was beautiful herself as she said it.

'Precisely; and is she fair or dark?'

The child kept gazing at me. '*Bionda-bionda*,' she answered, looking about into the golden sunshine for a comparison.

'And is she young?'

'She is not young—like me. But she is not old like—like—'

'Like me, eh? And is she married?'

The little girl began to look wise. 'I have never seen the Signor Conte.'

'And she lives in Via Ghibellina?'

'*Sicuro*. In a beautiful palace.'

I had one more question to ask, and I pointed it with certain copper coins. 'Tell me a little—is she good?'

The child inspected a moment the contents of her little brown fist. 'It's you who are good,' she answered.

'Ah, but the Countess?' I repeated.

My informant lowered her big brown eyes, with an air of conscientious meditation that was inexpressibly quaint. 'To me she appears so,' she said at last, looking up.

'Ah, then she must be so,' I said, 'because, for your age, you are very intelligent.' And having delivered myself of this compliment I walked away and left the little girl counting her *soldi*.

I walked back to the hotel, wondering how I could learn something about the Contessa Salvi-Scarabelli. In the doorway I found the innkeeper, and near him stood a young man whom I immediately perceived to be a compatriot and with whom, apparently, he had been in conversation.

'I wonder whether you can give me a piece of information,' I said to the landlord. 'Do you know anything about the Count Salvi-Scarabelli?'

The landlord looked down at his boots, then slowly raised his shoulders with a melancholy smile. 'I have many regrets, dear sir—'

'You don't know the name?'

'I know the name assuredly. But I don't know the gentleman.'

I saw that my question had attracted the attention of the young Englishman, who looked at me with a good deal of earnestness. He was apparently satisfied with what he saw, for he presently decided to speak.

'The Count Scarabelli is dead,' he said, very gravely.

I looked at him a moment; he was a pleasing young fellow. 'And his widow lives,' I observed, 'in Via Ghibellina.'

'I daresay that is the name of the street.' He was a handsome young Englishman, but he was also an awkward one; he wondered who I was and what I wanted, and he did me the honour to perceive that, as regards these points, my appearance was reassuring. But he hesitated, very properly, to talk with a perfect stranger about a lady whom he knew, and he had not the art to conceal his hesitation. I instantly felt it to be singular that though he regarded me as a perfect stranger, I had not the same feeling about him. Whether it was that I had seen him before, or simply that I was struck with his agreeable young face—at any rate, I felt myself, as they say here, in sympathy with him. If I have seen him before I don't remember the occasion, and neither, apparently, does he; I suppose it's only a part of the feeling I have had the last three days about everything. It was this feeling that made me suddenly act as if I had known him a long time.

'Do you know the Countess Salvi?' I asked.

He looked at me a little, and then, without resenting the freedom of my question—'The Countess Scarabelli you mean,' he said.

'Yes,' I answered; 'she's the daughter.'

'The daughter is a little girl.'

'She must be grown up now. She must be—let me see—close upon thirty.'

My young Englishman began to smile. 'Of whom are you speaking?'

'I was speaking of the daughter,' I said, understanding his smile. 'But I was thinking of the mother.'

'Of the mother?'

'Of a person I knew twenty-seven years ago—the most charming woman I have ever known. She was the Countess Salvi—she lived in a wonderful old house in Via Ghibellina.'

'A wonderful old house!' my young Englishman repeated.

'She had a little girl,' I went on; 'and the little girl was very fair, like her mother; and the mother and daughter had the same name—Bianca.' I stopped and looked at my companion, and he blushed a little. 'And Bianca Salvi,' I continued, 'was the most charming woman in the world.' He blushed a little more, and I laid my hand on his shoulder. 'Do you know why I tell you this? Because you remind me of what I was when I knew her—when I loved her.' My poor young Englishman gazed at me with a sort of embarrassed and fascinated stare, and still I went on. 'I say that's the reason I told you this—but you'll think it a strange reason. You remind me of my younger self. You needn't resent that—I was a charming young fellow. The Countess Salvi thought so. Her daughter thinks the same of you.'

Instantly, instinctively, he raised his hand to my arm. 'Truly?'

'Ah, you are wonderfully like me!' I said laughing. 'That was just my state of mind. I wanted tremendously to please her'. He dropped his hand and looked away, smiling, but with an air of ingenuous confusion which quickened my interest in him. 'You don't know what to make of me,' I pursued. 'You don't know why a stranger should suddenly address you in this way and pretend to read your thoughts. Doubtless you think me a little cracked. Perhaps I am eccentric; but it's not so bad as that. I have lived about the world a great deal, following my profession, which is that of a soldier. I have been in India, in Africa, in Canada, and I have lived a good deal alone. That inclines people, I think, to sudden bursts of confidence. A week ago I came into Italy, where I spent six months when I was your age. I came straight to Florence—I was eager to see it again, on account of associations. They have been crowding upon me ever so thickly. I have taken the liberty of giving you a hint of them.' The young man inclined himself a little, in silence, as if he had been struck with a sudden respect. He stood and looked away for a moment at the river and the mountains. 'It's very beautiful,' I said.

'Oh, it's enchanting,' he murmured.

'That's the way I used to talk. But that's nothing to you.'

He glanced at me again. 'On the contrary, I like to hear.'

'Well, then, let us take a walk. If you, too, are staying at this inn we are fellow-travellers. We will walk down the Arno to the Cascine. There are several things I should like to ask of you.'

My young Englishman assented with an air of almost filial confidence, and we strolled for an hour beside the river and through the shady alleys of that lovely wilderness. We had a great deal of talk: it's not only myself, it's my whole situation over again.

'Are you very fond of Italy?' I asked.

He hesitated a moment. 'One can't express that.'

'Just so; I couldn't express it. I used to try—I used to write verses. On the subject of Italy I was very ridiculous.'

'So am I ridiculous,' said my companion.

'No, my dear boy,' I answered, 'we are not ridiculous; we are two very reasonable, superior people.'

'The first time one comes—as I have done—it's a revelation.'

'Oh, I remember well; one never forgets it. It's an introduction to beauty.'

'And it must be a great pleasure,' said my young friend, 'to come back.'

'Yes, fortunately the beauty is always here. What form of it,' I asked, 'do you prefer?'

My companion looked a little mystified; and at last he said, 'I am very fond of the pictures.'

'So was I. And among the pictures, which do you like best?'

'Oh, a great many.'

'So did I; but I had certain favourites.'

Again the young man hesitated a little, and then he confessed that the group of painters he preferred on the whole to all others was that of the early Florentines.

I was so struck with this that I stopped short. 'That was exactly my taste!' And then I passed my hand into his arm and we went our way again.

We sat down on an old stone bench in the Cascine, and a solemn blank-eyed Hermes, with wrinkles accentuated by the dust of ages, stood above us and listened to our talk.

'The Countess Salvi died ten years ago,' I said.

My companion admitted that he had heard her daughter say so.

'After I knew her she married again,' I added. 'The Count Salvi died before I knew her—a couple of years after their marriage.'

'Yes, I have heard that.'

'And what else have you heard?'

My companion stared at me; he had evidently heard nothing.

'She was a very interesting woman—there are a great many things to be said about her. Later, perhaps, I will tell you. Has the daughter the same charm?'

'You forget,' said my young man, smiling, 'that I have never seen the mother.'

'Very true. I keep confounding. But the daughter—how long have you known her?'

'Only since I have been here. A very short time.'

'A week?'

For a moment he said nothing. 'A month.'

'That's just the answer I should have made. A week, a month—it was all the same to me.'

'I think it is more than a month,' said the young man.

'It's probably six. How did you make her acquaintance?'

'By a letter—an introduction given me by a friend in England.'

'The analogy is complete,' I said. 'But the friend who gave me my letter to Madame de Salvi died many years ago. He, too, admired her greatly. I don't know why it never came into my mind that her daughter might be living in Florence. Somehow I took for granted it was all over. I never thought of the little girl; I never heard what had become of her. I walked past the palace yesterday and saw that it was occupied; but I took for granted it had changed hands.'

'The Countess Scarabelli,' said my friend, 'brought it to her husband as her marriage-portion.'

'I hope he appreciated it! There is a fountain in the court, and there is a charming old garden beyond it. The Countess's sitting-room looks into that garden. The staircase is of white marble, and there is a medallion by Luca della Robbia set into the wall at the place where it makes a bend. Before you come into the drawing-room you stand a moment in a great vaulted place hung round with faded tapestry, paved with bare tiles, and furnished only with three chairs. In the drawing-room, above the fireplace, is a superb Andrea del Sarto. The furniture is covered with pale sea-green.'

My companion listened to all this. 'The Andrea del Sarto is there; it's magnificent. But the furniture is in pale red.'

'Ah, they have changed it then—in twenty-seven years.'

'And there's a portrait of Madame de Salvi,' continued my friend.

I was silent a moment. 'I should like to see that.'

He too was silent. Then he asked, 'Why don't you go and see it? If you knew the mother so well, why don't you call upon the daughter?'

'From what you tell me I am afraid.'

'What have I told you to make you afraid?'

I looked a little at his ingenuous countenance. 'The mother was a very dangerous woman.'

The young Englishman began to blush again. 'The daughter is not,' he said.

'Are you very sure?'

He didn't say he was sure, but he presently inquired in what way the Countess Salvi had been dangerous.

'You must not ask me that,' I answered; 'for, after all, I desire to remember only what was good in her.' And as we walked back I begged him to render me the service of mentioning my name to his friend, and of saying that I had known her mother well, and that I asked permission to come and see her.

9*th*.—I have seen that poor boy half-a-dozen times again, and a most amiable young fellow he is. He continues to represent to me, in the most extraordinary manner, my own young identity; the correspondence is perfect at all points, save that he is a better boy than I. He is evidently acutely interested in his Countess and leads quite the same life with her that I led with Madame de Salvi. He goes to see her every evening and stays half the night; these Florentines keep the most extraordinary hours. I remember, towards 3 A.M., Madame de Salvi used to turn me out. 'Come, come,' she would say, 'it's time to go. If you were to stay later people might talk.' I don't know at what time he comes home, but I suppose his evening seems as short as mine did. Today he brought me a message from his Contessa—a very gracious little speech. She remembered often to have heard her mother speak of me—she called me her English friend. All her mother's friends were dear to her, and she begged I would do her the honour to come and see her. She is always at home of an evening. Poor young Stanmer (he is of the Devonshire Stanmers—a great property) reported this speech verbatim, and of course it can't in the least signify to him that a poor grizzled, battered soldier, old enough to be his father, should come to call upon his *inammorata*. But I remember how it used to matter to me when other men came; that's a point of difference. However, it's only because I'm so old. At twenty-five I shouldn't have been afraid of myself at fifty-two. Camerino was thirty-four—and then the others! She was always at home in the evening, and they all used to come. They were old Florentine names. But she used to let me stay after them all; she thought an old English name as good. What a transcendent coquette! . . . But *basta così*, as she used to say. I meant to go tonight to Casa Salvi, but I couldn't bring myself to the point. I don't know what I'm afraid of; I used to be in a hurry enough to go there once. I suppose I am afraid of the very look of the place—of the old rooms, the old walls, I shall go tomorrow night. I am afraid of the very echoes.

10*th*.—She has the most extraordinary resemblance to her mother. When I went in I was tremendously startled; I stood staring at her. I have just come home; it is part midnight; I have been all the evening at Casa Salvi. It is very warm—my window is open—I can look out on the river, gliding past in the starlight. So, of old, when I came home, I used to stand and look out. There are the same cypresses on the opposite hills.

Poor young Stanmer was there, and three or four other admirers; they all got up when I came in. I think I had been talked about and there was some curiosity. But why should I have been talked about? They were all youngish men—none of them of my time. She is a wonderful likeness of her mother; I couldn't get over it. Beautiful like her mother, and yet with the same faults in her face; but with her mother's perfect head and brow and sympathetic, almost pitying, eyes. Her face has just that peculiarity of her mother's, which, of all human countenances that I have ever known, was the one that passed most quickly and completely from the expression of gaiety to that of repose. Repose, in her face, always suggested sadness; and while you were watching it with a kind of awe, and wondering of what tragic secret it was the token, it kindled, on the instant, into a radiant Italian smile. The Countess Scarabelli's smiles tonight, however, were almost uninterrupted. She greeted me—divinely, as her mother used to do; and young Stanmer sat in the corner of the sofa—as I used to do—and watched her while she talked. She is thin and very fair, and was dressed in light, vaporous black: that completes the resemblance. The house, the rooms, are almost absolutely the same; there may be changes of detail, but they don't modify the general effect. There are the same precious pictures on the walls of the salon—the same great dusky fresco in the concave ceiling. The daughter is not rich, I suppose, any more than the mother. The furniture is worn and faded, and I was admitted by a solitary servant, who carried a twinkling taper before me up the great dark marble staircase.

'I have often heard of you,' said the Countess, as I sat down near her; 'my mother often spoke of you.'

'Often?' I answered. 'I am surprised at that.'

'Why are you surprised? Were you not good friends?'

'Yes, for a certain time—very good friends. But I was sure she had forgotten me.'

'She never forgot,' said the Countess, looking at me intently and smiling. 'She was not like that.'

'She was not like most other women in any way,' I declared.

'Ah, she was charming,' cried the Countess, rattling open her fan. 'I have always been very curious to see you. I have received an impression of you.'

'A good one, I hope.'

She looked at me, laughing and not answering this: it was just her mother's trick.

'"My Englishman," she used to call you—"*il mio Inglese.*"'

'I hope she spoke of me kindly,' I insisted.

The Countess, still laughing, gave a little shrug, balancing her hand to and fro. 'So-so; I always supposed you had had a quarrel. You don't mind my being frank like this—eh?

'I delight in it; it reminds me of your mother.'

'Every one tells me that. But I am not clever like her. You will see for yourself.'

'That speech,' I said, 'completes the resemblance. She was always pretending she was not clever, and in reality—'

'In reality she was an angel, eh? To escape from dangerous comparisons I will admit then that I am clever. That will make a difference. But let us talk of you. You are very—how shall I say it?—very eccentric.'

'Is that what your mother told you?'

'To tell the truth, she spoke of you as a great original. But aren't all Englishmen eccentric? All except that one?' And the Countess pointed to poor Stanmer, in his corner of the sofa.

'Oh, I know just what he is,' I said.

'He's as quiet as a lamb—he's like all the world,' cried the Countess.

'Like all the world—yes. He's in love with you.'

She looked at me with sudden gravity. 'I don't object to your saying that for all the world—but I do for him.'

'Well,' I went on, 'he's peculiar in this: he's rather afraid of you.'

Instantly she began to smile; she turned her face towards Stanmer. He had seen that we were talking about him; he coloured and got up —then came towards us.

'I like men who are afraid of nothing,' said our hostess.

'I know what you want,' I said to Stanmer. 'You want to know what the Signora Contessa says about you.'

Stanmer looked straight into her face, very gravely. 'I don't care a straw what she says.'

You are almost a match for the Signora Contessa,' I answered. 'She declares she doesn't care a pin's head what you think.'

'I recognize the Countess's style!' Stanmer exclaimed, turning away.

'One would think,' said the Countess, 'that you were trying to make a quarrel between us.'

I watched him move away to another part of the great saloon; he stood in front of the Andrea del Sarto, looking up at it. But he was not seeing it; he was listening to what we might say. I often stood there in just that way. 'He can't quarrel with you, any more than I could have quarrelled with your mother.'

'Ah, but you did. Something painful passed between you.'

'Yes, it was painful, but it was not a quarrel. I went away one day and never saw her again. That was all.'

The Countess looked at me gravely. 'What do you call it when a man does that?'

'It depends upon the case.'

'Sometimes,' said the Countess in French, 'it's a *lâcheté*.'

'Yes, and sometimes it's an act of wisdom.'

'And sometimes,' rejoined the Countess, 'it's a mistake.'

I shook my head. 'For me it was no mistake.'

She began to laugh again. 'Caro Signore, you're a great original. What had my poor mother done to you?'

I looked at our young Englishman, who still had his back turned to us and was staring up at the picture. 'I will tell you some other time,' I said.

'I shall certainly remind you; I am very curious to know.' Then she opened and shut her fan two or three times, still looking at me. What eyes they have! 'Tell me a little,' she went on, 'if I may ask without indiscretion. Are you married?'

'No, Signora Contessa.'

'Isn't that at least a mistake?'

'Do I look very unhappy?'

She dropped her head a little to one side. 'For an Englishman—no!'

'Ah,' said I, laughing, 'you are quite as clever as your mother.'

'And they tell me that you are a great soldier,' she continued; 'you have lived in India. It was very kind of you, so far away, to have remembered our poor dear Italy.'

'One always remembers Italy; the distance makes no difference. I remembered it well the day I heard of your mother's death!'

'Ah, that was a sorrow!' said the Countess. 'There's not a day that I don't weep for her. But *che vuole*! She's a saint in paradise.'

'*Sicuro*,' I answered; and I looked some time at the ground. 'But tell me about yourself, dear lady,' I asked at last, raising my eyes. 'You have also had the sorrow of losing your husband.'

'I am a poor widow as you see. *Che vuole*? My husband died after three years of marriage.'

I waited for her to remark that the late Count Scarabelli was also a saint in paradise, but I waited in vain.

'That was like your distinguished father,' I said.

'Yes, he too died young. I can't be said to have known him; I was but of the age of my own little girl. But I weep for him all the more.'

Again I was silent for a moment.

'It was in India too,' I said presently, 'that I heard of your mother's second marriage.'

The Countess raised her eyebrows.

'In India then, one hears of everything! Did that news please you?'

'Well, since you ask me—no.'

'I understand that,' said the Countess, looking at her open fan. 'I shall not marry again like that.'

'That's what your mother said to me,' I ventured to observe.

She was not offended, but she rose from her seat and stood looking at me a moment. Then—

'You should not have gone away!' she exclaimed.

I stayed for another hour; it is a very pleasant house. Two or three of the men who were sitting there seemed very civil and intelligent; one of them was a major of engineers, who offered me a profusion of information upon the new organization of the Italian army. While he talked, however, I was observing our hostess, who was talking with the others; very little, I noticed, with her young Inglese. She is altogether charming—full of frankness and freedom, of that inimitable *disinvoltura* which in an Englishwoman would be vulgar, and which in her is simply the perfection of apparent spontaneity. But for all her spontaneity she's as subtle as a needle point, and knows tremendously well what she is about. If she is not a consummate coquette . . . What had she in her head when she said that I should not have gone away?—Poor little Stanmer didn't go away. I left him there at midnight.

12*th*.—I found him today sitting in the church of Santa Croce, into which I wandered to escape from the heat of the sun.

In the nave it was cool and dim; he was staring at the blaze of candles on the great altar, and thinking, I am sure, of his incomparable Countess. I sat down beside him, and after a while, as if to avoid the appearance of eagerness, he asked me how I had enjoyed my visit to Casa Salvi, and what I thought of the *padrona*.

'I think half a dozen things,' I said; 'but I can only tell you one now. She's an enchantress. You shall hear the rest when we have left the church.'

'An enchantress?' repeated Stanmer, looking at me askance.

He is a very simple youth, but who am I, to blame him?

'A charmer,' I said; 'a fascinatress!'

He turned away, staring at the altar-candles.

'An artist—an actress,' I went on rather brutally.

He gave me another glance.

'I think you are telling me all,' he said.

'No, no, there is more.' And we sat a long time in silence.

At last he proposed that we should go out; and we passed into the street, where the shadows had begun to stretch themselves.

'I don't know what you mean by her being an actress,' he said, as we turned homeward.

'I suppose not. Neither should I have known if any one had said that to me.'

'You are thinking about the mother,' said Stanmer. 'Why are you always bringing *her* in?'

'My dear boy, the analogy is so great; it forces itself upon me.'

He stopped, and stood looking at me with his modest, perplexed young face. I thought he was going to exclaim—'The analogy be hanged!'—but he said after a moment—

'Well, what does it prove?'

'I can't say it proves anything; but it suggests a great many things.'

'Be so good as to mention a few,' he said, as we walked on.

'You are not sure of her yourself,' I began.

'Never mind that—go on with your analogy.'

'That's a part of it. You *are* very much in love with her.'

'That's a part of it too, I suppose?'

'Yes, as I have told you before. You are in love with her, and yet you can't make her out; that's just where I was with regard to Madame de Salvi.'

'And she too was an enchantress, an actress, an artist, and all the rest of it?'

'She was the most perfect coquette I ever knew, and the most dangerous, because the most finished.'

'What you mean, then is that her daughter is a finished coquette?'

'I rather think so.'

Stanmer walked along for some moments in silence.

'Seeing that you suppose me to be a—a great admirer of the Countess,' he said at last, 'I am rather surprised at the freedom with which you speak of her.'

I confessed that I was surprised at it myself. 'But it's on account of the interest I take in you.'

'I am immensely obliged to you!' said the poor boy.

'Ah, of course you don't like it. That is, you like my interest—I don't see how you can help liking that; but you don't like my freedom. That's natural enough; but, my dear young friend, I want only to help you. If a man had said to me—so many years ago—what I am saying to you, I should certainly also, at first, have thought him a great brute. But, after a little, I should have been grateful—I should have felt that he was helping me.'

'You seem to have been very well able to help yourself,' said Stanmer. 'You tell me you made your escape.'

'Yes, but it was at the cost of infinite perplexity—of what I may call keen suffering. I should like to save you all that.'

'I can only repeat—it is really very kind of you.'

'Don't repeat it too often, or I shall begin to think you don't mean it.'

'Well,' said Stanmer, 'I think this, at any rate—that you take an extraordinary responsibility in trying to put a man out of conceit of a woman who, as he believes, may make him very happy.'

I grasped his arm, and we stopped, going on with our talk like a couple of Florentines.

'Do you wish to marry her?'

He looked away, without meeting my eyes. 'It's a great responsibility,' he repeated.

'Before Heaven,' I said, 'I would have married the mother! You are exactly in my situation.'

'Don't you think you rather overdo the analogy?' asked poor Stanmer.

'A little more, a little less—it doesn't matter. I believe you are in my shoes. But of course if you prefer it I will beg a thousand pardons and leave them to carry you where they will.'

He had been looking away, but now he slowly turned his face and met my eyes. 'You have gone too far to retreat; what is it you know about her?'

'About this one—nothing. But about the other—'

'I care nothing about the other!'

'My dear fellow,' I said, 'they are mother and daughter—they are as like as two of Andrea's Madonnas.'

'If they resemble each other, then, you were simply mistaken in the mother.'

I took his arm and we walked on again; there seemed no adequate reply to such a charge. 'Your state of mind brings back my own so completely,' I said presently. 'You admire her—you adore her, and yet, secretly, you mistrust her. You are enchanted with her personal charm, her grace, her wit, her everything; and yet in your private heart you are afraid of her.'

'Afraid of her?'

'Your mistrust keeps rising to the surface; you can't rid yourself of the suspicion that at the bottom of all things she is hard and cruel, and you would be immensely relieved if some one should persuade you that your suspicion is right.'

Stanmer made no direct reply to this; but before we reached the hotel he said—'What did you ever know about the mother?'

'It's a terrible story,' I answered.

He looked at me askance. 'What did she do?'

'Come to my rooms this evening and I will tell you.'

He declared he would, but he never came. Exactly the way I should have acted!

14*th.*—I went again, last evening, to Casa Salvi, where I found the same little circle, with the addition of a couple of ladies. Stanmer was there, trying hard to talk to one of them, but making, I am sure, a very poor business of it. The Countess—well, the Countess was admirable. She greeted me like a friend of ten years, towards whom familiarity should not have engendered a want of ceremony; she made me sit near her, and she asked me a dozen questions about my health and my occupations.

'I live in the past,' I said. 'I go into the galleries, into the old palaces and the churches. Today I spent an hour in Michael Angelo's chapel, at San Lorenzo.'

'Ah, yes, that's the past,' said the Countess. 'Those things are very old.'

'Twenty-seven years old,' I answered.

'Twenty-seven? *Altro*!'

'I mean my own past,' I said. 'I went to a great many of those places with your mother.'

'Ah, the pictures are beautiful,' murmured the Countess, glancing at Stanmer.

'Have you lately looked at any of them?' I asked. 'Have you gone to the galleries with *him*?'

She hesitated a moment, smiling. 'It seems to me that your question is a little impertinent. But I think you are like that.'

'A little impertinent? Never. As I say, your mother did me the honour, more than once, to accompany me to the Uffizzi.'

'My mother must have been very kind to you.'

'So it seemed to me at the time.'

'At the time only?'

'Well, if you prefer, so it seems to me now.'

'Eh,' said the Countess, 'she made sacrifices.'

'To what, cara Signora? She was perfectly free. Your lamented father was dead—and she had not yet contracted her second marriage.'

'If she was intending to marry again, it was all the more reason she should have been careful.'

I looked at her a moment; she met my eyes gravely, over the top of her fan. 'Are *you* very careful?' I said.

She dropped her fan with a certain violence. 'Ah, yes, you are impertinent!'

'Ah, no,' I said. 'Remember that I am old enough to be your father, that I knew you when you were three years old. I may surely ask such questions. But you are right; one must do your mother justice. She was certainly thinking of her second marriage.'

'You have not forgiven her that!' said the Countess, very gravely.

'Have you?' I asked, more lightly.

'I don't judge my mother. That is a mortal sin. My stepfather was very kind to me.'

'I remember him,' I said; 'I saw him a great many times—your mother already received him.'

My hostess sat with lowered eyes, saying nothing; but she presently looked up.

'She was very unhappy with my father.'

'That I can easily believe. And your stepfather—is he still living?'

'He died—before my mother.'

'Did he fight any more duels?'

'He was killed in a duel,' said the Countess, discreetly.

It seems almost montrous, especially as I can give no reason for it—but this announcement, instead of shocking me, caused me to feel a strange exhilaration. Most assuredly, after all these years, I bear the poor man no resentment. Of course I controlled my manner and simply remarked to the Countess that as his fault had been, so was his punishment. I think, however, that the feeling of which I speak was at the bottom of my saying to her that I hoped that, unlike her mother's her own brief married life had been happy.

'If it was not,' she said, 'I have forgotten it now.'—I wonder if the late Count Scarabelli was also killed in a duel, and if his adversary . . .

Is it on the books that his adversary, as well, shall perish by the pistol? Which of those gentlemen is he, I wonder? Is it reserved for poor little Stanmer to put a bullet into him? No, poor little Stanmer, I trust, will do as I did. And yet, unfortunately for him, that woman is consummately plausible. She was wonderfully nice last evening; she was really irresistible. Such frankness and freedom, and yet something so soft and womanly; such graceful gaiety, so much of the brightness, without any of the stiffness, of good breeding, and over it all something so picturesquely simple and southern. She is a perfect Italian. But she comes honestly by it. After the talk I have just jotted down she changed her place, and the conversation for half-an-hour was general. Stanmer indeed said very little; partly, I suppose, because he is shy of talking a foreign tongue. Was I like that—was I so constantly silent? I suspect I was when I was perplexed, and heaven knows that very often my perplexity was extreme. Before I went away I had a few more words *tête-à-tête* with the Countess.

'I hope you are not leaving Florence yet,' she said; 'you will stay a while longer?'

I answered that I came only for a week, and that my week was over.

'I stay on from day to day, I am so much interested.'

'Eh, it's the beautiful moment. I'm glad our city pleases you!'

'Florence pleases me—and I take a paternal interest in our young friend,' I added, glancing at Stanmer. 'I have become very fond of him.'

'*Bel tipo inglese*,' said my hostess. 'And he is very intelligent; he has a beautiful mind.'

She stood there resting her smile and her clear, expressive eyes upon me.

'I don't like to praise him too much,' I rejoined, 'lest I should appear to praise myself; he reminds me so much of what I was at his age. If your beautiful mother were to come to life for an hour she would see the resemblance.'

She gave me a little amused stare.

'And yet you don't look at all like him!'

'Ah, you didn't know me when I was twenty-five. I was very handsome! And, moreover, it isn't that; it's the mental resemblance. I was ingenuous, candid, trusting, like him.'

'Trusting? I remember my mother once telling me that you were the most suspicious and jealous of men.'

'I fell into a suspicious mood, but I was, fundamentally, not in the least addicted to thinking evil. I couldn't easily imagine any harm of any one.'

'And so you mean that Mr. Stanmer is in a suspicious mood?'

'Well, I mean that his situation is the same as mine.'

The Countess gave me one of her serious looks.

'Come,' she said, 'what was it—this famous situation of yours? I have heard you mention it before.'

'Your mother might have told you, since she occasionally did me the honour to speak of me.'

'All my mother ever told me was that you were a sad puzzle to her.'

At this, of course, I laughed out—I laugh still as I write it.

'Well then, that was my situation—I was a sad puzzle to a very clever woman.'

'And you mean, therefore, that I am a puzzle to poor Mr. Stanmer?'

'He is racking his brains to make you out. Remember it was you who said he was intelligent.'

She looked round at him, and as fortune would have it, his appearance at that moment quite confirmed my assertion. He was lounging back in his chair with an air of indolence rather too marked for a drawing-room, and staring at the ceiling with the expression of a man who has just been asked a conundrum. Madame Scarabelli seemed struck with his attitude.

'Don't you see,' I said, 'he can't read the riddle?'

'You yourself,' she answered, 'said he was incapable of thinking evil. I should be sorry to have him think evil of *me*.'

And she looked straight at me—seriously, appealingly—with her beautiful candid brow.

I inclined myself, smiling, in a manner which might have meant—

'How could that be possible?'

'I have a great esteem for him,' she went on; 'I want him to think well of me. If I am a puzzle to him, do me a little service. Explain me to him.'

'Explain you, dear lady?'

'You are older and wiser than he. Make him understand me.'

She looked deep into my eyes for a moment and then she turned away.

26*th*.—I have written nothing for a good many days, but meanwhile I have been half a dozen times to Casa Salvi. I have seen a good deal also of my young friend—had a good many walks and talks with him. I have proposed to him to come with me to Venice for a fortnight, but he won't listen to the idea of leaving Florence. He is very happy, in spite of his doubts, and I confess that in the perception of his happiness I have lived over again my own. This is so much the case that when, the other day, he at last made up his mind to ask me to tell him the wrong that Madame de Salvi had done me, I rather checked his curiosity. I told him that if he was bent upon knowing I would satisfy him, but that it seemed a pity, just now, to indulge in painful imagery.

'But I thought you wanted so much to put me out of conceit of our friend.'

'I admit I am inconsistent, but there are various reasons for it. In the first place—it's obvious—I am open to the charge of playing a double game. I profess an admiration for the Countess Scarabelli, for I accept her hospitality, and at the same time I attempt to poison your mind; isn't that the proper expression? I can't exactly make up my mind to that, though my admiration for the Countess and my desire to prevent you from taking a foolish step are equally sincere. And then, in the second place, you seem to me on the whole so happy! One hesitates to destroy an illusion, no matter how pernicious, that is so delightful while it lasts. Those are the rare moments of life. To be young and ardent, in the midst of an Italian spring, and to believe in the moral perfection of a beautiful woman—what an admirable situation! Float with the current, I'll stand on the brink and watch you.'

'Your real reason is that you feel you have no case against the poor lady,' said Stanmer. 'You admire her as much as I do.'

'I just admitted that I admire her: I never said she was a vulgar flirt; her mother was an absolutely scientific one. Heaven knows I admired that! It's a nice point, however, how much one is bound in honour not to warn a young friend against a dangerous woman because one also has relations of civility with the lady.'

'In such a case,' said Stanmer, 'I would break off my relations.'

I looked at him, and I think I laughed.

'Are you jealous of me, by chance?'

He shook his head emphatically.

'Not in the least; I like to see you there, because your conduct contradicts your words.'

'I have always said that the Countess is fascinating.'

'Otherwise,' said Stanmer, 'in the case you speak of I would give the lady notice.'

'Give her notice?'

'Mention to her that you regard her with suspicion, and that you propose to do your best to rescue a simple-minded youth from her wiles. That would be more loyal.' And he began to laugh again.

It is not the first time he has laughed at me; but I have never minded it because I have always understood it.

'Is that what you recommend me to say to the Countess?' I asked.

'Recommend you!' he exclaimed, laughing again. 'I recommend nothing. I may be the victim to be rescued, but I am at least not a partner to the conspiracy. Besides,' he added in a moment, 'the Countess knows your state of mind.'

'Has she told you so?'

Stanmer hesitated.

'She has begged me to listen to everything you may say against her. She prefers that; she has a good conscience.'

'Ah,' said I, 'she's an accomplished woman!'

And it is indeed very clever of her to take that tone. Stanmer afterwards assured me explicitly that he has never given her a hint of the liberties I have taken in conversation with—what shall I call it?—with her moral nature; she has guessed them for herself. She must hate me intensely, and yet her manner has always been so charming to me! She is truly an accomplished woman!

May 4th.—I have stayed away from Casa Salvi for a week, but I have lingered on in Florence, under a mixture of impulses. I have had it on my conscience not to go near the Countess again—and yet, from the moment she is aware of the way I feel about her, it is open war. There need be no scruples on either side. She is as free to use every possible art to entangle poor Stanmer more closely as I am to clip her fine-spun meshes. Under the circumstances, however, we naturally shouldn't meet very cordially. But as regards her meshes, why, after all, should I clip them? It would really be very interesting to see Stanmer swallowed up. I should like to see how he would agree with her after she had devoured him—(to what vulgar imagery, by the way, does curiosity reduce a man!) Let him finish the story in his own way, as I finished it in mine. It is the same story; but why, a quarter of a century later, should it have the same *dénoûment*? Let him make his own *dénoûment.*

5*th.*—Hang it, however, I don't want the poor boy to be miserable.

6*th.*—Ah, but did my *dénoûment* then prove such a happy one?

7*th.*—He came to my room late last night; he was much excited.

'What was it she did to you?' he asked.

I answered him first with another question. 'Have you quarrelled with the Countess?'

But he only repeated his own. 'What was it she did to you?'

'Sit down and I'll tell you.' And he sat there beside the candle, staring at me. 'There was a man always there—Count Camerino.'

'The man she married?'

'The man she married. I was very much in love with her, and yet I didn't trust her. I was sure that she lied; I believed she could be cruel. Nevertheless, at moments, she had a charm which made it pure pedantry to be conscious of her faults; and while these moments lasted I would have done anything for her. Unfortunately, they didn't last long. But you know what I mean; am I not describing the Scarabelli?'

'The Countess Scarabelli never lied!' cried Stanmer.

'That's just what I would have said to any one who should have made the insinuation! But I suppose you are not asking me the question you put to me just now from dispassionate curiosity.'

'A man may want to know!' said the innocent fellow.

I couldn't help laughing out. 'This, at any rate, is my story. Camerino was always there; he was a sort of fixture in the house. If I had moments of dislike for the divine Bianca, I had no moments of liking for him. And yet he was a very agreeable fellow, very civil, very intelligent, not in the least disposed to make a quarrel with me. The trouble of course was simply that I was jealous of him. I don't know, however, on what ground I could have quarrelled with him, for I had no definite rights. I can't say what I expected—I can't say what, as the matter stood, I was prepared to do. With my name and my prospects, I might perfectly have offered her my hand. I am not sure that she would have accepted it—I am by no means clear that she wanted that. But she wanted, wanted keenly, to attach me to her; she wanted to have me about. I should have been capable of giving up everything—England, my career, my family—simply to devote myself to her, to live near her and see her every day.'

'Why didn't you do it, then?' asked Stanmer.

'Why don't you?'

'To be a proper rejoinder to my question,' he said, rather neatly, 'yours should be asked twenty-five years hence.'

'It remains perfectly true that at a given moment I was capable of doing as I say. That was what she wanted—a rich, susceptible, credulous, convenient young Englishman, established near her *en permanence*. And yet,' I added, 'I must do her complete justice. I honestly believe she was fond of me.' At this Stanmer got up and walked to the window; he stood looking out a moment, and then he turned round. 'You know she was older than I,' I went on. 'Madame Scarabelli is older than you. One day, in the garden, her mother asked me in an angry tone why I disliked Camerino; for I had been at no pains to conceal my feeling about him, and something had just happened to bring it out. "I dislike him," I said, "because you like him so much." "I assure you I don't like him," she answered. "He has all the appearance of being your lover," I retorted. It was a brutal speech, certainly, but any other man in my place would have made it. She took it very strangely; she turned pale, but she was not indignant. "How can he be my lover after what he has done?" she asked. "What has he done?" she hesitated a good while, then she said: "He killed my husband." "Good heavens!" I cried, "and you receive him?" Do you know what she said? She said '*Che Vuole*?" '

'Is that all?' asked Stanmer.

'No; she went on to say that Camerino had killed Count Salvi in a duel, and she admitted that her husband's jealousy had been the occasion of it. The Count, it appeared, was a monster of jealousy—he had led her a dreadful life. He himself, meanwhile, had been anything but irreproachable; he had done a mortal injury to a man of whom he pretended to be a friend, and this affair had become notorious. The gentleman in question had demanded satisfaction for his outraged honour; but for some reason or other (the Countess, to do her justice did not tell me that her husband was a coward) he had not as yet obtained it. The duel with Camerino had come on first; in an access of jealous fury the Count had struck Camerino in the face; and this outrage, I know not how justly, was deemed expiable before the other. By an extraordinary arrangement (the Italians have certainly no sense of fair play), the other man was allowed to be Camerino's second. The duel was fought with swords, and the Count received a wound of which, though at first it was not expected to be fatal, he died on the following day. The matter was hushed up as much as possible for the sake of the Countess's good name, and so successfully that it was presently observed that, among the public, the other gentleman had the credit of having put his sword through M. de Salvi. This gentleman took a fancy not to contradict the impression, and it was allowed to subsist. So long as *he* consented, it was of course in Camerino's interest not to contradict it, as it left him much more free to keep up his intimacy with the Countess.'

Stanmer had listened to all this with extreme attention. 'Why didn't *she* contradict it?'

I shrugged my shoulders. 'I am bound to believe it was for the same reason. I was horrified, at any rate, by the whole story. I was extremely shocked at the Countess's want of dignity in continuing to see the man by whose hand her husband had fallen.'

'The husband had been a great brute, and it was not known,' said Stanmer.

'Its not being known made no difference. And as for Salvi having been a brute, that is but a way of saying that his wife, and the man whom his wife subsequently married, didn't like him.'

Stanmer looked extremely meditative; his eyes were fixed on mine. 'Yes, that marriage is hard to get over. It was not becoming.'

'Ah,' said I, 'what a long breath I drew when I heard of it! I remember the place and the hour. It was at a hill-station in India, seven years after I had left Florence. The post brought me some English papers, and in one of them was a letter from Italy, with a lot of so-called "fashionable intelligence." There, among various scandals in high life, and other delectable items, I read that the Countess Bianca Salvi, famous for some years as the presiding genius of the most agreeable *salon* in Florence, was about to bestow her hand upon Count Camerino, a distinguished Bolognese. Ah, my dear boy, it was a tremendous escape! I had been ready to marry the woman who was capable of that! But my instinct had warned me, and I had trusted my instinct.'

' "Insinct's everything," as Falstaff says!' and Stanmer began to laugh. 'Did you tell Madame de Salvi that your instinct was against her?'

'No; I told her that she frightened me, shocked me, horrified me.'

'That's about the same thing. And what did she say?'

'She asked me what I would have? I called her friendship with Camerino a scandal, and she answered that her husband had been a brute. Besides, no one knew it; therefore it was no scandal. Just *your* argument! I retorted that this was odious reasoning, and that she had no moral sense. We had a passionate quarrel, and I declared I would never see her again. In the heat of my displeasure I left Florence, and I kept my vow. I never saw her again.'

'You couldn't have been much in love with her,' said Stanmer.

'I was not—three months after.'

'If you had been you would have come back—three days after.'

'So doubtless it seems to you. All I can say is that it was the great effort of my life. Being a military man I have had on various occasions to face the enemy. But it was not then I needed my resolution; it was when I left Florence in a postchaise.'

Stanmer turned about the room two or three times, and then he said: 'I don't understand! I don't understand why she should have told you that Camerino had killed her husband. It could only damage her.'

'She was afraid it would damage her more that I should think he was her lover. She wished to say the thing that would most effectually persuade me that he was not her lover—that he could never be. And then she wished to get the credit of being very frank.'

'Good heavens, how you must have analysed her!' cried my companion, staring.

'There is nothing so analytic as disillusionment. But there it is. She married Camerino.'

'Yes, I don't like that,' said Stanmer. He was silent a while, and then he added—'Perhaps she wouldn't have done so if you had remained.'

He has a little innocent way! 'Very likely she would have dispensed with the ceremony,' I answered, dryly.

'Upon my word,' he said, 'you *have* analysed her!'

'You ought to be grateful to me. I have done for you what you seem unable to do for yourself.'

'I don't see any Camerino in my case,' he said.

'Perhaps among those gentlemen I can find one for you.'

'Thank you,' he cried; 'I'll take care of that myself!' And he went away—satisfied, I hope.

10*th*.—He's an obstinate little wretch; it irritates me to see him sticking to it. Perhaps he is looking for his Camerino. I shall leave him at any rate to his fate; it is growing insupportably hot.

11*th*.—I went this evening to bid farewell to the Scarabelli. There was no one there; she was alone in her great dusky drawing-room, which was lighted only by a couple of candles, with the immense windows open over the garden. She was dressed in white; she was deucedly pretty. She asked me of course why I had been so long without coming.

'I think you say that only for form,' I answered. 'I imagine you know.'

'*Chè*!what have I done?'

'Nothing at all. You are too wise for that.'

She looked at me a while. 'I think you are a little crazy.'

'Ah no, I am only too sane. I have too much reason rather than too little.'

'You have at any rate what we call a fixed idea.'

'There is no harm in that so long as it's a good one.'

'But yours is abominable,' she declared, with a laugh.

'Of course you can't like me or my ideas. All things considered, you have treated me with wonderful kindness, and I thank you and kiss your hands. I leave Florence tomorrow.'

'I won't say I'm sorry!' she said, laughing again. 'But I am very glad to have seen you. I always wondered about you. You are a curiosity.'

'Yes, you must find me so. A man who can resist your charms! The fact is, I can't. This evening you are enchanting; and it is the first time I have been alone with you.'

She gave no heed to this; she turned away. But in a moment she came back, and stood looking at me, and her beautiful solemn eyes seemed to shine in the dimness of the room.

'How *could* you treat my mother so?' she asked.

'Treat her so?'

'How could you desert the most charming woman in the world?'

'It was not a case of desertion; and if it had been, it seems to me she was consoled.'

At this moment there was a sound of a step in the ante-chamber, and I saw that the Countess perceived it to be Stanmer's.

'That wouldn't have happened,' she murmured. 'My poor mother needed a protector.'

Stanmer came in, interrupting our talk, and looking at me, I thought, with a little air of bravado. He must think me, indeed, a tiresome meddlesome bore; and upon my word, turning it all over, I wonder at his docility. After all, he's five-and-twenty—and yet, I *must* add, it *does* irritate me—the way he sticks! He was followed in a moment by two or three of the regular Italians, and I made my visit short.

'Good-bye, Countess,' I said; and she gave me her hand in silence. 'Do *you* need a protector?' I added, softly.

She looked at me from head to foot, and then, almost angrily—

'Yes, Signore.'

But, to deprecate her anger, I kept her hand an instant, and then bent my venerable head and kissed it. I think I appeased her.

BOLOGNA, 14*th*.—I left Florence on the 11th, and have been here these three days. Delightful old Italian town—but it lacks the charm of my Florentine secret.

I wrote that last entry five days ago, late at night, after coming back from Casa Salvi. I afterwards fell asleep in my chair; the night was half over when I woke up. Instead of going to bed, I stood a long time at the window, looking out at the river. It was a warm, still night, and the first faint streaks of sunrise were in the sky. Presently I heard a slow footstep beneath my window, and looking down, made out, by the aid of a street-lamp, that Stanmer was but just coming home. I called to him to come to my rooms, and, after an interval, he made his appearance.

'I want to bid you good-bye,' I said; 'I shall depart in the morning. Don't go to the trouble of saying you're sorry. Of course you are not; I must have bullied you immensely.'

He made no attempt to say he was sorry, but he said he was very glad to have made my acquaintance.

'Your conversation,' he said, with his little innocent air, 'has been very suggestive.'

'Have you found Camerino?' I asked, smiling.

'I have given up the search.'

'Well,' I said, 'some day when you find that you have made a great mistake, remember I told you so.'

He looked for a minute as if he were trying to anticipate that day by the exercise of his reason.

'Has it ever occurred to you that *you* may have made a great mistake?'

'Oh yes; everything occurs to one sooner or later.'

That's what I said to him; but I didn't say that the question, pointed by his candid young countenance, had, for the moment, a greater force than it ever had before.

And then he asked me whether, as things had turned out, I myself had been so especially happy.

PARIS, *December* 17*th*.—A note from young Stanmer, whom I saw in Florence—a remarkable little note, dated Rome, and worth transcribing:—

'My Dear General,—I have it at heart to tell you that I was married a week ago to the Countess Salvi-Scarabelli. You talked me into a great muddle; but a month after that it was all very clear. Things that involve a risk are like the Christian faith; they must be seen from the inside.—Yours ever, E.S.

'P.S.—*A fig for analogies—unless you can find an analogy for my happiness!'*

His happiness makes him very clever. I hope it will last!—I mean his cleverness, not his happiness.

LONDON, *April* 19*th*, 1877.—Last night, at Lady H—'s, I met Edmund Stanmer, who married Bianca Salvi's daughter. I heard the other day that they had come to England. A handsome young fellow, with a fresh, contented face. He reminded me of Florence, which I didn't pretend to forget; but it was rather awkward, for I remember I used to disparage that woman to him. I had a complete theory about her. But he didn't seem at all stiff; on the contrary, he appeared to enjoy our encounter. I asked him if his wife was there. I had to do that.

'Oh, yes, she's in one of the other rooms. Come and make her acquaintance; I want you to know her.'

'You forget that I do know her.'

'Oh, no, you don't; you never did.' And he gave a little significant laugh.

I didn't feel like facing the *ci-devant* Scarabelli at that moment; so I said that I was leaving the house, but that I would do myself the honour of calling upon his wife. We talked for a minute of something else, and then, suddenly, breaking off and looking at me, he laid his hand on my arm. I must do him the justice to say that he looks felicitous.

'Depend upon it, you were wrong!' he said.

'My dear young friend,' I answered, 'imagine the alacrity with which I concede it.'

Something else again was spoken of, but in an instant he repeated his movement.

'Depend upon it, you were wrong.'

'I am sure the Countess has forgiven me,' I said, 'and in that case you ought to bear no grudge. As I have had the honour to say I will call upon her immediately.'

'I was not alluding to my wife,' he answered. 'I was thinking of your own story.'

'My own story?'

'So many years ago. Was it not rather a mistake?'

I looked at him a moment; he's positively rosy.

'That's not a question to solve in a London crush.'

And I turned away.

22*nd.*—I haven't yet called on the *ci-devant.* I'm afraid of finding her at home. And that boy's words have been thrumming in my ears —'Depend upon it you were wrong. Wasn't it rather a mistake?' *Was* I wrong—*was* it a mistake? Was I too cautious—too suspicious—too logical? Was it really a protector she needed—a man who might have helped her? Would it have been for his benefit to believe in her, and was her fault only that I had forsaken her? Was the poor woman very unhappy? God forgive me, how the questions come crowding in! If I marred her happiness, I certainly didn't make my own. And I might have made it—eh? That's a charming discovery for a man of my age!

TEXTUAL VARIANTS

Introduction	
Benvolio	(1875/1879)
Four Meetings	(1877/1879/1909)
Théodolinde	(1878/1885)
Daisy Miller: A Study	(1878/1879/1909)
Longstaff's Marriage	(1878/1879)
An International Episode	(1878/1879/1908)
The Pension Beaurepas	(1879/1881/1908)

INTRODUCTION

In preparing this record of all substantive variants in the seven revised tales of the period some decisions of an editorial nature had to be taken: this introduction explains those decisions.

The variants listed below are keyed to the periodical versions of the tales—the original creations of which all later changes are, so to speak, offshoots—as reprinted in the present edition. I have taken all book editions of a tale published during James's lifetime and subjected them to textual comparison with the periodical text. The substantive variants revealed by the collation have been compiled in this record.

The overall authority of the revisions examined cannot be questioned: the five collections—*The Madonna of the Future, Daisy Miller: A Study, Stories Revived, Washington Square, Etc.*, and the New York Edition—where the revised versions of the tales first appeared, were all prepared by James himself. The authority, however, of individual instances of alteration is impossible to establish as none of the seven manuscript revisions has survived. In the absence of such evidence for comparison, the problem becomes a critical one. Needless to say, all substantive variants listed have been critically examined from the viewpoint of style and structure, and were found to conform to the context of meanings established in the originals. Remarkably few misprints have been noticed in the revised editions.

The decision to ignore all accidentals—variants of punctuation, contractions (I have/I've), expanded forms (I've/I have), paragraph division, spelling variants, etc.—is, of course, arbitrary. It is influenced by two factors. First, it is extremely difficult, if not altogether impossible, to record the variants of punctuation in a complex and large body of multiple texts such as the 112 tales of Henry James. Secondly, as readers of James know, in the matter of punctuation he was not very consistent. The difference between the early system of punctuation and that of the New York Edition is so great that the latter cannot be treated as anything but a new, highly idiosyncratic style. It was decided, therefore, to treat this aspect of the revisions separately in an essay to appear in the final volume of this edition. For the present it should suffice to say that the revised texts are lightly punctuated, and that most contractions there have been expanded. Although I have generally ignored the accidentals, punctuation variants in all substantively revised passages have been recorded.

Each of the seven lists opens with a brief headnote which singles out the texts that have been collated. The note does not mention that sample collations of all available reprints of the revised editions have been taken privately. For works with more than one revised form, capital letters of the alphabet have been used as identifying symbols for the various stages of revision. These symbols are explained in the first note and later appear against each entry. In most cases, the first note is followed by another set of notes which record the revised division of chapters, revised names of the characters, and similar other peculiarities of the revision.

For each entry the page and line references are to the text in the present edition. The usual square bracket divides the original from the revised form. Wherever possible, I have tried to divide the revisions into very small units of text, the original form of which is indicated preceding the square bracket. In the case of longer passages, however, three dots (. . .) have been used to cover the matter, of all lengths, left out. The ellipses cover not only substantive matter but also the punctuation, including full stops and quotation marks.

James often makes changes towards the end of his sentences and these usually add new matter. In recording such additions, the full stop coming at the end of the original sentence has *not* been indicated—unless the revised form closes with a different punctuation mark. The same treatment has been given to all punctuation marks coming *at the end* of a passage which has been revised without any change in the original punctuation mark.

A frequent, and significant, feature of the revisions is the readjustment of editorial directions in the dialogues—the changes made in the placing of such fictional props as 'he said', 'she said', etc. Since many of these alterations affect only the props, and not the speeches, a method had to be evolved in order to avoid long passages of unrevised matter. The following should explain the procedure adopted to deal with the problem. If, for example,

'No, I do not agree with you.'

is changed to

'No,' he said, 'I do not agree with you.'

the list would record the variant thus:

No, I do not] No,' he said, 'I do not

In other words, in the case of revisions involving dialogue, *only the relevant part* of the quotation marks has been indicated. And the same principle is employed in recording revisions where James has added something before or after a speech, or has omitted the stage direction. Also, in order to save space, the usual practice of transcribing dialogue in separate units has not been kept.

BENVOLIO

Note:

The variants recorded below are based on a collation of the original serial text of the tale (*Galaxy*, 1875) and its revised version in *The Madonna of the Future* (1879).

23 : 5	agreeable] profitable
9-10	He was . . . thirty-five] He was about to enter upon the third decade of our mortal span
11	property; he followed] property, and he followed
14-15	idea of . . . young man] ideal of manly beauty
24	dusky and ill-conditioned] perverse and dusky
31-2	sensitive] irritable
24 : 11-12	compounded . . . anomalies] a mixture of inconsistencies
13	absolute] om.
25	person] physiognomy
26-8	thrown . . . the machine] placed together to make the voyage of life in the same boat, and had agreed for convenience' sake to take the helm
28	machine] helm
30	kept . . . tune] worked very differently
40	moods] states of mind
25 : 5	trowsers] breeches
27-8	on either side] in either direction
42-3	cell . . . view] cell
26 : 3	came] had come
4	had seen] saw
6	pounded] rapped
12-13	square, and then] square. After this he would
15	a family] many relatives
16	sisters so] sisters were so
17	constantly] om.
19	an immense] a great
19	others] other moments
26-7	his hands . . . tight] he had a little golden ball and chain tied to his ankle
27-8	things was] things—life and love and art and truth—was
28-9	he satisfied . . . itself] his theory was to satisfy it as freely as might be
33-4	his imagination . . . worse] the gustatory faculty of his mind was loosing its keenness
34	glowing] savoury
36-7	pregnantly synthetic] comprehensive
38-41	such a . . . edges sharp] the mind can keep its freshness to the last, and that it is only fools that are overbored

41-3 certain possible . . . man's duty] way of never being bored, and the wise man's duty
27 : 5-6 (it might be concluded)] om.
6 occupations] occupation
10 entangle . . . human] multiply our relations with
10 get entangled] multiply his relations
11 pondered Benvolio] Benvolio reflected
12 ponder all this] reflect on this
14 cold] frigid
19 most] om.
19-20 entangle . . . sort] multiply his labours at least, and they should be very serious ones
21 handle] cultivate
36-7 way of . . . points out] relation with life which is a better antidote to ennui than any other—the relation established with a charming woman
28 : 1-2 categorically] in due form
7-8 pleased her] she listed
20 been the . . . time] played a part no less brilliant
26 dialogue] colloquy
26-7 unyielding, elegant] little oasis of luxury and
27 public] common
41-3 the number . . . announced] the effect upon the company of the announcement of their names
43 who liked] with his taste for
29 : 4 had herself refused] caused herself to be refused
16 a mutual] an answering
22 no idea . . . Now] not been thinking of changing her condition. But
23-5 had a great . . . other suitors] was perpetually thinking of it, and this negative quality in Benvolio was more present to her mind, gave her more to think about, than all the positiveness of her other suitors
32 mentally] om.
34 gone a-begging] never found a pair of wings
40-1 to be complete . . . her train] she valued him as a specimen of a rare and distinguished type
42-3 had it in . . . now,] appointed him to be her minstrel or her jester—it is to be feared that poor Benvolio would have figured rather dismally in the latter capacity; and at present
30 : 1 conveniently . . . of a] give such a man a place in her train as an illustrious
10 didn't care for her] was indifferent to her
10 did care] really cared
13 hiatus] lapse
31 : 30 have him] see that he was
32 : 17 constellations] firmament

20 strange] singular
20 stranger] more singular
42-3 I never . . . feeling it.] I assure you I don't resist it!
33 : 10 tribute] wooing
26 say] promise that
32 pack his bag] pay visits
34 expansive] inflated
34-5 the tide . . . in] he had begun to take in sail
37-8 school, suddenly] school, which had been suddenly
34 : 5 painted a couple] painted for a couple
6 one] remarkable work
9 glowed forth] bloomed out
29 she seemed . . . half-startled] there was something timid and tentative in her movements
42 had a fancy] formed a theory
35 : 8 in this . . . fashion] om.
8 really] during these hours
14 grey] grizzled
15 on] in
17 vine] creeper
18 fancy] suspect
29 befell] occurred
31 at . . . making] that her absence should make
31 with] for
32 didn't know] was ignorant of
40 broad] large
36 : 19 formulated the idea] devoted a formula to the idea
24 to take] for
29 on the corner] in the arcade
40 gentle] soundless
37 : 5 sciences . . . matters] sciences, matters, all of them, in which she seemed an expert
9 bibliophilist] old bibliophile
11 book] work
20 creeper] tendril
13-14 moment . . . or miss] moment—he had shaped it on the chance om.
15 was rightly aimed] would fit the case
16 of] who had been
38 : 9 quite still] motionless
10 movements] movement
11 fine sense] quick perception
12 cudgelled] tapped
21 on] in
25 He . . . it:] This he never noticed, however;
25-6 the great Place] all the arcades
31 would] should

39 : 10 most positively] om.
12-13 passion . . . degree] passion began to throb and flutter
22 we] you will
22 Very likely] Probably
31-2 steady-moving] softly-moving
43 old house] mansion
40 : 12 this one] his new abode
17 confess to] acknowledge
21 forgot] was capable of forgetting
26 finds] were to find
27-8 much high discourse] high colloquies
30 vowed] declared
32 thought otherwise] cared for more vulgar exercises
41 : 1-2 the appreciative . . . for] had not a charm, an interest, a character, for his appreciative mind
6 the charm] his entertainment
12 culture] intelligence
19 erudite, impressive, and] erudite and
20-1 sweet Scholastica] his devoted little daughter
25 and half-dimly] om.
33 certain] particular
37-8 her learning] her great learning
42 : 1 own] om.
3 learned maiden] little handmaid of science
6-7 clear . . . definite] perfect understanding—a mind as clear and still and natural as a woodland pool, giving back an exact and definite
7-10 presented to it . . . And] presented to it. And
14-15 For . . . organism] Benvolio said to himself that she was exquisitely constituted for helping a man
28-9 autumnal . . . the days] autumn afternoons began to grow vague
34-5 because . . . attentive] because she not only attended but she followed
35 had had women fix] had known women to fix
38 followed . . . him] gazed at him, but she understood him too
43 : 5 it] abstract science
7-8 was in . . . her a] suddenly found himself thinking of her as a
16-17 He found . . . of it] He left town and made his pilgrimage to her estate, where he found her holding her usual court and leading a merry life om.
18-19 of his life] he had ever known
20 nor] or
25 dozen . . . fire] hundred arrows in her quiver
27-8 that time . . . constant] such a time very assiduous
31 offered . . . setting] were a natural occasion
39-40 enjoyed . . . to maturity] greatly enjoyed his attempt to make a work of art of it

41 their proper mission] the proper mission of his faculties
43 bald . . . formulas] dry chopping of logic
44 : 2 act] don the buskin
2-3 she . . . talent] of her aptitude for the stage
6 the unexpected, the unforeseen] the unexpected
8 because] for
18 fairly] om.
19-20 paid . . . work] he saw or heard was grist to his mill
20-1 Life . . . becoming] Life on these terms became really
23-4 At . . . winter] When the winter nights had begun,
30 wrong conjectures] mistakes
32 his comedy . . . hands] the witticisms in his play and his comedy had begun to seem as mechanical
45 : 3 all summer] all the summer
10 cultivated] appealed to
17-18 in . . . fashion] for a fancy
20 at once, for all time] at once and for ever
21 could imagine] imagined
23 irresistibly] om.
23-4 it . . . He felt] a delicate resentment. Benvolio felt
28 in your fancy] om.
35 resentment] displeasure
37 chapter of] passage in a
39 dull . . . life] ignorance of the great world
41 about . . . reserve] very freely about the Countess
46 : 5 his way . . . for him] his way—it only seemed so at moments. For him
46-7 happiness . . . concentration.] real felicity was in the pleasure of study!
7 extreme pleasure] high satisfaction
9-10 with . . . to it] to cultivate so rare a faculty
16 perhaps . . . cruel] is perhaps most cruel
16 evade] escape
22 philosophical] philosophic
23 morning] evening
37 philosophy, history, and all] om.
47 : 1 alternation . . . contrast] alternation and contrast
4 point, it] point of choosing one thing or the other, it
11 away, which] away with a vague reproachfulness that was at the same time an encouragement, which
25 drew] banished
29 miserly] parsimonious
32-3 measured . . . made] measured out a part of his annual dole, made
43-48:1 the Countess] the Countess, with half a dozen of them in his pocket
48 : 8-9 impressive . . . in his finding] noble in his indifference, his want of eagerness, his finding

11 an account] an account with fame
19-20 little . . . and as she] syren, and as she
23 made . . . give] induced Benvolio to give
26 the room] a certain vestibule
49 : 1 estate] domain
14 for dinner] om.
17 light] blaze
23-4 fiddles] violins
25 petition] request
42 that quite satisfied] to satisfy
50 : 8 oddest] strangest
15 after his return] on reaching town
18 dingy little Quakeress] little dingy blue-stocking
21 blue-stocking] schoolmistress
23 could be so little] was so little to be
37 is] would be
43 the] om.
51 : 14 recur] often occur
15 caressing] genial
21-2 surrender . . . the more] pay our young man the tribute of her luxurious liberty. She admired him more
36 in] for
52 : 5-6 movements . . . fancied] movements were angular, her charming eye was dull
6 her] this charming
10 charm] great attraction
15-16 bade fair] promised
19 discretion] knowledge
23 ripened with] rejoiced in
27 and they] which
27 a vast] an immense
35 he] Benvolio
37-8 this pure] his
53 : 40 trifles . . . air] small accidents
6 proclaimed] replied
17 nothing] blankness
27 unfortunately] ridiculously
28 would] should
35 and to] and in order to
36 infernally . . . charge] ingenious calumny
38 the coldest civility] grim indifference
40 profoundly . . . indiscretion] furious at the mistake she had made
42 please] gratify
54 : 7-8 on . . . bench] in a dusky arbour
9 her . . . sadder] her sweet face was more joyless
13 affliction] mourning aspect

17 a boundless] the tenderest
23 high philosophical] philosophic
26 where she was] in her present abode
29 appealing] tender
30 secret] om.
30 her on] her again on
32 with . . . which] to be married to the Countess, and that this understanding
33 her] Scholastica
36 a great . . . enterprise] a useful and interesting task
43 about gossip] about vulgar gossip
55 : 9 was] were
16 little] om.
17 an ivory ball] a ball of ivory
21 stiver] penny
24 trowsers] breeches
30 forfeiture] relinquishment
36 his . . . walks] those long walks to which he had always been addicted
36 park] public gardens
56 : 6 our young . . . goings] the history of this amiable weathercock
15-16 And . . . talked of] And their talk, you may be sure, was not all technical; they touched on
17-18 forbade . . . sacred] felt obliged to be silent about those mundane matters as to which a
19 wholly] om.
25 this he had] this production he
32 double] complex
35 became . . . depressed] lost her peace of mind
40 making . . . her] a terrible thorn in her side
41 pleased her] she liked
57 : 3 that before] that he requested that before
8 silent] shrinking and unexpressed
17 befell] happened
19-20 unquenchable] imperious
22 for . . . purpose] to treat of a special question
36 she] the girl
38 was placed in] were placed before her in
58 : 7 returned] should return
7-8 his actual] his brilliant actual
12 at . . . bargain] for a very small sum
30-1 The . . . aversion] This repulsive proprietor, in spite of his constitutional aversion
37-8 intensely] woefully
39 old . . . garden] old brown room
39-41 He . . . he reflected] He only half succeeded in a fashion; it seemed dark and empty; doubly empty when he remembered

59 : 9	say] relate
13	said, his] said that his
14	this] it

FOUR MEETINGS

Notes:

1. The variants recorded below are based on a collation of the original serial text of the tale (*Scribner's Monthly*, 1877) and its two revised versions in *Daisy Miller: A Study* (1879)—hereinafter mentioned as A—and *The Author of Beltraffio, Etc.* (1909)—hereinafter mentioned as B.

2. In texts A and B the prologue is followed by four chapters, and not three as in the original version. The revised chapter division occurs at 124:29 thus dividing the original second chapter into two chapters.

3. The original Grimwinter is changed to North Verona in text B.

114 : 1	but four] only four A; but four B
2	an] her B
2	upon] on B
3	charming] touching B
3	type] type with which I had had other and perhaps less charming associations B
4	sorry] om. B
5	I will describe all] it will be of interest to take B
7	one took place] was B
7	little] small B
8	night. It . . . some] night of some B
10	persuaded . . . him] insisted on my company B
11-12	entertaining] full of savour—it had all the right marks B
15	perceived] inferred B
15-16	at Grimwinter . . . an effort] just those general rigours rendered any assembly offering the attraction of two gentlemen from New York worth a desperate effort B
23	standing] om.
24	mantel-shelf, and looking] mantel-shelf who looked B
24-5	small . . . somehow,] small vague smile, a discreet, a disguised yearning, which seemed somehow at odds B
26	said] chose B
115 : 3	rejoined] replied B
3-4	was, perhaps, not] wasn't perhaps B
4-5	already gone . . . to her] already, with a few steps, appealed to her participation B
6	she said, coming back. 'She is] my hostess came back to repeat; 'and she's B
7	then] om. B
8	Miss Caroline Spencer, and with this] Miss Caroline Spencer —with which B
9	exactly] quite B
9-11	she was a . . . and she had] was none the less, in her small odd way, formed to please. Close upon thirty, by every presumption, she was made almost like a little girl and had B

12 a very pretty head, and] also the prettiest head, on which B

13-14 though it . . . in plaster] though indeed it was to be doubted if she had ever seen a Greek bust AB

15-17 Grimwinter . . . Round her neck] the polar influences of North Verona could allow for such yearnings or could minister to them. Her eyes were perhaps just too round and too inveterately surprised, but her lips had a certain mild decision and her teeth, when she showed them, were charming. About her neck B

18 in] of B

20-2 a kind of . . . even a little] slow soft neatness, even without smiles showing the prettiness of her teeth, and she seemed extremely pleased, in fact quite B

27 copies] reproductions B

28 about] for B

29 with] om. B

29-30 under lip] under-lip and gently, yet, as I could feel, almost excitedly, rubbing it B

30-1 very softly,] without confidence, which would have been too much: B

32 traveller), and] traveller, though I was somehow particularly admonished not to swagger—and B

32-3 that she looked] her look B

34-5 she answered . . . whisper] she had answered 'No, no, no'—almost as much below her breath as if the image of such an event scarce, for solemnity, brooked phrasing B

37 was . . . bored] feared she was at last bored B

37 after] when B

38-9 I felt . . . bored] I rather guessed the exhibition really held her B

39 wished] wanted B

40 look at . . . there was] judge better and then saw B

41 was] kept B

42-3 upon the . . . the table] on the remainder of the collection, which leaned, in its receptacle, against the table B

116 : 1-2 asked . . . was agitated] quavered, drawing the long breath of a person launched and afloat but conscious of rocking a little B

3 you are not] you're really not B

4 'No, I . . . love it.'] 'Oh I'm not tired a bit. I'm just fascinated.' B

5 And . . . up the] With which as I took up the B

5 upon] on B

7 she asked.] om. B

8 that I had been] I had indeed been B

10 on] by B

11 Is it not] Isn't it B

15 was not where Bonnivard] weren't where Bonnivard B

15 was] had been B
16 and tried] trying B
16-17 some of . . . helpless] some of Byron's verses, but in this attempt I succeeded imperfectly A; Byron's verses, but not quite bringing it off B
19 flat . . . voice] flat voice but with charming conviction B
20 was blushing] was nevertheless blushing B
20 told] assured B
22 whether I was] if I might be B
25 asked] thereupon inquired B
27 I think] Well, I guess B
27 do it] go AB
27 within ten years] in *that* time B
27 very soberly] as if measuring her words B
28-9 'Well,' . . . And just] 'Then you'll enjoy it immensely,' I said; 'you'll find it of the highest interest.' Just B
31-2 a certain eloquence] considerable spirit B
33 in foreign lands] over there B
35 'Many years,' I said.] 'Well, it mounts up, put all the times together.' B
38 I] om. B
39 gave . . . gaze] turned on me her slow shy scrutiny B
40 And do] Do B
43 believe] imagine B
43 hard] so B
43 responded] answered B
117 : 1-2 listen,' she said.] listen.' B
2 after] on B
4 It is] Ah B
5 go very] go there very B
8 she hesitated . . . wonderful.'] her expression hovered—'as if you tell me a fairy-tale.' B
9 asked] put to me B
10 Which] And which B
11 country . . . others] I love beyond any B
12 She . . . softly] Her gaze rested as on a dim revelation and then she breathed B
13-14 looked at each other] communed over it B
15-16 analogy . . . which] resemblance she turned off blushing. It made a pause which B
18 have] om. B
19 said] laughed B
20 photographs] more views B
21 so dear] very dear B
22 Yes . . . charms] Well, one gets back there one's money. That's not the least of the charms B
23 all pretty dear] *all* very expensive B
26 I teach] I give lessons A; I teach, you know B

27 Of course] Oh of course B

27 said,] allowed; B

28 amount] amount judiciously spent B

29 laid . . . I am] saved and saved up, and I'm B

31 a kind of] om. B

32 a possibly] possibly an B

32-3 But it has not] You see it hasn't B

34 been] acted B

34 a mere] my B

36 been] come B

38 that such talking] such talk B

40 go; I . . . to her] go, but I'm always at her B

40 I tire] I think I must tire B

41 once] just the other day B

42 I should . . . certainly] She guessed I'd go crazy if I didn't sail, and yet certainly I'd go B

118 : 1 said] laughed B

1-2 gone yet . . . not crazy] sailed up to now—so I suppose you *are* crazy B

3-5 She looked . . . things that] She took everything with the same seriousness. 'Well, I guess I must be. It seems as if I couldn't think of anything else—and I don't require photo-tgraphs to work me up! I'm always right *on* it. It kills any interest in things nearer home—things B

7 The] Well then the B

7 to go,' I said.] just to go,' I smiled—'I mean the cure for this kind. Of course you may have the other kind worse,' I added—'the kind you get over there.' B

8 'I have . . . there.'] 'I have a faith that I shall go. I have a cousin in Europe!' she announced. A; 'Well, I've a faith that I'll go *some* time all right!' she quite elatedly cried. 'I have a relative right there on the spot,' she went on, 'and I guess he'll know how to control me.' B

9-13 We turned . . . would probably] I expressed the hope that he would, and I forget whether we turned over more photo-graphs; but when I asked her if she had always lived just where I found her, 'Oh no, sir,' she quite eagerly replied; 'I've spent twenty-two months and a half in Boston.' I met it with the inevitable joke that in this case foreign lands might B

15-24 think,' she said . . . shall know it all.'] think'—her earnest-ness resisted even that. 'I mean by reading—for I've really read considerable. In fact I guess I've prepared my mind about as much as you *can*—in advance. I've not only read Byron—I've read histories and guide-books and articles and lots of things. I know I shall rave about everything.'

'"Everything" is saying much, but I understand your

case,' I returned. 'You've the great American disease, and you've got it ''bad''—the appetite, morbid and monstrous, for colour and form, for the picturesque and romantic at any price. I don't know whether we come into the world with it—with the germs implanted and antecedent to experience; rather perhaps we catch it early, almost before developed consciousness—we *feel*, as we look about, that we're going (to save our souls, or at least our senses) to be thrown back on it hard. We're like travellers in the desert—deprived of water and subject to the terrible mirage, the torment of illusion, of the thirst-fever. They hear the plash of fountains, they see green gardens and orchards that are hundred of miles away. So we with *our* thirst—except that with us it's *more* wonderful: we have before us the beautiful old things we've never seen at all, and when we do at last see them—if we're lucky!—we simply recognize them. What experience does is merely to confirm and consecrate our confident dream.'

She listened with her rounded eyes. 'The way you express it's too lovely, and I'm sure it will be just like that. I've dreamt of everything—I'll know it all!' B

28-9 with a . . . eyes] as if quite shining and throbbing B

30 there,' I said,] there—one *has* to,' I said B

32-4 'I will tell . . . little straw fan] Yes, she fairly glittered with her fever of excited faith. 'Well, I'll tell you if I'm disappointed.' And she left me, fluttering all expressively her little straw fan B

35 returned to Europe] crossed the sea eastward again B

37 I] om. B

37 to Havre] to the Havre B

37 my sister and her husband,] a pair of relatives B

38 that] om. B

38-119:1 reaching . . . hours late] reaching the Havre I found the steamer already docked—I was two or three hours late B

119 : 1 relatives were already] travellers were duly B

2 disgusted] disabled AB

3 a wretchedly poor sailor,] a sadly incompetent sailor, A; the unsteadiest of sailors B

4 wished,] desired B

4-5 moment, for undisturbed] moment undisturbed B

5 unable] able B

5 for more than] but B

5-6 five minutes. It was agreed] five minutes; so it was agreed A; five minutes—long enough for us to agree B

6-7 that we . . . the next day] to stop over, restoratively, till the morrow B

7 who was] om. B

8-9 upon his . . . land-legs] on my taking him a walk for aid to recovery of his spirits and his land-legs B

10	was sufficiently entertaining] beguiling enough B
13	looked like] resembled B
17	white caps] white-capped women AB
18	street] vista B
19	brother-in-law] companion B
21	coming to] reaching B
24	nice] dear B
25	old fashioned] old-world B
26	with] who had B
27	who was] placed B
28	All this, however, I perceived] This, to be exact, I noted B
29	sitting] seated B
30-1	There was . . . quietly,] Something had been put before her, but she only leaned back, motionless and B
32	street, away] street and away B
32-3	only in something less than] but in diminished B
33-4	instantly . . . before] was sure I knew on the spot that we must already have met B
35	exclaimed my brother-in-law] my companion cried B
36	asked] asked with interest B
40	Are you] And are you B
41-2	I was too seedy] I wasn't in form to make up to ladies B
120 : 3	turned] had now turned B
4	to her] om. B
4	Then I said:] On this I decided. B
8	a whole winter's evening'] om. AB
9	And I] With which I B
9-11	her. She . . . startled] her, making her, as she turned to look at me, leave me in no doubt of her identity. Miss Caroline Spencer had achieved her dream. But she was less quick to recognize me and showed a slight bewilderment B
14-15	which betrayed recognition] and placed me B
16	Grimwinter!] North Verona. B
17	I feel as if it were] isn't it quite B
18	an official] the official B
20	so . . . exclaimed] so intensely happy!' she declared B
21	happy she] happy indeed she B
23	seemed before] struck me then as B
24	delicate] clear B
25	apparent] appealing B
26	was calling] called B
28	my companion] the gentleman with me B
30	seen him before] so much as seen him B
30	that] om. B
31	that] om. B
31	upon] on B
33	she] om. B
33	that she had] the contrary B

34 at the café door, and] on the little terrace of the café while B
35 said to Miss Spencer] remarked to my friend B
35 in] at B
36 was really very strange;] partook, among all chances, of the miraculous, B
38 as if I were] so much B
39 for] om. B
40-1 picturesque. I don't . . . delicious] delicious and romantic. I don't know whether the coffee has gone to my head—it's *so* unlike the coffee of my dead past B
42 said I] I made answer B
42 old] om. AB
43 shabby] om. AB
43 admiration] appreciation B
121 : 3 Italy!] Italy we talked about. B
5 day, saying] day—just saying B
6 dark, and old,] dark and strange—so old B
7-8 way,' . . . you not] way then,' I asked, 'how come you to be encamped in this odd place? Haven't you B
10 at a café door] on the edge of the sidewalk AB
11 here,' she answered] here and—a little while ago—left me,' she returned B
12 cousin in Europe. He] relation over here. He's still here—a real cousin. Well,' she pursued with unclouded candour, 'he B
12-13 morning.' 'It was] morning.' It was absurd—and the case moreover none of my business; but I felt somehow disconcerted. 'It was B
15 Miss Spencer] Caroline Spencer B
16 money.'] money.' I continued to wonder. B
18 She . . . laugh] She appeared seldom to laugh, but she laughed for the joy of this B
19 some] om. B
21 My cousin has them] In my cousin's pocket AB
22 very serenely uttered, but] uttered with such clearness of candour that B
23 certain] sensible AB
23-4 At the . . . I knew] At the moment I should have been utterly unable to give the reason of this sensation, for I knew A; I couldn't at all at the moment have justified my lapse from ease, for I knew B
24-6 cousin, and . . . uncomfortable at] cousin. Since he was her cousin, the presumption was in his favour. But I felt suddenly uncomfortable at A; cousin. Since he stood in that relation to her—dear respectable little person—the presumption was in his favour. But I found myself wincing at B
29 there] in Paris—I've always thought that so splendid B

32 he *is* very kind] he *is*,' said Caroline Spencer, 'very kind B

33-4 I instantly . . . this bright] I felt at once a strange eagerness to see this bright kind B

35 asked] enquired B

37 delicious] cunning B

40 haven't got] hadn't B

42 here, and] here—then B

122 : 1 It . . . fantastic] Her story was wholly lucid and my impression perfectly wanton B

1 he] the gentleman B

2 in my] in a B

2-3 Miss Spencer] my friend B

3-4 She was . . . in it] She was lost in the vision and the imagination of everything near us and about us—she observed, she recognized and admired, with a touching intensity B

5 the movement . . . before us] was brought before us by the movement of the street B

6 costumes] costume B

7 things. There] things, and there B

9 recognized and welcomed everything] sallied forth for the revel B

11 asked] went on B

12 She hesitated a moment] For this she had, a little oddly, to think B

16 that. My] that.' So far she was prepared. 'My B

18 said nothing more] had nothing to add B

19 her cousin] our absentee B

20-1 bright American] bright and kind American B

21 that Havre] that the Havre B

27 picturesque,] remarkable B

28 looked like a] figured a sort of B

28-9 St. Angelo . . . demolished.)] Saint Angelo. (I might really have foreknown that it was to be demolished.) B

30 she] om. B

34 until] till B

35 quickly] right off B

36 fortress. There is] fortress. Francis the First, did you say? Why, that's lovely. There's B

38-9 words. But . . . her eye] words, yet, looking at her with a purpose, I made out in her eyes, I thought, a tiny gleam of apprehension B

40 now] om. B

41-2 news!' 'I suspect] news!' She coloured as if convicted of a hidden perversity, but she was soaring too high to drop. 'Well, I guess B

123 : 1-2 I looked . . . came to see!'] I usurped an unscrupulous authority. 'Look here; you didn't come to Europe to listen—you came to *see*!' B

4 he certainly would come back] he certainly would turn up A; he'd infallibly turn up B
5-6 she told . . . From] told over the names as solemnly as a daughter of another faith might have told over the beads of a rosary; from B
11 religiously] scrupulously A; civilly B
11-12 kindling her suspicions] disturbing her sense of security B
14 upon] on B
14-15 felt . . . bright] knew he could but be the bright, if not the kind B
17-18 revealed . . . which,] displayed a stretch of throat that B
19 So much I had time to observe] These items I had time to take in B
21 umbrageous coiffure] romantic brim B
22 to him] om. B
22-3 Miss Spencer] Miss Spencer's, a character she serenely permitted me to claim B
23 little red] small sharp B
24 made] gave B
24 bow] wave, B
24 French] 'European' B
24 with his sombrero] of his rather rusty sombrero B
25 said] asked B
26 three] several B
28 solemnly] portentously B
29 it was] om. B
31 cousin . . . fellow] European protector was, by my measure, a very queer quantity B
32 naked] exhibited though not columnar B
33 was] were B
36 small, strange-coloured eyes] keen conscious strange-coloured eyes—of a brown that was almost red B
37 treacherous] too shifty B
38 cane] stick B
39 his cane] the stick B
40 remarked, softly] dropped with a certain flatness B
41 on] to B
41 side, and . . . half closed] side—he narrowed his ugly lids B
124 : 1 he] om. B
2 well,' . . . nice thing.'] well. Fine old tone. Make a nice thing.' B
3 strange, weak drawl] hard, vulgar voice A; charmless vulgar voice B
8-9 Still he . . . I asked] Still on this he continued to fix me, and then he named one of the greatest of that day; which led me to ask him if he liked his master B
10 said] returned B

11 kinds,' I answered.] kinds.' B

12 then he said—'*Je l'adore*!'] then he said—'*J'adore la peinture*!' A; with which he remarked: '*Je suis fou de la peinture*!' B

13 rejoined] replied B

13 Miss Spencer] Our companion B

14 upon her cousin's] on his B

14 little] small B

15-16 so . . . tongues] on such easy terms with foreign tongues B

16 Miss Spencer] her B

17 upon] on B

18 should] would B

19 honoured] favoured B

22 I . . . there] Well, that's the shop B

23 Caroline Spencer] Miss Spencer B

24 and] but B

25 upon] on B

26 said Miss Spencer] she returned B

26-7 *À la* . . .Cook] *À la Belle Normande* B

28-9 As I left . . . hat] 'I guess I know my way round!' her kinsman threw in; and as I left them he gave me with his swaggering head-cover a great flourish that was like the wave of a banner over a conquered field B

30 sister] relative B

31 Havre] the place B

32-3 sign of the 'Beautiful Cook.'] sign of the Fair Norman. A; establishment named to me by my friends B

33-4 my charming . . . telling her] the less attractive of these had been telling the other B

35 The *Belle Cuisinière*] The 'Belle Normande' A; The *auberge* of the Belle Normande B

40 statuette in] statuette set in B

125 : 2 perceived] distinguished B

3 saw that] was sure B

3-6 She was . . . her apricots] Supported by the back of her bench, with her hands clapped in her lap, she kept her eyes on the other side of the court where the landlady manipulated the apricots B

7 she was . . . apricots] that, poor dear, she wasn't thinking of apricots or even of landladies B

8 as I came . . . that she] on a nearer view I could have certified she B

9-11 I sat down . . . upon me] I had seated myself beside her before she was aware; then, when she had done so, she simply turned round without surprise and showed me her sad face B

12-13 changed. I] changed, and I B

14-15 news; you are in great distress] news. You've had a horrid time B

16-19 that she was . . . that she was] her afraid to speak lest her tears should again rise. Then it came to me that even in the few hours since my leaving her she had shed them all—which made her B

19-20 softly stoical and composed] softly stoical—intensely composed A; intensely, stoically composed B

21 is in distress] has been having one B

21 said] replied B

21 His news was bad] He has had great worries. His news was bad B

22 brief hesitation] dismally conscious wait B

22 terrible] dreadful B

24 that] om. B

24 honestly . . . money] honourably of course. Mine *is* all—well, that's available B

25 'And] Ah, it was as if I had been sure from the first! 'And B

26 She hesitated . . . glance,] Again she hung fire, but her face B

29 I have always remembered] I recall B

30-1 piece of . . . jumped up] bit of human utterance I had ever listened to; but then, almost with a sense of personal outrage I jumped up A; human sound I had ever listened to—which is exactly why I jumped up almost with a sense of personal outrage B

32 'Good . . . honestly?'] 'Gracious goodness, madam, do you call that his getting it "honourably"?' B

31 But] om. AB

32 blushed deeply] coloured to her eyes B

33 it,' she said.] it.' B

35 answered, sitting down] declared as I dropped beside her B

36 friend; it] friend—upon my word I'm your protector; it B

36-7 your cousin] this extraordinary person B

38 'He is] She was perfectly able to say. 'He's just badly B

39 doubt] doubt he is B

39 fitness . . . debts] propriety of your—in such tearing haste!—paying for that B

40 He] Well, he B

40 story . . . for him] story. I *feel* for him so much B

41 am I] do I, if you come to that B

41 hope he will] hope,' I roundly added, 'he'll B

41 you back] you straight back B

42 'Certainly] As to this she was prompt. 'Certainly B

42 will; as soon as] will—as soon as ever B

43 When] And when the deuce B

126 : 1 'When] Her lucidity maintained itself. 'When B

2 'My dear] It took me full in the face. 'My dear B

2 confound] damn B

3 unhappy cousin] voracious man B

4 She . . . answered.] It was as if she must let me feel a moment that I did push her!—though indeed, as appeared, he was just where he'd naturally be. 'He's having his dinner.' B

6 There, alone] There, sure enough, alone B

6-7 I perceived . . . bright young] was the object of my friend's compassion—the bright, the kind young B

9-10 observant attitude] air of observation B

11 lank] meagre AB

12 lightly brushing by] brushing lightly by B

13 exclaimed] wailed B

15 do that . . . murmured] seem to arrange everything so nicely!' she simply sighed B

17 approve of . . . funds] think it right, do you think it decent, that that long strong fellow should collar your funds B

19 great long] long strong B

20 Excuse] Pardon B

21 is not . . . enough] hasn't, clearly, the rudiments of delicacy B

23 she answered; 'I] she obstinately said—'of course I B

25 upon] on B

27 extreme] real B

27-8 poor wife] poor young wife B

29 poor wife] poor young wife B

30 it,] om. B

30 confessed everything] made a clear breast of it B

33 Caroline . . . about her,] My informant took precautions B

34 softly . . . tone—] with low impressiveness: B

34 a] the B

37 you . . . eh] you—whom she has never seen—for money B

37-8 I pursued . . . irresistibly.] om. AB

39 said Miss Spencer] Miss Spencer spoke now with spirit B

40-127:2 disinherited by . . . in Provence.'] cruelly treated by her family—in consequence of what she has done for him. My cousin has told me every particular, and she appeals to me in her own lovely way in the letter, which I've here in my pocket. It's such a wonderful old-world romance,' said my prodigious friend. 'She was a beautiful young widow—her first husband was a Count, tremendously high-born but really most wicked, with whom she hadn't been happy and whose death had left her ruined after he had deceived her in all sorts of ways. My poor cousin, meeting her in that situation and perhaps a little too recklessly pitying her and charmed with her, found her, don't you see?'—Caroline's appeal on this head was amazing!—'but too ready to trust a better man after all she had been through. Only when her "people", as he says—and I do like the word!—understood she would have him, poor gifted young American art-student though he simply was, because she just adored him, her great-aunt, the old Marquise, from whom she had expectations of wealth which she could yet sacrifice for her love, utterly cast her off and wouldn't so much as speak to her, much less to *him*, in their dreadful haughtiness and pride. They *can* be haughty over here, it seems,' she ineffably developed—'there's no mistake about that! It's like something in some famous old book. The family, my cousin's wife's,' she by this time almost complacently wound up, 'are of the oldest Provençal noblesse.' B

127 : 3 I looked and listened, marvelling] I looked and listened, in wonder A; I listened half bewildered B

3-6 It really . . . meant for her] The poor woman positively found it so interesting to be swindled by a flower of that stock—if stock or flower or solitary grain of truth was really concerned in the matter—as practically to have lost the sense of what the forfeiture of her hoard meant for her B

7 said] groaned B

7-8 ruined . . . sake?] stripped of every dollar for such a rigmarole! B

9-14 'I shall not be . . . she answered.] She asserted, at this, her dignity—much as a small pink shorn lamb might have done. 'It isn't a rigmarole, and I shan't be stripped. I shan't live any worse than I *have* lived, don't you see? And I'll come back before long to stay with them. The Countess—he still gives her, he says, her title, as they do to noble widows, that is to "dowagers", don't you know? in England—insists on a visit from me *some* time. So I guess for *that* I can start afresh—and meanwhile I'll have recovered my money.' It was all too heart-breaking. 'You're going home then at once?' I felt the faint tremor of voice she heroically tried to stifle. 'I've nothing left for a tour.' B

16 home] back B

17-18 I gave . . . of her] I uttered, I think, a positive howl, and at this juncture the hero of the situation, the happy proprietor of my little friend's B

18 precious purse] sacred savings AB

18-19 hand . . . dining-room] infatuated *grande dame* just sketched for me, reappeared with the clear consciousness of a repast bravely earned and consistently enjoyed B

20 for] om. B

20 removing] extracting B

21 which . . . the table] he had fondly retained B

22 sojourn] gratefully dissolve B

22 gratefully,] om. B

23 dropped] thrust B

24 jacket] coat B

25 which] that B

25-6	seemed to designate] expressed AB
26-7	a strange . . . perverted] at once resignation and fascination —the last dregs of her sacrifice and with it an anguish of B
27	enthusiasm] exaltation A; upliftedness B
28	the creature . . . appealed] him, and destitute of every grace of plausibility, he had yet appealed B
29	but most innocent] and tender AB
29	profoundly] deeply AB
30	absolutely] om. AB
30	interfere. Besides, I] interfere, and at any rate I A; interfere, and at any rate B
32-4	The young . . . staircase.'] He waved his hand meanwhile with a breadth of appreciation. 'Nice old court. Nice mellow old place. Nice crooked old staircase. Several pretty things.' B
35	was too . . . Without] couldn't stand it; without A; couldn't stand it, and without B
36	Caroline Spencer] my friend B
37	expanded] rounded B
39	said,] sublimely pleaded; B
40	Europe] this dear old Europe AB
41	told her . . . goodbye,] refused, however, to take literal leave of her— B
42	the] om. B
42	cousin] awful kinsman B
128 : 1	with] upon A; on B
2	took my departure] hurried away B
3-4	The next . . . landlady] On the morrow early I did return, and in the court of the inn met the landlady B
5	said the landlady] said the hostess A; the good woman said B
8	away; the poor] off—I felt the tears in my eyes. The poor B
8	about] some B
9	was . . . longer] continued to sacrifice to opportunity as I myself met it B
10	period I] period—of some five years—I B
11	return] return to America B
12	Grimwinter to pay] North Verona on a B
13	I] om. B
15	praise] praises B
16	terminated] ended B
18	upon] to B
19	back] off B
24-5	retire . . . and take] retire, and I described myself as anxious for B
27	will walk to her house] think I'll call on her B
31	bedstead] bedstead swung in the air B
32	go and see] look up B

32 said Mrs. Latouche] Mrs. Latouche further enjoined B
36-7 'I mean . . . her phrase] 'To see, I mean, a charming visitor' —Mrs. Latouche amended her phrase B
38 of visitors] of charming visitors B
39 enjoined] returned B
39-40 glancing at me] with significant eyes on me B
129 : 1 inquired, perplexed] asked in my ignorance B
2 see] make out B
7 ironical] sarcastic B
8 She's a countess] "Madame la Comtesse" B
9 this word] these titular words B
10 countess's face] face of the lady they designated B
10-11 a moment,] om. B
17 frugal] withdrawn B
18 the picturesque] striking effects inexpensively obtained B
21 which] that B
22 way of a countess] shape of a Comtesse B
23 and] om. B
23 it] which B
24-5 on either side] right and left B
27 of chairs] of light chairs B
32 that] om. B
32 was very shabby. I] to be of the shabbiest and B
33 intrude, for] penetrate, since B
34 seemed . . . indelicate] failed of confidence B
34 hesitated] demurred B
36-7 looked at . . . me before] faced me as if we had never met B
38 and then . . . badinage] where I spoke with an attempt at friendly banter B
40-1 she asked . . . than before] she quavered, her innocent eyes rounding themselves as of old B
43 waited at Havre] I waited at the old French port B
130 : 1-2 She stared . . . and clasped] She stared harder, then recognized me, smiling, flushing, clasping B
3 now,' she said. 'I] now—I B
6 awkward . . . path] awkward while I poked at the path with my stick B
7 year,' I said.] year.' B
8 murmured Miss Spencer] she ruefully breathed B
12 for a moment] thus B
13 thought . . . one sees] caught the expression visible B
14 upon] on B
15 the] her B
16 behind her] om. B
16 she . . . intently,] her strained smile prevailed B
16 that] om. B
18 she asked . . . whisper] she lowered her voice to ask B
20 looking . . . smile] shining at me as she could B

21 opened] reopened B
21 again] om. B
24 she answered . . . ever] she wouldn't hear of it now B
26 went in, following her] followed her in B
31 very] om. B
31 that] om. B
34 in so graceful a fashion] with so touching a grace B
35 portion] section B
35 with] om. B
36-7 it would . . . as pretty] I needn't now have felt called to insist on the facts of her person B
37-8 thought her . . . touching] still thought them interesting, and at any rate I was moved by them B
38 evidently] peculiarly AB
40 memory] echo B
40-1 little friendship . . . Havre] concentrated passage in the old French port B
42 You are distressed] Again you're in distress B
131 : 3 at Havre] at the Havre B
4 She shook] She wonderfully shook B
6 'I] Ah was it? my manner of receiving this must have commented. 'I B
6 shocked,' I rejoined, 'as] shocked as B
7 set sail again] wretchedly retreated B
8 a moment; and then] an instant, after which B
10 asked] nevertheless went on B
11 I had gone away] my first start B
13-15 'Oh, yes!' . . . brutal] 'Every minute of the time.' I took it in; I didn't know what to say, and what I presently said had almost the sound of mockery. 'When then are you going to make that tour?' It might be practically aggressive B
16 the softness of her] her depths of B
18 fixed . . . upon] attached her eyes a moment to B
20-1 it. Presently . . . she said:] it. I waited, watching her with interest—as if she had still something more to give me. Well, presently, in answer to my last question, she gave it. B
23-4 'I hope . . . from me.] 'I hope at least your cousin repaid you that money,' I said. At this again she looked away from me. 'I don't care for it now.' B
26 For going] For ever going B
28 over; I] over. Everything's different. I B
30 He] The scoundrel B
30 exclaimed] cried B
32 she stopped] she had stopped B
33 rustling] rustle B
37 my glance to receive] me to rise to B
40-1 'Excuse my . . . company—the] '*Pardon, ma chère*! I didn't

know you had company,' she said, 'The B

42 she directed . . . again] she again gave me the benefit of her attention B

43 yet my . . . that] yet I was at once sure B

132 : 1-2 Then I . . . very much] Afterwards I rather put it that I had only seen ladies remarkably B

2-4 Grimwinter, and . . . seemed to] North Verona, and it was the oddest of all things to meet one of them in that frame. To what quite other scene did the sight of her B

5 mussy] greasy B

7 dressing-gown] wrapper B

8 Miss Spencer's visitor] My friend's guest B

8 woman] lady B

11 an agreeable smile] *le sourire agréable* B

11 all] old B

12 'Madame,'] the figure B

13 was holding it together] confined it B

16 agreeable smile] *sourire agréable* B

18-20 and he also . . . Adonis of Grimwinter] where he also stood revealed, though with rather less of a challenge. He was a gentleman of few inches but a vague importance, perhaps the leading man of the world of North Verona B

21 nose, a] nose and a B

21-2 chin, and, as I . . . diminutive feet] chin; also as I observed, the most diminutive feet and a manner of no point at all B

23 foolishly, with] foolishly and with B

24-5 who had . . . her cheeks] as if an army of cooks had been engaged in the preparation of it B

26-32 'It is well!' . . . she repeated] '*C'est bien*!' said her massive inmate. 'Find your bouk'—and this personage turned to the gaping youth. He gaped now at each quarter of the room. 'My grammar, d'ye mean?' The large lady, however, could but face her friend's visitor while persistently engaged with a certain laxity in the flow of her wrapper. 'Find your bouk,' she more absently repeated B

33-4 also gazing at me again] who also couldn't take his eyes off me B

35 bouk,' said his companion] bouk'—his companion reconsidered B

35 we will talk] we'll just talk B

36-7 interrupt. Come,' and she turned away] interrupt Mademoiselle's. Come, come'—and she moved off a step B

38 Miss Spencer] Mademoiselle B

39-133:9 Then she gave . . . the ground again.] After which she gave me a thin salutation, jerked a measured 'Monsieur!' and swept away again with her swain following. I looked at Miss Spencer, whose eyes never moved from the carpet, and I spoke, I fear, without grace. 'Who in the World's that?' 'The

Comtesse—that *was*: my *cousine* as they call it in French.' 'And who's the young man?' 'The Countess's pupil, Mr. Mixter.' This description of the tie uniting the two persons, who had just quitted us must certainly have upset my gravity; for I recall the marked increase of my friend's own as she continued to explain. 'She gives lessons in French and music, the simpler sorts—' 'The simpler sorts of French?' I fear I broke in. But she was still impenetrable, and in fact had now an intonation that put me vulgarly in the wrong. 'She has had the worst reverses—with no one to look to. She's prepared for any exertion—and she takes her misfortunes with gaiety.' 'Ah well,' I returned—no doubt a little ruefully, 'that's all I myself am pretending to do. If she's determined to be a burden to nobody, nothing could be more right and proper.' My hostess looked vaguely, though I thought quite wearily enough, about: she met this proposition in no other way. B

133 : 10 she said] she simply said B

11 I asked] I none the less persisted B

12 her time to him] him all her time B

13-14 At this . . . too grave] It might have set me off again, but something in my whole impression of my friend's sensibility urged me to keep strictly decent B

15-17 she presently . . . turning away] she at all events inscrutably went on. 'He's not very bright as—a pupil; but he's very rich and he's very kind. He has a buggy—with a back, and he takes the Countess to drive.' 'For good long spells I hope,' I couldn't help interjecting—even at the cost of her so taking it that she had still to avoid my eyes. 'Well, the country's beautiful for miles,' I went on. And then as she was turning away: B

18 I said] om. B

21 She looked . . . serenity] She seemed to wonder who there should be B

23-7 'Can she not . . . that day] 'Then can't I help?' After which, as she but looked at me, I bettered it. 'Can't she wait on herself?' Miss Spencer had a slow headshake—as if that too had been a strange idea. 'She isn't used to *manual* labour.' The discrimination was a treat, but I cultivated decorum. 'I see—and you *are*.' But at the same time I couldn't abjure curiousity. 'Before you go, at any rate, please tell me this: who *is* this wonderful lady?' 'I told you just who in France—that extraordinary day B

28 saw] saw there B

29 who was] om. B

31 cast her off] completely broken with her B

33 He is] My poor cousin's B

34 'And] I pulled up, but only a moment. 'And B

35 girl] thing B

35-6 there was . . . questions] I kept her on the rack B

37 she said wearily] she woefully said B

38 But I . . . a moment] I scarce know what it didn't prompt me to—but I went step by step B

39 came over here] at once came to you B

40 'Yes] It was as if she had had too often to describe it. 'Yes B

42 Two years] Two years and four months B

43 She] And B

134 : 1 Every moment] Ever since B

2 'How] I took it all in. 'And how B

3-5 'Not at all.' . . . Miss Spencer] 'Well, not *very* much,' said Miss Spencer divinely. That too I took in. 'And how do *you*—?' She B

8-12 I remained alone . . . young man] Left alone in the little parlour I found myself divided between the perfection of my disgust and a contrary wish to see, to learn more. At the end of a few minutes the young man in attendance on the lady in question reappeared as for a fresh gape at me. He was inordinately grave—to be dressed in such parti-coloured flannels; and he produced with no great confidence on his own side the message with which he had been charged B

11-12 weak-eyed] rudimentary A

13-14 out there?' he observed at last.] right out.' B feebly . . . stature] feebly—for I may claim to have surpassed him in stature and weight B

20 the countess sitting] his instructress seated B

21 little] small B

21-3 house. She . . . small table] house; where she was engaged in drawing a fine needle with a very fat hand through a piece of embroidery not remarkable for freshness B

23 her. I seated myself] her and I seated myself A; her and I sat down B

24 sat down in] accommodated himself on B

25-6 feet. He . . . countess to me] feet; whence he gazed upward more gapingly than ever and as if convinced that between us something wonderful would now occur B

27 speak] spick B

27-31 countess, fixing . . . most expressively] Countess, whose eyes were singularly protuberant as she played over me her agreeable smile. 'I do, madame—*tant bien que mal*,' I replied, I fear, more dryly. 'Ah voilà!' she cried as with delight B

33 long] considerable B

34-5 'You know . . . madame.'] 'You love it then, *mon pays de France*?' 'Oh it's an old affection.' But I wasn't exuberant. 'And you know Paris well?' 'Yes, *sans me vanter*, madame, I think I really do.' B

40 with his hand] om. B

43 said] mocked B

43 Here are] It's going on B

135 : 1-2 that I am . . . he won't] since I took him in hand. Don't put yourself out not to say he's *la bêtise même*,' she added in fine style. 'He won't in the least B

3 'I hope] A moment's consideration of Mr. Mixter, awkwardly sporting at our feet, quite assured me that he wouldn't. 'I hope B

3 are more . . . remarked] do you more honour,' I then remarked to my entertainer B

4 French is] French—or what anything else—is B

6 replied] could but reply B

7 went on drawing her] continued to draw the B

8 her little finger curled out] an elegant curl of her little finger B

9-11 eyes close to her . . . dishonest and] eyes, near-sightedly, closer to her work—this as if for elegance too. She inspired me with no more confidence than her late husband, if husband he was, had done, years before, on the occasion with which this one so detestably matched: she was coarse, common, affected, dishonest— B

11 caliph. 'Talk to] Caliph. She had an assurance—based clearly on experience; but this couldn't have been the experience of 'race'. Whatever it was indeed it did now, in a yearning fashion, flare out of her. 'Talk to B

11-12 Paris,' . . . How] Paris, *mon beau Paris* that I'd give my eyes to see. The very name of it *me fait languir*. How B

14 Two months] A couple of months B

15 Happy man] *Vous avez de la chance* B

16 boulevards] boulevard A; Boulevard B

19 eh] *hein* B

19 *cafés-concerts*] cafés-concerts? *sous ce beau ciel* B

20 in front of] before B

22 rejoin] return B

24 then she put] then put B

25 had a . . . aspect] struck me as having acquired even while we sat a dingier and more desultory B

26-9 inclination.' . . . 'Oh,] by—inclination.' After which she pursued: 'And by the saddest events of my life—as well as by some of the happiest, hélas!' 'In other words by a varied experience!' I now at last smiled. She questioned me over it with her hard little salient eyes. 'Oh B

29 that if] that, no doubt, if B

29-30 I never . . . experience had] *On en a de toutes les sortes*—and I never dreamed that mine, for example, would ever have B

30-1 pointed . . . bare] indicated with her large bare B

31-2 head, at . . . her—at] head all surrounding objects; B

33 at] the rapt B

34 'You are . . . smiling.] I took them all bravely in. 'Ah if you mean you're decidedly in exile—!' B

35-7 that I have . . . I think] of my *épreuve—elles m'en ont données, des heures, des heures*! One gets used to things'—and she raised her shoulders to the highest shrug ever accomplished at North Verona; 'so that I sometimes think B

38 over] om. B

39 'Do you] I so far again lent myself. 'Do you B

39 I inquired.] om. B

40 She tossed . . . measured me] Her eyebrows went up as high as her shoulders had done B

41 prefer me] propose to me B

42 *demi-tasse*] little cup AB

136 : 5-6 She's an excellent girl;] *C'est une fille charmante,* B

6 cognac,] '*fine*,' B

9 arrives] does arrive B

9-10 offer you any . . . I know] press it on *you*—though monsieur here sometimes joins me!—it's because B

11 boulevards] boulevard A; Boulevard B

12-20 this scornful treatment . . . it's his dream.] so critical a view of my poor friend's exertions, but I said nothing at all—the only way to be sure of my civility. I dropped my eyes on Mr. Mixter, who, sitting cross-legged and nursing his knees, watched my companion's foreign graces with an interest that familiarity had apparently done little to restrict. She became aware, naturally, of my mystified view of him and faced the question with all her boldness. 'He adores me, you know,' she murmured with her nose again in her tapestry—'he dreams of becoming *mon amoureux*. Yes, *il me fait une cour acharnée* —such as you see him. That's what we have come to. B

20 a] some B

22 the] a B

22 me the heroine!] me—such as I am, monsieur—*je ne sais quelle dévergondée*! B

23-35 Mr. Mixter had . . . like a waiting-maid.] Mr. Mixter may have inferred that he was to that extent the object of our reference; but of the manner in which he was handled he must have had small suspicion—preoccupied as he was, as to my companion, with the ecstasy of contemplation. Our hostess moreover at this moment came out of the house, bearing a coffee-pot and three cups on a neat little tray. I took from her eyes, as she approached us, a brief but intense appeal—the mute expression, as I felt, conveyed in the hardest little look she had yet addressed me, of her longing to know what, as a man of the world in general and of the French world in particular, I thought of these allied forces now so encamped on the stricken field of her life. I could only 'act' however, as they said at North Verona, quite impenetrably—only make no answering sign. I couldn't intimate, much less could I frankly utter, my inward sense of the Countess's probable past, with its measure of her virtue, value and accomplishments, and of the limits of the consideration to which she could properly pretend. I couldn't give my friend a hint of how I myself personally 'saw' her interesting pensioner—whether as the run-away wife of a too-jealous hairdresser or of a too-morose pastry-cook, say; whether as a very small bourgeoise, in fine, who had vitiated her case beyond patching up, or even as some character, of the nomadic sort, less edifying still. I couldn't let in, by the jog of a shutter, as it were, a hard informing ray and then, washing my hands of the business, turn my back for ever. I could on the contrary but save the situation, my own at least, for the moment, by pulling myself together with a master hand and appearing to ignore everything but that the dreadful person between us was a 'grande dame.' This effort was possible indeed but as a retreat in good order and with all the forms of courtesy. If I couldn't speak, still less could I stay, and I think I must, in spite of everything, have turned black with disgust to see Caroline Spencer stand there like a waiting-maid. I therefore won't answer for the shade of success that may have attended my saying to the Countess, on my feet and as to leave her: B

32 *coiffeur*] hair-dresser A

36 at Grimwinter] in these *parages* B

36-7 I said to the countess.] om. B

38-41 She gave a . . . the cognac!'] What passed between us, as from face to face, while she looked up at me, *that* at least our companion may have caught, that at least may have sown, for the after-time, some seed of revelation. The Countess repeated her terrible shrug. 'Who knows? I don't see my way—! It isn't an existence, but when one's in misery—! *Chère belle*,' she added as an appeal to Miss Spencer, 'you've gone and forgotten the "*fine*"!' B

42 Caroline Spencer] that lady B

42 looking] considering B

43 at the little table,] the small array B

43 turning away . . . delicacy] turning away to procure this missing delicacy A; about to turn off in quest of this article B

137 : 1-3 I silently gave . . . I was going] I held out my hand in silence —I had to go. Her wan set little face, severely mild and with the question of a moment before now quite cold in it, spoke of extreme fatigue, but also of something else strange and conceived—whether a desperate patience still, or at last some other desperation, being more than I can say. What was clearest on the whole was that she was glad I was going B

5-6 I reflected . . . something] I could feel how right my poor friend had been in her conviction at the other, the still intenser, the now historic crisis, that she should still see something B

6-7 of Europe] of that dear old Europe AB

THÉODOLINDE

Note:

The variants recorded below are based on a collation of the original serial text of the tale (*Lippincott's Magazine,* 1878) and its revised version in *Stories Revived* (1885).

Théodolinde] Rose-Agathe

138 : 17	restaurant. Then] restaurant. It had above it the sign, 'Anatole, Coiffeur;' these artists, in Paris, being known only by their Christian name. Then
22	was] is
29	*empressement*] eagerness
33-4	my table . . . there was] my table—there was
139 : 1-2	in the act of . . . Glancing] exposed to the titillation of a new influence. It was as if a bottle of the finest hair-oil had suddenly been uncorked. Glancing
4	took] supposed
17	*coifée* in the Rue de la Paix] *coiffée* by M. Anatole
140 : 16	rapt in contemplation] gaping like a rustic at a fair
42	duchess] Parisienne
141 : 2	unobstructed space] point of visual access
142 : 4	taste,' . . . That] taste for picking up pretty faces,' I rejoined. 'That
19	perhaps,' I said, 'is] perhaps, is
29	Parisianized,' . . . 'about] Parisianized about
29	mouth.'] mouth,' I rejoined.
39	see,' I said, 'how] see how
11	knickknacks] bibelots,
31	had] om.
40	seventeen] many
144 : 5-6	that which was] things that were
9	things] objects
14	fellow-country people] country-people
22	upon] on
42	fellow,' I urged, 'you] fellow, you
42	enough. In] enough,' I urged, 'In
145 : 5	*Je crois bien*!] Rather, my dear boy.
6	rather] a little
7-8	know,' he added, 'but] know but
9	before.'] before,' he added.
23	room] salon
146 : 5	suppose,' . . . 'that] suppose that
15	other . . . absurd;'] other, infatuations are always absurd,' I said;
22	Boston,' . . . 'that] our country, that

22	our] one's
28	window . . . through] window through
32-3	improvised a purchase] invented something to buy
147 : 10	stand there] remain
10-11	and I had . . . and stood] and, as I had exhausted my expedients, I was obliged to withdraw. I took a position
17	a plump little white hand] a small, fair, dainty hand
23	absorbed, contemplative droop] attentive, absorbed droop
40	Regrettable] Unadvisable
148 : 1	morning,' . . . ever.'] morning she is in great beauty,' he added, the next moment.
34	course,' . . . still—'] course that will be something,' I replied. 'But still—'
35	mean,' . . . 'that] mean that
36	pay] give
38	ardour and coolness] passion and reason
149 : 8	grand passion] audacious flame
9	glow with a fervour] blaze in a manner
10	most] om.
150 : 5-6	audacity] perversity
17	true,' . . . 'that she] true she
21	think,' . . . 'that she] think she
21	exercise.'] exercise,' I objected.
24	ver] om.
151 : 11	modest] *pudique*
19	Madame Théodolinde] Madame Anatole
29	trifling] inconsiderable
35	five thousand dollars more] fifty thousand francs more (for instance)
152 : 3	twenty thousand dollars] a hundred thousand francs
43	was smiling . . . And he] had an expression of pure bliis. There was something in her eyes. He
153 : 4	bit,' . . . 'but] bit, but
13	does herself.' I answered.] herself does!'

DAISY MILLER: A STUDY

Notes:

1. The variants recorded below are based on a collation of the original serial text of the tale (*Cornhill*, 1878) and its two revised versions in *Daisy Miller: A Study* (1879)—hereinafter mentioned as A—and *Daisy Miller, Etc.* (1909)—hereinafter mentioned as B.

2. The magazine version appeared in two parts: that division is omitted in texts A and B, where the tale is divided into four chapters. Chapter I begins at 154:1; II at 164:11; III at 176:21; IV at 188:8.

IN TWO PARTS] om. AB

PART I] I AB

Daisy Miller: a Study] *Daisy Miller* B

154 : 2 hotels; for] hotels, since B
9 little] small B
13-14 air . . . maturity] air both of luxury and of maturity B
14 region, in] region, through B
16 this period] that time B
17 which] that B
155 : 3 that are] om. B
18 now she was] she was now B
23 an] om. B
23 fellow, and universally] and generally B
25 affirmed] conveyed B
27 indeed] truly B
30 metropolis] capital B
31 and he had] and had B
31 gone to college] even gone, on trial—trial of the grey old 'Academy' on the steep and stony hillside—to college B
37-8 his breakfast . . . drinking] that repast, but was enjoying B
39 served to him] served him B
40 an *attaché*] *attachés* B
156 : 1 knickerbockers, with] knickerbockers and had B
1 which] that B
4 that] om. B
7 little] om. B
9 small] light B
11 think sugar is] think too much sugar B
18-19 pronouncing . . . manner] divesting vowel and consonants, pertinently enough, of any taint of softness B
20 perceived] gathered B
20-1 fellow-countryman] countryman B
24 My mother] Mother B

29 said] ventured B
33-4 asked Winterbourne] Winterbourne asked B
36 laughed Winterbourne] the young lad laughed B
38 Winterbourne's] his friend's B
39 declared] declared with assurance B
42 a second] another B
157 : 1 this age] the same age B
2 the child, in a moment] his young compatriot B
3 girl.] girl, you bet! B
5-6 said . . . companion] thereupon cheerfully remarked to his visitor B
7 declared] promptly returned B
12 She . . . but] Bareheaded, B
14-15 Winterbourne, straightening] our friend, who straightened B
15 prepared] ready B
17 little] small B
20 'Randolph,' . . . lady] 'Why Randolph,' she freely began B
21 replied] cried B
22 little] extravagant B
25 cried] proclaimed B
25 little hard] harsh little B
26 announcement] circumstance B
27 you had] you'd B
30 young girl] charming creature B
34 except] save B
36 coming and standing] coming to stand B
36 a garden] a garden with all the confidence in life B
37 however] whatever that might prove B
40 far; but he decided] far, but decided B
40-1 advance farther,] gallantly advance B
42 turned to . . . again] turned again to the little boy, whom she addressed quite as if they were alone together B
43 pole,' she said.] pole.' B
158 : 1 responded Randolph] Randolph shouted B
3 declared] rang out B
4 The young girl] She B
5 rested her eyes upon] gave her sweet eyes to B
6 she said,] she dropped B
7-8 inquired . . . respect] now decided very respectfully to enquire B
9 The young lady] She B
10 again] with lovely remoteness B
11 she replied] she then replied B
12 going over] thinking of B
13-14 Winterbourne . . . embarrassed] he pursued with a slight drop of assurance B

15 going over] thinking of B

16-18 'Going . . . said Randolph.] 'Thinking of?'—the boy stared. 'Why going right over.' 'Going to where?' he demanded. 'Why right down to Italy'—Winterbourne felt vague emulations. 'I don't know,' said Randolph. B

20 rejoined the young man] the young man laughed B

21 loudly inquired] asked of all the echoes B

27 upon] on B

28 embarrassed] in doubt B

29 was not . . . herself] was really not in the least embarrassed. She might be cold, she might be austere, she might even be prim; for that was apparently—he had already so generalized—what the most 'distant' American girls did: they came and planted themselves straight in front of you to show how rigidly unapproachable they were B

30-1 alteration . . . evidently] flush in her fresh fairness however; so that she was clearly B

31-2 fluttered. If she looked] fluttered. Only she was composed—he had seen that before too—of charming little parts that didn't match and that made no *ensemble*; and if she looked B

33 her manner. Yet, as] her manner, the result of having no idea whatever of 'form' (with such a tell-tale appendage as Randolph where in the world would she have got it?) in any such connection. As B

35 quite] wholly B

35-6 gradually gave] gradually, none the less, gave B

36 glance] attention B

37 this glance . . . unshrinking] act unqualified by the faintest shadow of reserve B

38-40 an immodest . . . pretty eyes;] a 'bold' front that she presented, for her expression was as decently limpid as the very cleanest water. Her eyes were the very prettiest conceivable, B

40 had not . . . long time] hadn't for a long time seen B

42-159:1 had a great . . . as regards] took a great interest generally in that range of effects and was addicted to noting and, as it were, recording them; so that in regard to B

159 : 2 but it . . . expressive] yet at the same time wasn't pointedly—what point, on earth, could she ever make?—expressive B

2-3 was eminently delicate, Winterbourne] offered such a collection of small finenesses and neatnesses he B

4-7 it very possible . . . no irony] nothing more likely than that its wearer would have had her own experience of the action of her charms, as she would certainly have acquired a resulting confidence; but even should she depend on this for her main amusement her bright sweet superficial little visage gave out neither mockery nor irony B

7 obvious that] clear that, however these things might be, B
8 towards] to B
8 told him] remarked to Winterbourne B
10 shouldn't] wouldn't B
11-12 German . . . especially] German—this flower was gathered as from a large field of comparison— especially B
14 that he had] om. B
14-15 met an . . . German] any American with the resemblance she noted B
15-16 should not . . . bench which] mightn't be more at ease should she occupy the bench B
17-18 standing up . . . sat down] hanging round, but she none the less resignedly, after a little, dropped to the bench B
19 is.' Winterbourne learned more about her] is'; but our friend really quickened this current B
22 your name, my boy,' he said] your honest name, my boy.' So he artfully proceeded B
23-4 'Randolph C. Miller,' . . . sister] 'Randolph C. Miller. And I'll tell you hers.' With which he levelled his alpenstock at his sister B
26 calmly] quite at her leisure B
27 said Winterbourne] Winterbourne made free to reply B
28 child] urchin B
30 said Miss Miller] Miss Miller quite as naturally remarked B
32 'Ask him . . . Winterbourne] It seemed, all amazingly to do her good. 'Ask him *his* now'—and she indicated their friend B
33 on] to B
35 Ezra B. Miller,' . . . 'My] Ezra B. Miller, My B
36 my father's] he's B
37 imagined . . . this was] for a moment supposed this B
160 : 2 young girl] girl, as with an artless instinct for historic truth B
8 'Mother thought] It tapped, at a touch, the spring of confidence. 'Mother thought B
22 said Winterbourne] Winterbourne hastened to reply B
29 passed by,] passed before her B
30 talked to Winterbourne] addressed her new acquaintance B
32 unknown young lady,] wandering maiden B
36 decidedly] distinctly B
37 history] report B
43 did not make this remark] made this remark B
161 : 3 sweet] entrancing B
6 friends that] friends who B
6 times] times, and that way she had got thoroughly posted B
9 said Winterbourne] Winterbourne smiled B

11 Miss Miller, without] Miss Miller at once and without B
18 a great deal] plenty B
25 lively] frank gay B
25-6 light, slightly monotonous] clear rather uniform B
28 amused . . . decidedly] amused and perplexed—above all he was B
29-30 seemed a kind . . . deportment] was to have at the same time some rather complicated consciousness about them B
31 of actual] of an actual B
32 *inconduite*] *arrière-pensée* B
32 felt that he] felt he B
33-4 that he had . . . dishabituated to the] as to have got morally muddled; he had lost the right sense for the young B
35-6 American girl of so pronounced] compatriot of so 'strong' B
37 deucedly sociable] extraordinarily communicative and how tremendously easy B
38 had a] had had a B
39-41 an unscrupulous . . . not help him] in short an expert young person? Yes, his instinct for such a question had ceased to serve him, and his reason could but mislead B
162 : 1-2 He was . . . was a flirt] He must on the whole take Miss Daisy Miller for a flirt B
3 any] om. B
3 young ladies of this category] representatives of that class B
7 relations were liable to] light commerce might indeed B
7 young girl] charming apparition B
11-12 most charming] finest little B
16 asked the young girl] the girl soon asked B
17 far-gleaming] far-shining B
23 said Winterbourne] the young man returned B
27-8 the young girl] she B
29 my] om. B
29-30 couldn't go. Randolph] couldn't any more go—!' But this sketch of Mrs. Miller's plea remained unfinished. 'Randolph B
33 inquired, smiling] indulgently asked B
34 'He says] He now drew her, as he guessed she would herself have said, every time. 'Why no, he says B
39 said Winterbourne] Winterbourne was thus emboldened to reply B
41 then, very placidly] then with all serenity B
163 : 1 Winterbourne hesitated a moment] He pretended to consider it B
3 asked the . . . same placidity] she asked without a shadow of emotion B
4 girl] person B
5-6 yet Winterbourne . . . thought] yet, conscious that he had

gone very far, he thought B

6 was offended. 'With] had drawn back. 'And with B

9 my] om. B

10 after all,' she said] —for *you*,' she smiled B

13 earnestly] earnestly I meant it B

16 inquired] echoed B

21 Daisy] om. B

21 programme] prospect B

22 agreeable for credence] good to believe B

24 the project] his chance B

25-6 whiskers, wearing] whiskers and wearing B

26 brilliant watch-chain] voluminous watch-guard B

27 Miss Miller] the young lady B

28 said Miss Miller] she said B

29 looked at] eyed B

30 the young lady] Miss Miller B

31 luncheon is upon the] luncheon's on B

32 Miss Miller] Mademoiselle B

32 Eugenio,' . . . 'I'm] Eugenio, I'm B

36 very] om. B

38 upon the . . . situation] on her position B

39 Winterbourne . . . very little] Winterbourne with the slightest blush B

40 she said.] om. B

43 an] om. B

164 : 1-3 stood looking . . . imputation] still stood there with an effect of offence for the young man so far as the latter saw in it a tacit reflexion on Miss Miller's behaviour and an insinuation B

6 said Miss Miller. And she] she beautifully answered; with which she B

8 looking after] watching B

9-10 gravel . . . princess] walk, he spoke to himself of her natural elegance B

13 the former] that B

14 upon] on B

14-15 the proper . . . observed,] a show of the proper solicitude about her health, asked if she had noticed B

16 and a little] and an obstreperous little B

17 And a courier] An obstreperous little boy and a preposterous big courier B

18 observed] noticed B

19 with a] of B

20 were not] hadn't been B

21 upon] on B

23 *rouleaux*] om. B

26-7 he was . . . perceived] guided by his taste, was rarely observed B

28 own] om. B

28 up] om. B

29-30 than those . . . to her] than, as she said, her very own B

31 must . . . one's aunt] must be irreproachable in all such forms B

32 she was greatly] was now greatly B

34-5 she gave . . . American capital] he could see she would like him to think, she exerted from her stronghold in Forty-second Street B

36 were acquainted] had been better acquainted B

41 immediately perceived,] at once recognized B

43 he said] he pursued in reference to his new friends B

165 : 1 very common,' Mrs. Costello declared] horribly common'—it was perfectly simple B

2 not—not accepting] just ignoring B

3 Ah, you . . . young man] Ah you just ignore them?'—the young man took it in B

4 can't, my] can't *not*, my B

4 I would . . . I can't] I wouldn't if I hadn't to, but I have to B

5 young] little

5 said Winterbourne,] he went on B

6 she's pretty . . . very common] she's very pretty. But she's of the last crudity B

6 said Winterbourne,] he allowed B

9 that] om. B

16 the courier . . . demanded] him?' Ah there it was B

17 Oh . . . as bad] There's no other name for such a relation. But the skinny little mother's just as bad B

17 like] as B

18 like a gentleman] as a gentleman and a scholar B

20 like a gentleman] *like* a gentleman—or a scholar B

21-2 garden, in the evening] garden of an evening B

22 smokes] smokes in their faces B

25 courier, and] courier and I didn't smoke in her face, and B

27 said] mentioned B

27 said Mrs. Costello] Mrs. Costello returned B

28 her acquaintance] her valuable acquaintance B

29 and we talked] and talked B

30 *Tout bonnement*! And pray what] By appointment—no? Ah that's still to come. Pray what B

33 I am much] Your admirable aunt's a thousand times B

34 respectability,' said Winterbourne.] respectability.' B

36-7 nice young girl] nice girl A; innocent girl B

38 observed] returned B

39 uncultivated] uneducated B

39 went on. 'But] acknowledged, 'but B

40 that] om. B

42 'You two] Mrs. Costello made a wondrous face. 'You two B

166 : 3 said Winterbourne, smiling] Winterbourne smiled B

4-6 'Dear me! . . . earnestly] 'Then she's just what I supposed.' 'And what do you suppose?' 'Why that she's a horror.' Our youth was silent for some moments. 'You really think then,' he presently began B

7 paused again] paused again while his aunt waited B

8 said his aunt.] om. B

10 later—to carry her off] later to—well, we'll call it carry her off B

12 think that] consider B

13 that are . . . call them] who are uneducated, as you mildly put it B

16-17 I am not . . . and curling] not so much as that comes to!' he protested with a laugh and a curl of B

19 to curl . . . meditatively] all thoughtfully to finger the ornament in question B

23 I think that] I've no doubt B

26 be shocked] be honestly shocked B

27 young girls in America] little American girls at home B

30 declared, grimly] then grimly returned B

31 upon] on B

32 that] om. B

32-3 New York were] New York, the daughters of this lady's two daughters, called B

34 margin] licence AB

34 ladies, it] women it B

35 that anything . . . of her] she did go even by the American allowance rather far B

36-7 he was . . . should not] it vexed, it even a little humiliated him, that he shouldn't by instinct B

38 he was] so B

38 her, he] her again he B

38-9 what he . . . about his] what ground he should give for his B

42-3 starlight, like an] starlight after the manner of B

167 : 3-4 Miss Daisy . . . the longest] His young friend frankly rejoiced to renew their intercourse; she pronounced it the stupidest B

5 he asked] he asked with no intention of an epigram and no effect of her perceiving one B

7 she answered] Miss Miller explained B

9-10 bed,' . . . 'She doesn't sleep] bed. She doesn't sleep scarcely any B

14 'Let us] The soft impartiality of her *constatations*, as Winterbourne would have termed them, was a thing by itself—exquisite little fatalist as they seemed to make her. 'Let us B

14 observed Winterbourne] he encouragingly said B

15 'She will] 'Well, she'll B

16 him,' . . . her fan] him': with which Miss Daisy opened and closed her fan B

17 he] Randolph B

19 It appeared that] Her detachment from any invidious judgement of this was, to her companion's sense, inimitable; and it appeared that B

21 strolled . . . young girl] attended her in her stroll B

23 his companion . . . 'She's] she resumed—'I guess she's B

24 Winterbourne's] his B

28 *table d'hôte*] common table B

33 Well, we] Well, I guess we B

34 every] any B

35 know] meet B

36 embarrassed] embarrassed—he could but trump up some evasion B

36-7 happy,' he . . . will interfere] happy, but I'm afraid those tiresome headaches are always to be reckoned with B

38 The young girl] The girl B

38 the dusk] the fine dusk B

38 But I] Well, I B

39 day,' she said, sympathetically.] day.' B

40-1 Winterbourne . . . what to say] He had to make the best of it. 'She tells me she wonderfully does.' He didn't know what else to say B

42 Daisy] om. B

43 was opening and closing] kept flapping to and fro B

168 : 1 said, suddenly] then lightly broke out B

3 gave a little laugh] quite crowed for the fun of it B

4 fancied . . . voice] distinguished however a wee false note in this B

5-6 lady,' he . . . It's her] lady, she knows no one. She goes through life immured. It's her B

7 steps, laughing still] steps in the glee of the thing B

10 upon] on B

12-13 upon the . . . she *is*] at these great lights and shades and again proclaimed a gay indifference—'Gracious! she *is* B

13 she said.] om. B

14 whether she was] if she were B

16 attempt to] om. B

17-18 very . . . purposes] all accessible to a respectful tenderness at that moment B

18 then, for the instant,] om. B

19 admit that] acknowledge B

20 declare] make the point B

21 perilous] questionable B

25 darkness, and advancing] darkness; it advanced B
25-6 movement. Suddenly it] step and then suddenly B
27 distinguish her] make her out B
29 Well!' . . . laugh] Well,' the girl laughed B
32 to advance] now to approach B
37 the young . . . serenely] his companion placidly answered B
38 wear it] wear it if she didn't mind looking like a fright B
41 urged Miss Daisy Miller] the girl insisted B
43 Miss Miller gave him a serious] She gave him, he thought, the oddest B
169 : 5 the young . . . little soft,] Miss Miller added, in her small B
5 To introduce] Well, to introduce B
7 said Winterbourne] Winterbourne remarked B
9 Oh, dear;] Oh my— B
10 said his companion, with a laugh] cried his companion, much amused B
11 upon] on B
12 turning] presenting B
13 young] om. B
13 decision. Upon this] decision—upon which B
14-15 'Mr. Winterbourne,' . . . young man] 'Mr. Frederick Forsyth Winterbourne,' said the latter's young friend, repeating his lession of a moment before and introducing him B
15 was] might be B
16-17 it was . . . delicate] what provision was made by that epithet for her queer little native B
19 very . . . a large] scarce perceptible nose, and, as to make up for it, an unmistakeable B
19-20 decorated . . . a thin] decorated—but too far back, as Winterbourne mentally described it—with thin B
22 Winterbourne] the young man B
25 inquired; but] enquired—yet B
26 which] om. B
26 may imply] might have implied B
27 I don't] Well, I don't B
27 said . . . towards] and the new-comer turned to B
28 exclaimed] familiarly proceeded B
29 answered, with a little laugh] answered with a sound that partook for Winterbourne of an odd strain between mirth and woe B
30 asked the young girl] Daisy asked B
31 him' . . . very gently] him'—and Mrs. Miller seemed to confess to the same mild fatalism as her daughter B
33 was telling] was just telling B
33 young] om. B
36 said Winterbourne;] he concurred— B

38 turned] kept B
38 to] on B
39 she spoke] a sigh broke from her B
40 said Daisy Miller] Daisy at least opined B
41 asked] desired to know B
43 I know that] it seemed as if he couldn't budge B
170 : 1 half-past twelve,' . . . emphasis] half-past twelve when *I* gave up,' Mrs. Miller recorded with passionless accuracy B
2 'Does] It was of great interest to Winterbourne. 'Does B
2 Winterbourne demanded.] om. B
3 sleep much] sleep *very* much B
4 he would!] he just *would*! B
4 couldn't] *must* make it up somehow
5 I think he's real tiresome] Well, I guess it's we that make it up. I think he's real tiresome B
6 Then, for] After which, for B
7 said the elder lady, presently] the elder lady then unexpectedly broke out B
9-10 Daisy . . . retort] the girl, but with no sharpness of insistence B
11 He's] Well, he's B
11 urged Mrs. Miller] Mrs. Miller lucidly urged B
12-13 go to that . . . going there] go up to that castle anyway,' her daughter replied as for accommodation. 'I'm going up there B
14 mamma] parent B
15 granted that] granted on this that B
15-16 she deeply . . . excursion] she opposed such a course B
16 himself that she] himself at the same time that she B
18 take . . . displeasure] modify her attitude B
18 began;] therefore interposed, B
20 a sort of] an B
21 Daisy] her other companion B
22-3 said her mother] she then quite colourlessly remarked B
25 rejoined] returned B
26 been to] been up to B
27 said Winterbourne] he observed B
30 'We've] It was on this view accordingly that light was projected for him. 'We've B
30 going,' . . . 'but] going, but B
31 round] round everywhere B
40-1 impregnated . . . enterprise] that seemed to break under the burden of such conceptions B
42 there was] there's B
43 Oh, I think] Oh I'm pretty sure B
171 : 3 them, softly] them and softly B
4 undertake it] make the so interesting excursion B

	5	Daisy's mother] So addressed Daisy's mother B
	5	askance,] with a certain scared obliquity B
	8	Winterbourne observed to himself] It gave him occasion to note B
	14	murmured Daisy] she piped from a considerable distance B
	18	Of course] Why of course B
	18	said Daisy] she gaily returned B
	20-1	said Winterbourne . . . of guiding] he hereupon eagerly pleaded; so instantly had he been struck with the romantic side of this chance to guide B
	28	in the starlight] under the stars B
	29	said Daisy] Daisy laughed B
	30	ejaculated . . . again] the elder lady again gasped, as in rebuke of this freedom B
	34	said Winterbourne] Winterbourne replied B
	35	'Well;] 'Oh pshaw! B
	35	repeated] went on as if nothing else had been said B
	37	Winterbourne] her friend B
	37-8	were gleaming] gleamed in the darkness B
	38-9	No; it's . . . Winterbourne] No, he felt, it was impossible to be prettier than that B
	40-1	he said . . . which] and he pointed to a range of steps that B
172 :	1	Daisy] She B
	1-2	head and . . . laugh] head; she laughed as for the drollery of this B
	2	she declared.] om. B
	4	went on] agreeably mocked B
	7	remarked . . . gently] Mrs. Miller shyly pleaded B
	8	said to the young girl] persisted to Daisy B
	9	cried Daisy] she cried in reward B
	11	said Daisy.] om. B
	12	stood there laughing] remained an elegant image of free light irony B
	13	should think you had better] guess you'd better B
	13-14	interposed her mother] her mother impartially contributed B
	16	perceived] recognized B
	17-18	who was . . . ladies] he had already seen in attendance B
	19	out in] out with Mr. Winterbourne in B
	20	eleven o'clock, Mademoiselle] this hour of the night Mademoiselle B
	21	Mr. Winterbourne. This very] Mr. Winterbourne,' she repeated with her shining smile. 'I'm going this very B
	22	can't,' said Mrs. Miller] can't Eugenio,' Mrs. Miller said B
	24	Eugenio] the man B

	25	Heaven] goodness B
	25-6	so familiar] on such familiar terms B
	27	nothing] nothing, and she meanwhile added to his ground B
	27	proper!' Daisy exclaimed] proper! My!' she wailed B
	29	I am at] I'm nevertheless quite at B
	29	said Winterbourne] Winterbourne hastened to remark B
	30	asked Eugenio] Eugenio asked B
	32	answered Daisy's mamma] cried Daisy's mamma for reassurance B
	33	The courier] 'I *meant* alone with the gentlemen.' The courier B
	34	thought he was smiling] seemed to make out in his face a vague presumptuous intelligence as at the expense of their companions B
	34	solemnly, with] solemnly and with B
	36	'Oh, I] But Daisy broke off at this, 'Oh I B
	36	fuss!' said Daisy. 'I] fuss! I B
	38	I myself] Ah but I myself B
	39	And the young girl] With which she B
	41	gone to . . . frigidly] retired for the night!' the courier hereupon importantly announced B
	42	can go!' said] can go then!' cried B
	43	Daisy] Her daughter B
	43-173:1	Winterbourne . . . herself] their friend, all lighted with her odd perversity B
173 :	1	Good-night,' . . . 'I hope] Good night—I hope B
	3	her, taking . . . puzzled] her gravely, taking her by the hand she offered. 'I'm puzzled, if you want to know B
	8	Winterbourne . . . after] Winterbourne's eyes followed B
	8	puzzled] quite mystified B
	9	for] om. B
	9	turning over] baffled by the question B
	9-10	the mystery of the young girl's] of the girl's B
	13	afterwards] later B
	16	should . . . appointed it] would have chosen for a tryst, but she had placidly appointed it B
	18-19	in the . . . Winterbourne was] exactly in the way that consorted best, to his fancy, with their adventure. He was B
	20	say, sensibility] say, of sensibility B
	20-2	looked at . . . going forward] took in her charming air and caught from the great staircase her impatient confiding step the note of some small sweet strain of romance, not intense but clear and sweet, seemed to sound for their start B
	23	was going to elope] was *really* going 'off' B
	23-4	passed out with her among] led her out through B
	24	that were] om. B
	24-5	there . . . looking] —they all looked B

25 very] straight and B
26 Winterbourne's] His B
28-9 steamer; she . . . was always] steamer—there would be B
30 you saw] they should see B
31 to say a great many things] for many characteristic remarks and other demonstrations, not a few of which were, from the extremity of their candour, slightly disconcerting B
32-5 was so much . . . the same way] showed for so delightfully irregular and incongruously intimate that, even allowing for her habitual sense of freedom, he had some expectation of seeing her appear to find in it the same savour B
35 in this particular, he was] he was in this particular rather B
36 Daisy] Miss B
36 extremely] highly B
36 she was in charming] she was in the brightest B
37-8 apparently . . . fluttered] clearly not at all in a nervous flutter—as she should have been to match *his* tension B
39 blushed neither] neither coloured from an awkward consciousness B
39 felt] saw B
41 took much satisfaction] could at least take pleasure B
42 a little] privately B
42 that] om. B
43-174:1 move . . . good deal] more extravagantly about the boat B
174 : 2 upon] on B
2 moving] stirring B
4 garrulity] innocent prattle B
4-8 ever heard. He . . . turn] ever heard, for, by his own experience hitherto, when young persons were so ingenuous they were less articulate and when they were so confident were more sophisticated. If he had assented to the idea that she was 'common,' at any rate, *was* she proving so, after all, or was he simply getting used to her commonness? Her discourse was for the most part of what immediately and superficially surrounded them, but there were moments when it threw out a longer look or took a sudden straight plunge B
9 grave] solemn B
10 upon Winterbourne's] on her friend's B
11 grave]solemn B
13 funeral] prayer-meeting or a funeral B
18 murmured Winterbourne] Winterbourne returned B
19 and then . . . laugh] then let it renew her amusement B
21-2 the subjective . . . tripped] nothing could exceed the light independence of her humour. She tripped B
26 that] om. B
26 very] om. B
26-8 feudal . . . upon her] mediaeval history and that the grim

ghosts of Chillon loomed but faintly before her B

28 walk about] wander B

29 companionship] society B

29 the custodian] their guide B

30 this functionary] this companion B

31-2 The custodian] He B

34 not remarkable for] marked by no B

36 many pretexts in the] many, in the tortuous passages and B

36 Chillon] the place B

37 Winterbourne] her young man B

38 intentions—and] designs, and B

39 upon] on B

39-40 personality] situation B

40 intentions Miss Miller] designs the charming creature B

43-175:1 said to . . . history of] exclaimed after Winterbourne had sketched for her something of the story of B

175 : 3-4 Daisy . . . wished] this easy erudition struck her none the less as wonderful, and she was soon quite sure she wished B

5 they . . . case] they too in that case might learn something about something B

6-7 she asked. Winterbourne said] she asked; 'I guess he'd improve with a gentleman teacher.' Winterbourne was certain B

8-9 believe it!' said Miss Daisy] believe a speck of it!' she protested B

9 mean] mean now B

10 admitted] allowed B

11-12 force him to go back] necessitate his return B

12 said:] panted, B

14 pretty] interesting B

17 return ot Geneva] report myself there B

19 'Well . . . I think] She met it with a vivacity that could only flatter him. 'Well, Mr. Winterbourne, I think B

20 said Winterbourne] he quite sincerely pleaded B

22 cried the young girl] the girl cried B

22 the first.] the very first! B

26 announcement of his movements] mention of his personal plans B

28-9 upon the mysterious] on the special B

31 that . . . Geneva] of that agent of his fate in Geneva B

34 frankness of her *persiflage*] directness of her criticism B

35 seemed . . . this, an] struck him afresh, in all this as an B

37 asked Daisy, ironically] Miss Miller wished ironically to know B

39-40 come after] come right after B

41-2 Winterbourne . . . to feel] He began at last even to feel he had been wrong to be B

176 : 2 at last] towards the end B
3 in the] that B
4 said Winterbourne] he hastened to acknowledge B
5 for the winter] from January B
8 that the young man] he B
9 declared] promised her B
10 come . . . stopped] come, and after this she forbore from B
12 the young . . . quiet] the girl at his side, her animation a little spent, was now quite distractingly passive B
13 Winterbourne] he B
16 happily,' . . . 'the] happily the B
20 young person whom] little abomination B
23 for several weeks] a considerable time B
23-4 a couple of letters from her] from her a couple of characteristic letters B
28 some] various B
31-2 In the . . . presently have] Our friend would in the natural course of events, on arriving in Rome, have presently B
33 have] om. B
34 I think I may certainly] I certainly think I may AB
37 Of course a man] Of course you're not squeamish—a man B
39 it that happens] it then that "happens" B
40 demanded] asked B
177 : 1 The girl . . . foreigners] Well, the girl tears about alone with her unmistakeably low foreigners B
3 fortune-hunters, and] fortune-hunters of the inferior sort and B
4 to people's houses] to such houses as she may put *her* nose into B
4 party she] party—such a party as she can come to—she B
9 Winterbourne meditated a moment] Winterbourne thought them over in these new lights B
10 only. Depend upon] only, and utterly uncivilized. Depend on B
13 dislike] blush for B
15 Daisy Miller was surrounded] his little friend, the child of nature of the Swiss lakeside, was now surrounded B
22-3 Miss Miller . . . call upon] this young lady of his claim to her faithful remembrance, he called with more promptitude on B
27 the] om. B
29-30 came, in announcing] appearing in the doorway, announced complacently B
34 Mrs. Miller] the parent of the pair B
35 I] I guess I B
35 said Randolph] Randolph broke ground without delay B

36-7 exclaimed . . . the hand] —and his old friend clutched him all interestedly by the arm B
38 exchanging greetings very prettily] engaged in some pretty babble B
39-40 head. 'Well] head with a 'Well B
40 she said] which he met smiling B
41-2 know,' . . . smiling.] know.' B
43 said Miss Daisy] she answered B
178 : 1 to you] to you for that B
2 me!' said Daisy] me then,' Daisy went on as if they had parted the week before B
4 that!' . . . declared] any such thing!' the girl declared afresh B
6 upon] on B
7 said Randolph] Randolph hereupon broke out B
9 Mrs. Miller turned] Mrs. Miller, more of a fatalist apparently than ever, turned B
10 she murmured] she stated as for the benefit of such of the company as might hear it B
11 exclaimed] retorted B
13 Daisy . . . hostess;] As Daisy's conversation with her hostess still occupied her B
15 mother.] mother—such as B
15-16 Vevey,' he said.] Vevey.' B
20 it. I've got it] it bad. But I've got it B
20 most] worst AB
21 announcement] proclamation B
22 relieve her] soothe her by reconstituting the environment to which she was most accustomed B
23 she said] she amiably whined to Winterbourne B
26 should. Oh, at] *would.* Oh up in B
27 him] Dr. Davis B
29 cure it] get at it B
30 wouldn't try] wouldn't try, and I didn't care what he did to me if he only brought me relief B
30-1 new when we came off] new, and I just longed for it, when we came right off B
31 wanted] felt as if he wanted B
32 I wrote . . . get on] I couldn't help writing the other day that I supposed it was all right for Daisy, but that I didn't know as I *could* get on much longer B
39 answered] confessed B
42 'Ah] Winterbourne, however, abounded in reassurance. 'Ah B
42 become] grow B
42-3 it,' said Winterbourne] it.' B
179 : 2 said Winterbourne] his friend laughed B

3 No, I ain't] No I ain't—like any infant B
4 'You are . . . mother] 'Well, that's so, and you never *were*,' his mother concurred B
5 before] ahead of B
6-7 There's Zurich,' she concluded] There's Zurich—up there in the mountains,' she instanced B
7 Zurich is lovely] Zurich's real lovely B
11 his mother] Mrs. Miller B
13 I've seen] *I've* struck B
15-16 said . . . little laugh] said Mrs. Miller with strained but weak optimism B
17 found some gratification in] appreciated the so various interest of B
17-18 declared that] declared with some spirit that B
21 they have been very sociable;] they've all been very sweet— B
25-6 Winterbourne] Winterbourne, but in quite the same free form B
26-7 the young girl announced.] om. B
28-9 asked Winterbourne . . . of the] he asked, a trifle disconcerted, for all his superior gallantry, by her inadequate measure of the B
31-2 sentimental impatience] sweet appeal to his fond fancy, not to say to his finest curiosity B
32 that a cynical] how a cynical B
36 mean at] mean up at B
36 said Daisy] Daisy said B
37 do anything] do most anything B
38 My dearest] Dearest B
38 eloquence] generous passion B
39 to encounter your reproaches] only to be riddled by your silver shafts B
40-1 said Daisy . . . lady's dress] —and she gave an affectionate twist to a bow on her hostess's dress B
42 murmured Mrs. Walker, in] echoed Mrs. Walker more critically—quite in B
180 : 1 said Daisy . . . ribbons] —and the girl continued to finger her ribbons B
3 Motherr,' interposed] Say, mother-r,' broke in B
13 turning] who turned B
14-15 answered . . . to them!'] cried that lady, squirming in shy repudiation. 'It seems as if they didn't take to *me*—I never spoke to one of them!' B
16-18 said Daisy . . . little face] Daisy pursued without a tremor in her young clearness or a shadow on her shining bloom B
19 was silent a moment, she] had a pause and B
20 said] returned B

21 He's an Italian] He's just the finest kind of Italian B

22 mine—he's the] mine and the B

24 He . . . Americans] It seems as if he was crazy about Americans B

25 clever] bright B

26 brilliant personage] paragon B

28 go back] go right back B

28 she said] she remarked with a confessed failure of the larger imagination B

29-30 mother . . . said Daisy.] mother,' Daisy replied, 'but I'm just going to walk round.' B

31 walk] go it B

31 proclaimed] unscrupulously commented B

32 the Pincio,' said Daisy, smiling] go it on the pincio,' Daisy peacably smiled, while the way that she 'condoned' these things almost melted Winterbourne's heart B

35-6 think . . . Mrs. Walker] consider it's safe, Daisy,' her hostess firmly asserted B

37 I,' subjoined Mrs. Miller. 'You'll get] I then,' Mrs. Miller thus borrowed confidence to add. 'You'll catch B

39 some . . . Randolph] some of that medicine before she starts in,' Randolph suggested B

42 she said] she simply said B

181 : 1 getting the fever] catching the fever even it it *is* his own second nature B

3 Mr. Giovanelli?' asked the hostess] Mr. Giovanelli that's the dangerous attraction?' Mrs. Walker asked without mercy B

4 young] challenged B

7 answered] brought out all affirmatively and B

9-10 said . . . pleadingly,] —and, taking her hand, Mrs. Walker turned to pleading— B

10 walk] prowl B

12 English,' said Mrs. Miller] first-rate English,' Mrs. Miller incoherently mentioned B

13 exclaimed] piped up B

14 improper] that's going to affect my health—or my character either! B

14-15 She continued to glance at] Her eyes continued to play over B

15 distant] off B

17 walk with] walk right in with B

18 affirm] proclaim B

18 young] om. B

20 Winterbourne perceived] he saw B

30 upon] on B

31 foreign . . . upon his] woman of English race who passed through it, with some difficulty, on his B

33 expose] exhibit B
34 sense, apparently, was to] sense, was apparently to B
35 Winterbourne] om. B
36 resolved] he resolved B
37 asked Daisy] she meanwhile asked B
42 cried . . . laugh] she derisively cried B
182 : 9 quiet; I] quiet—in fact I B
9 awfully] deadly B
9 was sure] foresaw B
11 that explain] who explain B
22 front,' . . . 'where] front where B
24 'I] Winterbourne at this took a stand. 'I B
24 him,' Winterbourne declared.] him.' B
25 said Miss Daisy] Daisy said with spirit B
26 cried Winterbourne] he protested B
27 her little] her familiar little B
31 perceived] descried thereupon B
31-2 man standing . . . He had] figure that stood with folded arms and nursing its cane. It had B
32-3 an artfully poised hat] a hat artfully poised B
33 his] its B
34 Winterbourne looked at him] Daisy's friend looked at it B
35 man] thing B
38 said Winterbourne] the young man returned B
41 in her face;] om. B
41-2 but the . . . and her] in her face but her charming eyes, her charming teeth and her B
42-3 thought the young man] he thought B
183 : 1 said Daisy] she declared B
4 young] om. B
7 you have . . . Winterbourne] that's just where your mistake has come in,' he retorted B
9 Daisy began] At this she began B
9-10 gentlemen!' . . . 'Tell] gentlemen! Tell B
11 perceived] made out B
12 the young girl] Miss Miller B
13-14 companion . . . eye;] compatriot; he seemed to shine, in his coxcombical way, with the desire to please and the fact of his own intelligent joy, though B
17-18 Daisy . . . mentioned] She had clearly a natural turn for free introductions; she mentioned with the easiest grace B
19 along] forward B
19 each side of her] either hand B
22-3 nonsense . . . urbane] nonsense. He had the best possible manners B
24-6 upon that . . . disappointed] on that depth of Italian subtlety, so strangely opposed to Anglo-Saxon simplicity, which enables people to show a smoother surface in proportion as

they're more acutely displeased B

28 which] that B

29 that] om. B

30 not] anything but B

30 he is only a clever] he isn't even a very plausible B

32 Damn . . . looks] He's awfully on his good behaviour, but damn his fine eyes B

32-6 certainly a very . . . agreeable] indeed great advantages; but it was deeply disgusting to Daisy's other friend that something in her shouldn't have instinctively discriminated against such a type. Giovanelli chattered and jested and made himself agreeable according to his honest Roman lights B

37 brilliant] very skilful A; studied B

39 the question . . . was] the dreadful question of whether this *was* B

43 was it not impossible] wasn't it possible B

184 : 1 circumstances . . . cynicism] very circumstances as a proof more of vulgarity than of anything else B

2 young] om. B

4 vexed because] vexed precisely because B

5-7 perfectly . . . greatly to be] wholly unspotted flower—she lacked a certain indispensable fineness; and it would therefore much simplify the situation to be B

7 object] subject B

7-8 those . . . romancers] the visitations known to romancers as B

9 would help him] would have helped him B

10 and to] just as to B

10-11 would . . . less] would have made her less B

11 But . . . continued] Daisy at any rate continued on this occasion B

15-16 it seemed to Winterbourne] it after all struck one of them B

16 Mr. Giovanelli] the other B

18 perceived] noticed B

21-2 summons . . . excited air] summons—and all to find her flushed, excited, scandalized B

22-3 dreadful,' . . . 'That] dreadful'—she earnestly appealed to him. 'That crazy B

24 noticed] remarked B

25 Winterbourne . . . eyebrows] Winterbourne—suddenly and rather oddly rubbed the wrong way by this—raised his grave eyebrows B

28 said Winterbourne] he reasoned in his own troubled interest B

29-30 crazy!' . . . anything so] reckless!' cried Mrs. Walker, 'and goodness knows how far—left to itself—it may go. Did you ever,' she proceeded to enquire, 'see anything so blatantly B

32 save her] save them B

34-5 asked . . . smiling] Winterbourne uncomfortably smiled B

39-40 said . . . try] he said after reflexion, 'but you're at liberty to try B

41 Mrs. Walker tried] Mrs. Walker accordingly tried B

41 Miss Miller,] their young lady B

42 smiled at his interlocuter] smiled, from her distance, at her recent patroness B

42 interlocuter] interlocutrix A

43-185:1 and had . . . speak to her] and then had gone her way with her own companion. On learning, in the event, that Mrs. Walker had followed her, she B

43 her companion] her own companion A

185 : 1 steps with] steps, however, with B

2-3 declared . . . delighted] professed herself 'enchanted' B

3-4 Mrs. Walker. She] her good friend, and B

4-5 introduction, and declared that] introduction; declaring with it, and as if it were of as little importance, that B

5 Mrs. Walker's] that lady's B

7 this lady] her poor pursuer B

9 said Daisy] —Daisy knew her mind B

9 it much] it ever so much B

11 drive with] drive round *with* B

11 said Mrs. Walker] Mrs. Walker pleaded B

12-13 enchanting . . . glance at] fascinating just as I am!'—with which the girl radiantly took in B

14 enchanting] fascinating B

15 Mrs. Walker] the lady of the victoria B

15 her victoria] this vehicle B

17 said Daisy] Daisy imperturbably laughed B

19-20 the lady . . . losing] Mrs. Walker with a loss of B

21 exclaimed the young girl] the girl amusedly echoed B

22 that] om. B

23 added with a laugh] blandly added B

27 looked . . . intensely] wondered to extravagance B

30 her quickened glance] shining eyes B

32 very agreeably] irresponsibly B

33 thought . . . scene] thought the scene the most unpleasant possible B

34 said Daisy presently] the girl presently said B

35 Winterbourne wished that] Winterbourne only wished B

35 in] up B

36-7 lady did . . . told him.] lady, as she afterwards told him, didn't feel she could 'rest there.' B

38 demanded] accordingly asked B

39 Gracious] Gracious me AB

40 Winterbourne] her other companion B

40 little] small B
42-186:1 asked slowly . . . to foot] put to him with a wonderful bright intensity of appeal B
186 : 3-4 Winterbourne . . . strange] It really embarrassed him; for an instant he cast about—so strange was it B
5 must] had to B
6 simply] surely just B
7 Winterbourne] our young man B
8-10 Daisy Miller . . . gently,] his charming friend should listen to the voice of civilized society. He took in again her exquisite prettiness and then said the more distinctly: B
11 a violent laugh] the rein to her amazement B
13 must give me up] had better give me right up B
19 Mrs. Walker] the lady of the victoria B
21 in earnest . . . overtook] wound up. He accordingly hastened to overtake B
22 companion] more faithful ally B
22 the young girl] her B
23-7 an imperious . . . Mr. Giovanelli] a stringent claim on his presence. He had expected her to answer with something rather free, something still more significant of the perversity from which the voice of society, through the lips of their distressed friend, had so earnestly endeavoured to dissuade her. But she only let her hand slip, as she scarce looked at him, through his slightly awkward grasp; while Mr. Giovanelli, to make it worse B
28 a too-emphatic flourish] too emphatic a flourish B
30 in Mrs. Walker's victoria] beside the author of his sacrifice B
31 while] as B
32 wish] want B
33 wish to be *earnest*!] only want to be *true*! B
34 earnestness] truth B
34 her and] the strange little creature—it has only B
35 said Mrs. Walker] —Mrs. Walker accepted her work B
38 no harm] no great harm, you know B
38 rejoined] maturely opined
41 could] can B
187 : 1 goes away when visitors] melts away when the visitors B
2 said Winterbourne, laughing] laughed Winterbourne B
2-3 midnight] two in the morning B
5 all] om. AB
6 The servants be hanged] Ah we needn't mind the servants B
6 said Winterbourne angrily] Winterbourne compassionately signified B
7 that . . . uncultivated] her complete lack of education B
9 Mrs. Walker declared] Mrs. Walker, on her side, reasoned B
12 Fancy, then, her] Imagine then the taste of her B

14	Winterbourne was] He agreed that taste wasn't the strong point of the Millers—after which he was B
14	then he said,] but only at last to add: B
16	added . . . him] further noted that he should be glad to learn B
18	wished . . . cease] wanted to enjoin on you the importance of your ceasing B
18-20	Miss Miller . . . in short] Miss Miller; that of your not appearing to flirt with her; that of your giving her no further opportunity to expose herself; that of your, in short, letting her alone B
21	that,' said Winterbourne] anything quite so enlightened as *that,*' he returned B
21-2	extremely] awfully, you know B
23	that] om. B
24	There shall] Well, there shall B
24	her.'] her,' he was willing to promise. B
29	traversing] engaged in B
29	Garden that] Garden which A; drive which B
31	there] om. B
36-7	silence; then] silence and then B
37	she] om. B
37-8	Winterbourne stood there] He stood where he had alighted B
40-1	stood a moment] remained a little B
42	Giovanelli] the girl's attendant admirer B
42	upon] on B
188 : 1-2	Daisy's companion] the gallant Giovanelli B
4	it rest upon] it so rest on B
4	so] om. B
5	lingered a moment,] stayed but a moment longer; B
6-7	towards . . . towards] towards the couple united beneath the parasol, rather towards B
11-12	had the . . . them] was met by a denial B
13	frigidity of] final reserves that had marked B
14	the hostess Winterbourne] that social critic our young man B
15	American ladies] pilgrims from the younger world B
15	residing abroad] in contact with the elder B
17	her] om. B
18	fellow-mortals] humanity B
18	it were, as] might be, for B
19	Daisy Miller] the little person he desired most to find B
20	her mother] Mrs. Miller B
20	Mrs. Miller's] This lady's B
21	her exposed-looking] the dead waste of her B
22	Mrs. Walker] their hostess B
23	poor Mrs. Miller] Daisy's unsupported parent B

29 demanded . . . impressively] Mrs. Walker impressively enquired B

30 said Mrs. Miller,] Mrs. Miller testified B

33 she's got] she has B

34 the Italian] the handsomest of the Italians B

36 sings] does sing B

37 concluded . . . hopefully] Mrs. Miller hopefully concluded B

38 that way] that particular way B

38 said Mrs. Walker] Mrs. Walker permitted herself to observe B

39 that] om. B

40 responded] returned B

189 : 2 *Elle s'affiche*] *Elle s'affiche, la malheureuse* B

9 her. She came straight to] her while she floated up to B

17 audibleness] loudest confidence B

18-19 her shoulders] her very white shoulders B

19 asked] as undiscourageable asked B

20 pregnantly] as with a grand intention B

27-8 given . . . Daisy sat] set him in motion—this young lady being seated B

29-30 a high . . . going on] herself his musical patroness or guarantor, giving herself to gay and audible discourse while he warbled B

31 said] remarked B

33 Winterbourne answered;] he candidly returned. B

33-4 I don't dance] I'm incapable of a step B

35-8 you don't dance . . . 'But did you] you're incapable of a step,' the girl assented. 'I should think your legs *would* be stiff cooped in there so much of the time in that victoria.' 'Well, they were very restless there three days ago,' he amicably laughed; 'all they really wanted was to dance attendance on you.' 'Oh my other friend—my friend in need—stuck to me; he seems more at one with his limbs than you are—I'll say that for him. But did you B

39 cool as] cool,' Daisy demanded, 'as B

190 : 1 said Winterbourne;] Winterbourne decided to make answer to this: B

3 streets] streets of Rome B

4 cried Daisy] she cried B

5-6 streets, either; and I] streets either, I guess; and I besides B

7-8 poky . . . can learn] poky time of it, by what I can discover B

8 *them*] *such* stupids B

9 a flirt] a ruthless flirt B

10 gravely] with studied severity B

11-12 are,' . . . again] are!'—and she hoped, evidently, by the manner of it, to take his breath away B

15 'You're a] He remained grave indeed under the shock of her cynical profession. 'You're a B

16 only,' said Winterbourne.] only.' B

20 said Winterbourne] he resentfully remarked B

25 piano; they don't understand] piano. They don't,' he declared as in full sympathy with 'them', 'understand B

26 exclaimed Daisy] Daisy cried with startling world-knowledge B

29 Daisy declared] she retorted B

31-2 place . . . exist here] country. American flirting is a purely American silliness; it has—in its ineptitude of innocence—no place in *this* system B

34 interposed Daisy] and she made it beautifully unspeakable B

35 'Though you] Winterbourne had a touched sense for this, but it didn't alter his attitude. 'Though you B

37 said . . . vivacity] she returned B

38 flirting, we are] flirting—not a little speck. We're B

39 that; we are very] that. We're real B

40 'Ah . . . Winterbourne] He was to continue to find her thus at moments inimitable. 'Ah!' he then judged B

41 affair] affair altogether B

42 talk] speak B

43 expectation] thought B

43-191:1 this ejaculation . . . blushing] the force of his logic; yet she now none the less immediately rose, blushing B

191 : 1-2 to exclaim . . . in the world] mentally to exclaim that the name of little American flirts was incoherence B

3-4 said, giving . . . things to me] answered, sparing but a single small queer glance for it, a queerer small glance, he felt, than he had ever yet had from her—'Mr. Giovanelli never says to me such very disagreeable things B

5-6 Winterbourne . . . to Daisy] It had an effect on him—he stood staring. The subject of their contention had finished singing; he left the piano, and his recognition of what—a little awkwardly—didn't take place in celebration of this might nevertheless have been an acclaimed operatic tenor's series of repeated ducks before the curtain. So he bowed himself over to Daisy B

7 into] to B

7-8 asked, bending . . . smile] asked—offering Mrs. Walker's slightly thin refreshment as he might have done all the kingdoms of the earth B

8 ornamental] decorative A

9-10 turned to . . . inconsequent smile] at last turned on Winterbourne a more natural and calculable light. He was but the more muddled by it however, since so inconsequent a smile B

10-11 clear . . . that she had] clear—it seemed at the most to prove in her B
13-14 her little tormenting manner] her finest little intention of torment and triumph B
15 Winterbourne rejoined] the young man permitted himself to growl B
19 young people] conversers B
22 young . . . She] girl's arrival—she B
23 upon] on B
24 was standing] happened to be B
26 violation . . . forms] rupture of any law or of any deviation from any custom B
28 observance of them] conformity B
31 pale, grave face] small white prettiness, a blighted grace, B
35 said to] promptly remarked to B
36 'She never] But this lady's face was also as a stone. 'She never B
36 again,' replied his hostess.] again.' B
37 Winterbourne was] Winterbourne then, hereupon, was B
40 brilliant] polished A; glossy B
40-1 Roman was . . . Daisy alone] Roman, serene in success, but not unduly presumptuous, occupied with Daisy alone the florid salon enjoyed by Eugenio's care B
42 constantly] ever B
42-3 surveillance] solicitude B
192 : 1 never embarrassed or] neither embarrassed nor B
2 very] om. B
3-4 him; the . . . to expect] him and that he really liked, after all, not making out what she was 'up to' B
4-5 at her . . . being interrupted] for the interruption of her *tête-à-tête* with Giovanelli B
6-7 one; there was . . . puerility] one, and this easy flow had ever the same anomaly for her earlier friend that it was so free without availing itself of its freedom B
7-8 remarked to himself] reflected B
8-9 Giovanelli . . . should not] the Italian it was odd she shouldn't B
10 more] better B
11 apparently] om. B
11 good humour] gaiety B
12-18 seemed to him . . . of Daisy Miller] struck him as a young person not formed for a troublesome jealousy. Smile at such a betrayal though the reader may, it was a fact with regard to the women who had hitherto interested him that, given certain contingencies, Winterbourne could see himself afraid—literally afraid—of these ladies. It pleased him to believe that even were twenty other things different and Daisy should

love him and he should know it and like it, he would still never be afraid of Daisy B

19 sentiment] conviction B

19-21 Daisy; it was . . . young person] her: it represented that she was nothing every way if not light B

25 Winterbourne] her other friend B

26 little party] entertainment B

28-31 perceived Daisy . . . then she said] became aware that the young woman held in horror by that lady was strolling about the great church under escort of her coxcomb of the Corso. It amused him, after a debate, to point out the exemplary pair —even at the cost, as it proved, of Mrs. Costello's saying when she had taken them in through her eye-glass B

33 said the young man] he pleaded B

34 you are thinking] you're always thinking B

38 Winterbourne] he B

41 rejoined . . . pensiveness] he insisted with a hint perhaps of the preoccupation B

42 that] om. B

193 : 1 'I have heard] 'Well'—and Mrs. Costello dropped her glass —'I've heard B

3 very intimate,' said Winterbourne] as thick as thieves,' our exbarrassed young man allowed B

4-5 inspected . . . instrument] came back to them, however, after a little; and Winterbourne recognized in this a further illustration—than that supplied by his own condition—of the spell projected by the case B

5 He is very] He's certainly very B

6 gentleman] gentleman possible B

11 said Winterbourne] Winterbourne reasoned B

13 nothing. She goes] nothing at all. She romps B

15 vulgar. And] vulgar,' said Mrs. Costello, whose figure of speech scarcely went on all fours. 'And B

15-16 added Mrs. Costello] she added B

16 it that she may] it she may B

18 Giovanelli expects] Giovanelli really expects B

20 little Italian] shiny—but, to do him justice, not greasy—little Roman B

23 is] om. B

24 that] om. B

27 expensiveness] personal daintiness B

29 doubt that] doubt whether A

29 I rather . . . marrying her] Yes, he can't really hope to pull it off B

31 substantial Mr. Miller] substantial, a possibly explosive Mr. Miller B

32 dollars. Giovanelli knows] dollars and six-shooters. Giovanelli's but too conscious B

33-4 He must . . . the way] What on earth can he make of the way B
36 said Mrs. Costello.] om. B
40 that they are] them B
41 *avvocato*] *cavaliere* A; cavaliere avvocato B
41 can't believe it,' said Mrs. Costello] doesn't believe them!' cried Mrs. Costello B
194 : 1 Mrs. Costello] his relative B
2 little] small B
5 there was a great deal] much was B
9-10 he could . . . far indeed] the measure of her course struck him as simply there to take B
11 that she had] she had B
12 head] wits, B
12 hear] see B
13-14 assigned to . . . disorder] sink so low in human estimation B
18 talked . . . superb] 'went on' for some moments about the great B
19 which hangs] suspended B
20-1 had the . . . a picture] enjoyed sight of an image B
21 pretty American girl] little American who's so much more a work of nature than of art and B
23 pretty] little B
23-4 girl—prettier than] —prettier now than B
25 great] om. B
25 portrait was] presence is B
26 'Who was . . . Winterbourne] 'All alone?' the young man heard himself disingenuously ask B
27-8 A little . . . pretty] Alone with a little Italian who sports in his buttonhole a stack of flowers. The girl's a charming beauty B
30 answered] said B
31 Daisy . . . but five] the interesting pair but ten B
33 to him] om. B
35-6 Mr. Giovanelli,' . . . 'She's] Mr. Giovanelli. She's B
37 that . . . intimate] they're intimate indeed B
38 observed] concurred B
40-1 keep . . . engaged] guess I have the joke on Daisy—that she *must* be engaged B
42 what does Daisy say] how does your daughter *take* the joke B
43 she says] she just says B
43 engaged] om. B
43-195:1 impartial] philosophic B
195 : 2 *she* doesn't] Daisy don't B
3 shouldn't] wouldn't B
6-7 gave up . . . her guard] recoiled before the attempt to educate at a single interview either her conscience or her wit B
8 Winterbourne] he B

10-11 that she . . . too far] as to the length she must have gone B
11 and they intimated] intimating B
12 desired to express to] wished to make, and make strongly, for the benefit of B
12 great truth] point B
13-15 young American . . . as abnormal] pretty American girl all right, her behaviour wasn't pretty at all—was in fact regarded by her compatriots as quite monstrous B
16 towards] upon B
16-20 it annoyed him . . . perceived it] found himself suspecting with impatience that she simply didn't feel and didn't know. He set her down as hopelessly childish and shallow, as such mere giddiness and ignorance incarnate as was powerless either to heed or to suffer B
20 believed] couldn't doubt B
23 Daisy's defiance came] the defiance would come B
25-7 It must be . . . gallantry] Then it had to be admitted, he felt, that holding fast to a belief in her 'innocence' was more and more but a matter of gallantry too fine-spun for use B
28-31 angry at finding . . . had somehow] reduced without pleasure to this chopping of logic and vexed at his poor fallibility, his want of instinctive certitude as to how far her extravagance was generic and national and how far it was crudely personal. Whatever it was he had helplessly B
34-5 encountered . . . abode] came across her at that supreme seat B
38-9 was strolling . . . those] moved at her ease over the B
40-1 that Rome had never been] he had never known Rome B
41 stood looking off] looked off B
43 city, inhaling] city—he inhaled B
43 feeling] felt B
196 : 1 mysterious] deep B
2 seemed to him] struck him B
2-3 looked so pretty] showed to the eye for so utterly charming B
3 an observation . . . met her] his conviction on every occasion of their meeting B
4 was at] was of course at B
4-5 wore an . . . brilliancy] glowed as never before with something of the glory of his race B
6 said Daisy] she broke out upon the friend it would have been such mockery to designate as the latter's rival B
6 be lonesome] be quite lonesome B
7 asked Winterbourne] Winterbourne resignedly echoed B
10 said Winterbourne] he answered B
10 your companion] your gallant companion B
11 Giovanelli . . . Winterbourne] Giovanelli had from the first treated him B

13-14 seemed disposed . . . young man] attached such importance as he could find terms for to Miss Miller's cold compatriot B

16 your] any one's B

17-19 seemed to . . . him—to say] struck Winterbourne that he almost yearned at times for some private communication in the interest of his character for common sense; a chance to remark B

19 an] another B

20 bless you] bless him B

20 this] their B

21 delusive . . . hopes] confident—at least *too* confident and too delusive—hopes B

23 companion] charming charge B

25 said . . . Giovanelli] Daisy meanwhile observed B

27 her attendant] her discreet attendant B

28 said Winterbourne] was all Winterbourne found to reply B

29 Daisy exclaimed seriously] —she made this point with much expression B

30 believe it] believe a word of it B

32-3 disagreeably'] disagreeably,' he took on himself to state B

34 looked at him a moment] weighted the importance of that idea B

35 Winterbourne] he compassionately B

36-7 you were . . . first time I] you've no more ''give'' than a ramrod the first time ever I B

38-9 I am not . . . Winterbourne, smiling] at least that I've more ''give'' than several others,' he patiently smiled B

197 : 1 give] show B

5 Exactly!] Exactly as Mrs. Walker did the other night. B

5 said Winterbourne.] om. B

6 who was decorating himself] still titivating B

7 looking back at Winterbourne—] with her attention again on the important subject: B

8 she said.] om. B

9 he asked.] om. B

10 you would say] you'd want to say B

11 do say] do want to say B

11 he] Winterbourne B

11 I say that] I want to say that B

12 that] om. B

12 are] om. B

13 Well, she] Well, I guess she B

14 Winterbourne] The young man B

14-15 he asked.] om. B

16-17 anything,' . . . scepticism] anything.' This testimony to Randolph's scepticism B

17 hilarity] mirth B

18 observed] noticed B
19 too] as well B
20-1 Winterbourne looked at her;] He looked at her hard— B
22 He was . . . then] He asked himself, and it was for a moment like testing a heart-beat; after which B
23 'Well, then—I am not!'] 'But *if* you possibly do,' she still more perversely pursued 'well, I ain't!' B
24 The . . . cicerone] Miss Miller and her constant guide B
26 afterwards] later on B
28 charming,] perfect B
30-1 There was . . . and her] Above was a moon half-developed, whose B
31 she was] om. B
32 which] that B
33-4 (it was . . . Winterbourne] at eleven o'clock he B
34-6 it recurred . . . well worth] the sense of the romantic in him easily suggested that the interior, in such an atmosphere, would well repay B
42 shade . . . sleeping] shade while the other slept B
198 : 1-3 meditations . . . the doctors] meditation thereabouts was the fruit of a rich literary culture it was none the less deprecated by medical science B
3-4 historic . . . considered] air of other ages surrounded one; but the air of other ages, coldly analysed B
5 walked to] sought, however, towards B
6-7 to take a . . . to make] a further reach of vision, intending the next moment B
7-10 covered with . . . steps which] almost obscured; only as he drew near did he make it out distinctly. He thus also distinguished two persons stationed on the low steps that B
11 was standing in front of] hovered before B
14-15 were the . . . Daisy Miller] words were winged with their accent, so that they fluttered and settled about him in the darkness like vague white doves. It was Miss Daisy Miller who had released them for flight B
16-17 responded the ingenious Giovanelli] —the bland Giovanelli fell in with her humour B
18 stopped . . . horror;] felt himself pulled up with final horror now— B
19 a sort of] final B
19-21 as if a . . . had become] as if a sudden clearance had taken place in the ambiguity of the poor girl's appearances and the whole riddle of her contradictions had grown B
21-2 whom a . . . respect] about the *shades* of whose perversity a foolish puzzled gentleman need no longer trouble his head or his heart. That once questionable quantity *had* no shades—it was a mere black little blot B

23 companion] companion too B

24 visible] presented B

25-7 with himself . . . again, he] at all his shiftings of view—he felt ashamed of all his tender little scruples and all his witless little mercies. He was about to advance again, and then again B

27 that he was] of B

28-9 appearing . . . revulsion from] showing undue exhilaration for this disburdenment of B

32 cuts me] cuts me dead B

33-4 and how . . . played at] he was amply able to reflect at this, and how smartly she feigned, how promptly she sought to play off on him, a surprised and B

34 he . . . Winterbourne] nothing would induce him to cut her either 'dead' or to within any measurable distance even of the famous 'inch' of her life. He B

35 up;] up and B

37-8 craziness . . . in this nest] madness, on the ground of exposure and infection, of a frail young creature's lounging away such hours in a nest B

38-9 a clever little reprobate? that] the most plausible of little reprobates? That B

40 here] "fooling round" here B

40 almost brutally] with conscious roughness B

41-2 flattering . . . gently. . . .] sinister silver radiance, appraised him a moment, roughness and all. 'Well, I guess all the evening.' She answered with spirit and, he could see then, with exaggeration. B

43 pretty] quaint B

199 : 1 said Winterbourne] he returned B

1-2 Roman fever very pretty] a bad attack of Roman fever very quaint B

3 added, turning to] added to B

4 a terrible indiscretion] extraordinary rashness B

5 the handsome native] this seasoned subject B

5 am not afraid] have no fear B

6 am I . . . I am] have I—for you!' Winterbourne retorted in French. 'I'm B

7 lifted] raised B

7-8 brilliant . . . Winterbourne's] shining teeth, but he took his critic's B

8-9 told the Signorina] assured Mademoiselle B

9 the Signorina] Mademoiselle B

11 the Signorina] Mademoiselle B

13 shouldn't] wouldn't B

16 He has] Eugenio has B

17 advise you] advise you then B

19 'What you] Giovanelli smiled as for the striking happy thought. 'What you B

19 wise,' . . . 'I will] wise. I'll B

21-2 He . . . seemed] He tried to deny himself the small fine anguish of looking at her, but his eyes themselves refused to spare him, and she seemed moreover B

23-4 Winterbourne . . . about] He spoke no word; Daisy chatted over B

24 moonlight!' . . . good thing] moonlight—that's one thing I can rave about B

25 Winterbourne's] her companion's B

25-6 didn't speak] was so stiff—it had always been her great word B

26 answer . . . laugh] answer, but he felt his laugh an immense negation of stiffness B

28-9 the young American] her compatriot B

29 she asked] om. B

30 matter what] matter now what B

30-1 said . . . laughing] he replied with infinite point B

32 'Well, what] It was a wonder how she didn't wince for it. 'Well, what B

33 that] om. B

35-6 the young . . . to answer] her lighted eyes fairly penetrate the thick gloom of the vaulted passage—as if to seek some access to him she hadn't yet compassed B

37 Giovanelli . . . forward] Giovanelli, with a graceful inconsequence, was at present all for retreat B

37 quick,' . . . 'if] quick; if B

42 said . . . tone] she unexpectedly cried out for this B

43 Upon this] On which B

200 : 1 away over] across B

1 of the antique] of antique B

4-5 but nevertheless . . . was known] in spite of which deep discretion, however, the fact of the scandalous adventure was known a couple of days later, with a dozen vivid details, B

6 and commented] and was commented B

7 reflected . . . the hotel] judged thus that the people about the hotel had been thoroughly empowered to testify B

8 had been] would have been B

8 remarks] jokes B

9-10 was conscious] became aware B

10-11 that it had . . . regret to] of how thoroughly it had ceased to ruffle B

12-13 people, a day . . . to give] sources of current criticism a day or two later abounded still further B

13 ill] ill and the doctors now in possession of the scene B

17 by Randolph] by the all-efficient Randolph B

18 night,' . . . made her] night that way, you bet—that's what has made her so B

20 dark] dark over there B

20-1 here at . . . a moon] over here without the moon's right up B

21-2 there's always . . . was now] they don't go round by the moon!' Mrs. Miller meanwhile wholly surrendered to her genius for unapparent uses; her salon knew her less than ever, and she was presumably B

23 evident] clear B

24-7 went often to . . . good deal about] constantly attended for news from the sick room, which reached him, however, but with worrying indirectness, though he once had speech, for a moment, of the poor girl's physician and once saw Mrs. Miller, who, sharply alarmed, struck him as thereby more happily inspired than he could have conceived and indeed as the most noiseless and light-handed of nurses. She invoked a good deal of the remote shade of B

28-9 saying to . . . goose] taking her after all for less monstrous a goose. To this indulgence indeed something she further said perhaps even more insidiously disposed him B

29-30 day,' . . . 'Half] day quite pleasantly. Half B

32 told me to tell you that] wanted you to know B

33 Italian] Italian who was always round B

35 me that he] me he B

36-8 was angry with . . . scold him] hadn't approved of his being round with her so much evenings. Of course it ain't as if their evenings were as pleasant as ours—since *we* don't seem to feel that way about the poison. I guess I *don't* see the point now; but I suppose he knows I'm a lady and I'd scorn to raise a fuss B

38 says] wants you to realize

39 wanted you to know;] makes so much of it, B

41 went to] went up to B

43 I'm sure . . . know it] I guess I'm glad to realize it too B

201 : 1 said . . . very little] originally judged, the truth on this question had small actual relevance B

2-3 been a . . . grave was] been indeed a terrible case of the *perniciosa*. A grave was found for her B

3 cemetery, in an] cemetary, by an B

7 would have led you to expect] might have made probable B

8-10 Giovanelli . . . last he said,] Giovanelli, in decorous mourning, showed but a whiter face; his buttonhole lacked its nosegay and he had visibly something urgent—and even to distress—to say, which he scarce knew how to 'place'. He decided at last to confide it with a pale convulsion to Winterbourne. B

11 And then] To which B

12 And she was] Also—naturally!— B

13-14 looked at him . . . 'And the] sounded him with hard dry eyes, but presently repeated his words, 'The B

16 Winterbourne . . . angry] It came somehow so much too late that our friend could only glare at its having come at all B

18-19 Mr. Giovanelli's . . . then he said] Giovanelli raised his neat shoulders and eyebrows to within suspicion of a shrug B

20 she wanted to go] *she*—she did what she liked B

21-2 'That was . . . dropped his eyes] Winterbourne's eyes attached themselves to the ground. 'She did what she liked!' It determined on the part of poor Giovanelli a further pious, a further candid, confidence B

23 would never] never would B

23-4 me, I am sure] me B

25 'She . . . you?'] It had been spoken as if to attest, in all sincerity, his disinterestedness, but Winterbourne scarce knew what welcome to give it. He said, however, with a grace inferior to his friend's: 'I dare say not.' B

26 'For a] The latter was even by this not discouraged. 'For a B

26 sure] convinced B

27 listened to him] took it in B

28-9 away again . . . had retired] round again his fellow-mourner had stepped back B

30 Winterbourne] He B

31-2 Mrs. Costello . . . Vevey] Mrs. Costello extracted from the charming old hotel there a value that the Miller family hadn't mastered the secret of B

33 Daisy . . . manners] the most interesting member of that trio —of her mystifying manners and her queer adventure B

34 that] om. B

36 said Mrs. Costello] —that lady showed caution B

41-2 Is that . . . that she] She took an odd way to gain it! But do you mean by what you say,' Mrs. Costello asked, 'that she B

43-202:1 Winterbourne . . . presently said,] As he made no answer to this she after a little looked round at him—he hadn't been directly within sight; but the effect of that wasn't to make her repeat her question. He spoke, however, after a while B

202 : 3 parts.'] parts.' And this time she herself said nothing. B

4 he went] he soon went B

LONGSTAFF'S MARRIAGE

Notes:

1. The variants recorded below are based on a collation of the original serial text of the tale (*Scribner's Monthly*, 1878) and its revised version in *The Madonna of the Future* (1879).

2. In the revised text the name of Agatha Gosling is changed to Agatha Josling: only the first occurrence of this revision is recorded in the list of variants.

203 : 2	envy of] envy and despair of
9	Agatha Gosling] Agatha Josling
22	the lands . . . of] foreign lands
26	come together on] been united by
26-7	mother and the . . . of] mother, when the latter young lady took possession of
31	sufficient] all in all
204 : 1	stand . . . light-shafts] wander through the aisles
2	wander] wind
3	by . . . seas] on the shores of the blue lakes
9	she . . . them] they had filled her with contempt
11	disrelished] contemned
21	decency] propriety
24	had enough] had money enough
25	extensively] largely
205 : 20	But that] But for the fact that
26	consumptive people] pulmonary sufferers
31	inference . . . uncomfortable] induction from an embarrassing
37	being . . . defensive] turning her graceful back
38	her intimacy] their acquaintance
39	a best] her best
206 : 42	with . . . locks] and slightly dishevelled
43	this] his
207 : 9	furnishing] proposing to
11	should] would
35	it *was* Mr. Longstaff's lungs] Mr. Longstaff's complaint was pulmonary
36	most] quite
208 : 10-11	them, in . . . speaking otherwise] them. He would speak with the gravest courtesy—she could not fancy him speaking otherwise
19-20	small incidents . . . cast] accidents is to attribute to his behaviour a certain aggressiveness
21-2	something . . . impertinence] there was something scrupulous and subdued in his manner which made it perfectly discreet
209 : 5	rupture of] variation from
6	strong] sudden

8	deferred] accommodated herself
12	him] the young man
36	thus] so
210 : 13	appeal] have addressed himself
17	smaller] less formidable
211 : 3	didn't] hadn't
28	most] wonderfully
212 : 10	Then say] Then please say
34	lacking] deficient
36	most . . . contingency] very painful thing to see
213 : 3	believe] am sure
6-7	the Trois Frères Provençaux] a great restaurant
36	his interlocutress] the little lady
214 : 25	Diana] young lady
41	the Diana what he] your friend what my dear master
215 : 3-4	your beautiful friend] the signorina
5	most] very
11	that a] that an Italian
16	melt her down.] warm her up!
20-1	she came to a sense] it occurred to her
36	very] om.
216 : 2	cloudy] irritated
2	terribly handsome] more than ever like the easily-startled goddess of the chase
24	kind,' . . . 'as] kind as
24	nearer?'] nearer?' said Mr. Longstaff.
37	would] should
217 : 28	wept silently] silently let them flow
40-1	in this categorical fashion] so reasonably and consistently
43	delicate] discreet
218 : 3	perplexed] baffled
8	would] should
15	one of suspense] a critical one
31	get well] not die
35	along] upon
35	depended] was displayed
219 : 3-4	she . . . revolting] the scene had been revolting
5	suggest something in] make some vague
6	great] passionate
8	he had] this disgusting incident had
22	contentment] wanderings
24	charm] spell
26	evenness] generous mildness
37	this feeling] her opinion of it
39	*contretemps*] disaster
40	smile which] smile—a smile which
220 : 1	home, in] home, speaking of it in

Page : Line	Variant
5	conversation] intercourse
7	go and . . . country] go into the country and devote herself to her nearer kinsfolk
10-11	town gossip] town-talk
27	that she had broken off] that she was neither happy nor to be married. She had broken off
28	that] om.
29	and found] and she found
221 : 7	lent] thrown
7	to] into
19	acutely] greatly
21	removed] renewed
23	placidity] serenity
27	relished . . . rest] had much more taste for motion than for rest
31	lived] passed her days
34	would] determined to
34	So she] She
43	place] town
222 : 2	this fashion] this delightful fashion
5-6	extreme fatigue and determined] being very tired and prepared
22	the peopled pavement] the vast, peopled pavement
24-5	murmur . . . about] make remarks about the people around
30	point] occasion
30	found entertainment] found plenty of entertainment
33	and she] and then she
223 : 2	flush of colour] handsome colour
15	square of the] square, between the
29	noticed all the passers] looked at every one who passed her
38-9	possibility were a fact] belief of Diana's were true
224 : 3	mottled] freckled
9	pondered] thought of
9	resolved] made up her mind
10	sending for] to send for
18	disbelieved] found it impossible to believe
24	blooming manhood] blooming manhood. This last point there was no theory to explain
25	On this . . . unexplained.] om.
30	blooming, gallant, quiet,] quiet, blooming, gallant
37	Then she] She
40	I came back to strength] my strength came back to me
225 : 14	it once in] once to comfort her by
15	in] by
17-18	a renewed . . . she saw] that she herself admired him as much as ever—that the timid little flame which was kindled at Nice was beginning to shoot up again. Agatha saw

20-1	ingenuously murmured] pretended to murmur
38	investigate] interrogate
40	had] om.
226 : 1	palace] ancient
2	filled] adorned
18	wanted] wished
18-19	service read] service to be read
20	marvelling] in much surprise

AN INTERNATIONAL EPISODE

Notes:

1. The variants recorded below are based on a collation of the original serial text of the tale (*Cornhill*, 1878) and its two revised versions in *Daisy Miller: A Study* (1879)—hereinafter mentioned as A—and *Lady Barbarina, Etc.* (1908)—hereinafter mentioned as B.

2. Although substantive variants between the original and A are very few in number, there is one uniquely long interpolation in the first revised version which, after further alterations, is retained in B. This item is here recorded as a variant in A *and* B: the B forms are indicated within the passage in square brackets.

3. In A and B, the tale is divided into six chapters. Chapter I begins at 228:1; II at 237:26; III at 246:12; IV at 257:29; V at 270:14; VI at 280:37.

IN TWO PARTS] om. AB

PART I] I AB

228 : 4	fervid temperature of that city] high, the torrid temperature B
5	those] the B
5	which] that B
7	bumping, took] bumping they took B
8-10	not perhaps . . . interminable avenue] doubtless not the most engaging, though nothing perhaps could well more solicit an alarmed attention. Of quite other sense and sound from those of any typical English street was the endless rude channel B
12	each side . . . comfortable] either side at the rough B
13	sidewalks, the] sidewalks, at the B
13	architecture, the] architecture, at the B
14-15	façades, glittering . . . lettering, the] façades that, bedizened with gilded lettering, seemed to glare in the strong crude light, at the B
16	streamers, the] streamers, at the B
17	vehicles, the] vehicles, at the B
229 : 2	It seems a rum-looking] Awfully rum B
6	his friend] the clever man B
7	the other] his friend B
10	rejoined the other] the other returned B
12	was checked by] dropped on B
13	which had been] om. B
14	they made] they had made B
14	they became] they had become B
18-20	that his . . . from St. Louis] his 'partner' in earnest attendance on the wharf, with urgent claims on his immediate presence of mind B

Page	Line	Variant
	21	but] beyond B
	23	that] om. B
	23	was] om. B
	27	into] to B
	31	under any circumstances] in any connection B
	31	occasion] hour B
	32-3	something . . . themselves] much that ministered to ease in the general situation of our young men B
	33-4	extremely good-natured young men] formed for good spirits and addicted and appointed to hilarity B
	34-5	appeared; in a sort of] appeared; they were, in an B
	35-6	they . . . appreciative] capable of high appreciation B
	40-1	pavement, where there were] expanse studded with B
	42	trees . . . there was] trees—beyond which appeared B
	42	any] om. B
230 :	3	there] om. B
	5	a large proportion of] extremely frequent among B
	6	Within, the place] The place within B
	8	upon] on B
	12	rejoined] returned B
	15	Fancy] Ah but fancy B
	15	a club,] a London club! B
	16	young . . . little,] elder man stared B
	21	Well, you can't.] No more you can! 'B
	21	the elder . . . Englishmen] this candid critic B
	23	His companion . . . declaration] The other paid no heed whatever to his candour B
	24	he] the latter B
	26	understand them] make them out, you know B
	30-1	desultory observation . . . themselves] a desultory view of the mysteries of the new world bristling about them B
	33	of] as to B
	33-4	offered them a very long list] submitted to them a hundred alternatives B
	35-6	coming on] at hand B
	36	heat was still] heat still B
	37	travellers] visitors B
	42-3	Belgrave Square] Grosvenor Square B
	43	was] om. B
231 :	4	hotel seemed to be] hotel, figuring B
	5	flinging] flung B
	6	sort of] om. B
	9	with their legs stretched] their legs variously stretched B
	10	*queue*] cue B
	11	brilliantly . . . extent] vast marble altar of sacrifice, a thing shaped like the counter of a huge shop B
	13	very] om. B
	14	be rendering some mysterious] render mystic B

16 an absent] a cold B

18-19 an hotel-clerk . . . By bed time—] an hotel-clerk. 'I'm glad he didn't tell us to go there,' said one of our Englishmen, alluding to their friend on the steamer, who had told them so many things. They walked up the Fifth Avenue, where, for instance, he had told them that all [where he had for instance told them all B] the first families lived. But the first families were out of town, and our young travellers had only [our friends had but B] the satisfaction of seeing some of the second—or perhaps even the third—taking the evening air upon balconies and high flights of doorsteps, in the streets which radiate from the more ornamental thoroughfare [in streets at right angles to the main straight channel. B]. They went a little way down one of these side-streets, and they [and there B] saw young ladies in white dresses—charming-looking persons—seated in graceful attitudes on the chocolate-coloured steps. In one or two places these young ladies were conversing across the street with other young ladies seated in similar postures and costumes in front of the opposite houses, and in the warm night air their colloquial tones sounded strange [sounded strangely B] in the ears of the young Englishmen. One of our friends [of the latter, B], nevertheless—the younger one—intimated that he felt [—the younger—betrayed B] a disposition to intercept a few of these soft familiarities [intercept some stray item of this interchange and see what it would lead to; B] but his companion observed, pertinently enough, that he had better be careful. 'We must not begin with making mistakes,' said his companion [careful. They mustn't begin by making mistakes. B] 'But he told us, you know—he told us,' urged the young man, alluding again to the friend on the steamer. 'Never mind what he told us!' answered his comrade [his elder, B] who, if he had greater talents [had more years and a more developed wit, B] was also apparently more of a moralist. By bed-time [By bed-time B]— AB

24 had tossed upon the] had been tossed by B

26 England; and then it] England, but it then B

27 that] om. B

29 they wished] wishing B

30 they determined] resolved B

32 junior traveller] younger gentlemen B

38-9 He is a capital fellow] He's really very decent B

39 got] om. B

43 to him . . . circulation] him for the right kick-off B

232 : 1 got] om. B

3-4 a gentleman . . . depicted] so possible a benefactor B

8 we can . . . pursuit] can at once give chase B

13 upon] by B
18 London house] dirty London thing B
20 house] thing B
23 burning heavens] blaze of the sky B
27 sir,] om. B
34 two gentlemen] comrades B
35 languidly, to] languidly enough, to B
36 they] om. B
41 quickly] nimbly B
42 into this brilliant building] under portals that were as the course of a twofold torrent B
233 : 2 perceived them to be] recognized them as B
5-6 horizontal compartment] heaven, as it were, B
8 different] conjoined B
9 them] these B
10 which] om. B
14-15 with an expression . . . eye] a face suggesting one of the ingenious modern objects with alternative uses, good as a blade or as a hammer, good for the deeps and for the shallows. His forehead was high but expressive, his eyes sharp but amused B
16 mouth and made] mouth, made B
17 Lord Lambeth thought he looked] Relaxed though he was at this moment Lord Lambeth judged him on the spot B
19-20 he said, holding] —he held B
20 see] meet B
23 windows wide open beneath] where windows opened wide under B
24-7 Lord Lambeth . . . the air] his lordship felt high indeed in the air B
31 it won't last] I guess it will break B
31 very] om. B
32 nothing . . . over here] there's never anything bad over here but it does break B
34 will] shall B
35 didn't remember making] don't remember once mixing B
35 one day,] om. B
36 twenty] fifteen B
36-7 well; two . . . since then] well. I'd be glad to mix him some more B
38 right] right—and without *them* B
234 : 1 wiping] with a wipe of B
7 affirmed] was very positive B
16 upon] on B
17 fine] big things B
21-2 at him, narrowing his] him over with narrowed B
23 put you through] fix you all right B

25 had considerable practice,] been through a good deal with them B

26 right] true B

26 to] om. B

28 to] om. B

29-32 American, in his . . . professional—] American with his face of toil, his voice of leisure and his general intention, apparently, of everything; B

31 humourous] facetious A

34-5 coming over . . . across] to make this little visit, so I just came with him B

37 visit to the United States] time over here B

39 said Percy Beaumont] Percy Beaumont explained B

40 along] along for company B

235 : 1-2 said Mr. Westgate] Mr. Westgate threw off B

3-4 by way of . . . bringing a suit] just acting for some English shareholders by way of legal advice. Some of my friends—well, if the truth must be told,' Mr. Beaumont laughed—'have a grievance B

5-6 your railways . . . accordingly] your confounded railways, and they've asked me to come and judge, if possible, on the spot, what they can hope B

7 Mr. Westage . . . looks again] Mr. Westage's amused eyes grew almost tender

10 a little,] om. B

11-12 institutions,' . . . 'But] institutions. But B

14 barrister] emissary B

16-17 Some day . . . it square] I guess I can tell you more about it than most any one B

19-20 asked Percy Beaumont] Percy Beaumont appealed B

21-22 at home by . . . irrelevantly,] back early for *my* engagements,' said his companion irrelevantly B

23 hunting—] yachting or the hunting B

25 said Lord Lambeth, blushing a little] —and Lord Lambeth just amiably blushed B

26 rejoined Mr. Westgage] Mr. Westgate returned B

27 go down] go right down B

30 It isn't a train—it's a boat] You don't take any train. You take a boat B

32-4 It isn't a . . . cool; that's] It's a regular old city—don't you let them hear you call it a village or a hamlet or anything of that kind. They'd half-kill you. Only it's a city of pleasure—of lawns and gardens and verandahs and views and, above all, of good Samaritans,' Mr. Westgate developed. 'But you'll see what Newport is. It's cool. That's B

35 into] in B

35 hands] ones B

38 very fond of] half-crazy about B

40 an inquiring traveller] a collector of characteristic facts B

42 them. She has] them yet. You'll show her anyhow. She has B

236 : 1-2 believe,' . . . intellectual town] believe, is the most intellectual centre B

3 I believe . . . intellectual] Well, yes—Boston knows it's central and feels it's intellectual B

3-4 much,' responded his host] much—I stay round here,' Mr. Westgate more loosely pursued B

5 say, we] say, you know, *we* B

5 said Lord Lambeth] Lord Lambeth broke out B

11-14 Lord Lambeth . . . American humour] Lord Lambeth flushed himself, in his charming way, with wonder, though his friend glanced to make sure he wasn't looking too credulous—they had heard so much about American practices. He decided in time, at any rate, to take a safe middle course B

15 jolly,' . . . gentlemen.] jolly.' B

16 said Mr. Westgate] Mr. Westgate returned B

16 upon] on B

18-19 half the people in New York] many of our most prominent citizens and society leaders B

20 got] om. B

27 try] undertake B

28 expect] guess B

29 morning] om. B

30-1 make yourself comfortable] get into touch B

32 immediately send out] send right out B

35-6 will come . . . getting on] don't know but I'll come down myself and see how you are B

39 very good fellow] clear thinker B

40 upon] on B

41 it were—as if it hinted] might be, hinting B

42 possibly] om. B

237 : 6 he kept] he so kept B

6 so long] om. B

7 missing the steamer] miss their previous escape B

9 the wharf] embark B

18 spacious apartment,] luxurious retreat B

19 sculptured] florid B

20 that] om. B

25 you. I'll come . . . after you] you. Take it as it's meant. Renounce your own personality. I'll come down by and by and enjoy what's left of you B

27 steamer] ship B

28 an extraordinary . . . an hotel] a monstrous floating hotel or even as a semi-submerged kindergarten B

32 gas-light] gas-lights B

34 philosophic leisure] amused critcism B
36 discriminating black, our young men] blackamoor more closely related to the scene than his companions, our young friends B
37 some] om. B
38 in] from B
39 was playing] played B
39-40 were handing] handed B
40 as if they had been] in the manner of B
42 of the steamer,] om. B
43 in the vague starlight, to make] the vague starlight aiding, make B
238 : 1 The young Englishmen] Our travellers B
2 talked . . . talked] conversed, as they usually conversed B
4 people] a pair B
5 supply] guess B
5 missing phrases] sense B
5-6 people thoroughly] persons so B
6-8 so that a style . . . was all right] that missing links and broken lights and loose ends, the unexpressed and the understood, could do the office of talk B
10 word,] honour B
12 suppose] dare say B
16 cigars, we shall do very well] cigars I guess we shall muddle through B
17-18 'He seems a . . . occurred to him] 'I fancy he's awfully "prominent," you know, and I rather liked him,' Lord Lambeth pursued as if this appreciation of Mr. Westgate had but just glimmered on him B
19 'I say, we] His comrade, however, engaged in another thought, didn't so much as appear to catch it. 'I say, I guess we B
19-20 inn,' . . . 'I don't] inn. I don't B
20-1 don't . . . the house] rather object to turning in B
'I daresay] But it didn't rouse his friend, who only replied: 'I dare say B
25 really . . . Percy Beaumont.] really a bit think so.' B
27 declared . . . And then] his lordship humorously sighed. After which B
28 was devilish civil] *has* got us out of a hole B
29 'Nothing,] Percy Beaumont genially assented. 'Nobody B
29-30 civil,' . . . companion.] civil.' B
31 said Lord Lambeth] Lord Lambeth then contributed B
33 This American's—Mrs. Westgate] Our benefactor's. Mrs. Westgate B
33 J. L.'] J. L. It "kind of" sounds like a number. But I guess it's a high number,' he continued with freshened gaiety. B

34	Beaumont was silent a moment] The same influences appeared, however, with Mr. Beaumont to make rather for anxiety B
35	rather] a little B
36	asked his kinsman] his companion asked B
38-9	Percy Beaumont] the elder man B
40	'I don't care. I] His friend smoked acutely. 'Well, I B
42	Beaumont expounded] Mr. Beaumont allowed B
43	don't get entangled with her] keep free of her B
239 : 1	entangled] "free" B
2	hook] land B
3	Oh, bother] Oh rot B
4	clever,' urged his companion] cute,' the other urged B
5	the young man declared] said the young man B
6-7	game of . . . continued] wily game,' Mr. Beaumont developed B
8-10	England,' . . . 'you have] England you've B
12	began the young nobleman,] the youth began B
15	Percy Beaumont] his monitor B
17-18	said the . . . solicitude] cried Mr. Beaumont's charge B
19	rejoined the young barrister] the responsible party returned B
19-20	of a . . . a year—not] of—whatever it is you expect. Not B
22	our] the B
30	stone walls] stone dykes AB
33	casements] apertures B
37-8	jackets . . . about upon] jackets shuffled about on B
43	they] om. B
240 : 2	had relation to] took account of B
3	an] the B
4	a great . . . the hotel] copious diversion at their inn B
5	seemed to them that the] struck them the B
6	terribly deflowered] quite laid waste B
8	was blowing] freely blew B
10	seemed to float] floated B
10	long vistas with] endless vistas on B
10-11	like angels spreading] very much as angels spread B
11	upon] on B
13	lofty] high B
13	Englishmen] men B
22-3	the young . . . impulses] his social yearning B
24	care,' . . . 'or you will] care—else you'll B
28	kinsman] comrade B
29	perceive] see B
30	one's] their B
31	cried Lord Lambeth] he cried B
35	two] om. B
35	Englishmen] pair B

36 upon] on B
40 was brilliant and cool] shone and fluttered B
41 were smart . . . snug] stood up bravely in their smartness B
41-2 was very entertaining] turned all to confidence B
241 : 2 seemed to sparkle] sparkled B
3 to flash and twinkle] flashed and twinkled B
7 thick] fine B
8 young men] visitors B
10 they] om. B
11 very picturesque] many-pointed much-balconied B
12 *chalet* . . . perched upon] chalet, perched on B
14 around it] round B
15-16 in common] together B
20 dark] indistinct B
21 gloom, and a lady] gloom—a lady B
22 that] om. B
23 that she had heard them and] that, hearing them, she B
26-7 Mr. Beaumont,' she said. 'I have] Mr. Beaumont. I've B
27-8 would come . . . to see you] were coming. I make you warmly welcome B
28 visitors] guests B
29 visitors] guests B
29 had very good manners] made a gallant effort B
30 exclamations, and they] exclamations, they B
31 rejoined] returned B
32 upon] on B
34 said you were] says you're B
35 said Mrs. Westgate] she reported B
36 replied Percy Beaumont] —Percy Beaumont rose to it B
40 she was extremely] Mrs. Westgate was B
41 mind,' she said; 'and] mind, and B
43 you have arrived] you're really with us B
242 : 6 hand, tumbling] hand and tumbling B
7 it] om. B
8 use] employment B
9 moment] hour B
16-17 Percy Beaumont] the more guarded of our couple B
18 although] though B
19 it became cooler] everything turned to ease B
19-20 delicious . . . charming and] delicious and the view charming; B
20-1 there looked . . . comfortable] about looked fresh and fair B
21-2 ladies seemed . . . were slim, fair] younger ladies were clearly girls, and the gentlemen slim bright B
23 upon] on B
25 Beaumont] Percy B
25 one of the ladies] a lady B
27 Beaumont said it was] Percy pronounced it B

27 that] om. B
29 hear a] listen to a B
31 his] this B
33 perceived] saw B
34 the young Englishmen] their new recruits B
36 either of the visitors said] that dropped from either B
37 that] om. B
37 being made very] indeed made cordially B
38 them, and, talking a great deal] them, and while she talked continuously B
39-40 was as pretty . . . had promised] came up to their friend Littledale's promise B
41 and she was extremely light] and was light B
42-3 Mrs. Westgate . . . appeared always] Mrs. Westgate was, further, what she had occasion to describe some person, among her winged words, as being, all spontaneity. Frank and demonstrative, she appeared always B
243 : 1-2 after momentary hesitations] breaking out after momentary wonders B
5 a kind of joyous earnestness] her bland intensity B
8 a long . . . nice place] a nice long while. Newport's quite attractive B
13 ever so much attention. I] particluar attention—I B
15-16 a friend of Captain Littledale] friends of Captain Littledale's B
17 most] so B
18 here, and I am sure I] here that I B
18 stay. It] stay. That would have carried out his system. It B
19 England, for] England too—for B
21 am always on] always cling to B
23 that] —it B
32 have] om. B
36 that] om. B
39 Dover Street, in the] Dover Street and the B
244 : 2 in the season; I think] at the right season; I guess B
6 mean that they] mean they B
7 naturally . . . of course] naturally anything's a matter of course only B
8 But, of course, they are] But you'll say—oh yes you will, or you would if some of you ever did say much!—they're B
9 Of course, this isn't] You can't expect this to be B
18 bragging] "blowing" B
21 an old tablecloth] a table-cloth the worse for wear B
26 that] that—though I don't really know anything about them, because when I go over I always cling to the Continent B
32 succeeded. I suppose] succeeded. Perhaps that was only a part of *his* pleasant manners. I suppose at any rate B
34 fast] quick B

35 is] om. B

38 most charming] much more refined B

43-245:1 Newport society . . . interesting] the Newport phase—quite unique B

245 : 1 my husband] Mr. Westgate B

3 But] Only B

4-7 Mrs. Westgate's . . . such a stream] Mrs. Westgate's discourse was delivered with a mild merciless monotony, a paucity of intonation, an impartial flatness that suggested a flowery mead scrupulously 'done over' by a steam roller that had reduced its texture to that of a drawing-room carpet B

8-10 although he . . . deprecation] though he summoned to his aid such a show as he might of discriminating motions and murmurs B

12-13 seemed . . . moment; but] sometimes appeared to meet the case—any case; yet he felt he had never known such a case as Mrs. Westgate or as her presentation of *her* cases. But B

14 Mrs. Westgate] this exponent B

14 gracefully about in] fish-like through B

16 for she looked] since she looked B

17 Percy Beaumont,] Mr. Beaumont B

18 rather] measurably B

21 girl,] person B

21 case with] situation of B

22 girl] person B

23 hair was the] hair might be the B

24-5 which established] establishing B

27 in these days] on such days as these B

28 so very hot] very stuffy B

29 dreadful,' said the young girl] dreadful there,' said the pretty sister B

30 very busy,' . . . observed] immensely taken up,' the young man returned with a sense of conscientiously yearning towards American realities B

31 the young girl] his friend B

33 they? I daresay] they? Well, I dare say B

33 said her interlocutor] he hopefully threw out B

37-8 asked the young girl] the blue eyes and dark hair went on B

39 for a lark] for the joke of it B

40 Here . . . Lord Lambeth] Then occurred a pause, after which he B

40-1 Mr. Westgate . . . will not he] he *will* turn up here, won't he B

246 : 1 a little with . . . brown eyes] from handsome eyes that were brown B

2-3 urged him] pressed it B

4 Mr. Westgate's . . . and then—] The pretty girl treated this as rather an easy conundrum. B

5 answered] smiled B

6-7 'He was . . . he added.] 'Well, he was no end civil.' B

8 'He is a . . . And he is a] His young woman seemed much amused; this at least was in her eyes, which freely met Lord Lambeth's. 'He *would* be. He's a B

9 continued, smiling] confidently continued B

12-13 very friendly . . . jolly] pitched in a key of expression and emphasis rather new to him B

13-15 sooner or later . . . Two or three] the cool maidens not least, personally addressed him, and seemed to make a particular point of doing so by the friendly repetition of his name. Three or four B

16 seats and] seats, a B

16-20 all entered . . . very comfortable] took, individually, an interest in the visitors, putting somehow more imagination and more 'high comedy' into this effort than the latter had ever seen displayed save in a play or a story. These well-wishers feared the two Britons mightn't be comfortable B

20 that it was not] it being B

21 so private] not so private B

22 went on to . . . yet, perhaps] added that as yet perhaps, alas B

26 American . . . great deal] The life was really growing B

27 very much like England.] greatly to resemble European—which wasn't to be wondered at when two thirds of the people leading it were so awfully much at home in Europe. Europe, in the course of this conversation, was indeed, as Lord Lambeth afterwards remarked to his compatriot, rather bewilderingly rubbed into them: did they pretend to be European, and when had they ever been entered under that head? B

27-8 for instance, was] at all events, was described to them as B

28 Lord Lambeth would probably be] they would probably find themselves, when all was said, a good deal B

31 make visits;] 'visit round,' as somebody called it: B

32 case, they . . . deal] case would be constantly B

33 very] om. B

34 was a] was only a B

34-5 always away . . . very acute] never there—he being a tremendously fine man, one of the finest they had B

36 left his wife . . . as she liked] left his wife to play the social part. Well, she played it all right, if that was all he wanted B

37 seemed to] did B

37 extremely brilliant,] highly cultivated B

38 talker. Some people] converser—the sort of converser people would come miles to hear. But some B

39-40 sister; but . . . different; she] sister, who B

41 people] om. B

41 and . . . so sharp] but decidedly Miss Alden wasn't so smart B
42 style] style—the *quiet* Boston B
42-3 in Boston and she was] there and was B
44 propounded] intimated B
45 like English young ladies] on the English model B
247 : 1-2 this proposition; for on the] this last proposition; for, the B
6 she] Miss Alden B
6-7 to feel the . . . hospitality] conscious of the weight of expectation—unless she quite wantonly took on duties she might have let alone B
8-10 nature a reserved . . . moved slowly] habit rather grave and backward, perhaps even proud, with little of the other's free fraternizing. She might have been thought too deadly thin, not to say also too deadly pale; but while she moved B
11 with] om. B
11-13 looking gravely . . . thought her] and, seriously or absently, forgot expectations, though again brightly to remember them and to look at the summer sea as if that was what she really cared for, her companion judged her B
14-17 style the Boston . . . graceful] style, 'the quiet Boston,' it would do very well. He could fancy her very clever, highly educated and all the rest of it; but clearly also there were ways in which she could spare a fellow—could ease him; she wouldn't keep him so long on the stretch at once B
17 however] moreover B
17 that] om. B
19 world and from] world, from B
21 scattering themselves near] scattered about B
23-4 place, isn't it . . . jolly place] place for this sort of thing,' Lord Lambeth said. 'It must do beautifully B
25-6 'Very charming,' . . . cosy corners] 'It does indeed; there are cosy nooks and there are breezy ones, which I often try B
27-8 some of them . . . young men] a lot made,' he fell in B
29 Miss Alden . . . moment] She seemed to wonder B
30 It's pure] It's all pure B
32-3 be so jolly . . . went on] really be so jolly to ''develop'' the place,' he suggested B
34 'I am afraid] It made her thoughtful—even a little rueful. 'I'm afraid B
34-5 you,' said . . . thoughtfully.] you.' B
36 I daresay] Ah well, if B
36 saying] saying, there's nothing like that B
37 so grand, you know] awfully grand B
39-40 hereabouts was . . . of this fact] that contributed to the view melted away, but it too much lacked presence and character —a fact Miss Alden appeared to rise to a perception of B
41 rough,' . . . 'It's] rough. It's B

248 : 1 'Ah] He wouldn't let her, however, undervalue it. 'Ah B

1-2 it, you know,' . . . 'You] everything, you know. You B

3 were wandering about] wandered B

3 rocks, and they] rocks; they B

4 and looked down into] to look into B

6 there] om. B

7-8 young girl . . . when very young,] girl's eyes took in her companion, observing him attentively but covertly, as those of women even in blinking youth B

9 observation] contemplation B

12-16 look of intellectual . . . imaginaton; he] visible repose of mind, an inaccessibility to questions, somehow stamped in by the same strong die and pressure that nature, designing a precious metal, had selected and applied. It was not that he looked stupid, it was only, we assume, that his perceptions didn't show in his face for restless or his imagination for irritable. He B

17-22 a kind of appealing . . . further delay,] rather a constant appeal for delay in his waiting, his perfectly patient eye, this registered simplicity had its beauty as well and, whatever it might have appeared to plead for, didn't plead in the name of indifference or inaction. This most searching of his new friends B

24-5 was also . . . uncommonly pretty] had already made up his mind, quite originally and without aid, that she had a grace exceedingly her own B

27 for, if he was] since, though B

28 a sufficiency] a strict sufficiency B

29-30 on,' . . . 'There] on. There B

30-1 other things. You will] other pleasant things,' Bessie Alden explained. 'You'll B

32 It's very . . . say that] It will be very kind of you to let us see B

34 deal; but] deal, though B

35-6 sure,' . . . have so many] sure,' she said, 'that we haven't as many B

36 you have in] you in B

37 'Really!' exclaimed Lord Lambeth] He wondered—these so many prompt assumptions about his own country made him gape a little B

39-41 said the young . . . peculiar to her] she said—though she seemed to settle it for him with a quaver of interrogation B

42 seemed earnest and] sounded earnest indeed and B

43 seemed arch; but the] arch; the B

249 : 2 don't mean . . . laughing] don't really mean that,' her companion laughed B

3 I mean] I really mean B

3	the young girl declared] she returned B
6	her companion] Lord Lambeth, who appeared to cling to this general theory B
9	Oh, I *shall*] Ah what a blasphemous speech—I *must* B
9	Bessie Alden rejoined] our young woman protested B
10	them] om. B
11	Ah,] Oh B
11-12	said the young nobleman] —and her friend pleasantly bethought himself B
12	I haven't] I'm afraid I haven't B
13	know] knew B
14-15	know; they . . . they are] knew; they must have got up their subject. Good writers do, don't they? But those fashionable novels are mostly B
16	looked at] rested on B
16	with] om. B
17	and then] after which B
17	in] into B
18-19	Mrs. Gore . . . raising her eyes] Catherine Grace Gore, for instance?' she then more aspiringly asked B
20	'I am] But at this he broke down—he coloured, laughed, gave up. 'I'm B
20-1	either,' . . . 'I am] either. I'm B
25	it.'] it,' said Bessie Alden. B
26	always curious . . . jestingly] curious about everything?' he asked with continued hilarity B
27	But Bessie . . . seriously.] om. B
31-2	made conscious] advised B
33	just] close B
37	Lord Lambeth] he B
38	imagination,' said the young girl] imagination, and I *have* been to Paris,' she admitted B
39-40	repeated her . . . won't you] he repeated with gaiety—'fancy taking those brutes first! But you *will* come soon B
41	declared . . . smiling] Bessie Alden brightly professed B
42	But your sister] Your sister at any rate B
42	London] us B
250 : 1	The young . . . a moment] She appeared to take her view of this B
2	persons,' . . . 'She] persons. She B
3-4	several . . . English people] a little—not intimately. But she has met English people in other countries, and she arrives very quickly at conclusions B
5	'But] 'Ah I guess she does,' he laughed. 'But B
5	too,' said Lord Lambeth.] too.' B
6	'I don't think that] 'No—I don't think B
9	Lord Lambeth] the young man B
9-10	Attempts at impressiveness] The impressive B

11 he said.] om. B
14 young] om. B
14-15 she smiled . . . impressiveness] taking it more gaily B
15 that] om. B
15-16 beginning,' she said.] beginning.' B
19-20 is going to Europe,] expects to cross about then B
20 we go,] I do B
22 come in] come early in B
24 till] even till early in B
24 the young girl rejoined] his friend returned B
26 them] om. B
27 Miss Alden] the younger sister B
27 are going] go B
30-1 so handsome . . . his cousin's] of so handsome an effect as his comrade, though in the latter's B
31-2 might have . . . Englishman] might, with his manly stature and his fair dense beard, his fresh clean skin and his quiet outlook, have pleased by a due affirmation of the best British points B
33-4 eyes, which . . . colour, had] eyes had B
34 and] which B
35-7 rested them . . . every one alike] turned with some intensity on Lord Lambeth. Mrs. Westgate's beautiful radiance of interest and dissent fell meanwhile impartially everywhere B
39 about] for B
251 : 1 Beaumont, stroking] Beaumont, raising his eyebrows and stroking B
2 not thinking it] thinking it *not* B
3 'Oh, I say!' . . . again] 'Ah you *must* have been getting it!' cried his friend B
6 turned to] turned again to B
7 The phaeton is there] There must be something at the door for you B
9-10 At this point . . . kinsman; he tried] Mr. Beaumont, at this point, looked straight at his comrade, trying B
11-12 cried Bessie Alden] —Bessie Alden rose straight to their hostess's suggestion B
15 Beaumont] the elder man B
19 young] om. B
22 a] om. B
23 young lady] om. B
24 'I don't know] But even here Mrs. Westgate discriminated. 'I don't know B
24-5 should say . . . She is] should precisely say attractive. She's B
27-31 said Percy Beaumont . . . a great deal] said Percy Beaumont with evident wonder. And then as if to alternate with a certain grace the note of scepticism: 'I guess your shyness, in

that case, is different from ours.' 'Everything of ours is different from yours,' Mrs. Westgate instantly returned. 'But my poor sister's given over, I hold, to a fine Boston *gaucherie* that has rubbed off on her by being there so much. She's a dear good girl, however; she's a charming type of girl. She is not in the least a flirt; that isn't at all her line; she doesn't know the alphabet of any such vulgarity. She's very simple, very serious, very *true*. She has lived, however, rather too much B

33 She is] Bessie's B

34 cultivated . . . immensely and] cultivated and am called so only by those who don't know what true culture is. But Bessie does; she has studied Greek; she has B

36-7 'A rum sort . . . reflected] 'Ah well, it only depends on what one thinks *about*,' said Mr. Beaumont, who appeared to find her zeal for distinctions catching B

38 continued] pursued B

39 upon] on B

38 upon] on B

40-1 said Mrs. Westgate . . . of information] she declared, continuing to supply her guest with information and to do him the honours of the American world with a zeal that left nothing to be desired B

42 little basket-phaeton] light low pony-cart B

252 : 5 enormous cobble-stones] huge old cobbles B

6 proportion] allowance B

6 to be] om. B

8 them; and] them; while B

9 cobble-stones] round stones B

9 basket-phaetons] like or different carts B

12 demonstrative—] of the last effusiveness: B

13 exclamations and caresses] sounds and motions—obscure native words, shibboleths and signs B

15 phaeton] trap B

17 groom nor footman] other attendant B

18 ponies] pony B

18 although he was] though B

19 to entertain] harmlessly to divert B

20 the appearance of a kind of] an B

21 they were] om. B

23-4 Of course, before] And he felt by the time B

24-5 villa, he had . . . Bessie Alden] villa that he had made a stride in intimacy with Miss Alden B

27-8 what the French . . . new friends] the cultivation, right and left, far and near, of this celerity of social progress B

28 was extremely] was all extremely B

29-30 narrate minuetly the incidents] report the detail B

31 if it were] were it B

32 delectable] soothing B

34 brilliant mornings] early breezy shining hours B

35 girls] girls saying innumerable quaint and familiar things B

37 universal friendliness and frankness] a confidence that broke down, of a freedom that pulled up, nowhere B

38 they knew] they so knew B

38-9 and had . . . of ease] that they almost ached with reciprocity B

41 suppers] tea-tables B

43 Atlantic] Atlantic and amid irrelevant outbursts of clever minstrelsy B

253 : 2 with everybody] with everybody, and it was all the book of life, of American life, at least; with the chapter of 'complications' bodily omitted B

4 step to] step as to B

4-6 offered some . . . Bessie Alden] took up an attitude of mistrust apparently founded on some odd and just a little barbaric talk forced on him, he would have been tempted to say, and very soon after their advent, by Miss Alden B

7 had a good . . . her, for] been aware of her occasional approach or appeal, since B

9 upon] on B

9 he] om. B

10 clever] 'sharp' (Percy's critical categories remained few and simple) B

11 very nice] perfectly well-bred B

12 had said] funnily insisted B

13 very well] with an ease—! B

17 Percy Beaumont repeated] Percy's instinct was to speak as if he had never heard of such a matter B

20 said Beaumont] Percy pleaded B

20-1 it all set . . . I can do it] the whole matter in black and white, and upon my honour I know very little about it B

22-3 'He is a . . . is a Peer.'] The girl seemed to wonder at his innocence. 'You know at least whether he's what they call a great noble.' 'Oh yes, he's in that line.' 'Is he a "peer of the realm"?' 'Well, as yet—very nearly.' B

24-6 Lambeth,' . . . with interest.] Lambeth.' With which the fountain of Bessie's information appeared to run a little dry. She looked at him, however, with such interest that he presently added: B

27 Bayswater,' he added, presently.] Bayswater.' B

28 son] om. B

29 son] one B

31 Oh yes; if . . . living he] Naturally—as to his father. If *he* weren't living Lambeth B

32 his father] "the old lord" B

32 pursued Bessie Alden] —and the girl smiled B

33 a clever girl] one so 'sharp'— B

35 Percy Beaumont] their common friend B

38 Beaumont smiled a little] Percy seemed amused B

38 uncommonly robust.] built to last! B

254 : 2 Bessie Alden . . . a moment] Bessie entered into it all B

3 Beaumont] He B

7 try for you] have a go at you B

10 said Beaumont] his friend imperturbably pursued B

12 rejoined] returned B

13 observed . . . go, you go] said Percy, 'if you go straight into it, if you hurl yourself bang upon the spears, you do so B

15 exclaimed Lord Lambeth] the young man pronounced B

18 Beaumont] om. B

19-20 conscience, and] many scruples—in the direction in which he had any at all—and B

21 him] Mr. Beaumont B

23 that] such a B

24 of her] om. B

25 place] om. B

28 down as] down, I suppose, as B

30 invention, and] invention altogether and B

32 detest.'] detest,' said Lord Lambeth. B

33 a blue-stocking.] then rather a priggish American *précieuse*? B

34 'Is that . . . Miss Alden?'] Lord Lambeth took his time. 'Do you call Miss Alden all that?' B

37 I don't know . . . very clever] Well, why shouldn't she be? She's certainly very clever and has every appearance of a well-stored mind B

38-42 'Well,' said . . . held his tongue] Percy for an instant watched his young friend, who had turned away. 'I should rather have supposed you'd find her stores oppressive.' The young man, after this, faced him again. 'Why, do you think me such a dunce?' And then as his friend but vaguely protested: 'The girl's all right,' he said—and quite as if this judgement covered all the ground. It wasn't that there was no ground—but he knew what he was about. Percy, for a while further, and a little uncomfortably flushed with the sense of his false position—that of presenting culture in a 'mean' light, as they said at Newport—Percy kept his peace B

43-255:2 He was, as . . . proprieties of life] His conception of certain special duties and decencies, as I have said, was strong, and this step wholly fell in with it B

255 : 2 kinsman] companion B

2 a great deal of] much B

3 Bessie Alden] Miss Alden B

6 a house] one B
7 so frequently] so freely and frequently B
8 Percy Beaumont] their other guest B
10-11 bored him a little] did, according to Mr. Beaumont's term, a little oppress him B
12 said Bessie Alden,] —this had been one of them— B
14 cried Lord Lambeth] he returned B
16 you are a . . . the young girl.] you're natural members of Parliament.' B
21 an important] a very august B
22 said Lord Lambeth] Lord Lambeth smiled B
23 said Bessie Alden,] —she serenely kept it up, as the female American, he judged, would always keep anything up— B
26 It's a great humbug] There's a lot of humbug about it B
27 young girl] girl unconfusedly B
30 better,] better, I guess! B
30 affirmed] after a moment returned B
31 said Bessie Alden] —this at least she kept up B
33 was a little bored] felt a little the burden of her earnestness B
34 'Do you] But he took it good-humouredly. 'Do you B
34 he asked.] om. B
35 demanded] demanded as if the word were rich and rare B
36 a clergyman that is] a pet clergyman B
37 tell her that he had] plead guilty to his having, in prospect, B
40 describing . . . saying it was] a few pleasant facts about it and into pronouncing it B
41 and declared that] declaring B
42 Whereupon—] To which he charmingly made answer: B
43 there,' said Lord Lambeth] there, you know.' B
43-256:2 He took a . . . just recorded] It was not inconvenient to him meanwhile that Percy Beaumont hadn't happened to hear him make this general remark B
256 : 6-7 fingers, declaring . . . only hope the] fingers pronouncing it too 'fiendish' he should let his business so dreadfully absorb him that he could but platonically hope, as she expressed it, his two B
10 continued] kept up B
10 promenade] circulation B
12 leisure-class] leisure-class and that the universal passionate surrender of the men to business-questions and business-questions only, as if they were the all in all of life, was a tide that would have to be stemmed B
14 Beaumont] om. B
19-20 said Percy Beaumont] Mr. Beaumont however asseverated B
21 you] you flat B
22 before. She's] before. We have ours ever so much more on hand. She's B

23-4 Mrs. Westgate's . . . for Beaumont] The superlative degree so variously affirmed, however, was evidently a source of attraction in Mrs. Westgate, for the elder man B
26 Mr. Westgate] her husband B
27 Mr. Westgate's] that gentleman's B
28 certainly do things quickly] know how to put things—and put people—"through" B
29 he observed to his cousin] he subsequently and quite breathlessly observed to his comrade B
30 very uneasy . . . her visitor] markedly to fear his wife might suffer for loss of her guest B
36-9 On August 21st . . . annoyed. 'What the] August had still a part of its course to run when his lordship received from his mother the disconcerting news that his father had been taken ill and that he had best at once come home. The young nobleman concealed his chagrin with no great success. 'I left the Duke but the other day absolutely all right—so what the B
40 kinsman. 'What am I] comrade. 'What's a fellow B
41 annoyed as well] scarce less annoyed B
42 I have narrated, to write] we know, to report faithfully B
42 he] om. B
43 that] om. B
43 would] to B
43 upon] on B
257 : 1 is laid] is somehow, and rather suddenly, laid B
3 don't be alarmed] take it without alarm B
4 Lord Lambeth] This really struck Lord Lambeth as meaning that he essentially needn't take it, since alarm would have been his only good motive; yet he nevertheless, after an hour of intenser irritation than he could quite have explained to himself, B
4-5 but the few . . . have a place] in the course of which he exchanged a few last words with Bessie Alden that are the only ones making good their place B
6 you,' he said, 'that] you that B
7-8 the first . . . inform] the very first person notified B
9 Bessie Alden . . . smiled] She looked at him in that way she had which never quite struck him as straight and clear, yet which always struck him as kind and true B
10 London,' she answered, 'I] London I B
10 you would hear] you'd sufficiently hear B
11 returned . . . of duty] felt it his duty also to embark, and this same rigour B
13 Lord Lambeth] his friend B
13 suspected that the] suspected the B
13 was] to have been B

14 written to her] written her B
14-15 wrote to her] wrote her B
15 explicitly notified] distinctly warned B
15 promised to] promised in general to B
17 Lord Lambeth . . . and he] The young man, much upset by this avowal, B
18-19 simple language . . . young man, and I] strong and simple language of resentment. But if I have described him as inclined to candour and to reason I B
20 that he . . . companion at] of his being ready to face the truth by B
23 seriously] at all seriously B
23 in me] in poor me B
24 a little laugh] the rein to mirth and mockery B
25 your position] the position of ''poor'' you B
26-7 is a capital . . . on her] settles for me the question of what's the matter with you B
28-9 'She is not . . . his companion] Lord Lambeth's handsome eyes turned rueful and queer. 'Is anything so flagrantly the matter with me?' 'Everything, my dear boy,' laughed his companion, passing a hand into his arm for a walk. 'Well, *she* isn't interested—she isn't!' the young man insisted. 'My poor friend,' said Percy Beaumont rather gravely B
30 Percy Beaumont] the latter B
31 on the 18th of May] by the next mid-May B
32 she was not attended] unattended B
32-3 deprivation . . . was, however,] lost comfort of a husband respectably to produce, as she phrased it, she was now B
34-6 without him . . . conspicuous fact] under this drawback of looking ill-temperedly separated and yet of being thanklessly enslaved, and she still decently accounted for her spurious singleness to wondering friends on this side of the Atlantic by formulating the grim truth—the only grimness indeed in all her view— B
36 was] is B
258 : 1-2 be very . . . eyes upon] carry her away and counted on the joy of treating her eyes and her imagination to all B
3 about in the] of in B
5 retrospect, of mementoes] associations, of relics B
7 multitude] swarm B
14 oak-studded parks] oak-studded, deer-peopled parks B
15 the thousand] all the significant B
15-16 Mrs. Westgate's . . . keenness] Mrs. Westgate's reponse was of course less quick and less extravagant B
20 physical] in the least sensual B
21 England] London and perhaps in other parts of the celebrated island B

24 London] English B
26-7 Bessie Alden . . . day, as] was a remark that had one day dropped from Bessie while B
28 on a large blue rug] from under which spread conveniently a large soft rug B
29 asked] had then invited the girl to say B
30 whom] om. B
32 added Bessie Alden] the girl further mentioned B
34 Bessie] She B
34-5 to reflection. 'Well, yes] to fine reflexion. 'Well—to be nice B
38 asked Bessie] Bessie asked B
41 Bessie] our young lady B
42 'Shall] Mrs. Westgate had an ominous pause. 'Shall B
42 asked her sister.] om. B
259 : 1 what they do] what's frequently done B
4 gazing at] sat at gaze of B
14-15 him—they] him—the poor Butterworths—they B
28-9 Ascot Races, and there] Ascot Races—where B
38 you think it's] tell me you don't think it B
39 don't believe] don't think I believe B
39 young] om. B
40 Ah!] Ah then, B
40 you are . . . after all.] mademoiselle isn't of such an unspotted *candeur*! B
41 please; there is] like. There's at any rate B
260 : 1 because I shall not] for the simple reason that I shall never B
3 offensive] disobliging AB
4 Bessie . . . moment] Our young lady for a time said nothing B
5 she said] she then resumed B
8 think they are very] find them prodigiously B
10 said Bessie] Bessie brought up B
11 rejoined] returned B
11-12 it would . . . say that] so I think I'd rather put it B
13 Bessie Alden resumed] Bessie pursued B
15 added] wound up B
19-20 a large number of] numerous B
20-1 conversation . . . offered] enquiry and comment were only those supplied B
22-3 took an immense . . . metropolis] felt to intensity the many-voiced appeal of the capital of the race from which she had sprung B
23-4 young woman] person B
24-5 a considerable period] many days B
26 drive] roll B
27-8 a Hansom cab. To . . . picturesque life] the public con-

veyances. They presented to her attentive eyes strange pictures and figures B
29 which] in which the imagination of B
30 found so entertaining] lost itself B
33 made an . . . should be] desired they should, at whatever cost to convenience, be B
35 whether] if B
35 on the way] en route B
36 monument] relic B
37-8 disappointment; so that she] disappointment. She thus B
40 this line] the line of backward brooding B
42 She told] It was made clear to B
261 : 2 upon] in respect to B
2 sprinkled cold water] had the cold sense of complications B
5 Then] With which B
6 those that walked] those who walked B
6-7 those that did not] those who didn't B
9 answered Bessie, laughing] laughed Bessie, though all yearningly B
9-10 happen to prevent] happen arbitrarily to place B
13-14 Such was . . . appellation of] So was familiarly designated B
15-16 having . . . intimacy] enjoying some freedom of acquaintance B
20 who has just alighted] just installed B
21 slim, pale] slight mild B
21 of the . . . disposition] without high colour but with many elegant forms B
22 skill] authority B
22 Indeed] He was indeed B
23-4 this . . . believed to be] this fashionable frolic he was believed to be A; such evolutions, reckoned B
24-5 these terms that] those terms B
25 and that his identity was] and his pleasant identity B
26 gentlest . . . man it] most convenient gentle young man, for almost any casual light purpose, it B
26 he] om. B
30-1 always addressed] never addressed but B
32 conduct] guide B
32-3 Anne Boleyn's] Lady Jane Grey's AB
36 with young] with wild young B
37 often] often—not to call it so wildly B
37-8 observed Willie Woodley] the young man returned B
38 she] that she B
38 Hansom] jog-trot cab B
39 consider waltzing] consider public waltzing B
39-40 innocent pleasure] innocent, because the most guarded and regulated, pleasure B
41 a compliment] a jolly compliment B

41-2 exclaimed . . . of himself] Mr. Woodley cried with a laugh of the most candid significance B
43-262:1 said Bessie Alden] Bessie pursued B
262 : 3 murmured Willie Woodley] her friend applauded B
8 a faint . . . perhaps,] an asperity doubtless B
12-13 same week. An ingenious] same week; while an ingenious B
13 trace] have traced B
14 young girl's . . . privileges] girl's reference to her lack of social privilege or festal initiation B
15 lunch] luncheon B
16 said Bessie.] om. B
19 said that . . . gone to] believes Captain Littledale away in B
20 knew] knows B
21 Bessie Alden] Bessie B
23 'You] Her sister waited with a look at her. 'You B
23 Lord Lambeth,' said her sister.] Lord Lambeth.' B
24 was so] was—at Newport—so B
25 looked at . . . candour] prolonged the attitude of sisterly truth B
26 don't care] don't really care B
28 I am nice] I'm very nice B
29 'To every] Nothing indeed could have been simpler save perhaps the way Bessie smiled back: 'To every B
29 me,' . . . smiling] me.' B
30 her; then, at last,] her. B
31 she asked.] om. B
32 The young girl] Our young woman B
32-3 apparently too humorous] too unattended with any train B
33 blush] shy B
33-4 of,' she answered.] of.' B
37 declared Bessie, smiling] Bessie gaily insisted B
38 not nice] not really nice B
42 was silent a moment] seemed to cover much country in a few moments B
263 : 1 she blushed] blushing B
2 serious,' . . . 'we] serious we B
3 moments] minutes accordingly B
3 not mentioned again] shrouded in silence B
4 reverted to him] removed the ban B
5 will] shall B
5 here; because I] here. I B
9 with a little laugh] very simply B
10 added her sister] her companion added B
18 repeated her sister] echoed her sister a little impatiently B
18 what is your] what do you mean by better and what's your B
20 'How do you mean—] Bessie wondered. 'What do *you* mean by B
21 little] tiny speck B

22 was displeased; she] took it with still deeper reserve. She B
23 from her sister] om. B
24 so,' she said.] so.' B
28 and presently] after which B
29 that] om. B
31 'He is . . . declared.] Mrs. Westgate bethought herself. 'He's not clever.' B
32-3 said Bessie Alden] the girl said B
33 that] om. B
34 not stupid] no stupider than anyone else B
35 Not so . . . looks!] No stupider than he gives you warning of, B
35 exclaimed . . . smiling] her sister smiled B
36 Lord Lambeth,] him B
36 now, it] now,' Bessie returned, 'it B
40 young girl . . . room again] girl began once more to walk about B
41 sister] companion B
42 minutes,' she said, 'so] minutes so B
264 : 1 that] om. B
3 looked . . . instant] just hesitated B
4 Lord Lambeth] him B
5 Bessie Alden] Bessie B
5 like] much as B
6-7 rise from her chair] get up B
7 she demanded.] om. B
9 it,' said Bessie.] it.' B
11 this kind of thing] as many things as possible B
13 upon] on B
13-14 thought for a moment] could have believed B
15 she asked.] om. B
16 leave] let B
21 little laugh] persistence of private amusement B
23-4 Bessie Alden expected . . . from sitting] Bessie expected it would prove a rich passage to have sat B
25 trees, beside] trees and beside B
26 rendered . . . inaccessible] hampered this adventure B
29-30 half-past five . . . button-hole] half-past five adorned with every superficial grace that could qualify him for the scene B
31-2 said . . . her sister,] Mrs. Westgate mentioned B
32 Bessie Alden] Bessie B
33 her] om. B
33 was entertaining their visitor] had given their visitor the impression that she was particularly attuned B
36 asked Mrs. Westgate] Mrs. Westgate thereupon asked B
37 fun,' Willie Woodley affirmed] fun,' Mr. Woodley almost spoke as if the pleasure were attended with physical risk B
40 said Willie Woodley] cried the young man with elation B

41 Bessie Alden] Bessie B
42 trees, beside] trees and beside B
42 whose humours] the humours of which B
43 young] om. B
265 : 1-2 spectators, and the] spectators, as well as the B
2 were] om. B
3 brilliant] many-coloured B
3-4 Season at . . . she was able to] social pressure at its highest and it made our young woman think of more things than she could easily B
5 and] while B
6-8 let itself loose . . . preconceptions] kept pace with the deep strong tide of the exhibition. Old impressions and preconceptions became living things before the show B
8-9 herself fitting] herself, amid the crowd of images, fitting B
10 little] small B
11 expressed] delivered B
13-14 flounces,' said . . . *toilette*!'] flounces. Quelle toilette!' said Mrs. Westgage. B
15 said the young man] the young man was able to contribute B
16 the white] the queer white B
24 pursued] pursued to Bessie B
27 would appreciate] would particularly appreciate B
28 Willie Woodley] Their companion B
28-9 friend . . . who drove] mounted friend who drew B
31 ten] om. B
38 touching his hat a little] raising his hat afresh B
39 Bessie. 'Fancy] Bessie—'Fancy B
39 he said.] om. B
40 kind] note B
41 that] om. B
41 Bessie Alden's imagination] The girl's free fancy B
42 in exercise] in marked exercise B
42 that] om. B
266 : 3 he looked like] he somehow looked B
4 I say] Really B
4 man] fellow B
4-5 you were here] you've come B
7 asked Bessie, smiling] smiled Bessie B
8 cried Lord Lambeth] he insisted B
10 said Willie Woodley] this gentleman brought forth B
12 I'm a] I'm rather a B
13 said Bessie,] said Bessie after an instant, but choosing and conferring a grace on the literal— B
15 observed] pronounced B
15 are only tolerable] approach the normal only B

16 a chair] one B
24 observed Mrs. Westgate] the elder lady observed B
25 Lord Lambeth inquired] Lord Lambeth a little pointlessly enquired B
27 said] mocked B
31 'I say] He had but a brief wonder—he found something. 'I say B
31-2 humbug!' . . . 'I have] humbug! I've B
35 asked Mrs. Westgate] Mrs. Westgate fairly put to him B
36 'You] It found Willie Woodley at least ready. 'You B
36 Hurlingham,' said Willie Woodley.] Hurlingham.' B
38 said Lord Lambeth] he said B
40-1 cards,' said Bessie] a scrap of a card,' Bessie laughed B
42 'We are] Mrs. Westgate attenuated. 'We're B
42 quiet,' . . . 'We are] quiet. We're B
43 pursued] further mentioned B
267 : 7 speak if they tried] almost speak B
8 Lord Lambeth rejoined] his lordship returned B
9 that look . . . they tried,] who look a long way from that! B
11 Mrs. Westgate] the elder of the ladies B
12 Lord Lambeth] He B
12 round him] about B
13 Beaumont often] Percy sometimes B
14 into the crowd] or dast for it B
15 diving] of violent movement B
25 'Yes,' said Mrs. Westgate.] Mrs. Westgate practised the same serenity. 'Awful.' B
26 the people that] people who B
27 places] dens B
30 'Well, how] 'Well, and how B
32 'I think . . . Bessie Alden.] The girl was prompt. 'I think it grand.' B
33-4 exclaimed] recorded B
35 hope you are] hope then you're B
35 stay] stop B
36 said Bessie] Bessie replied B
37 where is Mr. Westgate] where's wonderful Mr. Westgate B
40 be tremendously clever] have staying power B
41 'I suppose . . . Mrs. Westgate.] She appeared to consider. 'Well, he stays ahead of everyone else.' B
268 : 1 Bessie Alden] the younger lady B
2 entertained] wasted a certain amount of effort to regale B
3-4 said very . . . thinking of] was sparing of effusion; she thought, on her guard, of B
5 in Lord Lambeth again, as] again in her English friend very much as B
6 her that . . . become] her he might here become B
8-10 and poor . . . picturesqueness] of all of which things poor

Bessie Alden, like most familiars of the overciphered *tabula rasa*, was terribly at the mercy B

11-12 at Newport . . . young man] back at Newport.' the young man candidly stated B

14 he] the old humbug B

16 like] om. B

18 Lord Lambeth rejoined,] he returned B

22 Her . . . a moment] He turned his cheerful brown eyes on her B

26-7 everything,' . . . but very] everything.' He appeared not quite to follow, but was clearly B

35 ideas,' . . . 'I want] ideas then. I want B

38 Lord Lambeth] He B

39 the] om. B

40 'Are] Bessie yearned. 'Are B

40 asked Bessie.] om. B

42 very] weirdly B

42 said Bessie] she said B

269 : 1 'I think] The girl rose to it. 'I think B

1-2 garden,' . . . 'We] garden. We B

3 Lord Lambeth] Her friend B

3 merriment] mirth B

3-4 Woodley,' . . . 'here's] Woodley, here's B

4 Gardens] Gardens! Hang it, they *are* "weird" B

9 believe you] believe that, to get your money's worth over here, you B

10 anywhere,' he cried.] anywhere!' B

13 cried the young man] he returned B

15-16 ladies,' . . . smiling.] ladies.' B

17 Bessie Alden] She B

17 awhile; smiling . . . shadow] from under the shade B

18 murmured] then quietly concluded B

20-1 said . . . still more] he cried with the note of sincerity B

24 consider it] regard it as B

26 said Lord Lambeth] the young man pleaded B

28 shall] should B

30 the young man] he B

31 Bessie Alden . . . again] Again, shadily, she took him in B

34 say,' said Lord Lambeth.] say.' B

35 asked Bessie Alden] she demanded B

36-7 down,' he said, 'as] down as B

42 House of Lords] Houses of Parliament AB

270 : 1 to make you] you to AB

4-5 What is Branches] And what may Branches be B

7 at this moment, were] were at this moment B

8-9 Lord Lambeth's] the other pair B

11 Mrs. Westgate] Mrs. Westgate hereupon B

12-13 Lord Lambeth] their English friend B

13 Mr. Woodley's conduct] conduct of their American B

15 instantly] at once B

17 when his kinsman informed him] on his kinsman's informing him B

17-18 their American friends] the two ladies B

19 remark] exchange B

20 What] And what B

20 demanded Lord Lambeth] the younger man had enquired B

22 added Percy Beaumont] Percy had added B

23 Her Grace] The Duchess B

24 said her Grace's son,] the Duchess's son had returned B

28 Percy Beaumont took a sombre] Mr. Beaumont took a subtle B

28-9 two ladies] fair strangers B

29 a man of the world] capable of a still deeper refinement B

31 at least, that was animated] animated at least B

32 made himself agreeable] appealed more confusedly B

34 expounding] discriminating B

271 : 3 well for] well arranged here for B

6 rejoined Beaumont] Percy plucked up spirit to answer B

9 outrageous;] unreasonable, B

12 heaven knows what!] really I can't make out quite what. B

13 received a] received in one way and another a B

15 come and see her] come and pay her my respects B

16 observed Percy Beaumont] Mr. Beaumont cried B

18 exclaimed] promptly pursued B

19 *naïveté*, I should] naïveté—of your blessed national lack of any approach to a sense of shades—I should B

21 and be told] to be told B

21-2 that is the] that the B

23 wicked] peevish B

24 critical, and] critical—it's the joy of my life—and B

27 that] om. B

29 'I hope] Percy mustered a rueful gaiety. 'I hope B

29-30 second-rate,' Beaumont interposed.] second-rate!' B

32 that] om. B

35 old lady; I assure] old lady—no, you mustn't look that way: I assure B

41 You seem] I should say she's not to mind, not a rap—though you seem B

42 Percy Beaumont exclaimed] Percy pursued B

272 : 3-4 retorted . . . expression because] retorted—an expression made use of, this last, because B

5 Percy Beaumont] Mr. Beaumont B

5-6 his country] the seat of his existence B

9-10 Bessie Alden] Bessie B
11-12 Mrs. Westgate] the elder lady B
12 though] even if B
20 Percy Beaumont] his comrade B
21 Bessie Alden told her sister] Bessie mentioned B
24 thither] all through the city B
24-5 communication,] news B
25 she] also B
26 mention] speak of B
27 I should venture] I'd make bold B
28 were] grew B
34 Bessie Alden] Bessie B
35 answered at last, curtly] at last answered with a certain dryness B
36 declared Mrs. Westgate] cried her sister B
37 her] om. B
40 'How should] The girl wondered. 'How should B
40 asked the young girl.] om. B
41-2 think . . . absorb] suppose you holding in thrall B
43 Bessie Alden, with] Our young lady, B
273 : 1 interrogate] examine it B
2 poised her answer] winged her shaft B
2 delivering] launching B
6 Bessie Alden . . . disgusted] Bessie showed again a coldness B
7 ideas?' . . . 'You have] ideas? You've B
7 strange] odd B
9 Kitty . . . enamoured of] But Kitty, unabashed, held to B
12 young . . . moment] girl turned it over B
12 that] om. B
13 upon] on B
15 mamma . . . life out] *materfamilias*—and when she's a Duchess into the bargain—is often a force to be reckoned with B
16-17 been intimated . . . scepticism] already been intimated that before certain appearances of strange or sinister cast our young woman was apt to shy off into scepticism B
20 a lively] quick B
21-3 be, to her . . . aloud was—] be no truth for her in the attribution to her of a vulgar identity. Only the form she gave her doubt was: B
24-5 her scheme . . . again] her own scheme, irradiated interest B
25-6 safe!' . . . 'When] safe! But when B
29-30 Bessie Alden . . . turned back] Bessie turned impatiently off—then at the end of a minute faced about B
30 she asked.] om. B
31 turned away] averted herself B

32 she also . . . again] met the case B
33 thing,' she said.] thing.' B
34 and] when B
36-7 duskier . . . metropolis] most fascinating, as Bessie called them, even though the duskiest districts B
37 which] that B
38-9 all descended . . . enclosure; and] alighted together to enter the famous fortress, where B
40-1 though there . . . information] ignoring the presence of other dependents on his leisure B
274 : 1-3 to the official . . . fascinating place] as he marshalled and directed them. Bessie appealed to this worthy—even on more heads than he seemed aware of; she overtaxed, in her earnestness, his learnt lesson and found the place, as she more than once mentioned to him, quite delirious B
4-5 he was . . . called the lark] his delirium at least was gay and he betrayed afresh that aptitude for the simpler forms of ironic comment that the girl had noted in him B
9 come back . . . questions—] do anything so weak. When it befell that Bessie's glowing appeals, B
10-11 history—the . . . appealed] history, but left the warder gaping she resorted straight B
12 But his . . . declared that] His lordship then pleaded gross incompetence, declaring B
13-14 thing, and . . . diverted] thing and greatly diverted, to all appearance, B
15 can't . . . know as] can't honestly expect people to know as awfully B
16-17 declared Bessie Alden] Bessie Alden returned B
18 'Women always] 'Well, women always B
19 that sort . . . rejoined] historical characters,' he said B
22 said Bessie] Bessie argued with all her freedom B
27 'Bessie is really . . . historical!'] 'Bessie really harks back too much to the dead past—she makes too much of it,' Mrs. Westgate opined, catching the sense of this colloquy. 'Yes, you hark back,' the young man laughed, thankful for a formula. 'You do make too much of the dead past.' B
33 were in blossom] blossomed to admiration B
34-5 quite entered . . . in ecstasies] found in Miss Alden the improving governess, he declared, of his later immaturity, as Mademoiselle Boquet, dragging him by the hand to view all lions, had been that of his earliest, pronounced the old red palace not half so beastly as he had supposed. Bessie herself rose to raptures B
36 exclaiming] 'raving' B
37 lovely,' . . . 'it's] lovely; it's B
39 little flocks of visitors] tinkling flocks B

40-1 upon the local antiquities] on the tough herbage of History B

42 Bessie Alden] our young woman B

42-275:1 applying . . . assistance] apply for judicious support B

275 : 1-2 But he again . . . his education] He, however, could but once more declare himself a broken reed and that his education, in such matters, B

4 unhappy,' he added in a moment] wretched,' he further professed B

5 very disappointing . . . she said] so disappointing you know,' she returned; but more in pity—pity for herself—than in anger B

6 that!' . . . 'That's] that! That's B

8 No,' she rejoined;] No'—she spoke with a sad lucidity— B

10 know. Give] know'—and he seemed to rejoice in a chance to demur. 'Give B

11 Well,' . . . 'that] Well, that B

12-13 place!' . . . 'you are] place!' he groaned. 'You're B

15-16 young girl . . . for a moment] girl gave him a look; he might have thought she coloured; and for a little B

17-18 she asked.] om. B

19 said, fearing, he had been] said as if fearing he had sounded B

22 about your being] of your future as B

23 a great many things.] so many things, oughtn't he? B

25 do legislate] *will* legislate one of these days—you may have to at any time B

25 don't] won't B

26 to] om. B

30 brilliant, and to know] brilliant—to be "up" in B

32 Lord Lambeth . . . moment] He turned on her his handsome young face of profane wonder B

32-3 something?' he asked. 'A young man] something? A young man B

34 interposed Bessie Alden] she interposed B

37 very well,] well enough at the worst—he muddles along B

39-40 said Bessie Alden, laughing] Bessie laughed B

41 been] om. B

42 Lord Lambeth declared] the young man man promptly brought out B

276 : 1 country,' said Bessie Alden] country then,' she as eagerly declared B

1 even] om. B

2 are so elevated!] make so for light. B

3-4 'Well, after all . . . make me out.'] He stopped short, with his slightly strained gaiety, as for the pleasantness of high argument. 'What it comes to then is that we're all here a pack of fools and me the biggest of the lot?' B

5 as that; but I] of a great people—and a great person. But I B

5-6 you are disappointing] you personally are—in your representative capacity that's to be—disappointing B

7 exclaimed the young man] he simply cried at this B

9 said . . . a smile] she beautifully smiled B

10 a good] om. B

10 she] om. B

12 extreme] prompt B

14 something of . . . to call to] a good deal of what she took great pleasure in calling to B

22 a] om. B

22 habitual] frequent B

25 sidereal bodies] bodies sidereal AB

26-7 had a good . . . disappointments] lost in this way certain fond illusions B

28-9 communicated . . . either class] laid bare the wealth of her emotions B

31 reflections . . . impart to] sentiments indeed she sought mildly to flash upon B

34 Mrs. Westgate's] this lady's B

36-7 Lord Lambeth] this particular friend of other days B

38 all the other irregularities] the remarked lapses B

39 them] the sisters B

39 he] om.

41 dinner] luncheon, to tea, to dinner, to supper even after the arduous German opera B

41-2 compatriots] countrywomen B

42 sister] companion B

277 : 3 one's going to a Drawing Room] her reception at Court B

4-5 declared that . . . ceremony on] expressed a hatred of Courts, but he had social privileges or exercised some court function—these undiscriminated attributes, dim backgrounds where old gold seemed to shine through transparent conventions, were romantically rich to our young heroine—that involved his support of his sovereign on B

7 which his lordship had sent] sent by his lordship B

7 had on] appeared in B

8 appearance] glory B

9 *her*] herself B

11 declaration] pronouncement B

13 seemed to her] struck her as B

15 was his disposition] was just his character B

15 answer] reply B

16-17 sister that she . . . wondered why] relative how much she liked him, and now that she liked him more she wondered at her excess B

17 disposition] clear nature B

18 When once] The truth was that when once B

20 her sister's] her subtle sister's B

20 about] on B

23-4 reality; and it . . . So she was] reality. Besides which there was her habit, her beautiful system, of consenting to know nothing of human baseness or of the vulgar side. There were things, just as there were people, that were as nought from the moment one ignored them. She was accordingly B

25 vulgar] low B

28 Bessie Alden] the girl B

29-31 dissimulate—to . . . belonged—the] dissimulate (to her finer intelligence) that 'appeal of type'—she had a ready name for it—to which her gallant hovering gentleman caused her wonderingly to respond. She was fully aware that she liked it, this so unalloyed image of the B

32-3 him as women . . . bravery (which] it as if she liked the man for it instead of her liking it for the man. She cherished the thought of his bravery, which B

34-5 tested), to . . . good looks] tested, enjoyed a fond view in him of the free and instinctive range of the 'gentlemanly' character, and was as familiar with his good looks as if she habitually handed him out his neckties B

36 that she liked to think of] of privately dilating on B

37-8 that her imagination . . . —opportunities] of the effect on her imagination of the large opportunities of so splendid a person; opportunities B

41 a kind of] an B

43 magnificent] grand B

43-278:1 Lord Lambeth's deportment,] her friends behaviour B

278 : 1 upon] over B

2 upon] on B

2 But] om. B

2-3 silhouette refused to coincide with] silhouette, however, refused to coincide at all points with B

3-4 image; and . . . When he] figure; a want of harmony that she sometimes deplored beyond discretion. It was his own affair she at moments told herself—it wasn't *her* concern the least in the world. When he B

5-7 seemed to her . . . amiable qualities] might have seemed sufficiently to unite high responsibilities with high braveries B

8-10 customary good . . . was heroic] usual effect of natural salubrity and mental mediocrity, she took the measure of his shortcoming and felt acutely that if his position was, so to speak, heroic B

10 but] om. B

10 the hero] that large line B

12 such] these B

12-18 seemed distinctly dull . . . him and measured] lagged ever so much behind it. He affected her as on occasion, dreadful to say, almost *actively* stupid. It may have been that while she so curiously enquired and so critically brooded *her* personal wit, her presence of mind, made no great show—though it is also possible that she sometimes positively charmed, or at least interested, her friend by this very betrayal of the frequent, the distant and unreported, excursion. So it would have hung together that a part of her unconscious appeal to him from the first had been in his feeling her judge and appraise B

20 been on the whole about as] passed for adventurously B

20-3 feel this . . . title and fortune—] be convinced of her 'cleverness' and yet also to be aware of her appreciation—when the cleverness might have been after all but dangerous and complicating—all made, to Lord Lambeth's sense, for convenience and cheer. Hadn't he compassed the satisfaction, that high aim of young men greatly placed and greatly moneyed, of B

23 himself.] himself? B

24 It is true that] It was true B

25 Yes; but not so very much] Ah not so very awfully *much* B

26 being like more] adding to that quantity B

27 seem, perhaps . . . true—] not seem to fit in—but the truth was strange— B

28-30 dull, devoted . . . because] 'deficient,' found herself aspiring by that very reason to some finer way of liking him. This was fairly indeed on grounds of conscience—because B

30 that] om. B

30 extremely] thoroughly B

31 because she reflected that it was] so deemed it B

32 This effort] The effort in question B

33 for] om. B

34 of it was . . . which expressed] being at moments an irritation, which, though consciously vague, was yet, with inconsequence, acute enough to express B

35-6 Bessie Alden went to some] Bessie went to B

36-7 she went] also B

37 his lordship] he B

37-8 potentially] imaginably B

38 on these latter occasions] at these latter B

41 Lord Lambeth] he B

41 it was a symbol] she might take it for a flat sign B

42 no poets and] neither poets nor B

42 in consequence] as a result B

279 : 1 strict consequence] direct result B

3 those] that B

3-4	said Lord Lambeth] he said B
5-6	Bessie Alden] she promptly B
7-8	said Lord Lambeth, gallantly] Lord Lambeth gallantly threw off B
11	see!' . . . 'In] see! In your so awfully clever B
12	in Boston . . . 'We] in our awfully clever Boston, but in our just commonly clever everywhere. We B
13	honour; they go to] honour,' said Bessie. 'It's they who go to B
15	Bessie Alden declared] she returned B
15-16	you good] you some good B
17	Lord Lambeth] the young man B
21	the young man] Lord Lambeth B
23	Bessie Alden] Bessie B
25	said Bessie] she suggested B
26	rejoined her companion] her companion allowed B
28	said Bessie] she went on B
29	Ah! well,] Don't they? Ah well B
30	Bessie was silent a moment] She had a pause B
30	the things] the few things B
31	England,' . . . 'your] England,—your B
36	Lord Lambeth . . . moment] All his pleasant face wondered—he seemed to take it as another of her rather stiff riddles B
41	repeated the young girl] Bessie earnestly contended B
42-280:2	other clever people, . . . many,' she said.] plenty of other clever people.' It was spoken with a fine simple faith, yet the tone of it made her laugh. '"Plenty?" How many?' B
280 : 3-4	told him that there was] mentioned B
8	'It isn't] She was to feel relieved at his not taking it solemnly. 'It isn't B
9	Lord Lambeth declared, laughing.] om. B
10-11	said Bessie] she insisted B
13	asked his lordship] Lord Lambeth asked B
14	that] om. B
15	thinking that] pretending B
15	that I cannot] I should grovellingly B
17-18	young lady . . . is beastly, but] person, either, for not "recognizing," let alone for not "grovelling." Everyone here has to grovel to somebody or to something—and no doubt it's all beastly. But one takes the thick with the thin, and B
18	trouble] trouble, by which I mean a lot of ugliness B
19	said Bessie] Bessie maintained B
20-1	asked Lord Lambeth] the young man asked B
21	last] last, you know B
25-6	observed Bessie . . . a young girl,] she cried with a charming but not wholly sincere ferocity. 'I'm a silly chit, no doubt, B

28 cried Lord Lambeth] he protested B
30 it,' . . . 'as] it—as B
32 said Bessie Alden,] —she clung as for consistency to her discrimination— B
33-4 rejoined Lord Lambeth,] Lord Lambeth said B
34-6 Bessie Alden could . . . extreme convenience] she couldn't induce him—amused as he almost always was at the effect of giving her, as he called it, her head—to join her in more formal reprobation of this repulsive custom, which he spoke of as a convenience she would destroy without offering a better in its place B
37 all this time had] had all this time B
38 noble kinsman] former fellow traveller B
39 upon] on B
40 although] though B
41 was sure that] made no doubt B
42-3 Lord Lambeth] his comrade B
281 : 1 said Percy Beaumont] Percy returned B
4 there,' he said; 'and] there yourself, confound you, and B
5 I don't] Well, I don't B
6 your—your reckless] your reckless B
8 Lord Lambeth . . . with] His friend turned on him B
9 nothing. 'It's not so obvious] nothing, presently, however, speaking a little stiffly. 'My passion doesn't make such a show B
9-10 suppose,' . . . 'considering] suppose, considering B
11 nothing] anything B
14 I know . . . it—that] I'm in complete ignorance, that B
17 You are devilish] Well, you're wonderfully B
17 said Lord Lambeth] the young man returned B
19 irritating] annoying B
22 that] om. B
27 that] om. B
30-1 little American girl . . . intimation by] little nobody of an American girl something may be supposed to be "up."' The young man met this remark with B
31 and] but B
32-4 said just now . . . curious to learn] told you just now that I cultivate my ignorance, but I find I can no longer stand my suspense. I confess I do want to know B
34 Miss Bessie Alden] Miss Alden B
35 interlocutor no immediate] questioner no prompt B
36 was musing, with a frown] only mused—frowningly, portentously B
36 Jove,' . . . 'they] Jove they B
38 Percy . . . laugh] Percy Beaumont, however, continued to aim at lucidity B

38	don't redeem your promises] don't, it's true, quite redeem your threats B
40	continued to meditate] just hung fire B
40	I asked] Well, I asked B
40-1	to call,' he said, simply.] to.' B
282 : 1	Percy Beaumont] Percy B
2	frightened I believe] scared I verily believe B
2	Lord Lambeth looked at him] His friend watched him on this B
4	she will] om. B
5-6	She will beg . . . measures] She'll try to get "at" her—to square her. She won't care what she does B
7-8	silence, and . . . watched him take] silence; he took B
8	then . . . 'I have] slowly returned. 'She had better take care what she does. I've B
9	Branches,' . . . 'and] Branches, and B
12	'Explicitly!'] Lord Lambeth indulged in one of his rare discriminations. 'I shall give them the opportunity.' B
13	set the Duchess off] touch the Duchess up B
13	suspect] "guess" B
16	Beaumont . . . Lambeth.] om. B
16	You do] Then do you B
17	sister, then] sister B
18	cried the young man] the young man cried B
20	said Percy Beaumont] Percy declared B
20-1	What *is*] What the devil's B
24	'That's] His friend looked at him harder. 'That's B
24	fellow; think . . . Beaumont.] chap. Think of *all* the bearings.' B
26-7	charming, intrinsically] more charming—in a very quiet way B
28	girls nearer home] girls—charming in all sorts of ways—nearer home B
28	I like] I particularly like B
28-9	observed . . . his cousin] said Bessie's admirer—almost as on a policy of aggravation B
32	seen that was not] seen,' Lord Lambeth explained, 'who hasn't seemed to me B
34	'How] Mr. Beaumont considered it. 'How B
34	that, if] she isn't dying if you haven't felt her pulse? I mean if B
36	me questions] *me*—over there—questions B
37	said Beaumont] Percy declared B
38-9	asked me . . . don't you know?] done that to me too—again and again,' his friend returned. 'But she wants to know about everything. B
40	Information? Ay,] Everything? Ah B

40 wanted it] wants to know B

41 as little] by the same law, B

43 'I shouldn't] It appeared to give the young man, for a moment, something rather special to think of. 'I shouldn't B

283 : 2 alone,' said Percy Beaumont.] alone.' Such was the moral drawn by Mr. Beaumont; which left him practically the last word in the discussion. B

4 Mr. Beaumont's] the latter's B

4 non-appearance of] non-appearance at their own door of B

5 professed] confessed B

5-6 derive more . . . circumstance] taking more pleasure in this hush of symptoms B

6 done from] taken in B

7 this] that B

7-8 most marked] unmistakeable B

8-9 most marked. It . . . miserable] delightfully unmistakeable; a most interesting sign that we've made them wretched B

9 Lord Lambeth] him B

10 fellow] boy B

12 not] om. B

12 his anxious mother] no near relation B

14-15 sense, possibly, morbidly] sense perhaps morbidly B

15 their absence] their hostile absence B

16-17 express myself . . . Bessie Alden;] work you up any further,' Bessie at last ventured to remark, B

20 looked at her sister,] rested deep eyes on her sister B

21 she said.] om. B

22 young girl continued] girl continued not to blench at her irony B

25 upon] on B

25 said Mrs. Westgate] Mrs. Westgate broke in B

28 upon . . . no more] on his ceasing relations with us B

30 now] at this point B

31 "now"?' asked Bessie Alden] "at this point"?' Bessie asked B

36 seen] watched B

37 said Bessie] Bessie declared B

38 My dear child] Ah you poor proud thing B

38 rejoined her sister] her companion returned B

39 'I know] The girl gave the matter, thus admonished, some visible thought. 'I know B

39 that,' . . . 'And] that. And B

42 exclaimed] commented B

43 Come, you would not] Do you pretend you wouldn't be glad to B

284 : 1 'Oh no,' said the young girl.] Again Bessie calmly considered. 'It would take a great deal more than is at all imaginable to make me marry him.' B

2-4 Mrs. Westgate . . . 'Because I don't] Her relative showed an impatience. 'And what's the great difficulty?' 'The great difficulty is that I shouldn't B
5 Percy Beaumont,] his own frankest critic B
7 his lordship] him B
9-10 the young nobleman said] his lordship went on B
11 so long] om. B
11 regrettably] accidentally B
12 acquaintance] acquaintance sooner B
12 Bessie Alden] Bessie at this B
16 obligation was] obligation's B
17 upon] on B
18 and] for B
18-19 Lord Lambeth's . . . her duties] her friend's parent now described the direction in which, according to her companion's observation, courtesy pointed B
24 wish to see] want really to find B
26-7 there was . . . of amenities] a solemn exchange of amenities took place B
31 she observed] she dropped—and from no towering nor inconvenient height B
35 says] tells us B
37 more comfortable] at home B
38-9 remarked . . . Bessie Alden] the visitor more heavily breathed, but as an overture, across to Bessie Alden B
40 'A very] Mrs. Westgate intercepted the remark. 'A very B
40 time,' said Mrs. Westgate.] time indeed.' B
41 look at Bessie] address her interest to Bessie B
285 : 3 'Very] The girl was prompt and clear. 'Very B
3 indeed,' said Bessie.] indeed.' B
5 comfortable,' said Bessie.] comfortable.' B
6 inquired Lady Pimlico,] lady Pimlico asked B
8 travelling,' . . . 'and] travelling, and B
11 the Countess of Pimlico, and] Lord Lambeth's sister, who B
16 perceived . . . look at her] felt herself now under the eyes of both visitors B
19 inspected . . . costume, she] taken in every item of that of the Duchess, she B
21-2 asked me to . . . Duchess] been so good as to tell me he expects me, but I'm not quite sure of what I can do,' the noble lady exhaled B
23-4 said Mrs. Westgate] Mrs. Westgate further contributed B
25 responded the Duchess] the Duchess went on B
26 Mrs. Westgate . . . 'I think it is] Her hostess melted to sweetness. 'I delight in it at all seasons. And I think it now above all B
29 moment] minute B

29 walked to] passed across the room with a great rustle and an effect of momentous displacement, reached B

30 young] om. B

31 little] om. B

35 'I daresay . . . she observed.] 'I suppose you go out immensely.' B

36 here for] for the local B

39-40 'It's charming,' . . . whom we like.'] 'I've known it of course duskier and dingier. But we only go to see a few people,' Mrs. Westgate added—'old friends or persons we particularly like.' B

41 said Lady Pimlico] Lady Pimlico conceded B

42 upon] on B

42 rejoined] returned B

286 : 1-2 said Bessie, smiling] our heroine smiled B

3-4 was not smiling . . . tranquil] took the case, clearly, as no matter for grimacing; there reigned in her large pink face a meridian calm B

4 susceptible,' . . . 'He] susceptible. He B

6 assented, smiling still] cheerfully assented B

7 looked at . . . then went on—] continued all serenely and publicly to appraise her. B

9 asked Bessie] Bessie echoed B

11 said Bessie;] the girl returned, B

12 he has] have found him so faithful. He has B

14 the Duchess] her Grace with a certain rich force B

15-16 little laugh . . . persistency] laugh of amusement as at such a contention from such a quarter B

17 Lord Lambeth's mother declared] said her massive monitress B

18 Well,' . . . 'we] Well, we B

19-20 The Duchess . . . more to say] The Duchess had a fine contemplative pause—evidently with more to say. She made, in the quantity, her next selection B

20-1 you,' she presently began.] you.' B

22 to see] with B

22-3 very kind,' said Bessie Alden] a ministering angel,' Bessie hastened to put on record B

26 kindness?' . . . smiling] angelic ministering?' the girl laughed again B

29-30 Lady Pimlico . . . attention] Lady Pimlico had allowed her to revert B

31 upon] on B

33 said Mrs. Westgate] Mrs. Westgate appealed B

34 upon] on B

35-6 the young men are] a young man's B

38 she added] —she gave their friends the benefit of the knowledge— B

40-1 was a little . . . while] took it, with a noble art of her own, as if she hadn't heard it; and while she was so occupied—for this involved a large deliberation— B

41-2 told us . . . Lady Pimlico.] has told us of your being so clever.' B

287 : 1 answered] returned B

1-2 says such things] treats you to such flights B

3-4 asked . . . young girl] abruptly asked of her B

5 'Lord Lambeth has asked] Bessie was to have afterwards a vivid remembrance of wondering what her Grace (she was so glad Duchesses had that predicate) would mean by 'long.' But she might as well somehow have wondered what the occupants of the planet Mars would. 'He has invited B

5 days,' said Bessie.] days.' B

6 I shall go,' the Duchess declared,] I think I must really manage it,' the Duchess declared— B

7 Bessie rejoined.] om. B

8 murmured] cried B

9 great] om. B

11 be most happy] give themselves up to you B

11 very] all B

12 want immensely] quite yearn B

12-13 said Bessie to the Duchess] Bessie went on to the larger lady B

15 inquired her Grace] —her Grace quite took it up B

16 Immensely!' replied the young girl] Of the idea of them—which is all I know—immensely.' And the girl's pale light deepened for the assurance B

18-20 a moment . . . very audacious] as if hardly knowing how to take such words, which, from the ducal point of view, had either to be very artless or very aggressive B

21 two great] noble B

23 asked Mrs. Westgate,] Mrs. Westgate sought to know B

23 were] had B

25 be polite,' said Bessie] do the friendly thing,' Bessie surmised B

28-9 grandeur, and] grandeur; they meant B

30-1 murmured Bessie Alden] the girl sighed as fairly for pain B

33 continued] substituted with confidence B

34 said Bessie] our young woman a little more helplessly allowed B

40 said the young girl] Bessie nevertheless persisted B

43-288:2 Bessie was silent . . . hypothesis] Her sister had a pause, but in a few moments claimed the possession of an excellent theory. 'They just came to look at me!' she brought out as with much ingenuity B

288 : 2 it] the idea B

3 most brilliant,] a credit to a fresh young mind; B
4 young] om. B
7-8 the morrow. On the] the morrow. She privately ached—almost as under a dishonour—with the aftersense of having been inspected in that particular way. On the B
8 had] having B
9 and] om. B
10-11 hotel, coming away] hotel and in the act of leaving it B
11 slightly] considerably B
11-12 he was certainly very grave] he certainly, she said to herself, had no spring B
14 No,' . . . 'I can't] No—I can't B
16 Mrs. Westgate,' . . . 'You have] Mrs. Westgate—you've B
17 look in] air on B
19 and she found] only to find B
19-21 that is . . . writing] find her, that is, seated at the table with the arrested pen in her hand. She put her question after a moment B
21-2 here,' . . . at last.] here?' B
23-4 face. She . . . her sister] face—bending it on her B
25 she] the girl B
27 displayed just a spark of irritation] gave a gasp of temporary disappointment B
28 she said with a smile] she nevertheless smiled B
28-9 Later, an] An B
29 said, 'Dear Bessie, I wish] spoke again. 'I do wish, you know, B
31 said Bessie, gently] said Bessie with the slowest gravest gentlest of headshakes B
32 an excellent fellow,' said Mrs. Westgate] really such a dear,' Mrs. Westgate pursued B
35 that] om. B
36 Bessie Alden] Our young lady B
38 significantly] with much point B
40 England,' she added.] England.' B
41 sister looked at her] sister's eyes studied her B
289 : 2 reflected a moment] lost herself for a little in this B
3 she said] she then said B
4 Percy Beaumont] that gentleman B
7 until] till B
9 Paris, and] Paris—when B
9 to that city] om. B
11 Bessie Alden seemed] Bessie Alden, strange and charming girl, seemed B

THE PENSION BEAUREPAS

Note:

The variants recorded below are based on a collation of the original serial text of the tale (*Atlantic Monthly*, 1879) and its two revised versions in *Washington Square, Etc.*, (1881)—hereinafter mentioned as A—and *Lady Barbarina, Etc.* (1908)—hereinafter mentioned as B.

290 : 2	moreover] further B
3-4	had a fancy for] was inclined to B
6	place] way B
7	by Stendhal] by the celebrated Stendhal B
8	have] om. B
10-11	it appeared to me that] easily believed B
22	a fountain. This fact] a generous cool fountain. That approach B
24	kitchen . . . odours] kitchen—amid the 'offices' and struck with their assault on your nostril B
25-7	there was . . . simple sort] things conformed frankly to their nature and the whole mechanism lay bare B
27	excellent] honest B
291 : 1	very] om. B
2	for forty] for more than forty B
4	seventy-three, she wore flowers] seventy-four she wore stacks of flowers B
5	tradition] legend B
5-6	pretended; that] pretended and that B
7	But I never] I never indeed B
7	theory; I am convinced] theory, convinced as I became B
9	was a philosopher . . . basis] dealt with the present and the future in the steady light of a long experience B
10	forty . . . asked of] nearly half a century and all her concern with B
11-12	make use . . . napkins] fold their napkins and make us of the door-mat B
13	care for] trouble about B
14	types, for categories] types and clear categories B
15	great number,] number of these B
15	was] become B
17	any] om. B
18	think] felt B
19	individuals, she] particular persons—once they conformed to the few rules—she B
25-6	contented . . . The line] contented herself with remarking that the proceeding was out of place. The line A; been satisfied to remark that this receptacle was not the place for

arsenic. She could have imagined it otherwise and suitably applied. The line B

29 had that illusion] so flattered myself B

31 upon] on B

31 But] Yet B

32 the more . . . themselves] take themselves the more B

34 had the little] fiercely bargained and had the cheapest B

39 for] as B

39-40 had no . . . methods] shrouded herself in no mystery and announced the day's fare, amid her fumes, quite with the resonance of the priestess of the tripod foretelling the future B

292 : 2 dinner] meals B

8 went on in a very] proceeded but in a B

9-10 the tone . . . sordid] we suffered from a sordid tone B

12-13 This is . . . reality] Nothing can be better than that principle when the rich real underlies it B

13 reality] rich real B

18 picturesque] local colour B

19 great word] grand term B

19 ingenuous; I] ingenuous and had B

21 I] om. B

21-2 that French . . . Swiss mouths] that it flourished by Lake Leman A; it to flourish by Lake Leman B

22 Academy, and] Academy, the nursing mother of the present University, and B

27 this was . . . approach] gave properest access B

28-9 middle, flanked] middle and flanked B

29-30 contained some] bristled with B

31 little] small B

33 and] together with B

33-4 tubs, with were deposited] tubs disposed B

37 There was] We enjoyed B

37 allotment] allowance B

38 there were only an] could boast but of a finished B

39 a young] an obscure young B

293 : 2 estimable town] well-perched place B

2 he] om. B

2 Paris, he] Paris, where he B

5 which] om. B

8 were] was B

9-10 with whom . . . metropolis] who might be more or less counted on to add to the resemblance B

11 large,] vast B

11 garden, reading with] garden and bent his eyes, with B

12 glass a] glass on a B

13 arrival at the Pension Beaurepas,] adoption of the retreat I describe B

15	went into] entered B
23	a hotel] an hotel B
24	rather] more B
26	which] these B
29	newspaper of] newspaper then of B
31	somewhat] sad and B
34	said] concluded B
36	it] this one B
42	in] at B
294 : 1	very much] infinitely B
2	began to feel] felt B
2-3	was not . . . jaded, faded] hadn't at all—as M. Pigeonneau, for instance, in his way, had it—the romantic note; he looked just a jaded faded absolutely voided B
5	unoccupied] helpless B
7	exercise] offer him B
7-8	said something to him] addressed him some remark founded on our passage of a moment before B
12	I should care] I'd want B
14	observed] dropped B
15-16	a dry, deliberate, kind-looking eye] an effect of bottomless wonder and deep despair B
17	answered, laughing] laughed B
19	in] om. B
25	Oh,' said I, 'you] Oh you B
25	immediately] at once B
27-8	I'm afraid . . . too simple] Well then I guess my two ladies will know right off what's the matter with it B
29	Everything is] Oh everything's B
29	went on] hastened to explain B
31	repeated meditatively] languidly echoed B
32	I asked.] om. B
32	very] om. B
34	blinking . . . manner,] absently blinking B
38	Yes, sir,' I replied,] Well, I guess I am, sir,' I felt it indicated to reply; B
39	presumed,' he said, 'that you] presumed you B
41	here?'] here?' he went on. B
295 : 1	declared] observed B
2	it's nice] it's superior A; it's really nice B
4	I rejoined] And then after I had rejoined B
4-5	and I . . . whether] and had inquired of him if B
6	long,' he said, 'but] long, but B
7	fourteen] nineteen B
8	asked] hazarded B
9-10	my companion . . . I at last] Once more he inclined his face to me—his face that was practically so odd a comment on my question, and I so felt his unspoken irony that I soon B

11 sir,' he . . . he repeated] sir. Not much, sir,' he added B

13 Excuse] Pardon B

13-14 said I, for . . . indiscreet] I said; for his desolation had a little the effect of a rebuke B

15 ejaculation] appeal B

17 like] enjoy B

19 confoundedly puzzled] confoundedly muddled A; plaguey muddled B

22 weakness] medical bankruptcy B

22 me to stop plaguing] to stop my run on B

23 me, and] me, as they had orginally pretended they did, and B

24 get out of it] get round it B

26 assented] could but assent B

27 asked] put to B

27 if he had] that I hoped he hadn't B

27-8 ill . . . delay] ill. He only shook his foot at first, for some time, by way of answer; but at last, 'I didn't get natural rest,' he wearily observed B

30 eat; I took] have a natural appetite—nor even an unnatural, when they fixed up things for me. I took B

31 hope you] guess you'll B

31 now,' I said] here,' I felt justified in remarking B

35 a holiday,' I observed] a good holiday,' I concluded B

38 In all] And in all B

38 have never . . . exclaimed, with] had never let up?' I cried in B

40 'Sundays,' he said at last.] 'I kind o' let up Sundays.' B

41-2 'No wonder . . . shouldn't have] 'Oh that's nothing—because our Sundays themselves never let up.' 'I guess they do over here,' said my friend. 'Yes, but you weren't over here.' 'No, I wasn't over here. I shouldn't have B

296 : 2-3 turned his . . . moment] bending, though a little hopelessly, about to me again B

4 went on again, slowly, softly,] proceeded slowly, mildly and B

9 observations have] fine talk has B

10 it was a good time] the time was good AB

11 neighbour] compatriot B

15-16 take,' . . . laugh] take.' To which he added a laugh as ghostly as a dried flower B

17 it's slightly illogical?' I remarked] there's a flaw in the reasoning?' I asked B

19-20 take a walk] recreation B

21 wants] requires AB

31 that,' said I. 'Simple] that. Simply B

35 My friend] He B

35-6 he looked . . . moments] his wan kind eyes considered me B

37 said presently,] only brought out: B

297 : 3 making . . . them] carrying out his offer B

7 looking about] where she looked about B

7 as I imagined] I inferred B

8-9 place, and . . . near] place. Old M. Pigeonneau meanwhile hovered near B

10-11 said my . . . me up] —my friend led me up B

12 large, plump,] ponderous B

13 elaborate coiffure] arrangement of hair, with forehead-tendrils, water-waves and other complications, that reminded me of those framed 'capillary' tributes to the dead which used long ago to hang over artless mantle-shelves between the pair of glass domes protecting wax flowers B

14-15 very small . . . brunette] tiny and pretty and lively, with no more maiden shyness than a feminine terrier in a tinkling collar B

16 attired] arrayed B

16-17 very much . . . elegance] much ruffled and flounced, and if elegance were *all* a matter of trimming they would have been elegant B

18 inquired] asked B

20 rough, but] rough,' I made answer, 'but B

20 comfortable,' I answered.] comfortable.' B

21 Mrs. Ruck pursued.] om. B

22 fame,' I said, smiling.] fame.' B

24 said Mrs. Ruck] Mrs. Ruck pursued B

25 quite a] quite in a B

26 was holding] held B

26 white little] small white B

27 she was tapping] tapped B

28 said Mrs. Ruck] said Mrs. Ruck, who looked considerably over my head and seemed to confide the truth in question, as with an odd austerity or chastity, a marked remoteness, to the general air B

30 whether this was] if this is B

32 We] Well, we B

32 thought] think B

33 said she was] say she's B

35 'Mr. and] Mrs. Ruck, at this, drew down a little. 'Mr. and B

36 them,' . . . pursued.] them.' B

41 Mother is . . . observed] Mother's death on comparing,' remarked B

42 am always . . . elder lady] like to study things and to see for myself,' the elder lady returned B

298 : 1 And . . . laugh] And, recovering her distance again, she seemed to impose this tax on the universe B

4 great decision] sharp affirmations B

5 'You like . . . affirmed.] Her father gave one of his ghostly grunts. 'You like the stores—that's what you like most, I guess.' B

7 remark] charge B

8 life!' exclaimed Mr. Ruck] life. He says you *can*!' Mr. Ruck proclaimed B

9 Mr. Ruck] Mr. Ruck then B

11-12 the husband . . . look] he retorted, but with his melancholy eyes on me B

15 'I don't . . . husband.] 'Well, lovey,' he sighed, 'I've had hitherto mainly to settle up!' B

16 exchange . . . *repartee*] clash between her parents B

17-18 seemed . . . colloquy] struck me as well out in the open—as leaning, subject to any swing, so to speak, on the easy gate of the house of life B

18 this young lady] her B

19 parents, after visiting] companions, after a visit to B

20-21 when she left] on quitting B

21-2 hotel,' said Miss Ruck; 'I] hotel—I B

22 And mother] And I guess mother B

24 she replied, promptly] —her promptitude was perfect B

26 many places] many other places B

28 said he had] claimed he had had B

30 said to him] took the ground B

31 leave him alone] let up on him B

33 of lucid] of the lucid B

35 father] sire B

37-8 voluminous . . . Mrs. Ruck] cold serenity of his companion B

39 young] om. B

41 'Have] I had an idea it was my duty to draw her out. 'Have B

41 I asked, jocosely.] om. B

299 : 1 principal things] most important ones B

1 back] right there B

6 plans?''] plans?' I continued, true to my high conception. B

9 care] see the point B

9 ill] bad B

9 bright, but] bright and natural, but B

17 Well, we have] Well, I guess we've B

19-20 the young lady] my young woman B

26 tell them!' he said.] *tell* them!' B

28 garments. 'Don't] garments. Then the girl put her mother a question. 'Don't B

28-9 the young . . . mother.] om. B

33-4 Mr. Ruck gave me another wink] he gave me another dry wink B

40 No, I thank you] Not much B
300 : 6-7 Sophy glanced . . . laugh] her little laugh, with which she glanced at me, was like the flutter of some gage of battle B
8 Her laugh . . . was pretty] The grace of this demonstration, in itself marked B
9-11 think I . . . paternal one] felt that the sharpest of the strain would come on the paternal B
12 'Come . . . Miss Ruck.] She took it sharply up. 'Come on, mother.' B
13 about] round B
13 explained the elder lady] the elder lady explained B
14 remarked . . . companions] their companion dropped as they B
15 a moment,] om. B
16 stood rubbing it a little,] rubbed it B
18-19 he was . . . querulous] him about to exhale some plaint B
20 very good-natured] a touching fatalist B
21 said] contented himself with recognizing B
22 Mr. Ruck] He B
23 a large portion] no small share B
35 middle] centre B
37 his time hung heavily upon] the time was heavy on B
38 sometimes . . . walk;] at times to propose him a walk, B
301 : 1 pedestrianism] any use of his legs other than endlessly dangling or crossing them B
1 own taste for it] direct employment of my own B
3 walk] stump B
8 contemplating] taking in, to vague ends, B
11 were . . . locomotion] lent themselves to complete displacement, however, much more B
16 deprived of] deprived, in the connection, of B
21 pension, at] pension bourgeoise at B
23 economy,' . . . 'They] economy. The B
26-7 *la mère*] *la maman* B
28 I reflected a moment] I considered the case B
31 Madame Ruck is] She's B
34 Madame Ruck] Madame Roque B
34-6 coquette.' . . . 'You suppose] coquette.' And then as I demurred: 'You suppose B
40 She is] *Toute menue* as she is she's B
43 Mademoiselle Ruck,] Mess Roque B
302 : 1 Mademoiselle] Miss B
7 flexibility of deportment] colloquial ease B
11 which is] om. B
16 inquired] was duly interested B
21 Pension Bonrepos,] Pension Chamousset AB
24 Madame Bonrepos may have invented] Madame Chamousset

may have invented. A; Madame Chamousset may dispense under that name B

31-2 this lady-like . . . residence] the source of these portents, who had presented herself at our door B

34 was disputing] now disputed B

35 among her boxes, on the steps] on the steps and among her boxes B

37 I] om. B

40 I] om. B

42 towards] to B

303 : 1-2 said . . . laugh] cried the cabman in high derision B

4 is] are B

7 if you are impolite] *si vous me manquez* B

11 addressed as 'Aurora'] so addressed B

13 she] om. B

14 manner, at] manner—looking at B

15 up] om. B

19 myself, below] myself and below B

24 to] om. B

24 and to remember] and remember B

29 seems hard] seems so hard B

31 expect] guess B

35 suspected] seemed to make out B

36 Pension Bonrepos] Pension Chamousset AB

40 she] om. B

304 : 6-7 puzzle . . . and her] puzzle; they were mystified beyond appeal by her frugal attire and B

8 very] om. B

10 very] om. B

11 into] to B

14 *fête*] *fête de nuit* A; *fête de nuit* B

14 undertaking] enterprise B

15 itself, consisting] itself on the lines B

17 festival] occasion B

20 Miss Ruck] Mees Roque B

22 occasion] scene B

23-4 Mademoiselle Ruck] Mees Roque B

26 Miss Church.] Mees Cheurche? B

27 name. There . . . which] name. *Ca veut dire "église," n'est-ce pas? Voilà* a church where B

29 Mrs. Church] the elder of the pair B

29-30 the latter lady sitting] that accomplished woman seated B

32 gazed at her with an air of] fairly glowered at her for B

33 said Mr. Ruck] he promptly observed to me B

34 go up] go right up B

42 expect] guess B

43 accomplished woman] devotee B

305 : 2-4 garden . . . 'are they] garden; and that young lady noted with interest the red paper lanterns. 'Good gracious,' she enquired, 'are they B

5-6 the other young girl rejoined] her companion returned B

6 Bonrepos] Chamousset AB

7 Bonrepos] Chamousset AB

8 darkness, lamenting] darkness and lamenting B

10 looked at me, smiling;] smiled at me— B

11 been awaiting] awaited B

16-17 said in . . . gave a little] dropped with a small B

18 with] om. B

19 if] om. B

25 manners,' murmured the old man.] manners.' B

28 there was . . . ardent] was a light of ardour B

28-9 mother, she was very] mother, though in a less degree, she was B

30-1 said Miss Sophy . . . companion's] —Miss Sophy explained to me her friend's B

32 answered, laughing] responsively laughed B

37 go to] om. B

38 go to] om. B

39 said Aurora Church, smiling] Aurora was at any rate not too spiritless to mention B

40-1 heard that there] heard there B

42 There] Oh there B

42 Americans,' . . . laughing.] Americans.' B

43-306:1 rejoined . . . new friend] cried Miss Ruck, ready, it seemed, for the closest comradeship B

306 : 2 young girl] attractive exile B

3 'She's] Miss Ruck, however, promptly answered for her. 'She's B

3 homesick,' . . . 'she's] homesick—she's B

4 I were you my mother] you were me,' she went on to her friend, 'I guess your mother B

6 I declare] om. B

6 dreadful!' cried] cold-blooded!' said B

7 a story] a weird story B

8-10 there was . . . a moment] Dresden was so awful a fate,' I ventured to interpose. Miss Ruck's eyes made light of me B

11 replied] smartly said B

12 go in] go right in B

14 said Miss Sophy] Miss Ruck at once returned B

16 angry] mad B

17 angry,' said Aurora, smiling] mad,' Aurora smiled B

18 rejoined] hastened to state B

19 Europe?'] Europe?' I added. B

20 Always] As long as I can remember B

21 Miss Sophy] Miss Ruck B
24 gave a little laugh] fairly snorted B
24 was saying] was just *saying* B
26 'Yes,] Well, I saw my way to admit it. 'Yes, B
27 looked . . . 'Well,] pounced straight. 'Then B
28 home,' . . . to you] home. We know how to treat your sort B
29 her companion] Aurora Church B
30 when I was] om. B
32 Miss Sophy] Miss Ruck B
33 It's the] The B
34-5 dear,' she said. 'If] dear. If B
37 'Don't] But Aurora lingered while she all appealingly put it to me. 'Don't B
37-38 Aurora asked, lingering.] om. B
39 Possibly . . . years] Well—as one may be tired of life B
40 'Father] 'Tired of life?' cried Miss Ruck. 'Father B
40 weeks,' said Miss. Ruck.] weeks.' B
42 with . . . speaking] as for some charming intelligence B
307 : 1 said Miss Ruck] Miss Ruck guaranteed B
3 that] om. B
4 cried Miss Sophy] said our companion B
9 hesitated a moment] consulted her reminiscences B
9 that there's] you can find B
11 Europe] Europe—say at some five or six hundred B
12 enough,' said Miss Ruck] enough!' Miss Ruck exhaled B
13-14 Europe,' . . . smile] Europe'—our friend rose to a bright high irony B
17 That's . . . Mamma means] That's so much beyond our mark that mamma means B
22-3 glancing . . . Mrs. Church] who had glanced through the window at Mrs. Church's concentration B
25 them] our vulgar life B
26-7 'Why . . . resentfully.] '"Vulgar"?' cried Miss Ruck. 'Why then does she skimp so?' This young woman had clearly no other notion of vulgarity. B
31 the young girl] she B
34 can't] could never B
38 the American] the natural American B
39 the American *toilette*] the natural American clothes B
39-40 looking . . . superior] in tribute to the other's B
42 said . . . laugh] our young lady laughed B
308 : 3 said the young girl] she said for the pleasantry of it B
4 askance . . . coquetry] askance and with no clear poverty of intention B
5 her, wondering] her and wondered B
7 that] that in that way B

7 an American] the American B
9 copy them] strike for freedom B
12-13 are so . . . I am] do come out so with things. I can't come out, I can't rush in, like that. I'm B
15-17 at least as . . . despondency. But] of an inspiration at least as untrammelled as her unexpatriated sisters, and her despondency in the true note of much of their predominant prattle. At the same time B
17-18 the American tone] what Miss Ruck called the natural American style B
18 her tone] her style B
18-19 fascination . . . audacity] fascination; there was something dainty about it, and yet it was decidedly audacious A; fascination—I knew not what (as I called it) distinction, and yet I knew not what odd freedom B
21 festival came to an end] conception of a 'high time' began to languish B
22 did not] failed to B
23-4 witness . . . attributed] see him off quaintly attributed by him B
28 But . . . I] But it was at least on the morrow that I B
30 with] om. B
31 she] om. B
37 to have some conversation] briefly to converse B
38 your] om. B
309 : 2 think . . . know] must have known in other days B
2 don't know] ask myself B
4 I know] I either know or desire to know B
6-7 added . . . the same] my patroness graciously added, 'there's no great difference B
7-9 a specimen . . . days of ours] a specimen—and I take you for a good one,' she imperturbably went on—'of modern young America. Tell me then what modern young America is thinking of in these days of ours B
11 near Mrs. Church] om. B
12 her bright little] her curiously bright and impersonal little B
13 treated . . . young America] taken for a superior specimen of modern young America B
14 summoned . . . alluded] expected to answer for looming millions B
16 an intense, melancholy] a dismal, a desperate B
17 went on] proceeded B
18 Speak, for the present] Speak just now B
19 with . . . design] to any intelligent conscious end B
20 Nothing] No great end B
20 I am studying] But I seem to feel myself study B
23 course. But you] course; but one B

23-4 little counts] little so counts B

25 rejoined gallantly] bravely answered B

27 Yes, I . . . fond of study] Ah yes, I go as straight as possible to the sources B

28-9 for facts . . . go with them] for digging up the facts and the evidence. For conclusions I frequently diverge B

30-1 can hardly . . . acquisitions] don't do much to spread the light B

32-3 of absentees] of impenitent absentees B

35 told me you had] tells me you've B

37 Mrs. Church smiled benignantly] She took it blandly B

37-8 long? We . . . leave it] long? You see it's *our* world, that of us few real fugitives from the rule of the mob. We shall never go back to that B

39 won't like . . . too] nevertheless fancies she yearns!' I replied B

310 : 1-2 a very charming . . . four languages] to do you honour.' I made answer. 'And I hear she speaks fluently four languages B

3-4 a tone which . . . of culture] the tone of one sated with fluencies and disillusioned of diplomas B

9 'You] She seemed to look at me a moment as for the tip of the ear of irony. 'You B

10 am able to] om. B

12 That is . . . daughter thinks] I should never dream of doubting it,' I returned, 'but your daughter nevertheless strongly holds that B

13-14 I began to . . . savoured of] I might have feared that these words would practically represent B

15 that they produced on] them produce in B

15-16 countenance] surface B

17 Mrs. Church] that lady B

18 illusions] small fond illusions and rebellions B

19-20 illusions? Aurora . . . Philadelphia] Sturm und Drang? Aurora says to herself—all at her ease—that she would be happier in their dreadful New York, in their dreary Boston, in their desperate Philadelphia B

21 is mistaken,] knows not what she babbles of— B

22-3 their illusions . . . over them] their yearning to make mistakes, mustn't we? But we must keep the mistakes down to as few as possible B

24-5 Although . . . positiveness] Her soft sweet positiveness, beneath which I recognized all sorts of really hard rigours of resistance and aggression somehow breathed a chill on me B

26 said] none the less threw off B

26 young girls] the female young B

27 asked Mrs. Church] she enquired B

27-8 young . . . from] generations reared in B

29 'Yes,' I said, resolutely.] 'Well,' I said resolutely, 'they're the nicest of all girls.' B

32 angel? But . . . uncivil] angel and one of the nicest of all? But I won't,' she amusedly added, 'force you to describe her as she deserves B

34-5 said I, 'at . . . much more] I at any rate pleaded, 'in America they've the easiest lot and the best of time. They've the most innocent B

36 for] om. B

37-8 there, so well] there down to the ground B

40-311:2 'I am afraid . . . delicately-uttered sentiment] 'To the effect, I see, of your holding them in horror,' I said a little roughly. Rude indeed as was my young presumption Mrs. Church had still her cultivated patience, even her pity, for it. 'We're very crude,' she blandly remarked, 'and we're proportionately indigestible.' And lest her own refined strictures B

311 : 3 that] om. B

5 little steps] the slow considerate steps to which a little dignity may still cling B

12 knowing where] knowing in the least where B

14 great] grand old B

14 observed,] returned B

15 could answer this inquiry] might have been able to meet her question B

16 which] that B

17 *little,*—just a *little*] wee bit—just a wee bit B

19 wait!] wait, to take breath. B

19 wish] want B

21-2 answered, laughing and getting] laughed as I got B

22 got up,] rose B

22-3 terminating . . . Mrs. Church's] terminating our interview, for I perceived Mrs. Church's A; closing our small discussion, for I felt my friend's B

26 meeting her mother's eyes] really facing her parent B

29 dear] om. B

29 young girl gently] girl with a sort of prompt sweet dryness B

31 was silent a moment] had a silence B

31 looked at her mother] met her mother's eyes B

33 to indulge in] om. B

34 be crude] be indigestibly raw B

35 inquired Mrs. Church] Mrs. Church serenely sighed B

312: 4 Do we not] Don't we find delightful things B

6 much] delightful B

6 young] om. B

6-7 a sort . . . submissiveness] her colourless calm B

9-10 was careful . . . manners] desired to testify to the interest at least with which she inspired me B

11 what you] what impression you B
12 said] again ventured B
12-13 what . . . there] of the impression you must have made there B
14 up] in motion B
21 of Calvin] of the dire Calvin B
22 Calvin] *ce monsieur* B
23 and] om. B
24 touch of originality] force of its own B
25 with, are you not] with it—aren't you B
26 Calvin] the evil genius of the Reformation B
27 mamma] mamma—very B
27 docility, while] docility—and also, as I thought, with subtlety—while B
32 told] remarked to B
33 cooks] domestic drudges B
33 poor] brave B
37-8 type do you call] type then,' I asked, 'do you pronounce B
313 : 4 very] awfully B
9 said, laughing] found myself moved to declare B
10 much; she's a] much; she's a *fine mouche*—a B
11 exclaimed. 'She's a charming girl] protested. 'She's no fool, but she's an honest creature B
12 Madame Beaurepas gave an elderly] My hostess gave an ancient B
15 little odd] shrewd politician B
15 position] case B
18 wishes] wants B
18-19 continued . . . 'She wishes] Madame Beaurepas so far confirmed me. 'She wants B
20 wishes] wants B
20 go] manage it B
22 rejoined] laughed B
25 said I] I cried B
27 forty years] nearly half a century B
31 here there is] there's here B
35 that fact that] my cold blood B
41 portion] stretch B
42 There] Here B
43 there is] om. B
314 : 2 promenade] high level B
3 very] om. B
3-4 and often . . . picturesque] resorting to it for stimulation of my sense of the social scene at large B
5 that] of B
6 was] om. B
6 with] om. B

7	brilliant and distinct] all radiant B
8-9	was staring] only stared B
10	proprietor] detainer B
13	transferred] moved B
13-14	high-featured . . . old houses] succession, the grey old high-featured house-masks, B
17	dusky,] 'mean' B
17	plunging their roots] that plunged its knotted roots B
19	suggest . . . delectable] strike a pleasanter note B
20	'That's . . . I observed.] 'The Alps, from here, do make a wondrous show!' B
21	Yes] Yes sir B
21	moving] a stir B
21	it] the Alps B
22	way,] way, the view B
25	they're just walking] I guess they're fooling B
27	shopping] an interest in the stores B
28	Are they shopping now] And are the stores what they're after now B
29	Well, if . . . They told] Yes—unless this is one of the days the stores don't keep. They regret them, but I wish there were more of them! They told B
30	walk round] have a look B
31	means. But] means—it's *their* form of scenery. But B
33	that] om. B
35	any way] anyway, stone by stone—and heard about it century by century B
39	eh] hey B
40	stopped] stepped B
42	a Herald] an old *Herald* B
43	I hope] Well, I hope B
43	said] returned B
315 : 1	D—d] Damned B
5	day] day, and two of them in our locality B
6	I hope . . . I said] I greatly hope they haven't inconvenienced you,' was all I could gratify him with B
7	they . . . much] I guess they haven't affected me quite desirably B
8	in your own street,] right where you live B
10-11	they've . . . to do] they get round to me B
11	blessed] blamed B
12-13	disturb me] break in B
19	I'm] You can't *make* me. I'm B
19	cathedrals; I'm] cathedrals. I'm B
20	beauties of nature. Come] way they used to chain you up in front of them—in those high old times. I'm thinking of the beauties of nature too B

21-4 'I'll think of . . . where?'] 'You can get killed over there I suppose also'—and he nodded at the shining crests. 'I'm thinking of going over—because, whatever the danger, I seem more afraid not to. That's why I do most things. How do you get over?' he sighed. 'Over to Chamouni?' B

29-30 and not in . . . Yes, Chamouni is] you can't tell the difference in these cars. 'Yes,' Mr. Ruck proceeded, 'Chamouni's B

30-1 a few nice shops] good stores B

31 Mr. Ruck] He B

31 certain] om. B

32-4 emphasis, and in . . . man who has] ring and with an irony more pointed than commonly served him. It was as if he had been wrought upon, and yet his general submission to fate was still there. I judged he had B

35 sudden, somewhat imaginative,] sudden sublime B

37 watch] look out B

37-8 walking round] taking a look B

39 hit on] struck B

316 : 2-5 rather exhausted . . . very expensive] jaded air. My companion watched them as they advanced. 'They're right down tired. When they look like that it kind o' foots up B

8 this] her unusually B

8 on the lady's part] om. B

9 a restless conscience] the less innocent aftertaste of her own late pastime B

10 Miss Sophy] Her daughter B

10 her . . . air of] the habit of straighter B

12 sitting] sneaking B

15-16 Miss Ruck . . . her mother's] If Miss Ruck was less conciliatory it would be scarcely, I felt sure, because she had been more frugal. It was rather because her conception of social intercourse appeared to consist of the imputation to as many persons as possible—that is to as many subject males—of some scandalous neglect of her charms and claims B

18 replied Miss Ruck,] she replied B

21-5 of a Sunday, but . . . her a while; then] for regular attendants, but it doesn't meet my idea of a really pleasant place of worship. Few of these old buildings do,' Mrs. Ruck further mentioned. 'Well, we discovered a little laceshop, where I guess I could regularly attend!' her daughter took occasion to announce without weak delay. Mr. Ruck looked at his child; then he B

26 gazed] gazing B

26-7 it was . . . contemplating] the place was certainly not expensive,' his wife said with her eyes also on B

28 said her husband] he pursued B

29 occasion . . . Chamouni] call for lace up there B

30-1 rejoined his wife] Mrs. Ruck returned B

31 a boarding-house] an old pension B

32 said Miss Ruck] her daughter reminded us B

36 Her father] Mr. Ruck B

43 declared the . . . sharp laugh] —the girl had unshaken confidence B

317 : 1 But her father] The subject of this serenity, however, B

4 Miss Sophy] Miss Ruck B

5 show it to] show it off to B

5 Mr. Ruck] he sociably B

7 talk . . . his wife] carry on!' his wife sighed B

8-9 going to] going up to B

10 You're restless;] You're real restless— B

11 got up] roused herself from her own repose B

14 sense whatever of homour] play of mind B

15 she said] she stated with a certain flatness B

16 Mr. Ruck] he B

16 his feet] match B

17 hesitate] let yourself suffer from want B

17-18 In for . . . pound] We can't be more than gay, and we can't be worse than broke B

19 Miss Ruck] Sophy B

20-1 carriage. 'In . . . and pounds] carriage, where the younger addressed her father. 'In your place Mr. Ruck, I wouldn't want to flaunt my meanness quite so much B

23 Poor Mr. Ruck] He B

23-6 observation . . . he was silent] rebuke, surely deserved by a man on whom the humiliation of seeing the main ornaments of his hearth betray the ascendancy of that character had never yet been laid. He flushed and was silent B

28 little] om. B

28 then, turning] turned B

28 rather] om. B

29 all,' he said, 'for] all, for B

31-3 proposed to . . . invitation] offered me the privilege of a walk in his company, but his invitation had hitherto, for one reason or another, always found me hampered B

33-5 perceived . . . demeanour] saw him go forth for a vague airing with an unattended patience B

36 a proceeding which] an overture that B

37-8 jovial . . . should bend] rejoicing a response that he at once proposed we should direct B

38-9 locality . . . occasion] scene less consecrated to social ease was worthy of our union B

318 : 1 bridge, beside] bridge and beside B

2-3 very pretty . . . persons sitting] always pretty and now was really recreative; a band played furiously in the centre and a number of discreet listeners sat B

4 strolling] strolled B
7 embellished the scene,] graced the prospect B
9 minds which was the] minds as to which might be B
10 as] om. B
10 game . . . at it] game in which I consented to take a hand B
11 M. Pigeonneau] my companion B
15 a vigilant mother] the most systematic of mothers B
16 exclamations;] transports— B
16-17 Miss Sophy Ruck] Miss Ruck B
19 We immediately] And then after we had B
20 scene] scene, he addressed himself to the special object of his admiration, Mees Roque B
21 admiration . . . even] enthusiasm to my young friend here even B
22 you,' said . . . Miss Ruck.] you, mademoiselle.' B
23-4 this young lady, presenting] Miss Sophy, who presented B
25 of] om. B
26-7 and of mine] to say nothing of mine B
28 out of] from B
29-30 looked at . . . revolve] inclined her head to the side and shone at me while her open parasol revolved on her shoulder B
31 gentleman? I wish] gentlemen that one picks up? I want B
33 'What mysterious . . . I inquired.] 'What perversity,' I asked, 'are you, with an ingenuity worthy of a better cause, trying to work out?' B
35 you, always!'] you,' she flirted at me—'always!' B
37 rejoined] cried B
39 cried] trumpeted B
39-40 smiling . . . inhumanity] all gallant urbanity and undiscouraged by her impertinence B
41 imposed his society upon] attached himself to B
42-3 was evidently . . . sublimely] treated her own lack even of the juvenile form of that attraction as some flower of alien modesty, and was ever sublimely B
319 : 5 any man] any clinging man B
6 very stupid] clinging enough B
6 but this] but I'm as stupid as you could wish, and this B
9-10 can steal] can kill and steal B
11 I don't know . . . things until] Well, it's a nice question. One doesn't know how those things are taken till B
13 that] om. B
15 out bad] out very bad B
16-17 The young . . . one of the] 'Ah,' she explained, 'you don't know the B
18-22 'Is your position . . . in every way] I was amused at her great formula. 'What do you mean by yours being one?' 'Oh I mean everything B
20 Actually] Distinctly B

	24	very] idiotically B
	25	very] in the least B
	26	'You don't pretend] This, however, was easy to meet. 'You don't in the least pretend B
	27	very] uncannily B
	28-9	am wise.' . . . to observe.] *am* uncannily wise. You could call it nothing more true.' I went along with her a little, rather thrilled by this finer freedom. 'You're essentially not an American girl.' B
	30	My companion] She B
	30-1	was a little flush in] came a flush to B
	32	I'm not] I've been hideously deprived of that immense convenience, that beautiful resource B
	33-6	went on. 'An . . . eagerness. 'How] pursued with interest. 'It would be utterly impossible to an American girl—I mean unperverted, and that's the whole point—to talk as you are talking to me now.' The expressive eagerness she showed for this was charming. 'Please tell me then! How B
	37	an American girl would] she'd B
	38	the things] most of the things B
	38	say] om. B
	41	that are] om. B
	43	permitted . . . hilarity] greatly enjoyed our intellectual relation B
320 :	1-2	are,' . . . are very] are, but, you know, I find you B
	3	that] om. B
	3-4	cried . . . just what] she quite comically wailed. 'See how my whole sense for such things has been ruined. False notes are just what B
	7	become . . . young lady] borne fruit. Miss Ruck B
	10	murmured] declared B
	11	There . . . pavilion or] We had come into view of a manner of pavilion or large B
	12	delicacies procurable] delicacies generally procurable B
	13-14	which were] om. B
	17	next to Aurora Church] next Aurora B
	19	was delighted with] rejoiced to extravagance in B
	20	all,' she said. 'I] all—I B
	21	strange men] strange and possibly depraved men B
	22	wrong we] wrong,' I returned, 'we B
	24	said the young girl] she cried B
	36	entwined] interlaced B
	38	looked at] watched B
	39	wonder . . . I suppose] wonder, no doubt, why I should care for her at all B
	41	about America] about her—your—everything but *my*—extraordinary country B

43	curious] devoured with curiosity B
43	Miss Ruck is very] Miss Ruck's so very B
321 : 3	Our friend] Ah but our friend B
3	to America] there B
4-5	the young . . . moment] my companion beautifully faced me on it B
6	a *maître de piano*] an outraged *maître de piano* B
9	that] who B
10	Street] Street near Fourth Avenue B
16	and I shall be lectured] and lectured B
23	who thinks] who the devil thinks B
24	nobody; she is] nobody; she's the dreariest of frumps; she's B
25	know Europe] know my Europe B
31	and] so that B
35	dull, stupid, second-rate] ugly stupid tenth-rate B
39	the English,] the most impossible English B
42-3	rise, with . . . from] rise—I fear with an undissimulated start—from B
322 : 3	Mr. Ruck] Mr. Ruck, whose high hat had never looked so high B
4	quest] search B
5	softer] more intimate B
7	Aurora Church] my young friend B
9-10	very serious, but] thoroughly resolute though B
10	fluttered] agitated B
11-12	looked all . . . without] took the rest of us in very fixedly and tranquilly and without B
13	to mention] om. B
18	feast] feast, on which she seemed somehow to shed at once the lurid light of the disreputable B
18	to ask] to appeal to B
19	puzzled;] much perplexed. B
20	puzzled] perplexed B
21	said] cried B
24	one. Come, my daughter] one; we'll enter it at once. Come, *ma fille* B
25-8	young girl . . . *lovely time*] girl had flushed for humiliation, but she carried it bravely off; and her grimace as she looked round at us all and her eyes met mine didn't keep her, I thought, from being beautiful. 'Good-bye. I've had a ripping time B
31	be charming] be even more charming B
34	hesitated . . . little gaze] covered him for a little with her coldest contemplation B
39	exclaimed] gasped B
323 : 1	that Mrs. Church would] a person of so much decision, and above all of so much consistency, would B

3 in the English Garden] by the most raffish part of the lake-side B
5 irresponsibility] practical detachment B
10 insufficient chaperonage] compromising countenance, as she regarded the matter, B
12 believe] consider B
12 members] inmates B
12-13 had the . . . understanding] was the best prepared for that exercise B
15 of] to B
17 book,] inveterate volume B
20 refined intellect] cultivated mind B
21 your studies] your deep studies B
21 ventured] didn't hesitate freely B
22 *Que voulez-vous*] *Que voulez-vous monsieur* B
23 boarding-house] boarding-house of this character B
25 seem] appear B
27 And she . . . secret:] And this treasure hung there a little temptingly before she revealed it. B
30 quiet little] little quiet persistent B
34 rejoined] pronounced B
324 : 1 art; every] art; sometimes into that of literature, politics, economics: every B
2 landscape, an] landscape, a mere B
7 perversely] hypocritically B
9-10 a moment . . . gravity,] an instant; taking it up, however, as one for whom discrimination was always at hand. B
13 kind] stamp B
14 said, laughing] ruefully laughed B
17 Oh, I see] Ah there you are beyond me B
18 'We have] 'Naturally'—she quietly assented. 'We have B
20 Miss Ruck . . . especially] Miss Ruck. To that of Miss Ruck in particular B
21 haven't . . . 'Don't] *have* no tone,' I pleaded. 'That's just the point of them. Don't B
23 'Tell me . . . are they] Well, she would see what she could do. But she bent grave eyes on me. 'Are they really B
27 calculate. And] calculate.' I used even a greater freedom. 'And B
28 very] so B
28 go] come B
29 Street] Street near Fourth Avenue B
32 declared . . . terrible] she declared, 'it's all too terrible B
33-4 Madame Bonrepos] Madame Chamousset AB
41 send a] send for a AB
325 : 1 'well . . . whether] She had thoroughly fixed it, as we said; but her large assumptions ruffled me. 'I nevertheless doubt,' I returned, 'if B

2 in a] great as might be the effect there of that B

4 regrets Wall Street, acutely] misses Wall Street all the time B

4 very] deplorably B

5 he has . . . Chamouni] I guess Chamouni won't quiet him B

7 Is it a] Is it, in its strange mixture of the barbaric and the effete, a B

7-8 an air of self-control] all the force of her noble appetite for knowledge B

10 suspect he is] think he must be B

11 selling; he] selling and watching prices, so that he B

13 buying; and] buying—with a considerable indifference to prices—and B

14 shop] 'store' B

19 and] while B

21 murmured Mrs. Church] my friend calmly sighed B

22 very—uncultivated] grossly illiterate B

23-4 They are . . . resources] We make a great talk at home about education, but see how little that ideal has ever breathed on them B

24 occupies . . . imagination] rides them like a fury B

25 idea—even] idea of any sort—not even B

26-7 extremely . . . a really] a mush of personal and private concession—I don't know what he may have been in the business world—strikes me as a really B

28 business is] affairs may be B

28 unable to stop it; he] unable, with his lost nerve, to apply himself; so he B

32-3 ruining themselves] marching to ruin B

38 Mrs. Church . . . meditation] Mrs. Church, with her cold competence, picked my story over B

39-40 be properly fed!] have a good *nourriture.* B

41 said, laughing] smiled B

43 'Why] She took it in—with its various bearings—and had after all, I think, to renounce the shrewd view of a contingency. 'Why B

43 *éprouvée*? Why] *éprouvée*?' From the moment nothing at all was to be got from the Rucks—not even eventual gratuitous board—she washed her hands of them altogether. 'Why B

326 : 3-5 'Pray . . . a moment] She challenged me nobly. 'Pray, do you mean that Aurora's such a hypocrite?' I saw no reason to hesitate B

5 ask me] enquire B

7-8 Mrs. Church . . . exultation: 'I never] 'I?'—she was shocked. 'I never B

9 rejoined] returned B

10 to go back to her own country] for her own great country B

13 her native shores] the paradise she imagines there B

15 Miss Ruck] such a person B

16 would] could B

17 upon] on B

17 logical] quickly-working B

17-18 repudiated . . . supposition] explained that I prescribed no such course B

19 *famille* Ruck] *famille* Roque B

21 serenely, and smiled at] lucidly—she found amusement in B

27 they . . . they] they pervade the place, they B

28 that] who B

28 said; 'go] said. 'There are plenty of Miss Rucks, and she has a terrible significance—though largely as the product of her weak-kneed sire and his "absorption in business." But there are other forms. Go B

31 daughter has] daughter,' Mrs. Church pursued, 'has B

35 go] proceed B

36 that] from which B

36 would omit,] can dispense himself— B

37 retire] retire from the field B

38 Dresden?'] Dresden?' I submissively echoed. B

41 my daughter] Aurora B

327 : 1-2 perceived . . . lounging in,] caught sight of Mr. Ruck, who lounged in B

6 said, slowly, as] said as B

9 precision] majesty B

11 she fixed . . . Mr. Ruck] looked at our luckless friend more in pity than in anger, though more in edification than in either B

12 Chamouni,' she said.] Chamouni.' B

13 replied Mr. Ruck] he made answer B

13 over] round B

14 leaving] called away B

15-16 and I wondered] and wondered B

16 the subject of my agitation] my wanton thought B

17-18 was a sudden . . . elucidated] mightn't be a mere extemporized and unestablished truth—a truth begotten of a deep desire; but the point has never been cleared B

28-30 said Mr. Ruck . . . take hold] he returned, 'I guess you know, and if I could *let* you fix me we'd probably have some big times. But I seem to strike opportunities—well, in excess of my powers. I don't seem able to respond B

32 which was an admirable] that was a perfect B

36 there?' he asked. 'Has] there? Has B

36 Mount Blank?'] Mount Blank?' Indeed in view of the way he had answered her I thought the dear man—to whom I found myself becoming hourly more attached—had beautiful manners. B

37 handed . . . elderly] held out to me with her own venerable B

39 informed her] let her know B
39-328:1 was apparently . . . my brother] appeared to call me away. My brother B
328 : 1 and proposed to me to] and he proposed I should B
3 cried the old woman] the old woman cried on this B
4 Ruck] Roque B
6 Church] Cheurche B
9-10 Ruck should . . . not an] Roque should take itself off. I assured her I was no such B
10 Ruck] Roque B
11 Madame Church, as] Madame Cheurche—quite as B
12 dish of cabbage] strong cheese B
13 Madame Church. I intimated to her] Madame Cheurche. I hinted B
16 you,' I said, 'to] you to AB
20 over it] om. B
20 that] om. B
26 entertaining,] enlivening B
29 there] om. B
29 a female figure] the figure of a female A; the figure of an apparently circumspect female, as they say in the old stories B
31 for] om. B
31 but] yet B
32 her] om. B
33 for a meditative stroll] to commune, like myself, with isolation B
35 young lady] slight but interesting figure B
36 light] rays B
37 It] My fellow solitary B
37-9 but she seemed . . . then she said,—] who acknowledged my presence with an impatience not wholly convincing. B
41 ought, I should] ought,' I replied, 'I should B
41 so,' I answered.] so.' B
43 time that] time then that B
329 : 2 said the young girl] she wailed to extravagance B
2-3 Then, quickly] Quickly, however B
3 Good] *Bon* B
7 replied] returned B
9 murmured Aurora Church] she all ruefully asked B
11 it was] I found B
12-13 looked . . . appearance was] took on an extreme interest, which was moreover B
15 her a . . . I felt] her charming, I thought her remarkable and felt B
16-17 her, those . . . her disposition] her the terms in which Madame Beaurepas had ventured to characterize her AB

20 looking out for a] in quest of an effective B
23 put into effect] render operative B
23 which was] charged B
23 charged] om. B
24 might] would B
27 sort] semblance B
28 and then] after which B
31-2 repeater . . . making] repeating watch and is, in his satisfaction, constantly taking it out of his pocket to hear B
34 the poor girl] my young friend B
38 immodest] indecent B
39 'That] I threw up hopeless arms. 'That B
39 note,' I said, laughing.] note!' B
43 I hesitated, and] On my hesitating B
330 : 3 voice] tone B
5-6 And . . . her voice] But she also gave a clear laugh, quite at variance with this stiffness. Suddenly I thought her adorable B
7 one has] people sometimes have B
18 out—and] out. There you'd be, monsieur—for I should B
19 'Where] I treated it as wholly thrilling, and indeed I quite found it so. 'Where B
25 I] om. B
28-9 upon . . . seemed to] on consular tenderness. It struck B
30 into] to B
34-5 that was . . . realistic] hostile to the romantic note. It was nothing less than the substantial B
40-1 only one . . . with Célestine] but one glance, the memory of which I treasure. Then she surrendered to Célestine, with whom she returned to the house B
42 found] learned B
43 departed] effectively quitted us B
331 : 1 having his coffee] drinking his *café-au-lait* B
4 Miss Aurora] Mees Aurore B
8 moderate] under control B
9-10 that young girl: she had] that attractive young person; she has B
11 that] om. B
12 wished to] wished so prodigiously to B
13 *femme austère*] *femme austère*—I made up my mind to that B
19 person,] form B
22-3 the handsome Madame Ruck,] *la belle* Madame Roque B
27 international comparison] ethnic studies B
33 absence of irritation] habit of forlorn patience B
36 epistolary] stack of postal B
37 I have taken it in] that I know where I am B
40 said] frankly pleaded B

41 news takes away] disappointments strike at the seat of B
42 that I . . . table] as not to be on show B
43 is always accusing] accuses B
332 : 3 breakfast] *déjeuner* B
3-7 he talked a great . . . philosophic] he still moved his lean jaws—he mumbled over his spoilt repast of apprehended facts; strange tough financial fare into which I was unable to bite B
5 or] nor A
8 do something for him,] ease him off; B
9 was] om. B
9 breakfasted, to] breakfasted was to B
12-13 are many . . . for which] prevail those shining shop-fronts of the watchmakers and jewellers for its long list of whom B
13-14 I always . . . windows,] I had always admired these elegant exhibitions B
14 glance] look B
16 suffered] attached B
16 wander along] om. B
18 made a discovery] recorded a fresh observation B
19 brilliant] irresistible B
19 establishments I perceived] repositories I distinguished B
25 looking at them] his eyes fixed on them B
25-6 The salesman was holding] A salesman was in the act of holding B
27 an irresistible] a winsome B
28 in, and I did] in; whereupon, feeling that I mustn't lose him, I did B
32-3 when Mr. Ruck . . . confusion] on the approach of their relative, opposing an indomitable front B
33-4 go home . . . remark, but she] get home to breakfast—that's what *you'd* better do,' his wife at once remarked. Miss Sophy resisted in silence; she only B
35 very fixedly. Mr. Ruck] all fixedly. My friend B
37 you have . . . wife; 'you] we've been here before, and you ought to know it.' Mrs. Ruck a trifle guiltily contended. 'We B
39 Miss Ruck . . . towards me] The younger lady held out to me the precious object in her hand B
40 she inquired.] om. B
42 She glanced . . . incredulous] She tossed her head as at a challenge to a romp B
333 : 1 just lovely] just too lovely B
1 Mrs. Ruck] her mother B
2 her daughter declared] piped Miss Ruck B
3 No, he won't] Not very much B
4 observed] returned B

5 going to] going up to B

7-8 Mr. Ruck . . . low tone] Her husband still turned his eyes over the shop, whistling half under his breath B

8 going to] going back to B

10 said Mrs. Ruck] she made answer B

15 said] observed all irrelevantly B

18 said Miss Sophy] was hereupon Miss Sophy's form of farewell to me B

19-20 remarked . . . proudly] her mother almost proudly attested B

21-22 was still . . . a little] was still vaguely inspecting the shop; he was still whistling a little A; still vaguely examined the shop; he still just audibly whistled B

22 said, softly,] took occasion to intimate B

23-4 him. 'Well, I] him; she had a brief but pregnant pause. 'Well, I must say I B

24 she exclaimed.] om. B

25 said] cried B

26 Mr. Ruck good-bye] her other parent good-bye B

30 the family] these interesting friends B

APPENDIX I

Some Contemporary Notices of the Tales

[The publication of 'Daisy Miller' created a minor furore on both sides of the Atlantic: readers were divided into two groups, 'Daisy Millerites and anti-Daisy Millerites'. Reprinted below is William Dean Howells's defence of James, and James's defence of himself. Also reprinted are two contemporary responses to 'An International Episode' and 'The Pension Beaurepas'.]

(A) Howells on 'Daisy Miller':

To read the silly criticisms which have been printed, and the far sillier ones which are every day uttered in regard to Mr. James's Daisy Miller would almost convince us that we are as provincial as ever in our sensitiveness to foreign opinion. It is actually regarded as a species of unpardonable incivism for Mr. James, because he lives in London, to describe an under-bred American family travelling in Europe. The fact that he has done so with a touch of marvellous delicacy and truth, that he has produced not so much a picture as a photograph, is held by many to be an aggravating circumstance. Only the most shiveringly sensitive of our shoddy population are bold enough to deny the truth of this wonderful little sketch. To those best acquainted with Mr. James's manner (and I believe I have read every word he has printed) Daisy Miller was positively startling in its straight-forward simplicity and what I can only call *authenticity*. It could not have been written—I am almost ready to say it cannot be appreciated—except by one who has lived so long abroad as to be able to look at his own people with the eyes of a foreigner. All poor Daisy's crimes are purely conventional. She is innocent and good at heart, susceptible of praise and blame; she does not wish even to surprise, much less outrage, the stiffest of censors. In short, the things she does with such dire effect at Vevey and at Rome would never for an instant be remarked or criticized in Schenectady. They would provoke no comment in Buffalo or Cleveland; they would be a matter of course in Richmond and Louisville. One of the most successful touches in the story is that where Daisy, astonished at being cut by American ladies, honestly avows her disbelief in their disapproval. 'I should not think you would let them be so unkind!', she cries to Winterbourne, conscious of her innocence, and bewildered at the cruelty of a sophisticated world. Yet with such exquisite art is this study managed that the innocence and loveliness of Miss Miller are hardly admitted as extenuating circumstances in her reprehensible course of conduct. She is represented, by a chronicler who loves and admires her, as bringing ruin upon herself and a certain degree of discredit upon her country-women, through eccentricities of behaviour for which she cannot justly be held responsible. Her conduct is without blemish, according to the rural American standard, and she knows no other. It is the merest ignorance of affectation, on the part of the anglicized Americans of Boston or New York, to deny this. A few dozen, perhaps a few hundreds, of families in America have accepted the European theory of the necessity of surveillance for young ladies, but it is idle to say it has ever been accepted by the country at large. In every city of the nation young girls of good family, good breeding, and perfect innocence of heart and mind, receive their male acquaintances *en tête-à-tête*, and go to parties and concerts with them, unchaperoned. Of course, I do not mean that Daisy Miller belongs to that category; her astonishing mother at once designates her as pertaining to one distinctly inferior. Who has not met them abroad? From the first word uttered by Miss Daisy to her rampant young brother in the garden at Vevey, 'Well, I guess you'd better be quiet', you recognize her, and recall her under a dozen different names and forms. She went to dine with you one day at Sceaux, and climbed, with the fearless innocence of a bird, into the great chest-nut tree. She challenged you to take her to Schonbrunn, and amazed your Austrian acquaintances whom you met there, and who knew you were not married. At Naples, one evening—*Eheu, fugaces labunter anni*; it is not worth while to continue the enumeration. It makes you feel melancholy to think she is doing the same acts of innocent recklessness with men as young and as happy, and what the French call as enterprising, as you were once.

. . . an American girl, like Daisy Miller, accompanied by a woman like Daisy's mother, brought up in the simplicity of provincial life in the United States, has no more chance of going through Europe unscathed in her feelings and her character than an idiot millionaire has of amusing himself economically in Wall Street. This lesson is taught in Mr. James's story,—and never was necessary medicine administered in a form more delightful and unobtrusive.

The intimacy with the courier is a fact of daily observation on the continent. A gentleman of my acquaintance, inquiring the other day for a courier he had employed some years before, was told that he was spoiled for any reasonable service by having been so much with American families, and that one family, after their tour in Europe was ended, had taken him home to South Boston as their guest, and had given a party for him!

('The Contributor's Club', the *Atlantic* (February 1879).)

(B) James on 'Daisy Miller':

[A minor English novelist, Mrs. Lynn Linton (1822-98), wanted James to explain his intentions; James answered in a letter—]

I will answer you as concisely as possible—and with great pleasure—premising that I feel very guilty at having excited such ire in celestial minds, and painfully responsible at the present moment.

Poor little Daisy Miller was, as I understand her, above all things *innocent*. It was not to make a scandal, or because she took pleasure in a scandal, that she 'went on' with Giovanelli. She never took the measure really of the scandal she produced, and had no means of doing so: she was too ignorant, too irreflective, too little versed in the proportions of things. She intended infinitely less with G. than she appeared to intend—and he himself was quite at sea as to how far she was going. She was a flirt, a perfectly superficial and unmalicious one, and she was very fond, as she announced at the outset, of 'gentlemen's society'. In Giovanelli she got a gentleman—who, to her uncultivated perception, was a very brilliant one—all to herself, and she enjoyed his society in the largest possible measure. When she found that this measure was thought too large by other people—especially by Winterbourne—she was wounded; she became conscious that she was accused of something of which her very comprehension was vague. This consciousness she endeavoured to throw off; she tried not to think of what people meant, and easily succeeded in doing so; but to my perception she never really tried to take her revenge upon public opinion—to outrage it and irritate it. In this sense I fear I must declare that she was not *defiant*, in the sense you mean. If I recollect rightly, the word 'defiant' is used in the tale—but it is not intended in that large sense; it is descriptive of the state of her poor little heart, which felt that a fuss was being made about her and didn't wish to hear anything more about it. She only wished to be left alone—being herself quite unaggressive. The keynote of her *character* is her innocence—that of her *conduct* is, of course, that she has little sentiment about Winterbourne, that she believes to be quite unreciprocated—conscious as she was only of his protesting attitude. But, even here, I did not mean to suggest that she was playing off Giovanelli against Winterbourne—for she was too innocent even for that. She didn't try to provoke and stimulate W. by flirting overtly with G.—she never believed that Winterbourne was provokable. She would have liked him to think well of her—but had an idea from the first that he cared only for higher game, so she smothered this feeling to the best of her ability (though at the end a glimpse of it is given), and tried to help herself to do so by a good deal of lively movement with Giovanelli. The whole idea of the story is the little tragedy of a light, thin, natural, unsuspecting creature being sacrificed as it were to a social rumpus that went on quite over her head and to which she stood in no measurable relation. To deepen the effect, I have made it go over her mother's head as well. She never had a thought of scandalizing anybody—the most she ever had was a regret for Winterbourne.

This is the only witchcraft I have used—and I must leave you to extract what satisfaction you can from it. Again I must say I feel 'really badly', as D. M. would have said, at having supplied the occasion for a breach of cordiality. May the breach be healed herewith! Believe in the very good will of yours faithfully, H. James

(August 1880)

(C) The *Atlantic* on 'An International Episode':

In ['An International Episode'] Mr. Henry James Jr., has given us some of his daintiest workmanship. His style is more than ever, in this elegant trifle, like a transparent vase, which lets perfectly be seen the swift, but seemingly aimless dartings of his brilliant mockery through the limpid medium of an intelligence absolutely uncoloured by preference or sympathy. The light satire of the present sketch is softly announced in its polysyllabic title. Mr. James is still, as in *The American, The Europeans,* and 'Daisy Miller', playing with the contrasts between New World and Old World types of character and codes of conduct; accumulating delightfully clever studies, and assorting or rearranging them in new combinations. It is the turn of his countrymen to be specially pleased with his last performance, because in it he has drawn, with his customary precision, the very best kind of American girl,—gentle, proud, high-minded, beautifully brought up, and fair to see, as a matter of course,—who cannot for her life love a British peer because he is a peer, though most amiably disposed towards himself, and keenly susceptible with regard to the picturesque accessories and historic dignity of his position. The comedy has two acts, the first which takes place in New York and New Port, where the Marquis of Lambeth and his cousin, Percy Beaumont, arrive in August, 'the season for watermelons and Englishmen', and are received and entertained with a lavish hospitality which is also uncalculating, although the noble visitors cannot believe it so. How admirable is the first conversation recorded of these two after their arrival in New York! [A lengthy quotation follows.]

Some such [as the New York passage quoted] bland apology seems equally requisite for the style of conversation of the ladies at Newport, with whom the Englishmen are presently domesticated. The lamentations of Mrs. Westgate over the fact that 'we have no leisure class in America' cover more pages with their vapid prolixity than any but the most reckless realist would have dared assign to them; and even Bessie Alden, destined to come out so nobly in England, does not so much more than vindicate her Boston training by making the inquiry of Lord Lambeth, 'Are you a hereditary legislator?'. To which he replies, naturally and appropriately, 'Oh, I say!—don't make me call myself such names as that.'

At the end of the first act of 'An International Episode', we confess to having thought, with Mr. James's premature admirers in England, that he meant his two countrywomen for delightful fools, but the events have proved that we did not know them nor their author. When the curtain rises upon them in England, they have undergone the most striking transformation: Mrs. Westgate has dropped her twaddle, and is full of spirit, *finesse*, epigram; Miss Bessie has developed into a model of maidenly dignity, capable of leading the story to the *dénoûment* foreshadowed above. And we heartly forgive our author this lack of artistic continuity in his female characters for the sake of the refined practical joke which he is thereby enabled to play upon his English readers.

In the pause between the two parts of the drama, when it seemed even to ourselves as if the balance of the laugh were to be against America, plaudits loud and long resounded the other side of the water. We read in the *Saturday Review* of 'a careful, clear, and subtle sketch of the American woman as she lives and flirts in the works of Mr. Henry James'; in the *Academy* of 'a piece of work so capable and original, so vigorous and to a certain point so telling, as to be worthy of equal praise and study', etc. But when the tables were turned,—and turned with what noiseless rapidity and smiling grace!—there was one moment of vacant bewilderment, and then a burst of something very different from applause. The *Cornhill Magazine* pronounces the episode 'thin, flimsy, and unsatisfactory', graciously adding that it would not withdraw its praise of the first part (how could it, by the way?), but that the conclusion is not equal to the prelude. The *Academy* protests, as it were with tears of wrath, that young English lords do *not* say 'filth' and 'beastly' to ladies. The British grandmother is ever slow to perceive herself smiled at, but by the time she had adjusted her reading-glass and slowly perused the account of the Duchess of Bayswater's call on the American adventurers, and the reflections and comments of the latter ('She won't even know how well I am dressed', was Mrs. Westgate's rueful observation), that abominable supposition had taken shape in her august mind. The British lion does not lightly own himself pervious to a thorn, but even so tiny and polished a one as Mr. James has insinuated into his paw is enough to make him shake that member in a terrible manner, and lift up howlings audible throughout two continents,—howlings however, which when heard at a certain distance, are harmless and even entertaining.

(June 1879)

(D) The *Atlantic* on 'The Pension Beaurepas':

Mr. James, as is well known, is the most brilliant of the discoverers of Europe, yet he has been quite as much interested in watching the movements of his fellow explorers. Indeed, his close familiarity with them and the Europeans among whom they pass has made him at times a little negligent of his country, and too much disposed, perhaps, to confine his portrayal of the American type to those varieties which have been seen in Europe. . . .

In 'The Pension Beaurepas', already known to the readers of the *Atlantic*, Mr. James has made us acquainted with two foreign Americans, who enable us to enter a little more easily into the perplexities of native Europeans, when they try to form their impressions of Americans from the specimens thrown up on their shores. Mrs. Church, the American mother, who has tried to efface her nationality with a wash of European culture of a severe order, and Miss Aurora Church, her daughter, who attempts a feeble revolt into the condition of free-born American girls, are individuals, but scarcely types. They amuse us as much as they must puzzle our European inquirers, and belong in the international museum of literature as examples of climatic and other effects upon the American genus, when undergoing voluntary or involuntary exile. The shade of distinction between Miss Ruck, the genuine American girl, and Miss Church, who makes desperate efforts at recovering her nationality, is a very nice one, and, with the help of a pretty vigorous treatment of Miss Ruck, is made clear and decisive.

(May 1883)

APPENDIX II

James's Preface to 'Four Meetings', 'Daisy Miller', 'An International Episode' and 'The Pension Beaurepas'

[Four of the ten tales in this volume were included in the New York Edition, to which James appended 'intimate' critical Prefaces. Two of the four, however, 'An International Episode' and 'Four Meetings', are completely ignored in the Prefaces: James has nothing to say about them. The other two, 'Daisy Miller' and 'The Pension Beaurepas', are treated more generously.

Section A below is an excerpt taken from volume xiv of the New York Edition, *Lady Barberina, Etc.*, where 'An International Episode' and 'The Pension Beaurepas' appear in their final textual state. In the opening paragraph of his Preface to that volume, James has some interesting general reflections on the international theme; these are followed by some reflections on 'The Pension Beaurepas'.

Section B reprints James's Preface to 'Daisy Miller', from volume xviii of the New York Edition. The volume receives its title from the tale, *Daisy Miller, Etc.*]

(A)

On the interest of *contrasted* things any painter of life and manners inevitably much depends, and contrast, fortunately for him, is easy to seek and to recognize; the only difficulty is in presenting it again with effect, in extracting from it its essence and its lesson. The reader of these volumes [the New York Edition] will certainly see it offered in no form so frequent or so salient as that of the opposition of aspects from country to country. Their author, I am quite aware, would seem struck with no possibility of contrast in the human lot so great as that encountered as we turn back and forth between the distinctively American and the distinctively European outlook. He might even perhaps on such a showing be represented as scarce aware, before the human scene, of any other sharp antithesis at all. He is far from denying that this one has always been vivid for him; yet there are cases in which, however obvious and however contributive, its office for the particular demonstration, has been quite secondary, and in which the work is by no means merely addressed to the illustration of it. . . .

'The Pension Beaurepas' is not alone, thanks to some of its associations, in glowing for me with the tender grace of a day that is dead; and yet, though the accidents and the accessories, in such a picture, may have been marked for change, why shall not the essence of the matter, the situation of Mr. Ruck and their daughter at old Geneva—for there is of course a new, a newer Geneva—freely recur? I am careful to put it as a question, and all for a particular reason that, to be frank, I find myself, before the vast diluvian occidental presence in Europe, with its remorseless rising tide and its positive expression of almost nothing but quantity and number, deprived, on definite and ample grounds, of the precious faculty of confidence. This confidence was of old all instinctive, in face of the 'common run' of appearances, the even then multitudinous, miscellaneous minor international phenomena, could effect a fairly prompt and easy notation; but it is now unmistakable to come forth, from whatever privacy, to almost any one of the great European highways, and more particularly perhaps to approach the ports of traffic for the lately-developed and so flourishing 'southern route' from New York and Boston, is to encounter one of those big general questions that sturdily brush away the multiplication of small answers. 'Who are they, what are they, whence and whither and why?' the 'critic of life', international or other, still, or more and more, asks himself, as he of course always asked, but with the actual difference that the reply that used to come so conveniently straight, 'Why, they're just the American vague variety of the dear old Anglo-saxon race', not only hangs fire and leaves him to wait and wonder, but really affects him as having for this act of deference (as to which he can't choose, I admit) little more than a conscious mocking, baffling, in fact a just all but sinister, grimace. 'Don't you wish you knew, or even *could* know?' the inscrutable grin seems to convey; and with resources of cynicism behind it not in the least to be disturbed by any such cheap retort as 'Don't you wish that, on your side, *you* could say—or even, for your own convenience, so much as guess?'

(B) 'Daisy Miller'

It was in Rome during the autumn of 1877; a friend then living there but settled now in a South less weighted with appeals and memories happened to mention—which she might perfectly not have done—some simple and uninformed American lady of the previous winter, whose young daughter, a child of nature and of freedom, accompanying her from hotel to hotel, had 'picked up' by the wayside, with the best conscience in the world, a good-looking Roman, of vague identity, astonished at his luck, yet (so far as might be, by the pair) all innocently, all serenely exhibited and introduced: this at least till the occurrence of some small social check, some interrupting incident, of no great gravity or dignity, and which I forget. I had never heard, save on this showing, of the amiable but not otherwise eminent ladies, who weren't in fact named, I think, and whose case had merely served to point a familiar moral; and it must have been just their want of salience that left a margin for the small pencil-mark inveterately signifying, in such connections, 'Dramatize, dramatize!' The result of my recognizing a few months later the sense of my pencil-mark was the short chronicle of 'Daisy Miller', which I indited in London the following spring and then addressed, with no conditions attached, as I remember, to the editor of a magazine that had its seat of publication at Philadelphia and had lately appeared to appreciate my contributions. That gentleman however (an historian of some repute) promptly returned me my missive, and with an absence of comment that struck me at the time as rather grim—as, given the circumstances, requiring indeed some explanation: till a friend to whom I appealed for light, giving him the thing to read, declared it could only have passed with the Philadelphian critic for 'an outrage on American girlhood'. This was verily a light and of bewildering intensity; though I was presently to read into the matter a further helpful inference. To the fault of being outrageous this little composition added that of being essentially, and pre-eminently a *nouvelle*; a signal example in fact of that type, foredoomed at the best, in more cases than not, to editorial disfavour. If accordingly I was afterwards to be cradled, almost blissfully, in the conception that 'Daisy' at least, among my productions, might approach 'success', such success for example, on her eventual appearance, as the state of being promptly pirated in Boston—a sweet tribute I hadn't yet received and was never again to know—the irony of things yet claimed its rights, I couldn't but long continue to feel, in the circumstance that quite a special reprobation had waited on the first appearance in the world of the ultimately most prosperous child of my invention. So doubly discredited, at all events, this bantling met indulgence, with no great delay, in the eyes of my admirable friend the late Leslie Stephen and was published in two numbers of 'The Cornhill Magazine' (1878).

It qualified itself in that publication and afterwards as 'a study'; for reasons which I confess I fail to recapture unless they may have taken account simply of a certain flatness in my poor little heroine's literal denomination. Flatness, indeed, one must have felt, was the very sum of her story; so that perhaps after all the attached epithet was meant but as a deprecation, addressed to the reader, of any great critical hope of stirring scenes. It provided for mere concentration, and on an object scant and superficially vulgar—from which, however, a sufficiently brooding tenderness might eventually extract a shy incongruous charm. I suppress at all events here the appended qualification—in view of the simple truth, which ought from the first to have been apparent to me, that my little exhibition is made to no degree in critical but, quite inordinately and extravagantly, in poetical terms. It comes back to me that I was at a certain hour long afterwards to have reflected, in this connection, on the characteristic free play of the whirligig of time. It was in Italy again—in Venice and in the prized society of an interesting friend, now dead, with whom I happened to wait, on the Grand Canal, at the animated water-steps of one of the hotels. The considerable little terrace there was so disposed as to make a salient stage for certain demonstrations on the part of two young girls, children *they*, if ever, of nature and of freedom, whose use of those resources, in general public eye, and under our own as we sat on the gondola, drew from the lips of a second companion, sociably afloat with us, the remark that there before us, with no sign absent, were a couple of attesting Daisy Millers. Then it was that, in my charming hostess's prompt protest, the whirligig, as I have called it, at once betrayed itself. 'How can you liken *those* creatures to a figure of which the only fault is touchingly to have transmuted so sorry a type and to have, by a poetic artifice, not only led our judgement of it astray, but made *any* judgement quite impossible?' With which this gentle lady and admirable critic turned on the author himself. 'You *know* you quite falsified, by the turn you gave it, the thing you had begun with having in mind, the thing you had had, to satiety, the chance of "observing": your pretty perversion of it, or your unprincipled mystification of our sense of it, does it really too much honour—in spite of which, none the less, as anything charming or touching always to that extent justifies itself, we after a fashion forgive and understand you. But why *waste* your romance? There are cases, too many, in which you've done it again; in which, provoked by a spirit of observation at first no doubt sufficiently sincere, and with the measured and felt truth fairly twitching your sleeve, you have yielded to your incurable prejudice in favour of grace—to whatever it is in you that makes so inordinately for form and prettiness and pathos; not to say sometimes misplaced drolling. Is it that you have after all too much imagination? Those awful young women capering at the hotel-door, *they* are the real Daisy Millers that were; whereas yours in the tale is such a one, more's the pity, as—for pitch of the ingenuous, for quality of the artless—couldn't possibly have been at all.' My answer to all which bristled of course with more professions than I can or need report here; the chief of them inevitably to the effect that my supposedly typical little figure was of course pure poetry, and had never been anything else; since this is what helpful imagination, in however slight a dose, ever directly makes for. As for the original grossness of readers, I dare say I added, that was another matter—but one which at any rate had then quite ceased to signify.

APPENDIX III

'Americans Abroad'—An Uncollected Essay by Henry James

[This little-known essay by James was published in the *Nation* of 3 October 1878, a few months after the appearance of 'Daisy Miller', and a couple of weeks before that of 'An International Episode'—two of his most controversial novellas on the theme of Anglo-Euro-American attitudes, to which the article might be seen to serve as a footnote. James was responding to a controversy—inspired, one is tempted to say, by some of James's own fictions on the subject—over the manners and behaviour of Americans abroad, which raged in the pages of the *Nation* in 1878. It is quite likely that James's title was meant particularly for the *Home Journal* of New York, where a pirated version of 'Daisy Miller' had appeared with a subtitle: 'Americans Abroad'.]

Some weeks ago (No. 668) there appeared in these columns a short account of the American colony in Paris, which called forth at the time a rejoinder, and upon which it has been our fortune to hear privately a good many comments. Some of these comments have been sympathetic; others have been highly dissentient. In every case, however, there was a discussion of the question raised—a discussion which, in the circle in which it took place, could not fail to be extremely interesting. However the question raised may in any case be settled—the question of Americans appearing 'to advantage' or otherwise in Europe—there is no doubt that nothing could be well more characteristic of our nationality than the sight of a group of persons more or less earnestly discussing it. We are the only people with whom such a question can be in the least what the French call an actuality. It is hard to imagine two or three Englishmen, two or three Frenchmen, two or three Germans comparing notes and strongly differing as to the impression made upon the civilized world by the collective body of their countrymen. In the first place, the Englishman or the Frenchman sees no reason to suppose that such an impression is in any way peculiar, or that one member of European society distinguishes himself noticeably from another. In the second place, if he were to be made aware that foreigners were criticizing him, he would be extremely indifferent to their verdict. He would comfortably assume that the standard of manners—the shaping influences—in his own country are the highest, and that if he is a gentleman according to these canons he may go his way in peace. The season is drawing to a close during which, chiefly, Americans disseminate themselves in foreign lands, and for the last three or four months the national character has had free play in European hotels and railway stations. The impression, whatever it is, produced upon the European community must have been sensibly deepened. In spite of the commercial tribulations at home, the number of American travellers abroad has been very large, and numerous also have been the Americans (more numerous every year) who have betaken themselves to Europe for an indefinite residence. Those observers of whom we just now spoke, who are always ready to be a party to national self-analysis, have probably, in many cases, collected some new ideas. They have encountered, for instance, a few more specimens of the unattached young American lady—the young lady travelling for culture, or relaxation, or economy—and, according to their different points of view, she has seemed to them a touching or a startling phenomenon. The writer of these lines feels that he has added to the number of his own observations; that the data upon which his general conclusions rest have been multiplied; and that, thanks to his having passed some weeks in a great city in which the American tourist is frequently met and easily recognized, he might, in such a discussion as was just now alluded to, be beguiled into giving an even indiscreet extension to remarks originally prompted simply by a friendly interest in that class of Parisians known as Americans.

Americans in Europe are *outsiders*; that is the great point, and the point thrown into relief by all zealous efforts to controvert it. As a people we are out of European society; the fact seems to us incontestable, be it regrettable or not. We are not only out of the European circle politically and geographically; we are out of it socially, and for excellent reasons. We are the only great people of the civilized world that is a pure democracy, and we are the only great people that is exclusively commercial. Add the remoteness represented by these facts to our great and painful geographical remoteness, and it will be easy to see why to be known in Europe as an American is to enjoy an imperfect reciprocity. It may be the Europeans who are the losers by this absence of reciprocity; we do not prejudge that point, and we do not know, indeed, who is to settle it. A great many Americans—by no means all—maintain that the Europeans *are* the losers, and declare that if they don't know us and don't care about us, so much the worse for them. This is in many ways a very proper and very natural attitude; but nothing can be more characteristic of our civilization than the fact that an American may be almost defied to maintain it consistently. Let him be even more patriotic than is necessary, he is constantly lapsing from it, and, when he is in company with Europeans who do nothing to ruffle his usually great good-nature, he constantly takes a tone which indicates that he values their good opinion and that he is rather flattered than otherwise by possessing it. This, however, is a matter to be discussed apart. We wish to mention the last fact which leads Europeans to look upon Americans as aliens—the fact that large and increasing numbers of them elect, as the phrase is, to spend large parts of their lives in foreign lands. When a European sees an American absentee settle down in the country of which he himself is a native it is not surprising that, in the face of this practical tribute, he should be found doubting whether the country the American has left is as agreeable, as comfortable, as civilized, as desirable a one to belong to as his own. The American may carefully explain that he is living abroad for such and such special and limited reasons—for culture, for music, for art, for the languages, for economy, for the education of his children; the fact remains that in pursuit of some *agrément* or other he has forsaken his native-land, and the European retains, ineffaceably, the impression that if America were really a pleasant place he would never do so. He would come to travel—yes, frequently and extensively; but he (or rather *she*, for as a general thing, in this case, that is the proper pronoun) would never take up an abode in a strange city and remain there year after year, looking about, rather hungrily, for social diversion and 'trying to get into society.' Such a spectacle makes the European take the American, as an American, by so much the less *au sérieux*. An Englishman, a Frenchman, a German finds his intellectual, his æsthetic ideal in living in his own country. A great many Englishmen live out of England for economy; a great many Germans emigrate to make a living. But the ideal in each of these cases is to be rich enough to live at home; the dream of felicity is to have a large income and spend it within one's native borders. If we perhaps except the Russians, who do not altogether come into our category, the Americans are the only highly-civilized people among whom the ideal takes another turn. It will probably never be the case that the country will lack a sufficient number of rich residents to 'run' it; but we shall probably for a long time continue to see numbers of Americans absenting themselves from the United States in proportion as fortune puts into their hands the means of what is called enjoying life. A great many of them prefer to enjoy life in Paris, where our correspondent who described the 'colony' gave a sketch of their situation. They are naturally a puzzle to many of the people they live among, who are at a loss to imagine the compensation that Americans find in a society with which they do not amalgamate for the forfeiture of those social advantages which, as is supposed, gentlemen and ladies enjoy in their own country. The compensation that comes from shops and theatres and restaurants seems insufficient to the average European mind, preoccupied as that mind is with the belief that nothing can be so agreeable as the *life* of one's native land—the animated circle of which one is a member as a matter of course. The average European mind can never understand that for many enriched Americans life at home has never been strikingly agreeable, and that public amusements in a European capital may not unfairly be held to outweigh the social advantages relinquished even in certain capitals of States.

Curiously combined with that argumentative national self-consciousness of which we began by speaking is a profound, imperturbable, unsuspectingness on the part of many Americans of the impression they produce in foreign lands. With this state of mind it is impossible to find fault; it has always been, we suspect, the mark of great nationalities. It has become a commonplace to say that the English are conspicuous for it, and it is highly probable that the ancient Romans—the *cives Romani*—were equally so. But it may sometimes provoke a smile, when the impression produced is a good deal at variance with European circumstances. There is the conscious and the unconscious American; for we, of course, do not mean that the two characters are combined in the same individual. The conscious American is apologetic, explanatory—a pessimist might sometimes say, snobbish. But perhaps, after having traversed a certain phase by a sort of Hegelian unfolding, this type is on its way to become unconscious again. Extremes meet, and that is a symptom of great experience as well as of great innocence. The great innocence of the usual American tourist is perhaps his most general quality. He takes all sorts of forms, some of them agreeable and some the reverse, and it is probably not unfair to say that by sophisticated Europeans it is harshly interpreted. They waste no time in hair-splitting; they set it down once for all as very vulgar. It may be added that there are a great many cases in which this conclusion hardly seems forced. A very large proportion of the Americans who annually scatter themselves over Europe are by no means flattering to the national vanity. Their merits, whatever they are, are not of a sort that strike the eye—still less the ear. They are ill-made, ill-mannered, ill-dressed. A very good way to get a collective impression of them is to go and sit for half an hour in the waiting-room of any European banker upon whom Americans hold letters of credit. During certain hours of the morning our compatriots swarm, getting their drafts cashed and asking for their letters—those letters which they apparently suspect the banker's clerks of a constitutional indisposition to surrender. The writer of these lines lately enjoyed on several occasions this opportunity of observation, and—from the point of view of amenity—the spectacle was not gratifying. *Are* we the worst-looking people in the world? the sophisticated spectator, on such an occasion, enquires; and lest he should be beguiled into giving an answer too monstrous he abstains from giving any at all. One American (of the 'conscious' class) has a way of explaining these things—the common facial types, the vulgar manners, the 'mean' voices, the want of acquaintance with the rudiments of the science of dress—to another. He says that in America 'every one travels,' and that the people at the bankers are much better than the corresponding class in Europe, who languish in downtrodden bondage and never have even a chance to show themselves to the world. The explanation is highly sufficient, for it is very certain that for many Americans a journey to Europe is the reward of a period of sordid toil. An American may take great satisfaction in this circumstance; he may be proud of belonging to a country in which the advantages of foreign travel are open to all, irrespective of 'social standing'; instead of being, as in Europe (according, at least, to his theory), only within the reach of the luxurious and the privileged. But the European only perceives that a great many American travellers are remarkably 'rough,' and quite fails to congratulate either his own country or theirs upon possessing them. The people in question neither know nor care what he thinks about them, and, having examined the antiquities of the Old World, they go westward across the Atlantic with a perfectly good conscience. The European critic, however, sometimes opens himself with striking candour to an American of the introspective class. It is a hundred to one that his tone is patronizing; but there are degrees of patronage. If it is grossly patronizing the American is offended, and invites him to keep his approbation for himself; but if it is subtly patronizing the American listens to it with a complacency decidedly at variance with the theory of his more exalted hours—the theory of the sufficiency of the great Republic in every way to itself.

It may be that we shall some day become sufficient to ourselves and lose the sense of being the most youthful, most experimental, and, somehow, most irregular of the nations. But until that time comes some of us may occasionally be caught listening without protest to compliments paid us at the expense of some others. It is only just to say, however, that the American in Europe often enters into what we have called the conscious phase by a great deal of irritation. He finds Europeans very ignorant of a country, very indifferent to a country which, in spite of irregularities, he may be pardoned for thinking a magnificent one. A few Englishmen and Germans know a good deal about the United States—a good deal more than most Americans do; but it is hardly too much to say that as a general thing, as regards this subject, the European mind is a perfect blank. A great many Americans are very ignorant of Europe, but in default of knowledge it may be said that they have a certain amount of imagination. In respect to the United States the European imagination is motionless; and it may well seem to an American that there is something ridiculous in a scheme of the universe which leaves out a country as large as an aggregation of European kingdoms. There are many anomalies and crookednesses in the lot of the conscious American, and not the least of them is the fact that the country on whose behalf he is expected to be humble and patient—to wait for further results and withhold inopportune boasts—is an affair which, at times and in certain lights, seems to make this sweet reasonableness an affectation. It is comparatively easy to confess yourself a provincial if you really come from a province; but if you have been brought up among 'big things' of every kind the admission requires an effort. On the whole, the American in Europe may be spoken of as a provincial who is terribly bent upon taking, in the fullness of ages, his revenge.

APPENDIX IV

'Daisy Miller': A Comedy in Three Acts—by Henry James

[In 1882, some four years following the publication of the story of Daisy Miller, James dramatized the fate of his heroine for the stage. The dramatized version was submitted to the Madison Square Theater in New York and to a theatre in London—and was rejected by both. The text reprinted below is the original magazine publication of the play in the *Atlantic* of 1883. Although there has been a recent, highly successful, film version of the story, the play by James has had little luck in the theatre. The play provides an interesting commentary on the novella.]

PERSONS REPRESENTED.

Frederick Winterbourne.	Mrs. Costello.
Charles Reverdy.	Madame de Katkoff.
Giacomo Giovanelli.	Alice Durant.
Eugenio.	Mrs. Walker.
Randolph Miller.	Daisy Miller.

A Waiter.

Act I.—*An Hotel on the Lake of Geneva.*
Act II.—*The Promenade of the Pincian, Rome.*
Act III.—*An Hotel in Rome.*

ACT I.

Garden and terrace of an hotel on the Lake of Geneva. The portico of the hotel to the left with steps leading up to it. In the background a low parapet dividing the garden from the lake, and divided itself by a small gate opening upon a flight of steps which are supposed to descend to a pier. Beyond this a distant view of mountains and of the lake, with the Château de Chillon. Orange-trees in green tubs, benches, a few small tables and chairs.

SCENE I. MADAME DE KATKOFF. EUGENIO.

MADAME DE KATKOFF, *coming in as if a little startled, with a French book in a pink cover under her arm.* I believe he means to speak to me! He is capable of any impertinence.

EUGENIO, *following slowly, handsomely dressed, with a large watch-guard, and a courier's satchel over his shoulder. He takes off his hat and bows obsequiously, but with a certain mock respect.* Madame does me the honour to recognize me, I think.

MME. DE K. Certainly I recognize you. I never forget my servants, especially (*with a little laugh*) the faithful ones!

EUGENIO. Madame's memory is perhaps slightly at fault in leading her to speak of me as a servant!

MME. DE K. What were you, then? A friend, possibly?

EUGENIO. May I not say that I was, at least on a certain occasion, an adviser?

MME. DE K. In the way of occasions, I remember only the one on which I turned you out of the house.

EUGENIO. You remember it with a little regret, I hope.

MME. DE K. An immense deal—that I hadn't dismissed you six months sooner!

EUGENIO. I comprehend the regret of Madame. It was in those six months that an incident occurred—(*He pauses.*)

MME. DE K. An incident?

EUGENIO. An incident which it is natural that Madame should not have desired to come to the knowledge of persons occupying a position, however humble, near Madame.

MME. DE K., *aside.* He is more than impertinent—he is dangerous. (*Aloud.*) You are very audacious. You took away a great deal of money.

EUGENIO. Madame appears still to have an abundance.

MME. DE. K., *looking at him a moment.* Yes, I have enough.

EUGENIO. *smiling.* Madame is to be congratulated! I have never ceased to take an interest in Madame. I have followed her—at a distance.

MME. DE. K. The greater the distance, the better!

EUGENIO. *significantly.* Yes, I remember that Madame was very fond of her privacy. But I intrude as little as possible. I have duties at present which give me plenty of occupation. Not so much, indeed, as when I was in the employment of Monsieur de Katkoff: that was the busiest part of my life. The Russians are very exacting—the Americans are very easy!

MME. DE K. You are with Americans now?

EUGENIO. Madame sees that she *is* willing to talk! I am travelling with a family from New York—a family of three persons.

MME. DE K. You have no excuse, then, for detaining me; you know where to find conversation.

EUGENIO. Their conversation is not unagreeable as that of Madame! (*With a slight change of tone.*) I know more about you than you perhaps suspect.

MME. DE K. I know what you know.

EUGENIO. Oh, I don't allude to Madame's secrets. I should never be so indiscreet. It is not a secret today that Madame has a charming villa on this lovely lake, about three miles from Geneva.

MME. DE K. No, that is not a secret.

EUGENIO. And that though she leads a life of elegant seclusion, suited to the mourning which she has never laid aside—though she has lightened it a little—since she became a widow, Madame does not entirely shut her doors. She receives a few privileged persons.

MME. DE K., *aside.* What on earth is he coming to? (*Aloud.*) Do you aspire to be one of them?

EUGENIO. I should count upon it the day I should have something particular to say to Madame. But that day may never come.

MME. DE K. Let us hope so!

EUGENIO. Let us hope so! Meanwhile Madame is in a position to know as well as myself that—as I said just now—the Americans are very easy.

MME. DE K. The Americans?

EUGENIO. Perhaps, after all, Madame doesn't find them so? Her most privileged visitor is of that nationality! Has he discovered—like me—that the Russians are very exacting?

MME. DE K., *looking at him a moment, then quickly, though with an effort.* The Russians, when their antagonists go too far, can be as dangerous as any one else! I forget *your* nationality.

EUGENIO. I am not sure that Madame ever knew it. I'm an Italian Swiss, a native of the beautiful city of Lugano. Is Madame acquainted with Lugano? If she should go that way, I recommend the Hôtel Washington: always our Americans, you see! The Russians? They are the most dangerous people I know, and we gentlemen who take charge of families know everything.

MME. DE K. You had better add frankly that you traffic in your knowledge.

EUGENIO. What could be more just? It cost us a good deal to get it.

MME. DE K., *to herself, after a pause.* It is best to know the worst, and have done with it. (*Aloud.*) How much do you want?

EUGENIO. How much do I want for what? For keeping quiet about Mr. Winterbourne, so that his family shan't think he's wasting his time, and come out from America to bring him home? You see I know even his name! He's supposed to be at Geneva for purposes of study.

MME. DE K. How much do you want to go away and never let me see you again? Be merciful. Remember that I'm not rich.

EUGENIO. I know exactly the fortune of Madame! She is not rich, for very good reasons—she was exceedingly extravagant in her youth! On the other hand, she is by no means in misery. She is not rich, like the American lady—the amiable Mrs. Miller—whom I have at present the honour to serve; but she is able to indulge herself with the usual luxuries.

MME. DE K. It would be a luxury to get rid of you!

EUGENIO. Ah, I'm not sure that Madame can afford that; that would come under the head of extras! Moreover, I'm not in want of money. The amiable Mrs. Miller—

MME. DE K., *interrupting.* The amiable Mrs. Miller is as great a fool as I?

EUGENIO. I should never think of comparing her with Madame! Madame has much more the appearance of one who is born to command. It is for this reason that I approached her with the utmost deliberation. I recognized her three days ago, the evening she arrived at the hotel, and I pointed her out to Mrs. Miller as a Russian lady of great distinction, whose husband I had formerly the honour to serve in a very confidential position. Mrs. Miller has a daughter even more amiable than herself, and this young lady was profoundly impressed with the distinguished appearance of Madame.

MME. DE K. Her good opinion is doubtless of great value; but I suppose it's hardly to assure me of that—

EUGENIO. I may add that I didn't permit myself to make any further remarks.

MME. DE K. And your discretion's an example of what you are capable of doing? I should be happy to believe it, and if you have not come to claim your reward—

EUGENIO. My reward? My reward shall be this: that we leave the account open between us! (*Changing his tone entirely.*) Let me speak to you very frankly. Some eight years ago, when you were thirty years old, you were living at Dresden.

MME. DE K. I was living at Dresden, but I was not thirty years old.

EUGENIO. The age doesn't matter—we will call it twenty, if you like: that makes me younger, too. At that time I was under your roof; I was the confidential servant, on a very exceptional footing, of M. de Katkoff. He had a great deal of business—a great deal of diplomatic business; and as he employed me very often to write for him—do you remember my beautiful hand?—I was not so much a servant as a secretary. At any rate, I was in a position to observe that you had a quarrel with your husband.

MME. DE K. In a position? I should think you were! He paid you to spy upon me.

EUGENIO. To spy upon you?

MME. DE K. To watch me—to follow me—to calumniate me.

EUGENIO, *smiling*. That's just the way you used to talk! You were always violent, and that gave one an advantage.

MME. DE K. All this is insupportable. Please to spare me your reminiscences, and come to the point.

EUGENIO. The point is this—that I got the advantage of you then, and that I have never lost it! Though you didn't care for your husband, you cared for some one else; and M. de Katkoff—with my assistance, if you will—discovered the object of your preferences. Need I remind you of what followed the day this discovery became known to you? Your surprise was great, because you thought yourself safe; but your anger was even greater. You found me for a moment in your path, and you imagined—for that moment—that I was a Russian serf. The mistake had serious consequences. You called me by the vilest of names—and I have never forgotten it!

MME. DE K. I thank you for reminding me of my contempt. It was extremely sweet.

EUGENIO. It made you very reckless. I got possession of two letters, addressed to the person I speak of, and singularly rash compositions. They bear your signature in full.

MME. DE K. Can there be any better proof that I have nothing to be ashamed of?

EUGENIO. You were not ashamed then, because, as I have already remarked, you were reckless. But today you are wise.

MME. DE K., *proudly*. Whatever I have said—I have always signed!

EUGENIO. It's a habit I appreciate. One of those letters I gave to M. de Katkoff; the other—the best—I kept for myself.

MME. DE K. What do you mean by the best?

EUGENIO. I mean—the worst!

MME. DE K. It can't be very bad.

EUGENIO, *smiling*. Should you like me to submit it to a few of your friends?

MME. DE K., *aside*. Horrible man! (*Aloud*) That's the point, then: you wish to sell it.

EUGENIO. No; I only wish you to know I have it.

MME. DE K. I knew that already. What good does it do you?

EUGENIO. You suspected it, but you didn't know it. The good it does me is this—that when, as sometimes happens to us poor members of a despised and laborious class, I take stock of my prospects and reckon up the little advantages I may happen to possess, I like to feel that particular one among them.

MME. DE K. I see—you regard it as a part of your capital. But you draw no income.

EUGENIO. Ah, the income, Madame, is accumulating!

MME. DE K. If you are trying to frighten me, you don't—very much!

EUGENIO. Very much—no! But enough is as good as a feast. There is no telling what may happen. We couriers have our ups and downs, and some day I may be in distress. Then, and only then, if I feel a pinch, I shall call on Madame. For the present—

MME. DE K. For the present, you only wish to insult me!

EUGENIO. Madame does injustice to my manners: they are usually much appreciated. For the rest of the time that we remain under the same roof—so to speak—I shall not again disturb your meditations.

MME. DE K. Be so good as to leave me.

EUGENIO. I wish Madame a very good morning! (*He goes into the hotel.*)

MME. DE K., *stands a moment, thinking.* That's what it is to have been a fool—for a single moment! That moment re-echoes through eternity. He has shaken my nerves, and in this wretched garden one is always observed. (*Exit into the hotel.*)

SCENE II. MRS. COSTELLO, MISS DURANT, CHARLES REVERDY. *They come out of the hotel as Madame de Katkoff passes into it, looking at her attentively.*

REVERDY, *who carries a camp-stool.* That's the biggest swell in the house—a Russian princess!

MRS. COSTELLO. A Russian princess is nothing very great. We have found one at every hotel.

REVERDY. Well, this is the best of them all. You would notice her anywhere.

MRS. C. The best bred people are the people you notice least.

REVERDY. She's very quiet, any way. She speaks to no one.

MRS. C. You mean by that that no one speaks to her.

REVERDY, *aside.* The old lady's snappish this morning: hanged if I'll stand it! (*Aloud.*) No one speaks to her, because no one ventures to.

MISS DURANT. You ventured to, I think, and she didn't answer you. That's what you mean by her being quiet!

REVERDY. She dropped her fan, and I picked it up and gave it to her. She thanked me with a smile that was a poem in itself: she didn't need to speak!

MRS. C. You needn't mind waiting on Russian princesses. Your business is to attend to us—till my nephew comes.

REVERDY, *looking at his watch.* As I understand you, he's already due.

MRS. C. He's a quarter of an hour late. We are waiting breakfast.

MISS D. I'm afraid the delay will bring on one of your headaches.

MRS. C. I have one already, so it doesn't matter!

REVERDY, *aside*. Very convenient, those headaches! (*Aloud.*) Won't you sit down, at least? (*Offering camp-stool.*) You know I don't come out for three minutes without our little implement.

MRS. C. I don't care for that; I'll sit on a bench.

REVERDY, *aside*. She insists on my bringing it, and yet she won't use it! (*The ladies seat themselves, and he places himself between them, astride the camp-stool. He continues, aloud.*) If Mr. Winterbourne is already due, my holiday has legally begun.

MISS D. You won't lose anything by waiting. After he comes you will be at perfect liberty.

REVERDY. Oh yes, after that you won't look at me, I suppose! Miss Durant is counting very much on Mr. Winterbourne.

MRS. C. And I am counting very much on Miss Durant. You are to be very nice to him, you know.

MISS D. That will depend on how I like him.

MRS. C. That's not what I brought you to Europe for—to make conditions. Besides, Frederick's a perfect gentleman.

MISS D. You seem to wish me to promise to marry him. I must wait till he asks me, you know.

REVERDY. He will ask you if Mrs. Costello bids him. He is evidently in excellent training.

MRS. C. I haven't seen him for ten years: at that time he was a model nephew.

REVERDY. I shouldn't wonder if he were to turn out a regular 'hard' one. That would be a jolly lark!

MRS. C. That's not his reputation. Moreover, he has been brought up in Geneva, the most moral city in Europe.

REVERDY. You can't tell anything from that. Here am I, brought up in New York—and we all know what New York is. Yet where can you find a more immaculate young man? I haven't a fault—I'm ashamed of myself!

MISS D. If Mr. Winterbourne is a little wild, I shan't like him any the less. Some faults are very charming.

REVERDY. Tell me what they are, and I'll try and acquire them.

MRS. C. My dear Alice, I'm startled by your sentiments. I have tried to form your taste . . .

MISS D. Yes, but you have only cultivated my dislikes. Those are a few of my preferences.

REVERDY. Tell us a few more of them—they sound awfully spicy!

MISS D. I'm very fond of a certain indifference. I like men who are not always running after you with a camp-stool, and who don't seem to care whether you like them or not.

MRS. C. If you like rude men, they are very easily found. If I didn't know you were a very nice girl, I should take you for—I don't know what!

REVERDY. Miss Durant's remarks are addressed to me, and between you two ladies it's hard to know what to do. You want me to be always at your elbow, and you make a great point of the camp-stool. Will you have it a little, for a change? (*Getting up and offering it. Mrs. Costello refuses with a gesture.*) I don't offer it to Miss Alice; we have heard what *she* thinks of it!

MISS D. I didn't speak of that piece of furniture: I spoke of the person who carries it.

REVERDY. The person who carries the camp-stool? Is that what I've come to be known by? Look here, my dear friends, you ought to engage a courier.

MRS. C. To cheat us out of our eyes? Thank you very much!

REVERDY. A courier with a gorgeous satchel, and a feather in his hat—like those ladies from Schenectady!

MRS. C. So that he might smoke in our faces, as he does in theirs, and have his coffee with us after dinner, as he does with them? They've ruined a good servant.

MISS D. They treat him as an equal; they make him their companion.

REVERDY. But they give him handsome wages—which is more than you do me!

MISS D. I've no doubt they give him little tokens of affection, and locks of their hair. But that makes them only the more dreadful!

MRS. C. I'm glad to see, my dear, that your taste is coming back to you!

REVERDY. Oh, if taste consists in demolishing Miss Daisy Miller, she can take the prize.

MISS D. Demolishing her? I should be sorry to take that trouble. I think her very vulgar: that's all!

MRS. C. Miss Daisy Miller? Is that her distinguished name?

REVERDY, *aside*. Ah, we can't all be named Costello!

MRS. C. They are the sort of Americans that one does one's duty by not accepting.

REVERDY. Ah, you don't accept her?

MRS. C. I would if I could—but I can't. One should let Europeans know—

REVERDY. One should let them know?

MRS. C. That we are not all like that.

REVERDY. They can see it for themselves: she's charmingly pretty.

MISS D. You are extremely impertinent.

REVERDY, *aside*. I put in one that time. (*Aloud.*) I can't help it; she's lovely.

MRS. C. And is the mamma lovely, too? Has any one ever seen the mamma?

REVERDY. She's sick in bed—she's always sick.

MISS D. The courier sits with her, and gives her her medicine.

REVERDY. I hope you call that devoted, then?

MRS. C. It doesn't matter, because the head of the family is the little boy. He orders the dinner; he has the best seat in the carriage.

REVERDY. He's the most amusing little specimen. He has the heart of a patriot in the body of a— (*Hesitates for a word.*)

MISS D. In the body of a grasshopper!

REVERDY. He hops a good deal, or, rather, I should say, he flies; for there is a good deal of the spread-eagle about him.

MISS D. He leaves his toys all over the hotel; I suppose you would say his plumes.

REVERDY. Well, he's a dauntless American infant; a child of nature and of freedom.

MRS. C. Oh, nature and freedom! We have heard too much of *them.*

REVERDY. Wait till you are stopped at the New York custom-house! The youthful Miller and I have struck up a friendship: he introduced me to his sister.

MRS. C. You don't mean to say you spoke to her!

REVERDY. Spoke to her? Yes, indeed—and she answered me.

MISS D. She was not like the Russian princess!

REVERDY. No, she's as little as possible like the Russian princess: but she's very charming in another style. As soon as Mr. Winterbourne arrives (and you must excuse me for saying that he takes a deuce of a time about it), I shall console myself for the loss of your society by plunging into that of the Millers.

MRS. C. You won't lose us, Mr. Reverdy: you can console yourself with *me.*

REVERDY. Oh, thank you!

MRS. C. Frederick will devote himself to Alice.

MISS D. We had better wait till he comes! I have no patience with this delay.

MRS. C. Neither have I, my dear; but I may as well take the opportunity of remarking that a young lady shouldn't seem too eager . . .

MISS D. Too eager?

MRS. C. For the arrival of a gentleman.

MISS D. I see what you mean—more reserve. But simply before you . . .

REVERDY. And before me, please. Am I nobody?

MISS D. Nobody at all!

REVERDY. Well, I don't care, for I descry in the distance the adorable Miss Miller!

MISS D. I'm glad she's in the distance.

REVERDY. Ah, but she's coming this way.

MISS D., *quickly.* I forbid you to speak to her.

REVERDY, *aside.* Ah, then I *am* somebody? (*Aloud.*) I can't cut the poor girl, you know.

MISS D. You needn't see her. You can look at me.

MRS. C. She's always wandering about the garden—the image of idleness and frivolity.

REVERDY. She's not as serious as we, nor as well occupied, certainly; but she's bored to death. She has got no one to flirt with.

MISS D. She shall not flirt with you, at any rate!

REVERDY. Do you wish me to hide behind a tree?

MISS D. No, you can sit down here (*indicating the bench beside her*), and take my parasol—so!—and hold it before your face, as if you were shading your eyes.

REVERDY, *with the parasol.* From Miss Daisy Miller? It's true she's very dazzling! (*Daisy enters from the right, strolling slowly, as if she has nothing to do, and passes across the stage in front of the others, who sit silent, watching her, Reverdy peeping for a moment from behind his parasol. 'She was dressed in white muslin, with a hundred frills and flounces, and knots of pale-coloured ribbon. She was bare-headed; but she balanced in her hand a large parasol, with a deep border of embroidery; and she was strikingly, admirably, pretty.'*[1] *She looks at the others as she passes them, and goes out on the*

[1] From the story.

left—not into the hotel. Reverdy continues.) Now, then, may I look out?

MISS D., *taking back her parasol.* She saw you, I'm happy to say.

REVERDY. Oh yes, I gave her a wink!

MRS. C. That's the way she roams about—

MISS D. Seeking whom she may devour!

REVERDY. Poor little creature! I'm the only tolerably good-looking young man in the hotel.

MRS. C. Mercy on us! I hope she won't get hold of Frederick!

REVERDY. Not if I can help it, dear Madam. I have never seen Frederick—but I mistrust Frederick.

MRS. C. He's not at all in your style. He's had a foreign education. He speaks a dozen languages.

REVERDY. *aside.* An awful prig,—I can see that.

MRS. C. Let us hope that, thanks to his foreign education, he will be out of danger. Such people as that can only disgust him.

REVERDY. I know the style of fellow you mean—a very high collar and a very stiff spine! He speaks a dozen languages—but he doesn't speak the language of Schenectady! He won't understand an American girl—he had better leave her alone.

MISS D. I'm very much obliged to you—for me!

Enter a waiter from the hotel.

REVERDY. Oh, you are not an American; you're an angel!

THE WAITER, *approaching with a bow.* The breakfast that Madame ordered is served.

MRS. C., *to her companions.* It's just twelve o'clock; we certainly can't wait any longer.

MISS D. I don't believe he's coming at all!

MRS. C. Ah, if I've only brought on a headache for nothing!

REVERDY, *aside.* Won't he catch it when he arrives? (*They pass into the hotel, the waiter leading the way.*)

SCENE III. EUGENIO, *then* WINTERBOURNE *and the* WAITER. *Eugenio comes out of the hotel, then looks about him and begins to call. He is without his hat and satchel.*

EUGENIO. Meester Randolph! Meester Randolph! Confound that infernal child—it's the fifth time this morning that I've chased him round the garden! (*Stands calling again.*) Meester Randolph! Meester Randolph! He is always there when he's not wanted and never when he is, and when I find him I haven't even the right to pinch his ear! He begins to kick like a little mule, and he has nails in his boots—for the mountains. Meester Randolph! Meester Randolph! Drat the little wretch—I'm a courier not a nurse! (*Exit to the right, while Winterbourne comes down from the hotel, followed by a waiter, the same who has just appeared, carrying a little tray with a service of black coffee.*)

WINTERBOURNE. I'll have my coffee here, it's so close in the hotel. (*The waiter places the tray on a small table, which he draws up to a bench. Winterbourne takes out a card, on which, on his pocket-book, he writes a few words.*) And please to take that card to the lady whose name I have written there, and ask her when it will be convenient for her to see me.

THE WAITER, *looking at the card.* The Russian lady who arrived three days ago? I will let you know, sir.

WINTERBOURNE, *seated at the little table.* Wait a moment. Do you know whether Mrs. Costello has breakfasted?

THE WAITER. Mrs. Costello? The lady with the young lady, and the gentleman also young?

WINTERBOURNE. I know nothing about her companions. A lady with her hair very high. She is rather—rather—

THE WAITER. Yes, sir, she is rather high altogether! When she gives an order—

WINTERBOURNE, *pouring out his coffee.* I don't ask you to describe her—I ask you if she has breakfasted.

THE WAITER. The party's at table now, sir. I conducted them myself, five minutes ago. I think they waited for you, sir; they expected you to arrive.

WINTERBOURNE. I arrived an hour ago, by the train; but I was dusty, and I had to have a bath. (*Lighting a cigarette.*) Then while I dressed to save time, I had my breakfast brought to my room. Where do they usually take their coffee?

THE WAITER. They take it in our beautiful garden, sir.

WINTERBOURNE. Very good. I will wait for them here. That's all (*The waiter re-enters the hotel. Winterbourne puffs his cigarette.*) There is no use in being in a hurry. I want to be eager—but I don't want to be *too* eager. That worthy man is quite right; when Aunt Louisa gives an order, it's a military command. She has ordered me up from Geneva, and I've marched at the word; but I'll rest a little before reporting at headquarters. (*Puffs his cigarette.*) It coincides very happily, for I don't know that, without this pretext, I should have ventured to come. Three days ago, the waiter said? A week ago, at the villa, they told me she had gone. There is always a mystery in that woman's movements. Yes, Aunt Louisa is rather high; but it's not of *her* I'm afraid! (*Puffs a moment in silence.*)

SCENE IV. WINTERBOURNE. RANDOLPH. *then* DAISY.

RANDOLPH. (*He comes in from the back, approaches Winterbourne, and stops. 'The child, who was diminutive for his years, had an aged expression of countenance, a pale complexion, and sharp little features. He was dressed in knickerbockers, with red stockings, which displayed his poor little spindleshanks; he also wore a brilliant red cravat. He carried in his hand a long alpenstock, the sharp point of which he thrust into everything that he approached,—the flowerbeds, the garden-benches. . . . In front of Winterbourne he paused, looking at him with a pair of bright, penetrating little eyes.'*[1] *Winterbourne, smoking, returns his gaze.*) Will you give me a lump of sugar?

WINTERBOURNE. Yes, you may take one; but I don't think sugar is good for little boys.

RANDOLPH. (*He steps forward and carefully possesses himself of the whole contents of*

[1] From the story.

the plate. From these he still more carefully selects the largest lump, depositing the others in his pocket. Biting, with a grimace.) Oh, blazes! it's hard!

WINTERBOURNE. Take care, young man. You'll hurt your teeth.

RANDOLPH. I haven't got any teeth to hurt; they've all come out. I've only got seven teeth. Mother counted them last night, and one came out afterwards. She said she'd slap me if any more came out. I can't help it—it's this old Europe. It's the climate that makes 'em come out. In America they didn't come out; it's these hotels!

WINTERBOURNE. If you eat all that sugar, your mother will certainly slap you.

RANDOLPH. She's got to give me some candy, then. I can't get any candy here—any American candy. American candy's the best.

WINTERBOURNE. And are American boys the best little boys?

RANDOLPH. I don't know. I'm an American boy!

WINTERBOURNE. I see you are one of the best.

RANDOLPH. That isn't what my mother says, you can bet your life on that!

WINTERBOURNE. Oh, your mother's too modest!

RANDOLPH, *astride his alpenstock, looking at Winterbourne.* She's sick—she's always sick. It's this old Europe! Are you an American man?

WINTERBOURNE. Oh, yes, a fellow-citizen. (*Aside.*) I wonder whether I was once like that!

RANDOLPH. American men are the best.

WINTERBOURNE. So they often say.

RANDOLPH, *looking off to the left.* Here comes my sister. She's an American girl.

WINTERBOURNE. American girls are the best girls.

RANDOLPH. Oh, my sister ain't the best. She's always blowing at me!

WINTERBOURNE. I imagine that's your fault, not hers. (*Daisy comes in from the left in the same manner as on her previous entrance, and on reaching the middle of the stage stops and looks at Winterbourne and at Randolph, who has converted his alpenstock into a vaulting-pole, and is springing about violently. Winterbourne continues, getting up.*) By Jove, how pretty!

DAISY. Well, Randolph, what *are* you doing?

RANDOLPH. I'm going up the Alps. This is the way!

WINTERBOURNE. That's the way they come down.

RANDOLPH. He's all right; he's an American man!

WINTERBOURNE, *aside.* It seems to me that I have been in a manner presented. (*Approaches Daisy, throwing away his cigarette. Aloud, with great civility.*) This little boy and I have made acquaintance.

DAISY. *She looks at him a moment serenely, and then, as if she had scarcely heard him, addresses Randolph again:* I should like to know where you got that pole!

RANDOLPH. The same way as you get your things. I made Eugenio buy it.

WINTERBOURNE, *aside.* With a little commission!

DAISY. You don't mean to say you're going to take that pole to Italy?

WINTERBOURNE, *same manner.* Are you thinking of going to Italy?

DAISY, *looking at him, and then looking away.* Yes, sir.

WINTERBOURNE. Are you going over the Simplon?

DAISY. I don't know—I suppose it's some mountain. Randolph, what mountain are we going over?

RANDOLPH. Going where?

DAISY. To Italy. (*Arranging her ribbons.*) Don't you know about Italy?

RANDOLPH. No, and I don't want to. I want to go to America!

WINTERBOURNE. Oh, Italy's a beautiful place.

RANDOLPH. Can you get any candy there?

DAISY. I hope not! I guess you have had candy enough, and mother thinks so too.

RANDOLPH, *still jumping about.* I haven't had any for ever so long—for a hundred weeks!

DAISY. Why, Randolph, I don't see how you can tell— (*She pauses a moment.*) Well I don't care! (*Looks down at her dress, and continues to smooth her ribbons.*)

WINTERBOURNE, *aside.* Does she accept my acquaintance or not? It's rather sudden, and it wouldn't do at Geneva. But why else did she come and plant herself in front of me? She is the prettiest of the pretty, and, I declare, I'll risk it! (*After a moment, aloud.*) We are very fortunate in our weather, are we not?

DAISY. Well, yes, we've got nice weather.

WINTERBOURNE. And still more fortunate in our scenery. (*Indicating the view.*)

DAISY. Well, yes, the scenery's lovely. It seems very mountainous.

WINTERBOURNE. Ah, Switzerland *is* mountainous, you know.

DAISY. I don't know much about it. We have only been here a week.

WINTERBOURNE, *smiling.* In a week one can see a good deal.

DAISY. Well, *we* haven't; we have only walked round a little.

WINTERBOURNE, *aside.* What a remarkable type! (*Aloud.*) You must be rather tired: there are plenty of chairs. (*Draws forward two of them.*)

DAISY, *looking at them a moment.* You'll be very clever if you can get Randolph to sit.

WINTERBOURNE. I don't care a fig about Randolph. (*Daisy seats herself. Aside.*) Oh, Geneva, Geneva!

DAISY, *smoothing her ribbons.* Well, he's only nine. We've sat round a good deal, too.

WINTERBOURNE, *seated beside her.* It's very pleasant, these summer days.

DAISY. Well, yes, it's very pleasant. But it's nicer in the evening.

WINTERBOURNE. Ah, much nicer in the evening. It's remarkably nice in the evening. (*Aside.*) What the deuce is she coming to? (*Aloud.*) When you get to Italy you'll find the evenings there! . . .

DAISY. I've heard a good deal about the evenings there.

WINTERBOURNE. In Venice, you know—on the water—with music!

DAISY. I don't know much about it. (*With a little laugh.*) I don't know much about anything!

WINTERBOURNE, *aside.* Heaven forgive her, she's charming! I must really ascertain . . . (*To Randolph, who has continued to roam about, and who comes back to them with his alpenstock, catching him and drawing him between his knees.*) Tell me your name, my beautiful boy!

RANDOLPH, *struggling.* Well, you drop me first!

DAISY. Why, Randolph, I should think you'd like it!

WINTERBOURNE, *aside*. Jupiter, that is a little strong!

RANDOLPH, *liberating himself*. Try it yourself! My name is Randolph C. Miller.

WINTERBOURNE, *aside*. Alarming child! But she doesn't seem to be alarmed.

RANDOLPH, *levelling his alpenstock at Daisy, who averts it with her hand*. And I'll tell you *her* name.

DAISY, *leaning back serenely*. You had better wait till you are asked.

WINTERBOURNE. I should like very much to know your name.

RANDOLPH. Her name is Daisy Miller.

WINTERBOURNE, *expressively*. How very interesting!

DAISY, *looking at him, aside*. Well, he's a queer specimen! I guess he's laughing.

RANDOLPH. That isn't her real name—that isn't her name on her cards.

DAISY. It's a pity that you haven't got one of my cards!

RANDOLPH. Her name is Annie P. Miller.

WINTERBOURNE. Oh, I see. (*Aside*.) That doesn't tell me much.

DAISY, *indicating Winterbourne*. Ask him *his* name.

RANDOLPH. Ask him yourself! My father's name is Ezra B. Miller. My father ain't in Europe. My father's in a better place than Europe.

WINTERBOURNE, *uncertain*. Ah, you have had the misfortune . . .

RANDOLPH. My father's in Schenectady. He does a big business. He's rich, you can bet your head!

WINTERBOURNE, *aside*. Oh, in Schenectady? I thought he meant in Paradise!

DAISY, *to Randolph*. Well you needn't stick your pole into my eye!

RANDOLPH, *to Winterbourne*. Didn't I tell you she was always blowing? (*Scampers away and disappears*.)

DAISY, *looking after him*. He doesn't like Europe; he wants to go back. He hasn't got any boys here. There's one boy here, but he's always going round with a teacher.

WINTERBOURNE. And your brother hasn't any teacher?

DAISY. Mother thought of getting him one, to travel round with us. But Randolph said he didn't want a teacher when school didn't keep; he said he wouldn't have lessons when he was in the cars. And we *are* in the cars most of the time. There was an English lady we met in the cars; her name was Miss Featherstone—perhaps you know her. She wanted to know why I didn't give Randolph lessons—give him instruction, she called it. I guess he could give me more instruction than I could give him! He's very smart—he's only nine.

WINTERBOURNE, *aside*. He might be ninety!

DAISY. Mother's going to get a teacher for him as soon as we get to Italy. Can you get good teachers in Italy?

WINTERBOURNE. Oh, it's the land of art—of science.

DAISY. Well, I guess he doesn't want to study art; but she's going to find some school, if she can. (*Pensively*.) Randolph ought to learn some more.

WINTERBOURNE. It depends upon what it is!

DAISY, *after a silence, during which her eyes have rested upon him*. I presume you are a German.

WINTERBOURNE, *rising quickly*. Oh dear, no! I shouldn't have ventured to speak to you, if your brother's mention of my nationality had not seemed a guarantee . . .

DAISY, *getting up*. I didn't suppose my brother knew. And you *do* speak queerly, any way!

WINTERBOURNE. I'm a countryman of your own. But I should tell you that I have spent many years in this Old Europe, as your brother says.

DAISY. Do you live here—in the mountains?

WINTERBOURNE, *aside*. Does she think I'm a goatherd? (*Aloud.*) No, I live just now at Geneva.

DAISY. Well, you *are* peculiar, anyhow!

WINTERBOURNE, *aside*. So are you, if you come to that. (*Aloud.*) I'm afraid I have got rather out of the way—(*pauses for a moment.*)

DAISY. Out of the way of what?

WINTERBOURNE. Of making myself agreeable to the young ladies.

DAISY. Haven't they got any over here? I must say I haven't seen any! Of course I haven't looked out much for them.

WINTERBOURNE. You've looked out more for the gentlemen!

DAISY. Well, at Schenectady I didn't have to look out.

WINTERBOURNE, *aside*. Queer place, Schenectady.

DAISY. I had so much society. But over here—(*She hesitates.*)

WINTERBOURNE. Over here?

DAISY. Well, you're the first gentleman that has been at all attentive.

WINTERBOURNE. Ah, you see, they're afraid!

DAISY, *continuing*. And the first I've cared anything about!

WINTERBOURNE, *aside*. And to think that, at the beginning, *I* was afraid! (*Aloud.*) If they knew how kind you are they would be much less timid.

DAISY. I hate gentlemen to be timid. That's only for us.

WINTERBOURNE, *aside*. 'For us' is enchanting!

SCENE V. DAISY. WINTERBOURNE. EUGENIO. *who comes in hastily from the right, wiping his forehead.*

EUGENIO. Mademoiselle, I have been looking for an hour for Meester Randolph. He must be drowned in the lake!

DAISY. I guess he's talking to that waiter. (*Serenely.*) He likes to talk to that waiter.

EUGENIO. He shouldn't talk to waiters, Mademoiselle.

WINTERBOURNE, *aside*. Only to couriers—the hierarchy!

DAISY. I want to introduce you to a friend of mine—Mr.—Mr.—(*To Winterbourne.*) I declare, I don't know your name.

WINTERBOURNE, *aside*. To the courier? Excuse me!

EUGENIO, *very proper*. I have the honour of knowing the name of Monsieur.

DAISY. Gracious, you know everything!

EUGENIO, *aside*. The lover of the Katkoff! (*Aloud.*) I found Meester Randolph, but he escaped again.

DAISY. Well, Eugenio, you're a splendid courier, but you can't make much impression on Randolph.

EUGENIO. I do what I can, Mademoiselle. The lunch is waiting, and Madame is at the table. If you will excuse me, I will give up the chase. (*Glancing at Winterbourne, aside.*) Is he leaving the Katkoff for the child?

DAISY. You needn't be so grand, need he? (*To Winterbourne.*) It's not the first time you've been introduced to a courier!

WINTERBOURNE, stiffly. The very first.

EUGENIO, *aside.* He has never kept one. (*Aloud.*) If Mademoiselle will pass into the hotel! (*Aside again.*) The child is not for every one.

DAISY. Tell mother to begin—that I'm talking to a gentleman.

WINTERBOURNE, *protestingly.* I shall be very sorry to incommode your mother.

DAISY, *smiling.* I like the way you say such things. (*Familiarly.*) What are you going to do all day?

WINTERBOURNE, *embarrassed.* I hardly know. I've only just arrived.

DAISY. I will come out after lunch.

WINTERBOURNE, *with extreme respect.* I shall be here, to take your commands.

DAISY. Well, you *do* say them! About two o'clock.

WINTERBOURNE. I shall not go far.

DAISY, *going.* And I shall learn your name from Eugenio.

EUGENIO, *aside.* And something else as well! He is not for the child. (*Follows Daisy into the hotel.*)

SCENE VI. WINTERBOURNE *alone, then* MADAME DE KATKOFF.

WINTERBOURNE. She's simply amazing! I have never seen them like that. I have seen them worse—oh, yes!—and I have seen them better; but I've never encountered that particular shade—that familiarity, that facility, that fragility! She's too audacious to be innocent, and too candid to be—the other thing. But her candour itself is a queer affair. Coming up to me and proposing acquaintance, and letting her eyes rest on mine! Planting herself there like a flower to be gathered! Introducing me to her courier, and offering me a rendezvous at the end of twenty minutes! Are they all like that, the little American girls? It's time I should go back and see. (*Seeing Madame de Katkoff.*) But I can hardly go while I have *this* reason for staying!

MME. DE K. (*She comes out of the hotel; she has still her book under her arm.*) They brought me your card, but I thought it better I should come and see you here.

WINTERBOURNE. I know why you do that: you think it's less encouraging than to receive me in-doors.

MME. DE K., *smiling.* Oh, if I could discourage you a little!

WINTERBOURNE. It's not for want of trying. I bore you so much!

MME. DE K. No, you don't bore me, but you distress me. I give you so little.

WINTERBOURNE. That's for me to measure. I'm content for the present.

MME. DE K. If you had been content, you wouldn't have followed me to this place.

WINTERBOURNE. I didn't follow you, and, to speak perfectly frankly, it's not for you I came.

MME. DE K. Is it for that young lady I just saw from my window?

WINTERBOURNE. I never heard of that young lady before. I came for an aunt of mine, who is staying here.

MME. DE K., *smiling again.* Ah, if your family could only take an interest in you!

WINTERBOURNE. Don't count on them too much. I haven't seen my aunt yet.

MME. DE K. You have asked first for me? You see, then it *was* for me you came.

WINTERBOURNE. I wish I could believe it pleased you a little to think so.

MME. DE K. It does please me—a little; I like you very much.

WINTERBOURNE. You always say that, when you are about to make some particularly disagreeable request. You like me, but you dislike my society. On that principle, I wish you hated me!

MME. DE K. I may come to it yet.

WINTERBOURNE. Before that, then, won't you sit down? (*Indicating a bench.*)

MME. DE K. Thank you; I'm not tired.

WINTERBOURNE. That would be too encouraging! I went to the villa a week ago. You had already left it.

MME. DE K. I went first to Lausanne. If I had remained there, you wouldn't have found me.

WINTERBOURNE. I'm delighted you didn't remain. But I'm sorry you are altering your house.

MME. DE K. Only two rooms. That's why I came away: the workmen made too much noise.

WINTERBOURNE. I hope they are not the rooms I know—in which the happiest hours of my life have been passed!

MME. DE K. I see why you wished me to sit down. You want to begin a siege.

WINTERBOURNE. No, I was only going to say that I shall always see with particular vividness your little blue parlour.

MME. DE K. They are going to change it to red. (*Aside.*) Perhaps that will cure him! (*Aloud.*) Apropos of your family, have they come to Europe to bring you home?

WINTERBOURNE. As I tell you, I haven't yet ascertained their intentions.

MME. DE K. I take a great interest in them. I feel a little responsible for you.

WINTERBOURNE. You don't care a straw for me!

MME. DE K. Let me give you a proof. I think it would conduce to your happiness to return for a while to America.

WINTERBOURNE. To *my* happiness? You are confounding it with your own.

MME. DE K. It is true that the two things are rather distinct. But you have been in Europe for years—for years and years.

WINTERBOURNE. Oh, I have been here too long. I know that.

MME. DE K. You ought to go over and make the acquaintance of your compatriots.

WINTERBOURNE. Going over isn't necessary. I can do it here.

MME. DE K. You ought at least to see their institutions—their scenery.

WINTERBOURNE. Don't talk about scenery, on the Lake of Geneva! As for American institutions, I can see them in their fruits.

MME. DE K. In their fruits?

WINTERBOURNE. Little nectarines and plums. A very pretty bloom, but decidedly crude. What book are you reading?

MME. DE K. I don't know what. The last French novel.

WINTERBOURNE. Are you going to remain in the garden?

MME. DE K., *looks at him a moment.* I see what you are coming to: you wish to offer to read to me.

WINTERBOURNE. As I did in the little blue parlour!

MME. DE K. You read very well; but we are not there now.

WINTERBOURNE. A quiet corner, under the trees, will do as well.

MME. DE K. We neither of us have the time. I recommend you to your aunt. She'll be sure to take you in hand.

WINTERBOURNE. I have an idea I shan't fall in love with my aunt.

MME. DE K. I'm sorry for her. I should like you as a nephew.

WINTERBOURNE. I should like you as a serious woman!

MME. DE K. I'm intensely serious. Perhaps you will believe it when I tell you that I leave this place today.

WINTERBOURNE. I don't call that serious: I call it cruel.

MME. DE K. At all events, it's deliberate. Vevey is too hot; I shall go higher up into the mountains.

WINTERBOURNE. You knew it was hot when you came.

MME. DE K., *after a pause, with significance.* Yes, but it's hotter than I supposed.

WINTERBOURNE. You don't like meeting old friends.

MME. DE K., *aside.* No, nor old enemies! (*Aloud.*) I like old friends in the autumn—the melancholy season! I shall count on seeing you then.

WINTERBOURNE. And not before, of course. Say at once you wish to cut me.

MME. DE K., *smiling.* Very good: I wish to cut you!

WINTERBOURNE. You give a charm even to that! Where shall you be in the autumn?

MME. DE K. I shall be at the villa—if the little blue parlour is altered! In the winter I shall go to Rome.

WINTERBOURNE. A happy journey, then! I shall go to America.

MME. DE K. That's capital. Let me give you a word of advice.

WINTERBOURNE. Yes, that's the finishing touch!

MME. DE K. The little nectarines and plums: don't mind if they *are* a trifle crude! Pick out a fair one, a sweet one—

WINTERBOURNE, *stopping her with a gesture.* Don't, don't! I shall see you before you go.

MME. DE K., *aside.* Not if I can help it! (*Aloud.*) I think this must be your family. (*Goes into the hotel.*)

SCENE VII. WINTERBOURNE. MRS. COSTELLO. MISS DURANT. REVERDY, *who come out of the hotel as Mme. de Katkoff enters it.*

REVERDY. We are always meeting the Russian princess!

MISS D. If you call that meeting her, when she never looks at you!

MRS. C. She doesn't look at you, but she sees you. Bless my soul, if here isn't Frederick!

WINTERBOURNE. My dear aunt, I was only waiting till you had breakfasted.

MISS D., *aside.* He was talking with the Russian princess!

MRS. C. You might have sat down with us: we waited an hour.

WINTERBOURNE. I breakfasted in my room. I was obliged on my arrival to jump into a bath.

MISS D., *aside.* He's very cold—he's very cold!

WINTERBOURNE. They told me you were at table, and I just sat down here.

MRS. C. You were in no hurry to embrace me—after ten years?

WINTERBOURNE. It was just because of those ten years; they seemed to make you so venerable that I was pausing—as at the entrance of a shrine! Besides, I knew you had charming company.

MRS. C. You shall discover how charming. This is Alice Durant, who is almost our cousin.

WINTERBOURNE, *smiling.* Almost? I wish it were quite.

MRS. COSTELLO. And that is Mr. Charles Reverdy.

REVERDY. Who is almost their courier!

WINTERBOURNE. I must relieve you of your duties.

REVERDY, *aside.* Oh, thank you, thank you! By George, if I'm relieved I'll look out for Miss Miller. (*Looks about him, and finally steals away.*)

MRS. C. My dear Frederick, in all this time you've not changed for the worse.

WINTERBOURNE. How can you tell that—in three minutes?

MISS D., *aside.* Decidedly good-looking, but fearfully distant!

MRS. C. Oh, if you are not agreeable, we shall be particularly disappointed. We count on you immensely.

WINTERBOURNE. I shall do my best, dear aunt.

MRS. C. Especially for our sweet Alice.

MISS D. Oh, Cousin Louisa, how can you?

MRS. C. I thought of you when I invited her to come to Europe.

WINTERBOURNE. It was a very happy thought. I don't mean thinking of me, but inviting Miss Durant.

MISS D., *to Winterbourne.* I can't say it was of you I thought when I accepted.

WINTERBOURNE. I should never flatter myself: there are too many other objects of interest.

MRS. C. That's precisely what we have been talking of. We are surrounded by objects of interest, and we depend upon you to be our guide.

WINTERBOURNE. My dear aunt, I'm afraid I don't know much about them.

MRS. C. You'll have a motive today for learning. I have an idea that you have always wanted a motive. In that stupid old Geneva there can't be many.

WINTERBOURNE. Ah, if there's one, it's enough!

MISS D., *aside.* If there's *one?* He's in love with some dreadful Genevese!

MRS. C. My young companion has a great desire to ascend a mountain—to examine a glacier.

MISS D. Cousin Lousia, you make me out too bold!

WINTERBOURNE, *aside.* She's not bold, then, this one, like the other? I think I prefer the other. (*Aloud.*) You should go to Zermatt. You're in the midst of the glaciers there.

MRS C. We shall be delighted to go—under your escort. Mr. Reverdy will look after *me!*

MISS D., *glancing about for him.* When he has done with Miss Daisy Miller!

WINTERBOURNE, *smiling.* Even among the glaciers, I flatter myself I can take care of both of you.

MISS D. It will be all the easier, as I never leave your aunt.

MRS. C. She doesn't rush about the world alone, like so many American girls. She has been brought up like the young ladies in Geneva. Her education was surrounded with every precaution.

WINTERBOURNE, *smiling.* With too many, perhaps! The best education is seeing the world a little.

MRS. C. That's precisely what I wish her to do. When we have finished Zermatt, we wish to come back to Interlaken, and from Interlaken you shall take us to Lucerne.

WINTERBOURNE, *gravely.* Perhaps you'll draw up a little list.

MISS D., *aside.* Perfectly polite, but no enthusiasm! (*Aloud.*) I'm afraid Mr. Winterbourne isn't at liberty; he has *other* friends.

MRS. C. He hasn't another aunt, I imagine!

WINTERBOURNE, *aside.* Fortunately not! (*Aloud to Miss Durant.*) It's very charming of you to think of that.

MISS D. Possibly we are indiscreet, as we just saw you talking to a lady.

WINTERBOURNE. Madame de Katkoff? She leaves this place today.

MRS. C. You don't mean to follow her, I hope? (*Aside.*) It's best to be firm with him at the start.

WINTERBOURNE. My dear aunt, I don't follow every woman I speak to.

MISS D., *aside.* Ah, that's meant for us! Mr. Reverdy is never so rude. I'd thank him to come back.

MRS. C. On the 1st of October, you know, you shall take us to Italy.

WINTERBOURNE. Ah! every one is going to Italy.

MISS D. Every one? Madame de Katkoff, perhaps.

WINTERBOURNE. Madame de Katkoff, precisely; and Mr. Randolph C. Miller and his sister Daisy.

MRS. C. Bless my soul! What do you know about that?

WINTERBOURNE. I know what they have told me.

MRS. C. Mercy on us! What opportunity?—

WINTERBOURNE. Just now, while I had my coffee.

MISS D. As I say, Mr. Winterbourne has a great many friends.

WINTERBOURNE. He only asks to add you to the number.

MISS D. Side by side with Miss Daisy Miller? Thank you very much.

MRS. C. Come, my dear Frederick, that girl is not your friend.

WINTERBOURNE. Upon my word, I don't know what she is, and I should be very glad if you could tell me.

MRS. C. That's very easily done: she's a little American flirt.

WINTERBOURNE. Ah! she's a little American flirt!

MISS D. She's a vulgar little chatterbox!

WINTERBOURNE. Ah! she's a vulgar little chatterbox!

MRS. C. She's in no sort of society.

WINTERBOURNE. Ah! she's in no sort of society!

MISS D. You would never know her in America.

WINTERBOURNE. If I should never know her in America, it seems to me a reason for seizing the opportunity here.

MRS. C. The opportunity appears to have come to you very easily.

WINTERBOURNE. I confess it did, rather. We fell into conversation while I sat there on the bench.

MRS. C. Perhaps she sat down beside you?

WINTERBOURNE. I won't deny that she did; she is wonderfully charming.

MISS D. Oh! If that's all that's necessary to be charming—

MRS. C. *You* must give up the attempt—mustn't you, my dear? My poor Frederick, this is very dreadful!

WINTERBOURNE. So it seems; but I don't understand.

MRS. C. What should you say at Geneva of a young woman who made such advances?

WINTERBOURNE. Such advances? I don't know that they *were* advances.

MRS. C. Ah! if you wish to wait till she invites you to her room!

WINTERBOURNE, *laughing*. I shan't have to wait very long.

MISS D., *shocked*. Hadn't I better leave you?

MRS. C. Poor child, I understand that you shrink . . . But we must make it clear.

MISS D. Oh yes, we must make it clear!

WINTERBOURNE. *Do* make it clear; I want it to be clear.

MRS. C. Ask yourself, then, what they would say at Geneva.

WINTERBOURNE. They would say she was rather far gone. But we are not at Geneva.

MRS. C. We are only a few miles off. Miss Daisy Miller is very far gone indeed.

WINTERBOURNE. Ah! what a pity! But I thought, now, in New York—

MRS. C., *sternly*. Frederick, don't lift your hand against your mother country!

WINTERBOURNE. Never in the world. I only repeat what I hear—that over there all this sort of thing—the manners of young persons, the standard of propriety—is quite different.

MISS D. I only know how *I* was brought up!

WINTERBOURNE, *slightly ironical*. Ah, that settles it.

MRS. C. We must take him back with us, to see.

WINTERBOURNE. *Not* to see, you mean—not to see my dear little friend!

MRS. C. In the best society—never.

WINTERBOURNE. Oh, hang the best society, then!

MRS. C., *with majesty*. I'm *exceedingly* obliged to you.

WINTERBOURNE. Oh, *you* are the best society! And the little girl with the naughty brother is the worst?

MRS. C. The worst *I*'ve ever seen.

WINTERBOURNE, *rather gravely, laying his hand on her arm*. My dear aunt, the best, then, ought to be awfully good!

MISS D., *aside.* He means that for an epigram! I'll make him go and look for Mr. Reverdy. (*Aloud.*) I wonder what has become of Mr. Reverdy.

MRS. C., *sharply.* Never mind Mr. Reverdy; I'll look after him. (*To Winterbourne.*) If you should see a little more of those vulgar people, you would find that they don't stand the test.

WINTERBOURNE. Oh, I shall see a little more of them—in a quarter of an hour. (*Looking at his watch.*) The young lady is coming back at two o'clock.

MRS. C. Gracious goodness! Have you made an appointment?

WINTERBOURNE. I don't know whether it's an appointment, but she said she would come back again.

MRS. C., *to Miss Durant.* My precious darling, *we* must go in. We can hardly be expected to assist at such a scene.

WINTERBOURNE. My dear aunt, there is plenty of time yet.

MISS D. Ah, no; she'll be before! Would you kindly look for Mr. Reverdy?

WINTERBOURNE, *extremely polite.* With the greatest of pleasure.

MRS. C. Later in the afternoon, if this extraordinary interview is over, we should like you to go with us into the town.

WINTERBOURNE, *in the same tone.* With the greatest of pleasure. (*Aside.*) They hate her ferociously, and it makes me feel sorry for her.

MRS. C., *to Miss Durant.* Quickly, my dear! We must get out of the way.

WINTERBOURNE. Let me at least see you into the house. (*Accompanies them into the hotel.*)

SCENE VIII. CHARLES REVERDY. RANDOLPH. *then* DAISY.

REVERDY, *coming in from behind with the child on his back.* The horrid little wretch! I'm like Sinbad the Sailor with the Old Man of the Sea! Don't you think youv'e had about enough?

RANDOLPH, *snapping a little whip.* Oh, no; I haven't had enough. I'll tell you when I've had enough.

REVERDY. Oh, come! I've galloped twenty miles; I've been through all my paces. You must sit still in the saddle a while. (*Pauses in front while Randolph bounces up and down.*) I'm playing horse with the brother to be agreeable to the sister; but he's riding me to death!

RANDOLPH, *still brandishing his whip.* I want you to prance about and to kick. Get up, sir; get up!

REVERDY, *aside.* It's the devil's own game—here at the door of the hotel! (*Aloud.*) I'll prance about so that you'll come off.

RANDOLPH, *firm in his place.* If you throw me off, I'll give you a licking! Get up, sir, get up!

REVERDY, *aside.* Damn the little demon! It was a happy thought of mine.

RANDOLPH, *kicking.* These are my spurs. I'll drive in my spurs! Get up, sir, get up!

REVERDY. Oh misery, here goes! (*He begins to imitate the curveting of a horse, in the hope of throwing Randolph off, but, seeing Daisy issue from the hotel, suddenly stops.*)

DAISY, *staring.* Well, Randolph, what are you doing up there?

RANDOLPH. I'm riding on a mule!

REVERDY, *with a groan.* A mule? Not even the nobler animal! My dear young lady, couldn't you persuade him to dismount?

DAISY, *laughing.* You look so funny when you say that! I'm sure I never persuaded Randolph.

RANDOLPH. He said if I would tell him where you were, he would give me a ride.

REVERDY. And then, when he was up, he refused to tell me!

RANDOLPH. I told you mother wouldn't like it. She wants Daisy and me to be proper.

REVERDY, *aside.* 'Me to be proper!' He's really sublime, the little fiend!

DAISY. Well, she does want you to be proper. She's waiting for you at lunch.

RANDOLPH. I don't want any lunch: there's nothing fit to eat.

DAISY. Well, I guess there is, if you'll go and see.

REVERDY, *aside.* It's uncommonly nice for me, while they argue the question!

DAISY. There's a man with candy in the hall; that's where mother wants you to be proper!

RANDOLPH, *jumping down.* A man with candy. Oh, blazes!

REVERDY, *aside.* Adorable creature! She has broken the spell.

RANDOLPH, *scampering into the hotel.* I say, old mule, you can go to grass!

REVERDY. Delightful little nature, your brother.

DAISY. Well, he used to have a pony at home. I guess he misses that pony. Is it true that you asked him that?

REVERDY. To tell me where you were? I confess I wanted very much to know.

DAISY. Well, Randolph couldn't tell you. I was having lunch with mother. I thought you were with those ladies.

REVERDY. Whom you saw me with this morning? Oh, no; they've got another cavalier, just arrived, on purpose.

DAISY, *attentive.* Another cavalier—just arrived? Do you mean that gentleman that speaks so beautifully?

REVERDY. A dozen languages? His English isn't bad—compared with my French!

DAISY, *thoughtful.* Well, he looks like a cavalier. Did he come on purpose for them?

REVERDY, *aside.* What does she know about him? Oh, yes; they sent for him to Geneva.

DAISY. To Geneva? That's the one!

REVERDY. You see, they want him to be always with them; he's for their own particular consumption.

DAISY, *disappointed, but very simply.* Ah, then he won't come out at two o'clock!

REVERDY. I'm sure I don't know. (*The bell of the hotel strikes two.*) There it is. You'll have a chance to see. (*Winterbourne, on the stroke of the hour, comes out of the hotel.*)

DAISY, *joyfully.* Here he comes! He's too sweet!

REVERDY, *aside.* Oh, I say, she had made an appointment with him while I was doing the mule!

SCENE IX. REVERDY, *for a moment*; DAISY, WINTERBOURNE.

WINTERBOURNE, *to Reverdy*. I'm glad to find you: Miss Durant has a particular desire to see you.

REVERDY. It's very good of you to be her messenger. (*Aside.*) That's what he calls relieving me!

WINTERBOURNE. You'll find those ladies in their own sitting-room, on the second floor.

REVERDY. Oh, I know where it is. (*To Daisy.*) I shall be back in five minutes.

DAISY. I'm sure you needn't hurry.

WINTERBOURNE. I have an idea they have a good deal to say to you.

REVERDY. I hope it isn't to complain of you! (*Goes into the hotel.*)

DAISY, *looking at Winterbourne a moment*. I was afraid you wouldn't come.

WINTERBOURNE, *aside*. She has a way of looking at you! (*Aloud.*) I don't know what can have given you such an impression.

DAISY. Well, you know, half the time they don't—the gentlemen.

WINTERBOURNE. That's in America, perhaps. But over here they always come.

DAISY, *simply*. Well, I haven't had much experience over here.

WINTERBOURNE. I'm glad to hear it. It was very good of your mother to let you leave her again.

DAISY, *surprised*. Oh, mother doesn't care; she's got Eugenio.

WINTERBOURNE, *startled*. Surely, not to sit with her?

DAISY. Well, he doesn't sit with her always, because he likes to go out.

WINTERBOURNE. Oh, he likes to go out!

DAISY. He's got a great many friends, Eugenio; he's awfully popular. And then, you know, poor mother isn't very amusing.

WINTERBOURNE. Ah, she isn't very amusing! (*Aside.*) Aunt Louisa was right: it isn't the best society!

DAISY. But Eugenio stays with her all he can: he says he didn't expect that so much when he came.

WINTERBOURNE. I should think not! I hope at least that it isn't a monopoly, and that I may have the pleasure of making your mother's acquaintance.

DAISY. Well, you *do* speak beautifully! I told Mr. Reverdy.

WINTERBOURNE. It was very good of you to mention it. One speaks as one can.

DAISY. Mother's awfully timid, or else I'd introduce you. She always makes a fuss if I introduce a gentleman. But I do introduce them—the ones I like.

WINTERBOURNE. If it's a sign of your liking, I hope you'll introduce me. But you must know my name, which you didn't a while ago.

DAISY. Oh, Eugenio has told me your name, and I think it's very pretty. And he has told me something else.

WINTERBOURNE. I can't imagine what he should tell you about me.

DAISY. About you and some one else—that Russian lady who is leaving the hotel.

WINTERBOURNE, *quickly*. Who is leaving the hotel! How does he know that?

DAISY, *with a little laugh.* You see it *is* true: you are very fond of that Russian lady!

WINTERBOURNE, *aside.* She is leaving the hotel—but not till six o'clock. (*Aloud.*) I haven't known you very long, but I should like to give you a piece of advice. Don't gossip with your courier!

DAISY. I see you're offended—and it proves Eugenio was right. He said it was secret—and you don't like me to know it.

WINTERBOURNE. You may know everything, my dear young lady, only don't get your information from a servant.

DAISY. Do you call Eugenio a servant? He'll be amused if I tell him that!

WINTERBOURNE. He won't be amused—he'll be furious; but the particular emotion doesn't matter. It's very good of you to take such an interest.

DAISY. Oh, I don't know what I should do if I didn't take some interest! You do care for her, then?

WINTERBOURNE, *a little annoyed.* For the Russian lady? Oh, yes, we are old friends. (*Aside.*) My aunt's right: they don't stand the test!

DAISY. I'm very glad she is going, then. But the others mean to stay?

WINTERBOURNE. The others? What others?

DAISY. The two that Mr. Reverdy told me about, and to whom he's so very devoted.

WINTERBOURNE. It's my aunt and a friend of hers; but you needn't mind them.

DAISY. For all they mind me! But they look very stylish.

WINTERBOURNE. Oh, yes, they are very stylish; you can bet your life on that, as your brother says!

DAISY, *looking at him a moment.* Did you come for them, or for the Russian lady?

WINTERBOURNE, *aside, more annoyed.* Ah, too many questions! (*Aloud.*) I came for none of them; I came for myself.

DAISY, *serenely.* Yes, that's the impression you give me: you think a great deal of yourself! But I should like to know your aunt, all the same. She has her hair done like an old picture, and she holds herself so very well; she speaks to no one, and she dines in private. That's the way I should like to be!

WINTERBOURNE. Ah, you would make a bad exchange. My aunt is liable to fearful headaches.

DAISY. I think she is very elegant—headaches and all! I want very much to know her.

WINTERBOURNE, *aside.* Goodness, what a happy thought! (*Aloud.*) She would be enchanted; only the state of her health . . .

DAISY. Oh, yes, she has an excuse; that's a part of the elegance! I should like to have an excuse. Any one can see your aunt would have one.

WINTERBOURNE. Oh, she has five hundred!

DAISY. Well, *we* haven't any, mother and I. I like a lady to be exclusive. I'm dying to be exclusive myself!

WINTERBOURNE. Be just as you are. You wouldn't be half so charming if you were different. (*Aside.*) It's odd how true that is, with all her faults!

DAISY. You don't think me charming: you only think me queer. I can see that by your manner. I should like to know your aunt, any way.

WINTERBOURNE. It's very good of you, I'm sure; but I'm afraid those headaches will interfere.

DAISY. I suppose she doesn't have a headache every day, does she?

WINTERBOURNE, *aside*. What the deuce is a man to say? (*Aloud.*) She assures me she does.

DAISY, *turns away a moment, walks to the parapet, and stands there thoughtful*. She doesn't want to know me! (*Looking at Winterbourne.*) Why don't you say so? You needn't be afraid; I'm not afraid. (*Suddenly, with a little break in her voice.*) Gracious, she *is* exclusive!

WINTERBOURNE. So much the worse for her!

DAISY. You see, you've got to own to it! Well, I don't care. I mean to be like that—when I'm old.

WINTERBOURNE. I can't think you'll ever be old.

DAISY. Oh, you horrid thing! As if I were going to perish in my flower!

WINTERBOURNE. I should be very sorry if I thought that. But you will never have any quarrel with Time: he'll touch you very gently.

DAISY, *at the parapet, looking over the lake*. I hope I shall never have any quarrel with any one. I'm very good-natured.

WINTERBOURNE, *laughing*. You certainly disarm criticism—oh completely!

DAISY. Well, I don't care. Have you ever been to that old castle? (*Pointing to Chillon, in the distance.*)

WINTERBOURNE. The Castle of Chillon? Yes, in former days, more than once. I suppose you have been there, too.

DAISY. Oh, no, we haven't been there. I want to go there awfully. Of course, I mean to go there. I wouldn't go away from here without having seen that old castle!

WINTERBOURNE. It's a very pretty excursion, and very easy to make. You can drive, you know, or you can take the little steamer.

DAISY. Well, we were going last week, but mother gave out. She suffers terribly from dyspepsia. She said she couldn't go. Randolph won't go, either: he doesn't think much of old castles.

WINTERBOURNE. *smiling*. Ah, your brother isn't interested in historical monuments?

DAISY. Well, he's generally disappointed. He wants to stay around here. Mother's afraid to leave him alone, and Eugenio can't be induced to stay with him, so that we haven't been to many places. But it will be too bad if we don't go up to that castle.

WINTERBOURNE. I think it might be arranged. Let me see. Couldn't you get some one to remain for the afternoon with Randolph?

DAISY, *suddenly*. Oh, yes; we could get Mr. Reverdy!

WINTERBOURNE. Mr. Reverdy?

DAISY. He's awfully fond of Randolph; they're always fooling around.

WINTERBOURNE, *laughing*. It isn't a bad idea. Reverdy must lay in a stock of sugar.

DAISY. There's one thing: with you, mother will be afraid to go.

WINTERBOURNE. She carries her timidity too far! We must wait till she has got used to me.

DAISY. I don't want to wait. I want to go right off!

WINTERBOURNE. Ah, you can hardly force her to come, you know.

DAISY. I don't want to force her: I want to leave her!

WINTERBOURNE. To leave her behind? What, then, would you do for an escort?

DAISY, *serenely.* I would take you.

WINTERBOURNE, *astounded.* Me? Me alone?

DAISY, *laughing.* You seem about as timid as mother! Never mind, I'll take care of you.

WINTERBOURNE, *still bewildered.* Off to Chillon—with you alone—right off?

DAISY, *eagerly questioning.* Right off? Could we go now?

WINTERBOURNE, *aside.* She takes away my breath! (*Aloud.*) There's a boat just after three.

DAISY. We'll go straight on board!

WINTERBOURNE, *aside.* She has known me for a couple of hours! (*Aloud, rather formally.*) The privilege for me is immense; but I feel as if I ought to urge you to reflect a little.

DAISY. So as to show how stiff you can be? Oh, I know all about that.

WINTERBOURNE. No, just to remind you that your mother will certainly discover . . .

DAISY, *staring.* Will certainly discover?

WINTERBOURNE. Your little escapade. You can't hide it.

DAISY, *amazed, and a little touched.* I don't know what you mean. I have nothing to hide.

WINTERBOURNE, *aside.* Ah, I give it up! (*Seeing Eugenio, who comes out of the hotel.*) And here comes that odious creature, to spoil it!

SCENE X. WINTERBOURNE. DAISY. EUGENIO.

EUGENIO. Mademoiselle, your mother requests that you will come to her.

DAISY. I don't believe a word of it!

EUGENIO. You should not do me the injustice to doubt of my honour! Madame asked me to look for you ten minutes ago; but I was detained by meeting in the hall a lady (*speaking slowly, and looking at Winterbourne*), a Russian lady, whom I once had the honour to serve, and who was leaving the hotel.

WINTERBOURNE, *startled, aside.* Madame de Katkoff—leaving already?

EUGENIO, *watching Winterbourne.* She had so many little bags that she could hardly settle herself in the carriage, and I thought it my duty—I have had so much practice—to show her how to stow them away.

WINTERBOURNE, *quickly, to Daisy.* Will you kindly excuse me a moment?

EUGENIO, *obsequious, interposing.* If it's to overtake the Russian lady, Madame de Katkoff is already far away. (*Aside.*) She had four horses: I frightened her more than a little!

WINTERBOURNE, *aside.* Far away—without another word? She can be hard—when she tries. Very good. Let me see if I can be the same!

DAISY, *noticing Winterbourne, aside.* Poor man, he's stiffer than ever! But I'm glad she has gone. (*Aloud.*) See here, Eugenio, I'm going to that castle.

EUGENIO, *with a certain impertinence.* Mademoiselle has made arrangements?

DAISY. Well, if Mr. Winterbourne doesn't back out.

WINTERBOURNE. Back out? I shan't be happy till we are off! (*Aside.*) I'll go anywhere—with any one—*now*; and if the poor girl is injured by it, it isn't my fault!

EUGENIO. I think Mademoiselle will find that Madame is in no state—

DAISY. My dear Eugenio, Madame will stay at home with you.

WINTERBOURNE, *wincing, aside.* If she would only not call him her 'dear'!

EUGENIO. I take the liberty of advising Mademoiselle not to go to the castle.

WINTERBOURNE, *irritated.* You had better remember that your place is not to advise, but to look after the little bags!

DAISY. Oh, I hoped you would make a fuss! But I don't want to go now.

WINTERBOURNE, *decided.* I shall make a fuss if you don't go.

DAISY, *nervously, with a little laugh.* That's all I want—a little fuss!

WINTERBOURNE, *aside.* She's not so easy as she would like to appear. She knows it's a risk—but she likes the risk.

EUGENIO. If Mademoiselle will come with me, I will undertake to organize a fuss. (*A steamboat whistle is heard in the distance.*)

WINTERBOURNE, *to Daisy.* The boat's coming up. You have only till three o'clock.

DAISY, *suddenly decided.* Oh, I can be quick when I try! (*Hurries into the hotel.*)

WINTERBOURNE, *looking a moment at Eugenio.* You had better not interfere with that young lady!

EUGENIO, *insolent.* I suppose you mean that I had better not interfere with you! You had better not defy me to do so! (*Aside.*) It's a pity I sent away the Katkoff! (*Follows Daisy into the hotel.*)

WINTERBOURNE, *alone.* That's a singularly offensive beast! And what the mischief does he mean by his having been in *her* service? Thank heaven she has got rid of him! (*Seeing Mrs. Costello, Miss Durant, and Charles Reverdy, who issue from the hotel, the ladies dressed for a walk.*) Oh, confusion, I had forgotten *them*!

SCENE XI. MRS. COSTELLO. MISS DURANT. CHARLES REVERDY. WINTERBOURNE. *then* DAISY.

MRS. C. Well, Frederick, we take for granted that your little interview is over, and that you are ready to accompany us into the town.

WINTERBOURNE. Over, dear aunt? Why, it's only just begun. We are going to the Château de Chillon.

MRS. C. You and that little girl? You'll hardly get us to believe that!

REVERDY, *aside, still with the camp-stool.* Hang me, why didn't I think of that?

WINTERBOURNE. I'm afraid I rather incommode you; but I shall be delighted to go into the town when we come back.

MISS D. You had better never come back. No one will speak to you!

MRS. C. My dear Frederick, if you are joking, your joke's in dreadful taste.

WINTERBOURNE. I'm not joking in the least. The young lady's to be here at three.

MRS. C. She herself is joking, then. She won't be so crazy as to come.

REVERDY, *who has gone to the parapet and looked off to right, coming back, taking out his watch.* It's close upon three, and the boat's at the wharf.

WINTERBOURNE, *watch in hand.* Not quite yet. Give her a moment's grace.

MRS. C. It won't be for *us* to give her grace: it will be for society.

WINTERBOURNE, *flattering.* Ah, but you *are* society, you know. She wants immensely to know you.

MRS. C., *ironical.* Is that why she is flinging herself at *you*?

WINTERBOURNE, *very gravely.* Listen to me seriously, please. The poor little girl has given me a great mark—a very touching mark—of confidence. I wish to present her to you, because I wish some one to answer for my honour.

MRS. C. And pray, who is to answer for hers?

WINTERBOURNE. Oh, I say, you're cruel!

MRS. C. I'm an old woman, Frederick; but I thank my stars I'm not too old to be horrified! (*The bell of the steamboat is heard to ring in the distance.*)

REVERDY. There's your boat, sir. I'm afraid you'll miss it!

WINTERBOURNE, *watch still in hand, aside.* Three o'clock. Damn that courier!

MRS. C. If she doesn't come, you may present her.

MISS D. She won't come. We must do her justice.

DAISY, *hurrying out of the hotel.* I say, Mr. Winterbourne[,] I'm as punctual as you! (*She wears a charming travelling-dress, and is buttoning her glove. Eugenio appears in the porch of the hotel, and stands there, with his hands in his pockets and with a baffled but vindictive air, watching the rest of the scene.*)

REVERDY. Alas, the presentation's gone!

DAISY, *half aloud.* Gracious, how they glare at me!

WINTERBOURNE, *hurriedly.* Take my arm. The boat's at the wharf. (*She takes his arm, and they hasten away, passing through the little gate of the parapet, where they descend and disappear. The bell of the steamer continues to ring. Mrs. Costello and her companions have watched them; as they vanish, she and Miss Durant each drop into a chair.*)

MRS. C. They'll never come back!

MISS D., *eagerly.* Isn't it your duty to go after them?

REVERDY, *between the two, as if to the public.* They'll be lovely company for the rest of the day!

ACT II.

A beautiful afternoon in the gardens of the Pincian Hill in Rome. A view of St. Peter's in the distance.

SCENE I. WINTERBOURNE. MADAME DE KATKOFF, *meeting from opposite sides. He stands before her a moment, and kisses her hand.*

WINTERBOURNE. When, at your hotel just now, they told me you had gone out, I was pretty sure you had come here.

MME. DE K. I always come here as soon as I arrive in Rome, for the sake of that view. It's an old friend of mine.

WINTERBOURNE. Have you no old friends but that, and wasn't it also—a little—for the sake of meeting one or two of them? We all come here, you know.

MME. DE K. One or two of them? You don't mean two—you mean one! I know you all come here, and that's why I have arrived early, before the crowd and the music.

WINTERBOURNE. That's what I was counting on. I know your tastes. I wanted to find you alone.

MME. DE K. Being alone with you isn't one of my tastes! If I had known I should meet you, I think I shouldn't have left my carriage.

WINTERBOURNE. If it's there, at hand, you might invite me to get into it.

MME. DE K. I have sent it away for half an hour, while I stretch myself a little. I have been sitting down for a week—in railway trains.

WINTERBOURNE. You can't escape from me, then!

MME. DE K. Don't begin that way, or you'll disappoint me. You speak as if you had received none of my letters.

WINTERBOURNE. And you speak as if you had written me a dozen! I received three little notes.

MME. DE K. They were short, but they were clear.

WINTERBOURNE. Oh, very clear indeed! 'You're an awful nuisance, and I wish never to hear of you again.' That was about the gist of them.

MME. DE K. 'Unless you promise not to persecute me, I won't come to Rome.' That's more how I should express it. And you did promise.

WINTERBOURNE. I promised to try and hate you, for that seemed to be what you wished to bring me to! And I have been waiting for you these three weeks, as a man waits for his worst enemy.

MME. DE K. I should be your worst enemy, indeed, if I listened to you—if I allowed you to mingle your fresh, independent life with my own embarrassed and disillusioned one. If you have been here three weeks, you ought to have found some profitable occupation.

WINTERBOURNE. You speak as if I were looking out for a job! My principal occupation has been waiting for you.

MME. DE K. It must have made you pleasant company to your friends.

WINTERBOURNE. My friends are only my aunt and the young lady who is with her—a very good girl, but painfully prim. I have been devoted to them, because I said to myself that after you came—

MME. DE K. You wouldn't have possession of your senses? So it appears. On the same principle, I hope you have shown some attention to the little girl who was at Vevey, whom I saw you in such a fair way to be intimate with.

WINTERBOURNE, *after a silence.* What do you know about her?

MME. DE K. Nothing but that we are again at the same hotel. A former servant of mine, a very unprincipled fellow, is now in her mother's employ, and he was the first person I met as I left my rooms today. I imagine from this that the young lady is not far off.

WINTERBOURNE. Not far off from *him*. I wish she were farther!

MME. DE K. She struck me last summer as remarkably attractive.

WINTERBOURNE. She's exactly what she was last summer—only more so!

MME. DE K. She must be quite enchanting, then.

WINTERBOURNE. Do you wish me to fall in love with her?

MME. DE K. It would give me particular pleasure. I would go so far as to be the confidant of your passion.

WINTERBOURNE. I have no passion to confide. She's a little American flirt.

MME. DE K., *aside.* It seems to me there is a certain passion in that!

WINTERBOURNE. She's foolish, frivolous, futile. She is making herself terribly talked about.

MME. DE K. She looked to me very innocent—with those eyes!

WINTERBOURNE. Oh yes, I made a great deal of those eyes—they have the most charming lashes. But they look at too many people.

MME. DE K. Should you like them to fix themselves on you? You're rather difficult to please. The young lady with your aunt is too grave, and this poor little person is too gay! You had better find some one who's between the two.

WINTERBOURNE. You are between the two, and you won't listen to me.

MME. DE K. I think I understand your countrypeople better than you do. I have learned a good deal about them from my observation of yourself.

WINTERBOURNE. That must have made you very fond of them!

MME. DE K. It has made me feel very kindly towards them, as you see from my interest in those young ladies. Don't judge them by what they seem. They are probably just the opposite, for that is precisely the case with yourself. Most people think you very cold, but I have discovered the truth. You are like one of those tall German stoves, which present to the eye a surface of smooth white porcelain, without the slightest sympton of fuel or of flame. Nothing at first could seem less glowing; but after you have been in the room with it for half an hour you feel that the temperature is rising—and you want to open a window!

WINTERBOURNE. A tall German stove—that's a very graceful comparison.

MME. DE K. I'm sure your grave young lady is very gay.

WINTERBOURNE. It doesn't matter: she has got a young man of her own.

MME. DE K. The young man who was always with them? If you are going to be put off by a rival, I have nothing to say.

WINTERBOURNE. He's not a rival of mine; he's only a rival of my aunt's. She wants me to marry Miss Durant, but Miss Durant prefers the gallant Reverdy.

MME. DE K. That simplifies it.

WINTERBOURNE. Not so very much; because the gallant Reverdy shows a predilection for Miss Daisy Miller.

MME. DE K. Ah, then he is your rival!

WINTERBOURNE. There are so many others that he doesn't count. She has at least a dozen admirers, and she knocks about Rome with all of them. She once told me that she was very fond of gentlemen's society; but unfortunately, they are not all gentlemen.

MME. DE K. So much the better chance for you!

WINTERBOURNE. She doesn't know, she can't distinguish. She is incredibly light.

MME. DE K. It seems to me that you express yourself with a certain bitterness.

WINTERBOURNE. I'm not in the least in love with her, if that's what you mean. But simply as an outsider, as a spectator, as an American, I can't bear to see a nice girl—if she *is* a nice girl—expose herself to the most odious misconception. That is, if she *is* a nice girl!

MME. DE K. By my little system, she ought to be very nice. If she seems very wild, depend upon it she is very tame.

WINTERBOURNE. She has produced a fearful amount of scandal.

MME. DE K. That proves she has nothing to hide. The wicked ones are not found out!

WINTERBOURNE. She has nothing to hide but her mother, whom she conceals so effectually that no mortal eye has beheld her. Miss Daisy goes to parties alone! When I say alone, I mean that she is usually accompanied by a foreigner with a waxed moustache and a great deal of manner. She's too nice for a foreigner!

MME. DE K., *smiling*. As a Russian, I'm greatly obliged to you!

WINTERBOURNE. This isn't a Russian. He's a Roman—the Cavaliere Giovanelli.

MME. DE K. You spoke of a dozen, and now you have settled down to one.

WINTERBOURNE. There were a dozen at first, but she picked them over and selected. She has made a mistake, because the man she has chosen is an adventurer.

MME. DE K. An adventurer?

WINTERBOURNE. Oh, a very plausible one. He is very good looking, very polite; he sings little songs at parties. He comes of a respectable family, but he has squandered his small patrimony, and he has no means of subsistence but his personal charms, which he has been hoping for the last ten years will endear him to some susceptible American heiress—whom he flatters himself he has found at last!

MME. DE K. You ought to advise her—to put her on her guard.

WINTERBOURNE. Oh, she's not serious; she is only amusing herself.

MME. DE K. Try and make her serious. That's a mission for an honest man!

WINTERBOURNE, *after a moment*. It's so odd to hear you defending her! It only puzzles me the more.

MME. DE K. You ought to understand your countrywomen better.

WINTERBOURNE. My countrywomen?

MME. DE K. I don't mean me: I mean Miss Daisy Miller.

WINTERBOURNE. It seems very stupid, I confess; but I've lived so long in foreign parts, among people of different manners. I mean, however, to settle the question today and to make up my mind. I shall meet Miss Daisy at four o'clock. I have promised to go to Mrs. Walker's.

MME. DE K. And pray who is Mrs. Walker?

WINTERBOURNE. The wife of the American consul—a very good-natured woman, who has a passion for afternoon tea. She took up Miss Daisy when they came; she used to call her the little Flower of the West. But now she's holding the little flower in her fingertips at arm's length, trying to decide to let it drop.

MME. DE K. Poor little flower! I must be four o'clock now.

WINTERBOURNE, *looking at his watch.* You're in a great hurry to get rid of me! Mrs. Walker's is close at hand, just beyond the Spanish Steps. I shall have time to stroll round the Pincian with you.

MME. DE K., *shaking her head.* I have had strolling enough. I shall wait for my carriage.

WINTERBOURNE. Let me at least come and see you this evening.

MME. DE K. I should be delighted, but I'm going to the opera.

WINTERBOURNE. Already? The first night you're here?

MME. DE K. It's not the first; it's the second. I'm very fond of music.

WINTERBOURNE. It's always bad in Italy.

MME. DE K. I have made provision against that in the person of the Russian ambassador, whom I have asked to come into my box.

WINTERBOURNE. Ah, with ambassadors I stand no chance.

MME. DE K., *smiling.* You're the greatest diplomatist of all! Good-bye for the present. (*She turns away. Winterbourne looks after her a moment.*)

WINTERBOURNE. You decide more easily than Mrs. Walker: you *have* dropped me!

MME. DE K. Ah, but you're not a flower! (*Winterbourne looks at her an instant longer; then, with a little passionate switch of his stick, he walks off. Just as he disappears, Eugenio comes in at the back.*) And now I shall have a quiet evening with a book!

SCENE II. MADAME DE KATKOFF. EUGENIO. *who enters hat in hand, with a bow.*

EUGENIO. It's the second time today that I have had the pleasure of meeting Madame.

MME. DE KATKOFF. I should like very much to believe it would be the last!

EUGENIO, *twirling his hat.* That, perhaps, is more than I can promise. We will call it the last but one; for my purpose in approaching Madame is to demand an interview—a serious interview! Seeing Madame, at a distance in conversation with a gentleman, I waited till the gentleman had retired, for I must do Madame the justice to admit that, with Madame, the gentlemen do usually, at last, retire!

MME. DE K. It's a misfortune to me, since they leave me exposed.

EUGENIO. Madame is not exposed. Madame is protected. So long as I have an eye on Madame, I can answer for it that she will suffer no injury.

MME. DE K. You protect me as the butcher protects the lamb! I suppose you have come to name your price.

EUGENIO. Madame goes straight to the point! I have come to name my price, but not to ask for money.

MME. DE K. It's very kind of you to recognize that I have not money enough.

EUGENIO. Madame has money enough, but the talents of Madame are still greater than her wealth. It is with the aid of these talents that I shall invite Madame to render me a service—a difficult, delicate service, but so valuable that it will release Madame from further obligations.

MME. DE K., *ironical.* It's delightful to think of being released! I suppose the service is to recommend you as a domestic. That would be difficult, certainly.

EUGENIO. Too difficult—for Madame! No; it is simply, as I say, to grant me an interview, when I can explain. Be so good as to name an hour when I can wait upon you.

MME. DE K. In my apartments? I would rather not see you there. Explain to me here.

EUGENIO. It's a little delicate for a public place. Besides, I have another appointment here.

MME. DE K. You do a great business! If you mean that I am to wait upon *you*, we may as well drop negotiations.

EUGENIO. Let us compromise. My appointment will end in a quarter of an hour. If at that time Madame is still on the Pincian—

MME. DE K. You would like me to sit upon a bench till you are ready to attend to me?

EUGENIO. It would have the merit of settling the matter at once, without more suspense for Madame.

MME. DE K., *thoughtfully, aside.* That would be a merit, certainly; and I'm curious about the exercise he wishes to offer my talents! (*Aloud.*) I shall stroll about here till my carriage comes; if you wish to take advantage of that—

EUGENIO. To take advantage is exactly what I wish! And as this particular spot is exceptionally quiet I shall look for Madame here.

MME. DE K., *as she strolls away.* How unspeakably odious!

EUGENIO, *alone a moment, looking after her.* She shall bend till she breaks! The delay will have the merit, too, of making me sure of Giovanelli—if he only keeps the tryst! I mustn't throw away a card on *her* before I've won the game of him. But he's such a deuced fine gentleman that there's no playing fair! (*Seeing Giovanelli, who comes in at the left.*) He is up to time, though. (*Bowing.*) Signor Cavaliere!

SCENE III. EUGENIO. GIOVANELLI.

GIOVANELLI, *very elegant, with flowers in his button-hole; cautious, looking round him.* You might have proposed meeting in some less conspicuous spot!

EUGENIO. In the Colosseum, at midnight? My dear sir, we should be much more compromised if we were discovered there.

GIOVANELLI. Oh, if you count upon our being discovered! . . .

EUGENIO. There is nothing so unnatural in our having a little conversation. One should never be ashamed of an accomplice!

GIOVANELLI, with a grimace, disgusted. Don't speak of accomplices, as if we were concocting a crime!

EUGENIO. What makes it a work of merit is my conviction that you are a perfect gentleman. If it hadn't been for that, I never should have presented you to my family.

GIOVANELLI. Your family? You speak as if, in marrying the girl, I should become your brother-in-law.

EUGENIO. We shall certainly be united by a very peculiar tie!

GIOVANELLI. United—united? I don't know about that! After my marriage, I shall travel without a courier. (*Smiling.*) It will be less expensive!

EUGENIO. In the event you speak of, I myself hardly expect to remain in the ranks. I have seen too many campaigns: I shall retire on my pension. You look as if you didn't understand me.

GIOVANELLI. Perfectly. You expect the good Mrs. Miller to make you comfortable for the rest of your days.

EUGENIO. What I expect of the good Mrs. Miller is one thing; what I expect of you is another: and on that point we had better be perfectly clear. It was to ensure perfect clearness that I proposed this little conference, which you refused to allow to take place either in your own lodgings or in some comfortable café; Oh, I know you had your reasons! You don't exhibit your little interior; and though I know a good deal about you, I don't know where you live. It doesn't matter, I don't want to know: it's enough for me that I can always find you here, amid the music and the flowers. But I can't exactly make out why you wouldn't meet me at a café. I would gladly have paid for a glass of beer.

GIOVANELLI. It was just your beer I was afraid of! I never touch the beastly stuff.

EUGENIO. Ah, if you drink nothing but champagne, no wonder you are looking for an heiress! But before I help you to one, let me give you a word of advice. Make the best of me, if you wish me to make the best of you. I was determined to do that when I presented you to the two most amiable women in the world.

GIOVANELLI. I must protest against your theory that you presented me. I met Mrs. Miller at a party, as any gentleman might have done.

EUGENIO. You met her at a party, precisely; but unless I wish it, Mrs. Miller doesn't go to a party! I let you know she was to be there, and I advised you how to proceed. For the last three weeks I have done nothing but arrange little accidents, little surprises, little occasions, of which I will do you the justice to say that you have taken excellent advantage. But the time has come when I must remind you that I have not done all this from mere admiration of your distinguished appearance. I wish your success to be *my* success!

GIOVANELLI, *pleased, with a certain simplicity.* I am glad to hear you talk about my success!

EUGENIO. Oh, there's a good deal to be said about it! Have you ever been to the circus?

GIOVANELLI. I don't see what that has to do with it!

EUGENIO. You've seen the bareback rider turn a somersault through the paper hoops? It's a very pretty feat, and it brings him great applause; but half the effect depends upon the poor devil—whom no one notices—who is perched upon the edge of the ring. If he didn't hold the hoop with a great deal of skill, the bareback rider would simply come down on his nose. You turn your little somersaults, Signor Cavaliere, and my young lady claps her hands; but all the while *I*'m holding the hoop!

GIOVANELLI. If I'm not mistaken, that office, at the circus, is usually performed by the clown.

EUGENIO. Take very good care, or you'll have a fall!

GIOVANELLI. I suppose you want to be paid for your trouble.

EUGENIO. The point isn't that I want to be paid: that goes without saying! But I want to be paid handsomely.

GIOVANELLI. What do you call handsomely?

EUGENIO. A commission proportionate to the fortune of the young lady. I know something about that. I have in my pocket (*slapping his side*) the letter of credit of the Signora. She lets me carry it—for safety's sake!

GIOVANELLI. Poor Signora! It's a strange game we're playing!

EUGENIO, *looking at him a moment*. Oh, if you doubt of the purity of your motives, you have only to say so. You swore to me that you adored my young lady.

GIOVANELLI. She's an angel, and I worship the ground she treads on. That makes me wonder whether I couldn't get on without you.

EUGENIO, *dryly*. Try it and see. I've only to say the word, and Mrs. Miller will start tomorrow for the north.

GIOVANELLI. And if you don't say the word, that's another thing you want to be paid for! It mounts up very fast.

EUGENIO. It mounts up to fifty thousand francs, to be handed to me six months after you are married.

GIOVANELLI. Fifty thousand francs?

EUGENIO. The family exchequer will never miss them. Besides, I give you six months. You sign a little note, 'for value received.'

GIOVANELLI. And if the marriage—if the marriage—

EUGENIO. If the marriage comes to grief, I burn up the note.

GIOVANELLI. How can I be sure of that?

EUGENIO. By having already perceived that I'm not an idiot. If you don't marry, you can't pay: I need no one to tell me that. But I intend you *shall* marry.

GIOVANELLI, *satirical*. It's uncommonly good of you! After all, I haven't a squint!

EUGENIO. I picked you out for your good looks; and you're so tremendously fascinating that even when I lose patience with your want of everything else I can't afford to sacrifice you. Your prospects are now very good. The estimable mother—

GIOVANELLI. The estimable mother believes me to be already engaged to her daughter. It shows how much she knows about it!

EUGENIO. No, you are not engaged, but you will be, next week. You have rather too many flowers there, by the way: you overdo it a little. (*Pointing to Giovanelli's button-hole.*)

GIOVANELLI. So long as you pay for them, the more the better! How far will it carry me to be engaged? Mr. Miller can hardly be such a fool as his wife.

EUGENIO, *stroking his moustache*. Mr. Miller?

GIOVANELLI. The mysterious father, in that unpronounceable town! He must be a man of energy, to have made such a fortune, and the idea of his energy haunts me!

EUGENIO. That's because you've got none yourself.

GIOVANELLI. I don't pretend to that; I only pretend to—a—

EUGENIO. To be fascinating, I know! But you're afraid the papa won't see it.

GIOVANELLI. I don't exactly see why he should set his heart on a Roman son-in-law.

EUGENIO. It's your business to produce that miracle!

GIOVANELLI. By making the girl talked about? My respect for her is in proportion to the confidence she shows me. That confidence is unlimited.

EUGENIO. Oh, unlimited! I have never seen anything like that confidence; and if out of such a piece of cloth as that you can't cut a coat—

GIOVANELLI. I never pretended to be a tailor! And you must not forget that I have a rival.

EUGENIO. Forget it? I regard it as a particularly gratifying fact. If you didn't have a rival I should have very small hopes of you.

GIOVANELLI. I confess I don't follow you. The young lady's confidence in Mr. Winterbourne is at least equal to her confidence in me.

EUGENIO. Ah, but *his* confidence in the young lady? That's another affair. He thinks she goes too far. He's an American, like herself; but there are Americans and Americans, and when they take it into their heads to open their eyes they open them very wide.

GIOVANELLI. If you mean that this American's a donkey, I see no reason to differ with you.

EUGENIO. Leave him to me. I've got a stick to beat him with!

GIOVANELLI, *uneasy*. You make me shiver a little! Do you mean to put him out of the way?

EUGENIO. I mean to put him out of the way. Ah, you can trust me! I don't carry a stiletto, and if you'll excuse me I won't describe my little plan. You'll tell me what you think of it when you have seen the results. The great feature is simply that Miss Daisy, seeing herself abandoned—

GIOVANELLI. Will look about her for a consoler? Ah, consolation is a specialty of mine, and if you give me a chance to console I think I shall be safe.

EUGENIO. I shall go to work on the spot! (*Takes out his pocket-book, from which he extracts a small folded paper, holding it up a moment before Giovanelli.*) Put your name to that, and send it back to me by post.

GIOVANELLI, *reading the paper with a little grimace.* Fifty thousand! Fifty thousand is steep.

EUGENIO. Signor Cavaliere, the letter of credit is for half a million!

GIOVANELLI, *pocketing the paper.* Well, give me a chance to console—give me a chance to console! (*Goes off at the back, while, at the same moment, Madame de Katkoff reappears.*)

SCENE IV. EUGENIO. MADAME DE KATKOFF.

EUGENIO, *perceiving her, aside.* The Katkoff—up to time! If my second little paper works as well as my first, I've nothing to fear. (*Aloud.*) I am quite at the service of Madame.

MME. DE K. My carriage has not come back; it was to pick up a friend at St. Peter's.

EUGENIO. I am greatly indebted to Madame's friends. I have my little proposition ready.

MME. DE K. Be so good as to let me hear it.

EUGENIO. In three words it is this: Do me the favour to captivate Mr. Winterbourne! Madame starts a little. She will pretend, perhaps, that Mr. Winterbourne is already captivated.

MME. DE K. You have an odd idea of my pretensions! I would rather pay you a sum of money than listen to this sort of thing.

EUGENIO. I was afraid you would be a little shocked—at first. But the proposal I make has the greatest recommendations.

MME. DE K. For Mr. Winterbourne, certainly!

EUGENIO. For Mr. Winterbourne, very plainly; but also for Madame, if she would only reflect upon the facility—

MME. DE K. What do you know about facility? Your proposal is odious!

EUGENIO. The worst is already done. Mr. Winterbourne is deeply interested in Madame.

MME. DE K. His name has no place in our discussion. Be so good as not to mention it again.

EUGENIO. It will be easy not to mention it: Madame will understand without that. She will remember, perhaps, that when I had the honour of meeting her, last summer, I was in the service of a distinguished family.

MME. DE K. The amiable Mrs. Miller? That name has stuck in my mind!

EUGENIO. Permit me to regard it as a happy omen! The amiable Mrs. Miller, as I then informed Madame, has a daughter as amiable as herself. It is of the greatest importance that this young lady should be detached from the gentleman whose name I am not allowed to mention.

MME. DE K. Should be detached?

EUGENIO. If he is interested in Madame, he is also a little interested in the Signorina. You know what men are, Madame!

MME. DE K. If the Signorina is as amiable as you say, I can imagine no happier circumstance.

EUGENIO. From the point of view of Madame, who is a little tired of the gentleman; but not from my own, who wish the young lady to make another marriage.

MME. DE K. Excuse me from entering into your points of view and your marriages!

EUGENIO, *abruptly*. Ah, if you choose to terminate the discussion, it wasn't worth while to wait. (*A pause.*)

MME. DE K., *aside*. It was worth while to wait—to learn what a coward I am! (*Aloud, after a moment.*) Is Miss Miller in love with Mr. Winterbourne?

EUGENIO, *smiling*. I thought Madame would come to the name! (*Aside.*) It was the idea that fetched her! (*Aloud.*) Miss Miller is not, perhaps, exactly in love with Mr. Winterbourne, but she has a great appreciation of his society. What I ask of you is to undertake that for the next two months she shall have as little of it as possible.

MME. DE K. By taking as much of it myself? You ask me to play a very pretty part.

EUGENIO. Madame would play it to perfection!

MME. DE K. To break a young girl's heart—to act an abominable comedy?

EUGENIO. You won't break anyone's heart, unless it be Mr. Winterbourne's—which will serve him right for being so tiresome. As for the comedy, remember that the best actresses receive the highest salary.

MME. DE K. If I had been a good actress, you never would have got me into your power. What do you propose to do with your little American?

EUGENIO. To marry her to a Roman gentleman. All I ask of you is to use a power you already have. I knew that of late it has suited your pleasure not to use it: you have tried to keep Mr. Winterbourne at a distance. But call him a little nearer, and you will see that he will come!

MME. DE K. So that the girl may see it too? Your ingenuity does you great honour. I don't believe in your Roman gentleman.

EUGENIO. It is not necessary that you should believe. Believe only that on the day the Signorina becomes engaged to the irreproachable person I have selected I will place in your hands the document which I hold at your disposition.

MME. DE K. How am I to be sure of that?

EUGENIO, *aside.* They all want to be sure! (*Aloud.*) Nothing venture, nothing have!

MME. DE K. And if she never becomes engaged?

EUGENIO. Ah, then, I confess, I must still hold the document. (*Aside.*) That will make her work for it! (*Aloud.*) Why should you trouble yourself with irrelevant questions? Your task is perfectly definite. Occupy Mr. Winterbourne, and leave the rest to me.

MME. DE K. I must tell you—disagreeable as it may be to me to do so—that I shall have to make a very sudden turn.

EUGENIO. It will be all the more effective (*Complacently.*) Sudden turns are the essence of fascination!

MME. DE K., *aside.* It's insufferable to discuss with him! But if there's a hope—if there's a hope . . . (*Aloud.*) I told Mr. Winterbourne, not an hour ago, that I wished never to see him again.

EUGENIO. I can imagine no more agreeable surprise to him, then, than to be told, half an hour hence, that you can't live without him! You know the things the ladies say! Don't be afraid of being sudden: he'll think it the more romantic. For you those things are easy, Madame (*bowing low*); for you those things are easy. I leave the matter to your consideration (*Aside, as he goes off*). She'll do it (*Exit.*)

MME. DE K., *alone a moment.* Those things are easy—those things are easy? They are easier, perhaps, than paying out half one's fortune. (*Stands a moment thoughtful, then gives a little nervous gesture, as of decision.*) If I give him leave to come to the opera, I must go myself—to Italian music! But an hour or two of Donizetti, for the sake of one's comfort! . . . He said he would come back—from the wife of the consul. (*Looking about her, she goes out.*)

SCENE V. DAISY, *then* GIOVANELLI.

DAISY, *coming in with a certain haste, and glancing behind her.* It's a pity you can't walk in Rome without every one staring so! And now he's not here—he's not where he said he would be. I don't care. He's very nice, but I certainly shan't go and look for him. I'll just wait a little. Perhaps, if I don't walk round, they won't stare at me so much. I didn't say good-bye to Mrs. Walker, because she was talking to Mr. Winterbourne, and I shan't go near Mr. Winterbourne again till he comes near me. Half an hour in the room, and never within ten yards of me! He looks so pleasant when he talks—even when he talks to other girls. He's always talking to other girls, and not even to girls—to old women, and gentlemen, and foreigners. I've done something he doesn't like, I'm very sure of that. He doesn't like anything—anything that *I* do. It's hard to know what he *does* like! He's got such peculiar tastes—from his foreign education; you can't ever tell where you'll find him. Well, I haven't had a foreign education, and I don't see that I'm any the worse for that. If I'd had a foreign education, I might as well give up! I shouldn't be able to breathe, for fear I was breathing wrong. There seem to be so many ways, over here; but I only know one way, and I don't see why I should learn the others when there are people who do like—who do like—what I do. They say they do, at any rate, and they say it so prettily! The English say it very nicely, but the Italians say it best. As for the Americans, they don't say it at all, and Mr. Winterbourne less than any of them! Well, I don't care so much about the Americans: I can make it all right with the Americans when I get home. Mr. Winterbourne isn't an American; I never saw any one like *him* over there. If I had, perhaps I shouldn't have come away; for over there it would all be different. Well, it isn't different here, and I suppose it never will be. Everything is strange over here; and what is strangest of all is one's liking people that are so peculiar. (*Stands thoughtful a moment, then rouses herself.*) There's Mr. Giovanelli—a mile off. Does he suppose I wish to communicate with him by signs? (*Giovanelli comes in, hat in hand, with much eagerness.*)

GIOVANELLI. I have looked for you everywhere!

DAISY. Well, I wasn't everywhere; I was here.

GIOVANELLI. Standing all alone, without a protector!

DAISY. I wasn't more alone than I was at Mrs. Walker's.

GIOVANELLI, *smiling, slightly fatuous.* Because *I* was not there?

DAISY. Oh, it wasn't the people who were *not* there! (*Aside.*) If they had known I was coming, I suppose there wouldn't have been any one!

GIOVANELLI, *in an attitude of the most respectful admiration.* How can I sufficiently thank you for granting me this supreme satisfaction?

DAISY. That's a very fine name to give to a walk on the Pincian. You had better put on your hat.

GIOVANELLI. You wish to escape notice? Perhaps you are right. That was why I didn't come to Mrs. Walker's, whose parties are so charming! I thought that if we slipped away together it might attract attention.

DAISY. Do you mean they would have thought it improper? They would have thought it still more improper to see me leaving alone; so I didn't say a word to any one—only mother.

GIOVANELLI. Ah, you told your admirable parent? She is with us, then, in spirit.

DAISY. She wanted to get away herself, if that's what you mean; but she didn't feel as if she could leave till Eugenio came for her. And Eugenio seems to have so much to do today!

GIOVANELLI. It's doubtless in your interest. He's a very faithful servant.

DAISY. Well, he told mother she must stay there an hour: he had some business of importance.

GIOVANELLI. Let us hope that his business is done, and the the patient Mrs. Miller is released.

DAISY. She was patient enough when I told her I shouldn't come to dinner.

GIOVANELLI, *starting, with an air of renewed devotion.* Am I to understand that you have consented to my little fantasy?

DAISY. Of dining at that old tavern, where the artists go?

GIOVANELLI. The renowned and delightful *Falcone,* in the heart of ancient Rome! You are a person of delicious suprises! The other day, you wouldn't listen to it.

DAISY. I don't remember the other day: all I know is, I'll go now (*Aside.*) The other day Mr. Winterbourne spoke to me!

GIOVANELLI. My dear young lady, you make me very happy!

DAISY. By going to eat maccaroni with you?

GIOVANELLI. It isn't the maccaroni; it's the sentiment!

DAISY. The sentiment is yours, not mine. I haven't any: it's all gone!

GIOVANELLI. Well, I shan't complain if I find myself at table with you in a dusky corner of that picturesque little cook-shop, where the ceiling is black, and the walls are brown, and the floor is red!

DAISY, *watching him as he describes it.* Oh dear! it must be very lovely.

GIOVANELLI. And the old wine-flasks, covered with plaited straw, are as big round—are much bigger round—than your waist!

DAISY. That's just what I want to see. Let's go there at once!

GIOVANELLI, *consulting his watch.* Half past four. Isn't that rather soon to dine?

DAISY. We can go on foot through the old streets. I'm dying to see them on foot.

GIOVANELLI, *aside.* That will be cheaper than a cab! (*Aloud.*) We should get there at five—a little early still. Mightn't we first take a few turns round this place?

DAISY, *after a pause.* Oh, yes, if you like.

GIOVANELLI, *aside.* I should like my creditors to see! (*Aloud.*) Perhaps it doesn't suit you: you're a little afraid.

DAISY. What should I be afraid of?

GIOVANELLI, *smiling.* Not of meeting your mother, I know!

DAISY. If I had been afraid, I shouldn't have come.

GIOVANELLI. That is perfect. But let me say one thing: you have a way of taking the meaning from the favours you bestow.

DAISY. The meaning? They haven't got any meaning!

GIOVANELLI, *vaguely.* Ah! (*Mrs. Costello, Miss Durant, and Charles Reverdy appear.*)

DAISY, *looking at Mrs. Costello and Miss Durant.* Unless it be to make those dreadful women glower! How d'ye do, Mr. Reverdy?

GIOVANELLI, *smiling.* I see you are not afraid! (*He goes out with her.*)

SCENE VI. MRS. COSTELLO. MISS DURANT. CHARLES REVERDY.

MISS D. She has grown to look very hard.

MRS. C. The gentleman looks soft, and that makes up for it.

MISS D. Do you call him a gentleman?

MRS. C. Ah, compared with the courier! She has a different one every time.

REVERDY, *with the camp-stool, aside.* A different one every time, but never, alas, *this* one!

MRS. C. There's one comfort in it all: she has given up Frederick.

MISS D. Ah, she goes too far even for him!

REVERDY. Too far with other men: that's the trouble! With him she went as far as the Castle of Chillon.

MRS. C. Don't recall that episode. Heaven only knows what happened there.

REVERDY. I know what happened: he was awfully sold. That's why he let you carry him off.

MRS. C. Much good it did us! I'm very much disappointed in Frederick.

MISS D. I can't imagine what you expected of him.

MRS. C. I expected him to fall in love with you—or to marry you, at any rate.

MISS D. You would have been still more disappointed, then, if I had refused him.

MRS. C., *dryly.* I should have been surprised.

REVERDY, *sentimentally.* Would you have refused him, Miss Durant?

MISS D. Yes, on purpose to spite you. You don't understand? It takes a man to be stupid! If Mr. Winterbourne were to marry some one else, it would leave Miss Daisy Miller free.

REVERDY. Free to walk about with the native population? She seems to be free enough already. Mrs. Costello, the camp-stool is at your service.

MRS. C. Give it to me, and I'll go and sit in the shade. Excuse me, I would rather carry it myself. (*Taking the camp-stool, aside to Miss Durant.*) If he proposes, mind you accept him.

MISS D. If who proposes?

MRS. C. Our young companion! He is manœuvring to get rid of me. He has nothing but his expectations, but his expectations are of the best. (*She marches away with her camp-stool, and seats herself at a distance, where, with her eyeglass raised, she appears to look at what goes on in another part of the garden.*)

MISS D., *aside.* Am *I* one of his expectations? Fortunately, I don't need to marry for money. (*Aloud.*) Cousin Louisa is furious with me for not being more encouraging to Mr. Winterbourne. I don't know what she would have liked me to do!

REVERDY. You have been very proper, very dignified.

MISS D. That's the way I was brought up. I never liked him, from the first.

REVERDY. Oh, he's a stupid stick!

MISS D. I don't say he's stupid—and he's very good looking.

REVERDY. As good looking as a man can be in whom one feature—the most expressive—has been entirely omitted. He has got no eyes in his head.

MISS D. No eyes?

REVERDY. To see that poor little creature is in love with him.

MISS D. She has a queer way of showing it.

REVERDY. Ah, they always have queer ways!

MISS D. He sees it, but he doesn't care.

REVERDY. That's still worse,—the omission not of a feature, but of an organ (*tapping his heart and smiling*), the seat of our purest and highest joys!

MISS D., *aside*. Cousin Louisa was right! (*Aloud.*) Do you mean that he has no heart?

REVERDY. If he had as big a one as the rosette on your shoe, would he leave me here to do all the work?

MISS D., *looking at her foot*. The rosette on my shoe is rather big.

REVERDY, *looking as well*. It isn't so much the size of the rosette as the smallness of the shoe!

MISS D., *aside*. Cousin Louisa is certainly right! (*Aloud, smiling.*) Yours, I suppose, is bigger than that.

REVERDY. My shoe? I should think so—rather!

MISS D. Dear, no! I mean your heart. Though I don't think it's at all nice in you to complain of being left with us.

REVERDY. When I'm left with you, I don't complain; but when I'm left with *her!* (*Indicating Mrs. Costello.*)

MISS D. Well, you're not with her now.

REVERDY. Ah, *now* it's very pleasant. Only she has got the camp-stool.

MISS D. Do you want it for yourself?

REVERDY. Yes; I have been carrying it for the last six months, and I feel rather awkward without it. It gives one confidence to have something in one's hand.

MISS D. Good heavens! What do you want to do?

REVERDY. I want to make you a little speech.

MISS D. You will do very well as you are.

REVERDY. I'll try it. (*In an attitude.*) Six months ago I had moments of rebellion, but today I have come to love my chains! Accordingly—(*Mrs. Costello starts up and hurries forward, the camp-stool in her hand.*) By Jove! if she hears me, she'll rivet them faster!

MRS. C., *seizing Miss Durant's arm*. My poor, dear child, whom do you think I've seen?

REVERDY. By your expression, the ghost of Julius Cæsar!

MRS. C. The Russian woman—the princess—whom we saw last summer.

MISS D. Well, my dear cousin, she won't eat us up!

MRS. C. No, but she'll eat Frederick!

REVERDY. On the contrary, her appetite for Frederick is small. Don't you remember that, last summer, she left the hotel as soon as he arrived?

MRS. C. That was only a feint, to put us off the scent. He has been in secret correspondence with her, and their meeting here is prearranged.

MISS D. I don't know why you call their correspondence secret, when he was always going to the post-office!

MRS. C. Ah, but you can't tell what he did there! Frederick is very deep.

REVERDY. There's nothing secret, at any rate, about her arrival here. She alighted yesterday at our own hotel, in the most public manner, with the landlord and all the waiters drawn up to receive her. It didn't occur to me to mention it.

MRS. C. I don't really know what you are with us for!

MISS D. Oh, Cousin Louisa, he is meant for better things than that!

MRS. C., *to Miss Durant, aside.* Do you mean that he has proposed?

MISS D. No, but he was just going to.

MRS. C., *disappointed.* Ah, you've told me that before!

MISS D. Because you never give him time.

MRS. C. Does he want three hours?

MISS D. No, but he wants three minutes!

REVERDY, *who has strolled away, observing them, aside.* Happy thought, to make them fight about me! Mutual destruction would ensue, and I should be master of the situation. (*Aloud.*) I am only a man, dear Madam: I am not a newspaper.

MRS. C. If you only were, we could stop our subscription! And, as a proof of what I say, here comes Frederick, to look after his Russian. (*Winterbourne comes in, with Mrs. Walker.*)

REVERDY. With the wife of the consul, to look after him!

SCENE VII. MRS. COSTELLO. MISS DURANT. REVERDY. WINTERBOURNE. MRS. WALKER.

MRS. WALKER. Oh, you dreadful people, what are you doing here, when you ought to be at my reception?

MRS. COSTELLO. We were just thinking of going; it's so very near.

MRS. W. Only round the corner! But there are better reasons than that.

MISS D. There can hardly be a very good one, when you yourself have come away!

MRS. W. You'd never imagine what has brought me! I've come in pursuit of little Daisy Miller.

MRS. C. And you've brought my nephew to help you!

WINTERBOURNE. A walk in such charming company is a privilege not to be lost. Perhaps, dear aunt, you can give us news.

MRS. C. Of that audacious and desperate person? Dear me, yes. We met her just now, on the arm of a dreadful man.

MRS. W. Oh, we're too late then. She's lost!

MRS. C. It seems to me she was lost long ago, and (*significantly, at Winterbourne*) that this is not the first rendezvous she has taken.

WINTERBOURNE, *smiling.* If it does her no more harm than the others. Mrs. Walker had better go back to her teapot!

REVERDY, *to Miss Durant.* That's an allusion to the way he was sold!

MRS. W. She left my house, half an hour ago, without a word to any one but her goose of a mother, who thought it all right that she should walk off to the Pincian to meet the handsome Giovanelli. I only discovered her flight just now, by a lady who coming in at the moment that Miss Daisy, shaking out her little flounces and tossing up her little head, tripped away from my door, to fall into the arms of a cavalier!

MISS D. Into his arms? Ah, Mrs. Walker!

MRS. W. My dear young lady, with these unscrupulous foreigners one can never be sure. You know as well as I what becomes of the reputation of a girl who shows herself in this place, at this hour, with all the rank and fashion of Rome about her, with no more responsible escort than a gentleman renowned for his successes!

REVERDY, *to Miss Durant.* It's as if you were here with me, you know!

MRS. W. This idea came over me with a kind of horror, and I determined to save her if I could.

MRS. C. There's nothing left of her to save!

MRS. W. There is always something left, and my representative position makes it a duty. My rooms were filled with guests—a hundred and fifty people—but I put on my bonnet and seized Mr. Winterbourne's arm.

WINTERBOURNE. You can testify that I didn't wince! I quite agree with you as to the importance of looking her up. Foreigners never understand.

REVERDY, *aside.* My dear fellow, if they understand no better than you! . . .

MRS. W. What I want of you dear people is to go and entertain my visitors. Console them for my absence, and tell them I shall be back in five minutes.

MISS D. It will be very nice to give a reception without any trouble.

MRS. C. Without any trouble—scarcely! But there is nothing we wouldn't do—

MRS. W. For the representative of one's country! Be charming, then, as you can so well. (*Seeing Daisy and Giovanelli come in.*) I shall not be long, for by the mercy of Heaven the child is guided to this spot!

REVERDY. If you think you have only to pick her up, we won't wait for you! (*He goes out with Mrs. Costello and Miss Durant.*)

SCENE VIII. MRS. WALKER. WINTERBOURNE. DAISY. GIOVANELLI.

WINTERBOURNE, *as the two others slowly come in together, not at first seeing him.* We shall have a seige: she won't give him up for the asking.

MRS. WALKER. We must divide our forces, then. You will deal with Daisy.

WINTERBOURNE. I would rather attack the gentleman.

MRS. W. No, no; there'll be trouble. Mr. Giovanelli, I should like a little conversation with you.

GIOVANELLI, *starting, and coming forward; very polite.* You do me great honour, Madame!

MRS. W. I wish to scold you for not coming to me today; but to spare your blushes, it must be in private. (*Strolls away with him, out of sight.*)

DAISY, *aside.* They have come to take me away. Ah, they are very cruel!

WINTERBOURNE. I had no chance to speak to you at Mrs. Walker's, and I've come to make up for my loss.

DAISY, *looking at him a moment.* What is Mrs. Walker doing here? Why doesn't she stay with her guests?

WINTERBOURNE. I brought her away—to do just what she has done.

DAISY. To take away Mr. Giovanelli? I don't understand you.

WINTERBOURNE. A great many people think that you understand, but that you don't care.

DAISY. I don't care what people think. I have done no harm.

WINTERBOURNE. That's exactly what I say—you don't care. But I wish you would care a little, for your friends are very much frightened. When Mrs. Walker ascertained that you had left her house alone, and had come to meet a gentleman here—here, where all Rome assembles at this hour to amuse itself, and where you would be watched and criticized and calumniated—when Mrs. Walker made this dicovery she said but three words—'To the rescue!' But she took her plunge, as if you had been drowning.

DAISY. And you jumped overboard, too!

WINTERBOURNE. Oh, dear, no; I'm standing on the brink. I only interpret her sentiments. I don't express my own.

DAISY. They would interest me more than Mrs. Walker's; but I don't see what either of you have to do with me.

WINTERBOURNE. We admire you very much, and we hate to see you misjudged.

DAISY. I don't know what you mean, and I don't know what you think I want to do.

WINTERBOURNE. I haven't the least idea about that. All I mean is that if you could see, as I see it, how little it's the custom here to do what you do, and how badly it looks to fly in the face of the custom, you would be a little more on your guard.

DAISY. I know nothing about the custom. I'm an American; I'm not one of these people.

WINTERBOURNE. In that case, you would behave differently. Your being an American is just the point. You are a very conspicuous American, thanks to your attractions, to your charms, to the publicity of your life. Such people, with the best intentions in the world, are often very indiscreet; and it's to save the reputation of her compatriots that the fairest and brightest of young American girls should sacrifice a little of her independence.

DAISY. Look here, Mr. Winterbourne, you make too much fuss: that's what's the matter with you!

WINTERBOURNE. If I make enough to persuade you to go home with Mrs. Walker, my highest ambition will be gratified.

DAISY. I think you are trying to mystify me: I can tell that by your language. One would never think you were the same person who went with me to that castle.

WINTERBOURNE. I am not quite the same, but I've a good deal in common with him. Now, Mr. Giovanelli doesn't resemble that person at all.

DAISY, *coldly*. I don't know why you speak to me about Mr. Giovanelli.

WINTERBOURNE. Because—because Mrs. Walker asked me to.

DAISY. It would be better if she should do it herself.

WINTERBOURNE. That's exactly what I told her; but she had an odd fancy that I have kind of influence with you.

DAISY, *with expression*. Poor Mrs. Walker!

WINTERBOURNE. Poor Mrs. Walker! She doesn't know that no one has any influence with you—that you do nothing in the world but what pleases yourself.

DAISY. Whom, then, am I to please? The people that think such dreadful things of me? I don't even understand what they think! What do you mean, about my reputation? I haven't got any reputation! If people are so cruel and wicked, I am sure I would rather not know it. In America they let me alone, and no one ran after me, like Mrs. Walker. It's natural I should like the people who seem to like me, and who will take the trouble to go round with me. The others may say what they like. I can't understand Italian, and I should never hear of it if you didn't come and translate.

WINTERBOURNE. It's not only the Italians—it's the Americans.

DAISY. Do you mean your aunt and your cousin? I don't know why I should make myself miserable for *them*!

WINTERBOURNE. I mean every one who has ever had the very questionable advantage of making your acquaintance—only to be subjected to the torment of being unable either to believe in you or to doubt of you.

DAISY. To doubt of me? You are very strange!

WINTERBOURNE. You are stranger still. But I didn't come here to reason with you: that would be vain, for we speak a different language, and we shouldn't understand each other. I only came to say to you, in the most respectful manner, that if you should consult your best interests you would go home with Mrs. Walker.

DAISY. Do you think I had such a lovely time there, half an hour ago, when you didn't so much as look at me?

WINTERBOURNBE. If I had spoken to you, would you have stayed?

DAISY. After I had an engagement here? (*With a little laugh.*) I must say, you expect a great deal!

WINTERBOURNE, *looking at her a moment.* What they say is true—you're a thorough-going coquette!

(*Mrs. Walker reappears, with Giovanelli.*)

DAISY. You speak too much of what they say. To escape from you, I'll go anywhere!

MRS. W., *to Winterbourne, while Giovanelli speaks to Daisy.* He's very accommodating, when you tell him that if Mrs. Miller gets frightened she will start off for America.

WINTERBOURNE. It's more than I can say of Miss Daisy!

MRS. W. Have you had no success?

WINTERBOURNE. I have had my ears boxed!

MRS. W., *to Daisy.* My precious child, you escaped from my drawing-room before I had half the talk we wanted.

DAISY. Are they all waiting there to see me brought back?

MRS. W. Oh dear, no; they've plenty to think about—with Mrs. Costello and Miss Durant.

DAISY. Ah, those ladies are there? Then I certainly shan't go back.

MRS. W., *alarmed.* Hush! They're relations of Mr. Winterbourne.

DAISY. All the more reason for my hating them!

MRS. W., *to Winterbourne.* You must excuse her; she is very wicked today! (*To*

Daisy.) If you won't go home, then I'll stay with you here. Mr. Giovanelli, you promised me you would go to my house.

GIOVANELLI. I am at the orders of Mademoiselle.

DAISY. You may do what you please till dinner-time.

WINTERBOURNE, *aside.* Gracious heavens! is she going to dine with him? (*Aloud, to Daisy.*) We were interrupted, but I have a great deal more to say.

DAISY. More of the same sort? It will be a pleasure to here that!

WINTERBOURNE. What's coming is a great deal better.—Do you dine at your *table d'hôte*?

DAISY. Oh, yes. Randolph likes the table d'hôte.

WINTERBOURNE. I will ask for a place there this evening, and, with your permission, it shall be next to yours.

DAISY. I'm very sorry, but I'm not sure of this evening.

WINTERBOURNE, *gravely.* That's a great disappointment to me. (*A short silence.*)

MRS. W., *to Giovanelli.* You promised me you would go to my house!

GIOVANELLI. As a man of honour, then, I must go. But I assure you, Mademoiselle (*to Daisy*), that I soon return.

DAISY. As soon as you like! (*Giovanelli walks away. To Winterbourne.*) Can't you come some other night?

WINTERBOURNE. Oh, yes, by waiting a little. But with the uncertainty of your stay in Rome, this would be always something gained.

DAISY. What will you do after dinner?

WINTERBOURNE. With you kind permission, I will adjourn with you to your mother's sitting-room.

DAISY. You are very devoted, all of a sudden!

WINTERBOURNE. Better late than never!

DAISY. You are just as you were at that castle!

WINTERBOURNE. So are you—at this moment. We can dream we are in that happy place!

DAISY, *aside.* He can do with me what he will. (*Aloud, quickly.*) I'll tell them to keep you a seat!

WINTERBOURNE. I shall be indebted to you forever!

DAISY. Oh, if I don't see about it, they'll put you at the other end.

WINTERBOURNE. Next [to] you—that's the point.

DAISY. Between me and Randolph! At half past six!

WINTERBOURNE. At half past six.

MRS. W., *to Winterbourne.* You can go about your business. I have something to say to her alone.

DAISY. Don't forget half past six!

WINTERBOURNE. Never in the world. At half past six! (*Walks away.*)

MRS. WALKER, *alone with Daisy.* And now may I be permitted to inquire whether you had arrange to dine with that Italian?

DAISY, *smiling.* In the heart of ancient Rome! But don't tell Mr. Winterbourne what I gave up!

MRS. WALKER, *aside.* I'll get you out of Rome tomorrow! (*Aloud.*) I must show you to the crowd—with *me.* (*Goes out leading Daisy.*)

SCENE IX. REVERDY. RANDOLPH.

REVERDY, *coming in just as the others pass out, and completing Mrs. Walker's phrase.* The wife of the American consul! The American consul is all very well, but I'll be hanged if I'll carry on the business! It's quite enough to do odd jobs for Mrs. Costello, without taking service at the consulate. Fifty carriages before the door, and five hundred people up-stairs. My companions may get up if they can! It's the first time today I've had a moment for a quiet smoke. (*Lights a cigar, and while he is doing so Randolph comes in.*) O Lord, the Old Man of the Sea!

RANDOLPH, *planted before Reverdy.* I say, Mr. Reverdy, suppose you offer me a cigar.

REVERDY. My poor child, my cigars are as big as yourself!

RANDOLPH. There's nothing fit to smoke over here. You can't get 'em as you can in America.

REVERDY. Yes, they're better in America (*smoking*); but they cost a good deal more.

RANDOLPH. I don't care what I pay. I've got all the money I want.

REVERDY. Don't spend it; keep it till you grow up.

RANDOLPH. Oh, I ain't going to grow up. I've been this way for ever so long. Mother brought me over to see if I wouldn't start, but I haven't started an inch. You can't start in this old country.

REVERDY. The Romans were rather tall!

RANDOLPH. I don't care for the Romans. A child's as good as a man.

REVERDY, *aside.* The future of democracy! (*Aloud.*) You remind me of the infant Hannibal.

RANDOLPH. There's one good thing: so long as I'm little, my mother can't see me. She's looking all around.

REVERDY. I was going to ask you if she allowed you to mingle in this human maze.

RANDOLPH. Mother's in the carriage, but I jumped out.

REVERDY. Imprudent little man! At the risk of breaking your neck?

RANDOLPH. Oh, we were crawling along—we haven't American trotters. I saw you walking about, and when mother wasn't looking I just dropped. As soon as she missed me, she began to howl!

REVERDY. I am sorry to be the occasion of a family broil.

RANDOLPH. She thinks I am run over; she has begun to collect a crowd.

REVERDY. You wicked little person! I must take you straight back to her.

RANDOLPH. I thought you might like to know where my sister is.

REVERDY. At the present moment my anxiety is about your mother.

RANDOLPH. Daisy's gone on a bender. If you'll give me a cigar, I'll put you up to it.

REVERDY. You're a vulgar little boy. Take me instantly to your mother.

RANDOLPH, *very sarcastic.* Wouldn't you like to carry me on your back?

REVERDY. If you don't come. I'll take you under my arm. (*Starts to seize him.*)

RANDOLPH, *dodging.* I won't come, then!

REVERDY. Blast the little wretch! I *must* relieve his mother. (*Makes another attempt to capture Randolph, who escapes, while Reverdy gives chase, and they disappear.*)

SCENE X. WINTERBOURNE. *then* MADAME DE KATKOFF.

WINTERBOURNE, *coming in alone.* Remarkable family, the Millers! Mrs. Miller, standing up in her carriage, in the centre of a crowd of Italians, and chattering to them in her native tongue. She falls upon my neck when she sees me, and announces that the gifted Randolph is no more. He has tumbled out of the vehicle, and been trampled to death! We institute a search for his remains, and as it proves fruitless she begs me to come and look for him here. (*Looking round him.*) I don't perceive any remains! He has mingled in the giddy throng, and the giddy throng may bring him back! It's the business of that ruffian of a courier! (*Seeing Madame de Katkoff, aside.*) Is *she* still here? (*Aloud.*) To meet you again is better fortune than I hoped.

MME. DE KATKOFF, *strolling in slowly, with an air of deliberation, and standing a moment thoughtful.* Will you do me the favour to dine with me tonight?

WINTERBOURNE, *startled.* To dine with you tonight?

MME. DE K. You stare as if I were a ghost! It's very simple: to dine with me tonight, at seven o'clock, at the *Hôtel de Paris*?

WINTERBOURNE, *aside.* It's a little awkward. (*Aloud.*) Do you dine at the *table d'hôte*?

MME. DE K. At the *table d'hôte*, with that rabble of tourists? I dine in my own apartments.

WINTERBOURNE. I supposed you had left the Pincian; I had no idea you were lingering.

MME. DE K. Apparently I had a purpose, which you seem quite unable to appreciate. You are very slow in accepting!

WINTERBOURNE. To tell you the honest truth, I have made an engagement.

MME. DE K. An engagement? A moment ago you were dying to spend the evening with me.

WINTERBOURNE. A moment ago you wouldn't listen to me.

MME. DE K., *after a pause.* My dear friend, you are very stupid. A woman doesn't confess the truth at the first summons!

WINTERBOURNE. You are very strange. I accepted an invitation just after we parted.

MME. DE K. Send word you can't come.

WINTERBOURNE. It was from the young lady you recommended me so strongly to turn my attention to.

MME. DE K. Ah, she gives invitations?

WINTERBOURNE. I confess I asked for this one. They are also at the *Hôtel de Paris*, and they dine at the *table d'hôte*.

MME. DE K. A charming place to carry on a courtship!

WINTERBOURNE. It's not a courtship—however much I may have wished to please you.

MME. DE K. Your wish to please me has suddenly diminished. Apparently, I am to understand that you refuse!

WINTERBOURNE. Even when you are kind, there's something cruel in it!—I will dine with you with pleasure.

MME. DE K. Send word, then, to your little American.

WINTERBOURNE. Yes, I'll send word. (*Aside.*) That's uncommonly rough! (*Aloud.*) After dinner, I suppose, you'll go to the opera.

MME. DE K. I don't know about the opera. (*Looking at him a moment.*) It will be a splendid night. How should you like a moonlight drive?

WINTERBOURNE. A moonlight drive—with you? It seems to me you mock me!

MME. DE K., *in the same tone.* To wander through the old streets, when everything is still; to see the solemn monuments wrapped up in their shadows; to watch the great fountains turn to silver in the moonshine—that has always been a dream of mine! We'll try it tonight.

WINTERBOURNE, *affected by her tone.* We'll see the great square of St. Peter's; we'll dip our hands in the Fountain of Trevi! You must be strangely beautiful in the moonlight.

MME. DE K. I don't know. You shall see.

WINTERBOURNE. What will you do with the Russian ambassador?

MME. DE K. Send him about his business.

WINTERBOURNE. An ambassador! For me?

MME. DE K. Don't force me to say it; I shall make you too vain.

WINTERBOURNE. I'm not used to being treated so, and I can't help feeling that it may be only a refinement of cruelty.

MME. DE K. If I've been cruel before, it was in self-defence. I have been sorely troubled, and I don't pretend to be consistent. Women are never so—especially women who love!

WINTERBOURNE. I ask no questions; I only thank you.

MME. DE K. At seven o'clock, then.

WINTERBOURNE. You are very strange; but you are only the more adorable. At seven o'clock!

MME. DE K. You are not to come with me; my carriage is there. (*Aside, as she leaves him.*) Ingenuous young man!

WINTERBOURNE, *alone, standing a moment in thought.* 'Women are never consistent—especially women who love!' I've waited three years, but it was worth waiting for! (*Mrs. Walker comes in with Daisy, without his seeing them.*)

SCENE XI. WINTERBOURNE. MRS. WALKER. DAISY. *then* EUGENIO AND GIOVANELLI.

DAISY. Well, Mr. Winterbourne, is that the way you look for my brother? You had better not come to dinner unless you find him.

WINTERBOURNE. I was just wondering which way I had better go.

MRS. WALKER. Mrs. Miller has pressed us into the service, and she wants every one to go in a different direction. But I prefer (*significantly*) that Daisy and I should stick together.

DAISY, *happily.* Oh, I don't care now. You may take me anywhere!

WINTERBOURNE, *aside.* Poor little thing! And I've got to disappoint her! (*Aloud.*) I suppose I had better separate from you, then.

EUGENIO, *arriving hastily.* Mr. Randolph has been found—by Mr. Reverdy! (*To Daisy.*) If I leave your mother a moment, a misfortune is sure to arrive.

MRS. W., *aside.* The misfortune, indeed, is his being found! (*To Daisy.*) If you will join your mother, I will go back to my guests (*seeing Giovanelli*)—whom Mr. Giovanelli has already deserted.

GIOVANELLI, *coming in.* Your guests have deserted me, Madame. They have left your house in a caravan: they couldn't stand your absence.

MRS. W., *to Daisy.* I have offended all my friends for you, my dear. You ought to be grateful.

DAISY. The reason they left was not because you came away, but because you didn't bring me back. They wanted to glare at me.

GIOVANELLI, *with a little laugh.* They glared at me a good deal!

MRS. W. I'll admit that they don't like you. (*To Daisy.*) Let me place you in your mother's hands.

EUGENIO, *with importance.* I will take charge of my young lady, Madame.

WINTERBOURNE, *to Daisy.* Before you go just let me say a word.

DAISY. As many as you please—only you frighten me!

WINTERBOURNE, *aside.* I'm rather frightened myself. (*Aloud.*) I'm very much afraid I shall not be able to dine tonight.

DAISY. Not be able—after your promise?

WINTERBOURNE. It's very true I promised, and I'm greatly ashamed. But a most unexpected obstacle has sprung up. I'm obliged to take back my word—I'm exceedingly sorry.

MRS. W., *in a low voice to Winterbourne.* Ah, my dear sir, you're making a mess!

DAISY. Your obstacle must have come very quickly.

WINTERBOURNE. Only five minutes ago.

EUGENIO, *aside.* The Katkoff's as good as her word!

DAISY, *much affected.* Well, Mr. Winterbourne, I can only say I too am very sorry.

WINTERBOURNE. I'll come the very first evening I'm free.

DAISY. I didn't want the first evening; I wanted this one.

WINTERBOURNE. I beg you to forgive me. My own loss is greater than yours.

GIOVANELLI, *aside.* My friend the courier is a clever man!

DAISY, *thoughtful for a moment.* Well, it's no matter.

MRS. W., *to Eugenio.* Please take her to her mother.

EUGENIO. I must act at my convenience, Madame!

DAISY. I'm not going to my mother. Mr. Giovanelli!

GIOVANELLI, *with alacrity.* Signorina?

DAISY. Please to give me your arm. We'll go on with our walk.

MRS. W., *coming between the two.* Now don't do anything dreadful!

DAISY, *to Giovanelli.* Give me your arm. (*Giovanelli passes behind Mrs. Walker, and gives Daisy his arm on the other side. She continues, with a sudden outbreak of passion.*) I see nothing dreadful but your cruel accusations! If you all attack me, I've a friend to defend me.

GIOVANELLI. I will defend you always, Signorina!

MRS. W. Are you going to take her to that drinking-shop?

DAISY. That's our own affair. Come away, come away!

WINTERBOURNE. I have done you a greater injury than I supposed.

DAISY. The injury was done when you spoke to me that way!

WINTERBOURNE. When I spoke to you? I don't understand.

DAISY. Half an hour ago, when you said I was so bad!

GIOVANELLI. If people insult you, they will answer to *me*.

WINTERBOURNE, *to Giovanelli*. Don't be rash, sir! You will need all your caution.

MRS. W. High words between gentlemen, to crown the horrors! (*To Eugenio.*) Go straight and ask Mrs. Miller if she consents.

EUGENIO, *smiling*. Mrs. Miller consents to everything that I approve.

DAISY. Come away, Mr. Giovanelli!

GIOVANELLI, *aside*. I shall have to take a cab! (*They walk up the stage.*)

MRS. W. Mercy on us! She is lost!

WINTERBOURNE, *sternly*. Leave her alone! She only wants a pretext!

DAISY, *who has heard him, turning as she reaches the top of the stage, and looking back a moment*. Thank you, Mr. Winterbourne! (*She goes out with Giovanelli.*)

MRS. W., *to Winterbourne*. Yes, my dear sir, you've done a pretty piece of work!

EUGENIO, *with his hands in his pockets, as at the end of the first act, watching the scene complacently*. My little revenge on the journey to the castle!

WINTERBOURNE, *looking at his watch, to himself*. Well, *I* shall have that moonlight drive!

ACT III.

Rome. Public parlours at the Hôtel de Paris; evening. Wide windows at the back, overlooking the Corso, open upon a balcony, which must be apparent, behind light curtains, to the audience. The Carnival is going on outside, and the flare of torches, the sound of voices and of music, the uproar of a popular festival, come into the room, rising and falling at intervals during the whole act.

SCENE I. MRS. COSTELLO. MISS DURANT. CHARLES REVERDY. *He comes in first at the left, holding the door open for the others to follow.*

REVERDY. You can see very well from this balcony, if you won't go down into the street.

MRS. C. Down into the street—to be trampled to death? I have no desire to be butchered to make a Roman holiday.

REVERDY, *aside*. They would find you a tough old morsel! (*Aloud.*) It's the last night of the Carnival, and a peculiar licence prevails.

MRS. C. I'm happy to hear it's the last night. Their tooting and piping and fiddling hasn't stopped for a week, and my poor old head has been racked with pain.

MISS D. Is it very bad now? You had better go to our own quiet parlour, which looks out on the back.

MRS. C. And leave you here with this youth?

MISS D. After all—in the Carnival!

MRS. C. A season of peculiar licence—as he himself confesses. I wonder you don't propose at once to mingle with the populace—in a fancy dress!

MISS D. I should like to very much! I'm tired of being cooped up in a balcony. If this is the last night, it's my only chance.

MRS. C., *severely*. Alice Durant, I don't recognize you! The Carnival has affected you—insidiously. You're as bad as Daisy Miller.

REVERDY. Poor little butterfly! Don't speak harshly of *her*: she is lying ill with Roman fever.

MRS. C. Since her visit to the Colosseum, in the cool of the evening, with the inveterate Giovanelli?

MISS D. I suppose he'll marry her when she recovers—if she does recover!

REVERDY. It was certainly idiotic, from the point of view of salubrity, to go to enjoy the moonlight in that particularly mouldy ruin, and the inveterate Giovanelli, who is old enough to know better, ought to have a thrashing. The poor girl may never recover. The little Flower of the West, as Mrs. Walker says, is withering on the stem. Fancy dying to the music of the Carnival!

MRS. C. That's the way I shall die, unless you come now and take your last look, so that we may go away and have done with it. (*Goes to the window.*) Good heavens, what a rabble! (*Passes out on the balcony.*)

REVERDY, *to Miss Durant, remaining behind.* Will you give her the slip, and come out with me?

MISS D., *looking at him, and listening to the music.* In a fancy dress?

REVERDY. Oh, no; simply in a mask. I've got one in my pocket. (*Takes out a grotesque mask and holds it to his face a moment, shaking his head at her.*) How d'ye do, lovely woman?

MISS D. Dear me, how very hideous!

REVERDY. If *you* put it on, I shall be as handsome as ever.

MISS D., *aside.* If he should propose out there, it would hide my blushes!

MRS. C., *from the balcony.* Young people, what are you doing? Come out here this minute!

REVERDY. There she is again! (*Aloud.*) Are you afraid they will pelt you with flowers?

MRS. C. A gentleman has already kissed his hand to me!

REVERDY. A season of peculiar licence! (*To Miss Durant.*) We can't escape from her now, but it won't be long! (*They rejoin Mrs. Costello on the balcony, Reverdy holding the mask behind him. While they remain there, apparently absorbed in the spectacle in the street, Eugenio and Giovanelli come in.*)

SCENE II. EUGENIO. GIOVANELLI: *then* REVERDY. MISS DURANT.

EUGENIO. You must come in here; we can't talk in the hall.

GIOVANELLI, *with a bouquet of flowers.* I have come for news of the dear young lady. I'm terribly nervous.

EUGENIO. You think you may lose her? It would serve you right!

GIOVANELLI. If I lose her I shall never try again. I am passionately in love with her.

EUGENIO. I hope so, indeed! That was part of our agreement.

GIOVANELLI. If you begin to joke, I see she's better.

EUGENIO. If I begin to joke? I'm as serious as you. If she's better it's no thanks to you—doing your best to kill her on my hands.

GIOVANELLI. It was no fault of mine. She had her own way.

EUGENIO. The Colosseum by moonlight—that was a lovely invention! Why didn't you jump into the Tiber at once?

GIOVANELLI. We are not the first who have been there. It's a very common excursion.

EUGENIO. By daylight, of course; but not when the miasma rises.

GIOVANELLI. Excuse me: it is recommended in the guide-books.

EUGENIO. Do you make love according to Murray?—or, perhaps, according to Baedeker? I myself have conducted families there, to admire the general effect; but not to spend the evening.

GIOVANELLI. I was afraid for myself, Heaven knows!

EUGENIO. 'Afraid for yourself' is good— with an American heiress beside you!

GIOVANELLI. I couldn't induce her to come away, the moon was so bright and beautiful! And then you wanted her to be talked about.

EUGENIO. Yes: but I wanted you to take her alive. She's talked about enough today. It was only a week ago, but the whole town knows it.

GIOVANELLI. *Per Bacco*! That solemn fool of a Winterbourne has spread the story.

EUGENIO. The further the better! But I thought I had given him something else to do.

GIOVANELLI. I don't know what you had given him to do; but, as luck would have it, he turned up at the Colosseum. He came upon us suddenly, and stood there staring. Then he took off his hat to my companion, and made her the lowest of bows.

EUGENIO. Without a word?

GIOVANELLI. Without a word. He turned his back and walked off.

EUGENIO. Stupid ass! But it is all right: he has given her up.

GIOVANELLI. He gave her up that day on the Pincian; he has not been near her since.

EUGENIO, *aside*. The Katkoff is really perfect!—though he comes to ask about her every day. (*Aloud*.) Yes, but he wanted a reason: now he has got his reason.

GIOVANELLI, *pretentiously*. I'll give him a better one than that!

EUGENIO. He's perfectly content with this one; and it must be admitted it would suit most people. We must hope it will suit Mr. Miller.

GIOVANELLI, *gloomily*. Ah, Mr. Miller? I seemed to see him there, too, in the moonlight!

EUGENIO. You're afraid of him, and your fear makes images. What did Miss Daisy do?

GIOVANELLI. After the American had left us? She held her tongue still till we got home.

EUGENIO. She said nothing about him?

GIOVANELLI. Never a word, thank goodness!

EUGENIO, *thoughtful a moment.* Cavaliere, you're very limited.

GIOVANELLI. I verily believe I am, to stand here and answer your questions. All this time you have told me nothing about my adored!

EUGENIO. She is doing very well; it has been a light attack. She has sat up these three days, and the doctor says she needs only to be careful. But being careful doesn't suit her; she's in despair at missing the Carnival.

GIOVANELLI, *tenderly.* Enchanting young person! Be so good as to give her these flowers. Be careful of them, you know!

EUGENIO. I should think so—why I pay for them myself.

GIOVANELLI. And ask if I may come up and see her.

EUGENIO, *looking at the bouquet.* You get 'em handsome, I must say.—I don't know what the doctor would say to that.

GIOVANELLI, *smiling.* Let me be the doctor. You'll see!

EUGENIO. You're certainly dangerous enough for one. But you must wait till we go out—the mother and the brother and I.

GIOVANELLI. Where are you going, at this hour?

EUGENIO. To show that peevish little brat the illumination.

GIOVANELLI. Mrs. Miller leaves her daughter—at such a time?

EUGENIO. Master Randolph's the head of the family.

GIOVANELLI. I must get *his* consent to the marriage, then?

EUGENIO. You can get it with a pound of candy.

GIOVANELLI. I'll buy him a dozen tomorrow.

EUGENIO. And charge it to me, of course.

GIOVANELLI, *stiffly.* Please to open the door. I'll wait in the hall till you go out. (*Eugenio opens the door, looks at him, and then passes out first. Giovanelli follows. When they have left the room, Reverdy and Miss Durant come in from the balcony.*)

REVERDY, *his fingers on his lips.* Hush, hush! She's looking for the gentleman who kissed his hand.

MISS D. When she kissed hers back, she frightened him away!

REVERDY. I can't stand that balcony business! I want to dance and sing, in the midst of it, with a charming creature on my arm!

MISS D. I forbid you to touch any of your creatures!

REVERDY. In the Carnival one may touch any one. All common laws are suspended.

MISS D. Cousin Louisa won't listen to that.

REVERDY. She's a great deal worse than we herself—having an affair with a perfect stranger! Now's our chance to escape; before she misses us, we shall be a mile away.

MISS D. A mile away is very far! You make me feel dreadfully like Daisy Miller.

REVERDY. To be perfect, all you want is to be a little like her.

MISS D. Oh, you wretch—I never!

REVERDY. There, now, you're just like her!

MISS D. I certainly am not used to being a wall-flower.

REVERDY. A plant in a balcony's even worse. Come, come! here's the mask.

MISS D. It's very dreadful. I can't bear to look so ugly!

REVERDY. Don't I know how pretty you are?

MISS D., *taking his arm, aside.* He can do anything with me he wants! (*Exeunt. Enter Daisy on the opposite side.*)

SCENE III. DAISY *alone; then* WINTERBOURNE. *a* WAITER; MRS. COSTELLO.

DAISY. *She wears a light dressing-gown, like an invalid, and it must be apparent that she has been ill, though this appearance must not be exaggerated. She wanders slowly into the room, and pauses in the middle.* Ah, from here the music is very distinct—and the voices of the crowd, and all the sound of the fête. Upstairs, in our rooms, you can hear it just dimly. That's the way it seemed to me—just faint and far—as I lay there with darkened windows. It's hard to be sick when there's so much pleasure going on, especially when you're so fond of pleasure as poor silly me! Perhaps I'm too fond; that's one of the things I thought of as I lay there. I thought of so many—and some of them so sad—as I listened to the faraway Carnival. I think it was this that helped me to get better. I was afraid I had been bad, and I wanted to live to be good again. I was afraid I should die, and I didn't want to die. But I'm better now, and I can walk and do everything I want. (*Listening again.*) Every now and then it grows louder, as if the people were so happy! It reminds me of that poetry I used to learn at school, 'There was a sound of revelry by night.' That's a sound I always wanted to hear. This is the last night; and when mother and Randolph went out, I couldn't stay there alone. I waited a little; I was afraid of meeting some one on the stairs. But every one is in the streets, and they have gone to see the illumination. I thought of that balcony: just to look out a little is better than nothing. (*Listens again a moment.*) Every now and then it increases. (*Goes to the window, but seeing Mrs. Costello outside comes back.*) Ah, there's some one there; and with this old wrapper . . . (*Looking at her dressing-gown.*) Perhaps the night air isn't good for me; the doctor forbids the night air. Ah, what a pity it's the last evening! (*Goes to the window again, and while she stands there a waiter throws open the door and ushers in Winterbourne, who at first does not see her.*)

THE WAITER. The ladies are here, sir. (*Surprised not to find them.*) Excuse me. I saw them come in with Mr. Reverdy, but they have gone out again.

WINTERBOURNE. It's not those ladies I want. Please to ask Madame de Katkoff if she can see me.

THE WAITER. Won't you go up to her sitting-room? She has a great many guests.

WINTERBOURNE, *annoyed.* A great many guests?

THE WAITER. A party of friends, who have come to see the fête from one of her windows. Her parlour is in the Square, and the view is even finer than from here.

WINTERBOURNE. I know all about her parlour. (*Aside.*) It's hateful to see her with a lot of others! (*Aloud.*) Ask her if she will kindly speak to me here.

THE WAITER. Ah, you lose a great deal, sir! (*Exit.*)

WINTERBOURNE. The servants in this place are impossible; the young Randolph has demoralized them all! That's the same fellow who, last summer, wanted to give me a definition of my aunt. (*Seeing Daisy.*) Ah, that poor creature! (*Aloud.*) I'm afraid I'm intruding on you here.

DAISY, *coming forward.* You have as good a right here as I. I don't think I have any.

WINTERBOURNE. You mean as an invalid? I am very happy to see you better.

DAISY. Thank you. I'm very well.

WINTERBOURNE. I asked about you every day.

DAISY. They never told me.

WINTERBOURNE. That was your faithful courier!

DAISY. He was so frightened at my illness that he couldn't remember anything.

WINTERBOURNE. Oh, yes, he was terribly afraid he should lose you. For a couple of days it was very serious.

DAISY. How do you know that?

WINTERBOURNE. I asked the doctor.

DAISY, *aside.* He's very strange. Why should he care?

WINTERBOURNE. He said you had done what might kill you.

DAISY. At the Colosseum?

WINTERBOURNE. At the Colosseum.

DAISY. Why didn't you tell me that, when you saw me there?

WINTERBOURNE. Because you had an adviser in whom you have much more faith.

DAISY. Mr. Giovanelli? Oh, it's not his fault. He begged me to come away.

WINTERBOURNE. If you didn't mind him, you wouldn't have minded me.

DAISY. I didn't care what happened. But I noticed, all the same, that you didn't speak to me.

WINTERBOURNE. I had nothing to say.

DAISY. You only bowed, very low.

WINTERBOURNE. That was to express my great respect.

DAISY. I had never had such a bow before.

WINTERBOURNE. You had never been so worthy of it!

DAISY, *aside.* He despises me! Well, I don't care! (*Aloud.*) It was lovely there in the moonlight.

WINTERBOURNE. I was sure you found it so. That was another reason I didn't wish to interrupt you.

DAISY, *playing indifference.* What were you doing there, all alone?

WINTERBOURNE. I had been dining at a villa in that part of Rome, and I simply stopped, as I walked home, to take a look at the splended ruin.

DAISY, *after a pause, in the same manner.* I shouldn't think you'd go round alone.

WINTERBOURNE. I have to go as I can; I haven't your resources.

DAISY. Don't you know any ladies?

WINTERBOURNE. Yes; but they don't expose themselves . . .

DAISY, *with quick emotion.* Expose themselves to be treated as you treated me!

WINTERBOURNE. You're rather difficult to please. (*Re-enter the waiter.*)

THE WAITER. Madame de Katkoff will come in about ten minutes, sir.

WINTERBOURNE. Very good.

THE WAITER. She's just pouring out tea for the company.

WINTERBOURNE. That will do.

THE WAITER, *smiling*. You know the Russians must have their tea, sir.

WINTERBOURNE. You talk too much.

THE WAITER, *going out*. He's very sharp tonight! (*Exit Waiter.*)

DAISY, *who has turned away a moment, coming down*. If you expecting some one, I'll go away.

WINTERBOURNE. There's another public room. I'll see my friend there.

DAISY. I've nothing to do here. (*Goes towards the door, but stops half-way, looking at him.*) You see a great deal of Madame de Katkoff. Doesn't *she* expose herself?

WINTERBOURNE, *smiling*. To dangerous consequences? Never!

DAISY. *She comes down again, as if unable to decide to leave him. Aside.* I'm determined to know what he thinks. (*Aloud, in a different tone.*) I was going out on the balcony, to see what's going on.

WINTERBOURNE. Aren't you afraid of the night air?

DAISY. I'm not afraid of anything!

WINTERBOURNE. Are you going to begin again?

DAISY. Ah, I'm too late! It's nearly over. (*At the moment she speaks, Mrs. Costello appears in the window, from the balcony. Re-enter Mrs. Costello.*)

MRS. C., *to Winterbourne*. Merciful powers! I thought you were Mr. Reverdy! (*Looking at Daisy.*) And that this young lady was my Alice!

DAISY. Something very different, you see! Now I can have the balcony. (*She passes out of the window.*)

MRS. C. What are you doing with that girl? I thought you had dropped her.

WINTERBOURNE. I was asking about her health. She has been down with the fever.

MRS. C. It will do her good—make her reflect on her sins. But what have you done with my young companions?

WINTERBOURNE. Nothing in the world. The last I saw of them they were frolicking in the Corso.

MRS. C. Frolicking in the Corso? Alice and Mr. Reverdy?

WINTERBOURNE. I met them as I was coming from my lodgings to the hotel. He was blowing a tin trumpet, and she was hiding behind a mask.

MRS. C. A tin trumpet and a mask! Have they gone to perdition?

WINTERBOURNE. They are only taking advantage of the Carnival.

MRS. C. Taking advantage of my back; I had turned it for three minutes! They were on the balcony with me, looking at this vulgar riot, and they slipped away to come in here.

WINTERBOURNE. You never give them a chance: they hunger and thirst!

MRS. C. A chance to masquerade? Think of their education!

WINTERBOURNE. I'm thinking of it now. You see the results.

MRS. C. I said to myself that I was perhaps too vigilant, and I left them here a moment to talk things over. I saw through the window a young lady and a gentleman, and I took it for granted it was they.

WINTERBOURNE. Ingenuous aunt! They were already a mile away!

MRS. C. It's too horrible to believe. You must immediately bring them back.

WINTERBOURNE. Impossible just now. I have an engagement here.

MRS. C. I'll go and look for them myself!

WINTERBOURNE, *laying his hand on her arm.* Don't, don't! Let them have a little fun!

MRS. C. I never heard of anything so cynical!

WINTERBOURNE. Don't you want them to marry?

MRS. C. To marry, yes; but not to elope!

WINTERBOURNE. Let them do it in their own way.

MRS. C. With a mask and a tin trumpet? A girl I've watched like that!

WINTERBOURNE. You've watched too much. They'll come home engaged.

MRS. C. Ah, bring them, then, quickly!

WINTERBOURNE. I'll go down into the street and look; and if I see them, I'll tell them what's expected of them.

MRS. C. I'll go to my room; I feel a headache coming on. (*Before she goes out, to herself, as if a thought has struck her.*) Had they bribed that monster to kiss his hand? (*Exeunt.*)

SCENE IV. GIOVANELLI. DAISY. *He enters the room, and she comes in from the balcony at the same moment. He advances with a radiant smile, takes both of her hands, holds them for a moment devotedly, then kisses each of them.*

GIOVANELLI. *Carissima signorina!* When I see you restored to health, I begin to live myself!

DAISY. Poor old Giovanelli! I believe you *do* care for me!

GIOVANELLI. Care for you? When I heard you were ill, I neither ate nor slept. I thought I, too, should have to have the doctor.

DAISY, *laughing.* I should have sent you mine if I had known it. You must eat a good supper tonight, for I am all right now.

GIOVANELLI. You look still a little pale.

DAISY. I look like a fright, of course, in this dreadful dress; but I'm only a convalescent. If I had known you were coming, I should have worn something better.

GIOVANELLI. You look like an angel, always. You might have been sure I would come, after so many days. I was always at your door, asking for news. But now, I think, we shall never again be separated.

DAISY. Never again? Oh, don't talk about the future! What were you doing there in the street?

GIOVANELLI. When I looked up and saw you on the balcony, bending over like a little saint in her shrine? It was that vision that made me come up again.

DAISY. You had gone out to enjoy the Carnival?

GIOVANELLI. I had come here to see you; but I learned from your excellent Eugenio that your mother and your brother were going out in a carriage. They appeared at that moment, and I went down with them to the door, to wish them a happy drive. Little Randolph was greatly excited.

DAISY. He insisted on mother's going she'll do anything for Randolph. But she didn't want to leave me.

GIOVANELLI, *smiling.* She has left you to me!

DAISY. Did Eugenio go with them?

GIOVANELLI. Oh, yes; he got into the carriage. (*Aside.*) The cheek of that man!

DAISY. They have left me alone, then.

GIOVANELLI. I am almost of the family, dear Miss!

DAISY, *apparently not hearing him, listening to the sounds from without.* They oughtn't to have left me alone—when I'm sick, when I'm weak.

GIOVANELLI, *anxiously.* You are not so well, then, as you say?

DAISY, *looking at him a moment, with a little laugh.* You look so scared at the idea of losing me! Poor old Giovanelli! What should you do if you were to lose me?

GIOVANELLI. Don't speak of it—it's horrible! If you are not well, you should go to your room.

DAISY. Oh, I'm all right. I only wanted to frighten you.

GIOVANELLI. It isn't kind—when you know how I love you!

DAISY. I don't know it, and I don't want to know it, as I've told you often. I forbid you to speak of that.

GIOVANELLI. You will never let me mention the future.

DAISY. I hate the future; I care only for the present!

GIOVANELLI. The future is the present, when one sees it as we see it.

DAISY. I don't see it at all, and I don't want to see it. I saw it for a moment, when I was sick, and that was enough.

GIOVANELLI. You have suffered much; but it was not my fault.

DAISY. I don't blame you, Giovanelli. You are very kind. Where are they going, mother and Randolph?

GIOVANELLI. Up and down the Corso; wherever there is something to see. They have an open carriage, with lots of flowers.

DAISY. It must be charming. Have you been going round?

GIOVANELLI. I have strolled about a little.

DAISY. Is it very, *very* amusing?

GIOVANELLI. Ah, you know, I'm an old Roman; I have seen it many times. The illumination is better than usual, and the music is lively enough.

DAISY. Listen to the music—listen to it!

GIOVANELLI, *smiling.* You mustn't let it go to your head. (*Daisy goes to the window, and stands there a moment.*) She has never been so lovely as tonight!

DAISY, *coming back, with decision.* Giovanelli, you must get me a carriage.

GIOVANELLI, *startled.* A carriage, signorina?

DAISY. I must go out—I *must*!

GIOVANELLI. There is not a carriage to be had at this hour. Everything is taken for the fête.

DAISY. Then I'll go on foot. You must take me.

GIOVANELLI. Into the air of the night, and the crowded streets? It's enough to kill you!

DAISY. It's a lovely night, as mild as June; and it's only for five minutes.

GIOVANELLI. The softer the night, the greater the danger of the malaria. Five minutes, in your condition, would bring back the fever.

DAISY. I shall have the fever if I stay here listening, longing, fidgeting! You said I was pale; but it's only the delicacy of my complexion.

GIOVANELLI. You are not pale now; you have a little spot in either cheek. Your mother will not be happy.

DAISY. She shouldn't have left me alone, then.

GIOVANELLI. You are not alone when you're with me.

DAISY. Of what use are you, except to take me out?

GIOVANELLI. It's impossible to contradict you. For five minutes, then, remember!

DAISY. For five minutes, then; or for ten! I'll go and get ready. Don't mind about the carriage: we'll do it better on foot.

GIOVANELLI, *at the door.* It's at your own risk, you know. I'll try for a cab.

DAISY. My own risk! I'm not afraid.

GIOVANELLI, *kissing his hand to her.* You are awfully beautiful! (*Exit Giovanelli.*)

DAISY, *alone.* I'm not afraid—I don't care. I don't like him tonight; he's too serious. I would rather be out-of-doors with him than shut up here. Poor Giovanelli; if he thinks I love him, after all I've said to the contrary . . . I can dress in three minutes. (*She is going to the door opposite to the one through which Giovanelli has made his exit when Madame de Katkoff comes in, meeting her.*)

SCENE V. DAISY. MADAME DE KATKOFF. *They stand a moment, looking at each other.*

MME. DE KATKOFF, *very kindly.* I have not the pleasure of knowing you, though we have spent half the winter in the same hotel; but I have heard of your illness, and you must let me tell you how glad I am to see you better.

DAISY, *aside.* Why does she speak to me? I don't like her, nor want to know her. (*Aloud.*) Thank you, I'm better. I'm going out.

MME. DE K. You must be better, indeed: but (*with interest*) you look a little flushed.

DAISY. It's talking with a stranger. I think I must go.

MME. DE K. Perhaps you can tell me something first. A gentleman sent me his name, and I was told I should find him here. May I ask you whether you have seen such a person?

DAISY. If you mean Mr. Winterbourne, he was here just now; but he went away with his aunt.

MME. DE K. I suppose he'll come back, then. But he oughtn't to keep me waiting.

DAISY, *very coldly.* I haven't the least idea what he ought to do. I know nothing whatever of his movements.

MME. DE K., *aside.* Poor little thing, she hates me! But she doesn't hate *him.* (*Aloud.*) I'm a stranger as you say; but I should be very glad to become a little less of one.

DAISY. Why should you want to know me? I'm not of your age.

MME. DE K., *aside, smiling.* She hates me indeed! (*Aloud.*) I should be tempted to say that we might know each other a little as mother and daughter—if I hadn't heard that you are already the devoted daughter of a devoted mother.

DAISY. She's good enough for me—and I'm good enough for her.

MME. DE K., *more and more gracious.* I envy you both, and I am happy to have the opportunity of saying so. One doesn't know how pretty you are till one talks to you.

DAISY. If you are laughing at my dress, I am just going to change it.

MME. DE K. Laughing at your dress? It has always been my admiration.

DAISY, *aside.* What does she mean by that? It's not as good as hers. (*Aloud.*) I can't stay with you. I'm going to the Carnival.

MME. DE K. It will last all night; you have plenty of time. I have heard Mr. Winterbourne speak of you.

DAISY. I didn't suppose he ever did that.

MME. DE K. Oh! very often. That's why I want to know you.

DAISY. It's a strange reason. He must have told you pretty things of me.

MME. DE K. He has told me you're a charming young girl.

DAISY, *aside.* Oh, what an awful story! (*Aloud.*) I don't understand what you want of me.

MME. DE K., *aside.* I can hardly tell her that I want to make up to her for the harm I have done her, for I can't do that unless I give up everything. (*Aloud, as if struck by an idea.*) I want to be kind to you. I want to keep you from going out.

DAISY, *smiling.* I don't think you can do that.

MME. DE K. You are barely convalescent: you mustn't expose yourself.

DAISY. It won't hurt any one but me.

MME. DE K. We all take a great interest in you. We should be in despair if you were to have a relapse.

DAISY. You all despise me and think me dreadful; that's what you all do!

MME. DE K. Where did you learn that remarkable fact?

DAISY. Mr. Winterbourne told me—since you speak of Mr. Winterbourne.

MME. DE K. I don't think you understood him. Mr. Winterbourne is a perfect gentleman.

DAISY. Have you come here to praise him to me? That's strange—for you!

MME. DE K. You know at least that I consider him an excellent friend.

DAISY. I know nothing whatever about it. (*Aside.*) She wants to torture me—to triumph!

MME. DE K., *aside.* She's as proud as she's pretty! (*Aloud.*) Are you going out alone?

DAISY. No, indeed. I have a friend.

MME. DE K., *aside.* A friend as well as I. (*Aloud.*) My dear child, I am very sorry for you. You have too many wrong ideas.

DAISY. That's exactly what they say!

MME. DE K. I don't mean it as other people may have meant it. You make a great many mistakes.

DAISY. As many as I possibly can! In American I was always right.

MME. DE K. Try and believe you are in America now. I'm not an American, but I want to be your friend.

DAISY. I'm much obliged to you, but I don't trust you.

MME. DE K. You trust the wrong people. With whom are you going out?

DAISY. I don't think I'm obliged to tell you.

MME. DE K., *gently*. I ask for a very good motive.

DAISY, *aside*. She may be better than I think. (*Aloud.*) With Mr. Giovanelli.

MME. DE K., *smiling*. A mysterious Italian—introduced by your courier!

DAISY, *with simplicity*. Oh, no; Eugenio got some one else!

MME. DE K., *aside*. Adorable innocence! (*Aloud.*) That's all I wanted to know.

DAISY. I hope you've got nothing to say against him.

MME. DE K. Nothing but this: he's not a gentlemen.

DAISY. Not a gentleman? Poor old Giovanelli!

MME. DE K., *aside*. 'Poor old Giovanelli?' Good! (*Aloud.*) If he were a gentleman, he wouldn't ask you to do what you tell me you are on the point of doing.

DAISY. He never asked me. He does what I wish!

MME. DE K., *aside*. She doesn't care a fig for him—and I should like to exasperate the courier. (*Aloud.*) It's none of my business; but why do you wish, in your condition, to go out?

DAISY. Because it's the last night of the Carnival, and I have no one else to take me.

MME. DE K. Excuse me; but where is your mother?

DAISY. Gone out with my brother.

MME. DE K., *aside*. Extraordinary family! (*Aloud.*) Let me make you an offer: I will order out my carriage, and take you myself.

DAISY, *staring*. Take me yourself? (*Then abruptly, ironically.*) Pray, what would become of Mr. Winterbourne?

MME. DE K., *aside*. She adores him! (*Aloud.*) Ah, you don't care for Giovanelli!

DAISY. Whether I care for him or not, I mustn't keep him waiting. (*Exit Daisy, hastily.*)

MME. DE K., *alone*. She's trembling with agitation, and her poor little heart is full. She thought I wished to torment her. My position is odiously false! And to think I hold her happiness in my hands! (*Winterbourne comes in.*) His, too, poor fellow! Ah, I can't hold it any longer!

SCENE VI. MME. DE KATKOFF. WINTERBOURNE.

WINTERBOURNE. I am afraid I have kept you waiting. I was carried away by my aunt.

MME. DE K. Is she keeping the Carnival, your aunt?

WINTERBOURNE. No, but her companions are. They are masquerading in the Corso, and she's in despair. She sent me to hunt them up, but they are lost in the crowd.

MME. DE K. Do you mean the young lady whom you described as so prim? If that's a specimen of her primness, I was right in my little theory.

WINTERBOURNE. Your little theory?

MME. DE K. That the grave ones are the gay ones.

WINTERBOURNE. Poor Miss Durant isn't gay: she's simply desperate. My aunt keeps such watch at the door that she has been obliged to jump out of the window.—Have you waited very long?

MME. DE K. I hardly know. I have had company—Miss Daisy Miller!

WINTERBOURNE. That must have made the time fly!

MME. DE K. She's very touching.

WINTERBOURNE. Very, indeed. She has gone to pieces.

MME. DE K. Gone to pieces?

WINTERBOURNE. She's quite impossible. You oughtn't to talk to her.

MME. DE K., *aside.* Ah, what a fool I've made of him! (*Aloud.*) You think she'll corrupt my innocence?

WINTERBOURNE, *after a moment.* I don't like you to speak of her. Please don't.

MME. DE K. She completes my little theory—that the gay ones are the grave ones.

WINTERBOURNE. If she's grave, she well may be: her situation is intensely grave. As for her native solemnity, you used to insist upon that when, for reasons best known to yourself, you conceived the remarkable design of inducing me to make love to her. You dropped the idea as suddenly as you took it up; but I'm very sorry to see any symptoms of your taking it up again. It seems to me it's hardly the moment.

MME. DE K., *aside.* It's more the moment than you think.

WINTERBOURNE, *rather harshly.* I was very sorry to learn, on coming here, that you have your rooms full of people.

MME. DE K. They have come to look out of my windows. It is not my fault that I have such a view of the Corso.

WINTERBOURNE. You had given me to understand that we should be alone.

MME. DE K. I didn't ask them; they came themselves.

WINTERBOURNE, *impatiently.* I wish to goodness they had stayed at home!

MME. DE K. Should you like me to turn them out?

WINTERBOURNE. I should like it particularly.

MME. DE K. The ambassador and all?

WINTERBOURNE. You told me a month ago that where I was concerned you didn't care a straw for the ambassador.

MME. DE K., *after a moment.* A month ago—yes!

WINTERBOURNE. If you intended to change so soon, you ought to have notified me at the moment.

MME. DE K. The ambassador is very considerate. When I have a few visitors, he helps me to entertain them.

WINTERBOURNE. That proves how little you have need of me.

MME. DE K. I have left my guests in his charge, with perfect confidence.

WINTERBOURNE. Oh, if you mean you are at liberty, that's just what I want.

MME. DE K. What does it occur to you to propose?

WINTERBOURNE. That you should drive out with me, to see the illumination.

MME. DE K. I have seen fifty illuminations! I am sick of the Carnival.

WINTERBOURNE. It isn't the Carnival; it's the drive. I have a carriage at the door.

MME. DE K. I have no doubt it would be charming; but I am not at liberty in that sense. I can't leave a roomful of people planted there! I really don't see why they should make you so savage.

WINTERBOURNE. I am not savage, but I am disappointed. I counted on this evening: it's a week since we have been alone.

MME. DE K. Do I appear to so little advantage in company? Are you ashamed of me when others are present? I do the best I can.

WINTERBOURNE. You were always strange—and you always will be! Sometimes I think you have taken a vow to torment me.

MME. DE K. I have taken a vow—that's very true! and I admit I'm strange. We Russians are, you know: you had warning of that!

WINTERBOURNE. Yes; but you abuse the national privilege. I'm never safe with you—never sure of you. You turn from one thing to the other.

MME. DE K., *aside.* Poor fellow, he's bewildered! (*Aloud.*) Will you do me a favour?

WINTERBOURNE. I'm sure it's something horrible!

MME. DE K. You say you have a carriage at the door. Take it, and go after that poor girl.

WINTERBOURNE. Oh, are you coming back to *her*? You try my patience!

MME. DE K. She has just risen from an attack of fever, and it strikes her as a knowing thing to finish her evening in the streets!

WINTERBOURNE, *starting a little.* She has gone out—looking that way?

MME. DE K., *aside.* That will touch him! (*Aloud.*) She won't come home alive.

WINTERBOURNE, *attentive.* Do you believe that?

MME. DE K., *aside.* It *has* touched him. (*Aloud.*) I think it's madness. Her only safety was to have left Rome the moment she could be moved.

WINTERBOURNE, *after a pause.* I'm not sure the best thing that can happen to her is not to die! She ought to perish in her flower, as she once said to me!

MME. DE K. That's a convenient theory, to save you the trouble of a drive!

WINTERBOURNE. You're remarkably pressing, but you had better spare your sarcasm. I have no further interest in the fate of Miss Daisy Miller, and no commission whatever to interfere with her movements. She has a mother—a sort of one—and she has other protectors. I don't suppose she has gone out alone.

MME. DE K. She has gone with her Italian.

WINTERBOURNE. Giovanelli? Ah, the scoundrel!

MME. DE K., *smiling, aside.* My dear friend, you're all right. (*Aloud.*) Gently, gently! It's not *his* fault.

WINTERBOURNE. That she is infatuated? Perhaps not.

MME. DE K. Infatuated? She doesn't care a straw for him!

WINTERBOURNE. And to prove her indifference, she lets him take her on this devil's drive? I don't quite see it.

MME. DE K. He's her convenience—her little pretext—her poor old Giovanelli. He fetches and carries, and she finds him very useful; but that's the end of it. She takes him to drive: he doesn't take her.

WINTERBOURNE. Did she kindly inform you of these interesting facts?

MME. DE K. I had a long talk with her. One woman understands another!

WINTERBOURNE. I hope she understands you. It's more than I do.

MME. DE K. She has gone out because she's unhappy. She doesn't care what becomes of her.

WINTERBOURNE. I never suspected her of such tragic propensities. Pray, what is she unhappy about?

MME. DE K. About the hard things people say of her.

WINTERBOURNE. She has only to behave like other girls, then.

MME. DE K. Like your friend, Miss Durant? A pretty model, this evening! You say you hope poor Daisy understands me. but she doesn't—and that's part of the misery. She can't make out what I have made of you!

WINTERBOURNE. A creature as miserable as herself! You might have explained: you had the opportunity.

MME. DE K. She left me abruptly—and I lost it forever!

WINTERBOURNE. All this is nothing to *us*. When will your friends leave you?

MME. DE K., *after a pause*. No, it's nothing to us.—I haven't asked my friends how long they mean to stay.

WINTERBOURNE. Till eleven o'clock—till twelve?

MME. DE K. Till one in the morning, perhaps—or till two. They will see the Carnival out. (*Smiling*.) You had much better join us!

WINTERBOURNE, *passionately*. Unfathomable woman! In pity's name, what did you mean by raising my hopes to such a point, a month ago, only to dash them to the ground?

MME. DE K. I tried to make you happy—but I didn't succeed.

WINTERBOURNE. You tried? Are you trying now?

MME. DE K. No, I have given it up: it's a waste of time!

WINTERBOURNE. Have you forgotten the day on the Pincian, after your arrival, and what you suddenly offered me—what you promised me—there? You had kept me at arm's length for three years, and suddenly the barrier dropped. The angel of justice has kept the record of my gratitude and eagerness—as well as of my surprise; and if my tenderness and respect were not greater than ever, it is because you had already had the best of them! Have you forgotten our moonlight drive through the streets of Rome, with its rich confusion of ancient memories and new-born hopes? You were perfect that evening, and for many days afterwards. But suddenly you began to change—to be absent, to be silent, to be cold, to go back to your old attitude. Tonight it's as if you were trying to make me angry! Do you wish to throw me over, and leave me lying in the dust? Are you only the most audacious of coquettes?

MME. DE K. It's not I who have changed; it's you! Of course I remember our moonlight drive, and how glad you were to take it. You were happy for an hour—you were happy for three days. There was novelty and excitement in finding that, after all, I had a heart in my bosom; and for a moment the discovery amused you. But only for a moment! So long as I refused to listen to you, you cared for me. From the day I confessed myself touched, I became a bore!

WINTERBOURNE. If you want to get rid of me, don't put it off on *me!*

MME. DE K. You don't really care for me; your heart is somewhere else. You are too proud to confess it, but your love for me is an elaborate deception.

WINTERBOURNE. The deception is yours, then, not mine!

MME. DE K. You are restless, discontented, unhappy. You are sore and sick at heart, and you have tried to forget it in persuading yourself that *I* can cure your pain. I *can* cure it; but not by encouraging your illusion!

WINTERBOURNE. If you thought it an illusion, why did you turn there and smile on me?

MME. DE K. Because I was vile and wicked—because I have played a part and worn a mask, like those idiots in the Carnival—because I'm a most unhappy woman!

WINTERBOURNE, *looking at her, surprised.* I assure you, I understand you less and less!

MME. DE K. I had an end to gain, and I thought it precious; but I have suddenly begun to loathe it! When I met that poor girl just now, and looked into her face, I was filled with compassion and shame. She is dying, I say, and between us we are killing her! Dying because she loves you, and because she thinks you despise her! Dying because you have turned away from her, and she has tried to stifle the pang! Dying because I have held you here—under compulsion of a scoundrel—and she thinks she has lost you forever! I read it all in her eyes—the purest I ever saw! I am sick of the ghastly comedy, and I must tell the miserable truth. If you'll believe me, it's not too late!

WINTERBOURNE, *amazed and bewildered.* Under compulsion—of a scoundrel?

MME. DE K. I have the misfortune to be in the clutches of one, and so has our little friend. You know that her mother's horrible courier was once in my husband's service. Thanks to that accident, he has some papers of mine which I wish to buy back. To make me pay for them, he has forced me to play his game.

WINTERBOURNE. His game? What has he to do with a game?

MME. DE K. I don't defend him: I explain. He has selected a husband for his young lady, and your superior attractions had somehow to be muffled up. You were to be kept out of the way.

WINTERBOURNE, *frowning.* Because I love her? (*Correcting himself.*) I mean, because he thinks so?

MME. DE K., *smiling.* You see I'm right! Because *she* loves you: he has discovered that! So he had the happy thought of saying to me, 'Keep Mr. Winterbourne employed, and if the young lady marries my candidate you shall have your letter.'

WINTERBOURNE. Your letter? What letter?

MME. DE K. A very silly—but very innocent—one that I wrote some ten years ago.

WINTERBOURNE. Why didn't you ask me to get it?

MME. DE K. Because I didn't want it enough for that; and now I don't want it at all.

WINTERBOURNE. You shall have it—I promise you that.

MME. DE K. You are very generous, after the trick I have played you.

WINTERBOURNE. The trick? Was it *all* a trick?

MME. DE K. An infamous, pitiless trick! I was frightened, I was tempted, I was demoralized; he had me in his power. To be cruel to you was bad enough: to be cruel to her was a crime I shall try to expiate!

WINTERBOURNE, *seated, his head in his hands.* You'll excuse me if I feel rather stunned.

MME. DE K., *sinking on her knees.* I ask your forgiveness! I have been living in a bad dream.

WINTERBOURNE. Ah, you have hurt me—more than I can say!

MME. DE K., *rising to her feet.* Don't think of yourself,—think of her! If I had only met her before, how much sooner *I* should have done that! We will go and find her together; we will bring her back; we will nurse her and comfort her, and make her understand!

WINTERBOURNE. It's all so extraordinary—and I have only your word for it.

MME. DE K. See if she contradicts me when you tell her you love her! You don't venture to deny that.

WINTERBOURNE. I have denied it to myself: why shouldn't I deny it to you!

MME. DE K. You have denied it to yourself? Who, then, had charged you with it?

WINTERBOURNE. You are not consistent, but you are perhaps more consistent than I! And you are very deep!

MME. DE K. I am deep enough to be very sure that from this moment forward I shall be nothing to you. If I have cured you of a baseless passion, that at least is a good work. Venture to say that for these three weeks I have satisfied you.

WINTERBOURNE, *turning away.* You are pitiless—you are terrible!

MME. DE K., *looking at him a moment.* My vanity bleeds: be that my penance! Don't lose time. Go to her now.

WINTERBOURNE, *in thought, gloomily.* Dying?—Dying?—Dying?

MME. DE K. That was a little for the sake of argument. She will live again—for you!

WINTERBOURNE, *in the same tone.* Gone out with that man? Always with him!

MME. DE K. My dear friend, she has her little pride, as well as you. She pretends to flirt with Giovanelli because her poor, swollen heart whispers to her to be brave!

WINTERBOURNE, *uncertain.* Pretends—only pretends?

MME. DE K., *impatient.* Oh, you've been stupid; but be clever now!

WINTERBOURNE. *after a pause.* How am I to know that this is not another trick?

MME. DE K., *clasping her hands, but smiling.* Have mercy on me! Those words are my punishment!

WINTERBOURNE. I have been an idiot—I have been a brute—I have been a butcher!

MME. DE K. Perhaps she has come back. For God's sake, go and see!

WINTERBOURNE. And if she's still out there? I can't talk of these things in the street.

MME. DE K. Bring her home, bring her home! Every moment's a danger. I offered to go with you; but you would rather go alone.

WINTERBOURNE, *takes up his hat.* Yes, I would rather go alone. You have hurt me very much; but you shall have your letter.

MME. DE K. I don't care for my letter now. There's such a weight off my heart that I don't feel that one. (*She leaves the room by the right, and Winterbourne is on the point of quitting it on the other side, when Mrs. Walker, Miss Durant and Charles Reverdy come in, meeting him.*)

SCENE VII. WINTERBOURNE. MRS. WALKER. MISS DURANT. REVERDY.

MRS. W. Pray, where is your aunt, Mr. Winterbourne? I have brought her back her truants.

WINTERBOURNE. She has retired to her room, to nurse a headache produced by the sudden collapse of her illusions.

MISS D. I thought she would be rather shocked; but Mr. Reverdy assured me that in the Carnival all common laws are suspended.

REVERDY. So we thought the law that governs Mrs. Costello's headaches might conform to the others.

WINTERBOURNE. What did you think about the law that governs her temper?

REVERDY. Nothing at all, because, as far as I have ascertained, there isn't any!

MRS. W., *to Winterbourne.* They were jostling along, arm in arm, in the midst of the excited populace. I saw them from my carriage, and, having the Consul with me, I immediately overhauled them. The young lady had a wonderful disguise, but I recognized her from Mr. Reverdy's manner.

MISS D. There, sir, I told you you had too much!

REVERDY, *aside.* One needs a good deal, when one's about to make an offer of one's heart. (*Aloud.*) It takes a vast deal of manner to carry off a tin trumpet! (*Winterbourne has listened to this absently; he appears restless and preoccupied; walks up, and goes out upon the balcony.*)

MRS. W., *noting Winterbourne.* What's the matter with him?—All I can say is that in my representative position I thought I must interfere.

REVERDY, *aside.* The wife of the Consul again? Our consuls ought to be bachelors!

MRS. W. You were dragging her along, with your arm placed as if you were waltzing.

REVERDY. That's very true; we were just trying a few rounds.

MRS. W. In that dense mass of people, where you were packed like sardines?

REVERDY. We were all turning together; it was all one waltz!

MRS. W., *to Miss Durant.* Mrs. Costello, my dear, will make you dance in earnest!

MISS D. I don't care for Mrs. Costello now!

REVERDY. Let me thank you for those noble words. (*Aside.*) You understood, then?

MISS D., *ingenuous.* Understood what?

REVERDY. What I was saying when she came down on us.

MISS D. Oh, yes, as far as you'd got!

REVERDY. I must get a little farther.

MRS. W., *who has gone up to Winterbourne, and comes down with him.* You may be interested to hear that I saw our little friend in the crowd.

WINTERBOURNE. Our little friend!

MRS. W. Whom we tried to save from drowning. I didn't try this time.

WINTERBOURNE. In the crowd, on foot?

MRS. W. In the thickest and roughest part of it, on Giovanelli's arm. The crush was so dense, it was enough to kill her.

MISS D. They are very good-natured, but you *do* suffocate!

MRS. W. She'll suffocate easily, in her weak state.

WINTERBOURNE. Oh, I can't stand this! Excuse me. (*Exit Winterbourne.*)

MRS. W. What's the matter with him, I should like to know?

MISS D. He has been like that these three weeks, rushing in and out—always in a fidget.

REVERDY, *to Mrs. Walker.* He's in love with Miss Durant, and he can't stand the spectacle of our mutual attachment.

MISS D., *gayly.* You horrid vain creature! If that's all that troubles him!

REVERDY, *aside.* She'll accept me! (*Aloud.*) Courage—the old lady! (*Enter Mrs. Costello.*)

SCENE VIII. MRS. WALKER. MISS DURANT. REVERDY. MRS. COSTELLO: *then* DAISY. WINTERBOURNE. GIOVANELLI. MME. DE KATKOFF.

MRS. C. (*She stops a moment, looking sternly from Miss Durant to Reverdy.*) Alice Durant, have you forgotten your education?

MISS D. Dear Cousin Louisa, my education made no provision for the Carnival!

REVERDY. That's not in the regular course; it's one of the extras.

MISS D. I was just going to your room, to tell you we had come back.

MRS. C. I've passed an hour there, in horrible torture. I could stand it no longer: I came to see if, for very shame, you hadn't reappeared.

MRS. W. The Consul and I picked them up, and made them get into our carriage. So you see it was not for shame!

REVERDY. It wasn't for ours, at least; it was for yours.

MRS. C., *with majesty, to Miss Durant.* We shall start for America tomorrow.

MISS D. I'm delighted to hear it. *There*, at least, we can walk about.

MRS. C. Ah, but you'll find no Carnival!

REVERDY. My dear Madam, we shall make our own.

MRS. C., *aside to Miss Durant.* This time, it's to be hoped, he has done it?

MISS D., *blushing and looking down.* He was on the very point, when Mrs. Walker interrupted!

MRS. C. I declare, it's beyond a joke—to take you back just as I brought you.

MISS D. It's very tiresome; but it's not my fault.

REVERDY, *who has been talking to Mrs. Walker.* Miss Alice, shall we try the balcony again?

MRS. C. It's past midnight, if you please; time for us all to retire.

REVERDY. That's just what I propose: to retire to the balcony!

MISS D., *to Mrs. Costello.* Just occupy Mrs. Walker!

REVERDY, *to Mrs. Walker.* Just keep hold of Mrs. Costello! (*Offers his arm to Miss Durant, and leads her to the balcony.*)

MRS. W., *looking after them.* I must wait till the Consul comes. My dear friend, I hope those young people are engaged.

MRS. C., *with asperity.* They might be, if it hadn't been for you!

MRS. W., *surprised.* Pray, how have I prevented? . . .

MRS. C. You interrupted Mr. Reverdy, just now, in the very middle . . .

MRS. W. The middle of a declaration? I thought it was a jig? (*As the door of the room is flung open.*) Bless my soul! what's this? (*Enter rapidly Winterbourne, carrying Daisy, in a swoon, in his arms, and followed by Giovanelli, who looks both extremely alarmed and extremely indignant. At the same moment Madame de Katkoff enters from the opposite side.*)

MME. DE K., *with a cry.* Ah, it's all over! She is gone!

WINTERBOURNE. A chair! A chair! Heaven forgive us, she is dying! (*Giovanelli has quickly pushed forward a large arm-chair, in which Winterbourne places Daisy with great tenderness. She lies there motionless and unconscious. The others gather round. Miss Durant and Reverdy come in from the balcony.*)

MRS. C., *seeing the two last.* Ah, they're interrupted again!

MRS. W. This time, she's really drowned!

GIOVANELLI, *much agitated, but smiling to Mrs. Costello and Mrs. Walker.* It will pass in a moment. It is only the effect of the crowd—the pressure of the mob!

WINTERBOURNE, *beside Daisy with passionate tenderness.* It will pass—because *she's* passing! Dead—dead—in my arms!

MRS. C.. *harshly.* A pretty place for her to be! She'll come to life again: they don't die like that.

MRS. W., *indignant, to Giovanelli.* The pressure of the mob? A proper pressure to subject her to!

GIOVANELLI, *bewildered and apologetic.* She was so lovely that they all made way; but just near the hotel we encountered one of those enormous cars, laden with musicians and maskers. The crowd was driven back, and we were hustled and smothered. She gave a little cry, and before I knew it she had fainted. The next moment this gentleman—by I know not what warrant—had taken her in his arms.

WINTERBOURNE. By the warrant of being her countryman! Instead of entertaining those ladies, you had better go for a doctor.

GIOVANELLI. They have sent from the hotel. Half a dozen messengers started.

REVERDY. Half a dozen is no one at all! I'll go and bring one myself—in five minutes.

MISS D. Go, go, my dear! I give you leave. (*Reverdy hurries out.*)

MRS. C., *to Miss Durant.* 'My dear, my dear'? Has he done it, then?

MISS D. Oh yes, we just managed it. (*Looking at Daisy.*) Poor little thing!

MRS. C. Ah, *she* hasn't a husband!

WINTERBOURNE, *angry, desperate, to the others.* Can't you do something? Can't you speak to her?—can't you help her?

MRS. W. I'll do anything in the world! I'll go for the Consul. (*She hurries away on the right.*)

MRS. C. I've got something in my room—a precious elixir, that I use for my headaches. (*To Miss Durant.*) But I'll not leave *you!*

MISS D. Not even now?

MRS. C. Not till you're married. (*They depart on the left.*)

WINTERBOURNE, *holding Daisy's hands and looking into her face.* Daisy!—Daisy! —*Daisy!*

MME. DE K., *who all this time has been kneeling on the other side of her, her face buried on the arm of the chair, in the attitude of a person weeping.* If she can hear that, my friend, she's saved! (*To Daisy, appealing.*) My child, my child, we have wronged you, but we love you!

WINTERBOURNE, *in the same manner.* Daisy, my dearest, my darling! Wake a moment, if only to forgive me!

MME. DE K. She moves a little! (*Aside, rising to her feet.*) He never spoke so to me!

GIOVANELLI, *a little apart, looking round him.* Where is he, where is he—that ruffian Eugenio?

WINTERBOURNE. In the name of pity, has no one gone for her mother? (*To Giovanelli.*) Don't stand there, sir! Go for her mother!

GIOVANELLI, *angrily.* Give your commands to some one else! It is not for me to do your errands.

MME. DE K., *going to him pleadingly.* Haven't you common compassion? Do you want to see the child die?

GIOVANELLI, *folding his arms.* I would rather see her die than live to be his!

WINTERBOURNE. There is little hope of her being mine. I have insulted—I have defamed—her innocence!

GIOVANELLI. Ay, speak of her innocence. Her innocence was divine!

DAISY, *stirring and murmuring.* Mother! Mother!

WINTERBOURNE. She lives, she lives, and she shall choose between us!

GIOVANELLI. Ah, when I hear *her* voice, I obey! (*Exit.*)

DAISY, *slowly opening her eyes.* Where am I? Where have I been?

MME. DE K. She's saved! She's saved!

WINTERBOURNE. You're with me, little Daisy. With me forever!

MME. DE K. Ah, decidedly I had better leave you! (*Goes out to the balcony.*)

DAISY, *looking at Winterbourne.* With you? With *you?* What has happened?

WINTERBOURNE, *still on his knees beside her.* Something very blessed. I understand you—I love you!

DAISY, *gazing at him a moment.* Oh, I'm very happy! (*Sinks back again, closing her eyes.*)

WINTERBOURNE. We shall be happy together when you have told me you forgive me. Let me hear you say it—only three words! (*He waits. She remains silent.*) Ah, she sinks away again! Daisy, won't you live—won't you live for me?

DAISY, *murmuring.* It was all for you—it was all for you!

WINTERBOURNE, *burying his head in her lap.* Vile idiot! Impenetrable fool!

DAISY, *with her eyes still closed.* I shall be better—but you mustn't leave me.

WINTERBOURNE. Never again, Daisy—never again! (*At this moment Eugenio strides into the room by the door opposite to the one through which Giovanelli has gone out.*)

SCENE IX. WINTERBOURNE. DAISY. EUGENIO. MADAME DE KATKOFF; *then* RANDOLPH. *and all the others.*

EUGENIO, *looking amazed at Daisy and Winterbourne.* What does this mean? What horrible thing has happened?

WINTERBOURNE, *on his feet.* You will learn what has happened quite soon enough to please you! But in the meanwhile, it is decent that this young lady should see her mother. (*While he speaks, Madame de Katkoff comes back and takes her place at Daisy's side, where she stands with her eyes fixed upon Eugenio.*)

EUGENIO. Her mother is not important: Miss Miller is in my care. *Cara signorina*, do you suffer?

DAISY, *vaguely.* Poor mother, poor mother! She has gone to the Carnival.

EUGENIO. She came home half an hour ago. She has gone to bed.

MME. DE K. Don't you think there would be a certain propriety in your requesting her to get up? (*Randolph comes in at this moment, hearing Madame de Katkoff's words.*)

RANDOLPH. She *is* getting up, you can bet your life! She's going to give it to Daisy.

MME. DE K. Come and speak to your sister. She has been very ill. (*She draws Randolph towards her, and keeps him near her.*)

DAISY, *smiling languidly at her brother.* You are up very late—very late.

RANDOLPH. I can't sleep—over here! I've been talking to that waiter.

EUGENIO, *anxious.* I don't see the Cavaliere. Where is he gone?

RANDOLPH. He came up to tell mother, and I came back ahead of him (*To Giovanelli, who at this moment returns.*) Hallo, Cavaliere!

GIOVANELLI, *solemnly, coming in.* Mrs. Miller is dressing. She will presently arrive.

MME. DE K., *to Randolph.* Go and help your mother, and tell her your sister is better.

RANDOLPH. I'll tell her through the door—or she'll put me to bed! (*Marches away.*)

GIOVANELLI, *approaching Eugenio, aside.* I shall never have the girl!

EUGENIO. You had better have killed her! (*Aside.*) He shall pay me for his flowers! (*Re-enter Reverdy.*)

REVERDY. The doctor will be here in five minutes.

MME. DE K. He won't be necessary now; nor even (*seeing Mrs. Costello come back with a little bottle, and accompanied by Miss Durant*) this lady's precious elixir!

MRS. C., *approaching Daisy, rather stiffly.* Perhaps you would like to hold it to your nose.

DAISY, *takes the phial, looking at Mrs. Costello with a little smile.* Well, I was bound you should speak to me!

REVERDY. And without a presentation, after all!

WINTERBOURNE. Oh yes, I must present. (*To his aunt.*) I present you my wife!

GIOVANELLI, *starting; then recovering himself and folding his arms.* I congratulate you, Mademoiselle, on your taste for the unexpected.

DAISY. Well, it *is* unexpected. But I never deceived you!

GIOVANELLI. Oh, no, you haven't deceived me: you have only ruined me!

DAISY. Poor old Giovanelli! Well, you've had a good time.

MRS. C., *impressively, to Winterbourne.* Your wife?

WINTERBOURNE. My dear aunt, she *has* stood the test!

EUGENIO, *who has walked round to Madame de Katkoff, in a low tone.* You haven't kept the terms of our bargain.

MME. DE K. I'm sick of your bargain—and of you!

EUGENIO. (*He eyes her a moment; then, vindictively.*) I shall give your letter to Mr. Winterbourne.

MME. DE K. Coward! (*Aside, joyously.*) And Mr. Winterbourne will give it to me.

GIOVANELLI, *beside Eugenio.* You must find me another heiress.

EUGENIO. I thought you said you'd had enough.

GIOVANELLI. I have been thinking over my debts.

EUGENIO. We'll see, then, with my next family. On the same terms, eh?

GIOVANELLI. Ah, no; I don't want a rival! (*Re-enter Mrs. Walker.*)

MRS. W., *to Daisy.* I can't find the Consul; but as you're better it doesn't matter.

DAISY. I don't want the Consul: I want my mother.

MRS. W. I went to her room as well. Randolph had told her you were better, and so—and so—(*Pausing, a little embarrassed, and looking round the circle.*)

DAISY. She isn't coming?

MRS. W. She has gone back to bed!

MRS. C., *as to herself and the audience.* They *are* queer people, all the same!

MISS D., *to Mrs. Costello.* Shall we start for America now?

REVERDY. Of course we shall—to be married!

WINTERBOURNE, *laying his hand on Reverdy's shoulder.* We shall be married the same day. (*To Daisy.*) Shan't we, Daisy—in America?

DAISY, *who has risen to her feet, leaning on his arm.* Oh, yes; you ought to go home!